AF848746

AUSTRALIAN FEMINIST JUDGMENTS

This book brings together feminist academics and lawyers to present an impressive collection of alternative judgments in a series of Australian legal cases. By re-imagining original legal decisions through a feminist lens, the collection explores the possibilities, limits and implications of feminist approaches to legal decision-making. Each case is accompanied by a brief commentary that places it in legal and historical context and explains what the feminist re-writing does differently to the original case. The cases not only cover topics of long-standing interest to feminist scholars – such as family law, sexual offences and discrimination law – but also areas which have had less attention, including Indigenous sovereignty, constitutional law, immigration, taxation and environmental law. The collection contributes a distinctly Australian perspective to the growing international literature investigating the role of feminist legal theory in judicial decision-making.

Australian Feminist Judgments

Righting and Rewriting Law

Edited by

Heather Douglas, Francesca Bartlett,
Trish Luker and Rosemary Hunter

·HART·
PUBLISHING
OXFORD AND PORTLAND, OREGON
2014

Published in the United Kingdom by Hart Publishing Ltd
16C Worcester Place, Oxford, OX1 2JW
Telephone: +44 (0)1865 517530
Fax: +44 (0)1865 510710
E-mail: mail@hartpub.co.uk
Website: http://www.hartpub.co.uk

Published in North America (US and Canada) by
Hart Publishing
c/o International Specialized Book Services
920 NE 58th Avenue, Suite 300
Portland, OR 97213-3786
USA
Tel: +1 503 287 3093 or toll-free: (1) 800 944 6190
Fax: +1 503 280 8832
E-mail: orders@isbs.com
Website: http://www.isbs.com

© The editors and contributors severally, 2014

The editors and contributors have asserted their right under the Copyright, Designs and Patents Act 1988, to be identified as the authors of this work.

Hart Publishing is an imprint of Bloomsbury Publishing plc.

All rights reserved. No part of this publication may be reproduced, stored in a retrieval system, or transmitted, in any form or by any means, without the prior permission of Hart Publishing, or as expressly permitted by law or under the terms agreed with the appropriate reprographic rights organisation. Enquiries concerning reproduction which may not be covered by the above should be addressed to Hart Publishing Ltd at the address above.

British Library Cataloguing in Publication Data
Data Available

ISBN: 978-1-84946-521-2

Typeset by Hope Services Ltd, Abingdon

FOREWORD

A judicial welcome is a quaint legal tradition. Having taken the oath or affirmation of office, the newly appointed judge sits, either alone or with one or more of her new judicial colleagues, and is addressed by lawyers representing those who will appear before her. Her life and achievements are rehearsed; for the first time, she is called Your Honour ('Your Honour was born at a young age, Your Honour's leadership qualities were apparent in kindergarten . . .'); levels of flattery and expectation are high. Then – and this will swiftly become her norm – she has the last say. For the first time, she hears her own voice projected from the bench towards those in the courtroom; she thanks the speakers and others who have contributed to her life and career, tells a self-deprecating tale or two and, perhaps, adds a few sentences of aspiration before the court is adjourned and the real work starts.

When I was welcomed to the Family Court of Australia in 1993 I joined a bench (in Victoria) of 11 men, two of whom sat with me. It had been five years since the Hon Peg Lusink, the first Victorian woman to be appointed to a court, had retired. I said (after the customary and sincere round of thanks) that at her welcome I had been cautioned against being the first judge to use the F-word – advice I had decided to ignore. The audience froze. To my right, then Chief Justice Alastair Nicholson sat, solid as a rock; he had weathered (and would again) too many storms to be worried by the prospect of profanity. But from the judge on his right came a sharp intake of breath and a stifled exclamation and to this day I am unsure whether he thought the word I then uttered – feminist – to be better or worse than the one he envisaged.

This was three years after Professors Reg Graycar and Jenny Morgan published *The Hidden Gender of Law*,[1] and three years after Justice Bertha Wilson, the first woman appointed to the Supreme Court of Canada, made a speech titled 'Will Women Judges Really Make a Difference?';[2] the Women's Electoral Lobby had been created 21 years earlier and there was a deal of writing and discussion about women's rights. But for a practising lawyer to call attention to the gendered nature of law and to declare herself a feminist was to risk being labelled anti-male, shrill and – antithetical to judging – biased. Indeed, Justice Wilson's speech brought down the wrath of the anti-feminist, conservative REAL women's organisation, which launched a complaint against her, alleging she was unfit to sit as a judge because of her feminist bias.

Did I, as a feminist, write feminist judgments? That's for others to determine, but the more interesting question is what *is* a feminist judgment? This book contains 24 of them, plus a chapter which addresses the impossibility of writing a 25th, and 25 commentaries on the judgments. The judgments are works of imagination, but they spring from recorded facts and legal principles: each is a rewriting of a published judgment, informed by feminist scholarship and reflection. In some, the feminist 'judge' reaches the same conclusion as the

[1] Reg Graycar and Jenny Morgan, *The Hidden Gender of Law* (Federation Press, 1st edn, 1990).

[2] This lecture was first presented at the Osgoode Hall Law School, York University, on February 8, 1990, and was subsequently published as: Bertha Wilson, 'Will Women Judges Really Make a Difference?' (1990) 28 *Osgoode Hall Law Journal* 507.

actual judge or judges but by a very different route; in some, the outcome is radically different from the original, a dissenting judgment of force and originality. Some reach conclusions which might surprise; for example, a feminist judge disagrees with the reasoning of the High Court which led it to find that a husband's immunity for prosecution for rape of his wife had ceased to be part of the common law of Australia by 1935. The rewritten decisions span almost eight decades and raise a range of issues, from sentencing principles to statutory interpretation, sexuality in refugee claims to the right of a lesbian to access artificial reproductive technology, propensity evidence to parental responsibility. The authors are feminist scholars from diverse backgrounds: three are Indigenous; some are young; all are creative. I had the privilege of working with many of them at workshops in 2013 and wished I had had the benefit of their scholarship and wit when I was writing judgments.

The book contains no definition of a feminist judgment, but consideration of the judgments and commentaries suggest common themes. The feminist judge strives to consider women's experience as well as men's; to resist assumptions about individuals' actions and capacities based solely on gender; to examine her own prejudices and biases; to focus on context; to consider the potential of judicial notice; to refuse to be gender-neutral when analysing gender-specific issues; to promote equality. There are questions of tone and of voice; decisions about who is to be named, and how; questions of audience and of the use of power.

And the point of it all? Perhaps the book will, as the editors write in their Introduction, reinvigorate interest and engagement with feminism in law school classes. Perhaps it may encourage practising lawyers to develop new ways of using classic tools of precedent and statutory interpretation to good effect, and push boundaries using new tools. But its central and stated aim is law reform through altering legal discourse. Law and text are inseparable. Judges write and their words change the lives of those before them and, sometimes, the lives of countless others. If more people who become judges are aware of the gendered nature of law and the overriding importance of equality, and more reflective about the fluidity of the judicial role and the effect of power on the operation of law, there will be more judgments which grapple with the concerns of these authors.

Finally (and perhaps heretically), read these judgments and commentaries for fun. Parody, imagination and the critique of law have rarely merged so seamlessly.

Hon Sally Brown AM
12 April 2014

ACKNOWLEDGEMENTS

This book is the result of the collaborative endeavour of a wonderful group of academics and practitioners and there are many people to acknowledge. First we thank the authors of the judgments and commentaries collected here. It was a great experience to work with you all and we appreciate your enthusiasm and patience on this journey. Our gratitude is extended to the Hon Sally Brown AM. Sally read and commented in detail on nearly all of the drafts of the commentaries and judgments in this collection. She attended workshops in both Sydney and Melbourne and gave warm and generous feedback to everyone involved. The collection is much better as a result of her efforts.

Several judges attended our workshops and shared their experiences and reflections about judgment writing with the project participants. In Victoria, we thank Justice Marcia Neave AO of the Victorian Court of Appeal and Justice Jennifer Coate of the Family Court of Australia. In Sydney, we thank Justices Elizabeth Fullerton and Lucy McCallum of the Supreme Court of NSW and Magistrate Margot Stubbs of the Local Court of NSW. In Brisbane, we thank President Margaret McMurdo AC of the Queensland Court of Appeal and Judge Fleur Kingham of the District Court of Queensland. Many others who are not represented in this collection also attended workshops and commented on the process of judgment-writing and on the drafts of judgments and commentaries. We thank them all for their support and valuable ideas.

In Melbourne, our workshops were hosted by the Melbourne Law School at the University of Melbourne and they would have been impossible to organise without the generous assistance of Associate Professor Wendy Larcombe. Our workshops in Sydney were hosted by the Faculty of Law at the University of Technology Sydney and in Brisbane by the TC Beirne School of Law at the University of Queensland. We thank these institutions for their support. We also thank the TC Beirne School of Law for providing seed funding for the project, which allowed us to hold an initial meeting of interested participants in 2010 to discuss the possibilities for feminist rewritings of Australian judgments.

Professor Kim Rubenstein provided a steady stream of articles of interest to the project, some of which have helped to inform the initial chapters of this collection. Thanks also to Professor Erika Rackley for reviewing and providing helpful comments on earlier drafts of Chapters 1 and 2. We also acknowledge the contribution of Charlotte Steer for suggesting the title for this collection. A number of hardworking research assistants have assisted us throughout the course of this project. Thanks to Sreedhevi Ramachandran, Ruth Walker, Catherine Carol, Kate Thomas, Rebekah Oldfield and Sian Littledale.

Thanks also to Madeleine Donovan for allowing us to use her image 'Two High, Shelving, 2003' (licensed by DACS, 2014) which appears on the cover of this book, and to Helen Maxwell for suggesting this work. We also thank Sofia Wood from *Shortie Designs* who designed the website we developed for the Australian Feminist Judgments Project http://www.law.uq.edu.au/the-australian-feminist-judgments-project. Finally we thank the Australian Research Council for funding this project under the Discovery Project scheme (DP12012375).

Any errors or omissions are the responsibility of the editors and contributors alone.

CONTENTS

Part III Crime and Evidence

Criminal Law

Evidence

Sentencing

Part IV Interpreting Equality

Family Law

NOTES ON CONTRIBUTORS

Isabella Alexander is an Associate Professor in the Faculty of Law, University of Technology Sydney.

Renata Alexander is a Senior Lecturer in the Faculty of Law, Monash University and a member of the Victorian Bar.

Thalia Anthony is a Senior Lecturer in the Faculty of Law, University of Technology Sydney.

Elisa Arcioni is a Senior Lecturer in the Sydney Law School, University of Sydney.

Paula Baron is Chair of Common Law in the LaTrobe Law School, La Trobe University.

Francesca Bartlett is a Senior Lecturer in the TC Beirne School of Law, University of Queensland.

Katherine Biber is an Associate Professor in the Faculty of Law, University of Technology Sydney.

Kathy Bowrey is a Professor in the Faculty of Law, University of New South Wales.

Kylie Burns is a Senior Lecturer in the Griffith Law School, Griffith University.

Annie Cossins is an Associate Professor in the Faculty of Law, University of New South Wales.

Mary Crock is Professor of Public Law in the Faculty of Law, University of Sydney.

Penny Crofts is a Senior Lecturer in the Faculty of Law, University of Technology Sydney.

Jonathan Crowe is an Associate Professor in the TC Beirne School of Law, University of Queensland.

Margaret Davies is a Professor in the Flinders Law School, Flinders University.

Heather Douglas is a Professor in the TC Beirne School of Law, University of Queensland.

Kirsty Duncanson is a Lecturer in Legal Studies in the Faculty of Humanities and Social Sciences, La Trobe University.

Rachael Field is an Associate Professor in the Faculty of Law, Queensland University of Technology.

Kate Fitz-Gibbon is a Lecturer in Criminology in the School of Humanities and Social Sciences, Deakin University.

Beth Gaze is an Associate Professor in the Melbourne Law School, University of Melbourne.

Katharine Gelber is a Professor in Public Policy in the School of Political Science and International Studies, University of Queensland.

Ann Genovese is an Associate Professor in the Melbourne Law School, University of Melbourne.

Paula Gerber is an Associate Professor in the Faculty of Law, Monash University.

Lee Godden is a Professor in the Melbourne Law School, University of Melbourne.

Reg Graycar is a barrister at St James Hall Chambers, Sydney and an Emeritus Professor in the Sydney Law School, University of Sydney.

Mary Heath is an Associate Professor in the Flinders Law School, Flinders University.

Adrian Howe is an Adjunct Research Fellow in the Griffith Law School, Griffith University.

Rosemary Hunter is Professor of Law and Socio-Legal Studies in the Law Department, Queen Mary University of London.

Isabel Karpin is a Professor in the Faculty of Law, University of Technology Sydney.
Wendy Larcombe is an Associate Professor at Melbourne Law School, University of Melbourne.
Heron Loban is a Torres Strait Islander woman and a Senior Lecturer in the School of Law, James Cook University.
Trish Luker is a Chancellor's Postdoctoral Research Fellow in the Faculty of Law, University of Technology Sydney.
JaneMaree Maher is an Associate Professor in the School of Social Sciences, Monash University.
Elena Marchetti is a Research Professor in the School of Law, University of Wollongong.
Jude McCulloch is a Professor in the School of Social Sciences, Monash University.
Jenny Morgan is a Professor at Melbourne Law School, University of Melbourne.
Wayne Morgan is a Senor Lecturer and Sub Dean LLB/JD Programs in the ANU College of Law, Australian National University.
Ngaire Naffine is Bonython Professor of Law, Law School, University of Adelaide.
Bronwyn Naylor is an Associate Professor in the Faculty of Law, Monash University.
Jennifer Nielsen is a Senior Lecturer in the School of Law and Justice, Southern Cross University.
Ann O'Connell is a Professor at Melbourne Law School, University of Melbourne.
Helen O'Sullivan served as judge on the District Court of Queensland 1991–2009.
Jacqueline Peel is a Professor at Melbourne Law School, University of Melbourne.
Janet Ransley is an Associate Professor and the Head of the School of Criminology and Criminal Justice, Griffith University.
Zoe Rathus is a Senior Lecturer in the Griffith Law School and Director of the Legal Clinic, Griffith University.
Kim Rubenstein is a Professor in the ANU College of Law, Australian National University.
Kerrie Sadiq is a Professor in the QUT Business School, Queensland University of Technology.
Mehera San Roque is a Senior Lecturer of Law and Director of the JD Program, University of New South Wales.
Lisa Sarmas is a Senior Lecturer at Melbourne Law School, University of Melbourne.
Nan Seuffert is a Professor of Law and Director of the Legal Intersections Research Centre, University of Wollongong.
Charlotte Steer is a Lecturer in the Faculty of Law, University of New South Wales.
Julie Stubbs is a Professor in the Faculty of Law, University of New South Wales.
Anita Stuhmcke is a Professor in the Faculty of Law, University of Technology Sydney.
Margaret Thornton is a Professor in the ANU College of Law, Australian National University.
Lesley Townsley is a Lecturer in the Faculty of Law, University of Technology Sydney.
Danielle Tyson is a Lecturer in the School of Social Sciences, Monash University.
Honni van Rijswijk is a Senior Lecturer in the Faculty of Law, University of Technology Sydney.
Irene Watson belongs to the Tanganekald and Meintangk First Nations Peoples. She is a Professor of Law in the David Unaipon College of Indigenous Education and Research, University of South Australia.
Nicole Watson is a member of the Birri-Gubba People and the Yugambeh language group. She is a Senior Researcher at the Jumbunna Indigenous House of Learning, University of Technology Sydney.

TABLE OF CASES

Australia

Canada

Europe

New Zealand

United Kingdom

United States of America

United Nations Human Rights Committee

TABLE OF STATUTES AND LEGISLATION

Australia

Commonwealth

Australian Capital Territory

New South Wales

Northern Territory

Queensland

South Australia

Tasmania

Victoria

Western Australia

Bangladesh

Canada

Europe

New Zealand

United Kingdom

International treaties and conventions

1

Introduction: Righting Australian Law

HEATHER DOUGLAS, FRANCESCA BARTLETT,
TRISH LUKER and ROSEMARY HUNTER

The Australian Feminist Judgments Project

The Australian Feminist Judgments Project aims to test new and enduring questions about the relationship between law and feminist ideas, approaches and objectives. We ask: is it possible to formulate a feminist judicial practice, and if so, what are the boundaries of this enterprise? What kinds of judicial practices and judgments 'count' as feminist? In this way, this book and the project contribute an Australian perspective to the growing international literature that investigates the role that feminist legal theory might play in judicial decision-making.[1]

This book collects 25 judgments which put into practice and test feminist ideas in real Australian legal cases. Bringing together the work of feminist academics and lawyers, this is a collection of 'alternative' judgments in Australian cases, where the authors have imagined the decision and the reasoning that might have been adopted if a feminist judge had heard the case.[2] This is done in a variety of ways: from adding another voice to an appellate decision of the High Court, to replacing the original decision at trial. The constraint imposed on authors was to write within the legal genre of decision-making to produce an 'authentic' and legally plausible judgment. Preceding each judgment, a commentary chapter, written by a different author, provides context, explanation and sometimes challenge.

The collection brings together many of the most eminent Australian feminist legal scholars who are experts in diverse areas of law, as well as contributions from new and emerging scholars. Importantly, the work of several Indigenous scholars is represented here. As we discuss in Chapter 2, several of the Indigenous authors challenged the Australian common law system as a way of deciding cases and as a genre of writing which is unable to tell their stories appropriately.

[1] See, eg, Rosemary Hunter, Clare McGlynn and Erika Rackley (eds), *Feminist Judgments: From Theory to Practice* (Hart Publishing, 2010); Ulrike Schultz and Gisela Shaw (eds), *Gender and Judging* (Hart Publishing, 2013); Ulrike Schultz and Gisela Shaw (eds), *Women in the Judiciary* (Routledge, 2012); Diana Majury, 'Introducing the Women's Court of Canada' (2006) 18 *Canadian Journal of Women and the Law* 1; Rosemary Hunter, 'The Power of Feminist Judgments?' (2012) 20 *Feminist Legal Studies* 135.

[2] We acknowledge at the outset that the concept of a 'feminist judge' is a contested idea which could take a number of forms, and we explore the challenges and possibilities this issue raises for the project below. See generally: Rosemary Hunter, 'Can *Feminist* Judges Make a Difference?' (2008) 15 *International Journal of the Legal Profession* 7; Beverley Baines, 'Must Feminist Judges Self-Identify as Feminists?' in Ulrike Schultz and Gisela Shaw (eds), *Gender and Judging* (Hart Publishing, 2013) 379; Beverley Baines, 'But Was She a Feminist Judge?' in Kimberley Brooks (ed), *One Woman's Difference: The Contributions of Justice Bertha Wilson* (UBC Press, 2009) 211.

We discuss the feminist approaches taken in relation to the judgments in this collection in Chapter 2. In this chapter, we consider the feminist judgments projects as an emerging movement, the concept of feminist judging, the context and methodology for the Australian Feminist Judgments Project, and the potential impact and application of the judgments in this collection.

An Emerging Movement?

While the idea of academics rewriting judgments is not new,[3] this project draws its main inspiration from two significant recent developments in feminist legal scholarship. In Canada and in England and Wales, feminist judgment-writing projects have emerged in which feminist academics, lawyers and activists have written alternative judgments in legal cases.[4] The Canadian project grew out of frustration experienced by feminists about how s 15 of the *Canadian Charter of Rights and Freedoms* – the equality provision – was being interpreted and applied by the Canadian Supreme Court.[5] As Diana Majury reports, despondency sparked action and energy with the revelatory question: 'so why don't we show them how it could have been done? . . . Why don't we rewrite these decisions that are so wrong?'[6] The resulting Women's Court of Canada is an on-going project which currently hosts a number of rewritten equality cases that 'show how it's done.'

In comparison to the Canadian project, the English project was broader in scope and set out to write 'missing' feminist judgments in a range of appellate cases relating to various areas of law. Their project set out to 'inaugurate a new form of scholarship, one which seeks to demonstrate, in a sustained and disciplined way, how judgments could have been rewritten and cases could have been decided differently'.[7] The English project resulted in a collection of 23 rewritten cases and associated commentaries.[8] In her review of the collection, Margaret Davies suggested that

> it is perhaps possible to say that the imaginative gap between the legal establishment and feminist legal theory is at last being reduced. Arguably, the judgments also represent the return of feminist scholarship to feminist activism through the socially engaged practice of judging.[9]

She also emphasised that the collection shows 'what is plausible and possible for the law in individual cases, but more importantly it constitutes a collective effort to shift the discourse and emphasis of law'.[10]

Other feminist judgments projects continue to emerge. For example, the Northern/Irish

[3] Jack Balkin (ed), *What Brown v. Board of Education Should Have Said: The Nation's Top Legal Experts Rewrite America's Landmark Civil Rights Decision* (New York University Press, 2002); Jack Balkin (ed), *What Roe v. Wade Should Have Said: The Nation's Top Legal Experts Rewrite America's Most Controversial Decision* (New York University Press, 2005).

[4] See the first six decisions of the Women's Court of Canada, available at <http://womenscourt.ca>. See also Hunter, McGlynn and Rackley, above n 1.

[5] Majury, above n 1.

[6] Ibid 2.

[7] Rosemary Hunter, Clare McGlynn and Erika Rackley, 'Feminist Judgments: An Introduction' in Hunter, McGlynn and Rackley, above n 1, 3.

[8] Hunter, McGlynn and Rackley, above n 1.

[9] Margaret Davies, 'The Law Becomes Us: Rediscovering Judgment' (2012) 20 *Feminist Legal Studies* 167, 168.

[10] Ibid 179.

Feminist Judgments Project emphasises the jurisdictional specificity of Irish decision-making and underlines the strong relationship between judicial decision-making and local political and cultural struggles and contestations.[11] A Feminist International Judgments project is currently being established, in part to address the silencing of women's voices in international law.[12] A United States Supreme Court edition of the feminist judgments project was also launched recently.[13] While in 2010, Davies hesitated to describe the various feminist rewriting projects around the world as a 'movement',[14] this collection, along with other emerging collections, arguably brings us a step closer.

Feminist Interventions in Law

Since the 1970s, feminist legal activism in Australia has focused on legislative reform;[15] feminist interventions in relation to judicial decision-making have largely taken the form of critique.[16] Margaret Thornton points out that the 1970s and 1980s represented a dynamic period of law reform 'that produced no-fault divorce, anti-discrimination legislation and a swag of egalitarian policies associated with the modernisation of the Australian state'.[17] These reforms were driven by feminist scholarship and activism. More recently, feminist engagement with institutional law reform projects has led to important changes, such as the decriminalisation of abortion in Victoria.[18] However, there are mixed views about the success of feminist engagements with legislative reform and participation in law reform commission references.[19] Some of the recent reforms, in particular the reformulation of homicide offences and defences leading to the abolition of provocation in several jurisdictions,[20] have been the subject of critique which has raised questions about whether they have been successful in addressing long-standing concerns about the legal responses to domestic homicide.[21] Others have noted the unintended or disappointing consequences

[11] See <www.feministjudging.ie>.

[12] Int Law Grrls, 'Invitation to Participate in the Feminist International Judgments Project' (16 January 2014) <http://ilg2.org/2014/01/16/invitation-to-participate-in-the-feminist-international-judgments-project/>. See also Eva Brems (ed), *Diversity and European Human Rights: Rewriting judgments of the ECHR* (Cambridge University Press, 2013).

[13] Bridget Crawford, 'CPF: U.S. Feminist Judgments Project' (11 August 2014) Feminist Law Professors <http://www.feministlawprofessors.com/2014/08/cpf-feminist-judgments-project/>.

[14] Davies, above n 9, 169.

[15] Reg Graycar and Jenny Morgan, *The Hidden Gender of Law* (Federation Press, 2nd ed, 2002) 442; Reg Graycar, 'Law Reform by Frozen Chook: Family Law Reform for the New Millennium?' (2000) 24 *Melbourne University Law Review* 737. See also Anne Summers, *The End of Equality: Work, Babies and Women's Choices in 21st Century Australia* (Random House, 2003).

[16] See generally: Graycar and Morgan, ibid; Margaret Thornton (ed), *Public and Private: Feminist Legal Debates* (Oxford University Press, 1995).

[17] Margaret Thornton, 'Post-Feminism in the Legal Academy?' (2010) 95 *Feminist Review* 92, 93; see also Margaret Thornton, *The Liberal Promise: Anti-discrimination Legislation in Australia* (Oxford University Press, 1990).

[18] Victorian Law Reform Commission, *Law of Abortion: Final Report*, Report No 15 (2008).

[19] See, eg: Reg Graycar and Jenny Morgan, 'Law Reform: What's in it for Women?' (2005) 23 *Windsor Yearbook of Access to Justice* 393; Marcia Neave, 'Institutional Law Reform in Australia: The Past and the Future' (2005) 23 *Windsor Yearbook of Access to Justice* 343; Patricia Easteal (ed), *Balancing the Scales: Rape, Law Reform and Australian Culture* (Federation Press, 1998).

[20] See, eg: Law Reform Commission of Western Australia, *Review of the Law of Homicide, Final Report*, Project No 97 (2007); Victorian Law Reform Commission, *Defences to Homicide: Final Report*, Report No 94 (2004).

[21] In relation to these reforms, see *R v Middendorp* in this collection. See also Jenny Morgan, 'Homicide Law

that sometimes flow from legislative reforms, in part because the impact of legislative change is dependent on wider cultural and social changes, and on implementation by often unsympathetic legal personnel.[22]

In terms of the appointment of women judges, Australia has been a leader in the field. Indeed, when Dame Roma Mitchell was appointed as a judge of the Supreme Court of South Australia in 1965, she was the first woman judge appointed to the office in the whole of the British Commonwealth.[23] However, despite the expectation that numbers would steadily increase, women remain under-represented in the ranks of judicial decision-makers.[24] Women are now represented on all Australian courts, but make up only around one third of the judiciary.[25] The disparity is highlighted by the fact that while women make up over 65 per cent of graduates from Australian law schools,[26] and indeed over half of Australian law school graduates have been women since the 1980s,[27] these statistics are not reflected in the appointments of senior legal professionals or judges.

We continue to see 'firsts' in the Australian judiciary, which may indicate a 'steady'[28] increase. The first Chief Justice of the Family Court of Australia, Elizabeth Evatt, was appointed in 1976 Over a decade later, in 1987, Justice Mary Gaudron was the first woman appointed to the High Court. In 1998, Justice Margaret McMurdo was the first woman to be appointed as the presiding judge of an appellate court in Australia, and in 2003, Justice Marilyn Warren became the first woman to be appointed as Chief Justice in any Australian state or territory. We are yet to see a woman Chief Justice of the Federal Court or the High Court.

The number of women judges is clearly of great symbolic value, and their presence and visibility enhances the democratic representativeness and legitimacy of the judiciary.[29] However, it is important to ask whether the presence of women in the judiciary makes any difference to the practice or substance of decision-making. We are aware that this is not a new question and that feminist legal scholars have debated issues around gender and its

Reform and Gender: Configuring Violence' (2012) 45 *Australian and New Zealand Journal of Criminology* 351; Kate Fitz-Gibbon and Julie Stubbs, 'Divergent Directions in Reforming Legal Responses to Lethal Violence' (2012) 45 *Australian and New Zealand Journal of Criminology* 318; Heather Douglas, 'A Consideration of the Merits of Specialised Homicide Offences and Defences for Battered Women' (2012) 45 *Australian and New Zealand Journal of Criminology* 367.

[22] Graycar and Morgan, above n 15, 442–5; Renee Romkens, 'Law as a Trojan Horse: Unintended Consequences of Rights-Based Interventions to Support Battered Women' (2001) 13 *Yale Journal of Law and Feminism* 265, 267; Rosemary Hunter, *Domestic Violence Law Reform and Women's Experience in Court: The Implementation of Feminist Reforms in Civil Proceedings* (Cambria Press, 2008).

[23] Shelley O'Connell, 'Dame Roma: Not One to be Excluded' (2011) 33(10) *Bulletin (Law Society of SA)* 26; see also Margaret Thornton, *Dissonance and Distrust: Women in the Legal Profession* (Oxford University Press, 1996). See also Mary Jane Mossman, *The First Women Lawyers: A Comparative Study of Gender, Law and Legal Professions* (Hart Publishing, 2006).

[24] Graycar and Morgan, above n 15, 422–3; Rosemary Hunter, 'Women in the Legal Profession: The Australian Profile' in Ulrike Schultz and Gisela Shaw (eds) *Women in the World's Legal Professions* (Hart Publishing, 2003) 87.

[25] Australian Institute of Judicial Administration, *Statistics* (2013) <http://www.aija.org.au/JudgesMagistrates 2013.pdf>. To compare with statistics from 1995, see Thornton, above n 23, 294.

[26] Margaret Thornton, 'The New Knowledge Economy and the Transformation of the Law Discipline' (2012) 19 *International Journal of the Legal Profession* 265, 267.

[27] Sharyn Roach Anleu, 'Women in the Legal Profession: Theory and Research' in Patricia Easteal and Sandra McKillop (eds), *Women and the Law: Proceedings of a Conference Held 24–26 September 1991* (Australian Institute of Criminology, 1993) 1.

[28] Michael Kirby, 'Women in Law – Doldrums or Progress?' (Speech delivered at the Women Lawyers of Western Australia Dinner, Perth, 22 October 2003).

[29] HP Lee and Enid Campbell, *The Australian Judiciary* (Cambridge University Press, 2013) 84–6.

effects on judging for at least 25 years.[30] Evidence from international research on whether women judges make a difference is equivocal, and tends to depend on the jurisdiction and the area of law being observed.[31] In their research on Australian judicial officers, Kathy Mack and Sharyn Roach Anleu identified gendered differences in the answers to survey questions by male and female magistrates and judges.[32] For example, they found that more female than male magistrates and judges thought interactive qualities of empathy, communication and being a good listener were essential skills for their work.[33] They found that this gender difference was more significantly pronounced at the magistrates' court level than in the higher courts. Furthermore, Mack and Anleu found that female magistrates were much more likely than male magistrates to report that legal knowledge was an 'essential' skill in their work. In explaining these differences, the study authors suggest that women magistrates' 'commitment to greater interactive qualities and more legal skills . . . may indicate an attempt to use knowledge and expertise as strategies of empowerment'.[34]

However, in the United States, Sally Kenney's research suggests that the more women there are serving on a court, the less compelled a woman judge may feel to 'articulate "a woman's point of view"'.[35] In another study of women judges in England and Wales, Hilary Sommerlad suggests that any impact is likely to be 'strictly constrained',[36] since judges 'are already socialised in the rules of the profession'.[37] This research suggests that simply 'adding women and stirring' is unlikely to make a difference.[38] As Lorraine Code points out:

> The admission of a few women to carefully controlled places, so that they can serve as 'role models' – those cardboard and ephemeral constructs – offers minimal revolutionary promise. The problem exists at a deeper level . . . It is about subjectivity and cognitive agency, about displacing entrenched thought structures.[39]

Feminist theory has, moreover, problematised the idea of a singular subject position 'woman' as a source of experience on which law might be based.[40] In her consideration of

[30] Susanna Sherry, 'Civic Virtue and the Feminine Voice in Constitutional Adjudication' (1986) 72 *Virginia Law Review* 543; Judith Resnik, 'On the Bias: Feminist Reconsiderations of the Aspirations for our Judges' (1988) 61 *Southern California Law Review* 1877; Bertha Wilson, 'Will Women Judges Really Make a Difference?' (1990) 28 *Osgoode Hall Law Journal* 507; Regina Graycar, 'The Gender of Judgments: An Introduction' in Margaret Thornton (ed), *Public and Private: Feminist Legal Debates* (Oxford University Press, 1995) 262; Sandra Berns, *To Speak as a Judge: Difference, Voice and Power* (Ashgate, 1999); Erika Rackley, *Women, Judging and the Judiciary: From Difference to Diversity* (Routledge, 2013).

[31] For a summary of the evidence, see Dermot Feenan, 'Editorial Introduction: Women and Judging' (2009) 17 *Feminist Legal Studies* 1. See also Jennifer L Peresie, 'Female Judges Matter: Gender and Collegial Decision-Making in the Federal Appellate Courts' (2005) 114 *Yale Law Journal* 1759. This research examined 556 cases of sexual harassment and sex discrimination decided in the United States between 1999 and 2001. It found that three-judge panels with at least one female judge decided cases for the plaintiff more than twice as often as did all-male panels.

[32] Kathy Mack and Sharyn Roach Anleu, 'Skills for Judicial Work: Comparing Women Judges and Women Magistrates' in Schultz and Shaw (2013), above n 1, 211, 227–9.

[33] Ibid 226–7.

[34] Ibid 229.

[35] Sally Kenney, 'Thinking about Gender and Judging' in Schultz and Shaw (2012), above n 1, 104.

[36] Hilary Sommerlad, 'Let History Judge? Gender, Race, Class and Performative Identity: A Study of Women Judges in England and Wales' in Schultz and Shaw (2013), above n 1, 372.

[37] Ibid 372. See also Thornton, above n 23, 2; Margaret Thornton, '"Otherness" on the Bench: How Merit is Gendered' (2007) 29 *Sydney Law Review* 391.

[38] Graycar and Morgan, above n 15, 422.

[39] Lorraine Code, *What Can She Know? Feminist Theory and the Construction of Knowledge* (Cornell University Press, 1991) 263.

[40] Ibid; Elizabeth V Spelman, *Inessential Woman: Problems of Exclusion in Feminist Thought* (Beacon Press, 1988); Judith Butler, 'Contingent Foundations: Feminism and the Question of "Postmodernism"' (1991) 11(2) *Praxis International* 150; Joan W Scott, 'Experience' in Judith Butler and Joan W Scott (eds), *Feminists Theorize the*

whether women judges make a difference, for example, Erika Rackley focuses on the need for diversity in the sense of differences from the established judicial 'norm', which includes people of different sex, ethnicity and sexuality. She argues that these different backgrounds and experiences of the world all bear on the way a judge performs her role.[41] Observing that rather than being about 'letting in', diversity is about 'letting go' (that is, of privilege and moral superiority), Rackley suggests that rather than being an end in itself, diversity is a process.[42] She explains that diversity 'acts as a catalyst for disruption; impacting upon the legal monotony, destabilising its taken-for-granted assumptions and uncovering alternative ways of seeing, understanding, and judging'.[43] In this way, sex is only one point of difference, as women judicial officers often bring a diverse set of backgrounds, experiences and perspectives to the role as compared to their 'benchmark' male counterparts.[44]

Arguably, the efforts of some Australian governments to achieve a greater gender balance in the judiciary have involved recognition that a more diverse judiciary will bring more diverse perspectives to bear on decision-making, which will improve the quality of justice dispensed by Australian courts.[45] These efforts at encouraging judicial diversity, including a diverse range of women, such as Indigenous women and women from immigrant or lower socio-economic backgrounds, are important. Some of the chapters in this collection illustrate that women who speak from an identity informed by an intersection of their sex and race,[46] or sex and sexuality,[47] may bring unique, and perhaps disruptive, ideas about judging and the meaning of justice. Rather than legitimising the current legal order,[48] such radical approaches provide new ways of thinking and acting in the judicial context. These ideas are explored further in Chapter 2, where we draw on the feminist judgment-writers' reflections on their approaches to decision-making and the influence of their backgrounds and experiences.

Political (Routledge, 1992) 22; Maggie Troup, 'Rupturing the Veil: Feminism, Deconstruction and the Law' (1993) 1 *Australian Feminist Law Journal* 63.

41 Rackley, above n 30, 28–9; Berns, above n 30, 8.

42 Erika Rackley, 'What a Difference Difference Makes: Gendered Harms and Judicial Diversity' in Schultz and Shaw (2012), above n 1, 49.

43 Ibid 37. See also Brenda Hale, 'Equality and the Judiciary: Why Should We Want More Women Judges?' [2001] *Public Law* 489; Brenda Hale, 'Making a Difference? Why We Need a More Diverse Judiciary' (2005) 56 *Northern Ireland Legal Quarterly* 281.

44 Thornton, above n 37.

45 In Queensland, the Honourable Matt Foley, the Attorney-General from 1998 to 2001, appointed an unprecedented number of women to the Queensland judiciary and to positions of legal authority. His appointments included Justice Margaret McMurdo as President of the Court of Appeal, Di Fingleton to the position of Chief Magistrate and Leanne Clare as Director of Public Prosecutions. His judicial appointments included women from immigrant and lower socio-economic backgrounds, and two Indigenous people: see Marg O'Donnell, 'Not Just Good Girls' (2008) 21 *Griffith Review* 111, 117–18. In Victoria, the Honourable Rob Hulls, Attorney-General from 1999 to 2010, had a deliberate policy of appointing more women judges. In his first seven years in office, 37 out of 80 appointments were women, including Chief Justice of the Supreme Court, Marilyn Warren: see Thornton, above n 37, 398. See also Sean Cooney, 'Gender and Judicial Selection: Should There Be More Women on Our Courts?' (1993) 19 *Melbourne University Law Review* 20.

46 See, eg, *Kartinyeri v The Commonwealth*; *ACCC v Keshow*; and *In the matter of Djaparri (Re Tuckiar)*, in this collection.

47 See, eg, *Appellant S395/2002 v Minister for Immigration and Multicultural Affairs* and *JM v QFG and GK*, in this collection.

48 As Sommerlad adds, there is a danger that a push for diversity becomes just a way of legitimising the current order, where we make a 'business case' for more women, rather than focus on important goals of diversity: Hilary Sommerlad, 'Diversity, Merit and the English Judiciary: The Lessons that Can be Learned from the Reform of Selection Processes, a UK Contribution' (2013) 40 *City Square, Fordham Urban Law Journal* 94.

Feminist Judging

Rosemary Hunter observes that the assumption that women judges will necessarily make a difference is 'at best naïve and at worst essentialist',[49] and instead argues that *feminist* judges are more likely (and indeed ought) to make a difference.[50] However, positivist method, with its claim to neutrality,[51] considers the political commitments of judges an improper point of reference for decision-making. The judicial role demands, at the very least, the appearance of neutrality and impartiality. Does this role, then, so restrict regard to political philosophy as to limit change and the possibility of a feminist approach? Indeed, is the subject position of a feminist judge an oxymoron? As Baroness Hale puts it in the Foreword to the English collection of feminist judgments: 'Is it possible to be both a judge and a feminist?'[52] Both Hunter and Hale have argued that there is ample scope for feminist judicial practice at all levels. This does not mean referring to feminist theorists as legal authorities, but rather, bringing a feminist consciousness to bear on one's understanding of litigants, facts, evidence and legal rules. Indeed, to the extent that feminists are committed to values of inclusivity and equality, these are also values that the law itself proclaims.[53]

Aside from judicial norms, however, the possibility or potential for feminist influence in current legal processes may be limited by law's deeply embedded structures and methods. As radical feminist writer Audre Lorde observed in her famous essay:

> What does it mean when the tools of a racist patriarchy are used to examine the fruits of that same patriarchy? It means that only the most narrow parameters of change are possible and allowable . . . For the master's tools will never dismantle the master's house. They may allow us temporarily to beat him at his own game, but they will never enable us to bring about genuine change.[54]

In the context of law, theorists such as Mary-Jane Mossman and Carol Smart have also insisted upon the imperviousness of law and legal method to feminist arguments, critiques and perspectives.[55] Smart has called for a 'de-centring' of law,[56] and Catharine MacKinnon advocates a complete dismantling of law's infrastructure to achieve appropriate outcomes for women.[57] Reg Graycar suggests that 'we will not have feminist judges or feminist adjudication until we have the opportunity to redesign the forums'.[58]

These critiques usefully remind us that projects engaging with the rewriting of legal decisions are inherently constrained by their methodology. But the extent of those constraints and the space that remains available for a feminist approach to decision-making are still being explored. Critical and postmodern legal scholars have observed that legal method is

[49] Hunter, above n 2, 7.

[50] Ibid.

[51] Code, above n 39.

[52] Brenda Hale, 'Foreword' in Hunter, McGlynn and Rackley, above n 1, v.

[53] Ibid; Hunter, above n 2; Rosemary Hunter, 'An Account of Feminist Judging' in Hunter, McGlynn and Rackley, above n 1, 30–5; Brenda Hale, 'Maccabaean Lecture in Jurisprudence: A Minority Opinion?' (2008) 154 *Proceedings of the British Academy* 319.

[54] Audre Lorde, *Sister Outsider: Essays and Speeches* (Crossing Press, 1984) 110–14.

[55] Mary Jane Mossman, 'Feminism and Legal Method: The Difference it Makes' (1987) 3 *Wisconsin Women's Law Journal* 147; Carol Smart, *Feminism and the Power of Law* (Routledge, 1989).

[56] Smart, ibid.

[57] Catharine A MacKinnon, *Towards a Feminist Theory of the State* (Harvard University Press, 1989).

[58] Reg Graycar, 'A Feminist Adjudication Process: Is There Such a Thing?' in Schultz and Shaw (2013), above n 1, 455.

considerably more open-ended and produces less determinate results than it might claim.[59] Moreover, feminist judgments projects aim to engage with the law as law *reform* projects, by demonstrating the ways decision-makers make choices about how to interpret and apply the law. For instance, the feminist judgments in this collection not only reason from the experience of women, but also importantly unmask seemingly neutral laws and show that prevailing approaches to fact-finding are contingent and often partial.[60] In this way, they achieve feminist goals within the parameters of existing legal principles and practice. As Ann Genovese points out in her commentary chapter for *Goode and Goode*:[61]

> By taking law's doctrines and techniques seriously, feminist jurists have shown many times that to change law – to reform its practice or alter its perceptions – does not necessarily involve a polemical position that would force feminists to sit outside the door of the court. Instead, the task has been to master law, to understand its rehearsed movements and its rules of interpretation, as well as to monitor its lived effects.

In Chapter 2, we consider in more detail how the authors in this collection apply legal method to create feminist judicial decisions.

In terms of a *feminist* method of decision-making, Hunter provides a checklist of approaches that a feminist judge may bring to the task. She suggests that a feminist judge should:[62]

- 'ask the woman question' and notice the gender implications of apparently gender-neutral rules, as well as the implications for other traditionally excluded groups;
- 'include women', writing women's experiences into the judgment (both as litigants and collectively) and in the construction of legal rules;
- challenge gender bias;
- contextualise and particularise, reasoning from context and making individualised rather than categorical or abstract decisions;
- seek to remedy injustice and improve the conditions of women's lives;
- promote substantive equality;
- be open and accountable about the choices made between competing interests; and
- draw on feminist scholarship to inform decisions.

It is notable that Hunter does not prescribe that a particular form of feminism be applied, and accepts that it is unlikely that there will be a singular feminist position on the issues arising in any given case. Rather, she points out that there are multiple feminisms which will have differing approaches and possible results when put into practice.[63] The kinds of feminist theoretical approaches adopted in the judgments in this collection are outlined in Chapter 2. As we discuss there, in the Australian project, there seems to have been less dispute between differing feminist positions than occurred in the English project.[64] This may

[59] See, eg, Hunter, above n 1, 139. Even earlier, Julius Stone in *Precedent and Law: The Dynamics of Common Law Growth* (Butterworths, 1985) at 97 argued that in appellate judgments and where points of law are disputed, the conclusion is rarely compelled; rather the materials leave open 'leeways of choice' within which judges must decide.

[60] See, eg, *Appellant S395/2002*; *Louth v Diprose*; *Phillips v R*; *R v Webster*; *R v Middendorp*; and *U v U* in this collection.

[61] See Ch 23 of this collection.

[62] Hunter, above n 2; Rosemary Hunter, 'Justice Marcia Neave: Case Study of a Feminist Judge' in Schultz and Shaw (2013), above n 1, 401.

[63] Indeed, this was one of the key lessons arising from the English Feminist Judgments Project: Hunter, McGlynn and Rackley, above n 7, 12–13.

[64] Ibid.

be due to the less controversial nature of the cases chosen, or the compelling arguments made in the draft judgments. In only a very few cases are alternative feminist approaches canvassed in the commentary chapters.[65]

Although a feminist approach will often make a difference to the outcome of a case, this will not always be true. In some instances the feminist contribution will be to provide different reasons for reaching the same result.[66] As discussed in Chapter 2, seven of the cases in this collection are concurring judgments, arriving at the same outcome as the original case but by means of a process of legal reasoning informed by feminist concerns. Finally, while feminist judgment projects illustrate feminist judicial methods and approaches in a concentrated way, they differ from the real world in two important respects. In reality, it cannot be assumed that a judge who identifies as a feminist will necessarily incorporate feminism into all her judgments (for a variety of reasons),[67] nor that a judgment reflecting feminist concerns would necessarily be written by a judge who thought of herself (or himself) as a feminist.[68]

The Australian Legal Context

When we began conceiving the parameters of the Australian Feminist Judgments Project, we were conscious that it would necessarily reflect a distinctive historical and political context, as well as a unique jurisprudence. As a result of the history of Australia's federated structure, the eight individual states and territories have law-making power in a number of key areas including criminal law, evidence and private law, with each state and territory maintaining its own court system and set of statutes. The Commonwealth has power to make laws with respect to matters such as family law, taxation and immigration. Furthermore, Australia differs from other countries, such as Canada and the United Kingdom,[69] in that it does not have a constitutional or statutory Bill of Rights.[70] Historically, however, the High Court has been called upon to protect both express and implied rights under Australia's Constitution, and pursuant to the common law and Australia's international treaty obligations. Several of the cases in this collection address rights issues in this way.[71]

As an Australian project, we recognised from the outset that the collection of feminist judgments must speak to the country's settler-colonial history. As the British settlers arrived in Australia from the end of the eighteenth century, they steadily began to impose their laws

[65] See, eg, *Lodge v Federal Commissioner of Taxation* and *U v U* in this collection.

[66] Hunter (2013), above n 62, 417–18.

[67] Ibid; Sommerlad, above n 36, 371–2.

[68] See, eg, Baines (2009), above n 2; Baines (2013), above n 2.

[69] *Canada Act 1982* (UK) c 11, sch B pt I ('*Canadian Charter of Rights and Freedoms*'); *Human Rights Act 1998* (UK).

[70] While in 2004 the Australian Capital Territory introduced a *Human Rights Act 2004* (ACT) and in 2006 Victoria introduced a *Charter of Human Rights and Responsibilities Act 2006* (Vic), neither gives individuals the right to bring complaints about breaches of human rights before the courts.

[71] See, eg, in this collection: *Dietrich v R* on the right to a fair trial; *R v Pearson; Ex parte Sipka* on the right to vote; *Re Minister for Immigration and Multicultural and Indigenous Affairs; Ex parte Applicants S134/2002* and *Appellant S395/2002* on the rights of refugees; *Kartinyeri v The Commonwealth* on Indigenous rights under cultural heritage legislation.

on the Indigenous people.[72] For over two centuries, the concept of *terra nullius*, or 'land belonging to no one', was used to justify dispossession and disregard of Indigenous sovereignty and laws. It was not until 1992, in the *Mabo* case,[73] that the concept of *terra nullius* was formally exposed by the High Court as a legal fiction. At the time, the *Mabo* decision seemed to open up new opportunities for the recognition of Indigenous sovereignty in Australia; however, successive attempts to achieve formal recognition through the courts have failed.[74] This history has encouraged some, like Aileen Moreton-Robinson, to reimagine notions of Indigenous sovereignty as separate from the political state, a project that is as yet unfinished.[75] This collection of feminist judgments includes a number of cases that speak to the unresolved relationship between Indigenous peoples and the white legal system in regards to legal issues including land rights, discrimination and criminal justice.[76]

Despite its Indigenous history, Australia is often described as a 'nation of immigrants'. Between 1945 (when immigration statistics began to be kept in Australia) and 2010, around seven million people settled in Australia.[77] The 2011 Census records that over one quarter of Australia's population was born overseas, with a further one fifth having at least one overseas-born parent.[78] Although Australia has a long history of, and economic reliance on, immigration, each year people who seek asylum in Australia are confronted by ever more punitive government approaches to refugee policy. Refugee cases have often become the subject of intense media and public scrutiny, and continue to attract controversy. Given this history, and present context, we recognised that it was important that an Australian collection include feminist judgments that address the impact of Australian laws on asylum-seekers.[79]

The collection also includes cases reflecting the diversity of federal jurisdiction, including tax law, environmental law, consumer law, family law and anti-discrimination law.

A Collaborative Approach

The idea of an Australian feminist judgments project was first discussed at a feminist legal theory reading group in Brisbane in 2010. Some of those present saw the project as an

[72] Around 2.5 per cent of Australians identify as Indigenous, and yet Indigenous people have a disproportionate level of contact with punitive legal systems in Australia: 26 per cent of people in custody are Indigenous people and Indigenous children are eight times more likely that other children to be removed from their families under child protection orders: Australian Human Rights Commission, *Face the Facts* (2012), ch 1 <http://www.humanrights.gov.au/publications/face-facts-2012/2012-face-facts-chapter-1>.

[73] *Mabo v Queensland (No 2)* (1992) 175 CLR 1 ('*Mabo*').

[74] Heather Douglas and Mark Finnane, *Indigenous Crime and Settler Law: White Sovereignty After Empire* (Palgrave Macmillan, 2012) 149–59; Phillip Falk and Gary Martin, 'Misconstruing Indigenous Sovereignty: Maintaining the Fabric of Australian Law' in Aileen Moreton-Robinson (ed), *Sovereign Subjects: Indigenous Sovereignty Matters* (Allen and Unwin, 2007) 33; Larissa Behrendt, 'The Power we Bring: Indigenous Sovereignty and Self-Determination in the Treaty Process' (2002) 5 *Balayi: Culture Law and Colonisation* 1.

[75] Aileen Moreton-Robinson, 'Writing off Indigenous Sovereignty' in Moreton-Robinson, ibid, 101–2.

[76] See: *Kartinyeri v The Commonwealth; ACCC v Keshow; In the matter of Djappari (Re Tuckiar); R v Morgan*; and *McLeod v Power* in this collection.

[77] Janet Phillips, Michael Klapdoor and Joanne Simon-Davies, 'Migration to Australia since Federation: A Guide to the Statistics' (Background Note, Parliamentary Library, Parliament of Australia, 2010) 2.

[78] Australian Bureau of Statistics, *Reflecting a Nation: Stories from the 2011 Census, 2012–2013* (2012) <http://www.abs.gov.au/ausstats/abs@.nsf/Lookup/2071.0main+features902012-2013>.

[79] See *Applicants S134/2002* and *Appellant S395/2002* in this collection.

opportunity to engage Australian academics interested in feminist theory in a collaborative project. A general invitation to an initial meeting was issued to feminist legal academics, women's legal services and legal practitioners, and around 25 academics and lawyers attended the first workshop in Brisbane in 2010. There was an enthusiastic response to the idea of creating a collection of Australian feminist judgments and, after successfully applying to the Australian Research Council for funds to support the project,[80] the next step was to elicit judgments appropriate for rewriting. Generally, participants came forward with judgments they wanted to rewrite. However, we were keen to ensure that we included cases from a wide variety of legal fields and some authors were specifically contacted and invited to rewrite a judgment in a particular area of law. Feminist academics with specific expertise were also contacted and invited to write commentaries for some cases. From the beginning, commentary and judgment writers were asked to work collaboratively, by discussing their approach to the task and providing feedback to each other along the way.

One of the challenges faced in Australia when co-ordinating a national project is the size of the country and the immense distances between us. Unfortunately, unlike the English project, participants were not all able to meet together at any single time. Despite the problem of distance, we are pleased that the project contributors are fairly geographically representative and include participants from Victoria, South Australia, New South Wales, Queensland and the Australian Capital Territory.[81] In order to bring participants together, once cases and commentary writers were identified, we held workshops on judgment-writing in Melbourne, Sydney and Brisbane. Participants, and their associated cases, were divided geographically rather than thematically, and everyone involved was asked to attend a workshop. Conscious that most of the judgment-writers are academics and therefore were unlikely to have experience in judgment-writing,[82] two or three currently serving feminist judges were invited to the workshops in each city to share their expertise and insights about judgment-writing. In particular, they were invited to comment on the craft and constraints of writing decisions. At the end of these workshops, the insights of the judicial decision-makers were collated and disseminated to project participants.

The judges who presented at the workshops identified several points that underline the differences between academic writing and judgment-writing. Notably, they emphasised that a judgment is not abstract and its content is likely to have a direct effect on the parties' lives. In this way, they stressed the importance of placing the people involved in the dispute at the centre of the decision. Some talked about the need to take care of parties, by being respectful of them, observing that the way the story is represented in the judgment is important in this regard.[83] The therapeutic potential of judgments was also highlighted, with some observing that a judgment may be able to provide solace to the party who has failed, acknowledge suffering,[84] or congratulate a victim of sexual assault for her courage in

[80] ARC Discovery Projects Grant: *Australian Feminist Judgments Project: Jurisprudence as Praxis* (DP 120102375).

[81] We actively sought participants from Tasmania, Western Australia and the Northern Territory, but ultimately were unsuccessful.

[82] Although one retired judge was involved and some other participants had experience in writing tribunal decisions.

[83] See, eg, Lisa Sarmas, 'Storytelling and the Law: A Case Study of *Louth v Diprose*' (1994) 19 *Melbourne University Law Review* 701.

[84] See, eg, Baroness Hale in *R (on the application of Gentle) v Prime Minister* [2008] UKHL 20 (where she expressed sympathy with mothers of soldiers killed in the Iraq war). On empathy and judges, see also Mitchell Crusto, 'Empathetic Dialogue: From Formalism to Value Principles' (2012) 65 *Southern Methodist Law Review* 845.

reporting the assaults.[85] Importantly, a judgment must ultimately result in a decision or orders; this clearly differentiates it from the rigours of critique associated with academic writing. Some judges conflated feminism with general principles of fairness as expressed in the judicial oath.[86] It was also suggested that while a feminist approach may not be explicitly identifiable in a judgment, it may nevertheless inform the judgment because the judge's background, personality, personal experience and world view have a particular influence in relation to fact-finding and assessments of credibility. In this way, a feminist judge perceives facts from a feminist perspective.[87]

There was significant discussion at the workshops about whether additional cases which were not cited in the original judgment could be discussed in the rewritten judgment, as well as the approach to referencing extrinsic or contextual material.[88] Generally, judges referred to the fair hearing rule,[89] that if a judge is going to refer to material not raised in submissions, it should be put to both parties so that they have the opportunity to comment. It was recognised that legal decision-makers must tread a fine line on the matter of judicial notice or statements of accepted social facts, with the suggestion that material such as research findings from academic literature could sometimes actually be introduced, but without acknowledgement of source.[90] The way the judgment-writers ultimately dealt with these issues is discussed in Chapter 2.

The judges who presented at the workshops also emphasised that writers should write simply and clearly: use short sentences and avoid the passive voice. One judge summarised this approach as the KISS principle: keep it short and simple.[91] The same judge suggested this could be adjusted to 'keep it simple sister' for the purposes of the project![92]

After the workshops, writers worked on their judgments alone or in collaboration with one or more other writers.[93] In many cases, authors closely collaborated with their

[85] 'A judge should never cause unnecessary hurt', Australasian Institute of Judicial Administration, *Guide to Judicial Conduct* (AIJA, 2nd ed, 2007) 19.

[86] See, eg, the Schedule to the *High Court of Australia Act 1979* (Cth): judges swear that 'I will do right to all manner of people according to law without fear or favour, affection or ill-will. . .'.

[87] Regina Graycar has emphasised the pivotal role of fact-framing in judicial decision-making: see 'The Gender of Judgments: Some Reflections on "Bias"' (1998) 32 *University of British Columbia Law Review* 1, 10–11. Justice Ruth McColl has referred to the 'subconscious factors' and 'underlying philosophy of life' that affect judicial decision-making, even though they may remain unnamed: see Justice Ruth McColl, 'The Art of Judging' (2008) 12 *Southern Cross University Law Review* 43, 51. The Hon Michael Kirby has noted also that 'hidden away in language may be a world of inappropriate attitudes and prejudice': see Michael Kirby, 'On the Writing of Judgments' (1990) 64 *Australian Law Journal* 691, 702–3.

[88] We explore these issues further in Ch 2.

[89] See generally *Antoun v R* (2006) 224 ALR 51.

[90] The issue of judges introducing their own materials into their decision-making has emerged as an important issue in recent Australian scholarship: see, eg, Zoe Rathus, 'A Call for Clarity in the Use of Social Science Research in Family Law Decision-Making' (2012) 26 *Australian Journal of Family Law* 81; Kylie Burns, 'The Way the World Is: Social Facts in High Court Negligence Cases' (2004) 12 *Torts Law Journal* 215; Kylie Burns, 'The Australian High Court and Social Facts: A Content Analysis Study' (2012) 40 *Federal Law Review* 317. Note also that the issue is not a new one – Smyth points out that Windeyer J was responsible for half of the citations to secondary sources during the 1960s High Court: see Russell Smyth, 'Other Than "Accepted Sources of Law"? A Quantitative Study of Secondary Source Citations in the High Court' (1999) 22 *University of New South Wales Law Journal* 19, 36.

[91] On the value of simplicity, see Kirby, above n 87, 705.

[92] Keeping judgments short is a particularly modern concern resulting from word processing, which allows large swathes of text to be copied and pasted from one place to another, as well as the increasing demands of the appeal process: see Matthew Groves and Russell Smyth, 'A Century of Judicial Style: Changing Patterns in Judgment Writing on the High Court 1903–2001' (2004) 32 *Federal Law Review* 255, 259–65; John Doyle, 'Judgment Writing: Are There Needs for Change?' (1999) 73 *Australian Law Journal* 737, 740.

[93] Six judgments were co-written: *R v Morgan; R v Taikato; Dietrich v R; Goode and Goode; PGA v R; R v Webster*; and in one case, written by a team of three: *R v Middendorp*.

commentary writer to ensure that, as far as possible, significant matters were covered. After authors completed their first drafts, all judgments and commentaries were subject to peer review. All work for the project was circulated to other participants for comment and extensive feedback was provided by the editors of the collection. A final set of workshops took place in Melbourne, Sydney and Brisbane in 2013, attended by the authors, as well as a retired judge.[94] In these workshops, we reality-tested each judgment and commentary chapter, and participants debated issues arising from them. Detailed written feedback was provided to all authors to assist them in preparing final drafts.

The authors were asked to write alternative feminist judgments under the same constraints that would have applied to the original decision-makers. They were asked to apply the law and theoretical knowledge available at the time the original judgment was written. Thus, the majority of the feminist judgments that appear in this collection,[95] could, at least theoretically, have been written at the time of the original judgment. We say 'theoretically' because the authors had arguable advantages that were not available to the original decision-makers. They had the obvious benefit of hindsight, in addition to being able to write on an area of particular academic interest on which many of them had been working for years. The authors also had up to two years to write their judgments, and thus did not write under the time constraints that usually affect working judges.[96] They were, however, subject to an intensive editing process and tight word-limit constraints.[97] While these points of difference may suggest inauthenticity, they may equally be considered to provide a firm foundation for legal decision-making. The feminist judgment authors had time, expertise, iterative feedback and strong encouragement to write in an economical and focused way, and so, it might be argued, could get the judgment 'right'.[98]

The Structure of the Book

Introductory Chapters

This chapter and the following chapter introduce and provide background to the feminist judgments. In this chapter, we locate the judgments within the literature on women judges, judicial diversity and feminist judging; outline the context and methodology for the Australian Feminist Judgments Project; and suggest ways in which the judgments may be used in legal education and legal and judicial practice. In Chapter 2 we draw on the reflections of the judgment authors to explore particular challenges they encountered in writing

[94] The Honourable Sally Brown also provided extensive review and feedback to authors on the final drafts of judgments and commentaries.

[95] Excluding *ACCC v Keshow* and *In the matter of Djappari (Re Tuckiar)*.

[96] Kathy Mack, Sharyn L Roach Anleu and Anne Wallace, 'Everyday Work in the Magistrates Courts: Time and Tasks' (2011) 21 *Journal of Judicial Administration* 34; see also Jason Payne, *Criminal Trial Delays in Australia: Trial Listing Outcomes* (Australian Institute of Criminology, 2007).

[97] Judgment-writers were asked to limit their contribution to 5000 words or less, and commentary writers to 2000 words or less.

[98] In the next chapter we describe what the judgment-writers said about their own work and the process of writing. Many of the authors indicated that the main task they saw themselves performing was correcting the law, in the sense that the original judgment had misapplied a statute or extended a principle incorrectly.

judgments and how those challenges were addressed. The chapter goes on to analyse the strategies adopted by the authors to rewrite existing cases from a feminist perspective.

Judgments

This collection includes 24 feminist judgments which are explicit rewritings of original cases and one essay by Irene Watson who explains why it was not possible to write a feminist judgment in the case of *Kartinyeri v The Commonwealth of Australia.*[99]

The collection draws on cases decided in a range of Australian jurisdictions and at various levels of the court hierarchy. It includes cases decided in the High Court, Federal Court, Family Court and the various state courts including Supreme Courts and Courts of Appeal. While the majority of cases were decided in the appellate jurisdiction of the High Court and Courts of Appeal, where judges usually sit together in groups of three or more, the collection also includes some single judge decisions. In the former cases, the author offers an extra voice on the court and in the latter cases, the author offers an alternative judgment. Although the context of federation in Australia may be expected to result in a collection of jurisdictionally specific judgments, most (17) of the judgments are decisions of the High Court which have precedent value throughout Australia, and four relate to issues of federal jurisdiction. Three sentencing cases rewrite state court decisions, but the feminist strategy they employ – of focusing on context and putting the victim's voice back into the judgment – could equally be applied in sentencing decisions in any jurisdiction. The final state court decision is a discrimination case – an area of shared federal and state jurisdiction – and again, the feminist strategy of interpreting the legislation purposively is equally applicable to discrimination cases anywhere.

The project intentionally sought out judgments not only in different courts, but also in different areas of law. In considering how law is taught, Graycar has lamented that 'most of the courses . . . accept and reproduce existing (but I would argue) artificial doctrinal boundaries. So we all recognize as "women's issues" sexual assault and family law, but not tax.'[100] With Graycar's comments in mind, the collection covers not only topics of long-standing interest to feminist scholars, such as family law, sexual offences and discrimination law, but also areas which have had less attention, including equity, immigration, taxation and environmental law.[101] The book is divided into four sections: public law, including cases in the areas of constitutional law, tax law, immigration law and environmental law; private law, including torts, consumer protection and equity; crime and evidence, including sentencing decisions; and interpreting equality, including family law, discrimination law and treaty law – the latter being an invented category for the future imagined by Nicole Watson in her judgment in *In the matter of Djappari (Re Tuckiar)*. While we acknowledge that traditional divisions of legal knowledge, specifically the public/private divide, have been subject to considerable feminist critique, we have adopted this structure in the hope that it will make the book easy to access for researchers, students and practitioners of law. We consider the

[99] (1998) 195 CLR 337.

[100] Regina Graycar, '"To Transform the Normative Tradition of Law. . .": A Comment on the Feminist Project in the Law School' (1986) 58 *The Australian Quarterly* 366, 369. See also Jenny Morgan, *Who Kills Whom and Why: Looking Beyond Legal Categories* (Occasional Paper, Victorian Law Reform Commission, 2002).

[101] See the Introduction in Graycar and Morgan, above n 15, for a discussion about the role of legal categories in constructing women's lives.

broad coverage of subject areas represented by the judgments to be a particular strength of the collection which indicates the extensive scope for feminist judgment-writing.

The collection includes decisions spanning 80 years, from the case of *Tuckiar v R*, originally heard in 1934 (but reimagined here as *In the Matter of Djaparri (Re Tuckiar)* and heard in 2035)[102] to the recent High Court case of *PGA v R*,[103] decided in 2012. While it was our aim to attract cases on a variety of areas of law, there was particularly strong interest from project participants in rewriting criminal law and evidence cases – areas classically of interest to feminist legal scholars – and there are eight cases in the collection that traverse this field.

Fittingly, the collection begins and ends with contributions by Indigenous authors. In the first chapter, Irene Watson points to the impossibility of an Indigenous feminist rewriting of a judgment about Indigenous knowledge within a white legal framework. Ending the collection, Nicole Watson provides scope for optimism with a futuristic vision of a new model of justice in an imagined First Nations Court of Australia, a court which 'critique[s] decisions that have had significant impacts on the ability of Aboriginal and Torres Strait Islander people to exercise their right to legal equality'.[104]

Commentaries

Each judgment is preceded by a chapter which provides commentary on the case. We deliberately sought additional authors to write these chapters, so that they could provide a critical perspective on the judgments. Writing the commentary chapter presented a more traditional academic task. The authors analyse the original judgment and examine and critique the relevant law. They also place the case in its social, policy and legal context, and consider how the original judgment was received, as well as the issues it was thought to raise at the time. Commentary chapters also consider what the feminist judgment does differently and the contribution the feminist judgment makes to the development of the law and feminist jurisprudence. These chapters aim to render the case and the feminist judgment accessible to non-specialist readers, including students or others not familiar with a particular area of law. We encourage readers of this collection to read the commentary chapter and judgment together. However, of themselves, the commentary chapters provide original scholarly appraisals of the law.

Applications and Implications

The process of rewriting existing legal judgments as feminist judgments is clearly an instructive activity which indicates that feminist approaches to legal decision-making may be learnt. Sexist attitudes among the judiciary are inculcated, inter alia, in the law school.[105] From the period of second-wave feminism in the 1970s, feminist legal scholars have endeavoured to challenge liberal legal ideologies of objectivity and neutrality. By the 1980s,

[102] (1934) 52 CLR 335.
[103] (2012) 245 CLR 355.
[104] *In the matter of Djaparri (Re Tuckiar)* [2035] FNCA 1.
[105] Australian Law Reform Commission, *Equality Before the Law: Women's Equality* (Report No 69, 1994) 91.

stand-alone feminist jurisprudence courses along the lines of 'Women and the Law' began to emerge in a number of Australian law schools.[106] However, by the end of the century, Rachael Field found that there had been 'virtually no progress' in the inclusion of subjects addressing issues for women and the law, suggesting that 'we seem to have gone backwards'.[107] In interviews conducted with legal academics in the mid-2000s in Britain, Canada, New Zealand and Australia, Margaret Thornton heard that women law students rejected feminism on instrumental grounds. She reported that they no longer wanted the word 'feminist' to appear on their transcripts, in case it might interfere with their employment prospects, observing that:

> [L]egal academics everywhere have recounted how merely mentioning the 'F-word' in class is enough for students to sigh and put down their pens. Feminism, the students believe, belonged to their mothers' generation and it had nothing to say to them. Furthermore, 'it was not going to be in the exam'![108]

Despite this discouraging state of affairs, feminist judgments projects in Canada and the United Kingdom have contributed to the reinvigoration of interest and engagement with feminism in legal education. In Canada, Jennifer Koshan and colleagues have reported on the value of teaching using some of the Women's Court of Canada decisions, particularly as a way of introducing feminist analysis into law school classes.[109] In the United Kingdom, an issue of the journal *The Law Teacher* is devoted to articles which reflect on the critical contribution of feminist judgments as teaching resources to be used in law school classrooms.[110] For example, Rosemary Auchmuty considers the role for feminist judgments in a core LLB subject in property law. She observes that most students do not take optional units in gender and the law, and emphasises the importance of including a consideration of 'the role of law in perpetuating gender (and other) inequities' in a core LLB module.[111] She also emphasises the importance of reading case reports, noting that 'good lawyers need to be able to read and *understand* cases', and yet increasingly students do not read cases.[112] Auchmuty's answer to these challenges was to set writing an alternative judgment as assessment for her students, and to use the English collection of judgments as a set of examples students could emulate, rather than focusing on a specific case.[113] Auchmuty believed that this approach would introduce students to new ideas, and help students to read cases as well as learn legal rules and problem-solving techniques.

Feminist judgments might also be used in legal theory modules.[114] Caroline Hunter and

[106] Margaret Thornton, 'The Development of Feminist Jurisprudence' (1998) 9 *Legal Education Review* 171, 172; Rachael Field, 'Women in the Law School Curriculum: Equality is About More than Just Access' (1999) 10 *Legal Education Review* 141, 147.

[107] Field, ibid, 144–5.

[108] Thornton, above n 17, 95.

[109] Jennifer Koshan et al, 'Rewriting Equality: The Pedagogical Use of Women's Court of Canada Judgments' (2010) 4 *Canadian Legal Education Annual Review* 121.

[110] *The Law Teacher* (2012) 46(3). The English project website also includes various teaching resources that could be adapted for use with the Australian feminist judgments in this book: Feminist Judgments Project, 'Teaching Resources' <http://www.kent.ac.uk/law/fjp/resources/teaching.html#resources>. See also Rosemary Hunter, 'Feminist Judgments as Teaching Resources' (2012) 2(5) *Onati Socio-Legal Series* 47.

[111] Rosemary Auchmuty, 'Using Feminist Judgments in the Property Law Classroom' (2012) 46 *The Law Teacher* 227, 227.

[112] Ibid 231.

[113] Ibid 229; Feminist Judgments Project, above n 110.

[114] Feminist Judgments Project, 'The Feminist Judgments Project in the Classroom' <http://www.kent.ac.uk/law/fjp/resources/classroom.html>.

Ben Fitzpatrick consider the role of the English collection of feminist judgments in a legal philosophy module that seeks to 'link theoretical principles and lived experiences of law'.[115] Cases are one of the key resources used in the module and feminist judging is included in a final section of the module called 'Critical Accounts of Law'.[116] As part of this module, students are asked to read a case and associated academic commentary and consider what a feminist voice can bring to judging. While the authors have not, so far, used judgments from the English project in their course, they suggest that a feminist judgment could be used in conjunction with the original case.[117]

Hunter has identified three ways in which rewritten judgments from the English project have been used as teaching resources.[118] First, they demonstrate how feminist theoretical ideas can be applied in the practice of legal decision-making. As she points out, students who are sceptical about whether this leads to bias or incoherence, or indeed whether it is actually possible, are able to see for themselves the ways a feminist judicial practice may be performed. Secondly, feminist judgments can be used to provoke critical thinking about judicial decision-making by 'exposing the contingency of the decisions made', highlighting judicial techniques of persuasion and the choices made in the construction of the 'facts' of the case, in this way directing students to reflect upon the relationship between the narrative and the facts.[119] Thirdly, feminist rewritten judgments can usefully be used to provoke critical thinking about the particular decision made, opening up the space for discussion of a different development of jurisprudence and suggesting the possibility of new directions in the common law.[120]

While this literature reflects a flourishing interest in the use of feminist judgments in legal education, such projects and publications also have a potential role to play in professional and judicial education. A presentation on the English Feminist Judgments Project at an International Association of Women Judges conference in London in 2012 attracted a large audience and lively debate. We have been encouraged by the interest expressed by members of the Australian judiciary in the Australian project, and hope that for practising lawyers and judges, this book will also be of value in demonstrating how case preparation, submissions and judgments may be done differently and in ways that are more sensitive and inclusive.

There is clearly a flourishing scholarship around feminist judging and the need for a diverse judiciary. This book contributes to both of these projects. The central aim of this project, as of other projects before it,[121] is law reform. As explored further in the following chapter, the feminist judgments in this collection rewrite law in order to right it.

[115] Caroline Hunter and Ben Fitzpatrick, 'Feminist Judging and Legal Theory' (2012) 46 *The Law Teacher* 255, 256.

[116] Ibid 259.

[117] Ibid 263.

[118] Rosemary Hunter, 'Introduction: Feminist Judgments as Teaching Resources' (2012) 46 *The Law Teacher* 214, 219.

[119] Ibid 220.

[120] Ibid.

[121] Hunter, McGlynn and Rackley, above n 7, 8.

2

Reflections on Rewriting the Law

HEATHER DOUGLAS, FRANCESCA BARTLETT,
TRISH LUKER and ROSEMARY HUNTER

In this chapter we draw on interviews undertaken with the authors of the feminist judgments in this collection to present both an overview of, and their reflections on, the judgments collected here. We consider the challenges the writers encountered and how they overcame those challenges and the strategies used to write feminist judgments in existing cases.

We conducted semi-structured interviews with the majority of the writers of the feminist judgments shortly after the final version of their judgment was submitted to us. In the interviews we aimed to capture the immediate reflections of the authors about how they approached the task of rewriting.

In the first part of this chapter we consider three of the challenges the writers commonly told us they grappled with in their writing process: the need to reach a decision; finding their judicial voice; and how, or whether, to refer to background information, such as academic writing and social facts, explicitly in their decisions.

In the second part of the chapter we consider the strategies used by the authors to write their feminist judgments. Many of the strategies adopted are similar to those employed by writers involved in the English Feminist Judgments Project and outlined by Rosemary Hunter in her analyses of feminist judging.[1] While we consider how the writers involved in the Australian project employ these previously observed strategies, there are two distinctive features of the Australian project which we also explore. The first is the invocation of legal formalism as feminist method. The second concerns the diverse and compelling ways Indigenous women have engaged with the rewriting process.

Challenges in Rewriting Judgments

The Need to Reach a Decision

Chief Justice French of the High Court of Australia has recently explained the distinctive role of judgment:

[1] Rosemary Hunter, Clare McGlynn and Erika Rackley (eds), *Feminist Judgments: From Theory to Practice* (Hart Publishing, 2010); Rosemary Hunter, 'Can *Feminist* Judges Make a Difference?' (2008) 15 *International Journal of the Legal Profession* 7; Rosemary Hunter, 'An Account of Feminist Judging' in Hunter, McGlynn and Rackley (eds), ibid; Rosemary Hunter, 'Justice Marcia Neave: Case Study of a Feminist Judge' in Ulrike Schultz and Gisela Shaw (eds), *Gender and Judging* (Hart Publishing, 2013). See also Ch 1 of this volume.

> It is an important feature of the judicial process that its focus is always upon the determination of the matter before the court. Where a judge writes reasons for decision he or she writes them by way of explanation for the decision in the particular case. A judge is not required to travel further than is necessary in order to determine the case.[2]

In judgment-writing, a judge must determine the case. She must make orders and dispose of arguments. In contrast, there is no requirement for scholarly writing to decide or to offer particular solutions to legal problems.[3] Academic critique can suggest alternatives and qualified conclusions. There is a significant difference between how academics and judges speak and make claims to truth.[4] Almost all of the writers involved in this project were academics, and some reported to us that they struggled with the requirement of making a decision.[5] While in a number of cases interviewees told us they knew what they would decide from the outset, others said that they tried to work through the law to its conclusion – a process that meant they did not know if they would, or could, decide as they hoped. Perhaps most compellingly, in *PGA v R* the feminist judgment decided *against* the complainant in relation to an accusation of rape within marriage. In this case the writers believed the law took them in a certain direction. The writers explained that one of the reasons they selected *PGA v R* was that it tested the limits of the common law. Mary Heath explained:

> [*PGA v R*] is a really rather poignant case from a feminist perspective, in that there are so many issues for feminists in here about what the complainant might hope for and what you might hope for her, to the impact on our understanding of the feminist activism of the 1970s, and so on.

In this case, the feminist judges highlighted the feminist activism which had inspired reform of the law to remove the common law immunity held by husbands who had raped their wives. However, this reform occurred after the rape alleged by the woman before the court. They found that the prosecution of a husband for the rape of his wife in the 1960s could not be sustained. The writers did not want to forget the woman involved or those women who had experienced similar sexual violence within their marriages and could not access the criminal law, and they took the unusual approach of giving an apology for the gendered violence perpetrated by the common law for so long.

Academics often work in the abstract in relation to a case, frequently critiquing the decided case with a view to influencing future legislation and decisions. In contrast, for a judge, the parties in a case demand a resolution of the specific conflict between them on the basis of a particular set of available legal arguments and evidence. They often have conflicting, but also compelling, arguments to make. Jennifer Nielsen reflected on these difficulties inherent in writing a judgment, observing that there was a

> complex set of interests that had to be met in writing one judgment. [This] was really quite illuminating I think, because it… put a lot of decisions in a different context to how you might assume – how I might have assumed – that they'd been drawn.

Nan Seuffert reported that, as an academic, she had been frustrated with the courts' limited approach to deciding asylum-seeker cases and the failure of judges to consider and

[2] Chief Justice Robert French, 'Judges and Academics: Dialogue of the Hard of Hearing' (2013) 87 *Australian Law Journal* 96, 101.

[3] Rosemary Hunter, Clare McGlynn and Erika Rackley, 'Feminist Judgments: An Introduction' in Hunter, McGlynn and Rackley (eds), above n 1, 17.

[4] Ibid 15.

[5] We note that a number of writers in this collection have been or are decision-makers, some sit on tribunals and one is a retired judge.

acknowledge feminist scholarship. However, after writing her judgment she explained she had

> a new appreciation for judges and what they have to do and the difficulty of being a feminist judge which we know theoretically, but maybe not so much in practice. We read the cases and we think oh, this is so limited compared to everything we know about this topic, and so little of feminist work has gotten into that judgment and why is that and why does it seem so narrow. I really have a new appreciation, I think, for the task . . . and for the limitations of the genre.

Most of the feminist judgments included in this collection come to a different conclusion to the original case or to the majority judgment.[6] In seven cases,[7] however, the feminist judgment-writers agree with the outcome of the original decision but take the opportunity to provide a different account of the facts or to adopt another understanding of applicable legal principle, or both. Lady Hale of the United Kingdom Supreme Court has observed that concurrences are a commonplace in the common law system, where a 'preference for plurality judgments would not rule out certain sorts of concurring judgment, which can enhance rather than detract from the power of the lead judgment'.[8] For example, Adrian Howe's feminist judgment in *Parker v R* concurs with the majority decision, which was later overruled by the Privy Council. Her emphasis on the historical development of the provocation defence through an examination of the precedents arguably strengthens the majority judgment. She explained: 'When the majority judgment, which I think was correct, was overruled in the Privy Council, it revealed that division within judicial thinking over time between taking a hard line and a soft excusatory line on provocation.'

Kylie Burns' judgment in *Cattanach v Melchior* also concurred with the majority, but her judgment provided an opportunity to address a gap in the majority reasoning in relation to whether pregnancy is a form of economic loss, or some other form of damage or harm. This again may be said to strengthen the majority judgment:

> In fact, when you read the case as a whole, there actually isn't a majority on whether . . . the kind of damage she suffered was economic or not. It's kind of left a little bit open. It's yes in some opinions, no in others, maybe. So for me that kind of damage is just not pure economic loss. It's clearly consequential and I think that has a feminist aspect to it. The disconnection of these damages, particularly related to women, from the harm is a feminist issue. So part of the judgment was talking about that aspect of it.

Nevertheless, not all concurrences have this effect. For example, Lisa Sarmas' judgment in *Trustees of the Property of Cummins v Cummins* (*Cummins*) is highly critical of the majority's reasoning in developing new principles of trust law. Jennifer Nielsen's judgment in *McLeod v Power* takes the opposite view from the original judgment on a key point of interpretation of racial vilification legislation. And while the feminist judge in *R v Webster*

[6] *Dietrich v R*; *Goode and Goode*; *JM v QFG & GK*; *Lodge v Federal Commissioner of Taxation*; *Louth v Diprose*; *Phillips v R*; *PGA v R*; *Re Minister for Immigration and Multicultural and Indigenous Affairs & Anor; Ex parte Applicants S134/2002*; *R v Middendorp*; *R v Morgan*; *R v Pearson*; *Ex parte Sipka*; *R v Taikato*; *RPS v R*; *State of New South Wales v Amery*; *U v U*; *Wildlife Preservation Society of Queensland Proserpine/Whitsunday Branch Inc v Minister for the Environment & Heritage & Ors.*

[7] *ACCC v Keshow*; *Appellant S395/2002 v Minister for Immigration and Multicultural Affairs*; *Cattanach v Melchior*; *McLeod v Power*; *Parker v R*; *R v Webster*; *Trustees of the Property of Cummins v Cummins.*

[8] Brenda Hale, 'Judgment Writing in the Supreme Court' (Paper presented at the Supreme Court First Anniversary Seminar, London, 30 September 2010) 4. See also in the Australian context Matthew Groves and Russell Smyth, 'A Century of Judicial Style: Changing Patterns in Judgment Writing on the High Court 1903–2001' (2004) 32 *Federal Law Review* 255, 275.

imposes the same sentence on the offender, her narration of the facts tells the victim's story and analyses the offender's actions quite differently from the original sentencing judgment.

Finding a Judicial Voice

Former High Court Justice Michael Kirby has observed that

> judges, with gifts of communication, writing in a simple, straightforward and 'magisterial' style tend to have the greatest influence because of their clarity of expression. On the other hand, rhetoric and the use of vivid phrases play an important part in persuasion.[9]

Australian judicial officers have often considered the question of what is an appropriate judicial voice,[10] and have tended to emphasise the importance of brevity and clarity of writing style,[11] as well as transparent reasoning.[12] Often, judges have described the task as an 'art'.[13] The persuasive and authoritative tone adopted in judgments is arguably quite different from the qualified approach of scholarly writing.

We asked interviewees to reflect on the question of judicial voice. A number of interviewees explained that maintaining the judicial voice was very difficult. In the workshops, participants often noticed where a judgment-writer had been equivocal in how they dealt with a point or that they had discussed an issue in the abstract without relating it to the issue at hand. Some of the writers commented specifically on the intellectual shift they had to make in order to write in a judicial voice. For example, in rewriting *PGA v R*, Wendy Larcombe observed:

> I think we realised [the difference] between the judicial voice and the academic voice. Initially we were wanting to work with the more familiar academic voice, in which you're used to bringing forward a lot of support for the propositions that you're putting forward. We had to cut that. As a result, the judicial voice sounds much more individualised.

Jennifer Nielsen explained that it was only in the second draft of her judgment in *McLeod v Power* that she found her voice. She explained:

> I started in my mind with an exercise of trying to actually rewrite [the original] judgment instead of writing my own judgment fresh. I probably followed it a little bit too much and I don't think I let my own voice come through as well as I should have in the original draft. But I was mindful of that in the redraft, in the second drafting, and this process to try and make my own voice the voice instead of the original message.

[9] Michael Kirby, 'On the Writing of Judgments' (1990) 64 *Australian Law Journal* 691, 705.

[10] See, eg, Ruth McColl, 'The Art of Judging' (2008) 12 *Southern Cross University Law Review* 43; Sir Frank Kitto, 'Why Write Judgments?' (1992) 66 *Australian Law Journal* 787; Sir Harry Gibbs, 'Judgment Writing' (1993) 67 *Australian Law Journal* 494; Sir Laurence Street, 'The Writing of Judgments: A Forum' (1992) 9 *Australian Bar Review* 130; LJ Priestley, 'The Writing of Judgments: A Forum' (1992) 9 *Australian Bar Review* 130; John Doyle, 'Judgment Writing: Are There Needs for Change?' (1999) 73 *Australian Law Journal* 737.

[11] Gibbs, ibid; Justice Susan Kiefel, 'Reasons for Judgment: Objects and Observations' (Speech delivered at the Sir Harry Gibbs Law Dinner, Queensland, 18 May 2012).

[12] See also Justice Roslyn Atkinson, 'Judgment Writing' (Speech delivered to Queensland Civil and Administrative Tribunal members, Brisbane, 6 February 2010).

[13] Lord Hope, 'Writing Judgments' (Speech delivered at the Judicial Studies Board Annual Lecture, London, 16 March 2005), cited in Erika Rackley, 'The Art and Craft of Writing Judgments' in Hunter, McGlynn and Rackley (eds), above n 1, 44. See also Kitto, above n 10, in which he laments that there is no formula that makes writing judgments easier as a judge matures.

In trying to find their own voice, several writers referred to judgments they admired or judges they thought wrote well. For example, in rewriting the judgment in *Cattanach v Melchior*, Kylie Burns explained:

> I was particularly influenced by . . . Lady Justice Hale, as she then was: some of the cases . . . where she'd written these beautiful, strong, feminist judgments in a kind of voice that I quite liked. I quite like the Kirby voice too. So I was thinking about [them] on the way through. I'd read examples of what I thought was quite good and I knew the ones I really didn't like too, from reading a lot . . . of close analysing of High Court cases.

In rewriting *Phillips v R*, Annie Cossins observed that she was influenced by the judgments of Canadian judges such as Justice Beverley McLachlin and Madame Justice Claire L'Heureux-Dubé, as she reflected:

> It was really about the voice . . . Of course, one has a voice. When you write anything, you have a voice, but that really made me think about, well, whose voice do I want to have? That's why I chose those Canadian judges. They were sitting on my shoulder. I still don't think I was as radical as them, or as eloquent.

In her rewriting of *R v Taikato*, Isabella Alexander explained she wanted to 'channel Lord Denning' because 'for all his failings' his 'narrative style of judgment brought people along with him and it was persuasive writing'. She observed that she saw the opportunity to rewrite a judgment as a law reform or legally persuasive exercise, where a conciliatory voice was adopted to 'bring everyone along', from academics to judges.

While judgment-writing may be described as an art of persuasion, many interviewees also emphasised the restraint needed in the judicial voice. For example, Anita Stuhmcke recounted that she initially had an angry reaction to the case of *JM v QFG & GK* – a case involving a lesbian couple's access to assisted reproductive technology – when it was handed down. She reflected:

> [I]t would have been really nice somewhere in that judgment just to say really what one thinks. But I mean whether that [was] the parameters of the project or the judicial voice that was adopted, it can't be done. So . . . in some ways the ranting that I had originally is still locked up deep inside me.

Several writers found adopting the judicial position empowering and liberating, because it was an opportunity to use a different language in writing the decision. Danielle Tyson, one of the authors of the sentencing judgment *R v Middendorp*, reflected on the powerful effect of judgments and of the language employed in a judgment:

> I wanted the judgment to be written not necessarily in the third person, so either in the first or second person. That was one of the things I was very keen on doing, because I think that that has a much more powerful effect . . . in the context of a courtroom, that can have a lot more symbolic power, and the court's quiet and you're addressing the accused, and you can really inflect your tone of addressing [the accused] sternly and in a condemnatory way – so that was one of the first things I set about doing in my part.

Drawing on Academic Scholarship, Social Facts and Empirical Research

In Australia, there has been very little judicial comment about whether it is appropriate to cite legal periodicals in reasons for judgment and, according to Russel Smythe's research, the issue seems to be a matter of judicial preference.[14] For example, Helen O'Sullivan, a retired District Court judge, commented that in rewriting *RPS v R*:

> I did not grapple with the thorny issue of using background literature because I had become accustomed to not doing this while I was still a Judge. However, I support the Canadian judges who do this, and I would like to see our appellate courts go the same way.

Chief Justice French lists what he considers 'impermissible use' of academic work in judgment-writing, as including:

> [T]he purely ornamental and the thoughtless padding out of references without direct relevance to the proposition which they are said to support. Reliance upon academic opinions cannot be a substitute for direct consideration of the relevant authorities and statutory provisions.[15]

In the project workshops there was significant discussion about when and where legal scholarship should and should not be cited. The judgment-writers in this collection, like judges generally, took a variety of approaches.

However, unlike judges, the writers in this project could rely on commentaries accompanying their judgments to reflect the scholarly sources by which they were influenced, including the influence of case law or scholarship *after* the case was decided. Some of the judgment-writers worked closely with commentary writers to ensure that important scholarly work they drew upon was acknowledged. For example, in rewriting *R v Webster*, the authors were informed by scholarship around masculinities,[16] yet Honni van Rijswijk observed:

> I didn't reference [this scholarship] mainly because I think my understanding of the sentencing judgment was that it wouldn't fit, so I sent those to [the commentary writer] and just gave her a list of what I thought she could include.

In the feminist judgment in *Louth v Diprose*, Francesca Bartlett was influenced by later critiques of the case,[17] a wider body of feminist critique[18] and developments in this area of private law, in rethinking the facts and whether they satisfied the unconscionability doctrine. However, she could not expressly refer to these influences or developments.

Feminist scholars and activists have long critiqued claims to neutrality and objectivity of legal decision-makers.[19] While it is now generally acknowledged that judges are people who have background experiences, knowledges and opinions, how far these 'extra-legal' sources should influence their decisions continues to be a controversial topic. Judges who have explicitly identified too strongly with a particular social position or experience have often

[14] Russell Smyth, 'Academic Writing and the Courts: A Quantitative Study of the Influence of Legal and Non-Legal Periodicals in the High Court' (1998) 17 *University of Tasmania Law Review* 164, 168.

[15] French, above n 2, 104. Rosemary Hunter makes the same point in relation to the use of feminist scholarship by feminist judges in 'An Account of Feminist Judging', above n 1, 42.

[16] See, eg, Felicity Holland and Jane O'Sullivan, '"Lethal Larrikins": Cinematic Subversions of Mythical Masculinities in *Blackrock* and *The Boys*' (1999) 13 *Antipodes* 79.

[17] Lisa Sarmas, 'Storytelling and the Law: A Case Study of *Louth v Diprose*' (1994) 19 *Melbourne University Law Review* 701; Bibi Sangha and Bob Moles, 'Gendered Stereotypes and Unconscionability – Can we Trust the Judges to Get it Right?' (1997) 1 *Flinders Journal of Law Reform* 145.

[18] See, eg, Richard Haigh and Samantha Hepburn, 'The Bank Manager Always Rings Twice: Stereotyping in Equity After *Garcia*' (2000) 26 *Monash University Law Review* 275; Paula Baron, 'The Free Exercise of Her Will: Women and Emotionally Transmitted Debt' (1995) 13(1) *Law in Context* 23.

[19] See Reg Graycar and Jenny Morgan, *The Hidden Gender of Law* (Federation Press, 2nd ed, 2002).

been accused of bias.[20] While judgments in this collection avoid explicit acknowledgement of background factors, overwhelmingly, when interviewed, the writers agreed that their background and experiences had influenced their judgment. For example, many of the judgment-writers said that it was their scholarship in the area of law and feminist jurisprudence which largely informed their approach. Many writers had previously written scholarly articles about the judgment they rewrote. In a few cases, the judgment-writer commented on personal connections to the facts of the case. For instance, a couple commented that the crime occurred in their home town. Kerrie Sadiq noted that the woman involved in a tax law decision had a child who was born around the same time as she was born. She commented on what she saw as a very specific context of the time in terms of gendered roles within a family:

> So it had a very personal sort of connection for me thinking, you know, here was this mother with a child the same age as me, and here I am actually not fighting to work. I am able to work. I'm able to earn an equal income ... [I]t kind of pulled me up too, on what a different kind of upbringing I had; Mum and Dad, and Dad went out to work, and Mum stayed at home – left [work] when she was pregnant with me – all the traditional kind of things, and here were these other women fighting cases.

Another writer was appalled at the offhand way in which sexual violence was described by the court and expressly 'put [herself] in the shoes' of the victims and drew on her experience as a woman when writing. Some authors also commented that their connection with the case was their experience as a student having studied the case with a sense of dismay. One interviewee said this was an empowering part of the project as a whole. This author explained that when she read feminist versions of some of the judgments she had previously studied she thought: 'thank God somebody has finally rewritten that [judgment] in a way that does justice to the victim'.

In several cases, the original judgment of the High Court, which has greater latitude to decide on matters of policy,[21] included express reference to extra-legal materials or there were earlier decisions in the case which contained reference to such materials. For example in *State of New South Wales v Amery*, Beth Gaze draws on extra-legal materials about women in the workforce and the gendered disadvantages they suffer which had been put in evidence before a series of tribunals and courts below. In some judgments, writers did not have the advantage of such background material being put before the court. Nevertheless, it was possible to include extra-legal knowledge or theory without expressly referencing it, by taking 'judicial notice' of a fact or consequence, in the sense that they stated it from the 'common sense' or social knowledge of the judicial officer.[22] The limits to the doctrine of judicial notice have been discussed by the High Court in *Thomas v Mowbray*: 'the inquiry must be into the "common knowledge of educated men" as revealed in "accepted writings", "standard works" and "serious studies and inquiries". . . In short, matters judicially noticed at common law must be indisputable'.[23]

[20] Reg Graycar, 'Gender, Race, Bias and Perspective: OR, How Otherness Colours Your Judgment' (2008) 15 *International Journal of the Legal Profession* 73; Martha Minow, 'Stripped Down Like a Runner or Enriched by Experience: Bias and Impartiality of Judges and Jurors' (1992) 33 *William and Mary Law Review* 1201.

[21] See Kylie Burns, 'The Australian High Court and Social Facts: A Content Analysis Study' (2012) 40 *Federal Law Review* 317.

[22] Hunter (2010), above n 1, 39–40; Hunter (2013), above n 1, 399–418.

[23] *Thomas v Mowbray* (2007) 233 CLR 307, citing Dixon J in *Australian Communist Party v Commonwealth* (1951) 83 CLR 1.

Not least because of its gendered expression and questionable logic, this approach is a significant shift away from the academic approach to writing which is required to be scrupulously well-referenced. It is a powerful statement to assume a position of authority to find a 'social fact' that requires no reference.[24] Appropriating this tool can be a site of resistance to persistent gendered norms in decision-making. Yet there are dangers to this approach. A judge can inform herself of things which may challenge gendered stereotypes, or perpetuate them. There was conscious use of judicial notice in a number of the feminist judgments. For example in *Dietrich v R,* which concerned the question of whether a person unable to afford legal representation is entitled to state-funded representation in order to ensure a fair trial on a serious criminal charge, Jenny Morgan and Reg Graycar state in their judgment: 'we are entitled to take judicial notice of the fact that the vast majority of legal aid for criminal trials goes to men as it is men who commit the vast majority of criminal offences, particularly serious criminal offences'.

Another approach adopted in the judgments was to use social science or empirically based material to support findings. Again this approach may risk appeal.[25] As Lady Hale observes in response to the question 'should judges be socio-legal scholars?': '[t]he short and easy answer to this question is "no, of course not"'. Hale advocates that judges should be *legal* scholars, although she suggests that 'even this can be dangerous if carried too far'.[26] However, there are a number of instances where the feminist judgments cite empirically based material. Zoe Rathus, who rewrote *Goode and Goode* with Renata Alexander, observed:

> I certainly think it's totally valid that we decided that we were going [to use extrinsic material] in the sense that that's the kind of decision that some judges on the Full Court [of the Family Court] have made . . . [T]he way that we've done it is very circumspect and rather than in any way endeavour to be very specific, [we said] . . . 'we are comforted by the fact that . . . there is significant social science literature which supports the statutory interpretation that we came to'.

In *Phillips v R*, a case involving the rape and sexual assault of six young women, Annie Cossins drew on statistical data. She commented:

> [O]ne [victim] was 14, 15, 16 . . . [The victims] are in places where they expect to be safe, going to a party. They're young, they're naïve . . . I looked at the . . . ABS stats on which age group was most vulnerable to sexual assault in Australia, and it was the 0 to 14 age group, or 0 to 16, and I said, we have to – well, I didn't say we, but I am going to take account of the vulnerability of this particular age group, because the complainants fell into that age group.

In deciding the case of *Cattanach v Melchior,* Kylie Burns commented that in obiter dicta she would have made further remarks about the development of the law in relation to the consideration of social facts:

> [T]he bit in the judgment where I talk about what the role of the policy is . . . we've recently in the High Court said we shouldn't be going on this perilous journey. Yes, let's not go on that perilous journey unless you've got good evidence. Probably if you had 10,000 words, you could have said

[24] For another discussion of use of social facts, see Claire L'Heureux-Dubé, 'Re-examining the Doctrine of Judicial Notice in the Family Law Context' (1994) 26 *Ottawa Law Review* 551; Zoe Rathus, 'Shifting Language and Meaning Between Social Science and the Law: Defining Family Violence' (2013) 36 *University of New South Wales Law Journal* 359; Kylie Burns, 'It's Not Just Policy: The Role of Social Facts in Judicial Reasoning in Negligence Cases' (2013) 21 *Torts Law Journal* 73.

[25] Where the material informs a reason for deciding, the test appears to be whether the material is available to the parties to present arguments to the court: *Aytugrul v R* [2012] HCA 15 (18 April 2012).

[26] Brenda Hale, 'Should Judges Be Socio-Legal Scholars?' (Paper presented at the Socio-Legal Studies Association 2013 Conference, University of York, 26 March 2013).

> . . . even if we go down the perilous journey, which is the preferable journey, then here's all the other stuff which also supports [the outcome] . . . [I]n some ways, if you go down that journey that would be a more transformative approach . . . I just think, for me, I think there were other things we could easily do to make it feminist without going there.

Other writers sought further information about the context of the dispute before them by obtaining transcripts of proceedings, and other documents filed by the parties. Information about the parties and what they said at trial, in addition to what is contained in the original judgments, was often referred to in the feminist judgment to bring out the story of one or several of the parties.[27]

Strategies of Feminist Judgment-Writing

Feminist Theoretical Approaches

Many judgment-writers told us that they did not feel the need to specifically refer to feminist scholarship, and few could specifically identify *a* feminist theoretical approach they had applied in rewriting. Some writers explained that they approached the role with a background of feminist activism or practice. For instance, Rathus commented that she and her co-writer, Renata Alexander, drew on '30 years of working with women'. Renata Alexander observed of her judgment in *Goode and Goode*: 'I didn't consciously adopt any of [my knowledge of feminist and queer theory]; it was more the practical implications of what it would mean for women and for children. So again, it was the application rather than the theory.'

Several judgments incorporate a notion of care and interconnection into their legal approach. In *Re Minister for Immigration and Multicultural and Indigenous Affairs & Anor; Ex parte Applicants S134/2002*, Charlotte Steer said she was influenced by a feminist ethic of care when she drew an expansive role for a decision-maker in asylum-seeker matters. In that case, the decision-maker did not read or was not aware of information in the files which indicated that the husband of the applicant and father of her children was in Australia and held a protection visa. Had the relevant tribunal member exercised care in understanding the position of the family, the outcome for the applicant for refugee status may have been different. Steer commented: '[m]y judgment follows the legal reasoning of the minority judgment, but it puts more emphasis on the importance of recognising family connections and of making a choice in statutory interpretation that promotes connection to networks of relationships'.

In the *Wildlife Whitsunday Case*, Lee Godden refers to an idea of 'eco-feminism' which emphasises the 'adoption of more holistic conceptions of the environment that emphasise the interconnectedness of all life forms and the need for a nurturing approach that creates a bond between people and nature'.[28] This case concerns a judicial review action brought in

[27] Appellate courts would have access to transcripts as well as other documents filed for the case. Indeed, as we describe in Ch 1, judges who spoke to participants in the workshops suggested that these resources were frequently useful to them as judges and could be legitimately drawn upon in writing reasons.

[28] Jacqueline Peel, commentary to *Wildlife Preservation Society of Queensland Proserpine/Whitsunday Branch Inc v Minister for the Environment and Heritage* in this collection.

the Federal Court by conservationists in relation to an environmental assessment of two proposed coal mines in Queensland. Godden, substituting her decision for that of the original judge and reversing the result, upholds the contention of the applicants that there are likely to be significant impacts on World Heritage sites when a cumulative and holistic approach to climate change and the environment is adopted.

Another approach of the feminist judgment-writers is to highlight the deleterious effects of the liberal legal dichotomy between public and private.[29] In *PGA v R*, the judgment emphasises the private realm of the home and marriage as unprotected by the common law, thus depriving women subject to violence in marriage of a legal remedy. The writers point out that we cannot just assume the common law will develop to address these entrenched gendered structures. *Appellant S395/2002* concerns the relationship between refugee status and persecution on the basis of sexuality. While this is a legitimate ground on which to claim asylum, in his commentary, Wayne Morgan observes decision-makers in Australia

> began to draw distinctions between gay men and lesbians who were 'discreet' about their sexuality, and those who were not. Decisions began to be made that, if the applicant concerned had been 'discreet' about their sexuality in the past, then they did not have a well-founded fear of persecution.[30]

The feminist judgment in this case, concerning a couple who had a same-sex relationship in Bangladesh and were subject to intimidation, but whom the tribunal felt were not in danger if they were 'discreet', corrects this privatising of their sexuality which operated to deprive them of the protection of the Refugee Convention.

Recognising Women's Stories and Gendered Experiences

Many of the judgments 'ask the woman question'.[31] In *Dietrich v R* the feminist judges decide, with 'judicial notice' of the reality that directing legal aid funding to those accused of serious crimes would have a gendered effect, that a trial should not generally be stayed in the absence of legal representation, unless there are exceptional circumstances. In discussing her rewriting of the case, Morgan commented: '[t]o a large extent we were doing that sort of very old-fashioned thing of just asking the gender question. What implications does this have for most women or particularly for poor women?' In *Cummins*, Lisa Sarmas employs a similar strategy to systematically expose and analyse the specific results of a presumption of formal equality between spouses in ownership of the family home under a resulting trust.

Several judgments also endeavour to include women by writing women's experiences into the judgment.[32] For instance, in *R v Pearson; Ex parte Sipka*, a constitutional law case about the right to vote, Kim Rubenstein foregrounds women's role in the constitutional debates prior to Australian federation in her first words. She begins her judgment: 'Listening closely to the women of the 1890s who were the first with an electoral voice in Australia'.

[29] There is a large feminist literature critiquing the public/private distinction. For a recent summary, see Rosemary Hunter, 'Contesting the Dominant Paradigm: Feminist Critiques of Liberal Legalism' in Margaret Davies and Vanessa E Munro (eds), *The Ashgate Research Companion to Feminist Legal Theory* (Ashgate, 2013) 13–30.

[30] Wayne Morgan, commentary to *Appellant S395/2002* in this collection.

[31] Katherine T Bartlett, 'Feminist Legal Methods' (1990) 103 *Harvard Law Review* 829.

[32] See also Australasian Institute of Judicial Administration, *Guide to Judicial Conduct* (AIJA, 2nd ed, 2007) 19 regarding sensitivity towards the parties, and others, in describing them and their actions in a judgment.

Reflecting on this approach, Rubenstein observed:

> I just spend a lot more time on the role of those women at the time of federation, and give a lot more voice to them . . . I think placing the women's stories at the centre of what I was doing was what I felt was my feminist tone and approach. So storytelling their experience being a significant part of [it], then thinking about the constitutional principles that were at play.

In a similar vein, Penny Crofts' and Isabella Alexander's judgment in *Taikato v R* begins with the statement: 'One night, Jo-Anne Taikato and her husband returned home to find an intruder in the process of breaking into their house.' While Jo-Anne Taikato was charged with an offence relating to carrying formaldehyde in her handbag in a public place, her experience of home invasion contextualises her safety concerns and helps explain why she might carry such a substance. Isabella Alexander explained that:

> [O]ur approach was generally one . . . of bringing in the defendant's experiences, and specifically her experiences as being a woman who had suffered a home intrusion and being on the street. So in that sense it kind of . . . played into all the Take Back the Night movement and other movements and community responses to the issue of violence against women such as White Ribbon Day.

In *ACCC v Keshow*, Heron Loban emphasises the concern shown by Indigenous mothers for their children's education as a legally recognisable vulnerability. In *Appellant S395/2002*, Nan Seuffert carefully considers the lived experience and personal histories of the applicants for asylum. She commented: 'I tried to . . . put in a bit more context and make [the applicants] seem a bit more human, and I think those are feminist things to do in a judgment.'

Several of the judgments involving criminal law focus on how the victim is represented, and try to write her voice more clearly into the judgment. For example, in *R v Morgan*, Elena Marchetti commented that a way in which her and Janet Ransley's feminist judgment is different from the original is that they are

> also bringing the victim back in [to the Court of Appeal judgment], because the original [County Court] judgment I think was quite effective at doing that, and she seemed to get a little bit lost again in the appeal judgment.

Danielle Tyson, one of the feminist judges in the sentencing judgment for defensive homicide in *R v Middendorp* explained that:

> I've been following an exemplary judge who has been making particular statements around the impact of the crime and the sentencing process on the victim's family and acknowledging that that can never take away the worth of their loved one and so on, and that was something that I thought was very powerful, and I wanted to have in the judgment.

While this was a common strategy of writers involved in the project, not all were satisfied with how far they were able to go. For example, Mary Heath who co-wrote *PGA v R*, observed:

> [T]he lives of women should be central in the judgment, not peripheral to it – that they should be a relevant consideration rather than a peripheral consideration, and I think we have ended up with a judgment where that underpinning principle is there and it's sketched in, but it is only sketched in, and I think we would probably both prefer that were different.

Furthermore, as some of the judgments show, a feminist judgment may not simply be about writing the woman victim into the judgment, although this is important. It could also be about how men and masculinity are represented. Tyson observed: 'I've been interested in

... how judges use language, the kinds of adjectives used that can minimise understandings of domestic violence, that can construct the subjectivity of the defendant, and the deceased in particular ways.' The feminist judges Honni van Rijswijk and Lesley Townsley, in *R v Webster*, another sentencing case, also demonstrate this approach. As Townsley commented:

> What's really loud in the narrative [of the original judgment] ... it was about masculinities, but the masculinities were construed in a particular kind of way which I found a bit offensive ... When I think of feminism ... I always think of how masculinity is presented.

Some of the judgment-writers give names to the participants to give them identity. For example in family law cases, which are subject to statutory restrictions on identifying the parties, children are typically referred to only by letters ('A', 'K', etc), and parties' names are also initialised or pseudonymised. In the two family law cases in this collection, *U v U* and *Goode and Goode*, however, parties and children are given full pseudonyms to avoid dehumanisation. In relation to *Goode v Goode*, Renata Alexander explained: 'the Full Court never talks about real children and their age and their names and things, so we've tried to humanise it from that point of view'. Similarly, in *R v Middendorp*, Tyson explained: '[w]e didn't call her "the deceased" or "the victim" in the case ... we wanted to call her by her name the whole time.'

Many of the cases in this collection attempt to contextualise and particularise the circumstances of the case and to present a judgment that is practical in its reasoning rather than abstract.[33] For example while the majority judges of the High Court in *Dietrich v R* claimed that a decision to stay a case where there was no legal representative was not the same as demanding that legal aid be applied to the case,[34] the feminist judges reject this idea as a 'distinction without a difference'.[35] Similarly in *State of New South Wales v Amery* the feminist judge, Beth Gaze, rejects the idea that women necessarily make a choice between full-time and casual work. She points out that in reality the women respondents in the case actually had little choice. In her interview Gaze explained she wanted

> to be able to try and personalise it so a person reading it could see how limited the choices were that were available to these women and how they got constrained into being paid less for essentially the same work as the male teachers were doing.

In *Cattanach v Melchior*, a central issue was whether a pregnancy which occurred after a negligent sterilisation could be considered a harm for which damages could be claimed. In this case the feminist judge, Kylie Burns, describes the parental relationship in a very concrete and contextualised way. She described her approach:

> So getting that story bigger and clearer, so that the female plaintiff, the mother, doesn't just disappear. Because that was one of the original critiques I'd made of the case when it came out, that everything was parenting and parent and the two roles were put together, even though the main damage is predominantly suffered by the mother ... I was re-writing it to make her story fuller, to weave her story further through the facts. But also to try and do it in a way that was relevant.

Several of the criminal law judgments are distinguishable from the original judgments in their careful particularisation of the use of violence against women by male perpetrators.[36]

[33] See Hunter (2008), above n 1, 12.
[34] See, eg, Deane J in *Dietrich v R* (1992) 177 CLR 292, 332.
[35] See also the feminist judgment in *JM v QFG & GK*.
[36] See *R v Webster*; *R v Middendorp*; and *Phillips v R*.

Challenging Gender Bias, Remedying Injustice and Promoting Substantive Equality[37]

Gender bias inherent in some of the original decisions is challenged in feminist judgments in this collection. For example, in relation to *RPS v R*, Helen O'Sullivan commented, with reference to her previous experience as a District Court judge, that:

> I enjoyed the challenge of writing the judgment so that it followed normal judgment-writing protocols but also reflected feminist jurisprudence. I welcomed the opportunity to examine important concepts such as a fair trial, the role of the jury, the privileging of the accused, and the silencing of victims.

In her judgment she challenges the traditionally limited conception of a fair trial and asks: fair trial for whom? (especially in the gendered context of sexual offences). Her judgment finds that the concept of a fair trial should be understood not just from the defendant's perspective but from the victim's perspective as well.

Phillips v R involved the sexual assault and rape of six young women, with the issue being whether the trials should be heard together. In deciding that they should be heard together, the dissenting feminist judge, Annie Cossins, finds that the evidence of the victims is relevant as similar-fact evidence in the trial.[38] She observed:

> I remember [the judges'] phrase [from the original judgment], that what the six complainants had suffered was a type of sexual behaviour at the hands of the defendant that was entirely unremarkable. I thought, 'goodness me . . . so you can be sexually assaulted and it is entirely unremarkable?' 'So therefore, what's the problem?' That was almost what I felt they were saying . . . As a woman, I've always felt that sexual assault was entirely remarkable. That's an experiential thing that probably really most men are never going to have to go through.

In *Louth v Diprose*, Francesca Bartlett disputes the interpretation in the original judgments of female self-interest as unusual, suspect and predatory and the mirror inference that male irrationality and weakness is 'bizarre' and must have been induced. Indeed, she noted that she was concerned to show that it was only by employing these stereotypes that the trial (and later) judgment filled in the evidentiary gaps to produce a particular legal result of the woman acting unconscionably. Once freed of these gendered tropes, the feminist judgment finds no evidence of victimisation and also makes room for a more understanding account of the woman's story (as neither the victim nor the aggressor).

In discussing his judgment in *U v U*, Jonathan Crowe observed that 'at the appellate level, [there is a tendency for] just summarising the facts. But the way the facts are presented is always selective, always has some sort of preparing the ground.' He also suggested that the original judgment perpetuated a narrative that there was 'a natural sort of process' of producing parenting proposals. In contrast, his rewritten judgment paints a picture which emphasises that 'it's not really a natural process. There are presumptions operating about the role of the different parents in parenting.'

While most of the cases in this collection seek to remedy injustice and improve the conditions of women's lives, one particularly original example of this strategy is the apology presented by the feminist judges in *PGA v R*. In this case the feminist judges, unusually,

[37] These are strategies of feminist judging suggested by Hunter (2008), above n 1.
[38] To be admissible in Australia, this type of evidence requires 'striking similarity' between the similar facts.

apologise to women injured as a result of the common law rule that afforded husbands immunity for marital rape. Wendy Larcombe and Mary Heath observed that:

> [T]his just became glaring, that you had no way for the common law to review its rules in this area and to update those rules to . . . reflect changing social attitudes. So the apology was on behalf of the court, recognising that it, as the custodian if you like of the common law in Australia, had not been able to deliver justice to married women because its processes were flawed. [Larcombe]

> You need other forms of recognition, of recompense, of social acknowledgement of the wrong that married women were subjected to across most of the 20th century, so some other form of therapeutic or corrective justice beyond the decision that we were able to make. [Heath]

Several of the judgments in this collection attempt to promote substantive equality. For example, in *Cummins*, Sarmas rejects the formal equality reasoning of the majority judges, who adopt an inference of equal beneficial ownership in the family home through a resulting trust. She observes that while this inference may provide just results for some (heterosexual) couples, in many cases this inference of equality will result in a loss of rights for the woman in a relationship. Sarmas argues that without a solid empirical or policy basis, which was not argued in the case, there is no reason to extend trust principles beyond their traditional basis which often provides substantive equality to parties.

In her judgment in *Lodge v Federal Commissioner for Taxation*, a case concerning the tax-deductibility of childcare expenses, Kerrie Sadiq makes her decision on the basis that there should be equal treatment of claims for expenses by taxpayers whether they are men or women, and without regard to whether they are occupying traditionally gendered roles. She observed: 'pragmatically, I was coming from an equity point of view and equality point of view first of all'. Nevertheless, this is one of a handful of judgments which may be contested by feminists writing now, as its outcome would produce a taxation system which would benefit high income earners more than low income mothers.

In this context, Hunter suggests that a feminist judge should be open and accountable about the choices made between competing interests.[39] The feminist judges in several cases in this collection point to the difficult choices they must make and carefully weigh the reasons for their choices.[40] In the family law relocation case of *U v U*, Jonathan Crowe considers the reality that it continues to be women who are usually the primary caregivers to children. Although he accepts that the mother has interests in her own right, he also finds that the best interests of the mother and child are interconnected. If the mother's relocation is in her best interests it also follows that it is likely to be in the best interests of the child:

> [I]f you acknowledge all the rights and issues, and say you're weighing the interests, there's a substantive decision to be made. You can't just take it for granted it comes out a particular way. That's one way of acknowledging the robust interests that children and the different parents have, and making sure they're all acknowledged.

Legal Formalism as Feminist Method

Several of the judgments in this collection explicitly use 'the master's tools'[41] of formal legal method to achieve what they consider to be more just and appropriate results. This occurs

39 Hunter (2008), above n 1, 14.
40 See, eg, *Cummins*; *Phillips v R*; *State of New South Wales v Amery*.
41 Audre Lorde, *Sister Outsider: Essays and Speeches* (Crossing Press, 1984) 110.

in the context of both common and statute law. The potential rationale and effectiveness of such an approach was adverted to by Annie Cossins:

> I was aware of Justice Gaudron . . . I thought she would do the black letter law stuff just to make sure that it all held up. As a feminist judge, you don't want to let the side down so that the blokes come along and go, well, phfff – see, there you go, female judges, they don't know anything, or they don't know what they're talking about.

In common law cases, this approach is manifested in close attention to precedent and/or the exercise of judicial restraint. For example, Adrian Howe's judgment in *Parker v R* traces the history of the doctrine of provocation and identifies a number of older cases which might have been cited by the High Court and may have encouraged the law on provocation to develop in a different way. In particular, her history demonstrates that the notion of what constituted legally sufficient provocation had been progressively and unjustifiably widened, with gendered consequences in cases in which men killed their wives on suspicion of adultery. She observed: 'I had the precedents. The 1946 *Holmes* case is the classic, the high point of judicial resistance to expanding provocation. There's nothing better after that, not even in the 21st century.'

In *Cummins*, the feminist judgment adopts 'traditional trust principles' (of a common intention constructive trust) to decide the case, rejecting the majority's extension of the doctrine of resulting trust as unprincipled and unhelpful, both doctrinally and empirically. Similarly, in *Dietrich v R*, the feminist judgment rejects the judicial activism of the majority of the High Court and declines to extend the substantive right to a fair trial in serious criminal cases, on the basis that to do so would impermissibly violate the separation of powers between the judiciary and the executive. In all three cases, the more conservative or restrained approach is one which, in the view of the feminist judges, is more likely to benefit women than the alternative. The feminist judgment in *PGA v R* also falls within this category of judicial restraint, with the feminist judges, as discussed earlier, considering it inappropriate to retrospectively rewrite the common law so as to abolish the marital rape immunity. Larcombe commented that:

> When I read people who critique our position or who accept the position of the majority in the High Court, I find their preparedness to exonerate the common law process and the courts that apply it from any responsibility at all for that situation to be quite profoundly unsatisfying.

Carefully applying the rules of statutory interpretation is a strategy used by other feminist judges in this collection to correct the outcome of a case or a misunderstanding about the meaning or import of a legislative provision. Notably, three of these cases are in the area of discrimination law, where highly restrictive interpretations of anti-discrimination legislation by appellate courts have, arguably, undermined the purposes of the legislation and made it extremely difficult for complainants to succeed.[42] The feminist judgments, by contrast, are concerned to give full effect to the legislation by reference to its stated objectives. For example, Beth Gaze commented: 'I actually wanted to [rewrite the judgment in *State of New South Wales v Amery*] by following what I regarded as a correct and clear legal method.' She said that she believed this, itself, could be a feminist strategy:

> [D]o you necessarily have to flag it as being about women's interests when you're writing a feminist judgment? Or is it enough actually to just be really quite legalistic on the legal method and the

[42] In the federal context, see Beth Gaze and Rosemary Hunter, *Enforcing Human Rights in Australia: An Evaluation of the New Regime* (Themis Press, 2010).

precedent that you're dealing with and to reach the particular result that you think is right? To set the precedents up in a way that's actually fully respectful of the interests of women?

Similarly, in *JM v QFG & GK*, which concerns refusal of access to assisted reproductive technology services for lesbian women, Anita Stuhmcke relies on careful consideration of the purpose underlying the legislation. She observed:

So if I had been sitting there . . . as that fourth person [on the court] . . . I wanted them, the other [judges], to take note of the fact that within the same paradigm at black letter law they could reach a different decision . . . That's why . . . the end result . . . was perhaps a more clinical piece than what I would have cathartically wanted to engage in, because to make them understand that the decision that they were coming to was wrong in law, I felt I had to engage with them there.

As discussed below, in the third discrimination case, *McLeod v Power*, the feminist judge finds, on the plain meaning of the words in the statute, that 'white' does constitute a race, colour, or national or ethnic origin.

The last judgment taking a strict approach to statutory interpretation is the family law case of *Goode and Goode*. In this case, the issue was about how to interpret a complex set of new provisions introduced into the *Family Law Act 1975* (Cth) by the *Family Law Amendment (Shared Parental Responsibility) Act 2006* (Cth). While the majority of the Full Court of the Family Court appeared to focus on the political intentions behind the amendments, the feminist judges engage in a careful reading of the new provisions themselves, finding that, rather than being compelled to divide children's time equally between their parents, the court retains the capacity to decide each case in the best interests of the relevant children. This is an important message in a context in which the amendments had generated expectations and misapprehensions about parental rights to equal time with their children. Rathus observed 'the extent to which men arrive in their various offices thinking that they have a right to equal time . . . The women arrive thinking that the fathers have a right to equal time', and continued by noting 'the irony, that to be good feminist judges, what Renata and I did was engage in straightforward statutory interpretation, which is actually what the Full Court failed to do.'

These judgments demonstrate that feminist judicial method does not necessarily involve pushing the boundaries of legal method, but in some instances may call for a more traditionally 'black letter' approach.

Indigenous People, Feminism and the Law

Five judgments in the collection are in cases involving Indigenous people. Two of these cases, *R v Morgan* and *McLeod v Power*, were rewritten by non-Indigenous contributors who felt able to rewrite the judgments within the constraints originally set by the project, while drawing on critical whiteness theory[43] and the theory of intersectionality, which recognises that gendered identity intersects with other identities such as race and class.[44] In *McLeod v Power*, Nielsen challenges the concept of whiteness as not-raced when she interprets racial

[43] See generally: Aileen Moreton-Robinson (ed), *Whitening Race: Essays in Social and Cultural Criticism* (Aboriginal Studies Press, 2004); Aileen Moreton-Robinson, *Talkin' Up to the White Woman: Indigenous Women and Feminism* (University of Queensland Press, 2000).

[44] See Emily Grabham et al, 'Introduction' in Emily Grabham et al (eds), *Intersectionality and Beyond: Law, Power and the Politics of Location* (Routledge, 2009) 1.

discrimination legislation.[45] The case arose from a complaint of racial vilification lodged by a white male prison officer against an Aboriginal woman, Samantha Power, who had come to visit her partner who was in custody. Ms Power had arrived at the prison, after a long bus journey with her four young children to discuss the threatened removal of one of them by social services, only to be denied entry. She swore at the officer when being ejected and referred to him using the word 'white'. While Nielsen agrees with the original decision that Ms Power's remarks did not constitute racial vilification, she takes issue with the assumption that there is no white race. When asked how race and gender intersect in the judgment, Nielsen said:

> [T]o me an interrogation and analysis of power and how power is used to oppress or privilege, to me is kind of the heart of a feminist . . . approach. Typically I suppose a feminist lens would tend to highlight gender and the influence of gender. But not only. I think that feminism has broader reach and I think that . . . it has developed much more sophisticated capacities to analyse across a range of sites.

In *R v Morgan* the feminist judges consider the role of Indigenous sentencing courts, emphasising the need for intersectional methodology to underpin these courts, and highlighting the victim's voice and experience and the Indigenous elders' views as key considerations in sentencing. While the original sentencing occurred before an Indigenous sentencing court where Indigenous elders were involved in the process, the feminist judges, Elena Marchetti and Janet Ransley, present an extra voice on the Court of Appeal. They reinstate the original sentence of the Indigenous sentencing court. Marchetti explained:

> I guess we pay more attention to recognising the fact that in the original sentencing decision, there would have been the elders present, and just being mindful of the fact that we couldn't move too far away from what that original decision was, if it wasn't incorrect in law, because the original sentencing judge had the benefit of that cultural input, which was about a domestic violence issue.

In contrast to these writers, the three Indigenous authors, Irene Watson, Heron Loban and Nicole Watson, wanted to extend the legal genre in various ways. Loban sits as a second, Indigenous, judge in the Federal Court, where usually a single judge would sit to hear a trial. As the Indigenous judge in *ACCC v Keshow*, she focuses on retelling the stories of the Indigenous women – quoting them directly – as mothers living in remote communities concerned about their children's education.

In the cases of *Kartinyeri v The Commonwealth* considered by Irene Watson and *Tuckiar v R* rewritten as *In the matter of Djaparri (Re Tuckiar)* by Nicole Watson,[46] the sovereignty of Australian law, and thus its courts, is itself questioned. Australian law is found to be, at best, limited in its capacity to recognise and account for Indigenous perspectives and laws, especially Indigenous women's perspectives and laws.

Each writer, in different ways, draws on Indigenous people's traditions of storytelling. In her response to *Kartinyeri v The Commonwealth*, Irene Watson opens the collection with a chapter which rejects the common law judgment form; she enacts the oral tradition of the land and people to show how Aboriginal women's law has been misinterpreted and suppressed. Such an articulation of stories in a sovereign First Nations legal system is, she argues, not possible within the Australian common law system. She concludes that the rewriting of *Kartinyeri v The Commonwealth* was impossible, as the methodology of the

[45] *Racial Discrimination Act 1975* (Cth) ss 18B–18F.

[46] *Kartinyeri v The Commonwealth* (1998) 195 CLR 337; *Tuckiar v R* (1934) 52 CLR 335.

project 'would not prise open spaces for Nunga women because the rewriting needs to be done from "another space", outside the jurisdiction of the Australian common law and the sovereignty of the Australian state'.

In the final judgment in this collection, *In the matter of Djaparri (Re Tuckiar)*, Nicole Watson observed that she needed 'latitude' so she could 'bring this alternative history [of the case] and ... shine a light on how the entire society in 1930s Darwin was raced and law was but one instrument of that racial oppression'. She draws on Indigenous peoples' storytelling traditions and on critical race theory. In her judgment, she imagines a more reconciled Australian future where there is a treaty between an Australian Republic and a Confederation of Aboriginal and Torres Strait Islander Nations. In this future world there is also a new healing court, the First Nations Court of Australia, tasked with casting light on the lived experience, the stories, of Aboriginal and Torres Strait Islander people. Watson explained that she employed:

> [A] form of outsider storytelling that critical race theorists describe and that's really influenced a lot of my scholarship, particularly Richard Delgado's work. So it was a tool for injecting this outsider narrative next to the established High Court judgments ... I think critical race theorists have – well the early critical race theorists like Richard Delgado, Derrick Bell, Mari Matsuda, they're the people who really influence my work and ... they were obviously people from oppressed backgrounds, similar to mine, but they're all legal scholars so I found a particular resonance I guess in their work.

Conclusion

The Australian Feminist Judgments Project has allowed space for a diverse group of Australian feminist academics and practitioners to come together to discuss the theory and application of feminism in legal decision-making. The contributors employ a wide variety of techniques and strategies to rewrite existing judgments as feminist judgments, demonstrating the potential and possibilities for feminist approaches to judgment-writing and feminist praxis more widely. Of particular interest in this collection is that a number of the judgments show how legal formalism may be co-opted as feminist method. Through careful statutory interpretation, vigilant attention to the doctrine of precedent and a deeply considered exercise of discretion, a judgment can reflect feminist aspirations and concerns. Nevertheless, the essay and judgments written by the Indigenous authors represented here show there are limitations to the feminist judgments project methodology and that these limitations are not easily overcome. The jurisdiction of Australian law is deeply contested by Indigenous people and new spaces, forums and forms of law are needed if the sovereignty of Indigenous people is to be properly recognised.

Importantly, both the scope and limits of the project force us to think about how legal judgments are written, what is taken for granted and what could be done differently. In doing so, we hope they will prove instructive, not only for academic feminists, but also for law students, legal practitioners and judges.

Part I

Public Law

Constitutional Law

3

Commentary on *Kartinyeri v The Commonwealth*

KATHY BOWREY

Introduction

Lawyers commonly characterise *Kartinyeri v Commonwealth of Australia*[1] (*Kartinyeri*), as a constitutional law case involving the 'race power' of the *Australian Constitution*. The plaintiffs, Doreen Kartinyeri and Neville Gollan, sought a declaration from the High Court that an Act of the Commonwealth Parliament, the *Hindmarsh Island Bridge Act 1997* (Cth) (*Bridge Act*), was unconstitutional under s 51(xxvi), because, in seeking to exclude specified places from the scope of the *Aboriginal and Torres Strait Islander Heritage Protection Act 1984* (Cth) (*Commonwealth Heritage Act*), it was not a law for the benefit of Aboriginal people. However this constitutional challenge was, in reality, nestled amongst an extraordinary array of related litigation and Parliamentary interventions encompassing numerous legal categories: contract, property rights, administrative law, heritage protection and specific laws affecting Aboriginal people. In these other cases, the legal status of 'secret women's business' was under discussion. To focus on one part of the dispute, stripped of a relationship to the surrounding political and legal interventions that were designed to avoid the implications of adhering to federal and state laws protecting Aboriginal heritage, diverts attention too narrowly to discrete technical legal issues at the expense of a consideration of the persistence of colonial practices, effected through a wide array of contemporary Australian legal categories and political processes.

The Broader Legal Context of *Kartinyeri*

Hindmarsh Island, or Kumarangk, sits in Lake Alexandrina near where the Murray River flows into the sea adjacent to the Southern Ocean below South Australia. There was a cable ferry to the island. Property developers, Tom and Wendy Chapman, had planning permission for a marina dating from the 1980s and it had been partially built. However planning assessment advised there was a problem with access using a cable ferry and so there was no permission to go beyond the initial stage of the development. The Chapmans sought to replace the ferry with a bridge and build a marina on the island.

[1] (1998) 195 CLR 337.

The Chapmans lacked the finances to build the bridge themselves. The Westpac bank agreed to put up the money for the marina expansion if the State government paid for the bridge. With a bridge constructed, the State government would save the costs associated with the running of the public ferry. Discussions between the State Premier, Mr Bannon, and the managing director of the Westpac bank, Stewart Fowler, led to the Chapmans, the Westpac bank and the South Australian State Labor Government entering into a financing arrangement whereby the State government agreed to build the bridge, half the cost of which was to be repaid by the developers later on. Personal letters were exchanged between the Premier and Westpac that also made the government liable for additional costs if the bridge was not constructed. In effect, the State government became guarantors for the Westpac loan to the Chapmans, and had to reimburse Westpac for losses from the loan to the Chapmans if Stages 2–4 of the development, including completing the marina, did not proceed.[2] The potential liability was estimated at hundreds of millions of dollars. This unusual arrangement had been entered into in a climate where the South Australian State Bank had recently collapsed. The State Labor government, coming into an election period, was very keen to be seen to be sponsoring major developments.

The bridge and marina development came under South Australian planning and heritage laws. The Chapmans appointed an expert to compile an archaeological report for the Aboriginal Heritage Branch of the South Australia Department of Environment and Planning. The expert's report noted there were stories of mythical associations with the area but no evidence of contemporary resonance. The developers were consequently asked to consult with traditional owners, known as the Ngarrindjeri people. There were some discussions, but this did not conclude anything. The Chapmans, having engaged in some consultation with Aboriginal persons, considered they had complied with the planning requirement.

However concerns over the development continued to emerge, pushed along by island residents, heritage and conservation groups. The South Australian Government sought another survey by the State's Chief Archaeologist, Mr Neil Draper. He identified different significant Aboriginal sites to those noted previously. He recommended these be protected under the State heritage legislation. He also noted that the beliefs associated with the site could not be disclosed, for cultural reasons, as they related to women's 'beliefs'.

By this time there had been a change of government and Dr Draper's report was presented to an incoming Liberal government. At first the new conservative government sought to avoid the legal obligation to finance the bridge, but the State could not find a way to step back from the agreement. The State Minister for Aboriginal Affairs then authorised damage to any heritage sites as was necessary to enable construction of the bridge.

Australia has a federal system of government. The *Australian Constitution* grants the Australian Commonwealth power under s 51(xxvi) to make special laws for people of any race ('the race power'). The Aboriginal Legal Rights Movement, which is based in South Australia, applied to the Federal Minister for Aboriginal Affairs, Hon Robert Tickner, on behalf of some affected women, seeking an urgent order banning construction of the bridge under the *Commonwealth Heritage Act.* This Act required the Minister to appoint a reporter to investigate the heritage claims. The Minister was aware that there were claims that the bridge would affect Ngarrindjeri culture and that it involved secret or sacred information

[2] This view was based on advice received by Samuel Jacobs QC, who was appointed by Premier Brown to determine the legal responsibilities arising out of the contracts entered into.

that was confined to women and could not be disclosed to men. He appointed Professor Cheryl Saunders, a University of Melbourne constitutional law expert, as reporter. Professor Saunders cited the cosmological significance of the area. Her report had appended to it two envelopes containing 'secret women's business'. The envelopes were only read by the Minister's female advisor. She informed the Minister there was nothing in the evidence in the envelopes that conflicted with the report. The Minister then issued an emergency declaration to stop work on the bridge.

The Chapmans appealed this decision under the *Administrative Decisions (Judicial Review) Act 1977* (Cth), claiming lack of procedural fairness, including bias, a failure to take relevant considerations into account in the making of decisions (including the evidence of men) and unreasonability. The Chapmans succeeded on the ground that the Ministerial delegation of the obligation of reading some of the evidence to a woman was a breach of his obligation under s 10 of the *Commonwealth Heritage Act.* O'Loughlin J found that 'it was not a proper exercise of a power on the part of the Minister to rely so heavily on the subject of women's business, yet deny himself access to the contents of the secret envelopes.'[3]

Arising from these proceedings, another group of 'dissident women' came forward claiming the secret women's business was fabricated. The South Australian Government set up a Royal Commission to inquire into the authenticity of secret women's business. It found the evidence of 'secret women's business' was fabricated.[4] However the Ngarrindjeri women who had initiated the original inquiries and were at the centre of the allegations refused to appear and be subjected to the State inquiry.

At the same time as the State Royal Commission was proceeding, a further application was made to the federal Minister for Aboriginal Affairs to ban the bridge. Another report was initiated, this time to be investigated by Justice Jane Matthews of the Federal Court. Her appointment was then challenged on the grounds that appointing a judge to conduct an inquiry contravenes the separation of powers doctrine.[5] The report was not released because of this. Apparently it found the undisclosed information was significant but not sufficient for a declaration under the Act.[6]

There was then a change of federal government. The new Liberal Government enacted the *Bridge Act,* which excluded the operation of the *Commonwealth Heritage Act* in the vicinity of the island altogether, in order to permit the building to proceed. *Kartinyeri* proceeded on the grounds that the *Bridge Act,* in seeking to exclude specified places, including Hindmarsh Island and an adjoining bank of the river in which it lies, from the scope of the *Commonwealth Heritage Act* was unconstitutional under the race power of the *Constitution.*

The High Court found the *Bridge Act* valid, deciding, in relation to the rules of construction, that paramountcy has to be given to the laws of the Commonwealth or of a State over international law and obligations, including international human rights obligations. The Court further failed to agree whether the race power of the *Constitution* restricted the Commonwealth Parliament to making laws for the *benefit* of the 'Aboriginal race'.

[3] *Chapman v Tickner* (1995) 55 FCR 316 .

[4] South Australia, Hindmarsh Island Bridge Royal Commission, *Report* (1995). Based on the Royal Commission report, there was further action for damages in the Federal Court against Robert Tickner, Cheryl Saunders and others associated with the Tickner report. These claims were dismissed. See *Chapman v Luminis Pty Ltd (No 4)* (2001) 123 FCR 62; *Chapman v Luminis Pty Ltd (No 5)* [2001] FCA 1106 (21 August 2001).

[5] *Wilson v Minister for Aboriginal and Torres Strait Islander Affairs* (1996) 189 CLR 1.

[6] Alexander Reilly, 'Finding an Indigenous Perspective in Administrative Law' (2009) 19 *Legal Education Review* 271, 284.

Accordingly it was found that the government could in fact enact laws to the *detriment* of any particular race.

Watson's response to *Kartinyeri* does not engage with the legal technicalities or intricacies of the reasoning in the High Court decision, because Australian legal taxonomies, associated jurisprudence and evidentiary requirements systematically mutilate and distort Aboriginal voices. Aboriginal women's law, in particular, is degraded by the demand, first, that the judge not be excluded because of his gender, and secondly, that a judge should be appointed to determine the veracity and significance of women's law for the women. The Australian legal order insists that Aboriginal male and female bodies, souls, laws and lands be opened up for general inspection, resulting in perverse legal readings of the original demands being articulated. Confinement within the legal framework and conformity with Australian legal narrative conventions imprisons acts of Aboriginal resistance to colonialism, blunting the capacity to effect progressive legal change. To understand the High Court challenge from an Aboriginal women's perspective, and in particular to appreciate Watson's response to it, it is necessary to go beyond the singularity of the conventional legal framework.

Patriarchy, Colonialism and Australian Law

As well as comprising a complex and bewildering sequence of legal actions, the litigation and political counter-actions surrounding the *Kartinyeri* litigation is an instalment in the 'history wars'.[7] In Australian popular culture the history wars followed the *Mabo* decision[8] that overturned the doctrine of *terra nullius* in relation to determining native title claims.[9] Following this decision and other 'advances' in Aboriginal rights, academic disagreement about the historical record crossed over into media debates about Australian identity, with discussion centring on the patriotic need to dispense with what then Prime Minister Howard termed 'black armband views' of history. The history wars entailed an antagonistic discourse around reconciliation, the truth about the 'settlement' of Australia, its impact on Aboriginal peoples and the appropriate role of the court in settling and correcting the historical record. Legal debate surrounding the constitutionality of the *Bridge Act* also encompasses concern for judicial activism and the extent of legal obligations to respect Aboriginal cultural beliefs. In so doing, *Kartinyeri* speaks directly to matters at the heart of the history wars and to the role of law in redressing injustice.

Watson's response to *Kartinyeri* rejects the conventional framing of the case as being about the race power, secret women's business, the truth of history or redressing past injustice. It is not written in the form of a legal judgment. Instead, she reinstates the priority of the oral traditions of the land and the peoples whose culture and heritage was at the heart of the dispute. In showing how different stories and different versions of stories of the land have been handed down, retold, distorted, misinterpreted, and the peoples misnamed, Watson shows how Aboriginal women's law has been contained and suppressed throughout Australian history. In so doing she reveals intimate connections between

[7] Stuart Macintyre and Anna Clark, *The History Wars* (Melbourne University Press, 2004) 151–3, 196–7.

[8] *Mabo v Queensland (No 2)* (1992) 175 CLR 1.

[9] It should be noted the foundational significance of *terra nullius* to Australian settlement is disputed by some Australian historians. See Andrew Fitzmaurice, 'The Genealogy of Terra Nullius' (2007) 129 *Australian Historical Studies* 1.

patriarchy, colonialism and Australian law. It is the naturalness and pervasiveness of these close connections that led to Watson's rejection of the methodology of the Australian Feminist Judgments Project and which informs her incisive critique of Australian legal jurisprudence. To understand what is at stake we need to hear an Aboriginal woman's voice, in her own terms.

First Nations Stories, Grandmother's Law: Too Many Stories to Tell

IRENE WATSON*

Kaldowinyeri[1]

Where to begin? From the beginning, the sisters were running and running away from the man Ngurrunderi; they ran past our country at the edge of the Coorong, the end of Tangane country, towards a place called Thangul, the land of the Tanganekald. They are First Nations Peoples and to whom I belong. The sisters ran away from Ngurrunderi[2] who was chasing his 'claimed women', his two wives.

Then Ngurrunderi came along to that same place and he was stopped by our ancestor Paramapari; Ngurrunderi and Paramapari fought right on the beach, where the Coorong lands end. Now this is a place where the old rocks come up out of the sea, the place where the grandmothers sit. Ngurrunderi fought Paramapari because he would not tell Ngurrunderi if he had seen the sisters and what direction they were heading in. There are different versions of what happened; one version tells of Paramapari falling following a fatal blow from Ngurrunderi's club and to make sure that he was dead Ngurrunderi placed Paramapari's body on a fire which burned for days and days. The granite boulders on the beach are said to represent his body. That same place is also where the sisters ran past, running along the Coorong, running to escape Ngurrunderi. As the sisters ran, they called out to each other; they laughed and stopped and ate fish, danced and sang songs as they laid down their story. They ran away from Ngurrunderi.[3]

One True God

Why was Ngurrunderi chasing his two wives? Also, why was his story privileged as the one true story, over the stories of Paramapari and the sisters? In contemporary times, the history of Ngurrunderi is retold as *the* story, the story which has constructed the Aboriginality of the First Nations Peoples of the River Murray and Coorong region.[4] Now some have called me Ngarrindjeri, but when the old people knew the land and its peoples there was no such name. We knew ourselves as Tanganekald, Yaraldi, Ramindjeri, among others. But today

* I would like to thank Kathy Bowrey for both her commentary and comments in general; thanks also to the editors for their feedback, Skye Krichauff for assistance in double checking historical references and Jo Bird for editorial assistance.

[1] A time when the land formed and the stories of country and dreaming emerged.

[2] The spelling of Aboriginal languages historically has undergone many changes. Ngurrunderi is now the most common pronunciation, while in the 1850s onwards Taplin used 'Nurunderee'. There are a number of variations on the pronunciation of Ngurrunderi.

[3] This version of the story is recorded by Norman Tindale, (1934–37) 2 *Journal of Researches in the South East of South Australia* 58 (Anthropology Archive, South Australian Museum).

[4] This is part of the coastal formation of the south-east of South Australia.

the privileged 'Ngarrindjeri' is a name which dominates native title jurisprudence, and its adherents claim the lands of the Tanganekald, Yaraldi and Ramindjeri among other groups as their own. Ngarrindjeri is a name which first became big when the missionary man George Taplin put the story down in its written form, and then it was expanded upon.[5]

Reverend Taplin's story went like this:

> Ngurrunderi was a man God who chased his two wives all along the Coorong and back again; he hunted them for days and days because they had eaten a food taboo to women and then fled his camp. For this he chased them along the Coorong and back again and all the way around past the Bluff at Victor Harbour where he threw his club at the sisters. Further to the west, he sang to cause the sea to rise and drown them and their bodies became the Pages Islands sitting out there, sticking up out of the sea between Kangaroo Island and the mainland. The club of Ngurrunderi now lies on the land, stretching out to sea.[6]

The story by Taplin is a tale endorsed by a British missionary. It reinscribes patriarchy while also introducing a christian patriarchal way of being into the lives of the newly colonised First Nations Peoples. The story of Ngurrunderi became privileged over the telling of many other stories about the land and how we lived with country. Many of these other stories came from a much earlier time than the time of Ngurrunderi. For example, the many different language groups and traditional identities of our ancestors had arrived well before Ngurrunderi. Our diverse languages were birthed from the body of Wururi, a female spider

> who roamed about at night, scattering fires while people slept – a dangerous practice – and she further exercised her bad temper by 'growling' that is, condemning others . . . When she died, there was much happiness and the people gathered to feast and celebrate. The Ramindjeri ate of her flesh first and, as other groups arrived from the north and the east, they too ate, each devouring different parts of the body and each then speaking a distinct language.[7]

Anthropologist Diane Bell interprets the story of Wururi as being evidence of the wholeness of a nation of the Ngarrindjeri.[8] In that act of retelling the story, Bell inadvertently inflates and centres Ngurrunderi as the hero-being that supports the construct of an overarching Ngarrindjeri entity. It is a construct which is best understood from a western eurocentric viewpoint informed by centuries of experience dominating and absorbing smaller peoples' identities into larger political identities. The Australian state subsumed First Nations Peoples into a patriarchal governance model. The coming into being of the Ngarrindjeri nation, for example, occurred at the expense and exclusion of the Tanganekald, Yaraldi, Ramindjeri and other First Nations Peoples; we were to be absorbed into a Ngarrindjeri identity. Bell reinscribes the work of early missionaries Meyer and Taplin on Ngarrindjeri identity, and many Nungas[9] living within and in connection to the mission experience of Point McLeay have also adopted that identity. But it is an identity which

[5] *Observer* (Adelaide), 19 November 1859, 3AB. The Congregationalist Reverend George Taplin founded Point McLeay Aboriginal mission in 1859, and at the first anniversary meeting to establish the Aboriginal Friends Association, the Bishop of Adelaide called upon the Association to provide for the 'spiritual and moral requirements of the aborigines'.

[6] George Taplin, *Journal: Five Volumes* as typed from the original by Mrs Beaumont (Mortlock Library, 1859–79) 25 June 1859, 13; 20 October 1859, 26; 18 November 1861, 139. There are as many versions of this story as there are differences in location and country.

[7] The story lives on in the oral traditions of the Ramindjeri people and was initially recorded by Norman Tindale in 1937. This version is cited in Dianne Bell, *Ngarrindjeri Wurruwarrin: A World That Is, Was and Will Be* (Spinifex Press, 1998) 137–8.

[8] Ibid 136–44.

[9] 'Nungas' means First Nation People. It is used extensively across southern South Australia.

comes at the expense of more ancient ones. Bell considers the capacity for Ngarrindjeri to act as a unified system of governance as follows: 'spider body as the origin of language is another way of thinking about the relationship between different entities. But what is the nature of this unity symbolically represented in the body of the spider?'[10]

Bell's question: 'what is the nature of this unity symbolically represented in the body of the spider?' is a good question. It is her response, however, which is closed to any other possibilities beyond the overarching Ngarrindjeri nation identity. Ngarrindjeri is what the early missionaries and colonists called us when they knew nothing of the complexity and depth of our stories and our laws; they named us in the same way that they called our country *terra nullius*, a way which excluded our pre-colonisation identities as both First Nations Peoples and also as law-full women. The invaders and the missionaries could only see and know us in the frame of their own experiences and knowledge systems – all about a male creator whom they represented as god to us all. The construction of Ngurrunderi as an all-powerful creator provided the missionaries with a storyline into the culture and minds of Nungas. The missionary Taplin became engaged in learning what he called the Ngarrindjeri language for the purpose of translating the bible. The 'Ngarrindjeri' were to come to hear and read about themselves in the context of christian myth and stories. Meanwhile, our Aboriginal ruwi-land became demonised, and we were seen instead to be in need of clothing, and to become 'civilised' just like the invaders. Reverend Taplin wrote in his Journals about Aboriginal law and its ceremonies as being 'barbaric': 'I find that most of the corroborees are very beastly and shall henceforth set my face against them, indeed I have always done so to some extent. I shall now enforce that no Christian shall go to a corroboree.'[11]

Bare Life – On the Margins

Within 10 years of the original invasion, the region of the south-east of South Australia was a war zone, with the guns of the Europeans inflicting devastation. Our Peoples who did not conform were called 'myall', or wild blacks, living outside the towns and missions of the settler. They were the old people who were left exposed to the frontier violence of massacres and poisoning by colonists. Their stories were mainly left untold. How can you speak with your tongue cut out, how can you speak the language of the old people when it has been stripped away because you have been locked away in the dormitories and prison chains of the coloniser? How might women *be* women without the knowledge to be? Can we only then perform as their slaves left to masquerade as women in the one true story of men?

Though sheltering people from the murderous frontier, Taplin still argued strongly for the destruction of First Nations culture. 'I told all the blacks plainly this morning, that they obeyed the devil, and that Jehovah would send them to hell with the devil if they did not cease to obey him'.[12] The christianising mission was to clothe Nungas and 'move forward': 'Many young adult natives, who would have belonged to the most degraded portion of the

[10] Bell, above n 7, 137.
[11] Taplin, above n 6, 7 March 1862, 96.
[12] Ibid, 2 November 1859, 28.

human family, are now clothed and in their right minds sitting at the feet of Jesus.'[13] The missionary vision was to strip away our connections to the natural world – to our land, our families and our culture. Our children were taken from their families and placed in dormitories where they were forbidden to speak our languages or practise our culture and law, and the stories and voices of women became subdued – just like the voices of white women. Reverend Taplin wrote in his journal in 1859:

> This horrid rite [ceremonial law] is much calculated to throw them back into barbarism, whatever good instruction they may have received in youth. Whatever sense of cleanliness, or love of European clothes may have been acquired is by this rite completely swept away. This custom must be done away with.[14]

Those who did not seek the sanctuary which Taplin provided at Point McLeay ended up dead, or nearly so. The following letter written by the police officer Armstrong at Meningie describes the conditions of our old people who lived away from the mission station of Point McLeay. It was written on 8 September 1891, more than 50 years after South Australia was established:

> Mrs Robb of Woods Well reported that old natives were in a very bad state near her place and they had asked her . . . to inform the police. I visited their camp on the 7th September and found that there are about 5 or 6 old people that are really in want of clothing, two old women are blind and are also unable to walk as far as I could ascertain. One old woman had nothing to cover her except a shirt and a blanket and another had not any clothing except a surge [*sic*] dress. They appear to be suffering from a sort of mange no doubt from their dogs, which are numerous. I advised them to go to Pt McLeay, but they state that the water there does not agree with them.[15]

Many of the old people did resist the constraints and limitations of living on the mission, despite the rigours of fringe-dwelling. My ancestors lived on the fringes from the earliest time of the invasion, and came to hold a different view of the world to the people who stayed at Point McLeay mission. At the time of the invasion the invaders knew nothing about who we were, but they deployed methods to annihilate our Nunga being – open warfare, genocide, separation and assimilation. Their coming to our lands was theoretically underpinned by *terra nullius*, the idea that we do not exist and that we could only come to exist through their ways of knowing and of coming to their god and their laws. So the Nunga survivors of colonialism return to places which now have colonial names and colonial translations of Nunga history and law. Since colonial times only one law is 'known' to exist, and the story of Ngurrunderi has become a part of the colonising mission, part of the one 'true' story retold over and over so as to weave the life of the First Nation who call themselves Ngarrindjeri more solidly into the life of the invader and becoming their object of Australian law.

The colonising mission continues to aim at dismantling our cultures and laws. Our stories were marginalised, proscribed and some lost to living memory (yet to be dreamed back). Through the power of colonisation and the agency of the missionaries, Ngurrunderi became the one god of the Ngarrindjeri; the word God was used to describe the creative powers of the ancestors and their role in creating landscape, the natural world, laws and

[13] John Harris, *One Blood: 200 Years of Aboriginal Encounter with Christianity* (Albatross Books, 1994) 530–1.
[14] Taplin, above n 6, 7 March 1862, 96.
[15] South Australian Government, *State Government Records*, GRG 52/1/1891/280.

customs.[16] The word God made invisible all other creative processes. The early reverence for Ngurrunderi as a god-identity was established through the subversive use of our languages. God is a word which brings with it a one-dimensional world view, a word which refutes the feminine and proscribes the natural world and its animal life. The world becomes viewed through a patriarchal christian lens. This approach has led to, for example, the demonising of the women in the story of Prupi, and the forgetting of Thukapi the tortoise, and Kondoli the whale. Animals could not be gods.

In more contemporary times Hemming, Jones, and Clarke, the curators of the South Australian Museum exhibit 'Ngurrunderi' represented 'the' creation story, as the 'text' on all things: identity, language, culture, and laws of the Ngarrindjeri. The curators noted 'the over-arching importance of Ngurrunderi as law-giver and as the main shaper of the distinctive landscape in which Ngarrindjeri people still live today.'[17]

Before the invasion, we had no hierarchy of gods looking down and over the people: our stories placed as much importance in our animal and female beings and the way their stories wove our being into existence as they did the stories of the men. Once the colonisers had embedded the agency of the missionary and christianity had established itself, Ngurrunderi himself was replaced with the myth of Jesus.

Out with the Old

The mission experience provided a framework and a home for the new Ngarrindjeri identity.[18] Point McLeay (or Raukkan) was the place where the new mission home emerged in response to the impact of colonialism and the massive decline in population of the different First Nations, including Yaraldi, Ramindjeri and Tanganekald nations. The emerging single Ngarrindjeri nation was to take form from the belly of genocide. In the early colonial frontier times after the invasion, many of our peoples living along the Coorong were massacred.[19] Those who survived had the power to govern their lives removed, and had their connections to their land and the space, and the language to articulate a world view that centred Nunga ways of being in the world, disrupted. Our stories seemed lost in the new world of the invader and the missionary man of God. The latter told stories of the laws of the invader, while stories of the coming of language and the death of the spider woman were marginalised. Patriarchy was imposed and with it came another law way, one which buried the laws of the land and the laws of women. All those law stories which were learned through oral tradition became known as something else. Colonising myths told the story of Nunga women being without authority and status in traditional societies, as a vehicle for a crusade against Nunga men as well as the old laws. They were, of course, not true. First

[16] While Rev George Taplin saw Ngurrunderi as a 'vile character' and held the idea of God in the image of Jehovah, Ngurrunderi would be transformed and assimilated into that same Christian image. See Taplin, above n 7.

[17] Steven Hemming, Philip Jones and Philip Clarke, *Ngurunderi: An Aboriginal Dreaming* (South Australian Museum, 1989) 4.

[18] The word Narrinyeri was to become Ngarrindjeri and derives from the word Kornarrinyeri, meaning 'belonging to men'; unlike Yaraldi, Ramindjeri or Tanganekald, Ngarrindjeri is not ruwe-land-location specific.

[19] SD Lendrum, 'The Coorong Massacre: Martial Law and the Aborigines at First Settlement' (1977) 6 *Adelaide Law Review* 26 provides a historical account of the South Australian colonial government's management of the massacre, including the use of martial law.

Nations women of Australia have a law known to women, as do the men have law known to them. White male anthropologists have tended to reflect a patriarchal ideology of colonial Australian culture upon us, and in imposing their own values they created the idea that Nunga women were oppressed (in the same way their own societies had oppressed women, but more so).

The Hindmarsh Island Bridge Royal Commission found Nunga women's law to not exist in the River Murray lower lakes Coorong region, and further to have been fabricated by those who argued for its existence. The Commission was established to enquire into the existence of women's law, but women's law could not be presented in the way the government wanted it to be told, that is, within a legal framework that set about to interrogate the laws of women, within an environment that was open to the public and to men and also to the flashing lights of the media. The story that was told by a group of First Nations women who argued against the existence of women's law was one mixed up with colonisation and the effects of christianity upon Nunga ways of being.

Sovereignty, Law-full Women and the New

From a critical Nunga perspective, the Australian legal system is without jurisdiction to determine the laws of the First Nations Peoples of what is now called Australia. The question remains alive: 'by what lawful authority did the invader invade our lands?'[20] Determinations of sovereignty by the Australian legal system and the state were made under the unethical framework of *terra nullius*. The British have never attempted to enter into any treaty agreements with any sovereign First Nations Peoples of Australia – including the Tanganekald and Meintangk Peoples – while we have become displaced, and our lands occupied and developed without our consent. The doctrine of *terra nullius* was used to legally annihilate Nungas, and this position has not been altered post-*Mabo (No 2)*[21] and the native title legislation.[22] The question of foundation still requires an answer. It is illogical to assume that, because there were no juridical relations between First Nations Peoples and colonial powers, the situation should result in a differentiation between respective rights.[23] The question remains relevant because while the theory of *terra nullius* has been rejected in *Mabo (No 2)*, it remains embedded as a legitimating principle for the foundation of the state.[24] The underlying principle of foundation of Australian law remains unchallenged, even though Article 2.4 of the *Charter of the United Nations* provides that contemporary international law must reject rights which are secured via unethical means.[25] I put

[20] For a more detailed discussion of these issues see Irene Watson, 'The Tanganekald and Meintangk Peoples', Submission to the United Nations Office of the High Commissioner for Human Rights at the Seminar on Strengthening Partnership between Indigenous Peoples and States: Treaties, Agreements and Constructive Arrangements, Geneva, 16–17 July 2012.

[21] *Mabo v Queensland (No 2)* (1992) 175 CLR 1 ('*Mabo (No 2)*').

[22] *Native Title Act 1993* (Cth); *Native Title Amendment Act 1998* (Cth).

[23] Miguel Alfonso Martinez, Special Rapporteur, *Final Report on the Study on Treaties, Agreements and Other Constructive Arrangements between States and Indigenous Populations*, 51st sess, UN Doc E/CN4/Sub.2/1999/20 (22 June 1999) [285].

[24] *Mabo (No 2)* (1992) 175 CLR 1, 30.

[25] Martinez, above n 23 [287].

the question again: by what lawful authority do you bring my native body into your law from the outside while keeping me out there?

Is there one true story to tell, and one law, and one way of being? The dominant story has already been made out; it is a story which was implanted by force, made legitimate by *terra nullius*, and remains a process which goes unchallenged post-*Mabo*. Is it possible for other stories of law and culture to co-exist, beyond one just cut to fit into the dominant narrative? Where might my Tanganekald creation story become sovereign in the retelling of a time when our elders saw the sea and called out:

Guru'nulun'and	'wardand	'wanunj ganji
'goronjkanjal	'lei a' meinjg	'nainj'gara'nal
'guru'nulun'and	'wardand	'terto:'lin
(h')end 'barum ai!	'walanjala	talanja'leir
r'einamb	'maranj'gara'nal.[26]	

The song sang our beginnings, when the ancestors travelling from the north, coming close to the Coorong and the sea, heard the crashing sound of the ocean. It made the old people frightened. they stood still, and some wanted to return to the north, but they agreed to stay and settle down. One of the people called out 'Tanjo'walo'njan', 'what will you do now?' The name of the Tangane or Tanganekald was created from this call.[27]

In a colonised space, woman's law risks erasure; within the colonising white patriarchal frame, one law claims to represent law for all. In the old days, the law stories of women lived in the land and held a place in the lives of the peoples they belonged to, but now the law-full woman is diminished by the dominant narrative of male gods and their laws. Our stories of women are often sacred and secret, and there is a reason for this, for we can see the danger of women's stories becoming subverted and becoming something else when they are retold within patriarchal frameworks; we saw where Australian law took those narratives and how it was a christian narrative which prevailed in the Hindmarsh Island Bridge Royal Commission. The matter of *Kartinyeri*[28] came about as a result of the events before the Hindmarsh Island Royal Commission, but the opportunity in *Kartinyeri* to include First Nations women's law narratives was not realised, and nor could be, as the issue before the court concerned the constitutional validity of the *Hindmarsh Island Bridge Act*. The question of women's law was never raised. Instead, the High Court entrenched the *terra nullius* narrative by allowing the Australian *Constitution* to remain unchallenged and its inherent white patriarchal privilege to remain intact.

The idea of there being one true story has come to frame all things, including the jurisprudential traditions of the common law. They are traditions drawn from a white patriarchal position and thinking about what constitutes the legal order and that which is excluded from that order. At the time of the invasion and early colonial frontier violence, First Nations were legally entirely excluded by the doctrine of *terra nullius*. Now we are known to have

[26] The song was sung by Milerum and recorded by Norman Tindale, above n 3, 108–9.

[27] Ibid.

[28] Those who opposed the building of the bridge from the mainland to Kumarangk applied to the Commonwealth Minister Tickner in April 1994, for a declaration to prevent construction. The *Aboriginal and Torres Strait Islander Heritage Protection Act 1984* (Cth) provides 'protection' for a site which is a significant Aboriginal area, in accordance with Aboriginal tradition and as interpreted and translated by the State Minister. See *Kartinyeri v The Commonwealth* [1998] 195 CLR 337.

existed at the time of Cook's coming, but we are now known to be peoples without any subjectivity in international law or sovereignty. I have disputed the myth of there being First Nations Peoples without law, and argued instead that we are nations of many laws – including the laws of women.

The rewriting of the judgment of *Kartinyeri* in accordance with the methodology of this project would not prise open places for Nunga women because the rewriting needs to be done from 'another space', outside the jurisdiction of the Australian common law and the sovereignty of the Australian state. The jurisdiction of Australian law is contestable due to its being imposed without lawful foundation beyond the unethical one of *terra nullius*. Therefore the option of rewriting within Australian law is not likely to return ruwe to sovereign First Nations legal systems that are inclusive of co-existing women's and men's laws.

4

R v Pearson; Ex parte Sipka: Feminism and the Franchise

ELISA ARCIONI

Introduction

On 3 February 1983, the Australian Prime Minister, Malcolm Fraser, called a snap federal election. The procedural wheels of electoral law began to turn, including the closing of the electoral rolls the next day. In order to vote in a federal election, a person must be both eligible to vote (which usually means that the person is an adult citizen)[1] and have their name on the electoral roll. The quick closure of the rolls meant that thousands of eligible electors, who were not yet enrolled, would be prevented from voting in the 1983 election held on 5 March 1983.[2] The Public Interest Advocacy Centre (PIAC) decided to challenge the early closure of the rolls, relying on s 41 of the *Constitution*, which states:

> No adult person who has or acquires a right to vote at elections for the more numerous House of the Parliament of a State shall, while the right continues, be prevented by any law of the Commonwealth from voting at elections for either House of the Parliament of the Commonwealth.

On its face, this section seemed to mean that all State electors should be able to vote in the federal election. The PIAC identified four individuals who represented categories of eligible electors. They commenced proceedings in the High Court to force the Australian Electoral Commission to allow federal enrolment of any person who was eligible to vote in their State. So began constitutional proceedings in *R v Pearson; Ex parte Sipka* ('*Sipka*'),[3] which would end with a section of the *Constitution* being interpreted as a dead letter. Significantly, it is one of the few parts of the *Constitution* which has a strong feminist history, in the sense that it was inserted into the text in order to protect the votes of, amongst others, women.

Social, Political and Legal Context

The 1983 election campaign raised a number of issues; the closing of the rolls was only one, and not the most prominent. The Tasmanian Franklin Dam controversy was significant,

[1] For the detail of eligibility and grounds for disqualification, see *Commonwealth Electoral Act 1918* (Cth).

[2] Estimates varied from 50,000 to 500,000: see Richard McGregor, 'Electoral Office Says Most People Are on the Roll', *Sydney Morning Herald* (Sydney), 8 February 1983, 11.

[3] (1983) 152 CLR 254.

leading to another great constitutional case concerning the federal Parliament's power to make laws implementing international conventions.[4] This election also saw the rise of Bob Hawke as Labor leader, replacing Bill Hayden. The Ash Wednesday fires in Victoria and South Australia on 16 February distracted the nation's attention away from the election, as did the proceedings in the Azaria Chamberlain case.[5]

In this context, limited attention was given to the closure of the electoral rolls. Newspaper articles noted the issue, with some writers highlighting the perceived disproportionate effect on young voters and other groups, suggesting, in turn, a cynical motivation on the part of the government.[6] Similar comments regarding the effect of the closure of the rolls were aired in more recent times, when the Howard Government enacted legislation in 2006 to shorten the timeframe to enrol to vote after the calling of a federal election.[7] These two events are linked.

Following the 1983 election, federal parliament passed legislation to require a period of seven days between the issue of the writs for an election and the closing of the rolls.[8] The Second Reading speech identified one of the reasons for the change as being:

> to make it easier for electors to get on the rolls and stay on the rolls . . . For example, the Bill provides that there must be a sufficient time between the announcement of an election and the close of rolls for that election.[9]

As noted in the case of *Rowe v Electoral Commissioner*:[10] '[t]he seven-day period of grace then introduced operated for eight subsequent federal elections', until 2006, when the Howard Government shortened the timeframe once more.[11] By contrast to *Sipka*, in *Rowe* in 2010, the High Court decided that the 2006 amendment was invalid, as it imposed too great a burden on the ability of 'the people' to exercise their constitutional choice of Members of Parliament. The High Court in that case relied on ss 7 and 24 of the *Constitution*, which require that federal Members of Parliament be directly chosen by 'the people'. Section 41 had no role to play in either case, despite its drafting history demonstrating concerns for the protection of the right to vote in federal elections.

[4] *Commonwealth v Tasmania* (1983) 158 CLR 1.

[5] In August 1980, Azaria Chamberlain, a two-month old baby, disappeared near Uluru in central Australia. Her parents claimed she had been taken by a dingo, but they were both charged and convicted over her alleged murder. In February 1983, a much-publicised appeal commenced over those convictions in the Federal Court: see *Chamberlain v R* (1983) 72 FLR 1 (29 April 1983). The convictions were later quashed and the Northern Territory coroner concluded in 2012 that Azaria had been taken by a dingo. For more discussion of the 1983 election, see Anne Summers, *Gamble for Power: How Bob Hawke Beat Malcolm Fraser: The 1983 Federal Election* (Thomas Nelson, 1983).

[6] See, eg, Shaun Watson, Letter to the Editor, 'Young Voters Frozen Out', *The Australian* (Sydney), 14 February 1983, 10.

[7] See Joint Standing Committee on Electoral Matters, Parliament of Australia, *Report on the Conduct of the 2007 Federal Election and Matters Related Thereto* (2009) 46–49; *Rowe v Electoral Commissioner* (2010) 243 CLR 1, 33 [67] (French CJ), 63 [174], 74 [214] (Hayne J), 90 [271] (Heydon J).

[8] Commonwealth Electoral Legislation Amendment Act 1983 (Cth).

[9] Commonwealth, *Parliamentary Debates*, House of Representatives, 2 November 1983, 2216 (Kim Beazley).

[10] (2010) 243 CLR 1, 31–2 [60] (French CJ) ('*Rowe*').

[11] *Electoral and Referendum Amendment (Electoral Integrity and Other Measures) Act 2006* (Cth).

The History of Section 41

The *Constitution* documented the unification of the six Australian colonies and their peoples into the Australian federal Commonwealth. In drafting the *Constitution*, numerous compromises were reached in order to obtain the support of each of those colonies. Section 41 of the *Constitution* was one such compromise. In 1891, the date of the first draft of what would become the *Constitution*, no woman in any Australian colony had the right to vote. In 1895, women in South Australia were enfranchised;[12] Western Australia followed suit in 1899.[13] During the drafting debates of 1897–98, the position of South Australia was that it would not agree to federate without ensuring the protection of its voters' right to vote in future federal elections. Frederick Holder, from South Australia, proposed an amendment to the *Constitution* such that: 'Every man and woman of the full age of twenty-one years, whose name has been registered as an elector for at least six months, shall be an elector.'[14] His proposal was defeated 23:12.[15] Opposition came from the colonies which only enfranchised men, objecting to being forced into enfranchising all adults. The tenor of the debates was that a universal adult franchise was something for the future federal parliament to address, and that each colony's particular franchise should be left untouched by the constitutional drafting process.

The refusal to include such a broad franchise in the *Constitution* led to Holder proposing the ultimate compromise, that anyone who had a vote at federation should retain that vote, leading to the enactment of s 41. However, the wording of s 41 was not completely clear, with at least three different interpretations being outlined even in 1901.[16] The High Court had touched on the meaning of the section in two cases,[17] before finally addressing its application directly in 1983. How did the Court arrive at its interpretation in *Sipka*, maintained in later cases, which meant that s 41 no longer protects any person's right to vote? Could greater emphasis on the feminist history of the section have led to an alternative outcome?

The Reasoning of the Court

In *Sipka*, a majority of the High Court concluded that s 41 had exhausted its effect; Murphy J dissented. The majority relied upon the text of the *Constitution*, and the drafting history of various sections, in order to read s 41 as having no more work to do. Sections 8 and 30 of the *Constitution* meant that the federal franchise was to be that which applied in each State

[12] See *Constitution Amendment Act 1894* (SA) ('*Adult Suffrage Act*'), effective from 20 March 1895.

[13] See *Constitution Acts Amendment Act 1899* (WA), which consolidated a number of amendments to the Constitution of that colony, including granting women the vote, but note that not all women in that State were thereby enfranchised. By s 15, women (and men) over 21 were entitled to vote subject to property qualifications, which required either owning property or being a 'householder' of a property of a certain value. Aboriginal natives 'of Australia, Asia, or Africa', and persons 'of the half-blood' were excluded.

[14] *Official Record of the Debates of the Australasian Federal Convention*, Adelaide, 15 April 1897, 715 (Frederick Holder).

[15] Ibid 725.

[16] See John Quick and Robert Randolph Garran, *The Annotated Constitution of the Australian Commonwealth* (LexisNexis Butterworths, 1901) 486.

[17] *Muramats v Commonwealth Electoral officer (WA)* (1923) 32 CLR 500; *King v Jones* (1982) 128 CLR 221.

until the federal Parliament enacted a uniform franchise. The federal Parliament did so in 1902.[18] The majority concluded that the protection of s 41 was to apply only in the intervening period. Only those who had a right to vote in their State 'before the passing' of that federal law were covered by s 41. Given that it was unlikely that any such person was still alive by 1983, the practical effect of s 41 was spent.

The majority concluded that s 41 was only of transitional value, prioritising the uniform federal franchise which took effect from 1902. After that time, any historical compromises made by the colonies, which became the States, were overtaken by the will of the federal Parliament. The majority was keen not to allow the States to jeopardise the uniformity of the franchise. No concern was displayed for the impact on individuals or groups, even those who were at the heart of the framing of s 41. Thus, the feminist history of s 41 was relegated to a discrete period of time, with no ongoing constitutional importance.

Murphy J took a different approach, in which the same history was used to opposite effect. Like the majority judges, Murphy J looked to the words of the *Constitution*, but adopted a more literal interpretation of s 41. He disagreed regarding the ongoing import of the section, because of a difference of approach with respect to the detail of the drafting history of the section. The majority preferred the 'restricted interpretation' of s 41, in line with the view of Quick and Garran in their influential text on the *Constitution*.[19] Murphy J disagreed with that view of the convention debates, referring to detail of those debates ignored by the majority.[20] His reasoning is also imbued with concerns for representation and democracy.

Aftermath of *Sipka*

There was not a huge political fall-out from the decision in *Sipka*. The case was noted in the media,[21] but the public's attention then moved on to other matters. A proposal to delete s 41 and insert an explicit protection of the right to vote was defeated in 1988.[22] However, the decision in *Sipka* has been criticised by scholars,[23] despite ongoing support from the High Court.[24]

[18] See *Commonwealth Franchise Act 1902* (Cth).

[19] Quick and Garran, above n 16, 486–7; *Sipka* (1983) 152 CLR 254, 262 (Gibbs CJ, Mason and Wilson JJ), 278–9 (Brennan, Deane, and Dawson JJ).

[20] See *Sipka* (1983) 152 CLR 254, 272.

[21] See, eg Verge Blunden, 'Action by Four who Missed the Vote Fails', *Sydney Morning Herald* (Sydney), 25 February 1983, 11.

[22] See *Constitution Alteration (Fair Elections) 1988* and note the earlier proposal which would have entrenched voting rights in 1974: *Constitution Alteration (Democratic Elections)*.

[23] For the most detailed critical analysis, see Anne Twomey, 'The Federal Constitutional Right to Vote in Australia' (2000) 28 *Federal Law Review* 125, esp 138–41. See also Peter Hanks, *Constitutional Law in Australia* (Butterworths, 2nd ed, 1996) 15; Adrian Brooks, 'A Paragon of Democratic Virtues: The Development of the Commonwealth Franchise' (1993) 12 *University of Tasmania Law Review* 208, 246–8.

[24] The *Sipka* interpretation of s 41 has never been challenged by a majority of the High Court: see *Holmdahl v Australian Electoral Commission (No 2)* [2012] SASCFC 110 (24 September 2012) [11]–[12]; *McGinty v Western Australia* (1996) 186 CLR 140, 244, 282; *Muldowney v Australian Electoral Commission* (1993) 178 CLR 34, 38–9; *Mulholland v Australian Electoral Commission* (2004) 220 CLR 181, 235; *Roach v Electoral Commissioner* (2007) 233 CLR 162, 195 (*Roach*); *Snowdon v Dondas* (1996) 188 CLR 48, 71–2. Even in the more detailed analysis of *Sipka* in *Rowe*, the ultimate conclusion reached in *Sipka* was not in doubt: *Rowe* (2010) 243 CLR 1, 13–14, 27–8, 31–2, 41, 48, 79–81, 113–14.

The majority reasoning is intriguing, as much for what it does say, and how it says it, as for what it omits. The majority took a very limited approach to s 41 and its history. This makes sense to some extent, because the date of the judgment preceded the famous case of *Cole v Whitfield* ('*Cole*'),[25] in which the High Court finally stated that it is legitimate to refer directly to the constitutional drafting debates in the course of understanding the meaning of the constitutional text. Prior to that date, the High Court used the drafting history at the same time as being ambivalent about directly citing the published records of the proceedings. This perhaps explains the restrained use of those debates by the majority, as compared to the slightly more extensive use made by Murphy J. While the Court was directed to various possible interpretations of the history during argument, it was framed in general terms regarding the 'envisagement' or 'speculation' as to what the drafters intended.[26]

Taking a broader view of the debates also assists in understanding why the majority reached their ultimate conclusion. Their judgment reinforces the preference expressed in those debates for parliamentary control of electoral rules and rights, rather than explicit rights protections within the *Constitution*. The debates revealed the overall view that the Parliament should decide, and the majority is consistent with that approach. It is only in more recent times that the High Court has become increasingly interventionist with respect to the operation of representative government.[27] Section 41 is understood in this context as a stop-gap sufficient to protect pre-existing rights, until the federal parliament expresses its will, being the will of the electors who choose their representatives.

None of the original judgments demonstrates feminist inclinations. The majority dismiss the feminist advocacy prior to federation as relevant to the ongoing meaning of s 41. Murphy J gives more attention to that history, but only slightly more. What is the outcome if more detailed and nuanced attention is given to the story of women's fight to retain and maintain their political participation in the new federal Commonwealth?

Alternative Feminist Judgment

The feminist judgment, written by Kim Rubenstein, provides a dissenting judgment to add to Murphy J's original dissenting judgment. As outlined above, Murphy J gave greater attention to the drafting history of s 41 than the majority, and emphasised the democratic nature of the system of representative government under the *Constitution*. Rubenstein places even further emphasis on the political context of the case, relying on the narratives of the women of South Australia who were responsible for the insertion of s 41 in the *Constitution*. That section is viewed as the basis for the protection of the right to vote of women and other groups, thus being a section with democratic, feminist and federalist foundations. The federal element is seen in Rubenstein's response to the majority's privileging of a federal uniform franchise. Rubenstein identifies the value of allowing the States to experiment with voting rights, in order to enrich the democratic experience across the country.

[25] (1988) 165 CLR 360.

[26] Transcript of proceedings, *R v Pearson; Ex parte Sipka* (High Court, Gibbs CJ, Mason, Murphy, Wilson, Brennan, Deane, and Dawson JJ, 17 February 1983) 34–40 (see particularly statements of Wilcox QC).

[27] See *Roach* (2007) 233 CLR 162; *Rowe* (2010) 243 CLR 1.

Rubenstein's judgment is distinctive for two reasons. First, she explicitly describes the involvement of women in politics prior to the *Constitution*, including the roles played by key individuals and colonies in the advancement of women's political equality. Rather than relying simply on the convention debates, Rubenstein delves deeper into the historical materials. Thus, she highlights the stories of women at federation, rather than allowing their involvement only to be understood through the debates of the all-male delegates to the federal conventions. Women's voices and stories are heard directly.

Second, Rubenstein uses those materials not only to allow a recording of the past that is absent in the original judgments, but also to inform the method of interpretation to be applied to s 41. Rubenstein adopts some of the orthodox elements of constitutional interpretation – text, history and underlying structural or policy arguments. She identifies the key difference between her approach and that of the majority judges: should the history be read to mean that only the rights of women at federation are protected by s 41, or is 'a broader commitment to the right to vote' to be derived from that material, thus extending the protection of voting rights beyond that temporally limited group? Rubenstein opts for the latter, demonstrating that judges can exercise choice in the way they identify materials to be used in constitutional interpretation, as well as how they reach their ultimate conclusion based upon the chosen materials.

This last point feeds into the contested use of history by the High Court in constitutional cases.[28] While the Court has often referred to a variety of historical sources, it has expressly justified reference to the drafting debates for the limited purposes of determining the 'contemporary meaning of language used, the subject to which that language was directed and the nature and objectives of the movement towards federation from which the compact of the *Constitution* finally emerged'.[29] The Court expressly rejected use of historical sources for the purpose of determining the 'subjective' intentions of the framers. Rubenstein's reference to historical materials seems to straddle the divide between subjective and objective intentions, as well as challenging whose words are relevant in interpreting the meaning of the *Constitution*. By referring to the broader history of women's fight for political participation, Rubenstein challenges the orthodox understanding which focuses on the intentions of the 'founding fathers'[30] by extending our gaze to the actions and beliefs of those who could be counted as amongst the *Constitution's* founding mothers.

[28] See Helen Irving, 'Constitutional Interpretation, the High Court and the Discipline of History' (2013) 41 *Federal Law Review* 95.

[29] *Cole* (1988) 165 CLR 360, 385.

[30] Note Irving's response to the use of this phrase in Irving, above n 28, 109, fn 72.

[HIGH COURT OF AUSTRALIA.]

THE QUEEN
AGAINST
PEARSON;
EX PARTE SIPKA.

THE QUEEN
AGAINST
PEARSON;
EX PARTE KLEPPICH.

THE QUEEN
against
PEARSON;
EX PARTE CHAPMAN.

THE QUEEN
against
PEARSON;
EX PARTE WALTERS.

RUBENSTEIN J. Listening closely to the women of the 1890s who were the first with an electoral voice in Australia, I join in dissent with Murphy J. This case and the Court's interpretation of s. 41 reflect the importance of a democratic system to a constitutional order. The objectives of those women who were instrumental to the insertion of s. 41 in the Constitution are relevant to the outcome of this matter.

Section 41 states plainly:

> "No adult person who has or acquires a right to vote at elections for the more numerous House of the Parliament of a State shall, while the right continues, be prevented by any law of the Commonwealth from voting at elections for either House of the Parliament of the Commonwealth."

Lying at the heart of the interpretation of this section is the tension between federalism and representative democracy in our Constitution. The claims of the women of the 1890s assist us in hearing the prosecutors in this matter and the argument being made by them before the Court. Those trailblazing women's actions are relevant to how best to resolve a continuing tension in our foundational political document, the Australian Constitution, in favour of representative democracy.

The context for this case coming before the court. Each constitutional case brought before this Court ultimately affects individuals with lives influenced by government and government activity. There are also significant political issues underpinning this matter, which comes to the Court during a period of heightened political activity. The 32rd Federal Parliament first met on 25 November 1980 and would have continued until 25 November 1983, save for the provision

H.C. OF A. 1983

THE QUEEN v. PEARSON; EX PARTE SIPKA.

Rubenstein J.

in s. 32 of the Constitution enabling the Governor-General in Council to "cause writs to be issued for general elections of members of the House of Representatives . . . within 10 days from the expiry of the House of Representatives *or from the proclamation of a dissolution thereof*" (emphasis added). While the Prime Minister, The Honourable Malcolm Fraser, was reported in the media on several occasions during the past few months as saying there would not be an early election (1), on that same day he announced that on his advice, the Governor-General had agreed to a double-dissolution of the Senate and the House of Representatives. This is the fifth double dissolution in the history of this Commonwealth, pursuant to s. 57 of the Constitution.

The practice until this election has been that when a federal election is imminent (according to the three-year electoral term), many of the people who have become qualified since the last election to vote (those turning 18; those who have become Australian citizens; those who have moved house or have no fixed address – all of whom are eligible under the *Commonwealth Electoral Act* 1918) can ensure they are enrolled before the writs are issued, as provided for by s. 42 of the *Commonwealth Electoral Act*. And while s. 32 of the Constitution states that writs are to be issued within ten days of the expiry of the House, the writs were issued for this forthcoming election *on the day following* the proclamation of the dissolution, 4 February 1983, with the date for nominations for the election fixed for 19 February 1983 and polling day set for 5 March 1983, with the return of the writs on or before 5 May 1983.

I have gone into some detail about the timing because it is crucial to why this case is before the Court. The four prosecutors were not enrolled on either the roll of the electors for the Commonwealth election at the time of the calling of the election, nor for that of a State. They were unable to enrol on the Commonwealth roll due to s. 45(a) of the *Commonwealth Electoral Act*, which states that "claims for enrolment or transfer of enrolment which are received by the Registrar after six o'clock in the afternoon of the day of the issue of the writ for an election shall not be registered until after the close of the polling at the election." They subsequently placed themselves on the State electoral roll.

While, as Murphy J. also points out, the issuing of the writs on the same day as the proclamation of the dissolution was done for the 1914 double dissolution, the practice since then has been to allow a space of some days between the proclamation of a double dissolution and the issue of the writs for the elections to enable people who are entitled to vote to be sure of having their names on the electoral roll. The Commonwealth Gazettes in 1951, 1974 and 1975 each shows a period of either nine or six days to enable people to do so.

The four prosecutors who bring this case to the Court will be excluded from participating and exercising their democratic rights in the forthcoming Federal election if their case is unsuccessful.

Mrs. Jarka Sipka became an Australian citizen on 2 December 1982. In contrast to her previous status as an alien living in Australia, she is now, in principle, in a position to exercise one of her duties as an Australian citizen. Mr. Murray Paul Chapman is an Aboriginal student and has been entitled to vote since 21

(1) See *The Australian* (Sydney), 3 February 1983.

December 1977. Ms. Sarah Jane Walters and Mr. Rudolph Kleppich both had significant events occur on 15 February 1983 (the day before our first day of hearing this matter) and a date that is between the closure of the electoral rolls and the election. Ms Walters turned 18, the minimum voting age in this country, and Mr. Kleppich became a citizen on that day, and, like Mrs. Sipka, is now in a position to be placed on the electoral roll as a result of his Australian citizenship. The four of them stand with many others who are entitled to be on the electoral roll. However, they were not yet enrolled and could not be enrolled between the calling of the election on 3 February 1983 and the closing of the writs on 4 February 1983.

Each of these people has been precluded by s. 45(a) of the *Commonwealth Electoral Act* 1918 (Cth) in that they had not enrolled by 6 p.m. on 4 February 1983 and could not be registered until after the close of polling. Each of the four prosecutors then placed their names on the electoral roll of New South Wales that is a joint Commonwealth/State roll (2). They are therefore now in a position to claim, pursuant to s. 41 of the Australian Constitution that "[n]o adult person who has or *acquires* a right to vote at elections for the more numerous House of the Parliament of a State shall, while the right continues be prevented by any law of the Commonwealth from voting at elections for either House of the Parliament of the Commonwealth" (emphasis added). They come to this Court to seek relief in the form of a writ of mandamus to direct the Electoral Commission to enable them to vote in the forthcoming election.

I will return later in my judgment to the specific issue of whether Ms. Walters falls within the definition of an adult given she is 18 and not 21. My first point is that, on its face, and in particular, due to the reference to a person having or "*acquiring a right to vote*", this section plainly provides the prosecutors with a clear and unambiguous constitutional entitlement to be enrolled and counted in this forthcoming election. This plain reading is also bolstered by inquiring further into the motives of those women of the 1890s who ensured that s. 41 would be part of the Constitution.

The history of s. 41. The history of s. 41 relates entirely to the history of women's voting rights in Australia and the less democratic antecedents of colonial Australia prior to Federation. The first piece of legislation in the colonies to give the vote to women was in South Australia, and not only did it give those women the vote, it also gave them the right to sit in Parliament.

This came after much work on the part of women in South Australia. A public meeting in support of women's suffrage was held in the Albert Hall in South Australia in 1893, under the auspices of the Women's Suffrage League, Woman's Christian Temperance Union and [Working] Women's Trades Union. Miss Catherine Helen Spence moved "[t]hat as no country can be called free where one half of its people are disenfranchised, in the opinion of this meeting the time has arrived when the suffrage should be granted to the women of South Australia" (3).

(2) See Arrangement between the Governor-General and the Governor of New South Wales making provision for a Joint Electoral Roll in New South Wales, Commonwealth, *Gazette*, 19 February 1930.

(3) *The Adelaide Register* (Adelaide), 15 March 1893.

H.C. OF A. 1983

THE QUEEN v. PEARSON; EX PARTE SIPKA.

Rubenstein J.

The *Adult Suffrage Bill* 1894 (S.A.) involved controversial debate in the Parliament, including statements from opponents that what would flow from giving women the vote, was "the dissolution of marriage and the institution of free love" (4). Despite this and other concerns, the Bill was passed on 18 December 1894 and became effective following proclamation on 20 March 1895. From that day, women in South Australia became the first in the world to have the right to vote *and sit in Parliament*. The New Zealand legislation that had been the first to give women the right to vote in 1893 had not given them the right to sit in Parliament (5). In 1899, Western Australia followed South Australia in allowing women the right to vote, but not the further step of allowing them to become members of Parliament.

The other colonies were slower off the mark. Victoria was the last Australian State after Federation to enfranchise women explicitly in 1908 (6). I use the term explicitly because, ironically, Victoria had actually empowered women to vote just seven years after the opening of the first Parliament of Victoria. In a piece of faulty legislative drafting, the *Electoral Act of 1863* (Vic.) enfranchised all ratepayers listed on local municipal rolls. By some oversight, the Parliament overlooked earlier local government legislation that had permitted women to be added to the municipal rolls for local government elections. Those women therefore had the vote and proceeded to use it in the general election of 1864 before those in New Zealand.

However, shocked and embarrassed by their oversight, members of the Victorian Legislative Assembly hastily amended the offending clause early in 1865 by restricting the vote for parliamentary elections strictly to male ratepayers. Women's enfranchisement in Victoria was therefore very short lived, leaving a period of another 43 years before it came to true fruition. The Tasmanian Parliament enfranchised women for their elections in 1903 (7) and Queensland's legislation was passed in 1905 (8).

This situation throughout the country meant that the women of South Australia were the only women voters in the country at the time of the Constitutional Convention debates at which the Constitution was drafted (9); this is where the story of s. 41 begins its journey.

By virtue of South Australia's world first, the women of South Australia were the first able to run for Parliament. While no woman ran in the first South Australian elections post enfranchisement, Catherine Helen Spence did run for the first Federal elections, which were those held to determine attendance at the Constitutional Conventions of the 1890s. Spence became the first woman in Australia to run for political office when she sought to represent South Australia at the Convention debates. She had been an active campaigner for social and electoral reforms before she had the vote, and experienced prejudice as a woman

(4) South Australian Parliament Debates, 11 December 1894, col. 2950.

(5) See Patricia Grimshaw, *Women's Suffrage in New Zealand*, Auckland University Press, 1963.

(6) *Adult Suffrage Act* 1908 (Vic.).

(7) *The Constitution Amendment Act* 1903 (3 Edw VII, No. 17) (Tas.).

(8) *Elections Acts Amendment Act of* 1905 (5 Edw. VII, No. 1) (Qld.).

(9) The Debates of the Australasian Federal Convention of 1897–1898 were: First session, Adelaide, 22 March–5 May 1897; Second session, Sydney, 2–24 September, 1897; Third session, Melbourne, 22 January– 17 March 1898.

for most of her life. Indeed, she provides an account in her autobiography of writing to the press for 30 years anonymously, because of her sex (10).

It was Spence's determination to see the *fairest voting system* possible as part of the new Commonwealth that led her to believe that she could not leave it to the men, and that she should run as a candidate in order to be present in Adelaide and Melbourne in the planned 1897–1898 debates. When her nomination became public, she was listed as one of the "ten best men" selected by a Liberal organization to appear, and one newspaper reported her nomination as evoking "an expression of approval" (11). Despite this, many people raised doubt as to whether she could, in fact, participate at a Federal level, given that the law in the United Kingdom did not recognize women as persons for the purpose of political representation. While she polled a credible 7383 votes, it was nowhere near the number needed. She wrote: "Had Mr. Kingston not asserted both publicly and privately that, if elected, I could not constitutionally take my seat, I might have done better" (12).

While not physically present at the Conventions, Catherine Helen Spence and the many women involved in the suffrage movement and the move to Federation certainly exerted their political will. The South Australian women were able to impress upon their representatives that they would not vote in favour of Federation if their vote was not protected and later, the Western Australian women were in a similar position. While uniform suffrage may not have been guaranteed by Federation itself, those South Australian women maintained their commitment to voting rights.

But was the commitment of those South Australian women sufficient to limit, as the majority does in this case, the purpose of the section *only* to those with the vote at Federation, or was it, and indeed can it be, a broader commitment to a right to vote?

If those South Australian women had not lobbied and obtained the right to vote in the first place, they would not have had the electoral power to urge their representatives at the Constitutional Convention debates to have s. 41 inserted. In other words, the power of voting rights underpins the section's presence, and that power is one that a democratic constitution must guarantee. If that is not the case, then individuals who hold power within the Parliament, such as in this current electoral cycle, can alter the system to exclude others from voting and thereby exercising meaningful voting power. That would undermine any constitutional democratic foundation to a society. If Spence's drive was to see the *fairest voting system* in place – and this led to s. 41 appearing in the Constitution – then using this section to deny people a fair voting system would result in an unnecessary hypocrisy in interpretation.

The tension between federalism and representative democracy. The majority judgments, while appreciating and referring to the suffrage issue, effectively find that s. 41 cannot be given its full and plain meaning because this would allow each of the States greater power to alter the federal franchise in a way that might benefit one State over the other States. In other words, a diverse and plural

(10) Catherine Helen Spence, An Autobiography (Jeanne Young (ed.), reprinted from the Register, 1910), p. 41.

(11) Ibid at p. 41.

(12) Ibid at p. 81.

H.C. OF A. 1983

THE QUEEN v. PEARSON; EX PARTE SIPKA.

Rubenstein J.

expression of voting rights, as existed in States and continued to exist in States as distinct from the Commonwealth until 1908 when Victoria finally gave women the right to vote, is rejected in favour of a single federal franchise. In the majority's view, a preference for a single federal franchise guides their interpretation of s. 41.

When a proposition was placed before the Constitutional Convention that universal suffrage be introduced into the Constitution (which would have precluded the need for s. 41) universal suffrage was rejected on the basis that, as some colonies were *opposed* to suffrage for women, federation would be jeopardised (13).

In this sense, States' rights were given greater weight than individual rights and the Women's Suffrage Movements needed s. 41 and its effect to propel the other States into action after Federation. Having s. 41 in the Constitution ensured that it would not be long before there was a uniform federal women's franchise in 1902. I use the term "women's franchise" rather than universal suffrage because it was not truly universal until 1962. As Murphy J. also discusses in greater detail in his judgment, *most* Indigenous Australians were not entitled to vote (although some were, due to different State franchise provisions) until amendments were made to the *Commonwealth Electoral Act of 1962*.

The majority's concern about the power of the States to alter the uniform nature of the franchise underpins their interpretation of the limited life of s. 41 of the Constitution and they draw also from the concern of the delegates at the Convention debates. In particular, they highlight the discussion around the amendment provision of the Constitution in s. 128. There was a heated discussion about those States with universal franchise having an unfair advantage in any federal election to change the Constitution. To protect against this, the third paragraph reads:

> "When a proposed law is submitted to the electors the vote shall be taken in such manner as the Parliament prescribes. *But until the qualification of electors of members of the House of Representatives becomes uniform throughout the Commonwealth, only one half the electors voting for and against the proposed law shall be counted in any State in which adult suffrage prevails*" (emphasis added).

Interestingly, those italicised words were *not* placed in s. 41. If that were meant to have been the case, then s. 41 *could* have said plainly:

> "*Until the qualification of electors of members of the House of Representatives becomes uniform throughout the Commonwealth*, no adult person who has or acquires a right to vote at elections for the more numerous House of the Parliament of a State shall, while the right continues, be prevented by any law of the Commonwealth from voting at elections for either House of the Parliament of the Commonwealth".

Given these words are not included in s. 41, and given there are also numerous other references throughout the Constitution to "Until the Parliament otherwise provides", it is harder to see why this Court would be inclined to interpret the provision narrowly.

(13) *Convention Debates*, Adelaide 1897: Mr Wise 3, 717; Mr Howe 3, 719; Mr Fraser 3, 720; Mr Glynn 3, 720; Mr Trenwith 3, 722–723.

Representative democracy is foundational to any democratic constitutional system. If a Parliament can easily change the core make-up of its electoral roll by simply closing the rolls in a way that stops those entitled to vote from doing so – even when there is a clear section enabling those individuals to be included through a Constitutional provision such as s. 41 protecting their voting rights – it would be undermining our democratic system and in my view, we must err on the side of protection of voting rights.

The voices of the women and men supporting universal suffrage who were behind s. 41 also provided for other forms of representative democracy in the Constitution. Sections 7 and 24 clearly protect the involvement of the people through the use of the words "directly chosen by the people". If there are people who are entitled to be enrolled in a State, then we must ensure that ss. 7 and 24 are also upheld by those voters "directly" choosing their representatives.

If in the future one State chooses to enfranchise its 16 year-olds (or others not yet entitled to vote in a federal election), it could also highlight a further value of our federal system; competition around different State policies. This occurs when States are encouraged (but not forced) to consider altering policy (in this case their voting rights) to make the system uniform. Rather than seeing such a possibility as undermining our uniform federal system, this could be heralded as a positive attribute of federalism, encouraging healthy democratic engagement with varying State views and policies. This would be another example of how a federal system can be said to further enhance democracy, rather than undermine it.

Applying this approach to the case at hand. Three of the four prosecutors, Mrs. Sipka, Mr. Kleppich and Mr. Chapman are over the age of twenty-one and are clearly "adult persons" under the terms of s. 41 of the Constitution. Ms. Walters turned eighteen on 15 February 1983. If we were fixed to the meaning of adult as it was in 1901, she would not qualify to vote, as an adult at that time was twenty-one years of age. In 1973, however, the *Commonwealth Electoral Act* 1918 was amended to give 18 year-olds the right to vote and for all relevant legal purposes, this is now seen as the age of adulthood.

In my opinion, the words of the Constitution should be interpreted according to their current meaning. While not denying the value of looking to history (as I have done in this judgment), I believe that history should be used to inform our understanding rather than to restrict it. This is in the spirit of interpreting our Constitution as a living document. As stated by O'Connor J.:

> "Where the question is whether the Constitution has used an expression in the wider or in the narrower sense, the Court should, in my opinion, always lean to the broader interpretation unless there is something in the context or in the rest of the Constitution to indicate that the narrower interpretation will best carry out its object and purpose" (*Jumbunna Coal Mine v Victorian Coal Miners' Association (No 2)* (14)).

Ms. Walters is clearly an adult in terms of the law of 1983 and should therefore be fully protected by s. 41. Indeed, in the spirit of the words of O'Connor J., my

(14) (1908) 6 C.L.R. 309, at p. 368.

H.C. of A.
1983

The Queen
v.
Pearson;
Ex Parte
Sipka.

Rubenstein J.

interpretation of s. 41 also leans to the broader interpretation. This best carries out the object and purpose underpinning s. 41 of the Constitution which was enlivened by a desire by those seeking universal suffrage that Australia protect and promote the *fairest voting system* possible as part of the new Commonwealth.

All four prosecutors have been placed on the New South Wales electoral roll and there is no administrative difficulty in permitting them to vote in the current election. They clearly fall within the protection of s. 41 of the Constitution, and they, and all individuals in a position to place themselves lawfully on their respective State rolls, will be entitled to vote at the forthcoming election.

The writ of mandamus should issue to direct the electoral commissioners who are the respondents in this matter to permit Mrs. Jarka Sipka, Mr. Rudolf Kleppich, Mr. Murray Paul Chapman and Ms. Sarah Jane Walters to vote in the forthcoming elections in the Senate and the House of Representatives.

5

Commentary on *Dietrich v R*

MARGARET DAVIES

Introduction

Olaf Dietrich was convicted in 1988 for trafficking heroin. After he had appealed unsuccessfully to the Victorian Supreme Court, the High Court accepted his argument that his trial had been unfair because he was unrepresented.[1] The decision reiterated the principle that an accused has a right to a fair trial and has a right to be represented. This does not necessarily mean that the state must provide representation, but it does mean that where the accused cannot afford representation (is 'indigent') and the offence is a serious one, a judge may be obliged, in order to ensure a fair trial, to stay proceedings until representation is appointed. The practical effect is that courts can force the state's hand, and ensure that legal representation is available to the accused.

Dietrich was released from prison in 1990 while his appeal to the High Court was still in process. Shortly after being released Dietrich changed his name to Hugo Alistair Rich and, in 1991, committed two armed robberies and various other offences, for which he was convicted. He spent late 1991 until October 2004 in prison.[2] In 2005 he committed another armed robbery and this time murdered a security guard (a 'senseless and callous killing'),[3] offences for which he was convicted in 2009. In the course of these various trials, Rich showed contempt for the court, its officers, and the law, as illustrated in the sentencing remarks of Lasry J in the 2009 trial:

> On any view, you have an appalling history. It began in 1971 when you were aged 19 years and although they were motor vehicle offences they involved dishonesty. Over the ensuing years you were convicted of offences which included handling stolen goods, theft, numerous counts of obtaining property by deception . . . false pretences, forgery. In total your criminal history consists of 80 charges arising from 15 court appearances . . .[4]
>
> . . .
>
> In 1995 and again in 2000 you were convicted of counts of armed robbery . . . One offence concerned an armed robbery on an Armaguard van and the other was on a branch of the National Australia Bank. Arising out of these matters were further convictions for threatening to kill and two

[1] *Dietrich v R* (1992) 177 CLR 292 ('*Dietrich*').

[2] See *R v Rich* [2009] VSC 515 (13 November 2009) [18] (Lasry J).

[3] Ibid [25].

[4] The catalogue of offences listed by Lasry J does not include trafficking heroin, which was the subject of *Dietrich*. Presumably this is because, as a result of the successful appeal, a new trial was ordered, but did not eventuate as Dietrich had already been released from prison. See John Silvester, 'Hugo Rich Chose the Low Road', *The Age* (Melbourne) 10 June 2005; see also Andrew Rule and John Silvester, 'Rich Man, Poor Man', *The Age* (Melbourne) 13 November 2009.

> counts of contempt. These counts of contempt involved threats by you addressed to a trial judge and a Crown prosecutor.[5]
>
> . . .
>
> In this case you have . . . treated the Court with the contempt as you did in that case. Apart from your abusive remarks directed to myself and to the Crown you at least endeavoured to manipulate the process by threatening to dismiss your counsel and actually doing so from time to time apparently in the belief that I would be in some way intimidated by having to deal with you unrepresented. . . . I regard you as irredeemable and reject your counsel's submission that there is any prospect of rehabilitation.[6]

Rich, then 57, was sentenced to life imprisonment for the murder of Mr Kastenberger, and 20 years on the count of armed robbery. A non-parole period of 30 years was set.

It would be difficult to estimate the cost of Rich's 2009 trial, which lasted for five months and involved 30 interlocutory hearings. He was represented by two barristers and instructing solicitors, presumably funded by the Victorian legal aid budget. The cost of the trial itself is unavoidable but the inevitable question, admittedly posed with the benefit of hindsight, is whether his case merited a considerable state expenditure on his legal representation. Many vulnerable and impoverished women and men are denied comparatively simple legal assistance for potentially life-altering situations, so should the state be spending tens of thousands of dollars on one 'irredeemable' recidivist? Can a price be put on a fair trial? Or, is there a point where, in a context of necessarily limited resources and unlimited levels of demand, extreme levels of spending on one area of justice itself constitutes a broader societal injustice?

The Case

The case which is the subject of the feminist judgment was decided in the High Court of Australia in 1992.[7] In the original judgment, the High Court held that while a defendant in a criminal trial has a right to have a legal representative appear in court for him or her, the state is not obliged to provide that legal representation and the court cannot direct the state to provide legal representation. However, the majority of the Court also held that the trial of an indigent unrepresented defendant for a serious criminal offence is likely to be unfair, except in 'exceptional' circumstances.[8] Since the right to a fair trial is undisputed, this means that a trial court ought to exercise its discretion to stay proceedings in such cases until representation is found. Failure to do so, as occurred in this case, would lead to a miscarriage of justice (except in the 'exceptional' circumstances where such a trial was not unfair). The dissenting judges, Brennan and Dawson JJ, gave greater emphasis to the inability of the

[5] Threats addressed to the prosecutor included the following: 'I don't care how long it takes, 25 years bitch, I'll have a go at you. One go, that's all I want and you think by locking me up for 25 years, I don't have legs and arms out there. I've a bank account overseas and even without the money, we'll be able to get you any time, slut, I'm telling you. All I ever wanted is a fair go. You've pulled every dirty, filthy trick under the book': *Attorney-General (Vic) v Rich* [1998] VSC 41 (21 August 1998) [9].

[6] *R v Rich* [2009] VSC 515 (13 November 2009) [17], [18] and [28]. Footnotes have been added to this quotation and are not in the original.

[7] The facts of the case are summarised in the feminist judgment.

[8] *Dietrich* (1992) 177 CLR 292, 311 (Mason CJ and McHugh J).

court to interfere in executive government decisions about distribution of public money.[9] They thought that the disadvantage of being unrepresented can be ameliorated to a degree by the trial judge,[10] that a mere lack of representation did not necessarily lead to a miscarriage of justice,[11] and that a refusal by the courts to exercise their jurisdiction by indefinitely adjourning a trial where there is no abuse of process 'is inconsistent with their constitutional duty'.[12]

While the decision in *Dietrich* has, in practical terms, been widely understood as enshrining a right to legal representation for serious criminal trials, it has been the subject of considerable reading down and distinguishing, including by the High Court itself. In fact it has never been applied outside the context of representation in a serious criminal trial. In *New South Wales v Canellis*,[13] the High Court refused to stay an inquiry under the *Crimes Act 1900* (NSW) until legal representation was provided for witnesses and noted that 'there is no suggestion in [*Dietrich*] that a court could exercise a similar jurisdiction in civil proceedings . . . nor do [the majority judgments] suggest that such a jurisdiction could be exercised in favour of an indigent person charged with a criminal offence which is other than serious'.[14]

The Full Federal Court has held that a person facing deportation is not entitled to legal representation,[15] and despite concerns expressed by Nicholson CJ in *T and S*,[16] there is no right for a person facing a dispute about parenting orders (ie a mother who might lose her child) to have legal representation provided at public expense.[17]

Immediate Consequences and Critique

The practical effect of *Dietrich* has been that people accused of serious criminal offences who cannot themselves afford to pay for representation can have representation provided at public expense, not through any formal legal right but rather via what amounts to a substantive right afforded to an indigent accused. As an abstract principle of justice, this seems intuitively fair, especially when we think about the significance we normally attach to liberty, to the presumption of innocence, and especially (as feminists) to the desirability of addressing power imbalances created when institutional or systemic authority is pitted against vulnerable individuals.

Whatever the intuitive fairness of the result, however, the case is set in a practical context and has some less than ideal consequences. *Dietrich* was criticised by feminists, including

[9] Ibid 323 (Brennan J); 349–50 (Dawson J); see also 335 (Deane J); 357 (Toohey J); 365 (Gaudron J).

[10] Ibid 345 (Dawson J), citing Brennan J in *Jago v District Court (NSW)* (1989) 168 CLR 23, 47.

[11] Ibid 343 (Dawson J).

[12] Ibid 324 (Brennan J).

[13] (1994) 181 CLR 309.

[14] Ibid 328 (Mason CJ, Dawson, Toohey and McHugh JJ).

[15] *Nguyen v Minister for Immigration and Multicultural Affairs* (2000) 101 FCR 20.

[16] [2001] FamCA 1147.

[17] For further consideration of *Dietrich* see, eg, *R v Marchi* (1996) 67 SASR 368 (meaning of 'indigence'); *Craig v South Australia* (1995) 184 CLR 163 (fault in not finding representation); *Attorney-General (NSW) v Milat* (1995) 37 NSWLR 370 (*Dietrich* does not extend to setting the rate of remuneration for a legal team chosen by the defendant). More recently, some Victorian cases have applied *Dietrich* where insufficient legal aid representation was offered (in the form of a barrister but very limited instructing solicitor time). See *R v Chaouk* [2013] VSCA 99 (2 May 2013) and *MK v Victoria Legal Aid* [2013] VSC 49 (18 February 2013) where the limited availability of an instructing solicitor resulted in a stay of proceedings on the basis that the fairness of the trial could not be assured.

the feminist judgment writers, and others in the years following the decision.[18] Legal aid funding was already severely restricted in 1992, and heavily favoured assistance for criminal law rather than civil matters or family law.[19] This meant that legal aid spending was gendered, men being much more likely to be involved in criminal matters than women. Women are more likely to seek legal aid in family law matters, a symptom of the fact that when a relationship breaks down, women are generally left in a worse financial position than men, and can more easily pass the means test upon which all legal aid grants rest.[20] Then, as now, criminal legal aid cases far outnumbered civil and family cases.[21] On top of this situation came *Dietrich* which in effect (if not in law) gave those accused of a serious crime a right to legal representation. Since serious crimes are even more likely to be committed by men than by women, compared to other crimes, the potential for the decision to intensify even further the gendering of legal aid was very apparent.

The gender implications of *Dietrich* were only one of a number of criticisms of the decision. It was also criticised because it represented an intrusion of the courts into decisions about public expenditure.[22] The restriction of the right to a fair trial to serious criminal cases was seen as illogical, since serious consequences can flow from civil and family cases, migration cases, as well as from relatively minor criminal matters.[23] The need for courts to work out who could not afford to pay for their own representation and was therefore 'indigent' was also seen as problematic.[24] A Senate Committee queried whether it would result in a reduction of guilty pleas and add further pressure to legal aid budgets.[25] Despite these concerns, the idea that people have a right to a fair trial and that it is desirable for legal aid to be available to indigent defendants in serious criminal cases is not really in doubt. What is extremely problematic is that *Dietrich* elevates serious crime over all other types of legal matters that are dealt with by courts, and fails to appreciate the real and often devastating consequences of lack of representation in these other contexts.

[18] Reg Graycar and Jenny Morgan, 'Disabling Citizenship: Civil Death for Women in the 1990s' (1995) 17 *Adelaide Law Review* 49; Sally Kift, 'The Dietrich Dilemma' (1997) 13 *Queensland University of Technology Law Journal* 211–34. See also Gideon Boas, 'Dietrich, the High Court and Unfair Trials Legislation: A Constitutional Guarantee?' (1993) 19 *Monash University Law Review* 256; Nicholas Cowdery, 'Dietrich: Why Should the Prosecution Worry?' (1997) 9 *Current Issues in Criminal Justice* 163; Karen Fletcher, 'Legal Aid: Right or Privilege?' (1993) 18 *Alternative Law Journal* 21; Frances Gibson, 'Legal Aid: A Decade After Dietrich' (2003) 41 *Law Society Journal* 52.

[19] Graycar and Morgan, above n 18, 53–4.

[20] Ibid 57.

[21] Current data is patchy, but see Commonwealth, Senate Legal and Constitutional References Committee, Inquiry into Legal Aid and Access to Justice, *Final Report* (2004) 46; *National Statistics*, National Legal Aid <http://www.nationallegalaid.org/home/national-statistics/>. A recent study has found that of the 50 highest users of legal aid services in NSW, 74 per cent were male, and 80 per cent were 19 or younger. All used legal aid for criminal matters, and many fewer used legal aid also for civil and family law matters. See Pia van de Zandt and Tristan Webb, 'High Service Users at Legal Aid NSW' (Legal Aid NSW, 2013).

[22] See, eg comments by Boas, above n 18, 270; Commonwealth, Senate Legal and Constitutional References Committee, Inquiry into the Australian Legal Aid System, *Second Report* (1997) ch 4 'Effects of the *Dietrich* Decision'.

[23] Kift, above n 18, 212.

[24] Justice Badgery-Parker, 'The Criminal Process in Transition: Balancing Principle and Pragmatism – Part I' (1995) *Journal of Judicial Administration* 171, 181–5; Kift, above n 18, 216–18.

[25] Commonwealth, Senate Legal and Constitutional References Committee, 'Effects of the *Dietrich* Decision', above n 22.

The Feminist Judgment

The feminist judgment rejects the abstract approach of the majority judgments and states that a trial should not generally be stayed in the absence of legal representation, while leaving open the possibility that there might be exceptional cases where a stay would be appropriate.

In the course of coming to this conclusion, the feminist judges tackle several aspects of the original judgments, which range from being difficult to accept, to being illogical and/or indefensible. The first of these deals with what the feminist judges have aptly termed the 'distinction without a difference' in the majority reasoning: that is, that an accused does not have a right to be provided with legal representation, but does have a right to a fair trial, and therefore has the right to have their trial stayed until legal representation is appointed. This distinction represents an exemplary exercise in legal formalism. From a feminist perspective the distinction without a difference is very problematic: it refuses an explicit right to be provided with representation on the one hand, while liberally providing a substantive right on the other. As feminists are only too aware, a formal right (eg to equality) does not normally amount to a substantive right (to be provided with the conditions which would make equality possible). The result in *Dietrich* means that defendants do not have a formal right, but do have a more valuable substantive right. It is precisely the kind of decontextualised and abstract reasoning employed by the High Court which leads to a result that systemically advantages men and disadvantages women. The feminist approach on this and other points refuses to see the issue purely in the abstract, and takes a much more concrete and practical approach both to the decision at hand and to its broader consequences.

This more practical feminist approach is also reflected in the feminist judges' discussion of the broad-scale distribution of public money and the separation of powers. They reject the proposition that the courts can effectively force public expenditure in a particular area, rather than allowing the government to determine the most appropriate distribution of finite funds. 'Justice' cannot be decontextualised: where funds are limited, trying obsessively to ensure justice for one person will quite likely lead to injustice for others. Within the context of legal aid, it is surely preferable that decisions about funding be made, as they always have been made, by the application of a means test and a merits test, and distributing funding so that the broader interests of justice are served.[26]

The gendered implications of the majority view are considered specifically by the feminist judges, who take judicial notice of the fact that men are overwhelmingly the perpetrators of crime, particularly serious crime. They do this because there was no evidence before the court about this matter. A court may judicially notice a fact whenever it 'is so generally known that every ordinary person may be reasonably presumed to be aware of it'.[27] The doctrine of judicial notice was considered by McHugh J in *Woods v Multi-Sport Holdings Pty Ltd*[28] in the context of accident data. His Honour held that it was in accordance with

[26] See also the additional reasons of former Family Court Chief Justice Alastair Nicholson on what he described as matters that 'were not the subject of argument at the hearing of this appeal'; ie, the difficulties experienced by women who have suffered serious domestic violence in presenting their cases 'unaided in family law proceedings': *T v S* [2001] FamCA 1147 [201]–[226].

[27] *Holland v Jones* (1917) 23 CLR 149, 153 (Isaacs J).

[28] (2002) 208 CLR 460 ('*Woods*').

long-standing authority and practice to refer to these statistics because they fell into the class of 'legislative' facts that a court may judicially notice and use to define the scope or validity of a legal principle.[29] More recently, in *Victorian Women Lawyers Association v FCT*,[30] French J (as he then was) took judicial notice of the 'historical and persisting disadvantage of women in relation to their participation and career advancement within the legal profession'.[31]

While the decisions in *Woods* and the *Victorian Women Lawyers* case clearly post-date *Dietrich*, there was, by 1992, well-established authority for taking judicial notice of the fact that men commit more serious crimes than women. While the feminist judges refer to the gendered incidence of crime, they do not refer to the detailed data on the gendered provision of legal aid, because this would go beyond the doctrine of judicial notice. However, as noted above, it has been demonstrated that litigation legal aid was (and remains) seriously skewed in favour of men.[32]

Finally, the feminist judgment leaves open the possibility that a stay of proceedings until representation is found might be appropriate in exceptional cases. The feminist judges do not elaborate on this possibility, but one could speculate that it might occur where systemic factors exacerbate the usual power difference, for instance, if a person is new to the country and unfamiliar with the legal system, a person whose language skills are not adequate to the task of understanding a trial, a person with an intellectual or other relevant impairment, an Indigenous person, and possibly – depending on the circumstances – a person who has not before appeared in court.

Conclusion

In an ideal world, government funding would be sufficient to provide adequate legal assistance to everyone who cannot afford to pay for it. However, the available legal aid funding competes with many other social purposes while, within legal aid, there are many ways of choosing which areas and individuals are most worthy of support. As the feminist judgment illustrates, *Dietrich* inappropriately constrained government choice in these matters and did so in a way which promoted those accused of serious crimes over those who require legal assistance for civil and family law matters. Given that serious crime is overwhelmingly a male activity, and women's legal requirements are more likely to arise in family and civil law, the gendered implications of the result are clear. A more defensible approach would have limited court intervention to the most extreme cases, determined by reference to the circumstances of the individual defendant.

[29] This is by contrast with an 'adjudicative fact' which is a fact in issue or relevant to a fact in issue: see ibid [64].

[30] (2008) 170 FCR 318.

[31] Ibid [116].

[32] See nn 18–21, above. See also Rosemary Hunter, Tracey De Simone and Louise Whitaker, *Women and Legal Aid: Identifying Disadvantage* (Legal Aid Queensland and Griffith University Socio-Legal Research Centre, 2006); Office of Legal Aid and Family Services, Attorney-General's Department (Cth), *Gender Bias in Litigation Legal Aid* (1994).

DIETRICH . . . . . . APPELLANT;

AND

THE QUEEN . . . . . RESPONDENT.

ON APPEAL FROM THE SUPREME COURT OF VICTORIA.

H. C. OF A. 1992.

DIETRICH v THE QUEEN.

Graycar J. Morgan J.

GRAYCAR AND MORGAN JJ. The applicant, Mr. Dietrich, is seeking special leave to appeal from the Court of Criminal Appeal of the State of Victoria and seeks to have set aside his conviction for one count of importing into Australia not less than a trafficable quantity of heroin in contravention of s. 233B(1)(b) of the *Customs Act* 1901 (Cth) on the basis that his lack of legal representation caused his trial to miscarry. He argues that this Court should declare that a trial for a serious criminal offence cannot be fairly conducted without the defendant being represented by counsel, and if the defendant is unable to afford such representation, that such representation be publicly provided. It follows, according to the defendant, that as he was not represented, his trial has miscarried and thus his conviction should be set aside.

The applicant was convicted by the County Court in Victoria on charges relating to the importation and possession of heroin. While he was charged on four counts, counts two and three were (lesser) alternatives to count one. He was convicted on count one ("importing into Australia not less than a trafficable quantity of heroin") and thus it was not necessary for the jury to consider counts two and three, but he was acquitted on count four ("possession of heroin which was not the subject of the importation offence"). The key ground of the appeal to the Victorian Supreme Court and the basis of his application to this Court is his claim that the original trial had been unfair because he had been unrepresented. The applicant had been offered legal aid if he were to plead guilty, but he refused to do so, wishing to contest all charges against him. Before this court, the applicant argued that the right to a fair trial, the existence of which is axiomatic (and is not the subject of any dispute between the parties), necessitates that a person accused of a serious criminal offence actually be legally represented. If the accused person cannot afford such representation then, so the argument goes, that representation must be provided at public expense. It was argued before us that in the absence of legal representation, the failure of the trial judge to stay the proceedings until such time as representation could be made available, resulted in a miscarriage of justice.

For the reasons that follow, we would grant special leave to appeal but dismiss the appeal.

H. C. OF A. 1992.

DIETRICH v THE QUEEN.

Graycar J. Morgan J.

Separation of powers

As the other judgments clearly demonstrate, a considerable amount of time was spent during the course of argument on international jurisprudence, considering the possibilities of implied rights, searching for principles derived from Chapter 3 of the Constitution, and interpreting Australian law by reference to international conventions. None of this in our view is of any assistance in resolving the matter before us.

This case raises important questions about the respective roles of the three branches of government. The applicant's claim amounts, in effect, to an assertion that a Court has both a responsibility and a power to direct the executive branch of government as to how to allocate its resources. We reject any such broad principle to that effect. However, we also acknowledge the possibility that there may from time to time be exceptional cases in which, in the absence of legal representation, a Court would be required to stay legal proceedings for manifest unfairness if it were apparent that the interests of justice required it to do so. As will become clear, however, this is not an issue that falls for decision on the facts before us.

We agree with Brennan J. that providing legal representation for a person facing a trial for a serious criminal offence is something only the legislature and the executive can undertake. This Court is not able, nor is it suited, to make decisions about the competing priorities that affect decisions about the allocation of public resources that are the subject of government appropriations. In order to accept the proposition put to this Court by the applicant, this Court would not only be required to direct the executive as to what proportion of public expenditure is allocated to legal aid, it would also be required to direct how, within that allocation, legal aid resources are directed at funding criminal trials as opposed to other kinds of litigation. If this Court were to engage in either exercise, it would, in our view, impermissibly breach the constitutional separation of powers.

Central to the judgment of Mason C.J. and McHugh J. are three key issues, which we summarize below. These approaches also appear in the judgments of other members of the court, all of which we have had the advantage of reading in draft form, but are expressed most succinctly by Mason C.J. and McHugh J. in their joint judgment.

Centrally, their Honours draw a distinction between a stay of proceedings because a trial is unfair as a result of a lack of legal representation on the one hand, and the court ordering a person to be provided with legal representation, on the other. In our respectful opinion, this is a distinction without a difference.

We further observe that the very limited nature of the argument put to the Court, and thus the limited factual substratum on which the majority's decision is based, may be due in part to the failure of the States' Attorneys (other than the Attorney-General for South Australia) to intervene, as well as a failure by the parties and by those who did intervene to lay out the full implications of decisions on the provision of legal aid. We are not persuaded by the process of reasoning adopted by their Honours, by which they appear to conclude that, in the absence of evidence that recognition of a right to counsel at public expense would impose an impossible financial burden, the Court is entitled to infer that it would not do so.

Finally, there is a consequent failure to consider the real implications of the relief sought, which must be that it involves the Court, notwithstanding its disavowal of this proposition, in ordering and reordering government priorities in a way that has clear gender implications.

We consider these issues in turn.

Distinction without a difference

Each of the judgments of our judicial colleagues draws a distinction between a "right" to legal representation, and a right to a fair trial, or between a "right" to counsel and a right to an adjournment or stay of proceedings. While a majority of the Court agrees that there is no unequivocal "right" to be legally represented at public expense (a view we share), there is said to be, by contrast, a right to a fair trial, the vindication of which may result in an (indefinite) stay of serious criminal proceedings where legal representation is not available to the defendant. To us this appears to rest upon what can only be described as a distinction without a difference.

For example, Mason C.J. and McHugh J. repeatedly stress that there is no right to counsel at common law and there is certainly no alternative statutory basis for any such right. Yet their Honours recognize that the effect of their decision will be that in a trial for a serious criminal offence, an accused will be represented by counsel at public expense.

Deane J. is meticulous in his presentation of the issue as to whether it is possible for there to be a fair trial of a serious criminal charge in the absence of legal representation, suggesting that this somehow differs from an "enforceable duty" to make free legal advice or representation available. His Honour makes it clear that there is no duty that could be enforced by, for example, an order in the nature of mandamus (and see also the reasons of Brennan and Toohey JJ.). However, the very broad finding by Deane J. that a trial of an indigent person accused of serious crime will be unfair if, because he cannot pay for it, he is denied legal representation, can mean only that legal aid agencies will be forced to reorder their priorities to ensure that funds are allocated for such a defendant's legal representation. The distinction that is sought to be maintained between a right to legal representation, on the one hand, and a right to a fair trial on the other, simply cannot be sustained once the reality of the situation is taken into account.

Even Brennan J. in his dissenting judgment seems to accept that there is a distinction between ordering the provision of legal representation at government expense and staying a proceeding. But a trial for a

H. C. of A. 1992.

Dietrich v The Queen.

Graycar J. Morgan J.

serious offence cannot be stayed indefinitely without, as his Honour points out, the court in effect failing to exercise its jurisdiction.

Rather, the whole purpose of the adjournment can only be to bring about a particular outcome: viz., the provision of legal representation to the accused. And that outcome in turn lies solely in the hands of the executive.

It is because we consider the approach of the majority and of Brennan J. to rest upon what we describe as a distinction without a difference that in our view, it is imperative that the Court undertake a practical and contextual appraisal of the effect of this Court's decision. It is not enough to rely on decontextualized assessments of legal technicalities, or the lack of enforceable rights. We are here dealing with the trial of a serious criminal offence. If such a trial were indefinitely stayed, it is not as if the accused would be, nor could he lawfully be, indefinitely detained. No doubt an immediate application for bail would be made and would be difficult to resist. The reality is that the legal aid agency would be required to provide legal representation of some sort, or the charges against the accused would have to be withdrawn, regardless of any concerns about a risk to the safety of the community. While the choice of which of those two courses is to be taken is ultimately a matter for executive decision, in our view (and this seems to be accepted by Mason C.J. and McHugh J.), the most likely outcome would be that the executive would be placed in a position where funding for legal representation would be provided. This is despite the fact that a majority of this Court agrees that there is no legal basis upon which can be founded a "right to legal representation" at public expense.

A financial burden

Together with Mason C.J. and McHugh J., we too are concerned that despite the States' Attorneys-General being given notice of the issues to be argued and being invited to participate, only the Attorney-General for South Australia (as well as the Commonwealth) chose to intervene to assist the Court in this matter. Given what was at stake, it is disappointing that the Court did not have the benefit of the views of the governments which would largely be affected by a decision that directly or indirectly has a clear impact upon the question of how much funding is allocated to legal aid. What is of even more concern is that none of the interveners, nor the Director of Public Prosecutions of the State of Victoria, truly raised resource allocation issues, issues that in our view are central to the resolution of this case.

Mason C.J. and McHugh J. observe that there was no argument made to us that any right to be represented by counsel paid for by the state would impose "an impossible financial burden". They then reason that, given that no such argument was put, it follows that such representation would therefore not impose such a burden. This form of reasoning requires the Court to adopt a starting point from which it is assumed, unless the contrary is proven, that it would not impose an impossible financial burden. But why this starting point? Why not commence the exercise, as we prefer to do, by assuming that requiring serious offenders to be represented by counsel at public expense would impose a financial burden on state-funded legal aid authorities, unless there is evidence to show that it would not do so? In our assessment, since no argument was put that it would not impose such a burden, we will assume that it will do so. It is surely at least as legitimate to take this approach as it is to take the one assumed by Mason C.J. and McHugh J.

Not a mere "re-ordering" of priorities

Mason C.J. and McHugh J. suggest that rather than imposing a serious financial burden on government, the majority's approach is likely to require no more than a "re-ordering" of the government's priorities on the allocation of legal aid funds. But what is not made clear are the consequences of any such re-ordering of priorities. If legal aid for court proceedings only is considered, this suggests a reallocation of resources away from civil law and family law and a redirection of those resources to criminal law. While this may sound entirely gender neutral, it in fact fails to take into account the gendered implications of such a reallocation. Although no argument was put to us about those implications (just as no argument was put about the financial burden that the Court's decision would impose on legal aid funding bodies), we are entitled to take judicial notice of the fact that the vast majority of legal aid for criminal trials goes to men as it is men who commit the vast majority of criminal offences, particularly serious criminal offences. We are also not convinced that a trial for a serious criminal offence, albeit that it carries a risk of a lengthy term of imprisonment, is necessarily more worthy of funding than, say, the loss of custody of one's children or the decision to deport a non-citizen with children who have lived all their lives in this country.

More generally, it is not immediately clear to us that legal aid, and in particular, funding for representation of people (mostly men) charged with serious criminal offences, is a priority over funding for education or funding to meet the support needs of people with disabilities or the care needs of an ageing population. Those are policy choices best made by governments and ones that this Court is ill-equipped to decide.

In our view, the clear implication of the relief sought by the applicant in this case is that the Court should, in effect, direct government as to how to utilize its resources and as to the priorities it ought to adopt in relation to government expenditure, a singularly inappropriate thing for this Court to do, as we noted in our opening comments. This means we cannot agree with Gaudron J.'s view that the consequences, including the financial consequences, of a decision are irrelevant.

It must also be recalled that the applicant, Mr. Dietrich, was not denied legal aid funding entirely; he was the subject of the application

H. C. OF A. 1992.
DIETRICH v THE QUEEN.
Graycar J. Morgan J.

of a merits test and he was offered representation if he were to plead guilty. He availed himself of an appeal to a legal aid appeal committee: that appeal was dismissed. The logical consequence of the majority's reasoning seems to be that when a defendant is charged with a serious criminal offence, a legal aid body may not undertake what is commonly known as a "merits test" where an assessment is made of the prospects of success when considering whether to grant legal aid.

Truly exceptional cases may require representation

It may be that there should be a power for a court to stay proceedings where a hearing is going to be inherently unfair due to a lack of representation. But any such principle must be stated, and operationalized, in such a way that we do not establish an underlying de facto assumption of a right to representation, which comes with all the difficulties we have noted.

As the Solicitor-General for South Australia rightly submitted, any such determination would require very careful examination of the facts and circumstances of a particular case rather than statements of broad abstract principle. In the interests of clarity, we compare our approach with that taken by our judicial colleagues in this case to justify our conclusion that, if there is ever a case in which a trial is unfair because of a lack of legal representation, the trial of the applicant was not such a case.

Both Deane and Gaudron JJ. find a very broad right to legal representation, stating in the widest possible terms that where there is a trial for a serious criminal offence, and the accused cannot afford representation, a trial is unfair. We fundamentally reject such an abstract approach for the reasons noted above: we cannot and will not disregard the funding consequences for governments.

Mason C.J. and McHugh J. suggest that they have decided the matter here by the nuanced, context-specific analysis we say is required. While their Honours are emphatic in their refusal to overturn the recent decision of this Court in *McInnis v. The Queen* (*McInnis*) (84), and expressly disavow the existence of any absolute right to publicly funded legal representation, their Honours distinguish *McInnis* to justify why, in their view, *in the particular circumstances of this case,* Mr. Dietrich's trial was, in their assessment, unfair.

It will be recalled that Mr. Dietrich was charged with four offences: one count of importation of heroin (packaged in condoms concealed inside his body), two counts of possession of heroin the subject of count one, which were alternatives to (and less serious than) the first count, and not further considered once he had been found guilty of the first more serious charge, and a fourth count involving the alleged possession of a separate quantity of heroin. He was found guilty on the first

(84) (1979) 143 C.L.R. 575.

count, and acquitted on the fourth. It was this apparent anomaly which led Mason C.J. and McHugh J. to find that the trial was unfair: the acquittal on one count apparently shows that there must have been a prospect of acquittal on the other. Their Honours concede that the evidence on all counts was strong, but note that Mr. Dietrich's defence was "disorganized and haphazard", and thus they find that the accused may have lost a real chance of acquittal.

There are a number of possible explanations, unrelated to the quality (or absence) of representation, or to any inherent unfairness, for why the jury might have reached different verdicts on the different counts. Most obviously, the evidence on the two counts was different. Alternatively, as King C.J. observed in *Reg. v. Kirkman* (85):

> "Sometimes juries apply in favour of an accused what might be described as their innate sense of fairness and justice in place of the strict principles of law. Sometimes it appears to a jury that although a number of counts have been alleged against an accused person, and have been technically proved, justice is sufficiently met by convicting him of less than the full number."

Thus we do not think it is reasonable to conclude that because of the apparent anomaly in the verdicts, the applicant lost a real chance of acquittal on the first charge. After all, even Mr. Dietrich did not allege there was any error or defect in his trial other than that he wanted to be represented, was refused representation and was obliged to represent himself.

This in turn leads to the question of whether the right to be represented in a serious criminal trial is a right to "adequate counsel" or merely a right to counsel, a matter raised by Mason C.J. and McHugh J. Is it correct to assume that an accused will be better off with inadequate counsel than he or she would be with no counsel? We see no reason to make such an assumption. A judge might be inclined to go out of his or her way to assist an accused if an accused is unrepresented. And of course it is well established that a prosecutor is no ordinary counsel: a prosecutor has a plethora of ethical duties that are directed at ensuring the fairness of a trial and has duties to the court that go well beyond any notion of merely seeking a conviction.

In our view, there is nothing that takes the applicant's case out of the ordinary, or makes it exceptional. While there may be cases which are truly exceptional, it is unnecessary for us to decide the matter now. We repeat that any such exception must be narrowly drawn, and is likely to involve consideration of aspects of disadvantage that pertain to the individual (accused) person which might warrant a stay, rather than a focus on any abstract principle about the fairness of a trial in general. In other words, the exceptional circumstances that might warrant a stay of a criminal or other proceedings in a particular case are to be found in the

(85) (1987) 44 S.A.S.R. 591, at p. 593.

H. C. OF A. 1992.

DIETRICH v THE QUEEN.

Graycar J. Morgan J.

concrete and material circumstances of the individual person who is claiming that his or her trial (and it is more likely to be his in a serious criminal trial) will be unfair rather than in attention to the broad nature of criminal trials.

The relief sought by the applicant in this matter is, in effect, an order that this court direct the executive government as to the manner in which the government is required to allocate and expend public resources. In our view, if the Court were to make the order sought, this would involve it impermissibly straying outside its judicial role. We would grant special leave to appeal but dismiss the appeal.

Tax Law

6

Commentary on *Lodge v Federal Commissioner of Taxation*

ANN O'CONNELL

Introduction

The availability of affordable childcare has broad social and economic significance. Affordable childcare assists parents with children to enter (or re-enter) the workforce. Since the 1960s there has been a significant increase in women's participation in the workforce. Yet, in Australia (and in most other developed economies) women are still seen as primarily responsible for the care of children,[1] and so are more likely to be impacted by the cost of childcare and related decisions about paid work.

One way in which childcare costs can be reduced is if the expense can be claimed as a tax deduction. The first significant claim for such a deduction arose in the 1972 case of *Lodge v Federal Commissioner of Taxation*[2] but was unsuccessful. Several other cases since, where it was argued that the decision in *Lodge* was wrong or could be distinguished, have also been unsuccessful.[3] In the feminist judgment of Kerrie Sadiq, the deduction would be allowed. In the absence of any binding authority Sadiq accepts that childcare expenses are incurred to enable the taxpayer to work, and to work more efficiently, and so deductible under the legislative regime at the time.

An important question is why, in the years following *Lodge*, was there not more of a concerted effort to have childcare costs recognised as tax-deductible? The answer to this question has something to do with the way Australia's income tax system operates, as described below. Before doing so it is useful to consider the social and political context at the time the case of *Lodge* arose.

The Social and Political Context

In 1972 Australia was about to experience significant political and social change. The conservative Liberal/Country Party Government had been in power for 23 years. The Labor

[1] See 'Gender Indicators, Australia, January 2013' (Catalogue No 4125.0, Australian Bureau of Statistics (ABS), 30 January 2013), 'Caring for Children'.

[2] (1972) 128 CLR 171 (*Lodge*).

[3] See *Martin v Federal Commissioner of Taxation* (1984) 84 ATC 4513 (Full Federal Court); *Hyde v Federal Commissioner of Taxation* (1988) 88 ATC 4748 (French J, Federal Court); *Jayatilake v Federal Commissioner of Taxation* (1991) 91 ATC 4516 (Full Federal Court).

Party won the election in December of that year, and women's issues and childcare became matters of political importance. The role of women in the workforce was also changing. In the post-war period the traditional roles of men working full-time and women staying at home with the children started to change. In 1970, women made up 38.6 per cent of the workforce, compared to 45.7 per cent in 2012.[4] The number of children per family was also decreasing and the possibility of part-time work was becoming more common.[5] As noted by Sadiq, the 'marriage bar', which required women to resign if they married, was only lifted in the Commonwealth public service in 1966, and the principle of 'equal pay for work of equal value' was established in decisions of the Commonwealth Conciliation and Arbitration Commission in 1969 and 1972.[6]

In that same year, a single judge in the High Court of Australia was asked to decide if the cost of childcare, incurred by a single mother in order for her to undertake paid work, was tax-deductible. The case of *Lodge* was not the first case in which a taxpayer had sought to deduct the cost of childcare, but it was the first case to be decided in the High Court, albeit as a case involving the original rather than the appellate jurisdiction of the Court. The case arose before the establishment of the Federal Court of Australia or the Administrative Appeals Tribunal. In 1971–72 the process for a taxpayer to object to an assessment initially involved consideration by the Commissioner of Taxation. If the objection was disallowed, the taxpayer could apply to a Board of Review for a review of the decision, or appeal the decision to a state Supreme Court or the High Court.[7]

The judge hearing the case was Anthony Mason (later Sir Anthony) who would become Chief Justice of the High Court. The case for Ms Lodge was argued by Keith Aicken QC, who would himself become a member of the High Court. The decision may have assumed particular persuasiveness as a result of these participants. Certainly, a number of later cases have been similarly decided without much further consideration or interpretation of the words of the Act.

Australia's 'Progressive' Income Tax System

The relevant section considered in *Lodge* was s 51(1) of the *Income Tax Assessment Act 1936* (Cth) (the general deduction provision), which has since been rewritten, without changing its meaning or application, as s 8-1 of the *Income Tax Assessment Act 1997* (Cth). The section is one of the most straightforward in the tax legislation. Essentially it provides that a taxpayer can deduct the cost of earning income. Income tax in Australia is imposed on a taxpayer's 'taxable income', which is 'assessable income' less 'deductions'. Assessable income includes ordinary income, that is, income according to judicial interpretation such as income for the provision of labour, income from business and income from investment. The general deduction provision allows a taxpayer to claim 'losses or outgoings incurred in

[4] See 'Labour Force, Australia, Dec 2012' (Catalogue No 6202.0, ABS, 17 January 2013).

[5] Glenda Strachan, 'Still Working For the Man? Women's Employment Experiences in Australia Since 1950' (2010) 45 *Australian Journal of Social Issues* 117, 121.

[6] *Equal Pay Case 1969* (1969) 127 CAR 1142; *Equal Pay Case 1972* (1972) 147 CAR 172.

[7] *Income Tax Assessment Act 1936* (Cth) s 187. The legislation was amended in 1973 to remove appeals from an objection decision to the High Court, and the Court now can only hear such matters on appeal from the Full Federal Court: *Income Tax Assessment Act (No 3) 1973* (Cth).

earning assessable income'. So, the test for determining whether a particular expense is deductible is whether it is incurred 'in' earning the income. Although there were no decided cases on childcare expenses before *Lodge*, there were cases that held that even though an expense had to be incurred in order to earn income, for example, the cost of travelling to and from work, it may not have a *sufficient* connection to the actual earning of income to be deductible. Travel expenses, and other expenses such as food and clothing costs, are said to put the taxpayer in the position to earn income but are not part of the income-earning process. The court in *Lodge* was being asked to determine whether the cost of childcare for a working parent was sufficiently related to the earning of income to be deductible or, alternatively, whether it was, like travel and food costs, just an expense that put the taxpayer in the position to earn income, and so was not deductible.

When are Expenses Deductible?

Section 51(1) included two positive limbs and (for the purposes of *Lodge*) a negative limb. The section provided that 'all losses or outgoings to the extent to which they are incurred in gaining or producing assessable income' (the first positive limb) or are 'necessarily incurred in carrying on a business for the purpose of gaining or producing assessable income' (the second positive limb) shall be allowable deductions 'except to the extent to which they are . . . private or domestic in nature' (the negative limb). The question for the High Court was whether the childcare expenses incurred by Ms Lodge, so that she could work (mostly) from home as a costs clerk, were deductible under this section. It should be noted that Ms Lodge was a contractor who was paid on a commission basis, not an employee, but the Court's analysis did not turn on this point. It can be assumed that the same result would have been reached if Ms Lodge had been an employee. However, the fact that Ms Lodge could be described as carrying on a business is significant because it raises comparisons with other business expenses.

Mason J decided against Ms Lodge on the ground that the expense was not incurred in gaining income, that is, it did not satisfy the positive limbs of s 51. He also described the expenses as 'private' in nature.[8] It was suggested in argument that the taxpayer (or perhaps her daughter) received other, presumably personal, benefits from placing her child in care, but this does not appear to have been part of the ratio of the decision. Sadiq addresses this argument by noting that the same could be said of a number of other allowable deductible expenses, and that there is a clear difference between using childcare to undertake social activities and using childcare to enable the taxpayer to undertake paid work. Indeed, Mason J accepted that Ms Lodge could not earn income without incurring the childcare costs. However, he decided that the expenses were not incurred 'in' deriving her income. On this point he followed the English case of *Halstead (HM Inspector of Taxes) v Condon*,[9] where the relevant provision required the expense to be 'in the performance of employment'. Although

[8] This accords with the view that the negative limbs are not true exceptions, but rather 'a way of saying that an expense was not sufficiently connected with the earning of income and thus not relevant': Ross W Parsons, *Income Taxation in Australia: Principles of Income, Deductibility and Tax Accounting* (Law Book Company, 1985) 459.

[9] (1970) 46 TC 289.

s 51 did not refer to performance of duties, Mason J assumed that the same conclusion was required because of the reference to expenses being incurred 'in' deriving income.

Sadiq's feminist judgment differs from that of Mason J in two important respects. First, Sadiq notes that the deduction in the English case was limited to expenses that were incurred in the *performance* of the employment, and is therefore not directly comparable to the provision before her. The second and perhaps most significant difference relates to Sadiq considering the social context in which the question of deductibility arises. This is sometimes described as the ambulatory approach to statutory interpretation, that is, that words are to be interpreted in accordance with their current meaning.[10] The 1972 context includes the changing role of women in the paid workforce and the growing appreciation of the need for equality between men and women as demonstrated by developments such as the lifting of the marriage bar and the equal pay decisions. Although Mason J did not reject such an approach, his conclusion suggests he did not really take these developments into account. The judgment of Sadiq is premised on *equality*, that is, equal treatment of claims for expenses by taxpayers whether they are men or women.

The Aftermath of *Lodge*

Canadian academic Claire Young reminds us that childcare should not be seen as just a women's issue.[11] The tax deductibility of the cost of childcare continues to be a contentious issue in Australia.[12] On the one hand, it is said that a deduction would provide recognition of the fact that childcare is a significant cost associated with earning of income. On the other hand, the value of a deduction increases with the level of income, so that deductions have an 'upside down' effect.[13] Taxpayers on a higher income (and therefore paying higher tax rates) get a greater benefit from a given amount of deduction. Those on lower incomes, who may have a greater need for assistance, will receive less money back through the tax system as a result of deductions for childcare expenses, and so pay more out of their own pocket for childcare. As noted above, Sadiq's decision is premised on equal treatment between men and women taxpayers, but cannot address the inequality built into the tax system between high-income and low-income earners. Indeed, it may disproportionately disadvantage women.[14]

Significantly, the first steps to provide affordable childcare in Australia did not rely on the tax system, but rather concentrated on the supply of government-funded childcare places. In 1985 the exemption for employers from fringe benefits tax on workplace-based childcare

[10] See Denis Pearce and Robert Geddes, *Statutory Interpretation in Australia* (LexisNexis Butterworths, 7th ed, 2011) 4.9.

[11] Claire Young, 'Child Care – A Taxing Issue?' (1994) 39 *McGill Law Journal* 539, 550.

[12] The Productivity Commission has been asked to consider future options for childcare and early childhood learning, with a focus on developing a system that supports workforce participation. See Commonwealth, Productivity Commission, *Childcare and Early Childhood Learning Inquiry* (2013) Terms of Reference.

[13] See Richard Krever, 'Tax Deductions for Charitable Donations: A Tax Expenditure Analysis' in Richard Krever and Gretchen Kewley (eds), *Charities and Philanthropic Institutions: Reforming the Tax Subsidy and Regulatory Regimes* (Australian Tax Research Foundation, 1991) 5–8.

[14] A recent report notes that that at all income levels Australian women earn significantly less than men. See Council of Australian Governments (COAG), *Tracking Equity: Comparing Outcomes for Women and Girls Across Australia*, Reform Council Report (2013) 6 which notes that in 2013, women's average weekly earnings were 17.5 per cent lower than men's (based on ordinary-time earnings)

was also focused on the supply side of the problem.[15] It was not until 2000 that the cost of childcare was addressed within the taxation system. In the current approach a rebate, arguably more equitable than a deduction,[16] is offered to people working or studying in relation to the cost of childcare expenses.[17]

[15] *Fringe Benefits Tax Assessment Act 1986* (Cth) s 47(8).

[16] A rebate reduces the amount of tax payable compared with a deduction which reduces the taxable income on which tax is payable. The amount of a deduction depends on the rate of tax payable. A $100 rebate has the same value regardless of the rate of tax payable.

[17] An eligible taxpayer is entitled to up to 50 per cent of 'out-of-pocket' childcare expenses up to $7500 per child per annum under *A New Tax System (Family Assistance) Administration Act 1999* (Cth). There is no separate income test for the rebate but the taxpayer must be eligible for payment of a Child-Care Benefit even if it is not claimed. For 2013–14 the maximum rate is payable if family income is less than $41 902 and cuts out at $145 642.

[HIGH COURT OF AUSTRALIA.]

LODGE . . . . APPELLANT;

AND

THE COMMISSIONER OF TAXATION OF THE COMMONWEALTH OF AUSTRALIA } RESPONDENT.

Cur. adv. vult.

H.C. OF A. 1972.

MELBOURNE, *Oct.* 3,16

Sadiq J.

SADIQ J. delivered the following written judgment: –

Ann Margaret Lodge is the mother of a daughter Deborah, born on 26th October 1968. During the income year in question she was also a law costs clerk for a partnership known as Law Cost. Miss Lodge was not an employee of the firm but rather earned a commission of four per cent on profit costs. For the income tax year ended 30th June 1971, Miss Lodge earned gross income of $3,521 of which $2,937 was remuneration from her primary work as a law costs clerk. In order to undertake a sufficient volume of work to enable Miss Lodge to earn a satisfactory income to support her and her daughter, she placed Deborah in childcare. In the income tax year in question, Miss Lodge incurred an amount of $647 in childcare fees. Miss Lodge returned a taxable income of $2,171. Her claim included a deduction for the childcare fees which was disallowed by the Commissioner of Taxation. She was subsequently assessed on a taxable income of $2,818. Miss Lodge objected to the rejection of her claim to the deduction and the Commissioner disallowed the objection. Pursuant to s. 187 of the *Income Tax Assessment Act* 1936–1971 (the Act), Miss Lodge subsequently requested the Commissioner to treat her objection as an appeal to this Court.

The claim of a deduction for childcare fees by Miss Lodge is based on the general deduction provision, s 51(1) of the Act. To qualify for the deduction Miss Lodge needed to satisfy the requirements of s 51(1) which provides that all losses and outgoings to the extent to which they are incurred in gaining or producing the assessable income, or are necessarily incurred in carrying on a business for the purpose of gaining or producing such income, shall be allowable deductions except to the extent to which they are losses or outgoings of capital, or of a capital nature, private or domestic in nature, or are incurred in relation to the gaining or producing of exempt income.

There is only one question before this Court and that is whether the childcare expenses incurred by Miss Lodge are deductible under s 51(1) of the Act. This question is simply one of statutory interpretation. However, it is precisely this question of whether childcare expenses are deductible under this provision that has not been dealt with previously by the Australian Courts.

In support of her appeal Miss Lodge gave oral evidence before this Court, which I accept. Her evidence was to the effect that she was unable to earn a sufficient income to maintain her establishment, herself and Deborah prior to the childcare arrangements being put in place. She also gave evidence that she could not be paid enough money to earn a living unless Deborah was in childcare. Under cross-examination Miss Lodge also gave evidence that there were ancillary benefits accrued to Deborah by reason of her attendance at childcare, in particular the company of other children that she would not otherwise have. However, on re-examination Miss Lodge indicated that she would have preferred to be at home with Deborah. As to this line of questioning by counsel for the respondent, I do not see that the ancillary benefits are of any relevance to the point at hand, that is, the deductibility of the childcare expenses as a loss or outgoing incurred in gaining or producing assessable income. This evidence is irrelevant except in so far as Miss Lodge clearly demonstrated that she wanted to provide the best environment and upbringing for her daughter, hence her difficult decision to place Deborah in childcare to ensure she could earn sufficient income to provide that environment. This line of reasoning is not traditionally raised in cases where the deductibility of an expense is in question.

Further, there are ancillary benefits to many expenses which are traditionally allowable deductions under s 51(1) of the Act. I view the case at hand as no different to the businessman who is allowed a deduction for entertainment expenses, such as a lunch, because they are incurred in the course of producing the taxpayer's assessable income. Nor is it any different to the businessman who is allowed a deduction for the annual golf club subscription where the club is used for business entertainment. The Court does not consider relevant the ancillary benefit of sustenance in the case of the business lunch, nor does it consider the recreational benefits of golf in the case of the annual golf club subscription. In fact, it may be pointed out that in the latter two examples the taxpayers may in fact gain not only the ancillary benefits from the events surrounding the deductible expenditure but also derive enjoyment from such events. Again, this has not previously been taken into account when deciding whether an expense is deductible under s 51(1). As I previously mentioned, Miss Lodge has made it clear that the ancillary benefits did not extend to any personal enjoyment from putting Deborah into childcare. As such, based on the law as it currently stands, I am of the view that the questions asked and evidence given under cross-examination are irrelevant to the case at hand and any ancillary benefit (and enjoyment) must be ignored in deciding the deductibility of childcare expenses.

As I have previously stated, the question of the deductibility of childcare expenses has not previously been decided by this Court. This may be for reasons alluded to below, as well as the fact that up until recently childcare has always been considered to be the responsibility of women through the private realm and via unpaid labour. The consequence of this lack of authority is that I am not currently bound by any previous cases of this Court except in so far

H.C. OF A.
1972.

MELBOURNE,
Oct. 3,16

Sadiq J.

as they provide broad guidance as to the interpretation of the legislative provision at hand. As a starting point, therefore, it is necessary to consider more broadly the claims for deductible expenses which have been allowed under s 51(1) of the Act. On this point, I turn to the settled law and I note with some interest that upon consulting the most recent Master Tax Guide (1970) it details the expenses listed under the category of a "professional man". To that extent, the deductibility of many of the expenses, such as private gentleman's club fees, which are considered relevant in a traditionally male dominated workforce, are well settled by this, and other, Courts. However, there is very little in the way of deductible expenses specifically for the professional woman. To date, the question of which costs associated with women working are a business expense has not been addressed by this, or other, Courts. It seems on this point that while over the last decade we have seen a period of significant social change, particularly with changes in attitudes to women in the workforce, along with their increased participation, the legislative interpretation of the income tax system has not kept pace. The increasing female participation in the workforce has been assisted by the lifting of the bar which required permanent female employees to resign on marriage. With the Commonwealth public service lifting its bar in 1966, many women now have the opportunity for a long term career whilst also raising a family. In addition, women are now also entitled to equal pay for equal work (1). These women are all participants in Australia's income tax system, each paying taxes equal to their male counterparts. With equal obligations come equal rights. This leads me to the conclusion that a decision in this case cannot be constrained by the principles established in a time when it was not contemplated that women would do more than raise children and keep house. I do not accept as a proposition that there are some kinds of expenses, such as childcare, which by virtue of their very nature are ordinary living expenses. In this case it has been determined that Miss Lodge has made the difficult choice to actively participate in the workforce while at the same time fulfilling the vital function of raising a child. However, the issue is much broader than simply the case at hand. We have recently seen women applying pressure to government to attain equal rights in all aspects of their lives. This must include the workplace and in particular extend to the consistent treatment of deductions for men and women for work related expenses under our income tax system.

Turning now to the particular issue at hand, that of whether the childcare expenses are an allowable deduction under s 51(1) of the Act, the question needs to be addressed as to whether the specific requirements of that provision are satisfied. This determination needs to be undertaken in the context of 1970 and not in line with an earlier era in which decisions were based on the "business man" claiming a deduction for what are traditionally viewed as income related expenses. These norms should not shape the interpretation of s 51(1), but rather the application of the income tax system to a given set of facts must be determined within the economic and social context which existed in the income tax year of 1970. To do anything else would be akin to suggesting that business men could not get a deduction for work related international aeroplane travel because traditionally international travel was undertaken by ship.

H.C. OF A.
1972.

MELBOURNE,
Oct. 3,16

Sadiq J.

To qualify as an allowable deduction under s 51(1) of the Act, the expenditure must be "incurred in gaining or producing assessable income" or necessarily incurred "in carrying on a business for the purpose of gaining or producing" such income. The meaning of these expressions is generally taken to be well settled with the first expression including most of the expenses covered in the second expression (2). As Miss Lodge is not an employee of Law Cost, it is reasonable to conclude that she is carrying on a business with expenses falling within the second positive limb. However, it is my view that it is only necessary for this Court to decide this point where it concludes that the expenditure is not deductible under the first positive limb. The question before me is simply whether the expenditure was incurred in preparing bills of cost. To that end, the decision in this case turns on two substantive points: first, whether the expense was incurred "in", or "in the course of", earning assessable income and second, whether it was relevant or incidental to the production of that income. These principles are well established in *Ronpibon Tin N.L. and Tongkah Compound N. L. v. Federal Commissioner of Taxation* (*Ronpibon*) (3). The passage on which reliance was placed for the appellant is:

> "For expenditure to form an allowable deduction as an outgoing incurred in gaining or producing the assessable income it must be incidental and relevant to that end."

This is immediately followed by the observation:

> "The words 'incurred in gaining or producing the assessable income' mean in the course of gaining or producing such income."

Later, it was said (4):

> "In brief substance, to come within the initial part of the subsection it is both sufficient and necessary that the occasion of the loss or outgoing should be found in whatever is productive of the assessable income or, if none be produced, would be expected to produce assessable income."

Turning first to whether the expenses were incurred "in" or "in the course of" earning assessable income, the distinction must be drawn between those expenses which are within the scope of s 51(1) of the Act and those which are outside because they are private or domestic in character. The distinction between childcare expenses which allow a person to participate in the workforce and childcare expenses which allow a person to partake in social activities is evident, with the latter, which involves discretionary spending, clearly not an allowable tax deduction. However, that is not what is in dispute in this case. There is no question that the spending was incurred for the purpose of allowing Miss Lodge to work, and as such, the question turns to whether it is considered private or domestic in the sense of placing Miss Lodge in a position to be able to work as opposed to expenditure incurred "in" gaining or producing assessable income. As Counsel for the appellant pointed out, the principal decision on what constitutes private or domestic expenditure is the decision of

(1) *Equal Pay Case* (1969) 127 C.A.R. 1142
(2) *Ronpibon Tin N.L. and Tongkah Compound N.L. v. Federal Commissioner of Taxation* (1949) 78 C.L.R. 47, at p. 56–57.
(3) (1949) 78 C.L.R. 47, at p. 56–57.
(4) (1949) 78 C.L.R. 47, at p. 174.

H.C. OF A.
1972.

MELBOURNE,
Oct. 3,16

Sadiq J.

this Court in *Lunney v. Federal Commissioner of Taxation* (*Lunney*) (5). In that case, the rejection of the claim that the expenses of travelling between home and work was an allowable deduction was based on the proposition that to say that expenditure on fares is a prerequisite to the earning of a taxpayer's income is not to say that such expenditure is incurred in or in the course of gaining or producing his income. This is a proposition with which I agree. However, it is a proposition that, when applied to the facts at hand, does not lead me to the conclusion that the childcare expenditure incurred by Miss Lodge is private or domestic.

Ultimately, *Lunney* is of little help in the current case, as it gives no guidance as to what is the essential quality of personal or domestic expenditure. *Lunney* is a decision based on a unique set of facts and circumstances where this Court was governed by authority established long before the general operation of s 51(1) was settled. Even if I felt bound by *Lunney*, which I do not accept is the case, in the current set of facts, the childcare expenses did not merely place Miss Lodge in the position to be able to work as the expenses of travelling to work do, but, as per her oral evidence, went further to enable her to work more efficiently, with greater speed and with more accuracy just as the expense incurred to employ a secretary may do for a business man. Had Miss Lodge employed a secretary to achieve the same purpose no one would doubt the deductibility of the wages paid to that secretary. Ultimately, it must be concluded that a secretary would perform functions which result in a similar outcome to that of childcare in the current case: to allow the taxpayer to gain or produce assessable income "in" or "in the course" of her work.

The Court's interpretation of s 51(1) of the Act, founded on the presence of the word "in", has its roots in the interpretation of Schedule E to the *Income Tax Act* 1952 (U.K.). Of particular relevance to this case is the English Court's decision in *Halstead (H.M. Inspector of Taxes) v. Condon* (*Halstead*) (6) where it was held that a taxpayer was not entitled to a deduction in respect of payments made to persons who minded his two children so as to enable him to work and earn an income. However, the relevant English provision was more narrowly expressed than the Australian provision because, as it was clearly explained by Megarry J. in *Halstead,* it only entitled an employee to a deduction if he was necessarily obliged "to expend moneys wholly exclusively and necessarily in the performance of the duties of his employment". The words of Megarry J. in that case are worth citing simply to illustrate the very different requirements of the two provisions. Megarry J. said (7):

"There is still the word 'in', governed as it is by 'wholly' and 'exclusively'. Even if one accepts the highest degree of inevitability in what the taxpayer did, in no conceivable sense can the expenditure be said to have been incurred by him 'in' the performance of his duties: it had nothing to do with the way in which he performed his functions as a clerk to the Borough Council."

(5) (1958) 100 C.L.R. 478.
(6) (1970) 46 T.C. 289.
(7) (1970) 46 T.C. 289, at p. 175.

In the present case, I am not restricted by the requirement that the monies be spent wholly exclusively and necessarily in the performance of the employment, and, in fact, Miss Lodge was not in a position of employee as envisaged by the narrowly drafted English provision but rather, had a contractual relationship with Law Costs. The question before me under the Australian provision is simply whether the expenditure was incurred "in" or "in the course" of earning assessable income; a question I resolve in the affirmative. I do so on the basis that the scope of what is considered a deductible expense has over the years expanded in Australia and childcare expenses should not be an exception. While Miss Lodge may not be considered to be participating in traditional business practices the reality of the diverse nature of business needs to be taken into account. Section 51(1) of the Act was introduced at a time when the traditional family structure of men working outside the home in paid labour and women working inside the home in unpaid labour was the norm. It is easy to imagine that s 51(1) was drafted at a time when childcare was not envisaged as a business expense.

However, a reading of the section itself in no way suggests that its application should be limited to such a view. Further, it is not my role to determine what expenses the drafters envisaged falling within the scope of the provision but rather to interpret that section in the context in which it presents itself today. In doing so, the contrary view is formed in that s 51(1) specifically refers to the activities involved in the earning of income and the connection required between the expenditure and that earning, not specific deductions or specific taxpayers. To deny Miss Lodge a deduction would be to deny the true intent of s 51(1) and place her at a distinct disadvantage compared to her "business man" counterpart who claims what are considered traditional business expenses.

A conclusion that results in Miss Lodge being denied a deduction for childcare expenses would also result in a narrower interpretation of s 51(1) of the Act than was otherwise ever anticipated. Such an interpretation may lead to a result which was clearly never intended by the drafters of the legislation. As Latham C.J. stated in *W. Nevill & Co. Ltd. v. Federal Commissioner of Taxation* (8) when determining the scope of the predecessor to s 51(1):

> "No expenditure, strictly and narrowly considered, in itself actually gains or produces income. It is an outgoing, not an incoming. Its character can be determined only in relation to the object which the person making the expenditure has in view. If the actual object is the conduct of the business on a profitable basis with that due regard to economy which is essential in any well-conducted business, then the expenditure (if not a capital expenditure) is an expenditure incurred in gaining or producing the assessable income."

Once it is established that an expense is incurred "in" producing assessable income, which I am of the view has been done in this case, the question turns to whether the expenditure is incidental and relevant to that end. This leads me to the second substantive point of whether the childcare expenses were relevant or incidental to the production of Miss Lodge's income. It is well settled

(8) (1937) 56 C.L.R. 290, at p. 301.

H.C. OF A. 1972.

MELBOURNE, *Oct*. 3,16

Sadiq J.

as to what is meant by "relevant or incidental" to the production of income. Again, turning to the decision of this Court in *Ronpibon* (9) it was said:

> "In brief substance, to come within the initial part of the sub-section it is both sufficient and necessary that the occasion of the loss or outgoing should be found in whatever is productive of the assessable income or, if none be produced, would be expected to produce assessable income."

This is a broad test which stresses the link between the expenditure and the production of income. However, these are merely attributes that need to be present and it is the essential character of the expenditure which must be examined. In *Lunney* the essential character of the travel expenditure was to place the taxpayer in a position to be able to work but unlike the case before me had no bearing on the taxpayer's ability to perform the work. In the present case the essential character of the expenditure is to gain or produce income in an efficient, speedy and accurate manner. Previous decisions have also made it clear that it is not the function of the Court to determine how a taxpayer should spend their money. Further, it is not the function of the Court to determine whether one type of expenditure which allows the taxpayer to work more efficiently, with greater speed and with more accuracy, is appropriate and therefore deductible, while another type of expenditure, which achieves the same result, is not appropriate and therefore not deductible. I am also of the view that it is the responsibility of this Court to distinguish between the legitimate needs of a business on the one hand and what have narrowly been defined as the needs of the "business man" on the other. Business expenses have and will continue to change over the years as work practices change and develop. As such, it is the Court's responsibility to determine simply whether an expense falls within the scope of s 51(1) of the Act and not to pass judgment on the type of expenditure incurred. It is clear in the case of Miss Lodge that she viewed the childcare expenses as a necessary part of her earning sufficient income. Unlike the types of expenditure in the cases which Counsel for the respondent relied upon, the expenditure incurred by Miss Lodge was for the sole and specific purpose of obtaining childcare to enable her to earn a sufficient income to support her and her daughter. As such, the expenditure is not merely necessary, as in the case of expenditure to travel to and from work, but is incurred "in" and is relevant and incidental to the gaining or producing of assessable income as required by the Court's decision in *Ronpibon*. Accordingly, Miss Lodge's claim for a deduction is upheld.

As I have concluded that the childcare expenses are a loss or outgoing incurred in gaining or producing assessable income, thereby satisfying the first positive limb, it is also necessary to mention the negative limbs of s 51(1) of the Act, in particular whether the expenditure is excluded by virtue of being private or domestic in nature. On this point, I again agree with Counsel for the appellant. Apart from circumstances where an apportionment of the expense is clearly called for, it is difficult to envisage a circumstance where expenditure would fall within one of the positive limbs but then be excluded by virtue of it being private or domestic in nature. This is a point which was conceded by

(9) (1949) 78 C.L.R. 47, at p. 56–57.

Counsel for the respondent during submissions in which he stated that once the exercise of categorising the expense in relation to the principal part of the section had been performed there would be little room for the exclusion to apply. As such, I have no need to expand on this point.

By concluding that the expenses are deductible under the first positive limb of s 51(1) of the Act it is not necessary for me to decide whether Miss Lodge was carrying on a business of preparing bills of cost as would be required under the second positive limb. As such, I do not agree with the submission made by Counsel for the respondent that Miss Lodge had no right to a deduction unless the expenditure related to a business expense. If I am wrong, however, I also find that Miss Lodge was carrying on a business and the expenses were incurred in carrying on the business of preparing bills of cost. Consequently, her claim for a deduction for the cost of childcare expenses would satisfy both the first and second positive limbs of s 51(1) of the Act.

For the foregoing reasons I allow the appeal. The assessment shall be remitted to the Commissioner for amendment in the manner which has been indicated.

Immigration Law

7

Roqia's Story: Refugees and Natural Justice in the Court of Public Opinion

MARY E CROCK*

Introduction

The majority's ruling in *Re Minister for Immigration, Multicultural and Indigenous Affairs; Ex parte Applicants S134/2002*[1] is spare on detail and brutal in its reasoning. The applicant and five of her children, we are told, were not persons to whom Australia owed protection obligations. They were *not* refugees. With Gaudron and Kirby JJ (and now Steer J) in vigorous dissent, the High Court ruled that the refusal of their applications was not impugned by a failure to consider that the applicants' husband and father *had* earlier been found to be a refugee.

This is a case about a troubled and troubling woman, stripped of her identity by operation of law.[2] She and her family were rightly described in 2004 as a 'kind of lightning-rod for the politics of asylum-seekers under the Howard Government.'[3] By the time her case came to be heard in the High Court, Roqia Bakhtiyari had become a *cause célèbre* for refugee advocates. For them, Roqia was a woman wronged by decision-makers ignorant of and/or insensitive to the experience of Afghan women living under Taliban rule. She and her children embodied the suffering generated by the policy of locking asylum-seekers away for long periods in harsh and inhospitable detention centres. For those opposed to asylum-seekers, she was the queue-jumper whose invocation of rights under international law offended Australian sovereignty and undermined border security. Denounced as mendacious and opportunistic, Roqia's failures assuaged a nation's guilty conscience and affirmed the wisdom of its punitive policies towards irregular migrants.

* I would like to acknowledge the assistance of Hannah Martin, Kerry Murphy, Nicholas Poynder, David Corlett and Mark Aronson, who assisted with research into this case. Thanks also to Ron McCallum, Frank Brennan and Mark Aronson for comments on the article in draft. Any errors that remain and views expressed are my own. Charlotte Steer would like to acknowledge the inspiration of Helen Carr and Caroline Hunter's feminist judgment in *YL v Birmingham City Council*, in Rosemary Hunter, Clare McGlynn and Erika Rackley (eds), *Feminist Judgments: From Theory to Practice* (Hart Publishing, 2010), which validated her ideas about *S134* and motivated her to contribute to the Australian Feminist Judgments Project.

[1] (2003) 211 CLR 441 ('*Applicants S134*').

[2] *Migration Act 1958* (Cth) s 91X (as amended in 2001) operates to prohibit the disclosure of the name of any person claiming protection as a refugee in Australia.

[3] See Editorial, *The Australian* (Sydney), 20 December 2004.

The Legal Issues

Applicants S134 was heard concurrently with *Plaintiff S157 v Commonwealth*.[4] Both involved the interpretation for the first time of the privative clause introduced into the *Migration Act 1958* (Cth) in September 2001.[5] The provisions in question appeared to strip all courts (including the High Court) of power to review decisions made under the Act.[6] Counsel for Plaintiff S157 focused attack on the constitutionality of the privative clause, arguing that the provisions offended against the guarantees enshrined in ch III of the *Constitution*.[7] In contrast, counsel for Mrs Bakhtiyari conceded that privative clauses could be interpreted so as to be within power of the federal legislature. They argued that the clause should be read down so as to do no more than limit judicial oversight of administrative decisions made *within* the limits of the law.[8] The High Court delivered its ruling on the constitutionality of the privative clause in *Plaintiff S157*. While it upheld the Minister on this point, it accepted the arguments put by Roqia's counsel, holding that judicial intervention involving a federal privative clause would thereafter turn on the identification of a 'jurisdictional error'.[9]

What is mystifying about the two cases is the way this principle was applied by the Court. It was Mrs Bakhtiyari's case that seemed to present the most obvious example of simple but profound legal error. That is, the Refugee Review Tribunal (RRT)'s failure to act upon material on the file before it by revealing information unknown to the applicants – that their husband and father was in Australia and had been granted refugee status. Yet it was in *Plaintiff S157* that the Court found denial of procedural fairness of sufficient gravity to constitute jurisdictional error. In Roqia Bakhtiyari's case the majority found no error at all. At its simplest, the majority's ruling illustrates the conclusory nature of the judicial function in identifying 'jurisdictional errors' in decision-making.[10] The majority had made up its mind about this illiterate mother of six, and was not going to provide a remedy.

Roqia's Story

Roqia Bakhtiyari claimed to have been born in Afghanistan in 1970 and to be married to Ali Asghar Bakhtiyari, born 1 January 1957.[11] She was mother to five Afghani children – Alamdar

[4] (2003) 211 CLR 476.

[5] *Migration Act 1958* (Cth) s 474 ('the Act').

[6] For a small selection of articles on the case, see, eg, Enid Campbell and Matthew Groves, 'Privative Clauses and the Australian Constitution' (2004) 4 *Oxford University Commonwealth Law Journal* 51; Caron Beaton-Wells, 'Restoring the Rule of Law – Plaintiff S157/2002' (2003) 10 *Australian Journal of Administrative Law* 125; Duncan Kerr, 'Deflating The Hickman Myth: Judicial Review After *Plaintiff S157/2002 v The Commonwealth*' (2003) 39 *Australian Institute of Administrative Law Forum* 7.

[7] *Australian Constitution* s 75(iii), (v). See *Plaintiff S157 of 2002 v Commonwealth S157/2002* [2002] HCATrans 351 (19 July 2002); [2002] HCATrans 352 (23 July 2002); [2002] HCATrans 354 (30 July 2002); [2002] HCATrans 420 (3 September 2002); [2002] HCATrans 423 (4 September 2002).

[8] See *Applicants S134/2002, Ex parte – Re MIMIA* [2002] HCATrans 288 (11 June 2002); [2002] HCATrans 353 (30 July 2002); [2002] HCATrans 421 (3 September 2002).

[9] See *Plaintiff S157/2002 v Commonwealth* (2003) 211 CLR 476 [92] ff; see, eg, James Spigelman, 'The Centrality of Jurisdictional Error' (2010) 21 *Public Law Review* 77.

[10] See, eg, Mark Aronson, 'Nullity' (2004) 40 *Australian Institute of Administrative Law Forum* 19.

[11] A good selection of newspaper clippings on the family is at <www.safecom.org.au/bakhtiari-files.htm>, best

(1988), Montazer (1990), Negina (1991), Samina (1993) and Amena (1997). A sixth child was born to the couple in Australia on 15 October 2003. Like many Afghan families of this era, the family's story was one of deprivation and flight. Typical of many Afghani women, Roqia had been raised in a repressive, patriarchal society. Her voyage to Australia (after losing touch with her husband) and the circumstances surrounding the rejection of her claims by the RRT on 26 July 2001[12] are set out by Steer J. While the RRT found Roqia to be lacking in credibility, this finding rested on gendered and ethnocentric assumptions about women's lives, capacity and agency that rendered her story unbelievable and her experiences apparently unimaginable.[13]

The Bakhtiyaris' misfortune may have gone largely unnoticed but for protest action taken by Roqia's brother. Mahzar Ali climbed on to the roof of one of the buildings in Woomera Detention Centre on 26 January 2002 – and jumped into the razor wire. The image was captured by a television camera and played to a national audience. Amazingly, he survived the fall and the hideous cuts to his stomach, legs and neck.[14] The gesture catapulted the Bakhtiyari family into the centre of the national debate around Australia's treatment of asylum-seekers.[15] However, it does not explain completely the chasm that developed between the family's supporters and their detractors. The real problem was that Roqia did not fit the expected stereotype of the vulnerable refugee woman.

Even before Mahzar Ali took his horrifying leap into the wire, Roqia and her boys had marked themselves as (violent) trouble-makers. Roqia responded to the rejection of her asylum claim by sewing her lips together and going on hunger strike. Her two boys, Alamdar (13) and Montezar (Monty) (12) both engaged in acts of self-harm including cutting their arms and legs and sewing their lips together. In early 2002 Alamdar carved the word 'Freedom' into his arm. Contemporaneous reports by psychologists and youth workers at the Woomera Centre suggest that both Roqia and her children descended into acute depression, the boys hugely traumatised by their experiences and by the violent contagion of the riots and protests within the Woomera Centre.[16]

Outside the wire, Ali Asghar Bakhtiyari had been used by the Refugee Action Coalition (RAC) in Sydney as the embodiment of the injustices perpetrated by the regime of mandatory detention and temporary protection visas that split refugee families.[17] Supported by a growing team of legal advisers, Ali Asghar travelled to Woomera and stayed near the centre for a week in March 2002, visiting his family for at least five hours each day. This was a period of huge unrest at the centre, with large numbers of detainees engaging in acts of self-harm: digging themselves mock graves; engaging in hunger strikes that brought many to the point of death; and engaging in riotous behaviour that left parts of the detention centre in ruins.[18]

accessed via the National Archives of Australia's Pandora web archive at <http://www.pandora.nla.gov.au/>. For a detailed account of the claims made by Ali Asghar Bakhtiyari, see David Corlett, 'Caught in the Crossfire', *Sending Them Home: The Fate of the Returned Asylum Seekers* (Black Inc, 2005) 13–15.

[12] *RRT Reference No V01/12921* (Unreported, Refugee Review Tribunal, Member Hamilton, 26 July 2001). Copy on file with author.

[13] See further Corlett, above n 11, 16–17.

[14] Ibid 20. See also *The Man Who Jumped* (Directed by Russell Vines, Prospero Productions, 2011).

[15] See Andrew West, 'Innocents in Centre of Storm', *Sydney Morning Herald* (Sydney), 10 February 2002; Andrew West, 'This Isn't a Camp, It's an Oven and We Are Burning', *Sydney Morning Herald* (Sydney), 17 February 2002.

[16] See Corlett, above n 11, 18–19.

[17] See, eg, Andrew West, 'Back to the Ruins', *Sun-Herald* (Sydney), 24 March 2002; Richard C Paddock, 'A Family Apart in Australia', *The Los Angeles Times* (Los Angeles), 10 April 2002.

[18] For a firsthand account of this traumatic period in Australian history, see Tom Mann, *Desert Sorrow: Asylum Seekers at Woomera* (Seaview Press, 2003).

At Easter 2002, activists from across Australia gathered at Woomera to protest, assisting rioting detainees to break out of the centre. The oldest Bakhtiyari boys were amongst those who escaped into the desert. Quickly recaptured, contemporary psychological reports on the children confirmed the depth of the on-going trauma they experienced.[19]

After the RRT rejected Roqia's claim in July 2001, her legal advisers did not at first attempt a legal challenge by way of judicial review. They opted instead to seek discretionary intervention[20] by the then Immigration Minister, Philip Ruddock MP. While this Minister had been known to intervene quietly in many difficult cases, he did not take kindly to aggressive and public opposition to the decisions and actions of his administrators. On 21 March 2002, he formally declined to exercise his discretion in the case of Roqia and her children.[21]

At this point, Sydney barrister Nick Poynder lodged a 'communication' on behalf of the Bakhtiyari family with the United Nations Human Rights Committee, pursuant to the First Optional Protocol to the International Covenant on Civil and Political Rights,[22] arguing that the detention of Roqia and her children put Australia in breach of this Convention. So began a chain of legal interventions that would ultimately involve close to 20 actions – most of which were ultimately unsuccessful.

The Bakhtiyari family became the international face of the fight against mandatory detention in June 2002, when Alamdar and Monty were involved in a second breakout from Woomera Detention Centre. This time the boys evaded recapture. Passed into the hands of activists, they disappeared into the South Australian desert. Transported to Melbourne, they claimed political asylum at the British Consulate.[23] The British Secretary for Home Affairs, Minister Jack Straw, intervened personally to reject the application. This set in chain a series of appeals in the British courts that were not finally resolved until late 2004.[24] Although unsuccessful, the actions highlighted the human cost to children of Australia's detention laws and drew biting criticisms from the British judiciary.

By this stage the Immigration Department had instituted an inquiry into Ali Asghar, emerging with allegations that his claim to be a farmer from a remote village in central Afghanistan was false. Rather, it was suggested that he was a plumber from Quetta in Pakistan. Andrew West, the journalist who had first highlighted Roqia's plight, took the lead in the media frenzy that followed, apparently being fed material by the immigration authorities.[25] Other journalists initiated their own investigations. The *Sun-Herald's* Matthew Benns joined a Pakistani journalist to claim that Ali Asghar was known in Quetta as a plumber.[26] Freelance journalist Alistair McLeod reported in the *Australian* that he had been unable to find anyone who could recognise a photograph of Ali Asghar in any of the towns cited as his places of birth or residence. The article was published on the front page, accompanied by a large photograph of a village elder looking quizzically at Ali's image.[27] The *Age's* Russell

[19] See Corlett, above n 11, 18–19, 29.

[20] Under *Migration Act 1958* (Cth) s 417.

[21] See *Applicants S134* (2003) 211 CLR 441, 452 [11].

[22] *Optional Protocol to the International Covenant on Civil and Political Rights*, opened for signature 19 December 1966, 999 UNTS 171 (entered into force 23 March 1976).

[23] Ewen MacAskill, 'Government Accused of Breaching Rights: Runaways Seeking Asylum Turned Away', *The Guardian* (London), July 2002.

[24] *R (on the application of B) v Secretary of State for Foreign and Commonwealth Affairs* [2005] QB 643.

[25] Andrew West, 'Have We Been Duped by a Pakistani Plumber?', *The Sun-Herald* (Sydney), 30 June 2002.

[26] See Matthew Benns and Saleem Shahid, 'He's From Pakistan and He Used to Repair Our Pipes', *The Sun-Herald* (Sydney), 28 July 2002.

[27] Alastair McLeod, John Zubrzycki and Ian Gerard, 'No Recognition in Afghanistan', *The Australian* (Sydney), 14 August 2002.

Skelton[28] was also unable to find anyone who would admit to knowing the man in the photograph he carried. His reports were again front-page news.[29]

The Appeal to the High Court

It was against the backdrop of this hugely damaging media maelstrom that Roqia's case came before the High Court in September 2002.[30] Her argument was simple. The file provided by the Department of Immigration when the initial (adverse) decision in her case went on appeal to the RRT contained two documents that should have made the RRT aware of both her husband's presence in Australia and his legal status as a Convention refugee. As a matter of statutory construction, she argued, this fact affected both her substantive and procedural entitlements. The unstated problem she faced was that a sizeable proportion of the Australian public believed by then that the RRT had been correct in its assessment of her national origin.

The judges on the High Court alluded to this identity question as a central problem as soon as Roqia's senior counsel, John Basten SC, rose to address the bench. McHugh J asked: 'How are we going to resolve this question of the disputed fact [ie the prosecutors' nationality] which is vital before you even reach these constitutional issues?' Basten made a valiant attempt to divert the focus from the troublesome issue of Roqia's identity, arguing that there were no disputed facts vital to Roqia's case, because the case did not turn on 'where the prosecutors come from'. At the time the case was heard, Ali Asghar still held a protection visa. But their Honours were not entirely diverted from the question of national origin, with Kirby J referring to nationality as the foundation on which 'the whole stack of cards' (the protection visa applications) was founded.[31]

In their judgments, however, the members of the High Court did not allude to the controversy surrounding the nationality of the prosecutors. The majority dealt with the issue by narrowing the focus of the inquiry required by the Act. It ruled that the fact that another application had been made by their husband and father, which had resulted in him gaining recognition as a refugee, was not relevant to their claim, since they had not made their application as secondary applicants to Ali Asghar. The majority's finding underscored the punitive effect of the temporary protection regime created by the government. It confirmed that family members arriving separately could not rely on the fact that an earlier member had been recognised as a refugee.[32]

In dissent, Gaudron and Kirby JJ (and Steer J) found a positive duty on the RRT to consider the prosecutors' refugee claims both independently *and* as 'members of the family unit'. The fact that the husband/father was not connected expressly to the family's claim did not make his status irrelevant to their case. For the dissenters, the failure to consider Ali

[28] See Corlett, above n 11, 25.

[29] See Russell Skelton, 'The Truth Behind Bakhtiyari', *The Age* (Melbourne), 23 August 2002; Russell Skelton, 'Looking For the Real Ali Bakhtiyari', *The Age* (Melbourne), 23 August 2002.

[30] *Applicants S134/2002; Ex parte – Re MIMIA S134/2002* [2002] HCATrans 419 (3 September 2002).

[31] Ibid.

[32] See *Applicants S134* (2003) 211 CLR 441 [18]–[26], [30]–[32] (Gleeson CJ, McHugh, Gummow, Hayne and Callinan JJ).

Asghar did indeed constitute a simple and profound error of law on the part of the RRT – a constructive failure on the part of the RRT to exercise the jurisdiction vested in it.[33]

The majority's ruling on the failure to consider the information on the Department's file is just as troubling. This information should have alerted the RRT to Ali Asghar's presence in Australia and his status as a refugee. The Court had acknowledged earlier that the failure by the Migration Review Tribunal to notice a key piece of correspondence on file rendered a decision by that Tribunal void by virtue of 'jurisdictional error'.[34] The majority distinguished the earlier decision on the basis that the documents in question in *Applicants S134* were not relevant to the RRT's task. They ruled that there could be no duty to disclose something of which the RRT was unaware, and that the information was not relevant anyway to the task at hand.[35]

Given the approach taken, there is some irony in the attention given in the majority judgment to the place of family unity under international law.[36] The case set the trend in the Australian jurisprudence to read the Act as a stand-alone document, unaffected by norms of international law. In a case involving the prosecution of asylum-seekers who had escaped from Woomera with the Bakhtiyari boys, the court ruled that the lawfulness of immigration detention was not affected by the conditions in which detainees were held. Again, norms of international human rights law were found to be of no relevance to Australia's domestic legal discourse.[37] The same Court rejected challenges to the mandatory detention of asylum-seeker children in general[38] and of the Bahktiyari children in particular.[39]

From the family's point of view, the High Court's ruling sealed the fates not only of Roqia and her children, but also of Ali Asghar and Mahzar Ali. All were returned to Pakistan on rudimentary travel documents issued by the Pakistani government. All moved to Kabul at the earliest opportunity. In spite of Minister Ruddock's threat to cancel the protection visas of 'up to 700' Afghan refugees suspected of being from Pakistan, the Bakhtiyari family was ultimately the only family group to be sent back involuntarily. Roqia and her children had become scapegoats – a lightning rod indeed for the fear and anger generated by the unwanted, uninvited asylum-seekers and refugees.

The Feminist Judgment

In her feminist judgment, Steer J puts the lived administrative experience of Roqia Bakhtiyari and her children centre-stage. She makes the point eloquently that this should have been the beginning and end of the case.

Steer J also uses the priority given to family unity and family reunion in international conventions as a means of redressing the systemic inequalities experienced by women and children in the asylum process. She writes:

[33] *Applicants S134* (2003) 211 CLR 441, 471–2 [86]–[92] (Gaudron and Kirby JJ).
[34] See *Minister for Immigration and Multicultural Affairs v Bhadwaj* (2002) 187 ALR 117.
[35] *Applicants S134* (2003) 211 CLR 441, 457–8 [33]–[34] (Gleeson CJ, McHugh, Gummow, Hayne and Callinan JJ).
[36] Ibid 454–5 [20]–[22].
[37] *Behrooz v Department of Immigration and Multicultural and Indigenous Affairs* (2004) 291 CLR 486.
[38] *Re Woolley; Ex parte M276/2003* (2004) 225 CLR 1.
[39] *Minister for Immigration and Multicultural and Indigenous Affairs v B* (2004) 219 CLR 365.

> It is a well-recognised fact that in times of war and other dangerous situations it is more often the men who flee and the women and children who stay behind, or leave later. A policy of family reunion to some extent ameliorates the disparities of opportunity for escape afforded to men and women.[40]

She thus reads s 36 of the Act to require family members to enjoy derivative status as refugees whenever (and wherever) one member is recognised as a refugee. The legislation on its face did not expressly require family members to be travelling together.

Steer J's treatment of the failure to notice material actually on the Department's file also acknowledges the feminist ethic of care – which by rights should underpin any notion of good administrative practice. For a tribunal styled as an investigative body, the finding that the RRT was under no legal obligation to be aware of documents that were actually in the file before it is indeed extraordinary. As Steer J stresses, the finding that the RRT had no obligation to notice, let alone to disclose, Ali Bakhtiyari's whereabouts (and status as a recognised refugee) is troubling because it entrenched Roqia's disempowerment. This situation illustrates the role for an extended feminist ethic of care. Although not yet applied outside of the law of negligence, it is known to Australian law that one person can be obliged to take care to protect the welfare of another. A feminist redefinition and broader application of this duty would see decision-makers allowed, even obliged, to be attentive to and responsible for the interests of another.[41] Steer J points out that there was a statutory foundation for the approach the RRT should have taken in s 420 of the Act. It does indeed beggar belief that a procedure could be 'fair' or 'just' where the decision-maker has failed to notice and disclose critically important information. Sadly, the High Court's jurisprudence on this aspect of s 420 places Steer J in the minority.

[40] See Steer's feminist judgment in this volume, p 110.

[41] See, eg, Joanne Conaghan, 'Tort Law and the Feminist Critique of Reason' in Anne Bottomley (ed), *Feminist Perspectives on the Foundational Subjects of Law* (Routledge Cavendish, 1996) 47–68; Daryl Koehn, *Rethinking Feminist Ethics: Care, Trust and Empathy* (Routledge, 1998).

RE MINISTER FOR IMMIGRATION AND MULTICULTURAL AND INDIGENOUS AFFAIRS & ANOTHER; EX PARTE APPLICANTS S134/2002

[2003] HCA 1

4 February 2003

HC OF A 2002–2003

Sept 3, 4 2002

Feb 4 2003

STEER J

103 STEER J. A family, separated by war, could have been reunited by a simple phone call. The crucial information, in the possession of the respondent Department, was not communicated to the family. When the information was passed on to the Refugee Review Tribunal ("the Tribunal"), the Tribunal also took no steps to communicate the information to the family. The majority of this Court hold there was no obligation on either the Department or the Tribunal to do so. Therefore, in similar cases of families separated by war, there will be no obligation on the decision-maker to disclose information that could assist the family's reunification. I disagree, for the reasons that appear below.

Factual Background

104 The proceedings were brought by the prosecutors in their capacity as persons who applied for protection visas and, thus, pursuant to s 91X of the *Migration Act* 1958 (Cth) (the Act), cannot be named by this Court. I will refer to them as Mrs B and her five children.

105 Submissions made to this Court indicate that in 1998, Mrs B, Mr B and their five young children were living in Afghanistan. Mrs B was approximately 28 years old, Mr B was 41 years old, and their children, all born in Afghanistan, were roughly 10, 8, 7, 5 and 1 year old. Following a series of incidents with local Taliban officials that left him in fear of his life, Mr B travelled to Quetta and Rawalpindi in Pakistan. Mrs B, escorted by her brother, her mother-in-law and the five children, followed Mr B to Pakistan. Mr B enlisted the aid of people smugglers to fly to Indonesia and then travel by boat to Australia. Mrs B and the children remained behind. Mr B arrived in Australia in October 1999. Taken into detention, he applied for recognition as a refugee on 29 May 2000, naming Mrs B, Mrs B's brother and his children as dependents who had remained behind in Pakistan. He was granted a temporary protection visa on 3 August 2000 and released from detention to live in the Australian community.

106 Escorted again by her brother, Mrs B and her five children arrived in Australia by boat from Indonesia on New Year's Day 2001. Mrs B applied for a protection visa on 21 February 2001 on behalf of herself and the children, stating that her husband, whom she named, had been missing for two years. Her claim was rejected on the basis that she failed to establish her identity as an Hazara woman and fugitive from Afghanistan. Mrs B exercised her right of appeal to the Tribunal. The Tribunal heard the case and

on 26 July 2001 upheld the decision of the Minister's delegate on the grounds that Mrs B's claim to have fled the Taliban in Afghanistan lacked credibility. While she accepted that Mrs B was an ethnic Hazara, the Tribunal relied on a language analysis of her speech that identified Mrs B's dialect and speech patterns as having their origin in Pakistan. The Tribunal found it implausible that Mrs B was unable to name the months of the Afghan calendar; that she could not identify or name the currency used in Afghanistan; that she could not describe her life in Afghanistan and the route taken from her village to Pakistan. Nor was she able to identify the Pashtun language spoken by the majority ethnic group in Afghanistan. The Tribunal found Mrs B's credibility "remarkably poor", describing as "facile" the responses given to questions about her husband's treatment at the hands of the Taliban and about her husband's whereabouts.

107 Whatever the merits of the Tribunal's assessment of Mrs B's claims, the matter that ultimately brought the case to this Court was that the Departmental file before the Tribunal contained two documents (or "folios") of critical importance. These identified the fact that Mrs B's husband, Mr B, was in Australia and that he had been granted a protection visa. Although the Tribunal member acknowledged that the Tribunal had been provided with the Departmental file, the Tribunal member appears to have conducted the hearing in ignorance of this information. It was not until two days after the Tribunal rejected her claim that Mrs B and Mr B discovered that they were both in Australia: Mrs B and the children in Woomera Detention Centre and Mr B in Sydney where he had taken work.

The Application

108 On 9 April 2002, Mrs B and her children instituted proceedings in this Court claiming relief by way of prohibition, certiorari, mandamus, injunction and declaratory order.

109 An order nisi for prohibition directed to the Minister to prevent him from acting either on the decision of the Tribunal or on his own decision, for certiorari to quash those decisions and for mandamus directed to the Minister and the Tribunal to reconsider, respectively, the applications for the exercise of the Minister's power and for review of the delegate's decision was granted on 11 June 2002. This is the return of that Order Nisi.

110 On the second day of the hearing before the Court, counsel for the prosecutors obtained leave to amend the order nisi. The principal grounds now relied upon in respect of the decision of the Tribunal are that it:

> "(i) constructively failed to exercise the jurisdiction vested in it, and the duty placed upon it by s 414(1) of the Act, by failing to consider a material fact, namely that the [first] Prosecutor's spouse held a temporary protection visa and was an applicant for a permanent protection visa;
>
> (ii) breached its obligation of procedural fairness in failing to disclose to the Prosecutor[s] the information it had about that material fact."

Issues

111 The application to this Court raises two issues. The first issue is whether the Tribunal's statutory duty to review the decision required the Tribunal to consider the application on the grounds of family reunion. The second issue is whether the decision-maker owed a duty to the applicant to disclose credible, relevant and significant information that would assist in her application.

Constructive Failure to Exercise Jurisdiction

112 Mrs B and her children submit that the Tribunal "constructively failed to exercise the jurisdiction vested in it, and the duty placed upon it by s 414(1) of the Act, by failing to consider a material fact, namely that the [first] Prosecutor's spouse held a temporary protection visa and was an applicant for a permanent protection visa".

113 The jurisdiction that the Tribunal has failed to exercise is the statutory duty under s 414(1) of the Act to "review the decision" of the delegate. The Tribunal must review the whole decision, not just the basis for the application as set out in an applicant's oral or written application. A narrow interpretation of "the decision", as the decision to refuse the prosecutors' applications on the ground that they did not have a well-founded fear of persecution in Afghanistan, is more likely to result in a decision adverse to the prosecutors. A wider view of "the decision", as the decision to refuse to grant a visa, is more likely to allow the applicants to succeed. The Act does not have a discernible policy for or against granting visas. The Act simply states that in some situations, subject to satisfaction of stated criteria, visas are to be granted.

114 Since "the decision" is a phrase with ambiguous meaning, the object or purpose of the Act should be considered. Where the words of a statute are ambiguous, the Court is required, pursuant to s15AA of the *Acts Interpretation Act* 1901 (Cth), to interpret the Act in a way that will "best achieve the purpose or object of the Act (whether or not that purpose or object is expressly stated in the Act)".

115 The object or purpose of the Act is to grant visas to those entitled to them, and to refuse visas to those not so entitled. Entitlement under the relevant provisions of the Act reflects the priority given in international conventions to family unity and to family reunion (93), as set out in the majority judgment. It is a well recognised fact that in times of war and other dangerous situations it is more often the men who flee and the women and children who stay behind, or leave later. A policy of family reunion to some extent ameliorates the disparities of opportunity for escape afforded to men and women. In this context, "the decision" should be given a wide ambit. The Tribunal is to review the decision to refuse a visa. The Tribunal is required to determine whether a visa should be granted.

(93) Being, respectively, the Convention Relating to the Status of Refugees done at Geneva on 28 July 1951 and the Protocol Relating to the Status of Refugees done at New York on 31 January 1967.

116 Gaudron and Kirby JJ note that paragraph 785.211(b) of Schedule 2 to the *Migration Regulations* 1994 (Cth) (the Regulations) (the "family reunion" ground) is ambiguous on its face. I agree with them that it can and should be read to require only that an applicant for a protection visa should claim to be a member of the same family unit as a person who, in fact, has made specific claims under the Convention and has, in fact, applied for a protection visa. Since Mr B had made specific claims under the Convention and had applied for, and been granted, a protection visa, all that Mrs B and her children were required to do in order to enliven their application on the family reunion ground, was to state that they were members of Mr B's family.

117 I therefore find that the decision under review was the decision to refuse a visa application made under paragraph 36(2)(a) and paragraph 36(2)(b) of the Act. The decision under review was not confined to the "protection" grounds stated in the application (paragraph 36(2)(a)) but extended to include the family reunion grounds (paragraph 36(2)(b)).

118 As the Tribunal has misunderstood or misconstrued the relevant legislation, there has been a constructive failure to exercise jurisdiction that constitutes jurisdictional error.

Failure to Take Into Account a Relevant Consideration

119 The reasons set out above support another ground of jurisdictional error, namely the failure to take account of a relevant consideration. The Tribunal failed to consider whether the prosecutors' membership of a family satisfied the criteria in Schedule 2 to the Regulations. If those criteria, and the other relevant criteria set out in the Act and the Regulations, were not satisfied, the decision-maker was required by the Act to refuse the relevant visa. Conversely, if all the relevant criteria were satisfied, the decision-maker was required by the Act to grant the relevant visa. The criteria were mandatory, and disregard of them amounts to jurisdictional error. By failing to take into account a relevant consideration, the Tribunal has fallen into jurisdictional error.

Procedural Fairness – the Hearing Rule

120 The content of the rule of procedural fairness requiring a fair hearing varies according to the statutory, or other, context. The most significant variation is between the content of the rules of procedural fairness in a court, as opposed to a tribunal. Courts must determine controversies between adversarial parties. In order to fulfill the requirement of impartiality, courts do not assist the parties to formulate or develop the bases of their arguments. A fair hearing in a tribunal may differ from that in a court room. Most tribunals perform a very different function from courts. Tribunals are not adversarial. The tribunal member does not judge. This is the reason for rules directing that tribunals can determine their own procedures, are not bound by the strict rules of evidence, and can inform themselves in any

manner they see fit (94). The Tribunal is not bound to look only at evidence and arguments raised by the parties. Tribunal members have a duty to all parties to make a fair decision. The duty requires the Tribunal to elucidate and consider all the relevant evidence and arguments raised by the material before the Tribunal.

121 Parliament has directed that the Tribunal, in reviewing "the decision", is to exercise all the powers and discretions conferred by the Act on the delegate. The Tribunal is to be given assistance by the Secretary to the Minister's Department, in that the Secretary is to give the Tribunal "documents in the Secretary's possession or control and considered by the Secretary to be relevant to the review" (95). The Secretary provided the departmental file, including the two folios that revealed the immigration status and whereabouts of Mr B.

122 The Tribunal member is required to review a decision of the Executive in order to determine the "correct or preferable decision" (96). The "correct or preferable decision" in the case of a visa application can only be made on the basis of a review of all the available grounds for the granting of a visa. This includes the grounds that are available based on a perusal of the documents provided by the parties. In this case, Mrs B's visa application revealed the identity of, and relationship to, Mr B. The Department's documents revealed Mr B's immigration status and whereabouts. The combined information forms the basis for an application for a visa. To fail to include the family reunion ground set out in paragraph 36(2)(b) of the Act is to negate Parliament's intention in directing the Secretary to provide the Tribunal with relevant documents. There would be no point in directing the provision of documents if the Tribunal was not required to read and consider them. Reading and considering the entirety of the material provided by the Secretary is the minimum required by the duty to "review the decision".

123 As the Tribunal has failed to comply with its statutory duty to "review the decision", there has been a failure to exercise jurisdiction that amounts to jurisdictional error.

Procedural Fairness – Disclosure

124 Mrs B and her children submit that the Tribunal "breached its obligation of procedural fairness in failing to disclose to the Prosecutor[s] the information it had about [a] material fact", "namely that the [first] Prosecutor's spouse held a temporary protection visa and was an applicant for a permanent protection visa".

(94) Section 353 of the Act refers to the "Tribunal's way of operating:
(1) The Tribunal shall, in carrying out its functions under this Act, pursue the objective of providing a mechanism of review that is fair, just, economical, informal and quick.
(2) The Tribunal, in reviewing a decision:
(a) is not bound by technicalities, legal forms or rules of evidence; and
(b) shall act according to substantial justice and the merits of the case".

(95) Section 418(3) of the Act requires the Secretary of the Department to "give to the Registrar [of the Tribunal] each other document . . . that is in the Secretary's possession or control and is considered by the Secretary to be relevant to the review of [a] decision".

(96) *Drake v Minister for Immigration and Ethnic Affairs* (1979) 24 ALR 577.

125 The issue is whether the Tribunal is under a duty to the prosecutors to disclose information that is before the Tribunal, and of which the prosecutors were unaware. The construction of the Act favoured by Gaudron and Kirby JJ and myself makes consideration of this argument unnecessary. However, the majority judgment takes a narrow view of "the decision" under review, confining "the decision" to the application made by the prosecutors on the basis of fears for themselves. The alternative basis for the visa, the family reunion, could only be considered by the Tribunal, according to the majority view, if Mrs B included this ground in an application. Mrs B could not do so, because she was unaware of the immigration status and whereabouts of Mr B.

126 Mrs B and her children had, through no fault or intention on any of their parts, lost contact with Mr B as a result of his immigration to Australia. The Department discovered a potential match to a person fitting the description of Mr B. This information was recorded in two folios in the Department file provided to the Tribunal. The Department did not advise Mrs B of the information that might enable her to locate Mr B. On review, the Tribunal also did not advise Mrs B of this important information.

127 The law as to the disclosure of adverse information is clear. The test laid down by Brennan J in *Kioa v West* is that "an opportunity should be given to deal with adverse information that is credible, relevant and significant to the decision to be made" (97).

128 There is no dispute as to the credibility of the information. It was obtained by the Department from its own records. The key concepts are therefore "relevance" and "significance". Information that might enable this family to be reunited is obviously, as a matter of common sense, highly relevant and significant to the prosecutors and to their ability to apply for a visa to which they may be entitled.

129 The majority in this case have taken the narrowest possible view of legal "relevance". They state that the information must be relevant to the applications made by Mrs B and her children. Since they had lost all contact with Mr B, they applied for protection visas only on the basis of fears for themselves. The immigration status of Mr B is irrelevant to that claim. However, if Mrs B had known that Mr B already held an Australian protection visa, they could have applied under the other limb of the same section, as a member of his family unit. The decision-makers could have told Mrs B what was on the file, and given her an opportunity to amend the applications. This makes the information legally relevant.

130 The duty to disclose adverse information is well-understood. The duty to disclose favourable information has received less attention in the cases. The development of the jurisprudence in this area may be skewed by the fact that the cases that have come before the courts have concerned prejudicial, rather than favourable information. However, the duty to disclose need not be limited to the disclosure of adverse information. The duty to disclose credible, relevant and significant information is based on the requirement of a fair

(97) (1985) 159 CLR 550 at 629.

hearing. In *Kioa v West,* Brennan J, having stated that "an opportunity should be given to deal with adverse information that is credible, relevant and significant to the decision to be made", added the following comment:

> "It is not sufficient for the repository of the power to endeavour to shut information of that kind out of his [sic] mind and to reach a decision without reference to it. Information of that kind creates a real risk of prejudice, albeit subconscious, and it is unfair to deny a person whose interests are likely to be affected by the decision an opportunity to deal with the information."(98)

131 The obverse is also true. By failing to consider favourable information that is credible, relevant and significant, the decision-maker will effectively "shut information of that kind out of . . . mind" and "reach a decision without reference to it". This creates "a real risk of prejudice, albeit unconscious", and it is "unfair to deny a person whose interests are likely to be affected by the decision an opportunity to deal with the information."

132 As the Tribunal has failed to disclose favourable information that is credible, relevant and significant, resulting in "a real risk of prejudice" to "a person whose interests are likely to be affected", there has been a failure to comply with the requirements of procedural fairness that amounts to jurisdictional error.

Conclusions

133 The decision of the Tribunal should be set aside for jurisdictional error. There was a constructive failure to exercise jurisdiction, namely a failure to comply with the statutory duty of review. The Tribunal misunderstood or misconstrued the relevant legislation, failed to take into account a mandatory consideration, and breached the rules of procedural fairness by not reading and considering all of the material before it, and by not disclosing information that was "credible, relevant and significant".

134 Prohibition should issue to prevent the Minister acting on the Tribunal's decision. Certiorari should issue to quash that decision. Mandamus should issue to the Tribunal requiring it to determine the prosecutors' review application in accordance with law.

Orders

135 I agree with the orders proposed by Gaudron and Kirby JJ.

(98) Ibid.

8

Commentary on *Appellant S395/2002 v Minister for Immigration and Multicultural Affairs*

WAYNE MORGAN

Background

The issue of refugee status and sexuality has been controversial since at least the 1980s in developed refugee receiving states. At that time, claims to refugee status on the basis of persecution suffered because of sexuality began to be examined by immigration officials, refugee tribunals and courts, raising questions for decision-makers; first, whether persecution on the basis of sexuality could even *be* a ground for claiming refugee status. Thankfully, by the mid-1990s, this question seemed to have been resolved affirmatively in most developed refugee receiving states, including Australia.[1]

However, even though this question was resolved positively, many controversies remained concerning how decision-makers approached questions of sexuality in refugee claims. In Australia, for example, many claims were denied on the basis that the applicant did not come from a country where gay men and/or lesbians were persecuted.[2] Very dubious sources were often relied upon by decision-makers to establish that the country concerned did not persecute sexual outsiders. Sometimes, these sources were diplomatic. Sparse information from the Department of Foreign Affairs and Trade might be relied upon to establish how a country might treat gay men and lesbians within its population. Sometimes, the sources were not diplomatic at all. For example, commentators such as Dauvergne and Millbank criticised the reliance on gay male travel publications, like the *Spartacus Guide*, to establish relevant country information.[3] Although obviously never intended to be used for such a purpose, if the *Spartacus Guide* listed gay bars and clubs as existing in the country concerned, decision-makers would often therefore conclude that gay men and lesbians were not persecuted in that country, even if homosexuality remained criminalised. Even more inappropriately, the *Spartacus Guide* was also used in claims brought by lesbians, even though the publication was directed exclusively at gay men.

[1] *Canada (Attorney General) v Ward* [1993] 2 SCR 689; *Applicant A v Minister for Immigration and Ethnic Affairs* (1997) 190 CLR 225; *R v Immigration Appeal Tribunal; Ex parte Shah* [1999] 2 AC 629. See Jenni Millbank, 'Fear of Persecution or Just a Queer Feeling?' (1995) 20 *Alternative Law Journal* 261; Kristen Walker, 'Sexuality and Refugee Status in Australia' (2000) 12 *International Journal of Refugee Law* 175.

[2] For an analysis of some of these cases, see Catherine Dauvergne and Jenni Millbank, 'Burdened by Proof: How the Australian Refugee Review Tribunal has Failed Lesbian and Gay Asylum Seekers' (2003) 31 *Federal Law Review* 299.

[3] Ibid 317–20.

It seemed that many decision-makers (whether they were immigration officials, tribunal members or judges) did not understand, nor sympathise, with refugee claims on the basis of sexuality. This lack of understanding was further manifested when immigration officials, tribunals and judges began to draw distinctions between gay men and lesbians who were 'discreet' about their sexuality, and those who were not.[4] Decisions began to be made that, if the applicant concerned had been 'discreet' about their sexuality in the past, then they did not have a well-founded fear of persecution under the Refugee Convention[5] and could be returned to their home country. In other words, you could not be persecuted for being gay if no one back home knew you were gay. The closet, apparently, is a very safe place. Gay men and lesbians were outraged by such decisions that showed complete ignorance of the nature of gay and lesbian oppression.

Thus, in a series of cases brought before the Refugee Review Tribunal (the Tribunal) and the Federal Court of Australia (FCA), it was established that a gay man or lesbian could not claim refugee status if there was evidence that they had been 'discreet' in the past and could be so again.[6] Such 'discreet' homosexuals would not suffer persecution if they were returned to their home country. With such precedents established, it would be necessary to take the issue to the High Court in order to have them overturned. The stage was now set for *Appellant S395/2002 v Minister for Immigration and Multicultural Affairs*.[7]

The Case in the High Court

The two gay men who were the applicants in *S395* came from Bangladesh. They were a couple who had lived together for four years before fleeing Bangladesh. They claimed that they had been ostracised by their families and to have been sentenced to death by a religious council. They stated that they feared death or serious harm if they were returned to Bangladesh. The original decision-maker, the Tribunal and the FCA all held that the two men were not refugees and should be returned to Bangladesh.[8]

The High Court in deciding this case split 3:4. Gleeson CJ and Callinan and Heydon JJ thought that the appeal should be dismissed. Luckily, the majority comprising McHugh, Kirby, Gummow and Hayne JJ thought otherwise.

The Chief Justice, in an application of strict legalism that would have made the famous Dixon CJ proud, avoided ruling on the actual issue in the case by ruling instead that the matter was not properly before him. In Gleeson CJ's view, the applicants were now putting their claims on an entirely different basis to that relied upon before the Tribunal. Before the Tribunal, the applicants relied on persecution and violence which they argued they had personally experienced. Their case was rejected by the Tribunal because it did not believe their claims. In rejecting them, the Tribunal stated that the applicants had not experienced

[4] Catherine Dauvergne and Jenni Millbank, 'Before the High Court: Applicants S396/2002 and S395/2002, a Gay Refugee Couple from Bangladesh' (2003) 25 *Sydney Law Review* 97.

[5] *Convention Relating to the Status of Refugees*, opened for signature 28 July 1951, 189 UNTS 150 (entered into force 22 April 1954) as amended by the *Protocol Relating to the Status of Refugees*, opened for signature 31 January 1967, 606 UNTS 267 (entered into force 4 October 1967).

[6] For an analysis of this line of cases, see Dauvergne and Millbank, above n 4.

[7] (2003) 216 CLR 473 (*S395*).

[8] *RRT Reference N99/28381*; *RRT Reference N99/28382* [2001] FCA 968 (Lindgren J); [2002] FCA 129 (Full Court of the Federal Court).

serious harm and would not experience serious harm on their return to Bangladesh *if they were discreet*. In Gleeson CJ's view, the applicants' lawyers had picked up on those four words and entirely refashioned their case into one that had not been put before the Tribunal. No argument was put to the Tribunal that the applicants wanted to behave less discreetly about their sexual relationship and that their inability to do so involved persecution. Thus, in Gleeson CJ's view, the appeal should have been dismissed.

Callinan and Heydon JJ in their joint judgment made similar findings to Gleeson CJ. Moreover, their judgment contains statements about sexuality which demonstrate a conservative and ill-informed approach to the issue. For example, the judgment analogises laws criminalising homosexuality with laws criminalising bigamy. It notes that countries like Australia and Canada criminalise bigamy and asks the rhetorical question: '[d]oes that mean that would-be polygamists in Australia, Muslim or otherwise, might seek refuge in other countries which are subscribers to the Convention where polygamy is not necessarily criminal?'[9] This demeaning statement obviously belittles the substantial abuse still experienced by lesbians and gay men around the world. Further, the judgment characterises the issue of 'discretion' as one of 'free choice'. That is, people *choose* whether or not to be 'discreet' about their sexuality. 'More likely . . . the appellants here regarded their sexual preference and activities as personal and not public matters, and ones therefore that required no public or overt expression.'[10] To characterise gay and lesbian decisions on whether to be 'in' or 'out' as ones of free choice, profoundly misunderstands the politics of the closet.

The four majority judges gave two separate joint judgments. The first, by McHugh and Kirby JJ, disagreed with the minority's characterisation of the case and the duties of the Tribunal in deciding it. They agreed with the minority that the applicants had not made the arguments before the Tribunal that they were now making before the High Court, and agreed that the Tribunal had placed no *obligation* on the two applicants to be discreet. However, McHugh and Kirby JJ noted that proceedings before the Tribunal were inquisitorial in nature. The Tribunal was entitled to go beyond the original arguments made by the applicants and had a duty to investigate whether Bangladesh was safe for them. The Tribunal had failed in this duty. Although the applicants did not argue that their 'living discreetly' in the past was caused by fear of persecution, this was likely. McHugh and Kirby JJ then explicitly stated:

> If it is an error of law to reject a Convention claim because the applicant can avoid harm by acting discreetly, the Tribunal not only erred in law but has failed to consider the real question that it had to decide – whether the appellants had a well-founded fear of persecution.[11]

They went on to decide that it is indeed an error of law to reject a refugee claim on the basis that harm can be avoided by acting discreetly, stating: 'persecution does not cease to be persecution for the purpose of the Convention because those persecuted can eliminate the harm by taking avoiding action within the country of nationality.'[12] They further decided that it was an error under the Refugee Convention to divide gay men and lesbians into two different groups: the discreet and the non-discreet.

The judgment of McHugh and Kirby JJ, in its *outcome*, is to be applauded. But it is still a heavily legalistic judgment in which the applicants themselves, their experience and histories, seem erased.

[9] *S395* (2003) 216 CLR 473, 512–13.
[10] Ibid 511.
[11] Ibid 489.
[12] Ibid.

Gummow and Hayne JJ also gave a majority joint judgment. They characterised the error of the Tribunal slightly differently, holding that the Tribunal's statement about being discreet could be read either as a simple statement of fact or as an attempt to place an obligation on the applicants. The error made by the Tribunal was that it did not ask why the applicants would live discreetly and did not investigate whether they lived that way in the hope of avoiding persecution. The Tribunal's decision thus contained either an error of law or an incorrect application of the law to the facts, and should be overturned.

The judgment of Gummow and Hayne JJ is perhaps more interesting than the other majority judgment because of the way it speaks about sexual identity. They recognise that sexuality is about more than just sex. In commenting on the Tribunal's use of the concept of 'discretion', they state:

> [T]he use of such language will often reveal that consideration of the consequences of sexual identity has wrongly been confined to participation in sexual acts rather than that range of behaviour and activities of life which may be informed or affected by sexual identity.[13]

They also state: '[t]hat two individuals engage in sexual acts in private . . . may say nothing about how those individuals would choose to live other aspects of their lives that are related to, or informed by, their sexuality.'[14] These statements may be more useful in disrupting the 'discreet/non-discreet' distinction than anything said in the judgment of McHugh and Kirby JJ.

S395 was welcomed by gay men and lesbians because of its outcome, and because a majority of the High Court clearly stated that refugee claimants could not be sent back to their country of origin on the basis that they would suffer no persecution if they were discreet. Expert commentary on the judgment was similar. The outcome was welcomed with caution, while noting that refugee claims on the basis of sexual identity would continue to be problematic.[15]

The Feminist Judgment

The judgment of Seuffert J in this case, adopting a feminist methodology and approach, addresses questions of sexual identity and its relationship with refugee claims. While rigorously applying the law, Seuffert J offers context not only with respect to sexual identity generally, but also with respect to the individual lives and histories of the applicants. She of course focuses on the concept of 'discretion' and its relationship with the requirement that a refugee should have a 'well-founded fear of persecution'. The fact that the applicants could not live openly in their country of origin suggests that the men did have such a fear, but the Tribunal erred in failing to consider this question. Seuffert J also comments on issues of credibility and how these were handled by the Tribunal. These comments are extremely apposite, given the developments in subsequent refugee case law.[16]

[13] Ibid 501.

[14] Ibid.

[15] Christopher N Kendall, 'Lesbian and Gay Refugees in Australia: Now that "Acting Discreetly" is No Longer an Option, Will Equality be Forthcoming?" (2003) 15 *International Journal of Refugee Law* 715.

[16] Nan Seuffert would like to acknowledge that her judgment draws on feminist scholarly analysis produced subsequent to the date of decision in *S395* which she cannot therefore reference in her judgment. Specifically:

Unfortunately, *S395* did not herald the end of controversy surrounding refugee claims by sexual outsiders and the gender-diverse. Indeed, it seems that decision-makers, tribunals and courts still deny such claims more often than they are upheld. Commentators examining refugee claims in the last decade have illustrated how decision-makers continue to be influenced by stereotypes and assumptions about sexual identity.[17] Further, the credibility of such claimants is often attacked and their evidence found wanting.[18] A trend seems to have emerged in these cases whereby the very claim to be a sexual outsider – claiming a gay, lesbian, bisexual or gender-diverse identity – will be disbelieved.[19] This indicates a disturbing trend that judgments such as those of Seuffert J might help to reverse.

Kendall, ibid; Laurie Berg and Jenni Millbank, 'Constructing the Personal Narratives of Lesbian, Gay and Bisexual Asylum Claimants' (2009) 22 *Journal of Refugee Studies* 195; Jenni Millbank, 'The Ring of Truth: A Case Study of Credibility Assessment in Particular Social Group Refugee Determinations' (2009) 21 *International Journal of Refugee Law* 1; Jenni Millbank, 'From Discretion to Disbelief: Recent Trends in Refugee Determinations on the Basis of Sexual Orientation in Australia and the United Kingdom' (2009) 13 *International Journal of Human Rights 391.*

[17] Berg and Millbank, ibid.

[18] Millbank, 'The Ring of Truth', above n 16.

[19] Millbank, 'From Discretion to Disbelief', above n 16.

APPELLANT S395/2002 ....APPELLANT;
APPLICANT,

AND

MINISTER FOR IMMIGRATION AND
MULTICULTURAL AFFAIRS ....RESPONDENT.
RESPONDENT,

APPELLANT S396/2002 ....APPELLANT;
APPLICANT,

AND

MINISTER FOR IMMIGRATION AND
MULTICULTURAL AFFAIRS ....RESPONDENT.
RESPONDENT,

[2003] HCA 71

ON APPEAL FROM THE FEDERAL COURT OF AUSTRALIA

HC OF A
2003

April 8; Dec 9
2003

Seuffert J

115 SEUFFERT J. In February 1999, the appellants, Mr Kabir and Mr Rahman, arrived in Australia from Bangladesh; within two weeks they applied for protection visas on the basis that they were refugees who feared persecution in Bangladesh by reason of their homosexuality. A non-citizen qualifies for a protection visa under s 36(2) of the *Migration Act* 1958 (Cth) (*Migration Act*), if, relevantly, he or she is a person to whom obligations are owed under the 1951 Convention Relating to the Status of Refugees (95) (the Convention). Under the Convention, obligations are owed to "refugees" as defined in Art 1.

116 In April 1999, a delegate of the Minister for Immigration and Multicultural Affairs refused the appellants' applications. The appellants applied to the Refugee Review Tribunal (the Tribunal) for review of the delegate's decisions. The Tribunal found that homosexual men in Bangladesh constituted a "particular social group" for the purposes of the Convention. The Tribunal found that if the appellants returned to Bangladesh and conducted themselves discreetly they would not suffer serious harm by reason of their homosexuality in the future (96). The Tribunal also found that the appellants did not have a well-founded fear of persecution if they returned to Bangladesh, and therefore were not refugees under the Convention and were not entitled to a protection visa under the *Migration Act*.

(95) The Convention Relating to the Status of Refugees done at Geneva on 28 July 1951 as amended by the Protocol Relating to the Status of Refugees done at New York on 31 January 1967.

(96) RRT Reference N99/28381; RRT Reference N99/28382, 5 February 2001.

117 The appellants applied under s 476(1) of the *Migration Act* for a review of the decision of the Tribunal. The Federal Court (Lindgren J) dismissed the application for review, stating that the Tribunal concluded that the "applicants are able to return to Bangladesh and to resume living there in a homosexual relationship as they did previously without a well-founded fear of being persecuted for reason of their homosexuality" (97). The Court held that there was no unreasonableness, illogicality or inconsistency in the Tribunal's reasons for decision and that the Tribunal gave reasons for not accepting the applicants' allegations of specific instances of persecution (98). Mr Kabir and Mr Rahman appealed against the decision of Lindgren J and the Full Court of the Federal Court (Black CJ, Tamberlin and Allsop JJ) held that all but one of the questions raised by the appellants were not matters that could be subject to review under s 476(1) of the *Migration Act*. The Full Court characterised the central question on appeal as "whether the material which led the Tribunal to the conclusions it reached was of itself demonstrative of persecution in demanding discreet behaviour from homosexual people, that is behaviour not likely to confront society" (99). It stated that the "overwhelming difficulty with this assertion is that it did not found the claims of these appellants before the Tribunal" (100) and concluded that "it would be wrong to allow it to be raised now in an appeal from an application for judicial review" (101). This court granted special leave to appeal against the order of the Full Court.

The findings of the Tribunal

118 The Tribunal found that Mr Kabir and Mr Rahman were "homosexual" males who had lived together in various places in Bangladesh from 1994 until their departure from the country in early 1999. They travelled to Australia for several months in 1998, and returned in February 1999, applying for protection visas in March on the ground that they had a well-founded fear of persecution in Bangladesh by reason of their homosexuality. The Tribunal accepted that "homosexual men in Bangladesh constitute a particular social group under the Convention." It relied on advice from Mr Khan, the Executive Director of the Naz Foundation, an international HIV/AIDS and sexual health agency, which stated:

> "[T]he consequences of being identified as homosexual vary enormously, from acceptance and tolerance, to harassment, physical abuse or expulsion from the community. Most of the harassment of males who have sex with males takes the form of extortion by local police and hustlers who threaten to expose them to their families if they do not cooperate."

119 The Tribunal also considered "country information" from the Department of Foreign Affairs and Trade, as well as other publications about

(97) [2001] FCA 968 at [19].
(98) [2001] FCA 968 at [21]–[22].
(99) [2002] FCA 129 at [19].
(100) [2002] FCA 129 at [20].
(101) [2002] FCA 129 at [22].

homosexuality and persecution, and made inquiries of various people and organisations. It found that "it is not possible to live openly as a homosexual in Bangladesh" and that to attempt to do so would mean facing problems ranging from being "disowned by one's family and shunned by friends and neighbours to more serious forms of harm . . . [including] the possibility of being bashed by the police" (102). The Tribunal accepted that the appellants were shunned by their families because of their homosexuality and may have been the subject of gossip and taunts from neighbours who suspected they were homosexuals. However, the Tribunal found that the shunning and any gossip or taunts did not constitute "serious harm amounting to persecution." The Tribunal rejected a number of claims made by the appellants that they had suffered persecution and serious harm in Bangladesh as a result of their homosexuality, finding that significant portions of the evidence of the appellants were not credible (103), and stated: "I found much of the evidence given by both men regarding the problems which they faced during their time together to be lacking in credibility" (104).

120 The Tribunal concluded that the appellants:

> ". . . did not experience serious harm or discrimination prior to their departure from Bangladesh and I do not believe that there is a real chance that they will be persecuted because of their sexuality if they return . . . they clearly conducted themselves in a discreet manner and there is no reason to suppose that they would not continue to do so if they returned home now."

121 The Tribunal also concluded there was no "real chance that they [the appellants] will be persecuted because of their sexuality if they return" as long as they conduct themselves in a "discreet manner."

Grounds of appeal

122 The appellants' single ground of appeal to this court is that the Full Court of the Federal Court should have found under s 476(1)(e) of the *Migration Act* that the Tribunal's decision "involved an error of law, being an error involving an incorrect interpretation of the applicable law or an incorrect application of the law to the facts as found" by the Tribunal. The issues are whether the Tribunal erred in determining whether the appellants were refugees under the Convention:

- by failing to correctly consider whether the appellants had a well-founded fear of persecution; or
- by considering the appellants' previous discreet behaviour in Bangladesh as relevant to the determination of whether the appellants had a well-founded fear of persecution.

123 Much of the argument in this court focused on the Tribunal's statement in its reasons that the appellants "clearly conducted themselves in a discreet manner and there is no reason to suppose that they would not continue to do so if they returned home now." The appellants argued that this finding

(102) RRT Reference N99/28381; N99/28382, 5 Feb 2001 at 6.
(103) RRT Reference N99/28381; N99/28382, 5 Feb 2001 at 16.
(104) RRT Reference N99/28381; N99/28382, 5 Feb 2001 at 15.

was central to the Tribunal's conclusions and that it had thereby *required* them to act discreetly on their return to Bangladesh; the Minister contended that this statement amounted to a finding of what the appellants would do upon their return to Bangladesh, supporting the conclusion that there was no real chance that they would be persecuted. Either way, the Tribunal failed to consider the correct question under the Convention, which was whether the appellants had a well-founded fear of persecution on the basis of their membership in their particular social group if they returned to Bangladesh. I have had the advantage of reading the draft judgments of McHugh and Kirby JJ, and Gummow and Hayne JJ, and I agree that the Full Court of the Federal Court erred in rejecting the appellants' claim for judicial review and that the Tribunal decision should be set aside and the matter returned to the Tribunal for redetermination. I will now outline my reasons for judgment.

The Convention relating to the Status of Refugees

124 The Convention provides that a refugee is a person who (105):

> "owing to well-founded fear of being persecuted for reasons of race, religion, nationality, membership of a particular social group or political opinion, is outside the country of his nationality and is unable or, owing to such fear, is unwilling to avail himself of the protection of that country . . ."

125 This Court has set out the issues for consideration by the Tribunal in determining refugee status (106):

- whether the group or class to which the appellants belong constitutes a particular social group for purposes of the Convention;
- whether the applicant is a member of the class;
- whether the applicant fears persecution;
- whether the fear is well-founded; and
- whether the fear is causally connected to membership in the particular social group.

126 This Court has recognised that "homosexuals" may constitute a particular social group for the purposes of the Convention (107). In *A v Minister for Immigration and Ethnic Affairs* (108) this Court recognised the analysis of

(105) Art 1A(2).

(106) *Dranichnikov v Minister for Immigration and Multicultural Affairs* (2003) 197 ALR 389 at 394-395 (*Dranichnikov*).

(107) *Gui v Minister of Immigration and Multicultural Affairs* S219/1999 [2000] HCA Trans 280 (26 May 2000) at line 365, per McHugh J: "The Federal Court accepted, correctly in our view, that homosexuals, whether in China generally or in Shanghai, are a particular social group within the Convention definition of 'refugees' "; at line 133–134, per Kirby J: "I do not think anybody now disputes that homosexuals are members of a particular social group"; see *Applicant A v Minister for Immigration and Ethnic Affairs* (1997) 190 CLR 225 at 265, 293–294, 303–304; *MMM v Minister for Immigration and Multicultural Affairs* (1998) 90 FCR 324 at 330; *R v Immigration Appeal Tribunal; Ex parte Shah* [1999] 2 AC 629 at 652; *Canada (Attorney General) v Ward* [1993] 2 SCR 689 (*Ward*).

(108) (1996) 190 CLR 225 (*Applicant A*). See Halley, "Sexual Orientation and the Politics of Biology: A Critique of the Argument from Immutability", *Stanford Law Review*, vol 46 (1994) 503.

the Canadian court in *Canada (Attorney-General) v Ward* (109), identifying three sub-categories of "particular social group", and the finding that sexual orientation falls within the first category of "groups defined by an innate or unchangeable characteristic" (110). Brennan CJ stated in this Court that he saw "no ground for holding that a characteristic must be 'innate or unchangeable' before it can distinguish a social group" and Kirby J stated that "some of the groups to whom the definition applies . . . involve immutable characteristics; others do not" (111). Other courts and tribunals have found that fear of persecution on the basis of sexual orientation may provide the basis for categorisation in a "particular social group" whether it is an innate characteristic or one "so fundamental to identity that it ought not be required to be changed" (112). The Federal Court has held that a person may be a member of a particular social group if that person "belongs to or is identified with a recognisable or cognisable group within society that shares some experience in common" (113) and in reliance on this definition the Tribunal has found that "homosexuals" constitute a particular social group (114). Recognition of sexual orientation as the basis for "membership of a particular social group" for purposes of the Convention definition of "refugee" should not require that sexual orientation is an innate or unchangeable characteristic. What is important for the purposes of the determination of refugee status is not whether a person is "innately" or "unchangeably" attracted to members of the same sex, but whether the person has been persecuted on the basis of his or her same-sex intimate relationships, sexual behaviour, or other characteristics related to sexual orientation.

127 A note on terminology is apposite here. The case law and tribunal decisions on refugee status determined on the grounds of membership of a particular social group based on sexual orientation have often used the term "homosexual" to denote the social group. This term has a Euro-centric historical origin as a gendered term referring specifically to men, and one with connotations of pathology (115). It continues to have connotations that are culturally and historically specific, as well as gender specific. Its use to refer to women is therefore problematic (116). Its use to refer to men who have sex with men in Bangladesh, where the term and its specific history may never have existed, or may have existed as a product of colonisation, is also problematic (117). While "gay men and lesbian women" may seem

(109) [1993] 2 SCR 689.

(110) *Ward* [1993] 2 SCR 689 at 739.

(111) *Applicant A* (1996) 190 CLR 225 at 236, 307.

(112) *Re GJ* (Refugee Status Appeals Authority, Refugee Appeal No. 1312/93, Auckland, 30 Aug 1995) at 25.

(113) *Morato v Minister for Immigration, Local Government and Ethnic Affairs* (1992) 111 ALR 417 at 432.

(114) RRT Reference N93/00846, 8 March 1994; RRT Reference N93/02240, 21 Jan 1994.

(115) See Moran, *The Homosexual(ity) of Law* (1996), pp 197-200.

(116) See Millbank, "Imagining Otherness: Refugee Claims on the Basis of Sexuality in Canada and Australia", *Melbourne University Law Review*, vol 26 (2002) 144, 157.

(117) See National AIDS Committee Bangladesh and its Technical Committee, *National Policy on HIV/AIDS and STD Related Issues* (October 1995), p 55, noting that the term homosexual does not have a direct equivalent in the Bangla language; Human Rights Watch, *Ravaging the Vulnerable: Abuses Against Persons at High Risk of HIV Infection*

preferable in Australia, these terms also arise from particular historical, cultural and political trajectories that may be irrelevant in Bangladesh and other refugee claimant countries of origin (118). This may explain Mr Khan's use of the phrase "males who have sex with males" in the quote above. While this phrase may be cumbersome, it avoids some of the pitfalls of "homosexual" and will therefore be used interchangeably with "homosexual" here.

128 The Tribunal found that "homosexual" men in Bangladesh constituted a "particular social group." The Tribunal also found that the appellants were "homosexual" males who had lived together in various places in Bangladesh from 1994 to 1999. The first two parts of the test for refugee status are met.

Fear of persecution

129 The Convention requires that a refugee have a "well-founded fear of persecution", and that this fear be causally related to the particular social group (119). This language creates a two-pronged test: the first part of the test requires the establishment of a subjective fear of persecution; the second part of the test requires that the fear be objectively "well-founded". While this Court has not specifically defined persecution, it has indicated that a systematic course of conduct is not required for a finding of persecution (120), and that disregard of human dignity may, in appropriate cases, constitute persecution (121). This Court has also held that there must be a "real chance" of persecution in order for the Convention test to be met(122).

130 In their statements filed in support of their applications for protection visas each appellant stated:

> "We realised Bangladesh is not a safe place for us at all. Our ideology and perceptions were wrong in the eyes of the 99% people [sic] in Bangladesh. We were captives in our homeland. There are no rights for us in the state Constitution . . . . I have a real fear of persecution. If I return to Bangladesh I will be killed. My life is not safe. I will be killed not only by the fundamentalists but also by the general masses."

131 The fact of previous persecution may be relevant to both whether the person claiming refugee status is afraid, and to whether that fear is well-founded. However, previous persecution by the person claiming refugee status is not required by the test. A well-founded fear of persecution may

in Bangladesh (2003), p 38 states that the expression "men who have sex with men" encompasses a range of gender identities including *hijras*, who take on feminine behaviour and dress and may live in distinct communities, *kothis*, who take on feminine mannerisms but do not live in distinct communities, and *panthi*, men who take on a masculine demeanour. The report also details extensive abuse of men who have sex with men, including sexual violence, physical abuse, extortion, theft and arbitrary arrest.

(118) See Stychin, *Governing Sexuality: The Changing Politics of Citizenship and Law Reform* (2003).

(119) *Dranichnikov* (2003) 197 ALR 389 at 394–395 [26]–[27], 403–404 [69]–[72].

(120) *Minister for Immigration and Multicultural Affairs v Ibrahim* (2000) 204 CLR 1 at 4 [1], 7 [16], 20 [60], 30 [95], 44 [133], 67 [192], 72 [203], 79 [223] (*Ibrahim*).

(121) *Chan v Minister for Immigration and Ethnic Affairs* (1989) 169 CLR 379 at 430 (*Chan*).

(122) *Chan* (1989) 169 CLR 379 at 388, 389, 398, 407, 408, 429.

result from other information in the possession of the refugee, such as, in the case of those belonging to a particular social group, knowledge of persecution of other people in that social group. The finding of the Tribunal that the appellants "did not experience serious harm or discrimination prior to their departure from Bangladesh" is therefore not determinative of their case. The question is whether they had a well-founded fear of persecution upon their return.

132 With respect to this question of potential persecution on the return of the appellants to Bangladesh, as noted above, the Tribunal heard from Mr Khan, considered "country information" from the Department of Foreign Affairs and Trade, as well as other publications about homosexuality and persecution, and made inquiries of various people and organisations. Based on this information, the Tribunal concluded that "it is not possible to live openly as a homosexual in Bangladesh" and that to attempt to do so would mean facing problems ranging from being "disowned by one's family and shunned by friends and neighbours to more serious forms of harm, for example, the possibility of being bashed by the police"; the evidence also referred to the risk of violence, robbery and extortion by "hustlers".

133 The Tribunal's finding that it is not possible to live openly as a homosexual in Bangladesh means that the only option for Mr Kabir and Mr Rahman if they return to Bangladesh is to hide their relationship and their sexual orientation from public view. This is indicated by the Tribunal's conclusion that there was no "real chance that they will be persecuted because of their sexuality if they return" as long as they conducted themselves in a "discreet manner." Hiding, silencing, or erasing same-sex attraction and desire has a long and infamous history in western societies and in the common law, evidenced perhaps most famously in Lord Alfred Douglas' phrase referring to same-sex attraction as "the love that dare not speak its name" (123). Legal recognition and some degree of societal acceptance of same-sex sexual orientation has required political action against violence, discrimination and pejorative social and cultural connotations, a struggle that is ongoing in Australia today. For many, in many parts of the world, "living discreetly", or hiding same-sex sexual orientation, has been the only option. The appellants' statement that their "ideology and perceptions" were perceived as wrong by the overwhelming majority of people in Bangladesh suggests not only that they felt that they had to live discreetly to avoid harm, but also that their perception of their sexual orientation encompassed more than sexual acts, and may have included, more broadly, ideas about how they lived their lives. I agree with Gummow and Hayne JJ that [s]exual identity is not to be understood in this context as confined to engaging in particular sexual acts or, indeed, to any particular forms of physical conduct. Appearing in public celebrating important events, going out for meals, to films, bars or for other social events may not involve physical contact, but may involve identification as a couple. Even mundane activities such as shopping for food or clothes, taking a car for servicing, or

(123) See Moran, *The Homosexual(ity) of Law* (1996), p 46.

engaging with tradespeople, can reveal a couple's status. When seen in this light, "discretion", if it means keeping one's intimate and domestic partner a secret, may require constant vigilance, and everyday self-monitoring (124). The Tribunal stated that "[m]en who conform outwardly to social norms, most importantly by marrying and having children, can get away with male to male sex provided it is kept secret," and the country evidence also suggested that living with someone of the same sex for a relatively long period may result in labelling as "homosexual" (125). In this context living "discreetly" in order to avoid persecution seems likely to preclude the possibility of living as a couple openly in a same-sex relationship.

134 The Tribunal failed to consider whether, if the appellants lived openly as a couple, or did not take steps to hide their sexual orientation and relationship, their fear of persecution would be well-founded, and whether they lived discreetly in the past due to the threat of persecution. The Tribunal's statement that it is not possible to live openly as a homosexual suggests that their fear may have been well-founded, but the Tribunal erred in law by failing to consider these questions.

135 The Tribunal found "much of the evidence given by both men regarding the problems which they faced during their time together to be lacking in credibility," rejecting a number of claims, which are detailed in the judgment of McHugh and Kirby JJ. Credibility in refugee claims generally is a crucial issue, and plays a central role in refugee determinations (126). Credibility assessments of applicants for refugee status may be difficult, with issues of cross-cultural communication and dangers in assessing truthfulness based on body language, particularly where applicants may have been abused or tortured by those in positions of authority, and there exists the perception that the Tribunal occupies a similar position of authority relative to the applicant (127). The United Nations High Commissioner for Refugees (UNHCR) Handbook notes that (128):

> "while the burden of proof in principle rests on the applicant, the duty to ascertain and evaluate all the relevant facts is shared between the applicant and the examiner. . . there may also be statements that are not susceptible of proof . . . [and] if the applicant's account appears credible, he should, unless there are good reasons to the contrary, be given the benefit of the doubt."

136 The UNHCR Handbook also states that "it is hardly possible for a refugee to 'prove' every part of his [sic] case and, indeed, if this were a

(124) A helpful analysis of the "discretion principle" in the Tribunal was provided in the Submissions of Amnesty International in Support of Application for Leave to be Heard as Amicus Curiae and Submissions on the Appeal provided to the Court in this case.

(125) RRT Reference N99/28381; RRT Reference N99/28382, 5 February 2001.

(126) Senate and Constitutional References Committee, Parliament of Australia, *A Sanctuary Under Review: An Examination of Australia's Refugee and Humanitarian Determination Processes* (2000), p 158.

(127) *Kathiresan v Minister for Immigration and Multicultural Affairs* (unreported; Federal Court of Australia; 4 March 1998) at 5–6.

(128) Handbook on Procedures and Criteria for Determining Refugee Status issued by the Office of the United Nations High Commissioner for Refugees, par [196] (UNHCR Handbook).

requirement the majority of refugees would not be recognised. It is therefore frequently necessary to give the applicant the benefit of the doubt" (129).

137 Establishing credibility in claims of membership of a particular social group based on sexual orientation may be particularly difficult. Speaking about one's sexuality to a stranger may, for anyone, in any culture, be uncomfortable. Persecution of refugees on the basis of their sexual orientation may include the persistent manifestation of homophobia, harassment, violent attacks and worse (130). Speaking about same-sex sexual attraction may therefore involve a host of powerful emotions including shame, confusion, self-hatred, anger at the responses of others, and feelings of affirmation in asserting a claim. Claimants may still be coming to terms with their sexuality, and attempting to repair their self-esteem; or they may be mired in self-loathing. As a result, claimants may be reluctant to speak about sexual acts. They may also be articulating this behaviour for the first time, which, combined with a lack of language to describe "the love that dare not speak its name" may result in halting, or apparently confused responses, in long pauses or a reluctance to speak at all. In this context it is particularly important for the Tribunal to consider the UNHCR Handbook guidance, where appropriate, about providing the claimant with the benefit of the doubt.

138 The Tribunal's finding that "while homosexuality is not acceptable in Bangladesh, Bangladeshis generally prefer to ignore the issue rather than confront it" (131) was, as Gummow and Hayne JJ state, one of three propositions underpinning the Tribunal's rejection of the appellants' claims. The conclusion that Bangladeshis prefer to ignore "homosexuality" was based in part on the Tribunal's interpretation of the circumstances of Mr Rahman's dismissal from his job:

> "When his [1980 or] 1981 dismissal was discussed, [he] said that he had lost his job because he had raped young men from the office who came to visit him in his room. These people had complained and he lost his job. I asked him to clarify that he had forced these men to have sex with him when they did not want to. He said that this was correct and confirmed that this was the reason that he had lost his job. He said that no other action had been taken against him."

139 The Tribunal concluded with respect to this issue:

> "I am extremely sceptical of the claim that [one of the appellants] was dismissed from his job in 1980 [or 1981] because he had raped a number of young men in his office. It seems most unlikely that someone who had raped a number of

(129) UNHCR Handbook, par [203]. A recent study of Tribunal decisions suggests that in some types of cases, the Tribunal "tends to focus upon credibility issues to discredit the applicant's whole version of events." Kneebone, "The Refugee Review Tribunal and the Assessment of Credibility: An Inquisitorial Role?" *Australian Journal of Administrative Law*, vol 5 (1998) 78 at 90.

(130) See Coffey, "The Credibility of Credibility Evidence at the Refugee Review Tribunal" *International Journal of Refugee Law*, vol 15 (2003) 377 at 386–389 noting at 389 that "a reluctance of trauma survivors to disclose trauma, especially in unfamiliar settings, and disturbance in memory that can affect such people to varying degrees, is well documented."

(131) RRT Reference N99/28381; N99/28382, 5 February 2001 at 19–20.

> young men would merely have been dismissed from his job and suffered no further consequences. On the other hand, if it is true, then his dismissal was for rape, and not because he is a homosexual, and the lack of more serious consequences suggests that Bangladeshis prefer to ignore the issue of homosexuality, even if it involves rape, rather than confront it."

140 In the paragraphs following this analysis, which are set out in the judgment of Callinan and Heydon JJ at paragraph 94, it appears that the Tribunal's rejection of the appellant's claims with respect to this incident are important in supporting the conclusion that Bangladeshis prefer to ignore rather than confront the issue of men who have sex with men; this rejection is then used to support rejection of other claims, and the conclusion that the appellant has a "tendency to exaggerate or concoct claims."

141 The Penal Code of Bangladesh, s 377 provides:

> "Whoever voluntarily has carnal intercourse against the order of nature with any man, woman or animal, shall be punished with imprisonment for life, or with imprisonment of either description for a term which may extend to ten years, and shall also be liable to fine."

142 The word "voluntarily" may provide the basis for another interpretation of this series of events. Is it possible that the appellant had sex with young men in his office, and both he and the young men were noticed and threatened with blackmail? Might the appellant have asserted or agreed that he raped the young men to spare them from blackmail and the stigma of labelling? Could this make sense of the fact that he was not prosecuted for rape? Might his dismissal from his job then appear as consistent with the lack of enforcement of s 377, but with societal and employment reprisal nevertheless?

143 It is not open to this Court to replace the findings of fact of the Tribunal with alternative findings. But it is part of the Court's role to provide the Tribunal with guidance in the performance of its inquisitorial task, which requires particular care and skill when dealing with claims of persecution on the basis of sexual orientation. The UNHCR Handbook states that "the duty to ascertain and evaluate all the relevant facts is shared between the applicant and the examiner." The UNHCR Handbook also states that untrue statements alone do not provide a justification for refusal of refugee status. It appropriately provides that the examiner, in this situation the Tribunal, has a "responsibility to evaluate such statements in the light of all the circumstances of the case" (132). In this matter a series of appropriate questions may have elicited an explanation for the seeming inconsistencies in the appellant's statements. Further, the Tribunal should hesitate to discredit an applicant's whole version of facts based on credibility assessments, or on one inconsistency, without attempting to find an explanation (133).

(132) Handbook on Procedures and Criteria for Determining Refugee Status issued by the Office of the United Nations High Commissioner for Refugees, par [196]. This Court has frequently referred to the UNHCR Guidelines and the Handbook in construing and applying the Convention. See, eg, *Ibrahim* (2000) 204 CLR 1 at 20 [61].

(133) See Handbook on Procedures and Criteria for Determining Refugee Status issued by the Office of the United Nations High Commissioner for Refugees, par [199].

Order

144 The appeal should be allowed with costs. The orders of the Full Court of the Federal Court in each case and of Lindgren J in the Federal Court should be set aside. The decisions of the Tribunal should be set aside and the matters remitted to the Tribunal for redetermination.

Environmental Law

9

Addressing Climate Change Inequities: The Contribution of a Feminist Judgment

JACQUELINE PEEL*

Introduction

Climate change is commonly thought of as a 'global problem': one to which every nation, community and household contributes through the release of greenhouse gases (GHG) into the atmosphere. For this reason, international law has sought a cooperative solution to the problem, based on the common responsibility of states for the causes and expected harms of climate change.[1] Yet climate change is also a problem characterised by deep inequities. The top 10 emitting countries account for nearly two-thirds of the world's emissions of carbon dioxide, the principal GHG.[2] Rich developed countries, including Australia, have built their industrial development and high standards of living upon a platform of GHG-intensive fuel sources but have been slow to curb emissions, arguing that a concerted global effort by all countries is required. Climate change impacts will hit hardest in some of the regions of the world that are already among the most vulnerable to poverty, famine, environmental degradation and social strife.[3] Within countries, climate change is also expected to have disparate impacts, disproportionately affecting the most vulnerable in the community, including women and children.[4] And emission levels now will leave a burden for future generations with the loss of iconic ecosystems like the Great Barrier Reef and the struggle to adapt to climatic changes that are already locked in by past levels of emissions.[5]

The tension between ideas of global, shared responsibility for climate change versus localised inequalities in the patterns of impacts suffered is one that reverberates through the

* I acknowledge funding support provided by ARC Discovery Project DP130100500, 'Transition to a Clean Energy Future: The Role of Climate Change Litigation in Shaping our Regulatory Path'.

1 *United Nations Framework Convention on Climate Change*, opened for signature 9 May 1992, 1771 UNTS 107 (entered into force 21 March 1994) preamble, arts 3(1) and 4(1) (UNFCCC). See also Kyoto Protocol, opened for signature 16 March 1998, 37 ILM 22 (entered into force 16 February 2005). Australia became a party to the Kyoto Protocol in December 2007, subsequent to the decision in the *Wildlife Whitsunday* case.

2 International Energy Agency (IEA), *CO2 Emissions from Fuel Combustion – Highlights* (IEA Statistics, 2012) 9.

3 Intergovernmental Panel on Climate Change (IPCC), *Climate Change 2007: Impacts, Adaptation and Vulnerability – Contribution of Working Group II to the Fourth Assessment Report of the Intergovernmental Panel on Climate Change* (Cambridge University Press, 2007). See also Michael B Gerrard and Gregory E Wannier (eds), *Threatened Island Nations: Legal Implications of Rising Seas and a Changing Climate* (Cambridge University Press, 2013).

4 See, eg, Fatma Denton, 'Climate Change Vulnerability, Impacts, and Adaptation: Why does Gender Matter?' (2002) 10 *Gender and Development* 10; United Nations Human Rights Council, *Report of the Office of the United Nations High Commissioner for Human Rights on the Relationship Between Human Rights and Climate Change*, 10th sess, Agenda Item 2, UN Doc A/HRC/10/61 (15 January 2009) 15–17.

5 IPCC, *Climate Change 2013: The Physical Science Basis – Summary for Policy-makers* (IPCC, 2013).

protracted international negotiations over climate change, as well as domestic debates over national climate change policy. Courts have not escaped this dilemma. Indeed, courts have become a focus for 'climate fights', as frustration with the slow progress and timid action taken by governments grows.[6] In Australia, litigation raising climate change concerns has often focused on the inequity created by domestic laws and policies that account only for GHG emissions occurring within Australia,[7] but which fail to take account of the nation's broader carbon footprint due to our significant exports of coal and other fossil fuels.[8] The case of *Wildlife Preservation Society of Queensland Proserpine/Whitsunday Branch Inc v Minister for the Environment and Heritage & Ors* ('*Wildlife Whitsunday*')[9] was one of the first Australian cases to bring this issue before a court, arguing that environmental approval processes for new large coal mines should take account of their 'indirect' climate change effects stemming from burning of the harvested coal.

Legal Context

The *Wildlife Whitsunday* case was a judicial review action brought in the Federal Court by activists of a North Queensland conservation group under the *Environment Protection and Biodiversity Conservation Act 1999* (Cth) (*EPBC Act*). At the heart of the *EPBC Act* lie its requirements for the assessment and approval of development projects that have, will have or are likely to have, a significant impact on matters designated by the *EPBC Act* to be 'matters of national environmental significance' – so-called 'controlled actions'.[10] The matters designated as being of national environmental significance in the *EPBC Act* do not include climate change or GHG emissions, despite the significant national-level environmental, social and economic implications of climate change for Australia.[11] Instead, the Act focuses on more discrete impacts such as the effects of actions on threatened species or particular protected areas such as world heritage properties.[12] Even so, many *EPBC Act* 'protected matters' will suffer 'indirect' adverse effects as a result of climate change. In the case of the Great Barrier Reef World Heritage Area, for example, climate change poses significant conservation challenges, including problems of coral bleaching, ocean acidification and biodiversity loss.[13]

[6] John Schwartz, 'Courts as Battlefields in Climate Fights', *New York Times* (online) 26 January 2010 <http://www.nytimes.com/2010/01/27/business/energy-environment/27lawsuits.html>.

[7] For example, the *National Greenhouse and Energy Reporting Act 2007* (Cth) requires reporting by certain corporations of their 'scope 1' (direct, onsite) emissions and 'scope 2' emissions (resulting from electricity consumption). The Clean Energy Act 2011 (Cth), which established Australia's carbon pricing mechanism, only required liable entities to acquire permits to cover scope 1 emissions. The Act has now been repealed.

[8] Climate Institute, *Unburnable Carbon: Australia's Carbon Bubble* (Carbon Tracker Initiative and Climate Institute, 2013) 12; Climate Commission, Commonwealth of Australia, *The Critical Decade 2013: Climate Change Science, Risks and Response* (2013).

[9] (2006) 232 ALR 510.

[10] *EPBC Act* s 67.

[11] Lisa Ogle, 'The Environment Protection and Biodiversity Conservation Act 1999 (Cth): How Workable Is It?' (2000) 17 *Environmental & Planning Law Journal* 468.

[12] *EPBC Act* ss 12 and 18.

[13] Chris McGrath, 'Regulating Greenhouse Gas Emissions from Australian Coal Mines' in Wayne Gumley and Trevor Daya-Winterbottom (eds), *Climate Change Law: Comparative, Contractual and Regulatory Considerations* (Thomson Reuters 2009) 217; Chris McGrath, 'Setting Climate Change Targets to Protect the Great Barrier Reef' (2007) 24 *Environmental & Planning Law Journal* 182.

Under the *EPBC Act*, decisions of the federal Environment Minister as to whether a project is a controlled action are governed by s 75, which requires consideration of 'all adverse impacts' the action has, will have or is likely to have, on matters of national environmental significance. In making this decision, the Minister is also required to take account of the precautionary principle – that 'lack of full scientific certainty should not be used as a reason for postponing a measure to prevent degradation of the environment where there are threats of serious or irreversible environmental damage'.[14] At the time of the *Wildlife Whitsunday* decision, the term 'impact' was not defined in the Act.[15] However, previous case law, including the Full Federal Court's decision in *Minister for Environment & Heritage v Queensland Conservation Council*, had interpreted the term broadly as encompassing 'the "indirect" consequences of an action'.[16] The applicants in *Wildlife Whitsunday* sought to extend this analysis. They argued that predicted climate change harm to the Reef was an indirect impact of the coal mines, which were expected to produce 18 million tonnes of coal for export over nine years.

Decisions by the Environment Minister under s 75 of the *EPBC Act* are judicially reviewable,[17] with applicants limited to procedural grounds relating to the conduct of the decision-making process. The applicant's case focused on the failure of the Minister to take account of a relevant consideration, namely the likely indirect adverse impacts on the Reef due to the mining, transport and use of the coal from the mines emitting a large amount of GHG contributing to global warming. The statement of reasons issued by the Minister's delegate in respect of his controlled action decision disclosed no information indicating consideration of these impacts. However, two weeks prior to the trial an affidavit was filed in which it was claimed that detailed consideration had in fact been given to GHG emissions from the mine but that the delegate had reached the conclusion that any impact on protected matters would be very small, speculative and therefore not significant.[18] Dowsett J did not seek to probe this evidence and stated that he 'derived little assistance from the cross-examination of Mr Flanigan' (the Minister's delegate) that sought to elucidate information as to the delegate's understanding of his assessment obligations under s 75.[19] In his Honour's view, Mr Flanigan's training and experience, and 'general views' on greenhouse gases and climate change impacts were sufficient to discharge the obligation of consideration, resulting in the dismissal of the applicant's main grounds of review.[20]

The judge also dealt rather summarily with other grounds of review. Dowsett J questioned the applicability of the precautionary principle[21] and the utility of interpreting s 75 in light of Australia's international obligations,[22] and rejected the relevance of assessing the cumulative impacts of the mines (ie how GHG emissions from the harvested coal

[14] *EPBC Act* s 391.

[15] Now see *EPBC Act* s 527E.

[16] (2004) 139 FCR 24, 38. See also *Booth v Bosworth* (2001) 114 FCR 39.

[17] *EPBC Act* s 487.

[18] Chris McGrath, 'Federal Court Case Challenges Greenhouse Gas Emissions from Coal Mines', *Environmental Law Publishing* (online) (2006) <http://www.envlaw.com.au/whitsunday19.pdf>.

[19] *Wildlife Whitsunday* (2006) 232 ALR 510 at 518.

[20] Ibid.

[21] Ibid 521.

[22] For instance, protective obligations arise under the *World Heritage Convention*, the *Biodiversity Convention* and the *UNFCCC*. Referring to art 3 of the *UNFCCC*, which requires Convention parties to take 'precautionary measures' in response to climate change, Dowsett J concluded that 'that provision, and the Convention generally, offer little assistance in the task of construing the EPBC Act'.

contribute to and exacerbate existing environmental threats).[23] While accepting the paucity of detail concerning greenhouse/climate change issues in the delegate's reasons, Dowsett J seemed to criticise the generality of the concerns raised by the applicant, pointing out: '[t] here was no suggestion that the mining of coal pursuant to these proposals would increase the amount of coal burnt in any particular year, or cumulatively'.[24] Then in a final obiter paragraph of the judgment, his Honour stated that he was 'far from satisfied that the burning of coal at some unidentified place in the world, the production of greenhouse gases from such combustion, its contribution towards global warming and the impact of global warming upon a protected matter' could be described as an 'impact' of the proposed coal mines.[25]

Contribution of a Feminist Perspective

Reflecting on the inequities created by climate change, a feminist rewriting of the *Wildlife Whitsunday* judgment offers scope for redressing at least some aspects of these and introducing a fairer decision-making process. A feminist perspective makes several distinct contributions.

First, it allows for the adoption of more holistic conceptions of the environment that emphasise the interconnectedness of all life forms and the need for a nurturing approach that creates a bond between people and nature.[26] In the feminist judgment, the underlying principles of environmental protection and sustainability that inform interpretation of the *EPBC Act*[27] are taken as the basis of a 'duty of care' for creatures (human and non-human) that are most vulnerable and closely dependent on a healthy environment. This would extend to women in developing countries who are heavily involved in tasks such as agriculture and water-carrying, which will become more difficult in changing climatic conditions.[28] The duty of care also extends to future generations, creating an inter-generational trust.[29] Applying this approach, the impacts of a project requiring environmental assessment are not to be evaluated in isolation, but should consider how impacts may accumulate and interact to cause harm, over space and time. Artificial boundaries between domestic and 'offshore' GHG emissions are de-emphasised in favour of looking at the overall impacts of such emissions on the local environment, communities and on biological diversity. This has parallels with the approach taken by Pain J of the New South Wales Land and Environment Court in the subsequent case of *Gray v Minister for Planning*. Pain J tied the need for a full assessment of the GHG emissions (both direct and indirect) associated with a coal mine proposal to the principles of precaution and inter-generational equity.[30]

[23] *Wildlife Whitsunday* (2006) 232 ALR 510, 522.
[24] Ibid 520.
[25] Ibid 524.
[26] Lee Godden and Jacqueline Peel, *Environmental Law: Scientific, Policy and Regulatory Dimensions* (Oxford University Press, 2010) 22.
[27] *EPBC Act* s 3A.
[28] Denton, above n 4.
[29] In environmental law, this is known as the principle of inter-generational equity: see Dinah Shelton, 'Equity' in Daniel Bodansky, Jutta Brunnée and Ellen Hey (eds), *The Oxford Handbook of International Environmental Law* (Oxford University Press, 2008) 639.
[30] *Gray v Minister for Planning & Ors* (2006) 152 LGERA 258, 293–7.

The feminist judgment gives meaning to these key environmental principles of sustainability by using them as part of an interpretative approach that focuses on the protective purpose of the *EPBC Act*[31] and the international obligations that it seeks to implement.[32] In contrast to Dowsett J's judgment, particular emphasis is given to the precautionary principle, and associated international obligations such as art 3 of the *Framework Convention on Climate Change*,[33] as requiring a fuller, more systemic investigation of potential harms, notwithstanding a lack of scientific precision on cause-and-effect relationships. This approach to interpretation of the precautionary principle can be read as a call for equitable risk-sharing that does not unduly burden the most vulnerable ecosystems and community members through exposure to threats of serious or irreversible harm.

Finally, a feminist rewriting of the *Wildlife Whitsunday* case gives a fair hearing to the serious environmental concerns raised by the applicant in the public interest. An important aspect of this is a careful evaluation of the available material regarding impacts, taking account of areas of uncertainty, and recognising the need for a wider evidential basis for assessment.[34] A feminist understanding of the precautionary principle acknowledges the role of values and alternative voices (rather than simply that of the dominant objective and rationalist scientific tradition) as a means for supplementing decision-making where environmental harms are potentially serious but available knowledge is uncertain. Giving a more prominent role to other voices and values, such as those of future generations and the carers for this generation, transforms questions regarding the implications of new coal mining development for climate change and its impacts from 'speculative' to substantive and meaningful considerations for the decision-making process under s 75 of the *EPBC Act*.

[31] See *EPBC Act* s 3.

[32] See *The Australian Environment Act – Report of the Independent Review of the Environment Protection and Biodiversity Conservation Act 1999*, Final Report (Commonwealth of Australia, 2009) 13-14.

[33] See above n 22.

[34] Jacqueline Peel, *The Precautionary Principle in Practice: Environmental Decision-making and Scientific Uncertainty* (Federation Press, 2005).

WILDLIFE PRESERVATION SOCIETY OF QUEENSLAND PROSERPINE/WHITSUNDAY BRANCH INC v MINISTER FOR THE ENVIRONMENT AND HERITAGE and Others

FEDERAL COURT OF AUSTRALIA

GODDEN J

28 October 2005, 15 June 2006 – Brisbane

[2006] FCA 736

Godden J.

Statutory Background

[1] The *Environment Protection and Biodiversity Conservation Act* 1999 (Cth) (the EPBC Act) was enacted to give effect to wide-ranging obligations under international law to protect the environment; to identify and protect Australian heritage (including indigenous cultural heritage); and to implement measures to protect matters of national environmental significance as agreed under the *Inter-Governmental Agreement on the Environment* (1992). The principal relevant provisions are to be found in Part 3, Division 1, EPBC Act.

[2] International treaties and conventions[1] articulate responsibilities for the Commonwealth Government to institute measures for a sustainable environment. As a national government entrusted with such responsibilities, the Commonwealth has a duty of protection, bearing in mind the holistic and interconnected nature of the environment. Obligations of this character have been conceptualised as a duty of care for future generations, or adopting the language of equity, as an intra-generational and inter-generational trust.[2] The necessity of protecting the environment as a fundamental basis for human life is important for communities who most closely depend on a healthy environment.

[3] Section 3A of the EPBC Act sets guiding principles. These objectives build upon the concept of sustainable development at international law.[3] Within Australia, the term adopted has been "ecologically sustainable development" to signify the priority to be accorded to ecological integrity and holistic environmental outcomes. These frameworks apply when assessing impacts upon Matters of National Environmental Significance ("MNES") listed in Part 3, EPBC Act.

---

[1] For example, *Convention on Biological Diversity*, opened for signature 5 June 1992, 31 ILM822 (entered into force 29 December 1993).

[2] Edith Weiss Brown, "The Planetary Trust: Conservation and Intergenerational Equity" (1984) 11 *Ecology Law Quarterly*, 495.

[3] See, eg, World Commission on Environment and Development, *Our Common Future* (1987).

[4] The primary mechanism is the prohibition of taking actions, without approval, "that have or are likely to have a significant impact" on identified MNES.[4] Section 12 prohibits actions which have, will have, or are likely to have a significant impact on the World Heritage values of a declared World Heritage property. Other sections in this Part contain similar provisions in respect of wetland sites of international importance, threatened species and communities, listed migratory species, National Heritage places (including indigenous heritage) and selected other MNES. MNES represent matters of national public interest and international significance, containing some of the most highly valued areas and places within Australia and the world. The loss of such values is not easily compensated, as they touch upon the sense of an enduring connection between humanity and the life-world. Other MNES comprise some of the creatures most at risk of extinction. Extinction represents an irretrievable loss and ruptures our duty of care for those creatures most vulnerable and dependent.[5] The special places and features of the environment hold strong cultural and spiritual values for many in our community; not least, Australia's Indigenous Peoples. Those values are expressed in international forums through constructs such as common heritage.

[5] The concept of an action is broadly defined.[6] Its use in defining development proposals is notable, as action is highly valued in our society. Action, as opposed to inaction, is associated with progress and success. Other views suggest that adoption of the terminology of development and action can be aligned to ideas of domination over nature.[7] In this context, the definition of action in the EPBC Act acknowledges that human activities are major factors in environmental degradation. Tensions between action and protection find expression in long-standing attempts to balance environment and development.

[6] Section 68 of the EPBC Act requires referral of any action that a proponent believes may be a controlled action. The Minister may require a referral. For any referred action, the relevant protected matters are to be identified and the Minister (or delegate) determines whether there is a controlled action. The identified MNES (controlling provisions) determine the intersection between the areas, creatures and values to be protected, and potential adverse impacts.[8] The controlled action decision under s 75 is an important one. It determines whether an action will require Commonwealth Government environmental assessment and approval.[9] Upon referral, the Minister must give notice to various persons and

---

[4] See EPBC Act ss 12–24.

[5] International Union for Conservation of Nature, United Nations Environment Program, World Wildlife Fund, *Caring for the Earth* (1991).

[6] The EPBC Act s 523 defines an action as – "(a) a project; and (b) a development; and (c) an undertaking; and (d) an activity or series of activities", and an alteration of any of the things mentioned above.

[7] Val Plumwood, *Feminism and the Mastery of Nature,* (Routledge, London, 1993).

[8] The EPBC Act s 75 relevantly provides: "Does the proposed action need approval? Is the action a controlled action?" (1)The Minister must decide: (a) whether the action that is the subject of a proposal referred to the Minister is a controlled action; and (b) which provisions of Part 3 (if any) are controlling provisions for the action.

[9] EPBC Act ss 136–140. Note the Commonwealth can accredit State government assessment and approval processes through bilateral agreements (ss 40-65).

invite public comment.[10] Where the Minister later gives approval, the prohibition against taking the action does not apply.[11]

[7] The EPBC Act is resonant with the language of control, suggesting a powerful agency, but the EPBC Act is not a robust command and control regime. The extent of Commonwealth protection for environmental matters is relatively limited. First it is constrained by the narrow range of MNES that carve out a small, albeit vitally important, subset of the environment. Secondly, any protection is heavily dependent upon the integrity of the Commonwealth decision-making process. That highlights the significance of the matter before the Court, being an application for judicial review of controlled action decisions for two proposed actions relating to coal mining projects. The Act, interpreted in light of its objectives of ecologically sustainable development, invokes the public interest through the Minister's regard to all adverse impacts when making the controlled action decision.

[8] Section 75 sets out the criteria against which the Minister must make the decision. Relevantly:

> Considerations and decision
>
> (2) If, when the Minister makes a decision under subsection (1), it is relevant for the Minister to consider the impacts of an action:
> (a) the Minister must consider all adverse impacts (if any) the action:
> (i) has or will have; or
> (ii) is likely to have;
> on the matter protected by each provision of Part 3; and
> (b) must not consider any beneficial impact the action:
> (i) has or will have; or
> (ii) is likely to have;
> on the matter protected by each provision of Part 3.

[9] Due to the pivotal role played by the controlled action decision, the Minister is directed to have regard to "all adverse impacts" and pursuant to s 75(2)(b) must not consider benefits from a proposal such as economic gains for example, in the construction industry. The Minister must have regard to the precautionary principle in construing "all adverse impacts" of the proposed action.[12] Having made a determination, the Minister is required to give notice, and to provide reasons.[13] In this instance, the Minister's delegate made controlled action decisions following referral of two proposed actions: Bowen Coal referred the Isaac Plains Project and QCoal referred the Sonoma Coal Project.

[10] The Wildlife Preservation Society of Queensland's application for judicial review is brought pursuant to the *Administrative Decisions (Judicial Review) Act* 1977 (Cth) (the ADJR Act). The applicant is a small conservation group run by volunteers, principally organised by Dympna and Ian Lee who have

---

[10] EPBC Act s 74.
[11] See EPBC Act pt 9. The proposed action may be subject to other Commonwealth laws and/or State environmental and planning legislation.
[12] EPBC Act s 391.
[13] EPBC Act s 77.

campaigned for many years for environmental protection. In each instance, the Minister's delegate decided that the referred action was not controlled under s 75 EPBC Act.

Isaac Plains Project

[11] Bowen Coal's referral (7 April 2005) indicated that: the immediate coal mine site did not contain MNES (with minor exceptions); remnant habitat was not critical species habitat; and only, "not of concern" vegetation was to be removed. In light of the proposed mitigation measures, the proponent concluded that, "it is not anticipated that the project will lead to significant impacts on rare, threatened or migratory species, communities or populations listed under the EPBC Act."

[12] Following public notification of the referral under s 74(3) of the EPBC Act, the applicant raised concerns, inter alia, about certain endangered species, threatened ecological communities, Ramsar wetlands, and water quality. The applicant argued more investigation was required to determine that there was no significant impact. Concerns were raised about World Heritage Areas,[14] specifically the impact on the Great Barrier Reef World Heritage Area and the Wet Tropics Heritage Area, which are within the region of the proposed mines. The applicant argued that a key fact that was overlooked was that over the proposed nine-year life of the mine, 18 million tonnes of coal would be extracted and exported, with the effect that:

> [t]he production of greenhouse gases is almost certain to occur as a result of the action and can reasonably be imputed as within the contemplation of the proponent of the action.

[13] Australia is particularly vulnerable to climate change impacts. Many in our community will be disproportionately affected by climate change, including the heightened probability of extreme weather events, and impacts on sensitive environmental areas.

[14] The applicant's argument was that while the precise contribution of burning coal from the mines to overall global warming would be difficult to calculate, notwithstanding any difficulties of calculation, the overall effects of greenhouse gas emissions on MNES, such as the Great Barrier Reef, must be considered in a decision that requires assessment of all adverse impacts.

[15] More specifically, the applicants argued that Australia's international obligations required evaluation of the impacts of greenhouse gas emissions on relevant MNES. The applicant also argued that the *Convention on Biological Diversity* proscribes nations from causing trans-boundary harm.[15] Finally, the applicant contended the project should be a controlled action.

---

[14] See EPBC Act ss 12–14.

[15] *Convention on Biological Diversity*, 31 ILM822 (1992), Art 3.

Initial assessment and reasons for the decision

[16] Following submissions, an officer of the Commonwealth Department prepared a minute advising the delegate of the Minister that the Isaac Plains project was not a controlled action. His evaluation was that mitigation measures would minimise potential effects on the relevant Ramsar wetland site. The officer also found that, "significant impacts on matters protected under the EPBC Act are not likely".

[17] In regard to "secondary or consequent impacts", the officer observed:

> . . . the impacts of climate change, as a consequence of the burning of coal produced from the mine, on the world heritage values of the Great Barrier Reef World Heritage Area should be considered. The nature of induced climate change from the referred coal mining operation, and impacts on world heritage values, are speculative.

The delegate accepted the officer's recommendations. It is of concern that an assessment of minimal impacts on MNES, and a finding that the consequential impacts of the coal mining operation on world heritage values were "speculative," were accepted without further evaluation or independent third-party verification. As a decision-maker must consider the precautionary principle, obtaining further evaluation may have been prudent to meet the objectives of environmental protection at this point in the impact assessment process.

[18] Subsequently, the applicant sought reasons pursuant to s 13 ADJR Act. The delegate supported his decision by reference to material such as departmental briefs, proponent-initiated consultancy reports and public comment on the referral. The appellants argued that the lack of express reference to the impacts from greenhouse gas emissions due to coal extraction suggested these matters were not considered. The delegate did refer to indirect impacts in a general sense; albeit while deeming them as speculative.

[19] The delegate has sworn an affidavit explaining his approach to coal extraction, greenhouse gas emissions and climate change in respect of the two decisions. The approach is founded on his expertise from a geography degree that covered topics such as geomorphology, climatology and ecology. An examination of the build-up of anthropocentrically produced greenhouse gases in the atmosphere was part of those studies. Allied to this scientific knowledge, he has experience in making delegated decisions. It can be inferred that on the basis of his training and experience, he has previously considered and formed general views about climate change.

[20] While reliance upon previous experience is not unreasonable, scientific knowledge can objectify relationships between humans and environment in a manner that fails to examine impacts in terms of broad interconnections. Instead, it may narrowly isolate action and effect, leading to a failure to give weight to "all adverse impacts" as required by the statute. Here it appears to have unduly narrowed the inquiry so as to discount the interconnected nature of the environment and the ripple effects of "small" impacts. In this context, the applicant argued that further investigation was necessary to establish whether the burning of 18 million tonnes of coal might indirectly produce an impact on MNES such as world heritage values. The decision-maker must always reflect on whether further examination is a precaution consistent with the criteria for decision articulated in s 75.

[21] At another level the reasoning adopts an overly linear form – one commonly associated with hierarchical modes of thought. This form of knowledge relies on the authoritative status of the source of the information, without adopting independent evaluation (the reproduction of "speculative" in the reasons for decision may be explained on this basis). This model of analysis can be contrasted with a view of knowledge as one where meaning arises contextually and where the impacts upon future generations are seen as relevant values for consideration. Recognition of these sources of value and knowledge would have allowed a more comprehensive inquiry to have been conducted around the concept of "all adverse impacts".

Sonoma Project

[22] On 13 April 2005 QCoal referred a proposal for a coal mine at Sonoma to the Minister. Again, the referral documentation was accompanied by a conclusion that this was not a controlled action, although it would involve some vegetation clearance. In response, the applicant submitted, "the need for further environmental assessment" of impacts on threatened species, and the indirect impacts upon world heritage values. A process similar to the Isaac Plains project was undertaken involving a departmental officer making findings.

[23] The officer evaluated the submission of the applicant about indirect impacts of coal extraction in contributing to climate change and consequential effects on, inter alia, the Great Barrier Reef. The conclusion was:

> [t]he nature of induced climate change from the referred coal mining operation, and impacts on world heritage values are speculative. The quantum contribution to induced climate change directly attributable to the referred action is minute and not likely to be measurable against the context of existing and reasonably foreseen contributors.

[24] This finding was the basis for the Minister's delegate concluding there was not a controlled action. The delegate's affidavit stated that the reasoning was the same as that adopted for the Isaac Plains project. The observations made above about such reasoning are relevant here. Subsequent cross examination of the delegate, which was limited, sought to evaluate whether the delegate's reasoning in the affidavit took place, and whether notations to a departmental minute were made in light of that reasoning (ie conclusions about burning large amounts of coal and the subsequent emissions produced). Given that this is a matter of public controversy, it is reasonable also to assume the witness would have previously formed a view about the matter.

The Applicant's Case

[25] The applicant raised a large number of grounds of review. The first seeks to rely on ss 5(1)(e) and 5(2)(b) of the ADJR Act (failure to take account of relevant considerations). In summary, the ground was that the decision-maker failed to consider the adverse impacts the Isaac Plains Coal Project and the Sonoma Coal Project are likely to have on the matters protected by Part 3 of the EPBC Act due to the mining, transport and use of the coal from the mines emitting a large amount of greenhouse gases contributing to global warming. There was a failure to address a relevant consideration and also a failure to address a relevant question.

[26] The second ground was that the decision-maker erred in law in the construction of s 72(2) by failing to consider "all adverse impacts", specifically, in excluding consideration of the contribution of coal production to global warming. The applicant also relied upon several other grounds under Part 5 ADJR Act. The grounds rest on the lack of detailed examination by the delegate of greenhouse gas emissions and climate change issues, despite a reference to indirect impacts of the actions upon world heritage values. There was general consideration of impacts by the delegate but these were categorised as "speculative" and only "theoretically possible".

[27] The arguments by the applicant centred on the contention that the two coal projects are likely to have a significant impact on MNES as a result of the mining, transport and burning of the coal, by emitting large amounts of greenhouse gases, thereby contributing to overall global warming and thus impacting MNES. The focus was the effect on the Great Barrier Reef World Heritage Area, although which MNES under Part 3 were not always clearly identified. Section 12 (World Heritage properties) is the relevant controlling provision. The applicant's submissions focussed on how greenhouse gas emissions from the burning of fossil fuels lead to climate change; noting that climate change will have long-term impacts upon the environment. Certain areas, such as the Great Barrier Reef, are particularly susceptible. It is not always possible to pinpoint the specific contribution to the deterioration of protected matters of any given action, but it is possible to identify general impacts of climate change on MNES that are not merely speculative.

[28] Indeed, "a causal relation between an action and a presumptive impact [is] capable of almost infinite extension".[16] In *Minister for Environment and Heritage v Queensland Conservation Council Inc*[17] it was accepted that the Minister or delegate in making a decision under s 75 is to give a literal meaning to all adverse impacts. The Full Federal Court defined impact as "the influence or effect of an action". In terms of its ordinary meaning, it "can readily include the 'indirect' consequences of an action and may include the results of acts done by persons other than the principal actor".[18] Pursuant to s 75(2) the task for the decision-maker is to "consider each way in which a proposed action will, or is likely to, adversely influence or affect the world heritage values of a declared World Heritage property".[19] The ordinary meaning of impact was held to include direct or indirect effects, including "effects which are sufficiently close to the action to

[16] *Fitzgerald v Penn* (1954) 91 CLR 268, 277.
[17] (2004) 139 FCR 24, [45].
[18] Ibid [53].
[19] Ibid.

allow it to be said, without straining the language, that they are, or would be, the consequences of the action on the protected matter".[20] In relation to the first ground of review, the question is whether the decision-maker has construed his task too narrowly, thereby failing to take account of relevant considerations by examining each way in which a proposed action such as a coal mine will adversely affect MNES, and in particular, the world heritage values of the Great Barrier Reef.

[29] All adverse impacts can comprehend, "each consequence which can reasonably be imputed as within the contemplation of the proponent of the action, whether those consequences are within the control of the proponent or not."[21] Failing to account for relevant considerations in this way entails reasoning from an earlier age where simplified models of causation isolated a primary cause for an event. By contrast, ecology, drawing on concepts around the care and protection of life, has developed a systemic approach that expands to examine multiple causes over longer time periods. It focuses on interconnection between the elements of an ecosystem, with humans an integral component. Thus, what will be a significant impact should comprehend systemic, interconnected effects of actions, known as cumulative impacts, as well as broadly-construed indirect impacts. If the integrated nature of the environment as a web of life is accepted, it is conceivable to posit enhanced risks of impact across many categories of MNES due to any single action, even if current scientific knowledge cannot precisely define the exact character of impact on MNES.

[30] In *Booth v Bosworth*[22] it was accepted that an action can have a significant impact on world heritage values, even though each element of what constitutes those values was not affected in the same manner (ie there is an impact on a "keystone species"). It highlights the importance that society places on these values. Therefore, it is possible to speak of a "significant impact" where a particular action and its consequences might affect all protected matters, albeit perhaps not in exactly the same way and to the same extent.

[31] With respect to the second ground of review, the question of how to consider all adverse impacts including indirect impacts is a complex one. The applicants submit that there is a risk that at some future time (dependent upon the level of increases in atmospheric warming) protected matters in Australia will be adversely and significantly affected by climate change. The predictions of impact refer to scientific degrees of probability, and to that extent are not fully certain. No direct effect on MNES is posited between coal production from either proposed mine; nor is it possible to quantify exactly which emissions from such mining, transportation and burning might aggravate the greenhouse gas problem. The applicant's case is based upon the contention that greenhouse gas emissions will have wide-ranging and indirect impacts on MNES. The impacts on MNES of actions undertaken by third parties but facilitated by the proposed action was examined in *Minister for Environment and Heritage v Queensland*

[20] Ibid.
[21] Ibid [57].
[22] (2001) 114 FCR 39 [102]–[104].

Conservation Council Inc.[23] In that context, consideration of third party actions was not deemed speculative but held to be integral to an examination of all adverse impacts.

[32] In the present situation, the indirect impact (categorised as additional) on global emissions from the coal extracted and burnt from the two proposed coal mines was regarded by the delegate as speculative or only having a small, and therefore, not significant impact. Given the relatively minimal examination of indirect impacts, the decision-maker's reasoning has not sufficiently considered all adverse impacts of greenhouse gases generated in the extraction, transportation and burning of coal from the mines. The decision-maker has not considered all adverse impacts as required under s 75(2).

[33] In light of the potential for loss of important values associated with the MNES, especially those of world heritage and cultural heritage, there has been a failure to properly address the relevant considerations in respect of s 75 EPBC Act. The finding of no significant impact by virtue of treating indirect impacts as small or speculative for the purposes of Part 3 also requires reconsideration. The applicant succeeds on each of the first two grounds for review.

Decision-making under the EPBC Act

[34] The other grounds of review are widely-drawn, seemingly to capture all plausible grounds under s 5 ADJR Act. They may have benefited from more careful articulation. As the applicant has succeeded on the first two grounds, I shall deal with the remaining grounds only briefly. Ground 3 argues that there was a failure to adopt a "common sense approach" to causation in terms of attributing legal responsibility for the impacts of greenhouse gas emissions in respect of the decision under s 75. The role of the decision-maker under s 75 is not one of determining responsibility but of identifying if there is a need for further assessment of the proposed action; accordingly ground 3 is not sustained.

[35] Grounds 4–12 largely relate to the interpretative approaches that the applicant argues should inform decision-making. The applicant proposes five factors appropriate to the task prescribed by s 75 EPBC Act.

[36] Ground 4 claims an error of law in that the delegate failed to treat the issue of causation generally, and failed to construe references to "a significant impact" appropriately. The particular manner in which causation is to be considered by the delegate under s 75 is not prescribed so long as matters relevant to the controlled action decision are taken into account. However, the question as to whether the action has or will have a significant impact on the action, as construed in light of s 3A of the EPBC Act, was not adequately considered.

[37] The applicants argued first that the *Acts Interpretation Act* 1901 (Cth) provides that in construing an Act a court may have regard to "any treaty or other international agreement that is referred to in the Act". Such "agreements" include the *Framework Convention on Climate Change* 1992 where Art 3, para 3 provides:

[23] (2004) 139 FCR 24.

> The parties should take precautionary measures to anticipate, prevent or minimize the causes of climate change and mitigate its adverse effects.

[38] It is accepted that the precautionary principle, and the Convention generally, offer assistance in construing the EPBC Act. Australia is part of a holistic system for dealing with climate change. To date, Australia has entered into obligations under the Framework Convention but not the associated Kyoto Protocol. A second pertinent factor is the existence of key objectives for the EPBC Act enunciated in s 3A(b):

> If there are threats of serious or irreversible environmental damage, lack of full scientific certainty should not be used as a reason for postponing measures to prevent environmental degradation . . .

These frameworks are augmented by express adoption of the precautionary principle in s 391 to guide critical areas of decision-making under the Act, including the controlled action decision. It is highly relevant to determining the circumstances in which an action has, will have, or is likely to have, a significant impact upon a protected matter under s 12 EPBC Act. In *Booth v Bosworth* the precautionary principle was closely identified with the meaning of "is likely to have".[24] Pertinently, the Court observed, ". . . that a lower standard is intended to be set by para 12(1)(b)".[25] The expression "likely" is to be construed, "in the sense of 'prone', 'with a propensity' or 'liable.'" Such an approach[26] would tend to

> avoid the risk to biological diversity and the environment generally which would flow from the need for scientific certainty or confidence about the potential impacts of actions concerning which there has been limited scientific study.[27]

[39] Adopting a precautionary approach suggests that while indirect impacts of the greenhouse gas emissions from the extraction of coal in the two proposed mines cannot be identified with absolute scientific precision, the principle requires careful consideration in a controlled action decision. Thus "likely" in s 12 should be understood as requiring a more comprehensive examination than that undertaken by the delegate. The delegate was required to adopt a precautionary approach, and at the very least to investigate further whether either project will indirectly cause serious or irreversible environmental damage. The applicant succeeds on ground 4.

[40] The applicant argues under ground 5 that the delegate "failed to consider the greenhouse impacts operating cumulatively with other contributors to global warming." The cumulative effect of each individual action, such as a mine, to global climate change should be evaluated, not just the impact of each action in isolation. In *Minister for Environment and Heritage v Queensland Conservation Council Inc,*[28] it was held necessary to have regard to cumulative impacts. This requirement is informed by growing ecological knowledge of the pervasive effects of the accretion of human activity on the environment. Accordingly, this

---

[24] (2001) 114 FCR 39, [97].
[25] Ibid.
[26] *Friends of Hinchinbrook Society Inc v Minister for Environment* (1997) 142 ALR 632 s677–679.
[27] *Booth v Bosworth* (2001) 114 FCR 39, [98].
[28] (2004) 139 FCR 24.

interpretation requires the delegate to bring a wide range of relevant considerations to the s 75 task. In this manner, the consideration of cumulative impacts is integral to decision-making under s 75. The error of law by the delegate that occurred with respect to narrowly construing the cumulative impacts of the two coal mine projects as "small" and "speculative" also relates to this ground. The delegate failed to adequately consider all adverse impacts as required under s 75, including impacts of greenhouse gas emission as part of co-contribution to global warming. The applicant succeeds on this ground.

[41] Grounds 6, 7 and 8 focus on the delegate's understanding of indirect impacts and probability in terms of gauging "a significant impact" upon MNES for the purposes of Part 3 EPBC Act. Ground 6 argues that there was an error of law in that the delegate equated a small impact with one which was insignificant. This conflation is evident in the reasons for decision and it indicates a failure to give proper consideration to "all adverse impacts". This ground of review succeeds.

[42] Ground 7 is based upon an argument that the delegate incorrectly assumed that climate change was a prerequisite for impacts upon MNES to occur, rather than something already in train. The reasoning was obscure, but there was no inference to be drawn that the delegate disregarded climate change processes as not already operative. This ground cannot be substantiated.

[43] Ground 8 rests on the applicant's argument that having conceded that the two projects would increase greenhouse gas concentrations in the atmosphere the delegate incorrectly concluded that there was no possibility of any impact on climate in the vicinity of matters protected by Part 3. The basis of this argument is closely connected with the discussion of whether the delegate adequately had regard to factors related to "likely" significant impact on MNES. Given the narrowness of the delegate's consideration of "likely significant impact" in terms of the decision under s 75, this ground of review is substantiated.

[44] In Ground 9, the applicant asserts an error of law in that the delegate required that impacts to be taken into consideration for the purposes of s 75 were those that were "measurable, specifically identifiable and demonstrable." The reliance by a decision maker on strictly quantifiable impacts rather than those of a probabilistic nature is understandable at one level. Nonetheless confining consideration to such narrowly-determined parameters exemplifies the strictures of the older model of scientific reasoning. Such reasoning has been widely disclaimed by modern scientific methodologies that now inform the understanding of "significant" impact. The limitations of the mode of reasoning adopted by the delegate in failing to account for statistically valid probabilities of impact are well-established. This ground of review succeeds.

[45] In Ground 10, the applicant's arguments in respect of the listing of climate change as a key threatening process under the EPBC Act, (and thus that the process must be taken into account in the controlled action decision), are more abstruse. These are not a matter to which the decision-maker is specifically directed under s 75. The applicant failed to establish the relevance of the threatening process to the decision under s 75 and therefore the applicant fails on this ground.

[46] The applicant argued in Ground 11 that the decision under s 75 is an initial threshold examination of the nature of impacts on the relevant MNES, and thus, the fact that later assessment of impacts of the action will occur requires the adoption of a more liberal approach to the controlled action decision at the initial stage. This reasoning relies on the integrity of later decision-making and is unavailable when seeking review of the initial controlled action decision. The argument that there was an improper exercise of the relevant power does not succeed.

[47] The basis of Ground 12, that there was no evidence upon which the delegate could have been reasonably satisfied that greenhouse gas emissions were not likely to have a significant impact on MNES, is not established. The delegate clearly had regard to factual evidence.

[48] In summary, the resolution as to whether greenhouse gas emissions consequent upon the burning of coal mined in the two proposed projects will have an indirect impact upon a protected matter, such as the world heritage values of the Great Barrier Reef, is a matter of compelling public interest. Decision-makers under s 75 of the EPBC Act are charged with the responsibility to uphold the integrity of controlled action decisions, and therefore to ensure that matters which raise questions of public interest can be examined in a manner that transcends sectional interests to embrace a perspective consistent with the articulated objectives of the legislation. In light of Australia's international obligations for protection of the ecosystems upon which life depends, a precautionary approach should be applied to such decisions. Accordingly, I am satisfied that the burning of coal (although occurring at specific places in the world) the potential for such combustion to contribute towards cumulative global warming and any potential for consequent indirect impacts upon a protected matter, should be considerations for a decision-maker under s 75(2). The requirement for the decision-maker to have regard to the precautionary principle reinforces the relevance of a widely-framed approach. Such an approach can take into account important values, such as intergenerational equity and care for vulnerable and unique parts of our continent. The applicant's concern is the possibility that in the not-too distant future, protected matters in Australia will be adversely and significantly affected by climate change (given the scientific calculation of the probability of such risks); such climate change having been caused by levels of greenhouse gases (derived from all sources) in the atmosphere. While there has been no suggestion that the mining, transportation or burning of coal from either proposed mine would *directly* affect any such protected matter, the controlled action decision in this instance must be interpreted to cover cumulative and indirect impacts.[29]

Orders

1. The application is allowed.

[29] Ibid.

2. The decision is remitted to the Minister for the Environment and Heritage for reconsideration under s 75 *Environment Protection and Biodiversity Conservation Act* 1999, taking into account all relevant adverse impacts upon protected matters, and having regard to the precautionary principle.

Part II

Private Law

Torts

10

The Economic Value of Human Relationships: *Cattanach v Melchior* Revisited

ISABEL KARPIN

The Case

In 1992, Kerry Melchior, a 40-year-old mother of two, decided, together with her husband Craig, that she had completed her family. She engaged the services of Dr Stephen Cattanach, an obstetrician and gynaecologist, to perform a tubal ligation. Acting on Melchior's advice that her right ovary and tube had been removed when she was 15, Cattanach clipped her left fallopian tube only. Four years later, at 44, Melchior became pregnant and gave birth to a 'healthy' baby in May 1997. A subsequent hysterosalpingogram revealed a functioning right fallopian tube. It appeared that an ovum from the left ovary had migrated across the abdominal cavity into the right fallopian tube. Kerry Melchior and her husband subsequently sued both Dr Cattanach and the State of Queensland, the authority responsible for the public hospital where the failed sterilisation was performed, on the basis that Dr Cattanach was negligent when providing advice about the risks of the proposed operation. The Melchiors were successful in the Queensland Supreme Court[1] and on appeal, first to the Queensland Court of Appeal,[2] and then the High Court of Australia.[3]

When the case went on appeal to the High Court there was no controversy over the issue of whether there had been a negligent act. That was accepted. The question was instead: what constituted the resulting harm for which damages could be claimed? Two components of the damages award were undisputed. These were Kerry Melchior's award for pain and suffering associated with the pregnancy, attendant loss of amenities and economic loss ($103 672.39), and Craig Melchior's award for loss of consortium ($3000). The High Court appeal concerned only the validity of the third award of damages, $105 249.33 for the costs associated with raising and maintaining the child until age 18.

The third claim had been upheld by the Queensland Court of Appeal but without unanimity. The Court split 2:1, with dissenting judge Thomas JA holding that parenting a healthy child was a benefit that could not be outweighed or undone by the financial costs and therefore it was not a loss to be compensated.[4] This kind of judicial statement is not unusual in so-called wrongful birth cases, and Melinda Jones surmises that the disturbing idea of a 'wrongful birth' has prompted some judges to offer their 'judicial opinion about

[1] *Melchior v Cattanach* [2000] QSC 285 (23 August 2000).
[2] *Melchior v Cattanach* [2001] QCA 246 (26 June 2001) ('*Melchior*').
[3] *Cattanach v Melchior* (2003) 214 CLR 1 ('*Cattanach*').
[4] *Melchior* [2001] QCA 246 (26 June 2001) [196].

the sanctity of life [and] the immeasurable love of parents of their children.'[5] The idea of 'wrongful birth' also fails to fully encompass the true extent and duration of the harm. For this reason, Nicky Prialux and others have suggested that a better description of the claim might be 'unsolicited parenthood'.[6] It is notable that, in the High Court *Cattanach* decision, McHugh and Gummow JJ describe the language of 'wrongful birth' as diverting attention away from the relevant wrongful act – the negligence of the doctor.[7]

The High Court Decision

The High Court ultimately decided the case in favour of the Melchiors, and Kylie Burns' feminist judgment agrees with the majority and dismisses the appeal. However the Court was split 4:3, with five separate judgments. The majority judges were Gummow, McHugh, Kirby and Callinan JJ, while Gleeson CJ, Hayne and Heydon JJ made up the minority. Even though, arguably, the High Court decision supported a view that the negligent curtailment of reproductive choice is a significant harm warranting compensation, the decision has attracted significant feminist commentary. Reg Graycar,[8] Natasha Cica[9] and Kylie Burns herself[10] have all been critical of the way in which some of the judgments reflected abstract personal values which were then framed as public policy.

Graycar describes the judgment of Heydon J, for example, as 'replete with exhortations to various values'[11] and the evidence to support this comment is not difficult to find. He states at paragraph 353 for example: 'It is wrong to attempt to place a value on human life or a value on the expense of human life because human life is invaluable – incapable of effective or useful valuation.' This is in stark contrast to the way Holmes J, at first instance, framed the issue contextually. She explicitly eschewed appeals to personal values, stating:

> Although there is a natural appeal in the assertion that a healthy child's birth should not be regarded other than as great good fortune, it is counsel for an ideal world. In reality, the context in which a child is born may profoundly affect the happiness to be derived from his or her existence. The introduction of an undesired child into the family may range in its effect from mild economic setback to catastrophe in emotional and financial terms.[12]

Graycar also notes that Heydon J criticises the Queensland Court of Appeal decision on the grounds that they took 'insufficient account of the law's assumptions about some key values in family life'.[13] In fact if we look at the judgment of McMurdo P we see that, like her

[5] Melinda Jones, 'Valuing all Lives – Even "Wrongful" Ones' in Marcia H Rioux, Lee Ann Basser Marks, and Melinda Jones (eds), *Critical Perspectives in Human Rights and Disability Law* (Martinus Nijhoff, 2011) 87.

[6] Nicky Prialux 'Joy to the World! A (Healthy) Child is Born! Reconceptualizing Harm in Wrongful Conception' (2004) 13 *Social and Legal Studies* 5, 7.

[7] *Cattanach* (2003) 214 CLR 1 [68].

[8] Reg Graycar, 'Judicial Activism or "Traditional" Negligence Law? Conception, Pregnancy and Denial of Reproductive Choice' in Ian Freckelton and Kerry Petersen (eds), *Disputes and Dilemmas in Health Law* (Federation Press, 2006) 436.

[9] Natasha Cica, 'Can't Buy Me Love – Public Policy Implications of *Cattanach v Melchior*' (2003) 10 *Agenda* 367.

[10] Kylie Burns, 'The Way the World Is: Social Fact in High Court Negligence Cases' (2004) 12 *Torts Law Journal* 1.

[11] Graycar, above n 8, 447.

[12] *Melchior v Cattanach* [2000] QSC 285 (23 August 2000) [51].

[13] *Cattanach* (2003) 214 CLR 1 [322].

lower court counterpart, she rejects an appeal to personal values and instead relies on an examination of actual harms. She states:

> Whilst recognising that only the crustiest of curmudgeons is not warmed by the miracle of new life, I am far from persuaded that the blessing of parenthood should prohibit or even limit a claim for the modest reasonable costs of rearing to majority the baby conceived as a result of medical negligence . . . The free choice of the individual or couple not to be blessed with a child has been taken away from them through negligence and they will consequently suffer economic loss.[14]

Natasha Cica, like Graycar, finds the judgment of Heydon J 'replete with speculative commentary'[15] but goes on to say that 'legal pronouncements of judges' cannot and should not 'be detached from the values of the society in which the law operates'.[16] Rather, quoting Kirby J in *Cattanach,* 'the common law . . . is expressed by judges to respond to their perceptions of the requirement of justice, fairness and reasonableness in their society.'[17] Arguing that many of the 'social fact' assumptions made by the minority judges in *Cattanach* were 'by their very nature value laden, highly contentious and contestable',[18] Burns too notes that the problem is not that social facts were used by these judges, but, that very little social scientific evidence was provided to support the social 'fact' statements.

The Feminist Judgment

Kylie Burns' feminist judgment articulates a strong view on the appropriate use of public policy concerns and argues for the inclusion of empirical research and scholarly commentary to support asserted social facts. Her judgment demonstrates how social facts might be appropriately incorporated, citing Australian Bureau of Statistics (ABS) data, amongst other literature, to support her claims. Specifically, she points to the comprehensive lawful availability of contraception and sterilisation to support the claim that reproductive choice is an assumed value that cannot be discounted. She refers to ABS data that demonstrates that mothers still bear the major share of the burden of the physical and emotional care of children and household chores and tasks, and she cites social science evidence of the impact of these facts on workplace participation and economic success. In her feminist judgment, Burns provides a resonant account of the physical, psychological and economic impact the negligent act has had and will continue to have on Kerry Melchior's life and thus firmly rejects the characterisation of the damages for the upbringing of the child as pure economic loss.

Burns also crafts her judgment so that the essential frame of the parental relationship is neither obscured (it is recognised as loving and caring) nor idealised (it is also full of obligation and responsibility). It is concretely and contextually realised. Interestingly, Gleeson CJ, in the minority, argues that the frame of the relationship forecloses the claim for damages. He states at paragraph 38: 'It is a human relationship regarded by domestic law and by international standards as fundamental to society. To seek to assign an economic value to

[14] *Melchior* [2001] QCA 246 (26 June 2001) [49].
[15] Cica, above n 9, 373.
[16] Ibid 374.
[17] *Cattanach* (2003) 214 CLR 1 [106].
[18] Burns, above n 10, 8.

the relationship, either positive or negative, in the ordinary case is neither reasonable nor possible.'

In fact, it is precisely because we perceive ourselves so fundamentally as existing inside these relationships that compensation is both appropriate and necessary. If the parent–child relationship did not matter, then the Melchiors would neither feel obligated to the child nor need to be compensated for its care. Feminist legal theorist Jennifer Nedelsky argues for a relational theory of law in which it is recognised that 'human beings are in a constant process of becoming in interaction with the many layers of relationship in which they are embedded' and that the role of law is to construct those very relationships in such as way as to enhance our autonomy within them.[19] She says we need a 'relational approach' to law that 'looks at not just how personal relationships shape autonomy but also how societal institutions, practices and beliefs structure relationships.'[20]

The idea of the relationship is useful here to argue that, although the wrongfulness is as Gummow and McHugh JJ state, the negligent act, the damage is also, as Gleeson CJ notes, attached to the enforced parental relationship. Thus a feminist relational approach would argue in favour of doing exactly what Gleeson CJ has argued is impossible – attaching notions of compensable harm and damage to the relationship.

In their joint judgment, McHugh and Gummow JJ state: 'the unplanned child is not the harm for which recompense is sought in this action; it is the burden of legal and moral responsibilities which arise by reason of the birth of the child that is in contention'.[21] Burdens or obligations of care and responsibility are intrinsic to the way the parent-child relationship operates. It is clear that the obligation to take care of one's children is real, but it is not necessarily repugnant. The recognition of that obligation does not degrade the nature or value of that relationship. Instead it justifies, as appropriate, the award of compensation for the costs that would not have been incurred had the negligence not intervened to undo the Melchiors' original decision not to take on further parental responsibilities.

The Aftermath of *Cattanach v Melchior*

Importantly, though it is not the issue here, there is a second kind of claim that is made, where the conception, pregnancy and birth of a healthy child are desired, yet negligence leads to the birth of a disabled child. Melinda Jones describes this as a case in which '*a child* is very much wanted, but the particular child's disability results in the *particular disabled child* being unwanted'.[22] It appears there is a greater willingness by legislatures and judges to countenance claims for the costs of raising this kind of child. There is not space to consider the question of disability-based discrimination and the value of life with a disability in detail here, however, it is worth noting that it was specifically referred to in both the Supreme Court and the Court of Appeal decisions with respect to and to further rebut the child as blessing or benefit argument. Holmes J at first instance notes:

[19] Jennifer Nedelsky, *Law's Relations: A Relational Theory of Self, Autonomy and Law* (Oxford University Press, 2011) 38.

[20] Ibid 176.

[21] *Cattanach* (2003) 214 CLR 1 [68].

[22] Jones, above n 5, 90 (emphasis in original).

> A further difficulty is the artificiality of the notion of the 'healthy child'. How does one distinguish between the healthy and the unhealthy; how many defects are required before the child loses the quality of being a blessing and becomes a burden? Does one compensate for the cost of rearing a child with cystic fibrosis, for example, but not for a child with mild hearing impairment? The drawing of such distinctions is unattractive.[23]

Similarly in the Queensland Court of Appeal, McMurdo P states:

> [S]ome would limit the benefit argument to the birth of a normal healthy child, but, as I have earlier noted, this offends the respect and value the law places on every life and undervalues the benefit from and the valuable contribution of those born with disabilities.[24]

It seems however, that the legislature does not agree. Since the *Cattanach* decision, Queensland, New South Wales and South Australia have introduced provisions in their *Civil Liability Acts* to foreclose claims for damages for the cost of raising a non-disabled child.[25] Furthermore there continues to be judicial disagreement, with some recent decisions drawing heavily on the dissenting opinions in *Cattanach.*[26]

[23] *Melchior v Cattanach* [2000] QSC 285 (23 August 2000) [52].

[24] *Melchior* [2001] QCA 246 (26 June 2001) [50].

[25] The *Civil Liabilities Act 2003* (Qld) ss 49A and 49B leave open the door for a claim where the child is born disabled because they preclude only those claims for loss arising out of the costs ordinarily associated with rearing or maintaining a child. The *Civil Liability Act 2002* (NSW) s 71 and the *Civil Liability Act 1936* (SA) s 67 preclude the costs of raising a child but make special exception for raising a child with a disability and the additional costs associated with that disability.

[26] See *Hamilton v Young* [2007] QSC 160 (6 July 2007); *G v Armelin* [2008] ACTSC 68 (24 July 2008); cf *G v Armelin* [2009] ACTCA 6 (1 May 2009).

CATTANACH AND ANOTHER .... APPELLANTS.
DEFENDANTS,

AND

MELCHIOR AND ANOTHER .... RESPONDENTS.
PLAINTIFFS,

[2003] HCA 38

ON APPEAL FROM THE SUPREME COURT OF QUEENSLAND

BURNS J

An unexpected pregnancy

HC OF A 2003

Feb 11–13; *JULY* 16 2003

Burns J

415 Mrs Kerry Melchior discovered she was pregnant in November 1996. She was forty-four years old. She and her husband Mr Craig Melchior were unsurprisingly shocked by the pregnancy not only because of her age (665) but because in March 1992 Mrs Melchior had undergone tubal ligation sterilisation surgery. The surgery was carried out by the first appellant Dr Stephen Cattanach, a specialist obstetrician and gynaecologist, at Redland Hospital. This was a public hospital operated by the Brisbane South Regional Health Authority, and later by its statutory successor the second appellant, the State of Queensland.

416 Jordan Melchior, the Melchiors' son, was born by caesarean section on 29 May 1997. This was far from an ordinary birth. It was not an intimate or private event. It was much more traumatic. In addition to medical staff caring for Mrs Melchior and her baby, medical experts retained by the parties were present. Following Jordan's delivery, Mrs Melchior's uterus was removed outside her abdominal cavity. The experts observed that her left fallopian tube had been clipped. Following dissection, it became apparent that Mrs Melchior had an unclipped right fallopian tube. Its presence was obscured by adhesions, it was convoluted and compressed, was attached by adhesions to its own supporting structure and to the uterus, and was displaced from its normal position. In consultations in November 1991 prior to the sterilisation surgery, Mrs Melchior advised Dr Cattanach that her right fallopian tube and ovary had been removed during appendectomy surgery when she was fifteen years old. At the time of the sterilisation surgery, Dr Cattanach recorded in his surgical notes that no right tube or ovary were visible. As became evident at the time of Jordan's birth, the right fallopian tube had not in fact been removed.

(665) Day, Sullivan, Ford & Lancaster, Australian Institute of Health and Welfare (AIHW), National Perinatal Statistics Series No 9, *Australia's Mothers and Babies 1997* (1999). The estimated median age of women giving birth in 1997 was 28.7 years. There were only 174 confinements of women in Australia aged 45 and over in 1997, 0.1% of all Australian births in that year (at p 54, Table, A5).

417 In September 1997, Mrs Melchior underwent a hysterosalpingogram. This is a painful and invasive procedure where dye is inserted into the uterus of a woman under pressure. The flow of dye through the fallopian tube is observed under X-ray to determine whether a fallopian tube is patent. Mrs Melchior's right fallopian tube was found to be patent. The medical experts concluded that Mrs Melchior conceived when an ovum from her left ovary transmigrated to her right fallopian tube. Mr Melchior subsequently underwent a vasectomy in June 1998 as a precaution against any further pregnancy.

418 Jordan Melchior is a much loved child. He is a valued member of his family. However, his birth and the financial and personal costs of raising him caused significant disruption and emotional, physical and financial stress to the Melchior family, particularly to Mrs Melchior. In April 1997 Mr and Mrs Melchior commenced proceedings against Dr Cattanach and the State of Queensland in both contract and negligence. Ultimately, only the claim in negligence was pursued. The State of Queensland admitted liability on the basis of vicarious liability should Dr Cattanach be found negligent. At the trial of the matter, Holmes J found Dr Cattanach and the State of Queensland negligent on the basis that Mrs Melchior was not informed of the possibility that the sterilisation could be ineffective due to the possibility of the right fallopian tube still being in existence, giving her an option to undertake further investigations (666). Mrs Melchior was awarded damages for her pain, suffering and loss of amenities in relation to the pregnancy, birth and subsequent effects on her health, a small amount of damages for loss of future earning capacity resulting from a condition related to the pregnancy, and an amount for future care and maternity wear. Mr Melchior recovered $3000 for loss of consortium. Mr and Mrs Melchior also recovered an amount of $105,249.33 jointly as compensation for the costs of raising Jordan.

419 Dr Cattanach and the State of Queensland appealed to the Court of Appeal against the findings in relation to negligence, causation and recoverability of damages (667). The appeal was dismissed by a majority (McMurdo P and Davies JA, Thomas JA dissenting). Special leave to appeal to this Court was granted by Gaudron and Kirby JJ only in relation to the question of the recoverability of damages for the costs of raising and maintaining Jordan. The question of whether the costs of raising a child born after a failed sterilisation constitutes a harm recognised by law is one that has troubled courts throughout the world. Many different and conflicting responses have been given. These are summarised in the judgments of other members of this Court (668). The House of Lords recently rejected a claim for the costs of raising a child in *McFarlane v Tayside Health Board* (669). There is scant Australian authority reflecting divergent judicial

(666) *Melchior v Cattanach* [2001] Aust Torts Reports ¶81-597 at 66,626 [33] (*Melchior*).
(667) *Melchior v Cattanach* [2001] QCA 246.
(668) Reasons of Kirby J at [103]–[132]; reasons of Hayne J at [186]–[187]; reasons of Callinan J at [283]–[290]; reasons of Heydon J at [313].
(669) [2000] 2 AC 59 (*McFarlane*).

approaches (670). This question has not previously been considered by this Court.

The nature of the harm

420 Most people regard babies and small children with genuine affection. Judicial pronouncements have identified the many benefits children bring to their families. Judicial reasons in cases like this one have, often influenced by religious or other moral values, focussed on the inherent value of human life to both society and the law and on the maintenance by the law of family relationships (671). The appellants submitted that in this case and those like it, the bringing into existence of another human being should not and cannot be considered "damage" or a legally compensable harm. However, this case does not concern a claim that human life, in this case Jordan's life, is of itself damage (672). The damages claimed by Mr and Mrs Melchior were for the physical, psychological and economic consequences of his unplanned and negligently caused birth, not for his life itself.

421 I do not agree that the damage at issue in this appeal, the economic costs of raising Jordan, should be characterised as a claim for pure economic loss (673). The duty of a medical professional in Australia is a single comprehensive duty covering diagnosis, treatment, information and advice (674). It is not to be divided into multiple separate duties, some to avoid physical harm and some to avoid economic loss. It is not in dispute in this Court that a duty of care was owed to Mrs Melchior and that the duty was breached. It is artificial to separate the physical consequences to Mrs Melchior of the breach of this duty from the consequential economic loss suffered including the costs of raising Jordan (675). This does not occur in other categories of personal injury claims. Rather, at least in the case of Mrs Melchior's claim, these losses along with Mrs Melchior's physical, psychological and other economic losses, must be seen as being intimately and directly connected to the invasion of Mrs Melchior's fundamental right to her own bodily integrity and autonomy. Some aspects of claims for the financial costs of raising a child, for example the costs of childcare, respond directly to a parent's loss of autonomy by facilitating some small measure of personal freedom and relief from childcare duties. Others respond to the

(670) *Melchior* [2001] Aust Torts Reports ¶81–597 at 66,626–66, 627 per Holmes J referring to *Dahl v Purnell* (1993) 15 QLR 33; *Veivers v Connolly* [1995] 2 Qd R 326; *CES* (1995) 38 NSWLR 47 (*CES*). See also reasons of Kirby J at [109]–[116]; reasons of Callinan J at [289]–[290].

(671) Reasons of Gleeson CJ at [6], [35], [39]; reasons of Heydon J at [323]–[337]; reasons of Kirby J at [135] citing *CES* (1995) 38 NSWLR 47 at 87 where Meagher JA cited John 16:21 in the Christian Bible. See also reasons of Kirby J at [140].

(672) Reasons of McHugh and Gummow JJ at [67]–[68]; reasons of Kirby J at [148]. cf Reasons of Gleeson CJ at [25]–[31], [35]–[39].

(673) Reasons of Kirby J at [148]–[149]. cf reasons of Gleeson CJ at [4], [9], [24]–[30]; reasons of Callinan J at [299]; *MacFarlane* [2000] 2 AC 59 at 76, per Lord Slynn; at 83–84, per Lord Steyn; at 89, per Lord Hope.

(674) *Rogers v Whitaker* (1992) 175 CLR 479 at 483 per Mason CJ, Brennan, Dawson, Toohey and McHugh JJ; at 492 per Gaudron J (*Rogers*).

(675) Reasons of Hayne J at [193].

financial loss suffered by parents directly connected to their moral and legal (676) obligations to raise the child.

422 The appellants have not argued that we must consider Mr Melchior's claim as distinctly different and separate to Mrs Melchior's claim. That may be an issue in future cases before this Court. Although it has not been argued here nor did it form part of the Melchiors' claim, it is apparent from the evidence given at trial that Mr Melchior did himself suffer an interference with his own physical integrity as a result of the failed sterilisation when he underwent a vasectomy following Jordan's birth to prevent further pregnancies. The appellants' negligent actions must be seen as causing Mrs Melchior to become pregnant, bear and raise a child against her will. Although Mrs Melchior and her husband have, as many parents have in similar circumstances, accepted Jordan into their family, loved him, cared for him, and accepted a financial obligation for his care, these are obligations that were thrust upon them as a result of the appellants' negligent action. They are intimately connected to the invasion of Mrs Melchior's bodily integrity and her autonomy. They are the very obligations that Mr and Mrs Melchior wanted to avoid when Mrs Melchior sought sterilisation surgery from Dr Cattanach (677).

423 In *Parkinson v St James & Seacroft University Hospital NHS Trust* (678) Hale LJ described the right to bodily integrity as (679):

> "the first and most important of the interests protected by the law of tort, listed in *Clerk & Lindsell on Torts,* 18th ed (2000), para 1-25. 'The fundamental principle, plain and incontestable, is that every person's body is inviolate': see *Collins v Wilcock* [1984] 1 WLR 1172, 1177. Included within that right are two others. One is the right to physical autonomy: to make one's own choices about what will happen to one's own body. Another is the right not to be subjected to bodily injury or harm. These interests are regarded as so important that redress is given against both intentional and negligent interference with them."

In medical cases, this Court has recognised a patient's right to make a decision in relation to whether their bodily integrity is intruded upon by medical treatment following appropriate advice and information (680).

424 In the trial and appeal of this matter reference was made to the decision of this Court in *Perre v Apand Pty Ltd* (681). Holmes J at trial (682) and McMurdo P and Davies JA in the Queensland Court of Appeal (683) applied considerations identified by various members of this Court in *Perre* as supporting a claim for pure economic loss by the Melchiors. These factors included reliance, vulnerability, control, defendant's knowledge of the risk

(676) eg, *Family Law Act* 1975 (Cth) ss 60B and 66C; *Criminal Code* (Q) ss 286 and 324; *Child Support (Assessment) Act* 1989 (Cth) s 3.
(677) *Melchior* [2001] Aust Torts Reports ¶81–597, 66, 626 [32].
(678) [2002] QB 266, 284 [56] (*Parkinson*).
(679) See also Balkin and Davis, *Law of Torts*, 2nd ed (1996) p 11.
(680) *Rogers* (1992) 175 CLR 479; *Chappel v Hart* (1998) 195 CLR 232; reasons of Hayne J at [190].
(681) (1999) 198 CLR 180 (*Perre*).
(682) *Melchior* [2001] Aust Torts Reports ¶81-597 at 66,631 [61].
(683) *Melchior v Cattanach* [2001] QCA 246 at [44] per McMurdo P; at [98] per Davies JA.

to the plaintiff, avoidance of interference with autonomy and avoidance of indeterminate liability. Thomas JA in dissent in the Queensland Court of Appeal held that he was not satisfied that application of those considerations led to legal liability in this case (684). While I do not consider that the principles in *Perre* are directly applicable to this case, if they were I would have agreed with Holmes J, McMurdo P and Davies JA, and with the reasons of Callinan J (685), that they favoured recovery by Mr and Mrs Melchior. *Perre* concerned a claim by growers of potatoes for economic loss suffered by them when the defendants introduced seed potatoes infected by bacterial wilt to their own growers in the same geographical region. Although neither the plaintiffs' potatoes nor their land were infected or physically damaged, they lost a valuable export market due to an exportation ban on potatoes grown in a 20 kilometre radius of bacterial wilt infection. This was clearly pure economic loss. The plaintiffs' property was not physically damaged. No aspect of their physical integrity was intruded upon. The nature of harm suffered by parents, particularly by a mother, following a failed sterilisation is of an entirely different character. Pregnancy, birth and subsequent obligations for the physical, emotional and financial care of a child into adulthood are in no way like the losses suffered when a potato, although undamaged, can not be exported.

425 The nature of harm in this case can only be properly determined by considering the whole context of Mrs Melchior's claim. When this is done, it becomes even more apparent that it is inappropriate to consider the nature of harm in this case as pure economic loss. As Holmes J noted at the trial of this matter, "there is inevitably a degree of pain, discomfort, and inconvenience associated with any pregnancy and birth" (686). Pregnant women may experience anywhere from minor physical discomfort to significant pain and infirmity. While a pregnancy may bring good health for many pregnant women, for others it may bring nine months of illness and pain. For women aged over 35, the health risks for both mothers and babies escalate (687). The nature of pregnancy and consequent medical investigations and interventions result in significant losses of privacy and direct intrusion on and into a woman's body. For many pregnant women, pregnancy interferes with their ability to continue in paid work at some stage of the pregnancy (688).

426 For all pregnant women, pregnancy impedes their free choice as to their individual actions and pastimes. It intrudes upon their choice to eat what they like and drink what they like, what medications they can take, and in what recreational activities they can engage (689). Pregnancy is tiring. Pregnancy may also bring anxiety, stress and in some women mental illness such as depression. Giving birth is a wonderful moment for many women.

(684) *Melchior v Cattanach* [2001] QCA 246 at [145]–[146], [170]–[174] per Thomas JA.

(685) Reasons of Callinan J at [299]. cf reasons of Gleeson CJ at [28]–[34].

(686) *Melchior* [2001] Aust Torts Reports ¶81–597 at 66, 631 [63].

(687) Australian Bureau of Statistics (ABS), *Australian Social Trends, 2001: Family Formation: Older Mothers*.

(688) *Parkinson* [2002] QB 266, 286 [67] per Hale LJ.

(689) *Parkinson* [2002] QB 266, 286 [67] per Hale LJ.

It can also be very painful, sometimes traumatic and women can take time to recover from birth physically and mentally (690). Some women do not fully recover and their bodies bear scars, physical damage and mental damage for years to come (691). Fortunately, in countries like Australia with good access to prenatal care and medical care, women now rarely die in pregnancy and childbirth. Regrettably, every year in Australia some women do die (692). While pregnancy may be enjoyed and sought by many women, these intrusions into personal autonomy are reasons why women may choose not to undertake an initial or subsequent pregnancy.

427 Pregnancy and birth are however just the start of the journey for parents, particularly mothers, following a negligent sterilisation. Pregnancy and birth cannot be artificially separated from the parental obligations that arise following the birth of a child (693). A child must be raised and parents must physically, emotionally and financially maintain and care for a child. In Australia, mothers still bear the major share of the burden for the physical and emotional care of children and household chores and tasks (694). This responsibility has very significant impacts on women's participation and progress in the workforce and their long-term financial position (695). Where parents' relationships break down, it is mothers who are still predominantly left to raise children (696). Women are also usually the primary carers of family members with a disability (697). Parenthood can be a joyful experience. However, it can bring intensely physical, emotional and financial burdens and sacrifice for parents. Women still bear a disproportionate share of these burdens and sacrifices in Australian families. It is for this reason that women, like Mrs Melchior, may seek to avoid an initial or subsequent pregnancy.

428 The appellants' submission that in cases of the present kind where a woman has sought a sterilisation "the mother's reason may simply reflect a desire to have sexual relations without the possibility of pregnancy, or may reflect a view that the mother does not wish to have children for economic or career reasons, or does not like children" is both an oversimplification and underestimation of what factors may lead women to desire no further pregnancies. The legality and availability of sterilisation and contraception in Australian society signals that Australian society accepts that it is appropriate that men and women decide they do not wish to undertake either the significant benefits or the significant obligations and onerous burdens of parenthood.

(690) *Parkinson* [2002] QB 266, 286 [68] per Hale LJ.
(691) *Parkinson* [2002] QB 266, 286 [68] per Hale LJ.
(692) AIHW, *Report on Maternal Deaths in Australia 1994–1996* (2001). In the years 1994–1996, 100 women died during pregnancy, birth or following birth. "The overall maternal mortality ratio was 13.0 per 100,000 confinements and was the highest reported since 1984" (at p 1).
(693) *Parkinson* [2002] QB 266, 287 [73] per Hale LJ.
(694) ABS, *Australian Social Trends, 2001: Unpaid Work: Time Spent on Unpaid Household Work*.
(695) ABS, *Australian Social Trends, 2001: Income Distribution: Women's Incomes*.
(696) ABS, *Australian Social Trends, 2001: Arrangements: Future Living Arrangements*.
(697) ABS, *Disability, Ageing and Carers, Australia: Summary of Findings* (1998).

429 It was submitted by the appellants in this case, and has been accepted by judges in like cases, that the costs of raising a child should not be recognised as legally compensable harm or damage because it should be assumed by the law that all children are an overwhelming benefit and blessing to their parents and to society (698). This should be rejected on several bases. First, the crux of these claims is not that a child itself as a human being constitutes damage to its parents. Rather, the claim is that the economic costs of raising the child result in financial loss to parents. Second, medical professionals who become defendants in these cases are well aware from the outset that the patient parents do not consider these economic costs of parenthood to be a benefit, because of the express decision of the parents to seek sterilisation. Thirdly, as Holmes J noted at trial "it entails a blunt invasion of the individual decision-maker's value system into legal reasoning" (699). The "blessing" argument in this case also ignores the specific facts of Mrs Melchior's claim, and the evidence accepted at trial. At trial, Mrs Melchior was awarded $103 672.39 in respect of her own loss including $30 000 for her pain and suffering and loss of amenities. That is not in issue in this Court. However, an elaboration of the circumstances of Mrs Melchior's claim serves to demonstrate the absurdity in suggesting the law must recognise that parenthood will be of such a benefit for all women and all parents that no damages should be recoverable in respect of the financial consequences of the upbringing of a child (700). It also ignores that the burdens of parenthood still fall disproportionately on the shoulders of mothers and that Australian law has recognised that it is inappropriate to discriminate on the basis of pregnancy, parental obligations and gender (701).

430 Mrs Melchior was faced with a pregnancy that was not desired and which she had taken active steps to prevent. She was faced with the obligation for the care and financial responsibility for a child, when she had desired to have more time and freedom for herself. It was not an easy pregnancy. Due to her age and the consequent increased risks of pregnancy and foetal abnormality, Mrs Melchior underwent extensive prenatal testing. She experienced the usual symptoms such as back aches, morning sickness and loss of agility during pregnancy. However, due to the circumstances of her pregnancy she also suffered emotionally. She was distressed, angry and depressed during the pregnancy. Mr Melchior gave evidence that she had been frustrated and upset since the pregnancy and this had affected their mutual happiness and sexual relations. She also suffered thrombophlebitis in her right leg. Her delivery of Jordan was via a caesarean section, major abdominal surgery which was exacerbated by the necessity for experts to carry out investigations immediately following Jordan's delivery to determine the cause of the failed sterilisation. In his evidence, Mr Melchior

(698) See reasons of Kirby J at [146]–[148]; reasons of Hayne J at [195]–[198] for discussion of the nature and origins of the "blessings" argument.

(699) *Melchior* [2001] Aust Torts Reports ¶81-597 at 66, 629 [51].

(700) *Melchior* [2001] Aust Torts Reports ¶81-597 at 66, 629[51].

(701) Reasons of Kirby J at [162]; *Sex Discrimination Act* 1984 (Cth); *Anti-discrimination Act* 1991 (Q).

described her as having horrific bruising from her neck to her pelvic area following the caesarean section and abdominal investigation. She later underwent a hysterosalpingogram, a painful and invasive investigatory procedure without sedation or anaesthetic.

431 Following the birth she developed deep venous thrombosis (702). Ten days after Jordan's birth she was readmitted to hospital with a very serious medical condition. A clot affected the deep veins of her left leg. Part of this clot became a pulmonary embolism; the clot travelled to her lungs and obstructed blood flow in the pulmonary arteries. This required her to take the medication Warfarin and undertake on-going blood testing. In March 2000 she was also diagnosed as suffering from incompetence of the saphenofemoral junction and the entire long saphenous vein from the groin to upper calf. This condition causes Mrs Melchior significant discomfort and swelling in the leg. As is not uncommon, Mrs Melchior also suffered depression following the birth which lasted for at least twelve to eighteen months with subsequent continuing vulnerability.

432 In the years following Jordan's birth, Mrs Melchior has had the primary responsibility for Jordan's care and will continue to have this responsibility. Due to her on-going health issues, Mr Melchior and the couple's two older daughters have also had to assist. At a stage in her life when she had wished to have more time for her own plans and activities, she was unable to do so due to childcare responsibilities for a small child. She experienced difficulties in physically keeping up with and managing an active toddler. Her housework load increased. She was unable to continue with social and physical activities she had enjoyed prior to her pregnancy. Due to on-going financial stress as a result of healthcare costs and the maintenance of Jordan, the family were unable to send their daughters to the private school they had selected. At the time of trial, Jordan was attending childcare for six hours one day a week which gave Mrs Melchior a small respite. This was all the family could afford at that time. While she loved her son, Mrs Melchior's own ability to live a life of her choice was severely curtailed. One cannot help but reflect that it is easy for some judges who have not been a primary carer of small children on a daily and on-going basis to make assumptions that the law should recognise blessings and benefits but ignore burdens and obligations. They have not experienced restrictions on their own autonomy, life choices, career or financial security, particularly in circumstances where those restrictions were not by choice. It is true that society as a whole benefits from the birth of children, and the raising of healthy and happy children. However, the price of that "benefit" is not equally paid by all members of society. It is paid by parents, and is disproportionately still paid by mothers.

The normal compensatory principles of negligence

433 The appellant conceded that "it was possible to say the negligence of the medical practitioner has resulted in the event which the procedure in

(702) *Melchior* [2001] Aust Torts Reports ¶81–597 at 66,632 [69].

question was intended to prevent namely pregnancy and birth of a child." The appellant also conceded that it was "reasonably foreseeable that one of the consequences of the negligence of the medical practitioner will be that there will be expenses likely to be incurred as costs of child rearing" and that if otherwise recoverable as damage such amounts could be calculated readily enough. The existence of duty, breach, causation and the calculability of damages were not in issue in this appeal. As Lord Steyn noted in *McFarlane*, on the normal compensatory principles of negligence, the consequential economic loss of raising a child born following a failed sterilisation would be recoverable as clearly foreseeable damage, unless there were some other basis upon which the law should reject the claim (703). The only basis upon which the appellant argues that the claim for damages for the upbringing of Jordan should fail is because the law should not recognise the claim for the costs of Jordan's upbringing as "damage". I explicitly reject the submissions of the Attorney General for South Australia intervening that the decision of a parent to keep a child rather than adopt it out, or not to terminate a pregnancy, should be said to be acceptance that the child was of such substantial benefit that damages should be reduced or offset. I also reject any argument that such decisions could be said to be a failure to mitigate or to break the chain of causation. To uphold such arguments would be to wrongfully characterise the plaintiffs' actions as borne of free will, and would deny their autonomy to make their own individual decisions in light of the appellants' negligence. This argument was not accepted by the House of Lords in *McFarlane* (704). It should not be accepted by this Court.

434 The appellants submitted that a finding that there was a legal harm or wrong had major policy and social consequences including the extension of liability to other categories of claim such as failed abortions and defective contraception, claims by mothers for lost income or career opportunities, and claims by other family members. The appellants also argued claims could be large in ambit. Extension of the entitlement to damages was said to extend the ambit of liability of medical practitioners and have potential impacts on medical insurance, availability of medical services, medical fees and the Medicare levy. The appellants submitted that there were also a range of policy and social reasons for rejection of liability in this area including that children should be recognised as innate benefits to both their parents and society more broadly, the protection of children from psychological damage caused by the knowledge they were initially unwanted or the subject of litigation, and the prevention of shifting of the burden of loss to medical practitioners and hospitals. These submissions were supported by the submissions of the Attorneys-General for South Australia and Western Australia (intervening).

(703) [2000] 2 AC 59 at 82. See also reasons of McHugh and Gummow JJ at [51]; reasons of Kirby J at [179]. See also *Nominal Defendant v Gardikiotos* (1996) 186 CLR 49 at 54.

(704) [2000] 2 AC 59 at 74 per Lord Slynn; at 81 per Lord Steyn; at 97 per Lord Hope; at 104 per Lord Clyde; at 112-113 per Lord Millett.

The role of public policy in the denial of compensation

435 This Court has recently considered the role of policy concerns in the determination of duty of care in *Sullivan v Moody* (705). In that case, the Court expressly rejected the three-stage approach of Lord Bridge of Harwich in *Caparo Industries Plc v Dickman* (706), requiring at its last stage a determination of what is considered fair, just and reasonable (707):

> "The question as to what is fair, and just and reasonable is capable of being misunderstood as an invitation to formulate policy rather than to search for principle. The concept of policy, in this context, is often ill-defined. There are policies at work in the law which can be identified and applied to novel problems, but the law of tort develops by reference to principles, which must be capable of general application, not discretionary decision-making in individual cases."

436 The Court also acknowledged in *Sullivan* that (708):

> "Developments in the law of negligence over the last 30 or more years reveal the difficulty of identifying unifying principles that would allow ready solution of novel problems. Nonetheless, that does not mean that novel cases are to be decided by reference only to some intuitive sense of what is 'fair' or 'unfair'."

437 While these comments were made in the context of the proper approach to determination of duty of care, they are equally applicable to the consideration of what constitutes legally compensable "damage". The development of the Australian common law, including tort law, has to some extent been influenced by policy concerns (709). However, the recent comments of this Court serve as a warning that where "policy" concerns are based only on judicial intuition, personal judicial values or judicial suppositions about what "ordinary people" on common modes of public transport (710) might consider appropriate, they should be given little or no weight. They should particularly be given little or no weight when they result in an effective immunity for a defendant who would be otherwise liable pursuant to the normal compensatory principles of negligence. In *McFarlane* the House of Lords rejected a claim for the costs of raising a child. Despite disavowal by their Lordships that their judgments were based on public policy grounds (711), it is clear to me that unsupported "policy" concerns lay at the heart of the respective judgments although disguised with varying labels such as distributive justice (712), fairness, justice and reasonableness (713) and "legal" policy (714). Given

(705) (2001) 207 CLR 562 (*Sullivan*).
(706) [1990] 2 AC 605 at 617–618.
(707) *Sullivan* (2001) 207 CLR 562, at 579 [43].
(708) (2001) 207 CLR 562, at 580 [53].
(709) Reasons of McHugh and Gummow JJ at [54], [65]; reasons of Hayne J at [223]–[242].
(710) [2000] 2 AC 59 at 82 per Lord Steyn cf *Parkinson* [2002] QB 266, at 290 [82] per Hale LJ.
(711) *McFarlane* [2000] 2 AC 59 at 76, per Lord Slynn; at 82-83 per Lord Steyn; at 95, per Lord Hope; at 100, per Lord Clyde; at 108, per Lord Millett.
(712) *McFarlane* [2000] 2 AC 59 at 82 per Lord Steyn.
(713) *McFarlane* [2000] 2 AC 59 at 94–92 per Lord Hope; at 105 per Lord Clyde.
(714) *Rees v Darlington Memorial Hospital NHS Trust* [2003] QB 20 at [13] per Hale LJ.

this, I do not find their Lordships' reasoning in *McFarlane*, to the extent that it ultimately rejected the plaintiffs' claim in that case, persuasive and would not follow it in this case.

438 I agree with Kirby J that despite what this Court said in *Sullivan*, it is clear that policy concerns are reflected in the judgments of other members of the Court in this case (715). It is preferable that when judicial reasoning rests on policy grounds, that those policy grounds are expressly articulated so that they might be open to scrutiny by the parties and by the public (716). However, it is clear following *Sullivan* that it is undesirable that judgments are based on social or public policy concerns which have no basis other than speculation, individual judicial discretion, or intuition. Where policy concerns are utilised in judicial reasoning in negligence cases, particularly when they are utilised to deny recovery contrary to the normal principles of negligence, it is desirable that they be based either on enduring "legal" concerns supported by precedent, for example coherency of the law or protection of bodily integrity, or on evidence ideally based on empirical research (717). Where intuitive or "common sense" public or social policy grounds or assumptions are relied upon to reject claims, outcomes can seem arbitrary and based on judges' own value systems. In addition, it is essential that unsupported social policy concerns and judicial intuitions in relation to "fairness" do not outweigh or override enduring legal concerns which lie at the heart of negligence law, such as protection of bodily integrity, autonomy and coherence of the law (718).

439 The dangers of over-reliance on unsupported social policy concerns can be seen in the "harm the child" argument. This argument suggests that children will be psychologically harmed by the knowledge that their parents have litigated to recover costs associated with their upbringing (719). It was articulated by Meagher JA in *CES v Superclinics (Australia) Pty Ltd*, in apparent reliance on intuitive assumptions about what constitutes good mothering and the propensity of women to maliciously gossip (720):

> "For all I know the child was in court to witness her mother's rejection of her. Perhaps, on the other hand, the plaintiff had the taste to keep her child out of court. Even if that be so, it does not mean the unfortunate infant will never know that her mother has publicly declared her to be unwanted. When she is at school some [âme] charitable – perhaps the mother of one of her 'friends' – can be trusted to direct her attention to the point. That a court of law should sanction such an action seems to me improper to the point of obscenity."

440 There was no empirical or expert evidence either admitted at trial in this matter, for example by a child psychologist, or submitted to this Court, for example peer reviewed empirical studies, in support of this "harm the child" argument. Even if it was accepted that there is some possibility of

(715) Reasons of Kirby J at [121].
(716) Reasons of Kirby J at [152]; reasons of Callinan J at [291].
(717) Reasons of Kirby J at [152].
(718) *Sullivan* (2001) 207 CLR 562.
(719) Reasons of Heydon J at [372]–[389]; reasons of Hayne J at [202]–[204].
(720) (1995) 38 NSWLR 47 at 86. The father of the child was also a plaintiff in this case.

harm to children as a result of litigation, it is not unusual that court proceedings in Australia in the spirit of open justice (721) involve the airing of private and potentially hurtful information concerning children and their families. This is an everyday occurrence across Australia in Family Court cases and in child protection cases. In those jurisdictions the legislature has not determined that because children may hear potentially private or hurtful information, cases simply cannot be brought and parties' legal rights should be restricted. Rather, other measures are taken such as the restriction on reporting the identity of parties to the proceedings or parties associated with or subject to the proceedings, restriction on publication of particular sensitive proceedings concerning children, and exclusion of non-interested parties from the court room (722). It would accordingly be incoherent and inconsistent to restrict parties' right of action in this case based on unproven arguments about possible harm to children (723).

441 Even if I were entitled to rely on unproven and speculative social or public policy arguments to allow the appeal in this case, I am unconvinced by any of the policy grounds advanced by the appellant or the interveners. I do not consider that there are therefore any grounds to disallow the Melchiors' recovery of the costs of raising their son Jordan.

Set-off

442 The alternative ground of appeal of the appellants was that if this Court were to allow an award of damages for the financial damage suffered by Mr and Mrs Melchior, the emotional and other benefits received by Mr and Mrs Melchior as a result of the birth of Jordan should be set-off against those damages. For the reasons given by McHugh and Gummow JJ (724) and Kirby J (725) there should be no such set-off.

Conclusion

443 For the reasons stated above, this appeal should be dismissed with costs.

(721) *Scott v Scott* (1913) AC 417; *Russell v Russell* (1976) 134 CLR 495 at 520 per Gibbs J; at 532 per Stephens J.

(722) See, eg, *Family Law Act* 1975 (Cth) s 121; *Child Protection Act* 1999 (Q) ss 192–194; *Childrens Court Act* 1992 (Q) s 20.

(723) Reasons of McHugh and Gummow JJ at [79]–[80]; reasons of Kirby J at [145].

(724) Reasons of McHugh and Kirby JJ at [84]–[91].

(725) Reasons of Kirby J at [173]–[175].

Consumer Protection

11

Unconscionability, Education and Indigenous Women: *ACCC v Keshow*

BRONWYN NAYLOR

Background Context

Australian Competition and Consumer Commission v Keshow[1] deals with unscrupulous financial transactions with Indigenous women from communities in remote areas of Australia. The case can be seen as a 'textbook' example of unconscionable conduct.

The *Trade Practices Act 1974* (Cth) (TPA), concerned in part with consumer protection, was amended in the late 1990s to address unconscionable conduct.[2] The vulnerability of particular groups to predatory financial agreements was at this time also gaining greater attention in a range of contexts.[3] Consumer protection, particularly in relation to Aboriginal and Torres Strait Islander communities, was being enforced by the Trade Practices Commission, and then by its successor the Australian Competition and Consumer Commission (ACCC), using the TPA provisions.[4] The National Indigenous Consumer Strategy Plan was launched in 2005 to 'improve consumer outcomes for Indigenous people' by improving Indigenous consumers' knowledge of their rights as consumers, improving the behaviour of traders and reducing detriment experienced by Indigenous consumers.[5] *ACCC v Keshow* sits in the intersection of these developments.

[1] [2005] FCA 588 (5 May 2005) ('*Keshow*').

[2] *Trade Practices Act 1974* (Cth) ss 51AA–51AC. These provisions were added to the TPA, which already prohibited conduct that is misleading or deceptive, or likely to be misleading or deceptive (s 52). The TPA has now been repealed and replaced by the *Australian Consumer Law*, scheduled to the *Competition and Consumer Act 2010* (Cth). However, the current Act retains the same specific prohibition of misleading or deceptive conduct (s 18) and unconscionable conduct (ss 20–22).

[3] For example, with the rapid expansion of technology, behaviours in breach of the TPA were commonplace in the marketing of mobile phone and internet contracts: see Chris Atmore, Derek Wilding and Elizabeth Beal, *Not So Special: Telecommunications Contracts, Disability and Unfair Practices* (Communications Law Centre, 2006).

[4] Allan Fels, '*Storecharter* and Indigenous Consumer Protection Issues' (Paper presented at Indigenous Consumer Protection Workshop, Alice Springs, 22 April 2002); Jon C Altman, S McDonnell and Sally Ward, 'Indigenous Australians and Competition and Consumer Issues: A Review of the Literature and an Annotated Bibliography' (Working Paper 12, Australian National University Centre for Aboriginal Economic Policy Research, 2002); Heron Loban, 'Unconscionable Conduct and Aboriginal and Torres Strait Islander Consumers' (Research Report, Indigenous Consumer Assistance Network Ltd, 2010).

[5] Ministerial Council on Consumer Affairs, *Taking Action, Gaining Trust: A National Indigenous Consumer Strategy Action Plan 2010–2013* (2010) 2.

The Facts of the Case

The case arose in relation to agreements entered into by Ramon Lal Keshow with eight Indigenous women to supply children's educational materials and household goods.[6] The specific facts – which were uncontested at the hearing – were that Keshow entered three Aboriginal communities outside Alice Springs, all communities requiring permission from the community council for entry, which he did not obtain. He approached the eight complainants in the case uninvited. Each woman had one or more children, and Keshow offered to provide them with educational materials, for which the women signed authorities for periodic deductions from their bank accounts. All but one spoke little or no English and all had limited or no English literacy skills. This activity occurred between 1998 and 2003, and in some cases, Keshow returned and entered into further financial arrangements with some of the women. Keshow had made similar arrangements with a total of 114 people in the Northern Territory, and many others in other States, during that period.

All eight women gave evidence at the hearing. The approaches to each of the eight women were discussed in detail in the judgment. Common patterns were: unsolicited visits to each woman at her home, offering educational materials 'that would help her children' without any inquiry about the ages of the children, asking the woman to sign a form to pay for the materials, and failing to leave any personal or business information about the transaction or about making contact with him. All the women were in receipt of benefits through Centrelink. Some women received some materials; others received nothing, or were given unrequested goods such as televisions and tape recorders (some of which did not work). Deductions in the thousands of dollars were made from most of the women's accounts, the largest sum being $10,400, and all amounts were greater than might have been the value of the materials provided (if any).

The women ultimately had the payments stopped. In some cases the police had been contacted, and in other cases the women themselves had the payments stopped.

The Decision of the Federal Court

The case was brought by the ACCC alleging misleading or deceptive conduct and unconscionable conduct by Keshow contrary to provisions of the TPA.

'Unconscionability' is an equitable concept defined in the Australian context by the High Court in *Commercial Bank of Australia v Amadio* as requiring proof of three elements.[7] These are the existence of a special disability or disadvantage (which affected the victim's capacity to conserve their interests); the existence of inequality between the parties; and the notion of the defendant 'taking advantage of' the disability (including the idea that the defendant had knowledge of the circumstances of disadvantage).

[6] The case also concerns Mr Keshow's other transactions with Indigenous consumers in the Northern Territory during 1998, in which he was also found to have engaged in conduct that was unconscionable under the TPA.

[7] (1983) 151 CLR 447.

'Unconscionability' is not defined in s 51AB of the TPA, but is recognised as going beyond the equitable doctrine. Section 51AB states that a corporation shall not 'engage in conduct that is, in all the circumstances, unconscionable', and lists factors that a court can consider when determining whether behaviour is unconscionable, including:

- 'the relative strengths of the bargaining positions' (s 51AB(2)(a));
- whether the consumer was 'required to comply with conditions that were not reasonably necessary for the protection of the legitimate interests of the corporation' (s 51AB(2)(b));
- 'whether the consumer was able to understand [the] documents' (s 51AB(2)(c)); and
- 'whether any undue influence or pressure was exerted on, or any unfair tactics were used against' the consumer (s 51AB(2)(d)).

In *Keshow*, Mansfield J adopted the 'ordinary meaning' of unconscionability as 'showing no regard for conscience, irreconcilable with what is right or reasonable'.[8] As discussed below, in her feminist judgment, Heron Loban specifically considers Keshow's conduct with reference to the factors above, and finds that all indicia were fulfilled. Mansfield J found that Keshow's conduct in respect of his dealings with each woman had breached these provisions of the TPA. The Court issued injunctions restraining Keshow for a period of three years from entering specific Indigenous communities for the purpose of selling goods or services, from using periodical payment forms or bank deduction authorities anywhere in Australia without providing specified disclosures, and requiring that he attend a trade practices compliance seminar. The feminist judgment of Loban, as an additional judgment to Mansfield J's, agrees with these conclusions and orders, but takes a different approach to the determination of the issues.

Making the Assessment of Unconscionability

The ACCC provided an anthropologist expert witness to speak to 'socio-economic, cultural, gender [and] age factors' relevant both to the individual consumers and also the group, their communities, and Indigenous consumers in remote Northern Territory communities generally. The expert witness gave evidence that 'each of the complainants as young Aboriginal women for cultural reasons would not directly question the respondent to elicit information from him.'[9] He highlighted 'the reticence of individual Aboriginal consumers in their dealings with older, non-familiar, non-Aboriginal males', and the preference not to respond 'especially but not only when dealing with strangers [as] a common mechanism to avoid difficult or embarrassing questions amongst Aboriginal people in remote or traditionally-oriented communities'.[10] These factors were considered by the witness to 'place Aboriginal people from these regions generally, and Aboriginal women in particular, at a significantly increased risk in commercial dealings such as those initiated by . . . Keshow.'[11]

[8] *Keshow* [2005] FCA 588 [97] citing *Australian Competition and Consumer Commission v Samton Holdings Pty Ltd* (2002) 117 FCR 301 [44].

[9] Ibid [85].

[10] Ibid [86].

[11] Ibid.

The Court considered that it was apparent – even without the expert evidence – that the individual women had 'limited commercial sophistication', and lacked English language skills 'to deal in an informed way with a commercial transaction, even a relatively simple one'.[12] Importantly, to indicate Keshow's awareness of their vulnerability, Mansfield J observed that the respondent would have seen that they were 'diffident and shy people' who would not have engaged in a conversation with him 'which might have exhibited any particular interest in what he was offering to sell or the normal interest or awareness of a consumer about matters such as cost or delivery, or the terms of the periodical payment forms.'[13] Mansfield J made it clear, however, that he found the conduct to have been unconscionable without reference to the broader cultural factors mentioned, and 'without attributing to the respondent an understanding of those cultural factors.'[14] He concluded that Keshow knew he had been overpaid, knew that he had not provided the goods agreed, and did not make efforts to remedy these problems, but used the funds as his own. In particular, he referred to the imbalance in educational and commercial literacy (showing disadvantage and inequality), and the fact that it was clear that the respondent had 'taken advantage': Keshow clearly understood the nature of the transactions and the matters about which 'a consumer with normal commercial acumen might inquire', but which these consumers did not.

The Significance of the Decision

The case is significant for the approach taken to the Indigenous context of the transactions. The Court gave specific consideration to the views of the relevant land councils, in support of injunctions addressed to excluding the respondent from a range of Indigenous communities. At the same time, the Court expressed concern to avoid the appearance of labelling Aboriginal people as, by definition, vulnerable consumers. Whilst accepting that the land councils supported a general injunction, Mansfield J denied any more general assumption of incompetence, saying: '[t]here are no doubt persons within those communities who could capably negotiate with the respondent'.[15]

After the decision of the Federal Court in *Keshow*, the ACCC ensured that the case was publicised as part of its mandate as a consumer protection agency. It issued press releases and used the fact situation as a warning story in publications aimed at the business community.[16] The fact situation was also publicised in the course of the investigation by Indigenous groups, warning communities of an 'Indian man and wife' who targeted women with children and whose 'mode of operation is to approach young women with children outside their homes'.[17]

[12] Ibid [84].

[13] Ibid.

[14] Ibid [87].

[15] Ibid [115].

[16] For instance, ACCC, *Business Snapshot – Don't Take Advantage of Disadvantage*, ACCC 03/11_44164_217, (2011).

[17] Paddy Stephenson, 'Message: AN ABORIGINAL WARNING!' on ACT Indigenous Network, *Yahoo Groups* (24 July 2005) <https://groups.yahoo.com/neo/groups/actindnetwork/conversations/topics/7351>.

The Feminist Judgment

Heron Loban's judgment is that of an Indigenous judge sitting with Mansfield J hearing and deciding the case. This is not the usual approach to hearing trials in the Federal Court under the *Federal Court Act of Australia 1976* (Cth). However, this small, imagined procedural adjustment allows Loban space to identify additional grounds for finding breaches of the TPA by closely attending to the women's stories.

The feminist judgment places the complainants at the centre, first as Indigenous women with specific cultural and language backgrounds, and second, by quoting their evidence to demonstrate the frustration and pressure they experienced in the transactions. On this basis, Loban highlights the value placed on education by the complainants. This made them more susceptible to the respondent's proposals, not only to purchase educational products, but to do so using an open-ended payment method. The educational priorities and values of the complainants were clearly relied on by the respondent when he approached them. It is rare for Indigenous women to appear as plaintiffs in civil cases, as opposed to victims of crime. The feminist judgment emphasises the determination of the complainants to challenge the unconscionable actions of the respondent.

AUSTRALIAN COMPETITION AND CONSUMER COMMISSION v RAMON LAL KESHOW
[2005] FCA 558

Mansfield and Loban JJ

Northern Territory District Registry

5 May 2005

LOBAN J

121 I sit in this case as an Indigenous judge in accordance with the practice of this court. In matters where Indigenous parties are involved the bench must include an Indigenous judge. Ingrid White, Roseanne Dixon, Deanne Williams, Louanne Patterson, Marlene Doolan, Rosina Dickson, Fiona Turner and Muriel Palmer (the 'complainants') are all Aboriginal women.

122 I agree with Mansfield J's detailed statement of the facts of the case. I further agree with his findings that the respondent, Ramon Lal Keshow, engaged in misleading and deceptive conduct and unconscionable conduct under the *Trade Practices Act 1974* (Cth) (TP Act). However, I have reached the conclusion of unconscionable conduct by Mr Keshow on some differing bases to Mansfield J.

123 The applicant in this matter alleges conduct by the respondent in contravention of the TP Act in respect of eight Aboriginal women resident in Aboriginal communities in remote central Australia. It further alleges that this conduct extended beyond those eight individuals to other people living in Aboriginal communities in the Northern Territory.

124 Between September 1998 and May 2003 the respondent is alleged to have engaged in misleading, deceptive and unconscionable conduct contrary to s 51AB in respect of the complainants, or alternatively s 51AA in respect of his conduct in dealing with people living in Aboriginal communities, and s 52 of the TP Act.

125 The proceedings were commenced with an application and statement of claim outlining the respondent's businesses, his dealings with the complainants and with Aboriginal communities more generally throughout the Northern Territory. These documents seek to outline characteristics of the Aboriginal communities in which the complainants lived and which are relevant to the circumstances of the dealings.

126 A defence was filed by the respondent. It set out a number of factual assertions. It did not address the allegations set out in the statement of claim or amended statement of claim in a methodical way. The respondent asserted in his defence that he treated the complainants and his other 'Indigenous customers' the same as any other customer. A number of assertions were made by the respondent about his educational materials.

127 The respondent acknowledged receipt of overpayments from the complainants.

128 Each of the complainants gave evidence. The transcript of an interview between the applicant and the respondent was tendered, as were bank records of the complainants together with an analysis of those records. A social anthropologist, Dr David Martin, gave evidence about the characteristics of remote Aboriginal communities and Aboriginal people who live in such communities. In the course of the proceedings I visited the communities where the women lived.

129 The circumstances in which expert evidence is admissible in such cases were considered in *Australian Competition and Consumer Commission v Lux Corporation* [2004] FCA 926 at [98] (*Lux*). I accept the expert witness as qualified to give evidence. However, I have not found the opinion of the expert witness essential in coming to my decision.

130 The evidence presented by the applicant at hearing was ultimately uncontested and as such there is no need to deal with all the evidence or opposing arguments.

Findings

The Respondent

131 The respondent is 63 years old and a trained teacher. He is not Aboriginal. He has been retired from classroom teaching for a number of years. In 1993 he formulated the idea of selling educational materials which he began to develop. In 1998 he registered two business names 'National Maths Academy' (NMA) and 'Drysdale Correspondence Schools' (DCS) as the sole registered proprietor of both. In 2002 he registered in his wife's name 'Easy Buying Services' (EBS), a business to provide household goods on layby. The respondent was principally responsible for the operations of EBS despite its registration in his wife's name. I conclude that all three businesses were within the scope of the respondent's authority.

132 The respondent estimated the cost of the educational materials offered by NMA was up to about $340. He charged $740 which included the cost of freight. Eight modules in total were offered as part of the NMA package. The modules were basic. They were not prepared for any particular age level. There was no evidence the materials were culturally appropriate or specifically developed for Indigenous families. In respect of DCS there is no evidence of the nature of its business or the educational materials it sought to sell. In respect of EBS there is no evidence of a proper business plan or detailed records of its transactions.

133 In about September 1998, the respondent, as part of his business, began entering remote Aboriginal communities in the Northern Territory to sell his educational materials through NMA. He also received orders for unspecified goods through DCS and for household goods through EBS.

Dealings with the Complainants

134 Ingrid White is an Aboriginal woman. She speaks Warlpiri and English. In about September 1998 the respondent approached Ms White at Little Sisters Camp in Alice Springs.

135 Roseanne Dixon is an Aboriginal woman. English is her first language and she speaks mainly English at home at Amoonguna. She can read and write English "a bit". In about September 1998 the respondent visited Ms Dixon at Santa Teresa.

136 Deanne Williams is an Aboriginal woman. She speaks Arrernte and English. She learned to speak English at school. Ms Williams can read and write some English. In about September 1998 the respondent visited Ms Williams at Santa Teresa.

137 Louanne Patterson is an Aboriginal woman. She speaks Amatjerra, Arrernte, Warlpiri and English. She can read and write some English. In about 1998 the respondent visited Ms Patterson at Amoonguna.

138 Marlene Doolan is an Aboriginal woman. She speaks Arrernte and English. In about 1998 the respondent visited Ms Doolan at Amoonguna.

139 Rosina Dickson is an Aboriginal woman. She speaks English as her only language. She can read and write some English. In about August 2000 the respondent visited Ms Dickson at Amoonguna.

140 Fiona Turner is an Aboriginal woman. She speaks Arrernte and English. She learned to speak English at school. Ms Turner was visited by the respondent at Santa Teresa about 15 May 2003.

141 Muriel Palmer is an Aboriginal woman. She speaks Arrernte and English. About 21 May 2003 the respondent visited Ms Palmer at Amoonguna.

142 The complainants were all residents of Aboriginal communities located near Alice Springs. Each of these was a closed community that required visitors to obtain permission from the community council in writing, or in the case of Amoonguna, permission granted in person at the council office. The respondent failed to obtain the necessary permission for any of his visits.

143 In respect of each of the complainants, the respondent attended upon them in their communities uninvited. In his interview with the applicant, he acknowledged that he was aware that most if not all of the complainants were on Centrelink benefits. I find that the respondent would have known that between $40-$60 each fortnight would take a significant portion of that person's income. He asked all of the complainants to sign an open-ended periodic payment form. I accept their evidence that none of the complainants read the form and that the respondent did not read its contents to them. I find that the complainants did not understand the details of the open-ended periodic payment form or what it authorised. None of the complainants were given a copy of a written contract, a copy of the payment form or invoices. There was no information given to them about the cost of the goods to be supplied.

144 The supply of educational materials and other goods to the complainants was haphazard. It ranged from one complainant who received no goods

whatsoever through to several receiving goods that were not sought and in one case an item that did not work. In respect of goods provided under the NMA, no assessment was made by the respondent as to the appropriateness of the educational materials for the ages of any of the children of the complainants. I also find that in most cases the evidence points to a lack of intention to supply goods or services promised.

145 The respondent's customers were based in the Northern Territory and Western Australia. He primarily promoted his businesses through rural towns and remote Aboriginal communities such that approximately 80 per cent of his customers were Aboriginal people. Living in remote Aboriginal communities the complainants would have had limited exposure to individuals such as the respondent selling goods and services.

Consideration

146 The applicant has sought declarations that the conduct of the respondent contravened s 51AB, or in the alternative s 51AA, of the TP Act and s 52 of that Act.

147 The respondent's conduct was within the meaning of trade and commerce and in connection with the supply or possible supply of goods to a person, and clearly falls within the scope of the Act.

148 The meaning of "unconscionable" is not defined in the TP Act. It has however been explained in a number of cases. In *Lux* [2004] FCA 926, French J said (at [98]):

> "It will be relevant whether advantage is taken of an innocent party who, though not deprived of an independent and voluntary will, is unable to make a worthwhile judgement as to what is in his or her best interests: *Commercial Bank of Australia v Amadio* (1983) 151 CLR 447 at 461 (*Amadio*)".

149 Section 51AB, which is not confined to this common law definition, provides instruction to the court as to what it ought to look to in determining whether there has been unconscionable conduct. For a breach to have occurred not all indicia need be met. The indicia are there to act as a guide to indicate whether unconscionable conduct has occurred. I find that the facts of this case satisfy *every* indicia of this section. The circumstances of particular relevance to my findings of the unconscionable nature of the respondent's dealings with each of the complainants are: 1) the offer being one of educational benefit; 2) the open-ended nature of the agreement; 3) Aboriginal languages as a first language; 4) the experience of pressure, referred to by the Aboriginal women as 'humbugging'; and 5) the availability of comparable goods elsewhere at a significantly cheaper price.

Offering educational benefit

150 Education holds a great value within Australian society. It is important not only because it is the means by which much knowledge is shared and gained but because it provides for opportunities to work and to have a livelihood. Paragraph (a) of s 51AB looks to "the relative strengths of the bargaining positions of the corporation and the consumer". For the

complainants, the educational benefit being offered by the respondent greatly affected their bargaining position, as I will explain.

151 The circumstances that contribute to the relative strengths of the bargaining positions of the corporation compared to the consumer are not defined in the TP Act. However, circumstances to which the court has referred in respect of unconscionable conduct in this regard are: unfamiliarity with English (*Amadio* (1983) 151 CLR 447), "poverty or need of any kind . . . age, sex . . . or other circumstances affect his [or her] ability to conserve his [or her] own interests, and the other party unconscientiously takes advantage of the opportunity thus placed in his [or her] hands" (*Blomley* (1956) 99 CLR 362 at 415).

152 A key circumstance which affected the bargaining position of the complainants was the nature of the goods being offered. The complainants were being shown educational materials and making decisions about the education of their children. Living, as they did, in remote Australia meant that public education services and facilities existed at a basic level. The complainants were not in circumstances where a range of educational materials were readily available. Their desire for a good education for their children in circumstances where choices and opportunities were limited placed them in a particular position of vulnerability when dealing with the respondent.

153 Marlene Doolan, Deanne Williams, Louanne Patterson, Ingrid White and Roseanne Dixon each signed an open-ended periodic payment form and cited the same reason for doing so – to help their children's education. Marlene Doolan recalled the respondent:

> ". . . introduced himself to me and told me that he was from a place where they give comunities and people who live in the bush education tools so their kids can learn properly. . . . He told me that it would help my kids to read and write numbers when they go to school. . . . I thought he was from the education in the government. . . . I signed the form because I thought it would help my kids to learn at home before they went to school".

Deanne Williams recalled that:

> "Mr Keshow told me that his name was Raymond and that he was from the National Maths Academy. He showed me a folder with books and tapes in it and said they were for children for learning. I thought he was a teacher or from a school because he had folders with him. . . . I'm not sure now why I signed the form. I just thought it would be a good thing to do".

Louanne Patterson recounted her dealings with the respondent as follows:

> "The man showed me a white folder which had some kids' tapes inside it about songs and maths. . . . The man told me that the folder was for my kids to help them learn maths and songs, and that they would learn much quicker. I thought that the folder looked good because I had not seen anything like it before. I thought it would be good for [my daughter] to help her learn".

Ingrid White similarly recalled that "Mr Keshow told me that the folder would be good for my kids and that it would help them with learning. . . . I signed the form because I thought the folders would be good for my kids for learning". Roseanne Dixon stated: "He said it was for my children for learning and that he could give me the files. . . . I signed that form because I thought it would be good for my kids to get some books and tapes".

154 I do not suggest that businesses should be prevented or dissuaded from marketing or selling their products to people living in remote Aboriginal communities. But, there is a balance to be struck between the opportunity to buy goods and services and the protective values of the regulatory framework. The purpose of the TP Act is to ensure that those businesses that do seek the custom of people living in remote Aboriginal communities act in accordance with community standards, enshrined in law, such as acting in good faith, with honesty and fairness.

155 In my opinion the respondent would have been aware of the poor level of educational services and resources available to people living in remote Aboriginal communities throughout the Northern Territory. I think this is apparent in his decision to actively sell educational materials of the type he did – a folder with tapes and books for use at home – to people living in remote Aboriginal communities. His knowledge of the limited educational facilities in the communities and the complainants' natural desire to provide the best for their children put the complainants at an overwhelming disadvantage in their dealings with the respondent. It created circumstances whereby the complainants' hopes as parents wanting the best for their children and their limited access to education services vastly impaired their ability to protect their own interests and greatly impacted on their interactions with the respondent.

Open-ended nature of agreement

156 The use of open-ended periodic payments as the means of securing payment from the complainants was excessive. Paragraph (b) of s 51AB looks to "conditions that were not reasonably necessary for the protection of the legitimate interests of the corporation". The respondent caused open-ended periodic payment forms to be signed by each of the complainants. I find that such payments were not reasonably necessary for the protection of his legitimate interests because they did not correspond with the cost of the goods or services to be supplied. The payments received from the open-ended periodic payments resulted in the respondent receiving far in excess of the value of the agreed goods from a number of the complainants. There was no attempt to specify an end date for payments or to calculate, or inform his customers of, the worth of the goods supplied. Compounding this was the limited access the complainants had to banks and banking services to query their statements, stop the payments or review their authorisation; this fact would have been evident to the respondent on his visits.

Aboriginal languages spoken by complainants

157 Understanding documentation provided as part of any consumer transaction is fundamental. All but two of the complainants spoke an Aboriginal language as their first language. Paragraph (c) considers "whether the consumer was able to understand any documents". Only one complainant, Rosina Dickson, spoke English only. In her evidence she stated that "I can read and write in English a little bit". Whilst the complainants provided

evidence of being able to speak some English it is not clear which dialect. On the basis of my observation of the complainants when they gave evidence, I concluded that the complainants' use of English may well be different from that of the wider Australian community.

158 The respondent would have been aware that the residents of the remote Aboriginal communities he visited in the Northern Territory to sell his goods in all likelihood spoke the Aboriginal language of their community as their first language. None of the complainants filled out the open-ended periodic payment form. He did this. The form was written in Standard Australian English. No interpreter was present or made available to the complainants. The respondent did not read the form out to them. He did not encourage them to read it before signing. The respondent's accent made it even more difficult for at least one of the women to understand him. Louanne Patterson recalled "a man coming to Rosina's house at Amoonguna in about 1998. He wasn't an Aboriginal man . . . He spoke English but it was in a funny way. It was hard to understand him".

159 This, of course, is not to say that any person who has an Aboriginal language (or any other non-English language) as their first language cannot contract. The complainants no doubt enter into contracts regularly that do not involve unconscionable conduct. However, there must be some expectation that businesses, when dealing with a person for whom English is a second, third or fourth language, can satisfy themselves that there is a reasonable understanding of the terms of the agreement, particularly where that agreement involves such terms as an open-ended periodic payment plan.

160 The cumulative evidence of the complainants leaves me satisfied that none of the complainants sufficiently understood the open-ended periodic payment form or the full nature of the transactions entered into by them.

The experience of pressure or "humbugging"

161 Humbugging is an unflattering term that relates to demanding or pressuring behaviour mainly in relation to money. The term "humbugging" was used by the complainants in their descriptions of the respondent. Paragraph (d) of s 51AB looks at "whether any undue influence or pressure was exerted on, or any unfair tactics were used against, the consumer". A number of the complainants referred to feeling pressure from the respondent to deal with him.

162 In her evidence Ingrid White said the respondent walked over to each house in the community and spoke only to the mothers. On her evidence, women were primarily sought out as potential customers. Muriel Palmer said the respondent was humbugging her. Rosina Dickson said the respondent came up to her and asked her if she had any children and was "sort of" humbugging her. Louanne Patterson felt pressured and forced to enter into her agreement with the respondent. In respect of a second visit by the respondent to Ms Patterson, she said she:

> ". . . felt more pressure from him than I did the first time I met him. He showed me his business card. When I walked away from him I did not get my keycard for him. I hid from him because I thought he wanted money for no reason. . . . I did not want to give this man this money. I think it is a rip-off. I only get $340 a fortnight and $680 is a lot of money for me".

163 Louanne Patterson's words indicate that humbugging can be more than a mere nuisance. Although, even a nuisance can be harmful. Whether this "humbugging" pressure was undue is less clear from the evidence but it was raised on a number of occasions by the complainants in their evidence. Whilst not as strong a vitiating circumstance as the others, I find it likely to have contributed to the actions of some of the complainants. It is further evidence that the complainants as Aboriginal women living in remote Aboriginal communities were vulnerable, and that this vulnerability was knowingly exploited by the respondent.

Availability of comparable goods

164 In respect of the availability of comparable goods, paragraph (e) of s 51AB refers to "the amount for which, and the circumstances under which, the consumer could have acquired identical or equivalent goods or services from a person other than the corporation". For the household items and educational materials offered for sale by the respondent, the prices the subject of the agreement were far in excess of the cost to purchase comparable items elsewhere, including in Alice Springs which is in reasonably close proximity to the three communities.

Conclusion

165 For these reasons, I find that the respondent engaged in unconscionable conduct contrary to s 51AB of the TP Act. I agree with the orders and declarations proposed by Mansfield J.

Equity

12

Give and Take: Unconscionability and the Pervasiveness of Gender Stereotypes

PAULA BARON

Introduction

In *Louth v Diprose*,[1] the common law doctrine of unconscionability was applied to allow a lawyer to recover the gift of a house he had made to a woman with whom he had been infatuated. The decisions in *Louth v Diprose*[2] have always been controversial and have attracted feminist critique[3] as denying women's experience[4] and stereotyping male and female roles.[5] As Otto observed of this case (and its predecessor on the doctrine of unconscionability, *Commercial Bank of Australia Ltd v Amadio*):[6]

> [T]he different, unequal and subordinate position of the women is rendered natural, uncontroversial and not legally cognizable. This results in a conceptualization of 'special disadvantage' that regards male experience as universal and is consequently blind to inequalities of gender.[7]

Louth v Diprose sparked a significant debate between feminist legal academic Sarmas[8] and Justice Heerey.[9] Sarmas argued that the judicial narratives in the case reflected and reinforced dominant ideas about gender and social class, and presented alternative stories which the judges might have told about the facts of the case. Justice Heerey argued that such criticism ignored the forensic constraints which restricted the presentation of the case to the

[1] (1992) 175 CLR 621. In authoring the feminist judgment, Francesca Bartlett acknowledges the feminist critique which immediately followed the decisions in *Louth v Diprose* described in this chapter. In particular, she is indebted to Lisa Sarmas and Bibi Sangha and Bob Moles for their identification of factual issues from evidence recorded in the trial transcript which was not contained within the decisions: Lisa Sarmas, 'Storytelling and the Law: A Case Study of *Louth v Diprose*' (1994) 19 *Melbourne University Law Review* 701; Bibi Sangha and Bob Moles, 'Gendered Stereotypes and Unconscionability – Can we Trust the Judges to Get it Right?' (1997) 1 *Flinders Journal of Law Reform* 145. Thanks also to Dr Warren Swain for feedback on a draft.

[2] *Diprose v Louth (No 1)* (1990) 54 SASR 438; *Diprose v Louth (No 2)* (1990) 54 SASR 450; *Louth v Diprose* (1992) 175 CLR 621.

[3] See, eg, Regina Graycar, 'Telling Tales: Legal Stories About Violence Against Women' (1996) 8 *Cardozo Studies in Law and Literature* 297; Dianne Otto, 'A Barren Future? Equity's Conscience and Women's Inequality' (1991–92) 18 *Melbourne University Law Review* 808; Sarmas, above n 1.

[4] Graycar, ibid.

[5] See further, Richard Haigh and Samantha Hepburn, 'The Bank Manager Always Rings Twice: Stereotyping in Equity After Garcia' (2000) 26 *Monash University Law Review* 275; Otto, above n 3; Sangha and Moles, above n 1; PD Baron, 'The Free Exercise of Her Will: Women and Emotionally Transmitted Debt' (1995) 13 *Law in Context* 23, 33–4.

[6] (1983) 151 CLR 447 ('*Amadio*').

[7] Otto, above n 3, 818.

[8] Sarmas, above n 1.

[9] Justice Peter Heerey, 'Truth, Lies and Stereotype: Stories of Mary and Louis' (1995) 1 *Newcastle Law Review* 1.

court, tended to replace one alleged stereotype with another, and sought to use litigation to correct perceived injustice within society, rather than applying justice to the parties in the particular case.

Despite Justice Heerey's assertions, it is hard to read *Louth v Diprose* without some level of disquiet, a disquiet shared by commentators such as Sangha and Moles, who comment on the gender stereotypes in this case: Diprose as a man rendered vulnerable by reason of his infatuation, despite being a lawyer; Louth as the manipulating woman, despite her troubled history and economic disadvantage. They argue that the case is susceptible to very different readings of the parties' behaviour.[10] As Haigh and Hepburn observe, the gendered stereotypes and colourful language highlighting the gender characterisations in the case were possibly used to explain the 'aberrant' behaviour of Diprose: '[t]he court could not regard Diprose's manner as consistent with that of an educated male solicitor and so targeted Louth as the cause of this aberrant behaviour'.[11] Similarly, Otto points to the assumptions in *Louth v Diprose* and *Amadio* that men should act in self-interest and women should act selflessly. The facts of this case go against those assumptions. Perhaps this explains the judges' description of the case as 'curious', 'unusual'[12] and 'most unusual';[13] the description of Diprose as 'a strange romantic character'[14] and his conduct as 'bizarre'.[15]

The Original Decision

Louis Diprose, a solicitor, met Mary Louth in Tasmania in 1981 and followed her to Adelaide when she relocated a few years later. Diprose claimed to be completely infatuated with Louth. Louth did not share those feelings for Diprose but the two did sustain a friendship. During their relationship, Diprose composed love poems for Louth and regularly provided her with gifts, including paying household bills from time to time.

When the house Louth was occupying in Adelaide was to be sold, Louth became distressed. Diprose purchased the house for her in her name. After their relationship came to an end, and some three years after the purchase of the house, Diprose wanted Louth to transfer the title of the house back to him. She refused, and Diprose brought proceedings to recover the gift, arguing unconscionability.

Rickett[16] traces the history of the doctrine of unconscionability to two sources: first, equity's special protection of heirs and expectants. Where an individual expected to inherit property, but then sold or mortgaged that interest, a rebuttable presumption was raised that the heir was entitled to be relieved of the obligation. The basis for equity's intervention was that the heir lacked sufficient judgement to make rational decisions about their long-term best interests. The second source arose from the principle that, where a plaintiff was under some disadvantage such that they could not expect to fend for themselves in dealings with

10 Sangha and Moles, above n 1.
11 Haigh and Hepburn, above n 5, 300.
12 (1990) 54 SASR 450, 451 (Jacobs ACJ).
13 Ibid 454 (Legoe J).
14 *Diprose v Louth (No 1)* (1990) 54 SASR 438, 443 (King CJ).
15 Ibid 439.
16 Charles Rickett, 'Unconscionability and Commercial Law' (2005) 24 *University of Queensland Law Journal* 73, 75–6.

others, equity would intervene. Such disadvantage originally lay in poverty, ignorance and lack of independent advice. The influence of both sources can be seen in the contemporary doctrine of unconscionability.

To recover the gift under the modern doctrine of unconscionability, Diprose had to show, first, that he was the weaker party, due to a 'special disadvantage'. The notion of a 'special disadvantage' is intended to 'disavow any suggestion that the principle applies whenever there is some difference in the bargaining power of the parties'.[17] The notion of special disadvantage as stated in *Blomley v Ryan*[18] is open-ended and said to include drunkenness, infirmity, lack of explanation or independent advice at the time of the transaction, poverty, age, sex,[19] and unfamiliarity with the English language.

Diprose then had to establish that this disadvantage affected his capacity to decide his best interests; and lastly, that Louth knew of, and exploited this disadvantage in a manner which, in the circumstances, was against conscience. If these elements could be established, a presumption of unconscionability would arise. Louth would then have the burden of proving that the transaction was 'fair, just and reasonable'.[20]

The trial judge, King CJ, found that Diprose was at a special disadvantage by reason of his infatuation and that Louth had exploited this by 'manufacturing an atmosphere of crisis' where none existed. It was thus unconscionable for Louth to retain the gift. The decision was affirmed on appeal to the Full Court of the Supreme Court of South Australia (Jacobs ACJ and Legoe J, Matheson J dissenting). Louth appealed to the High Court, but the decision was, again, upheld by majority, with only Toohey J dissenting, and the appeal was dismissed. A key aspect of the appeal decisions was a reluctance to interfere with King CJ's findings of fact:

> It is precisely because different people may come to different conclusions as to character, credit and disputed matters of fact that, in a forensic contest, findings as to those matters are entrusted to the trial judge . . . in accordance with rules and procedures that guarantee a considerable measure of finality.[21]

Yet, Sangha and Moles are critical of this view. They write:

> [M]ost of the findings by the trial judge were taken as 'findings of fact' by the appeal court and the High Court. However, we find that when we look at them more closely, there is little of a factual nature to them. The 'connective tissue' in these main findings by the judge was not comprised of facts at all, but of attributions and assertions. However, once the Appeal Court takes them to be findings of fact 'which this court ought not to disturb', then there is no possibility of the appeal being successful.[22]

[17] *Amadio* (1983) 151 CLR 447, 462 (Mason J).

[18] (1956) 99 CLR 362, 405 (Fullager J).

[19] In *European Asian v Kurland* (1985) 8 NSWLR 192, Rogers J held that being female was not, per se, a special disadvantage for the purposes of the doctrine. However, the so-called 'special equity' in *Yerkey v Jones* (1939) 63 CLR 649, which was used to defend from the equitable fraud caused by their husbands and/or third party creditors where the wife acts as surety or guarantor for her husband's debts, would later be upheld in *Garcia v National Australia Bank* (1998) 194 CLR 395. There are obvious overlaps between the special equity and unconscionability.

[20] *Amadio* (1983) 151 CLR 447.

[21] (1992) 67 CLR 95, 105 (Dawson, Gaudron and McHugh JJ). See also *Diprose v Louth (No 2)* (1990) 54 SASR 450, 453 (Jacobs ACJ).

[22] Sangha and Moles, above n 1, 179.

The Feminist Judgment

Bartlett J's feminist judgment seeks to acknowledge the counter-narrative in this case that views the facts of *Louth v Diprose* through the lens of women's experience. In Bartlett J's judgment, Diprose's infatuation is not disputed, but its legal impact is: Bartlett finds him not to be at a special disadvantage by reason of his infatuation, noting that, although emotional dependency had been found in earlier cases to constitute a special disadvantage for the purposes of unconscionability, in those cases the dependency is such as to render the judgement of the disadvantaged party seriously impaired, or to render them liable to manipulation. Diprose, however, evidenced no lack of understanding of his actions: he was a solicitor of considerable experience, had acted for Louth on a number of occasions, completed the conveyance of the house, applied on Louth's behalf for a home owner's grant and made a will which made no reference to the house as one of his assets. The transaction was not made in haste and, for some three years, Diprose did not dispute ownership of the property. Nor does Bartlett J find Diprose was emotionally dependent upon Louth. As she points out, Diprose did not rely upon Louth in his daily life, nor did he seek her advice in the conduct of his affairs. As Bartlett observes, 'he may have sought friendship and comfort from her, but that is not dependence'.

Nor does Bartlett J find, had she accepted that there was a special disability, that Louth exploited that disability. While accepting that Louth attempted suicide, she finds, given Louth's troubled history, that this was a 'self-evidently human reaction to a personally terrifying prospect' and was neither dishonest nor deceitful. Even if equity would intervene in situations where there is passive acceptance of a gift with knowledge of a special disability, she does not find the circumstances would warrant equity's intervention. There was no evidence that Diprose was at such a disadvantage that he could not perceive his own best interests; nor did Louth ask for the purchase price or mislead Diprose as to the legal result of the transaction. This was not an impulsive transaction; it was not soon regretted; and it was implausible that Louth might consider Diprose incapable of appreciating its legal effect.

The Aftermath of the Case

In the same year that *Louth v Diprose* was decided, nationally consistent laws on unconscionable conduct were introduced into the *Trade Practices Act 1974* (Cth) (now the *Australian Consumer Law*). Despite its legislative acceptance and extension to commercial transactions, the doctrine of unconscionability and its application remain controversial.[23]

Louth v Diprose remains the key case for considerations of special disadvantage in unconscionability cases,[24] though it is often distinguished on the basis that its facts are 'extreme'. A recent example of this is *Johnson v Mackintosh*.[25] In this case, as in *Louth v Diprose*, the issue

[23] See, eg, *Australian Competition and Consumer Commission v Berbatis Holdings* (2003) 197 ALR 153 and the flurry of academic comment this decision generated.

[24] See, eg, *Bridgewater v Leahy* (1998) 194 CLR 457; *Kakavas v Crown Melbourne Ltd* (2013) 298 ALR 35; *Violet Home Loans Pty Ltd v Schmidt* [2013] VSCA 56 (25 March 2013); *Herrod v Johnston* [2013] 2 Qd R 102.

[25] [2011] VCC 1400 (11 November 2011).

was whether gifts made by a man to a woman with whom he was infatuated were induced by unconscionable conduct.

Johnson was a wealthy and successful businessman. The object of his affection, Mackintosh, was a much younger woman who was in the process of separating from her husband. Their relationship was relatively short, and involved a number of separations and reconciliations. Mackintosh alleged sexual harassment, coercion and instances of aggression by Johnson on more than one occasion; Johnson alleged she initiated their sexual encounters. After the final breakdown of their relationship, Johnson sought recovery of money he had given Mackintosh and a house that he had bought in her name. Johnson alleged he was at a special disadvantage by reason of his age (at the time of the gifts he was 73), his loneliness and vulnerability, his desire for a companion, his infatuation with Mackintosh and, at the time of the purchase of the house, he was recovering from heart surgery.

The trial judge, Misso J, found the gift of the house to be unconscionable. The decision of Misso J echoes that of King CJ in *Louth v Diprose* in its gender stereotypes and its condemnation of female self-interest. Johnson is described by the trial judge as a 'generous man' who was 'captivated' by Mackintosh's 'overt signs of affection' and so infatuated that his judgement was 'clouded'.[26] Mackintosh is described as an unreliable witness and 'deceitful'; 'aggressive' in her showing of affection for the plaintiff; her interpretation of events 'perverse' and she is criticised for acceptance of Johnson's 'generosity'.[27] Despite the fact that the trial judge describes Johnson's actions as 'obsessed', and refers to his 'pursuit' of Mackintosh, *she* is at fault because she knew she could 'exploit and manipulate' the plaintiff's feelings'.[28]

Clearly, the legacies of gender stereotypes and assumptions, so evident in *Louth v Diprose*, live on. The Court of Appeal was to overturn the decision in *Mackintosh v Johnson*,[29] distinguishing *Louth v Diprose* as an extreme case. Yet even in the appeal decision, there are questions about the ways in which the parties are portrayed. Johnson's actions are 'a mere folly' (he is just a foolish old man); and failure by Mackintosh to reveal her true feelings, 'the stuff of ordinary . . . relationships'.[30]

[26] Ibid [135], [157], [162].
[27] Ibid [164], [159], [113], [139].
[28] Ibid [136], [160], [162].
[29] [2013] VSCA 10 (8 February 2013).
[30] Ibid [82], [84].

LOUTH . . . . . APPELLANT;
DEFENDANT,

AND

DIPROSE . . . . . RESPONDENT.
PLAINTIFF,

ON APPEAL FROM THE SUPREME COURT OF SOUTH AUSTRALIA.

Cur adv. vult.

BARTLETT J. The case that comes before us concerns whether the judge at trial erred in drawing certain inferences from evidence before him that there existed a relationship of influence of a woman upon a man, and that his resulting vulnerability was misused by her with the consequence that she unconscientiously received substantial property. It also concerns recognition by the trial judge, affirmed on appeal, of a situation of "emotional dependency" as sufficient to constitute a disability that the law will protect. The modern concept of unconscionable dealing on which this case rests is open to accept a range of relationships of imbalance or inequity within its scope. Equity is not fixed; but "fluid" (1) and infinitely various in its application. Nevertheless, it is appropriate that this Court pay close attention to what sort of relationships accord with the development of the doctrine, as well as the evidence required to establish such a disability in a court.

I begin by closely considering the parties, their relationship and how the dispute arose. This is particularly important when the conscience of equity provides a remedy. It thereby requires a "scrutiny of the exact relations established by the parties" to determine "the real justice of the case" (2).

The gift of the house

Mary Louth was given a house by Louis Diprose. Prior to this, she lived in this house as a tenant from 1982, when it was owned by her sister and brother-in-law. Ms. Louth acquired title to the house in July 1985. Mr. Diprose negotiated the price of sale, provided money for the full purchase price and completed all the paper work conveying title to her. (These matters are described in detail by Toohey J.) Ms. Louth signed the contract of sale in the presence of Mr. Diprose, and has ever since been the registered proprietor of the house. This has been Ms. Louth and her children's home for nearly ten years. Mr. Diprose has never lived there.

(1) Sir Anthony Mason, "Themes and Prospects" in P. Finn (ed) *Essays in Equity* (1985), p. 242.
(2) *Jenyns v. Public Curator (Qld)* (1953), 90 C.L.R. 113, at pp. 118–9.

Mr. Diprose currently resides in his own home with his three children. He is a practising solicitor. He has been married and divorced twice. He has a number of assets including his own home (with a mortgage), two cars and an old aeroplane.

Property rights to the house in which Ms. Louth lives are the subject of dispute between the parties here and in the courts below. It was the primary contention of Mr. Diprose at trial that title to the house was provided on the stipulation that it be held beneficially for him, and that she would retransfer the house to him at some stage. Much of his evidence – referring to this arrangement at least six times – was that the purchase money was provided, and conveyance of title, to Ms. Louth not as a "gift." However, the Chief Justice, with regard to the weight of other evidence given in the case, did not accept Mr. Diprose's evidence on this point and "accept[ed] [Ms. Louth's] evidence that [Mr. Diprose] told her that it was a gift and that there were no strings attached" (3).

Nevertheless, Mr. Diprose was successful in his action to receive beneficial ownership of the entire property on the basis of the principle of unconscionability. This was upheld on appeal by Legoe A.C.J. and Jacobs J. (Matheson J. dissenting) (4), albeit the nature of the orders was amended. The nature of the relationship between the parties and what occurred immediately prior to the purchase of the house are contested at this appellate stage, as they were in the courts below.

The antecedent relationship and events leading to the gift

The parties first met in late 1981 in Launceston where they were both living. They were both married but in troubled relationships which soon ended. In 1982, they had sexual intercourse twice, separated by eight months. They were otherwise not in a sexual relationship but on friendly terms and socialized regularly. In August 1982, Ms. Louth told Mr. Diprose that she was leaving Launceston to go to Adelaide as she had friends and family there and was in need of financial assistance. He asked her to stay and proposed marriage or a similar relationship. Ms. Louth gave evidence that he "had a contract, that he would give me so much money if I stayed", or a half interest in his house, and lived with him "as man and wife." Mr. Diprose confirmed this in his evidence. Ms. Louth refused the offer.

Mr. Diprose visited Ms. Louth in Adelaide in January 1983 and she told him that she would not enter an intimate relationship with him. When Mr. Diprose came to Adelaide to live in February 1983, he did not immediately make contact with her "so that she would not think that she was being harassed." However, around April, he sent her poems attesting to his love and sexual attraction to her entitled "The Mary Poems". In total, he sent her 91 poems written throughout their acquaintance. Sometime in April 1983, he visited her home but only

(3) *Diprose v. Louth [No. 1]* (1990), 54 S.A.S.R. 438, at p. 445.
(4) *Diprose v. Louth [No. 2]* (1990), 54 S.A.S.R. 450.

H. C. of A. 1992. LOUTH v. DIPROSE. Bartlett J.

spoke to a man, whom he had known from Tasmania. He was then contacted by Ms. Louth's brother-in-law, Arch Volkhardt, to tell him that Ms. Louth did not want to see him. Mr. Volkhardt testified that Ms. Louth was distressed by Mr. Diprose's decision to come to Adelaide.

Ms. Louth called Mr. Diprose twice in May 1983, but she refused to give him her telephone number which was unlisted. They met for lunch on 6 July. Mr. Diprose testified, and this aspect of his evidence was accepted and relied upon in the reasoning of the trial judge, that he told Ms. Louth that he wanted an intimate relationship with her to which she replied: "Oh well, if you don't try and hassle me, I would probably let you sleep with me occasionally, but I don't want any commitment." His evidence continues that he regarded this statement as "light hearted" and "didn't regard it as an inducement at all." Ms. Louth denied making this statement. Mr. Diprose also gave evidence that Ms. Louth said she was depressed and had considered suicide by slashing her wrists. Nevertheless, Ms. Louth did not give him her telephone number at this meeting or until November that year.

From the end of 1983, they spoke on the telephone or Mr. Diprose called at her house fairly regularly and their children sometimes stayed at the other's houses. At various times throughout 1984 until mid-1985, Mr. Diprose gave Ms. Louth gifts including jewellery, alcohol, paid household bills from time to time, and gave her household appliances. These gifts were apparently not requested by Ms. Louth, but they were accepted. She gave evidence that many of the gits were unwanted when they were accompanied by unwanted sexual advances: "he kept plying me with champagne and then trying to seduce me after."

The parties appear to have confided in each other and sought friendship and comfort from one another on occasion during this period. When Ms. Louth was charged with shoplifting in 1984, Mr. Diprose acted as her solicitor, and charges were not pursued by the police. On her behalf, he provided medical documentation as to her mental ill-health.

In September 1984, Ms. Louth's sister and brother-in-law separated. Their house, of which she was the tenant, was jointly owned by them, and would be subject to any property division agreed. Around this time, Mr. Volkhardt spoke to Ms. Louth telling her that "[M]aybe she should be paying more rent or maybe it would be a good idea to put her name down on the housing list because she couldn't assume she would live there forever." The nature of the discussions between Ms. Louth and Mr. Diprose that resulted are a point of dispute between the parties. The trial judge accepted Mr. Diprose's evidence in full. On this account, the parties spoke several times on the telephone in which Ms. Louth expressed her distress at the prospect of leaving her home. He offered her several options: to lend her the purchase price of the house or to buy the house and rent it to her. In respect of the offer to become her landlord, both testified that this offer was rejected "on the ground that it would give the plaintiff a hold over her which, in view of his sexual interest in her, was unacceptable"; Ms. Louth said "I would feel that he would be like threatening me if I did that." Mr. Diprose gave testimony about one conversation in which Ms. Louth told him about her bad experiences travelling around the country following her husband and that "since living at [her home in Adelaide] . . . she felt that she has some security and stability in her life." She expressed distress at having to move again and threatened to kill herself. Mr. Diprose said: "By the way she spoke about it, I had no doubt that she may well do it and certainly try." Ms. Louth denied that she threatened suicide in this conversation.

At the time of the gift, and for much of the time that she knew Mr. Diprose, Ms. Louth's income consisted of a Supporting Mother's pension. She was a qualified nurse, but needed to update her qualifications in order to pursue this occupation, which she has apparently done during these proceedings. It was never in contention that Ms. Louth was in an emotionally fragile state throughout her acquaintance with Mr. Diprose in South Australia, at least partially due to a number of traumatic events in her past including a brutal rape. She had attempted suicide after her marriage ended, and again shortly after having two surgical operations to remove a cancerous appendix and a complete hysterectomy. Both parties also testified that Ms. Louth made at least one serious attempt on her life *after* gaining ownership of the house, sometime in 1988. Mr. Diprose learned these personal details through the course of their friendship or in acting for Ms. Louth and her children as their solicitor in a number of matters before and after the purchase of the house.

From the time of purchase of the house until 1988, the relationship continued as it had been, including Mr. Diprose continuing to provide financial support to Ms. Louth and seeking to pursue a sexual relationship. In mid-1988, Mr. Diprose purchased the house that he now resides in, but was awaiting settlement and had to vacate his rental accommodation. Ms. Louth agreed to his son staying with her, and in August, to him staying for a period between 10 days to three weeks. Ms. Louth gave evidence that she was uncomfortable with this arrangement, and that Mr. Diprose used his temporary stay in her home to make sexual advances towards her. It is unclear from Mr. Diprose's evidence if this account is disputed. However, he acknowledged that his presence made Ms. Louth uneasy and uncomfortable. It appears Ms. Louth emphatically refused him. King C.J. concluded that it was at this stage that the "scales fell from his eyes" and Mr. Diprose no longer wished to pursue a relationship with Ms. Louth. At this point, in Ms. Louth's house, there was a violent dispute in which Mr. Diprose demanded that she return title to the house, and other chattels. When she refused, he left and sought legal assistance and eventually began this action.

H. C. of A. 1992. LOUTH v. DIPROSE. Bartlett J.

The trial judge's unconscionability findings

The Chief Justice found that Mr. Diprose was "deeply in love" and "deeply infatuated" with Ms. Louth since their first meeting in Tasmania in 1981, and that she was neither in love nor interested in pursuing an intimate relationship with him. King C.J. concluded of the relationship that Ms. Louth "tolerated [Mr. Diprose's] visits and his company because of the material advantages which resulted. The result of this toleration was to feed the flames of [Mr. Diprose's] passion and to keep alive his hopes that [Ms. Louth] would relent and that his devotion would be requited" (5). By reason of his infatuation, and findings about his demeanour as a "strange romantic character", Mr. Diprose was found to be "emotionally dependant" on Ms. Louth. King C.J. thereby found that Ms. Louth occupied a "position of great influence on his actions and decisions" (6).

The Chief Justice found that a particular vulnerability towards her "crucially" arose from comments in which Ms. Louth was found to have "created an atmosphere of crisis with respect to the house where none existed" as to the urgent need to leave the house, and "by making suicide threats." As Ms. Louth was found to know of Mr. Diprose's vulnerability towards her, her behaviour was found to have constituted a "fraud" that resulted in an unconscionable gift of the house.

The arguments before this court

Counsel for Ms. Louth has argued that in a number of ways King C.J.'s findings of unconscionability are unsound. For the reasons explained by Dean J., in order to be successful, Ms. Louth must convince this Court that there is a clear error in the process of applying the law or in finding facts. At this second appellate stage we must be cautious to observe the great advantage of the trial judge in hearing and seeing the parties when giving oral evidence. The case turns, it has been said, on such observations at trial as to the character and veracity of the parties' evidence because it is about their relationship.

Counsel for Ms. Louth has urged us to find an error in the Chief Justice's findings as to credibility when he disbelieved Mr. Diprose's evidence as to his beneficial ownership of the house but still found his evidence to be "truthful and reliable and to be preferred to that of the defendant" (7) in relation to the "circumstances and events leading to the house transaction." I find that this line of argument must fail for the reasons given by Dean J. and the joint judgment of Dawson, Gaudron and McHugh JJ. However, as Matheson J. said in the Full Court, I believe we are in "as good a position as the judge at trial" (8) to draw certain crucial inferences as to the nature of the relationship and whether it was exploited, on the basis of agreed or decided facts.

(5) (1990), 54 S.A.S.R. 438, at p. 447.
(6) ibid., p. 459.
(7) ibid., p. 448.

This Court has been asked to disturb the findings of facts made at trial and upheld on appeal on the basis of a lack of regard to certain underlying and undisputed facts, such as the unequal social and financial status of the parties. That is, Ms. Louth was a woman without professional status, earning capacity or knowledge of the law. She was also in an emotionally fragile state. It is argued that even if Mr. Diprose was emotionally vulnerable to her, as found by the judge at trial, their relationship as a whole was thereby one of "equal" status. In so far as the submission urges us to take a different view of Mr. Diprose's dependency on Ms. Louth and her consequential ability to exert influence over him, with regard to persistent structural and social factors impacting upon them, I find that a full regard to the factual matrix makes an unconscionability finding impossible.

Unconscionable conduct

The doctrine of unconscionable dealing provides relief for people who, by virtue of a "special disability," are vulnerable to and do in fact succumb to exploitation. It requires, at the least, constructive knowledge by the stronger party of the position of weakness of the other party. The stronger party then purposely exploits this weakness to their own advantage. In this way, the principle, in contrast to the closely related doctrine of undue influence (9), is concerned with the "victimisation" of a vulnerable person. The task of the court is to determine whether the whole course of dealing between the parties has been such that, with regard to their relationship, responsibility for the loss should be ascribed to the unconscientious behaviour of the other party.

The operation of the doctrine is so as to, when vulnerability and manipulation are evidenced, give rise to a presumption of an unconscionable result. This may be rebutted by proof of the fairness, justice and reasonableness of the transaction. Where the transaction is an improvident one for the weaker party, as found in this case, the onus will be difficult to discharge. This is as it should be, I believe, because it provides courts with a chance to measure the justice of the case in the form of an assessment of evidence of personal impact on the weaker party.

Nevertheless, the improvidence of the conduct does not create a presumption in law of victimisation. A lack of consideration provided is similarly not decisive (10). In *Allcard v. Skinner*, Lindley L.J. stated (11):

> "Courts of Equity have never set aside gifts on the ground of the folly, imprudence, or want of foresight on the part of donors.... It would obviously be to encourage folly, recklessness, extravagance and vice if persons could get back their property which they foolishly made away with ..."

(8) (1990), 54 S.A.S.R. 450, p. 65.

(9) It also differs from the notion of recognising an imbalance of bargaining power as suggested by Lord Denning in *Lloyds Bank Ltd. v. Bundy* [1975] Q.B. 326, at p. 339.

(10) *Brusewitz v. Brown* [1923] N.Z.L.R. 1106, at p. 1109, per Salmond J.

(11) (1887) 36 Ch.D. 145, at pp. 182–3.

H. C. of A. 1992. LOUTH v. DIPROSE. Bartlett J.

There is a balance to be observed, but the onus of bringing himself within the doctrine rests upon Mr. Diprose.

"Emotional dependence" of Louis Diprose

As to the first limb of the doctrine, Fullagar J. in *Blomley v. Ryan* lists categories of "weakness" that have given rise to relief as "special disabilities" under unconscionable dealing, including (12):

> "poverty or need of any kind, sickness, age, sex, infirmity of body or mind, drunkenness, illiteracy or lack of education, lack of assistance or explanation where assistance or explanation is necessary".

Mason J. in *Commercial Bank of Australia Ltd v. Amadio* (13) clearly states that there is no exhaustive list of "weaknesses" which may give rise to relief against unconscionable dealing. Nevertheless, those "situations mentioned" in that case, exemplifying the general principle, are quite unlike the one before us. These are personal disabilities of understanding, or they arise from institutionalized arrangements of social power in evidence within the relationship – such as class and sex (14). In *Amadio* there was evidence of a lack of understanding as to the nature of the document signed due to poor English and education, and a clear course of manipulation by the son which could be brought home to the third party (the bank) whose agent knew of the vulnerability leading to a lack of understanding and who consciously exploited it. *Wilton v. Farnsworth* (15) was a case concerning the execution of a deed by a man who was similarly unaware of the nature of the legal right conferred by reason of his lack of education or knowledge of the substantial financial benefit involved, whom the court described as "markedly dull-witted and stupid." Again, there was active manipulation by the stronger party, when he was knowingly rushed into signing, with no explanation of the nature of the document or rights foregone. *Blomley v. Ryan* (16) concerned an agreement procured from an alcoholic, in a state of intoxication, where the alcohol was brought by the other party to the signing of the document.

I do not accept that there are analogous facts here which satisfy the underlying principles as in the cases above. There is no authority, quite properly to my mind, which indicates that infatuation or sexual attraction is a sufficient disability on its own. This is not to be confused, even in the most poetic sense, with a mental illness that would require a solid evidential basis on which to make a finding of incapacity operating at the relevant time.

(12) (1956) 99 C.L.R. 362, at p. 405.
(13) (1983) 151 C.L.R. 447.
(14) I acknowledge what Rogers J. said in *European Asian of Australian Ltd. v. Kurkland* (1985) 8 N.S.W.L.R. 192, at p. 198, that "it seems anachronistic to be told that being female and a wife is, by itself, a sufficient qualification to enrol in the class of persons suffering a special disadvantage".
(15) (1948) 76 C.L.R. 646.
(16) (1956) 99 C.L.R. 362.

This is not to say that a person cannot be emotionally dependent on another person, so as to make their judgement seriously impaired or liable to manipulation. There have been a number of cases in which evidence of an "emotional condition" of a wife as vulnerable to the husband's will was legally recognisable (17). Under the doctrine of undue influence, cases concerning wives guaranteeing their husband's business loans have, in part, recognized the trust imparted by wives to husbands, and sometimes the "domination" of the husband over the wife in deciding financial matters (18). In such cases, the vulnerability within the relationship is consequently attended by a lack of information about or ability to comprehend the transaction. There is also a very great gap in bargaining power between a bank, as the party seeking to enforce and benefit from the transaction, and the wife as guarantor for the benefit of another person (the husband). On the other hand, it is appropriate that this Court have regard to a possible consequence that those falling into recognized categories of vulnerability be presumed to lack capacity to care for their own financial affairs. This is to be avoided and, for instance, no automatic presumption arises from the marriage contract (19). This is again not an analogous relationship. There is no evidence of Mr. Diprose reposing his trust as to his affairs or his well-being (or his children's) in Ms. Louth; nor are there any similarly operating structural factors such as traditional gendered roles that would influence his behaviour.

In this case, it was not open for the judge at trial to find that Mr. Diprose was emotionally dependent on Ms. Louth and that this constituted a "special disability." There is nothing in the evidence that indicates lack of understanding by Mr. Diprose of what he did. Mr. Diprose was a solicitor of considerable experience, including acting apparently with competence for Ms. Louth on a number of occasions. He completed the conveyance of the house, applied on her behalf for a home owner's grant and executed his will which made no reference to the house as one of his assets. While acting for her in a custody matter against her former spouse, he wrote to another solicitor to the effect that she lived in her own home which was free of encumbrances. It is not contested that he fully understood the financial and legal consequences of what he did. The transaction was not a rash one conducted hastily, and in three years after its purchase was not of concern to him. There is no evidence that he did not exercise his own free will, without any form of duress.

It is not necessary that Mr. Diprose establish that he was deprived of an independent and voluntary will, but I also cannot find any evidence

(17) *Page v. Horne* (1848) 50 ER 804; *K. v. K.* [1976] 2 N.Z.L.R. 31, per O'Regan J.; *Archer v. Cutler* [1980] 1 N.Z.L.R. 386.

(18) *Broadlands International Finance Ltd. v. Sky* (1987) 4 B.P.R. 97280; *Nolan v. Westpac Bank* (1989) 51 S.A.S.R. 496.

(19) *Yerkey v. Jones* (1940) 63 C.L.R. 649, at p. 675.

H. C. of A. 1992.

Louth v. Diprose.

Bartlett J.

pointing to his inability to make judgements as to his own best interests. He did not rely on Ms. Louth to assist im in the performance of any aspects of his daily life or ask her for advice in conducting his affairs. He may have sought friendship and comfort from her, but that is not dependence.

The Chief Justice observed Mr. Diprose to be a "strange romantic character". However accurate this characterisation is, it does not produce the necessary inference that he was dependent so as to be incapable of caring for his own interests when it came to Ms. Louth. To the contrary, there is ample evidence of Mr. Diprose courting Ms. Louth by sending her champagne and poetry and other gifts. As Jacobs A.C.J. opined (20):

> "in some respects this is but one more case in the annals of human relationships in which an infatuated but unrequited suitor has lavished gifts upon the subject of his infatuation, well knowing what he was doing and intending to do it, but in a sense allowing his heart to rule his head".

While his Honour concluded that the case moved beyond this "ordinary" one of romantic pursuit for reasons I will shortly address, I cannot agree that there is such evidence. I believe the undisputed evidence inevitably leads to a conclusion that Mr. Diprose's interests were in pursuing a sexual relationship. Throughout their relationship, Ms. Louth made it clear that she had no intention of entering into a relationship with him. Yet, he consistently pursued his interest by offering her financial incentives, which included unwelcome or unrequested gifts. He may have stopped giving her gifts, or stayed away from her (indeed he did stay away from her for a time in the course of his "infatuation" with her), but he chose not to. He had proposed a similar deal in 1982, in writing, that provided that he would transfer to her a half-interest in his house if she lived with him in a marriage-like relationship. These may be construed as romantic gestures made in folly. Or they may be understood as indicating something more sinister whereby Mr. Diprose's financial and professional advantage was used to gain access to Ms. Louth's life and to make unwanted sexual advances towards her. In either case, neither inference of fact satisfies the requirements of a special disability suffered by Mr. Diprose.

Exploitation by Mary Louth

As I find that no legally recognisable disability operated on Mr. Diprose toward Ms. Louth at the relevant time, the finding of unconscionable dealing must be set aside. However, it is not possible to separate the elements of this principle in an arbitrary way. Ms. Louth's conduct was found to be relevant to whether Mr. Diprose was able to resist giving her the house in the context of his love for her and the "atmosphere of crisis" about losing her home she was said to have manufactured.

(20) (1990), 54 S.A.S.R. 450, at pp. 451–2.

While the account of Ms. Louth, and other witnesses, differs substantially from Mr. Diprose's account, I am bound to accept King C.J.'s preliminary findings that Ms. Louth said that she would commit suicide if she was required to leave her house. I do not accept that Mr. Diprose was under any misapprehension that Ms. Louth was in imminent danger of losing her home, for the reasons described by Toohey J. Mr. Volkhardt's evidence establishes that Mr. Diprose, and probably Ms. Louth, was aware of the correct state of affairs. Thus, even if Ms. Louth made false statements about the urgency as to leaving her the house, this cannot be said to have caused Mr. Diprose to act.

King C.J. also placed great reliance on his finding that Mr. Diprose believed that Ms. Louth may attempt suicide. This finding was open to him in the context of accepting Mr. Diprose's evidence and evidence of Ms. Louth having made earlier attempts on her life. Indeed, there is no contest that Ms. Louth *was* in a depressive state (and she did make an attempt on her life later in 1988), and had good cause to be concerned about her family's security and safety. Her reaction was one that is eminently understandable on the basis of her background of which we have some picture as I have set out earlier. There was no evidence, even in the evidence of Mr. Diprose, that this was a concoction. Rather I find it a self-evidently human reaction to a personally terrifying prospect. I cannot see how this can be interpreted as dishonest or fraudulent.

There is authority for the proposition that equity will intervene even in cases of passive acceptance of a gift where it is received in the knowledge that it resulted from a disability (21). It was open for King C.J. to find that Ms. Louth knew that Mr. Diprose was not an extremely wealthy man, and that the purchase price of a house was a substantial expense for him. Whether or not she knew the exact nature of his finances, which is unclear from the evidence, she appears to have at least constructive knowledge of how affordable this house was for him. Yet there is no evidence that she acted on the basis that he was so emotionally dependent on her that he could not perceive his own best interests. Ms. Louth did not ask for the purchase price for the house or mislead him as to the legal result of the transaction. She knew it was not an impulsive act soon regretted. It was a proposal she had heard before. It is implausible that Ms. Louth would think him unable to appreciate its legal effect.

Ms. Louth may have thought Mr. Diprose intellectually competent but known him to be in her emotional thrall. However, the evidence does not support a picture of manipulation of emotional vulnerability, if it existed. It is not in contention that Ms. Louth made her feelings towards Mr. Diprose clear when it came to a sexual relationship. She did not behave deceitfully by concealing her true feelings for Mr. Diprose so as to encourage his attentions and efforts to establish this sort of relationship. She did not ask him for financial advantages. On the contrary, in many ways Ms. Louth did what she could to protect herself from

(21) *Hart v. O'Connor* [1985] All E.R. 880.

H. C. of A. 1992.

LOUTH v. DIPROSE.

Bartlett J.

unwanted advances on various occasions, for instance, by refusing to give him her telephone number for a period of time, or to enter into a relationship with Mr. Diprose as her landlord. She knew about his sexual attraction to her, but this does not mean she believed him to be sufficiently disabled by it.

Finally, the trial judge referred to Ms. Louth's "unexpressed wish[es]" to become the owner of the house, but there is no evidentiary basis on which to make this finding of intention. This is attribution rather than inference. I do not accept that we can fill the evidential gap with a story about a finely balanced course of sexual temptation, consisting of constant rejection over many years with nothing actually said to lead Mr. Diprose to a very specific course of conduct, executed as it was by him in formal legal documentation over a significant period. As the doctrine rests in the wrongful receipt of property, there must be some proof of her predatory state of mind. Indifference to the best interests of Mr. Diprose is not sufficient. Equally, while there may have been some self-interestedness on the part of Ms. Louth, it is not enough to constitute a considered course of victimisation.

I would allow the appeal.

13

Formal Equality and Third Party Interests in the Family Home: *Trustees of the Property of John Daniel Cummins, a Bankrupt v Cummins*

FRANCESCA BARTLETT

Introduction

Feminists have long engaged in the 'equality versus difference' debate in relation to the law's approach to women's economic disadvantage.[1] Some argue that a sameness approach removes a seemingly anachronistic distinction between the rights of men and women, entrenching women's right to earn the same wages for the same work,[2] and their capacity to contract and to manage their own financial affairs. Others point out that legal presumptions which take account of continued structural imbalances or vulnerabilities based on gendered norms can provide valuable protections and substantive equality.[3] The case of *Trustees of the Property of Cummins v Cummins*[4] raises some of these difficult questions in the area of trust law concerning beneficial ownership by spouses of a family home.

Lisa Sarmas's feminist judgment, written as an additional member of the High Court, applies traditional trust principles to the legal dispute. In doing so, Sarmas's decision reflects the profoundly gendered impact a rather subtle change in legal doctrine can make. In her judgment, she rejects the move by the other members of the Court to presumptively apply notions of formal equality between spouses.

The Issues to be Decided

In *Cummins*, the High Court heard an appeal by the trustees in bankruptcy of the estate of John Cummins. His former wife and the trustee of the Cummins family trust were the respondents. The High Court unanimously reinstated the original orders of the trial judge,

[1] Marcia Neave, 'From Difference to Sameness – Law and Women's Work' (1992) 18 *Melbourne University Law Review* 768; Jenny Morgan, 'Equality Rights in the Australian Context; A Feminist Assessment' in Phillip Alston (ed), *Towards an Australian Bill of Rights* (Centre for International and Public Law, 1994).

[2] See, eg, Carol Bacchi, 'Do Women Need Equal Treatment or Different Treatment?' (1992) 8 *Australian Journal of Law and Society* 80.

[3] See, eg, Peta Spender, 'Resurrecting Mrs Salomon' (1999) 27 *Federal Law Review* 217; Marcia Neave, 'The New Unconscionability Principle – Property Disputes between De Facto Partners' (1991) 5 *Australian Journal of Family Law* 185.

[4] (2006) 227 CLR 278 ('*Cummins*').

Sackville J,[5] which had been overturned by the Full Federal Court.[6] The High Court found that there had been no transfer by John Cummins to his wife of his legal or beneficial interest in their family home, or of shares in a company to the trustee of the Cummins family trust.[7] The result of this finding was to make these assets available to John Cummins's creditors – in this case, primarily the Australian Taxation Office (ATO). It was then necessary to determine the extent of John Cummins's share of the beneficial ownership of the family home.

Avoiding a Tax Debt

John Cummins was a barrister who went to the New South Wales Bar in 1961. He took silk in 1980. In 2000 he became bankrupt. The ATO instituted proceedings to recover $955,672.92 in unpaid income tax. The trustees of the property of Mr Cummins (the trustees) applied to the Federal Court for a declaration that John Cummins held an interest in one half of the family home. This meant that this share in the property was available to settle his tax debt. This was declared by Sackville J and finally by the High Court.

The Full Court of the Federal Court found differently. There was a lack of evidence as to John Cummins's earnings for all of the years of his professional practice (from 1955 until 2000). On this basis, the Full Court was prepared to accept that his earnings, even when acting as Queen's Counsel, could have been below the taxable threshold. However, the High Court emphatically disagreed, and held that it was reasonable for Sackville J to find that the ATO was a creditor.[8] It further accepted that Mr Cummins's purported transfer of his interest in the family home to Mary Cummins in 1987 was void, pursuant to s 121 of the *Bankruptcy Act 1966* (Cth). It was inferred that the 'main purpose' of the transfer was to 'prevent the transferred property becoming divisible' so as to be available to creditors, and was thereby ineffective.

The feminist judgment concurs with the High Court's decision that the transfers are void. The judgment also ultimately agrees that John Cummins had a beneficial interest in half of the family home that ought to be available to his creditors. It disagrees, however, with the rest of the Court's reasoning on the latter point. In addition, the feminist judgment alone considers whether equity should have regard to the nature of the creditor, being the ATO. That is, whether, as a matter of policy, the intentional defrauding of the public purse by the bankrupt ought to be a relevant factor in determining whether a trust arises in favour of the non-bankrupt spouse. Sarmas is cautious on this point, noting the impact of such a consideration on the personal property rights of those who have not participated in the fraud, as well as the possible effect of 'infecting' a wife with her husband's liability.[9]

[5] *Prentice v Cummins (No 5)* (2002) 124 FCR 67; *Prentice v Cummins (No 6)* (2003) 134 FCR 449.

[6] *Cummins v The Trustees of the Property of John Daniel Cummins, A Bankrupt* (2004) 209 ALR 521 (Carr and Lander JJ; Tamberlin J dissenting).

[7] The beneficiaries of this trust were Mary Cummins and the four children of Mr and Mrs Cummins. The trust owned John Cummins's law chambers in a prestigious Sydney location.

[8] Indeed, other courts found that John Cummins's non-payment of income tax was wrongful and deliberate. For instance, in separate proceedings, John Cummins was struck off the practising Roll because his actions 'brought the profession into disrepute': *NSW Bar Association v Cummins* (2001) 52 NSWLR 279.

[9] Sarmas is referring to the feminist-coined term, 'sexually-transmitted debt', which has been identified as arising within intimate relationships and recognised, to some degree, by the courts.

Beneficial Ownership of the Family Home: Presumption of Resulting Trust and Inference of Joint Ownership

The Cummins home was jointly owned (in legal title) by John and Mary Cummins from 1970 until 1987. In 1970, they bought vacant land at Hunters Hill, which they registered in their joint names. Mary Cummins contributed 76.3 per cent of the purchase price and John Cummins contributed the remaining 23.7 per cent. They obtained a mortgage and built the family home on the land. They sold another property they jointly owned in December 1971. The proceeds of that sale were paid into a joint account in December that year. Sackville J inferred that the proceeds of the sale of that property were intended to be paid to both John and Mary Cummins. Agreeing with Sackville J, the High Court found that the 'likely source of funds' for the building of the family home was from this bank account and was the joint resource of the Cummins'.[10] From this series of events, the High Court held that the presumption of a resulting trust favouring Mary Cummins was rebutted and that they were joint legal and beneficial owners of the property.

The High Court's construction of the facts affects the outcome, because a resulting trust arises *at the time of purchase* of the relevant property. If only the purchase of the land was the relevant transaction, then Mary Cummins would have a larger beneficial interest according to the proportion of her financial contribution (76 per cent of the value of the land).[11] However, the High Court found the relevant 'transaction' to be the purchase of the land and subsequent building and occupancy of the house. In contrast, Sarmas finds that later events cannot be properly considered part of the transaction, and cannot be relied upon to show actual intention of the parties at an earlier time.

The High Court decision found another basis to infer joint tenancy. The majority adopted Austin Scott's view that there was a legal inference of a one-half interest of married couples in the family home 'regardless of the amounts contributed by them' or in whose name title is drawn.[12] This approach assumes *equality* of interests (absent other evidence) as a starting point, seemingly displacing the traditional approach of finding a resulting trust based on financial contribution. Sarmas's decision also points out that the competing 'presumption of advancement', which entitles a wife to a beneficial interest equal to any legal interest given by the husband,[13] may be displaced by this new assumption of equality. This will leave some wives with less access to the assets of the relationship than under traditional equitable principles.[14] Thus, Sarmas cautions that the practical effect of this new inference, while it is formally 'equal', is that it may result in the wife being worse off.

Sarmas ultimately disagrees with the assumption of the other members of the Court that spousal equality is sufficiently established at law, and that it ought to be imposed on policy grounds. On this basis, she does not apply it, preferring to base her judgment on what she

[10] *Cummins* (2006) 227 CLR 278, 304.

[11] The High Court does overturn the well-established position that where there are tenancies in common, irrespective of legal title, proportional beneficial interests are indicated by financial contribution: *Calverley v Green* (1984) 155 CLR 242. This is the case unless the relationship raises the presumption of advancement.

[12] Austin Scott and William Fratcher, *The Law of Trusts* (Little, Brown, 4th ed, 1987) vol 5, §454, 197–8.

[13] This presumption does not work in the reverse in relation to a gift from wife to husband.

[14] Sarmas's judgment also argues for an extension of the advancement presumption to de facto wives which would 'neutralise' the effect of the majority decision in those relationships. Compare to the present distinction between wives and de facto couples: *Napier v Public Trustee (WA)* (1980) 32 ALR 153.

terms 'traditional trusts principles'. However, as a dissenting judgment, Sarmas accepts that this inference of joint tenancy is now part of Australian law. Therefore, she importantly takes the opportunity to expressly extend the inference to 'other marriage-like relationships'.

A 'Common Intention' Constructive Trust in the Family Home

In an academic examination of *Cummins*, Sarmas explains that '[p]recise factual circumstances that may determine that one type of trust will be imposed rather than the other have not been clearly articulated'.[15] The lack of clarity in the law is the basis for a differing approach taken by Sarmas in her feminist judgment, finding the existence of a 'common intention' constructive trust of joint ownership. The majority decision makes no mention of a constructive trust as potentially applicable to the facts. However, they do acknowledge what they call the 'practical and economic realities'[16] of uneven contributions by partners to relationship assets over time with an intention to benefit them in common. This is reminiscent of the *Baumgartner v Baumgartner*[17] 'unconscionability' constructive trust which recognises that it would be wrong for one party to deny a share of ownership by the other. As Sarmas's decision points out, where the facts concern differing types of contributions by a couple, a constructive trust approach is more common. She contends that the 'common intention' constructive trust provides a more appropriate consideration of all the facts in cases like *Cummins* as it may refer to subsequent actions of the parties to infer intention and reliance as to ownership.[18]

The Feminist Approach

Sarmas's judgment shows an understanding of the feminist dilemma in this area of law. Presumptions of resulting trust and advancement can work to entrench gendered stereotypes, positioning wives as dependent and non-contributing to relationship property.[19] On the other hand, if they are removed, there is an equal danger of disadvantaging some women due to the on-going 'structural inequalities and power differences that exist between men and women'.[20] Her judgment employs a feminist strategy of exposing these complexities and expressly weighing them in her legal reasoning. Her detailed analysis shows that the joint ownership inference may result in poorer results for wives than if traditional trust principles were applied.

[15] Lisa Sarmas, 'Trusts, Third Parties and The Family Home: Six years Since *Cummins* and Confusion Still Reigns' (2012) 36 *Melbourne University Law Review* 216, 219.

[16] *Cummins* (2006) 227 CLR 278, 301.

[17] (1987) 164 CLR 137.

[18] Absent legislation relating to separating de facto couples, the common intention constructive trust developed to have regard to non-financial contributions by a partner: *Allen v Snyder* [1977] 2 NSWLR 685.

[19] See Lee Holcombe, *Wives and Property: Reform of the Married Women's Property Law in Nineteenth Century England* (University of Toronto Press, 1983); Julie Dodds and Susan MacCallum, 'Bankruptcy and Matrimonial Claims – the Spouse as Competing Creditor' (1985) 15 *Melbourne University Law Review* 211.

[20] Sarmas, above n 15, 246.

This analysis is borne out by subsequent cases. Some lower courts have ignored the decision in *Cummins.*[21] But in cases applying the inference of joint tenancy, the result generally favours the trustee in bankruptcy to the detriment of the non-bankrupt wife.[22] And, despite obiter comments of the majority, the inference has not been extended to non-married couples.[23]

The Legislative Regime for Separating Couples

In her judgment, Sarmas notes that s 79 of the *Family Law Act 1975* (Cth) (*FLA*), allows the Family Court a wide, but directed, discretion to consider the family context when apportioning the assets of separating couples. At the time of deciding *Cummins*, that section did not extend to considering third party claims to assets, but a 2005 amendment to the *FLA* did so extend it. It seems, however, that courts have rarely used this provision since its introduction[24] and continue to apply trust principles in resolving cases like *Cummins*,[25] giving Sarmas's feminist judgment continuing relevance as to the effect of common law doctrine, and force to her suggestion that a legislative approach is preferable.

[21] Ibid 237–44. The academic commentators have also rarely noticed the inference or disagree that this is a change to Australian trust law.

[22] *Draper v Official Trustee in Bankruptcy* (2006) 156 FCR 53 [83].

[23] However, it should be noted that there is now legislation which governs the attribution of property rights between separated de facto, including same-sex, partners: *Family Law Amendment (De facto Financial Matters and Other Measures) Act 2008* (Cth).

[24] When principles of apportionment under s 79 have been applied, these tend only to be applied to the remaining assets of the separating couple, after the interests of third party creditors have been satisfied.

[25] See eg *Commissioner of Taxation & Worsnop* (2009) 40 FamLR 552; *Trustee of the Property of Lemnos v Lemnos* (2009) 41 FamLR 120.

THE TRUSTEES OF THE PROPERTY OF CUMMINS .... APPELLANTS;
APPLICANTS,

AND

CUMMINS AND ANOTHER .... RESPONDENTS.
RESPONDENTS,

[2006] HCA 6

ON APPEAL FROM THE FEDERAL COURT OF AUSTRALIA

HC OF A 2005–2006

Dec 6, 7 2005

March 7 2006

Sarmas J

77 SARMAS J. I concur with the orders proposed by Gleeson CJ, Gummow, Hayne, Heydon and Crennan JJ (the joint judgment). I agree with the joint judgment both as to the setting aside of the 1987 transfers and as to the entitlement of Mr Cummins' trustees in bankruptcy (the Trustees) to a one half interest in the family home of Mr and Ms Cummins. I give my own reasons for judgment in relation to the latter, as I differ as to the appropriate trusts principles that govern this important area.

78 The background and facts of the case are set out in detail in the joint judgment. I need not repeat them in detail here. Briefly, Mr Cummins was declared bankrupt for debts largely associated with his non-payment of tax for over 40 years while practising at the Bar. The Trustees seek declaratory and consequential relief pertaining to certain assets that they claim belong to him and that they therefore seek to recover on behalf of his creditors. Included in the assets claimed is a one half interest in the family home at Hunters Hill. The basis of this claim is that Mr and Ms Cummins share equally in the beneficial ownership of the home. Ms Cummins contests this claim. Ultimately, the resolution of this issue depends upon the application of relevant trusts principles to determine their respective beneficial interests in the home.

Trusts in a social policy context

79 I observe at the outset that the law of trusts is at best a blunt instrument for the determination of beneficial interests in family assets. In an article published in 1991, Professor Marcia Neave (as she then was) explained how the application of trusts principles in a domestic relationship context could lead to inequitable outcomes for women on the breakdown of those relationships (114). In the continuing context of gender pay inequality and women's greater contribution to the unpaid role of homemaker and parent (115), trust law's predominant focus on financial contributions and its doctrinal inability to consider the future needs of the parties can lead to results that disproportionately disadvantage women.

(114) Neave, "The Unconscionability Principle – Property Disputes Between De Facto Partners", *Australian Journal of Family Law*, vol 5 (1991), p 185.

80 The enactment of the *Family Law Act 1975* (Cth) (the FLA) essentially ended the use of resulting and constructive trusts in the resolution of property disputes between separating married partners (116). Section 79 of the FLA provides a statutory scheme for allocation of assets based on a structured discretion that requires the consideration of a range of factors including the parties' respective contributions to family assets, including contributions as homemaker and parent, and the future needs of the parties. This statutory scheme has also been criticised for failing to adequately take into account women's structural inequality, however it is broadly acknowledged as an improvement on the comparatively rudimentary doctrinal tools available under the law of trusts (117).

81 The law of trusts continues to play a role in the domestic relationship context when a third party makes a claim against the assets of one of the parties to the relationship. If legislation currently before the Parliament is enacted (118), the law of trusts may soon become redundant in cases where the third party is a creditor of one of the parties to the relationship, as in the present case. Until that time the Court is bound to apply the law of trusts to the determination of the dispute before it as it relates to the Trustees' interest in what was the family home of Mr and Ms Cummins.

The context of tax avoidance in the present case

82 Before embarking upon an application of the relevant trusts principles it is important to point out that the notorious factual backdrop of tax avoidance in the present case has no bearing upon the appropriate trusts principles to be applied. As noted in the joint judgment, the Australian Taxation Office (the ATO) is the largest creditor in Mr Cummins' bankruptcy, Mr Cummins having paid no income tax for the whole period in which he had practised as a barrister since 1961 (119). Thus, it is in effect the public purse (through the ATO) that stands to "lose" whatever beneficial interest is declared in favour of Ms Cummins as against Mr Cummins. From a doctrinal perspective, this broader context is irrelevant to

(115) See, for example, Australian Bureau of Statistics (ABS), *Australian Social Trends – Income Distribution: Female/male earnings*, Cat No 4102.2, 12 July 2005; ABS, *Australian Social Trends – Unpaid Work: Time spent on unpaid household work*, Cat No 4102.0, 6 June 2001.

(116) Various State-based statutory schemes have also, although to a lesser extent, reduced reliance on such trusts for separating *de facto* couples: see, eg, *Property Law Act 1958* (Vic) Pt IX.

(117) See, eg, Graycar and Morgan, *The Hidden Gender of Law*, 2nd ed (2002), pp 98–108.

(118) See *Bankruptcy and Family Law Legislation Amendment Bill 2005* (Cth) Sch 5. This Bill seeks to amend the FLA to give the Family Court jurisdiction to make orders regarding third party creditors' interests in property of a separating couple.

(119) Mr Cummins was removed from the Roll of Legal Practitioners for professional misconduct and for not being a fit and proper person to be on the Roll

the law of trusts unless it can be shown that a court should deny an equitable interest to a party on the basis of that party's own questionable conduct (120). No such conduct has been alleged against Ms Cummins.

83 It may be considered that, from a policy perspective, different trusts principles favouring the public purse as against the private wealth of the partner of a bankrupt should apply. It may, for instance, be considered that such principles should redistribute some of the proprietary rights of the individual (non-bankrupt) partner to the public, on the basis that the non-bankrupt partner has shared in the benefits enjoyed by the bankrupt at the expense of the public. As the application of any such principle would involve a significant change to existing doctrine and to existing proprietary interests, it would be for Parliament and not for the courts to consider such a change. It is Parliament and not this Court that is best placed to give appropriate consideration to the myriad of factors that must be considered and balanced before any such fundamental change to property rights is contemplated.

84 My observations in this regard should not necessarily be read as lending support for legislative intervention of this kind. A heavy onus lies on those who would argue for the taking away of established proprietary interests from a person on the basis that their bankrupt partner (not they) owes money to the public purse. It would also be incumbent on those who would seek such a change to show that it would not further entrench women's structural disadvantage by "infecting" women with the debts of their male partners, in terms similar to the phenomenon identified as "sexually-transmitted debt" (121).

The law of trusts and the respective beneficial interests of Mr and Ms Cummins

85 I now turn to a consideration of the relevant trusts principles. I concur with the conclusion in the joint judgment that Mr and Ms Cummins held both legal and beneficial title in their Hunters Hill home as joint tenants. That joint tenancy was severed on Mr Cummins' bankruptcy and the Trustee is entitled to his half interest.

86 In the joint judgment the majority of this Court is of the view that any presumption of resulting trust in favour of Ms Cummins, based on her greater contribution to the purchase price of the Hunters Hill property, namely 76.3 per cent, is rebutted by evidence of the parties' actual intentions. Those intentions, it is said,

of Legal Practitioners. The Court noted that his actions were such as to bring the entire legal profession into disrepute: See *New South Wales Bar Association v Cummins* (2001) 52 NSWLR 279 (Spigelman CJ, Mason P and Handley JA).

(120) *Parsons v McBain* (2001) 109 FCR 120 at [16] (Black CJ, Kiefel J, Finkelstein J) (*Parsons*).

(121) See, for example, Graycar and Morgan, *The Hidden Gender of Law*, 2nd ed (2002), pp 114–126.

are consistent with the joint legal title on the register. The majority of this Court also considers that in marriage at least, there is an inference of joint ownership of the family home, and on the facts of the present case that this inference is consistent with the actual intentions of the parties. I cannot agree with either of these two bases for decision, for the reasons given below.

Application of resulting trusts principles not based on previous authority

87 The joint judgment finds that any presumption of resulting trust over the Hunters Hill property in favour of Ms Cummins (as to 76.3 per cent) is rebutted by evidence that the parties intended that the beneficial ownership of the property would be held jointly. There is, however, insufficient evidence to rebut the presumption of resulting trust that arose in favour of Ms Cummins at the time of the purchase of the property in 1970. It is true that the property that was purchased at Hunters Hill at that time, and to which Ms Cummins contributed the majority of the purchase price, was vacant land, and that later, a house was built on the land funded from the joint resources of both Mr and Ms Cummins. It is also true that the couple treated the property as their home, and that Mr Cummins' attempt to transfer full legal title to Ms Cummins in 1987 (which, as the joint judgment finds, is void as an attempt to defraud creditors pursuant to s 121 of the *Bankruptcy Act 1966* (Cth)) had all the markings of a transaction that assumed that the parties considered themselves to be joint beneficial owners of the property at that time.

88 It is not open to rely on the subsequent indications that the parties ultimately came to view the Hunters Hill property as their "joint" property to rebut the presumption of resulting trust that arose in favour of Ms Cummins in 1970. The trust that arises under the doctrine of resulting trusts determines the beneficial interests of the parties in accordance with their intentions *at the time of the purchase.* Any changes of intention as to beneficial ownership are not appropriately considered under this doctrine. It is not the intentions of the parties as they change over the course of the relationship that go toward rebuttal or otherwise of any presumption that arises at the time of the purchase. Rather, the trust is formed as a result of the actual intentions of the parties *at the time of purchase* itself.

89 This analysis is further supported by the rule of evidence that applies to the determination of the parties' intentions as to beneficial ownership under the resulting trust. The "no subsequent evidence rule" admits as evidence of such intention any acts or statements of the parties before or at the time of the transaction, or so immediately after the transaction that it forms part of the transaction. Such evidence is admissible both for and against the party who did the act or made the statement. Subsequent acts and

declarations, however, are only admissible against the party making them (122). The point of the rule is to admit evidence that is most reliable in the determination of the parties' actual intentions as to beneficial ownership, *at the time of purchase*. This then sets their respective beneficial interests under the resulting trust.

90 For the purposes of this rule, the joint judgment considers that the relevant "transaction" in relation to the Hunters Hill property was a "composite" of the purchase of the property, the construction of a dwelling house and occupation as a matrimonial home for many years. This rather elongated view of the relevant "transaction" forms the basis upon which the majority considers evidence of subsequent events, long after the initial purchase of the property in 1970, as indicative of the parties' intentions "at the time of the transaction." This approach departs significantly from the established view that it is the time of purchase (or transfer) which fixes the parties' beneficial interests under a resulting trust.

91 To assert that the resulting trust arises from the intentions of those who contribute to the purchase price of property *at the time of purchase* is not to say that any changes of intention or any additional factors that may, for example, amount to unconscionable assertion of title, cannot be taken into account in the ultimate determination of beneficial ownership. As I find below, they clearly can; but they cannot be appropriately taken into account under the doctrine of resulting trusts.

No legal authority for an inference of joint ownership of the family home

92 There is a further basis upon which the majority of this Court finds that Mr and Ms Cummins are joint beneficial owners of the Hunters Hill property. The majority hold that, in marriage at least, there is an inference of joint ownership of the matrimonial home. There being no evidence of contrary intention to rebut the inference on the facts, the joint beneficial ownership of the parties is affirmed. For the reasons given below, I also cannot agree with this basis for the majority's decision.

93 There is insufficient authority to support an inference of joint ownership of the matrimonial home. Prior to the joint judgment in the present case, there are few judicial references to such an inference. There is an *obiter dicta* comment in 1970 by Lord Upjohn in *Pettitt v Pettitt* (123), and an *obiter* reference to the principle by Mason and Brennan JJ in *Calverley v Green* (124). There is also a reference to the principle in a passage in Professor Scott's work on the *Law of Trusts*, which asserts the existence of the principle without citing any supporting authority for it (125). These few ref-

(122) See *Shephard v Cartwright* [1955] AC 431; *Charles Marshall Pty Ltd v Grimsley* (1956) 95 CLR 353 at 364–366.
(123) [1970] AC 777 *at 815 (Pettitt)*.
(124) (1984) 155 CLR 242 at 259–60 (Mason and Brennan JJ) (*Calverley*).

erences do not amount to prior legal authority for the existence of such an inference in Australia.

94 Mason and Brennan JJ, in their *obiter dicta* comments in relation to the inference in *Calverley*, explicitly confine its operation to what they consider to be the "lifetime relationship" of marriage. Their Honours contend that it is inappropriate to apply the inference to the case before them on the basis that that case involved a de facto relationship (126). The case before us today involves a matrimonial relationship. Thus, in their application of the inference to the present context, the majority is not required to extend the scope of the inference beyond the marriage context.

95 If the inference is now part of the law of Australia, as it must be given the majority of this Court establishing the principle in this case, then I concur with the (*obiter dicta*) views expressed in the joint judgment that suggest that such an inference should not be confined to the context of formal marriage. I would go further and explicitly state that if the inference of joint ownership is to be part of Australian law, then it should extend beyond marriage, and cover other marriage-like relationships.

96 As I have indicated, I consider that there is no prior authority to support the existence of an inference of joint ownership in Australian law. The effect of the joint judgment is to introduce a new principle into the law of trusts in Australia. This Court undoubtedly has the power to do so (127). There must, however, be compelling reasons of principle and policy for this Court to depart from long-established doctrine and such departure is best openly acknowledged to ensure that the consequences of any change are fully contemplated.

97 In my opinion, there are no compelling reasons of principle or policy that support the introduction of this new principle. Such a change will lead, at best, to doctrinal inconsistency and confusion, and at worst it may also lead to unintended social consequences that may further disadvantage vulnerable women. Doctrinal inconsistency will result as courts may be faced with a number of competing and contradictory presumptions and inferences. In the context where there is insufficient evidence of the parties' actual intentions, the starting presumption or inference will ordinarily determine the outcome of the case. If, in the present case, the joint judgment had not found any positive evidence of an intention by the parties to hold the property jointly, each of the two bases for its decision would have resulted in a different outcome in the case. The application of the presumption of resulting trust would have produced an outcome giving Ms Cummins an interest of 76.3 per

(125) Scott and Fratcher, *The Law of Trusts*, 4th ed (1989) vol 5, pp 197–8 (footnote omitted).
(126) (1984) 155 CLR 242 at 259–60 (Mason and Brennan JJ).
(127) *John v Federal Commissioner of Taxation* (1989) 166 CLR 417 at 438–439.

cent (her initial contribution) whereas the application of an inference of joint ownership would have produced an outcome giving Mr and Ms Cummins a half beneficial interest each. As it turns out, the joint judgment has found sufficient evidence of intention to rebut the presumption of resulting trust and to affirm the inference of joint ownership, thereby producing a consistent result in the case. But this will often not be the case.

98 If facts exist that would give rise to the presumption of advancement of a wife by her husband, then a further contradiction would arise. Where, for example, a wife holds a legal interest greater than a joint tenancy, the presumption of advancement would presumptively (absent evidence of intention) entitle her to a beneficial interest equal to her greater legal interest. On the same facts, the inference of joint ownership would presumptively give rise to joint beneficial ownership. In *Calverley,* Mason and Brennan JJ alluded to this contradiction and to the disadvantage that would result to a wife as a result of the application of the inference rather than the presumption of advancement in these circumstances, but their Honours did not find it necessary to resolve the issue in the context of that case (128).

99 The inconsistency and contradiction in doctrine that results from the introduction of this new principle is enough to warrant extreme caution in regards to its adoption. Unless such issues of doctrinal consistency are dealt with, then the new principle is likely to lead to justified confusion in the lower courts. The joint judgment does not deal with these issues of inconsistency and for this reason alone I cannot concur with it.

Policy reasons against the introduction of a new principle of joint ownership

100 Neither do I consider that there is any justifiable policy basis for the introduction of a new inference of joint ownership of the family home. To the contrary, there are strong reasons of policy against the introduction of such a principle.

101 I have already noted that the introduction of such an inference would presumptively work to the disadvantage of a wife who holds a legal interest greater than a joint tenancy on the basis that the presumption of advancement that has traditionally applied from husband to wife would otherwise presumptively entitle her to a beneficial interest equal to her greater legal interest. The inference of joint ownership would also presumptively disadvantage a wife, such as Ms Cummins, who has contributed more than half of the purchase price, as the presumption of resulting trust that traditionally attaches to her contribution in this context would presumptively entitle her to an interest equivalent to her greater

(128) (1984) 155 CLR 242 at 259–60 (Mason and Brennan JJ).

contribution. In fact, as I have noted, had the traditional presumption of resulting trust been applied in the present case with its doctrinal integrity intact (129), the beneficial interest of Ms Cummins at the time of purchase would have been 76.3 per cent.

102 The only context in which the inference of joint ownership sets up a presumptive advantage for a wife as compared to the traditional presumptions is when title is taken out in the husband's name alone and the wife has made a lesser contribution to the purchase price than her husband. In such cases the inference presumes equal ownership whereas the presumption of resulting trust presumes that interests are commensurate with the parties' contributions. This particular ownership and contribution context reflects patriarchal models of home ownership and women's traditionally lower financial contributions. It may be argued, therefore, that at least the inference of joint ownership would serve to benefit the most vulnerable women, those who lack the means to make an equal financial contribution *and* also lack sufficient power to insist on being named on the legal title.

103 The beneficial effect of the application of the new inference to women in this particular context may, at first blush, appear to provide a policy justification for its introduction. Such cases are, however, usually and more appropriately dealt with under the principles of constructive rather than resulting trusts. Where the factual context involves substantial contributions of an indirect or non-financial kind, evidence of detrimental reliance on representations as to ownership, or unconscionable assertion of title (factors which are particularly pertinent to women in a traditional gendered relationship context) then a constructive rather than a resulting trust analysis is more appropriate and tends to be the doctrine of choice by courts (130). This is particularly the case for women who do not appear on the legal title to the family home and who have made significant non-financial contributions to the relationship. Where the factual context is predominantly confined to direct financial contributions to the acquisition of the home, then resulting trust principles tend to be applied by courts.

104 In factual contexts where a resulting trusts analysis is most likely to be applied by a court, the introduction of an inference of joint ownership sets up a presumptive disadvantage for married women in relation to beneficial ownership of the family home against

(129) That is, with a focus on whether there was any evidence to indicate that at the time of the purchase, the parties intended that beneficial ownership be otherwise than in accordance with their contributions to the purchase price.

(130) See, for example, *Baumgartner v Baumgartner* (1987) 164 CLR 137; *Parsons* (2001) 109 FCR 120; *Green v Green* (1989) 17 NSWLR 343. For a detailed discussion of the various types of constructive trust relevant to the family home, see Bryan, "Constructive Trusts and Unconscionability in Australia: On the Endless Road to Unattainable Perfection", *Trust Law International*, vol 8 (1994), p 74. See also my judgment below at [108]–[111].

third parties who claim through their husbands. This presumptive disadvantage applies where the presumption of resulting trust would otherwise operate in favour of a wife who makes a greater financial contribution to the acquisition of the home and in contexts where, traditionally, the presumption of advancement would operate from a husband to a wife. The latter presumption may, in this age of "identical treatment" between the sexes, appear to be somewhat paternalistic, yet its existence can also be viewed as a counterweight to the structural inequalities that women continue to suffer in our society (131). Until those structural inequalities are eliminated, there is a continuing basis in principle and policy for its existence. The presumption of advancement (and the presumption of resulting trust) should not be superseded by a principle of equal ownership. In my view this Court should not introduce a new principle that further disadvantages women, particularly when the principle affects ownership of the family home, an asset of central importance to the standard of living of the family as a whole.

105 It may be that, if the inference of joint ownership postulated by the majority of this Court is taken to extend to de facto relationships, then de facto wives may benefit from it on the basis that the presumption of advancement does not traditionally extend to their benefit. If, for example, a de facto husband contributes a greater share of the purchase price, then the presumption of resulting trust (as opposed to the presumption of advancement) would ordinarily apply to his contributions and he would presumptively hold a greater beneficial interest. The inference of joint ownership in this context would presumptively result in joint beneficial ownership. In *Calverley*, Gibbs CJ was the only member of this Court to hold that the presumption of advancement extended to de facto wives (132). In my view, his Honour was correct in so holding. There is no reason to draw a distinction between the presumptive wishes of men who are formally married to their partners and those men in couples who have chosen to live in a de facto relationship. If the presumption of advancement is extended to de facto wives, as it should be, then any presumptive disadvantage suffered by them as a result of the non-application of the inference of joint ownership would be neutralised.

106 It should also be noted that in the regulation of property disputes between separating partners, Parliament has followed the advice of the Australian Law Reform Commission (133) and has chosen not to implement a "community of property" regime such

(131) See Graycar and Morgan, *The Hidden Gender of Law*, 2nd ed (2002), pp 28–33; 44–48; 99–101.

(132) Gibbs CJ at 250–1; cf Mason and Brennan JJ at 259-61; Deane at 268–9.

(133) Australia, The Law Reform Commission, *Matrimonial Property*, Report (133) No 39 (1987), p xxxiv [24], 25 [53], 239 [513].

as that which exists in some jurisdictions (134). Such a regime presumes joint ownership of family assets, an approach that differs from the structured discretion applied under s 79 of the FLA. This Court should not, of its own accord, impose a de facto community of property regime through the introduction of an inference of joint ownership in the context of third party claims to the family home.

107 I have already noted that trusts law is a blunt tool for the resolution of disputes involving third party claims to the family home, and that legislative intervention in a form similar to s 79 of the FLA would be welcome. Until that legislative intervention occurs, this Court must make do with the trusts principles available to it. Of course, it is open to this Court to develop those principles, but such development should occur with caution lest there be unintended consequences, as noted above, of such development. For these reasons I prefer to rely on existing trusts principles to resolve the present case.

The "common intention" constructive trust

108 The resolution of this dispute can readily be dealt with through the use of traditional trusts principles. As there was no evidence to rebut the presumption of resulting trust that arose on the purchase of the Hunters Hill property in 1970, Ms Cummins and Mr Cummins initially each held a beneficial interest under a resulting trust of 76.3 per cent and 23.7 per cent respectively. Through their course of dealing with the property over time, including the building of a house on the land, its use as their family home over many years, and various other factors that indicated that they came to view the property as jointly owned, it is possible to infer that a common intention emerged that they were joint beneficial owners. Thus the initial resulting trust predominantly in favour of Ms Cummins was subsequently superseded by a constructive trust based on the common intention of the parties as it developed over time.

109 In *Allen v Snyder* (135), Glass JA traced the so-called "common intention" constructive trust to the judgments of the House of Lords in *Pettitt* (136) and *Gissing v Gissing* (137). His Honour noted that this constructive trust arose from the common intention of the parties as to how the beneficial interest is to be held and that such intention may be inferred from the conduct of the parties (138). Significantly, his Honour also noted that such common intention

(134) For example, in Washington and Texas in the United States of America.
(135) [1977] 2 NSWLR 685 at 688-696.
(136) [1970] AC 777.
(137) [1971] AC 886.
(138) [1977] 2 NSWLR 685 at 690.
(139) [1977] 2 NSWLR 685 at 691.

may arise after the acquisition of the home (139). There is also the notion that for the trust to be imposed there must be some detrimental reliance on the common intention such as the making of contributions or the provision of services (140).

110 In his article on the constructive trust in Australia (141), Michael Bryan notes that despite predictions that the so-called "common intention" constructive trust would be superseded and replaced by the emergence of the broad-based "unconscionability" constructive trust developed by this Court in *Baumgartner v Baumgartner* (142), the common intention constructive trust has in fact survived as an independent basis for relief and continues to be used by Australian courts. In *Parsons v McBain* the Full Court of the Federal Court imposed a common intention constructive trust in favour of the spouses of two brothers who had been declared bankrupt in a case involving a claim by the Trustee in bankruptcy to the full interest in each of their family homes (143). Each of the two spouses was found to have a one half beneficial interest in the family home, and such interests could defeat the claim of the Trustee. In *Green v Green*, the New South Wales Court of Appeal also held that a beneficial interest existed in the claimant based on the common intention constructive trust (144).

111 As these cases indicate, there is authority to support the continued existence of the common intention constructive trust in Australia. The present case can therefore be resolved through the imposition of a common intention constructive trust and without recourse to new doctrine or to the making of substantial changes to existing doctrine. Unlike the resulting trust, the doctrinal components of the common intention constructive trust permit evidence of, and give effect to, the intention of the parties as it develops and possibly changes over time. The evidence in the present case points to the existence of a common intention that the parties were joint beneficial owners of the Hunters Hill property. That common intention existed at least since 1987, when Mr Cummins attempted to transfer full legal ownership to Ms Cummins through actions that indicated that the parties at that stage considered themselves to be joint beneficial owners. That common intention may have existed as early as the building of the house on the property shortly after the initial purchase. It is unnecessary, however, to decide on the precise date at which the common intention as to joint beneficial ownership took effect as it was clearly manifest by 2000 when

(140) [1977] 2 NSWLR 685 at 691.
(141) Bryan, "Constructive Trusts and Unconscionability in Australia: On the Endless Road to Unattainable Perfection", *Trust Law International*, vol 8 (1994).
(142) (1987) 164 CLR 137.
(143) (2001) 109 FCR 120 (Black CJ, Kiefel and Finkelstein JJ).
(144) (1989 17 NSWLR 343 (Gleeson CJ, Priestley JA agreeing).

Mr Cummins was declared bankrupt. What is clear is that at the relevant time of his bankruptcy, Mr Cummins was a joint beneficial owner of the Hunters Hill property, and the Trustee is entitled to his interest therein.

Conclusion

112 For the reasons given above, I concur with the ultimate orders in the joint judgment. The resolution of issues such as those in the present case may ultimately come to be decided on a basis similar to the statutory structured discretion available for separating couples under s 79 of the FLA. Until that time, there is no reason of principle or policy that justifies the making of fundamental changes to traditional trusts principles. The consequences of such changes cannot be fully anticipated by this Court. Indeed, they may lead to results that are undesirable. This Court undoubtedly has the power to change existing doctrine, but it should only do so when fully cognisant of the effects of such change, particularly when it may result in further entrenching the disadvantage of vulnerable groups. In the present case the Court has not had the assistance of *amicus curiae* nor does it have the research expertise and resources of a law reform body. The Court should move with caution before re-writing so long-established an area of law.

Part III

Crime and Evidence

Criminal Law

14

Reconsidering Precedent: *Parker v R*

HEATHER DOUGLAS

Introduction

Parker v R[1] is a landmark Australian provocation case. Provocation is a partial defence to murder which, if successful, reduces murder to manslaughter, usually resulting in a lesser sentence for the accused. Legislative provisions dealing with provocation vary between jurisdictions, and in some jurisdictions the defence has been abolished.[2] The defence has three key ingredients: the accused must be provoked by the actions of the victim; as a result of the provocation he or she loses self-control and kills; and confronted with the same gravity of provocation, an ordinary person could have lost self-control and formed the intention to kill or do grievous bodily harm.[3]

In 1960, Frank Parker, his wife Joan and their six children moved to Jerilderie in New South Wales, so Frank could find farm work. Within a few weeks of arriving Frank Parker had noticed and commented on the fact that a farm hand, Daniel Kelly, had been spending time with his wife Joan. Around six weeks after her arrival at the farm, Joan Parker decided to leave with Kelly. The pair set off on a bicycle, with Joan Parker balanced on the handlebars. Some time later Frank Parker drove after them in his car, hitting both his wife and Kelly. His wife was badly injured as a result, and on Frank's account, 'I done my block, lost my temper',[4] leading to him hitting Kelly with a knuckleduster and stabbing him to death. Frank Parker was subsequently found guilty of murder by a jury. At the trial the judge refused to submit the issue of provocation to the jury for consideration. Parker appealed to the Court of Criminal Appeal on the basis that the jury should have been able to consider provocation. Sugerman J found that there was no evidence of provocation, and that Parker 'acted at the time in a fury of rage' and dismissed the appeal.[5]

Parker sought special leave, on the same grounds, to appeal to the High Court, but this was refused by the majority (Taylor, Owen and Menzies JJ; Dixon CJ and Windeyer J dissenting). One matter that all four judgments of the High Court accepted was that 'if a man kill[s] his wife, or the adulterer, in the act of adultery it is manslaughter, providing the husband has ocular inspection of the act'.[6] However there was disagreement between the

[1] *Parker v R* (1963) 111 CLR 610 ('*Parker*').

[2] There have been significant reforms to provocation law since *Parker* was decided; see the last section of this commentary.

[3] See generally *Stingel v R* (1990) 171 CLR 366 ('*Stingel*'); *Pollock v R* (2010) 242 CLR 233 ('*Pollock*').

[4] *Parker* (1963) 111 CLR 610, 620 (Dixon CJ).

[5] *Parker v R* (1963) 80 WN (NSW) 632, 640, 642 (Manning J concurred).

[6] *Parker* (1963) 111 CLR 610, 646 (Menzies J), 639 (Taylor and Owens JJ), 628 (Dixon CJ), 655 (Windeyer J). The Court referred to *R v Maddy* (1671) 1 *Ventris* 158; 86 ER 108 ('*Maddy*').

judgments on the key issue. Taylor and Owen JJ dismissed the appeal, finding that the realisation that Parker had injured his wife caused the loss of control, and that the nature and sequence of the acts which caused Kelly's death were not of a character that would have deprived the ordinary person of self-control. Menzies J also dismissed the appeal. He found that the deceased's conduct in 'taking away' the accused's wife could not amount to provocation in law.[7] Dixon CJ dissented. He observed:

> According to the standards governing our society in the later nineteenth century and the twentieth century the succession of events and the conduct of Dan Kelly brought a very strong provocation to an emotional nature, a provocation still in actual operation when Parker came upon Dan Kelly with his wife. That at all events is a view which the jury were entitled to adopt.[8]

Along with Dixon CJ, Windeyer J would have also ordered a retrial. He explained that the husband's discovery of his wife in the act of adultery was at one end of the scale (and provocation in law), and insulting words or gestures unaccompanied by a blow were at the other (and not considered provocation).[9] The actions of Kelly, Windeyer J suggested, had extended over the afternoon, during which time Parker's 'passions and emotions' were mounting. In his view Kelly's actions could be thought by a jury to be 'reasonably calculated to deprive an ordinary person of self-control'.[10]

Parker appealed to the Privy Council, where the dissenting judgment of Dixon CJ in the High Court was followed. As Leader-Elliot observes: 'It took a good story . . . told with judicious passion [by Dixon CJ] and embellished with references to Othello, to change the law of provocation in Australia.'[11] At the Privy Council, Lord Morris of Borth-y-Gest delivered the reasons of the Court. He noted that although there was an interval of time between the moment that Joan Parker and Kelly left the farm and the moment when Frank Parker confronted them and killed Kelly, 'a jury might well consider . . . that the deceased's whole conduct was such as might "heat the blood to a proportionable degree of resentment and keep it boiling to the moment of fact"'.[12] He observed that the jury might find that Parker was 'tormented beyond endurance' by his wife being 'lured away' and Kelly speaking with 'relish of his lascivious intents'.[13] Ultimately the Privy Council concluded that the appeal should be allowed, and that the case should be remitted back to the New South Wales Court of Criminal Appeal to either enter a verdict of manslaughter and impose an appropriate sentence or order a new trial.[14]

[7] *Parker* (1963) 111 CLR 610, 646.
[8] Ibid 628.
[9] Ibid 653.
[10] Ibid 663.
[11] Ian Leader-Elliot, 'Battered But Not Beaten: Women Who Kill in Self-Defence' (1993) 15 *Sydney Law Review* 403, 418.
[12] *Parker v R (New South Wales)* (1964) 111 CLR 665, 679, quoting from Edward Hyde East, *A Treatise of Pleas of the Crown* (Butterworth, 1803) 238.
[13] *Parker v R (New South Wales)* ibid; that is Kelly had, in effect, provoked his own demise. See Adrian Howe, 'Provoking Polemic-Provoked Killings and the Ethical Paradoxes of the Postmodern Feminist Condition' (2002) 10 *Feminist Legal Studies* 39, 42.
[14] *Parker v R (New South Wales)* ibid, 668.

The Impact of *Parker*

Despite the successful appeal to the Privy Council, all four of the judgments of the High Court in *Parker* have been regularly relied upon by subsequent High Court and state Court of Appeal decisions, many of which have involved men killing women when the woman has decided to leave the relationship, or killing other men as a result of sexual jealousy.[15] *Parker* has been cited as providing a helpful summary of the early history and development of provocation and as authority for a range of principles, including the relevance of social change to the development of the provocation defence; the importance of judges leaving provocation to the jury where there is 'sufficient' evidence even if the defence is not explicitly raised (and that 'sufficiency' may be interpreted differently by different judges); the need for an objective standard of self-control; the need to assess the whole of the circumstances; the onus of proof for provocation; the possibility of provocation accumulating over time and the requirement for an absence of a 'cooling off' period.[16]

The judgments of the High Court in *Parker* both underlined and sometimes exacerbated the problems with the provocation defence. Howe reflects the views of many commentators when she describes the provocation defence as 'an irredeemably sexed excuse for murder'.[17] While both men and women have relied on provocation in intimate partner homicides,[18] men have often successfully argued they were provoked to kill by their partner's alleged infidelity and/or their partner leaving or threatening to leave the relationship.[19] *Parker* has been a convenient case for defence lawyers to rely on, sometimes successfully, to support the narrative that a woman's decision to separate or to start a new relationship is a provocative act.[20] Morgan has noted the difficulty of displacing 'the cultural story that a woman leaving a man for another, taunting him about his sexuality, or otherwise being "provocative" excuses homicidal rage.'[21] In finding that provocation could accumulate over time, and in relaxing the requirement for suddenness in the loss of self-control,[22] *Parker* contributed to the High Court's increasingly expansive view of what might count as provocation to kill.[23]

[15] See eg, *Heron v R* (2003) 77 ALJR 908 ('*Heron*'); *Hart v R* (2003) 27 WAR 441 ('*Hart*'); *Stingel* (1990) 171 CLR 366; *R v Croft* (1981) 1 NSWLR 126; *R v Dutton* (1979) 21 SASR 356 ('*Dutton*'); *Moffa v R* (1977) 138 CLR 601 ('*Moffa*'); *R v Yasso* (2004) 148 A Crim R 369 ('*Yasso*').

[16] See *Van Den Hoek v R* (1986) 161 CLR 158, 166 (Mason J); *Moffa* (1977) 138 CLR 601, 621 (Mason J); *Johnson v R* (1976) 136 CLR 619, 634 (Barwick CJ), 652 (Gibbs J), 665 (Jacobs J); *Masciantonio v R* (1985) 183 CLR 58, 71 (McHugh J); *Heron* (2003) 77 ALJR 908, 913–14 (Kirby J); *Green v R* (1997) 191 CLR 334, 402 (Kirby J) ('*Green*'); *Pollock* (2010) 242 CLR 233, 250 (French CJ, Hayne, Crennan, Kiefel and Bell JJ). While the High Court's decision in *Parker* was primarily important for its comments related to the provocation defence, it is also thought to be the first case to declare the independence of the High Court from the English House of Lords: see Editorial, 'Current Topics' (1963) 37 *Australian Law Journal* 1.

[17] Howe, above n 13, 40, 44; see also Danielle Tyson, *Sex, Culpability and the Defence of Provocation* (Routledge-Cavendish, 2013) ch 1, where an overview of this literature is provided.

[18] Rebecca Bradfield, 'Is Near Enough Good Enough?: Why Isn't Self-Defence Appropriate for the Battered Woman?' (1998) 5 *Psychiatry, Psychology and Law* 71, 71.

[19] Graeme Coss, 'Provocative Reforms: A Comparative Critique' (2006) 30 *Criminal Law Journal* 138, 149.

[20] See, eg, *Yasso* (2004) 148 A Crim R 369; *Dutton* (1979) 21 SASR 356; *Moffa* (1977) 138 CLR 601. It is notable that such claims appear to have been less likely to succeed in more recent times: see, eg, *Hart* (2003) 27 WAR 441.

[21] Jenny Morgan, 'Homicide Law Reform and Gender' (2012) 45 *Australian and New Zealand Journal of Criminology* 351, 364.

[22] Leader-Elliot, above n 11, 458; Tyson, *above n 17*, 87.

[23] See, eg, *Green* (1997) 191 CLR 334, 344; *Pollock* (2010) 242 CLR 233, 246–7, 250. See also Adrian Howe, 'Provocation in Crisis Law's Passion at the Crossroads? New Directions for Feminist Strategists' (2004) 21 *Australian Feminist Law Journal* 12.

This shift led inexorably to the reduction of culpability for many violent men who killed.[24]

The Feminist Judgment

The feminist judgment in *Parker* joins the majority of the High Court in refusing leave to appeal. It finds, along with the majority, that the provocation defence was correctly not left to the jury to consider at trial. However, its detailed review of the history of the common law of provocation demonstrates that most of the authorities available at the time did not support an expansion of provocation to include suspected adultery. The feminist judgment cites different precedents, then available to, but not cited by, the High Court or the Privy Council, to uncover an alternative view of suspected adultery: that killing in response to it must be murder[25] or 'insanity',[26] but could not be manslaughter. The feminist judgment emphasises the unanimity of the decision of the House of Lords in *R v Holmes*,[27] and specifically the resistance of Viscount Simon's dicta in that case, to the idea that suspected infidelity could ground provocation to kill. It stresses that the preceding case law had been reluctant to expand the principle that for adultery to count as provocation, the accused must have had 'ocular inspection' of it.[28] The judgment identifies *Holmes* as the 'highpoint of judicial resistance' to expanding provocation beyond this.[29] In his High Court judgment Dixon CJ alluded to social changes to justify an expansion of the context in which provocation may be successfully argued (ie to include suspected adultery).[30] In contrast, the feminist judgment uses the same argument to find in the alternative; that the evolution of society should lead to a higher standard of self-control being expected, rather than an assumption of reduced self-control (and an associated expansion of the provocation defence). After reviewing the case law, the feminist judgment concludes that the law must recognise the 'legal right of women to leave unsatisfactory relationships without fear of serious or fatal violence' to themselves or to others.

Law Reform Since *Parker*

Since *Parker* was decided,[31] and particularly since the 1980s, significant feminist critique has repeatedly exposed the gender-biased operation of the provocation defence, and pressed for

[24] While women have also sometimes claimed provocation, their claims have often been made in a different context, involving a long history of abuse, and have often had more in common with a self-defence claim than with provocation: see Victorian Law Reform Commission, *Defences to Homicide: Final Report*, Report No 94 (2004) 29.

[25] *R v Kelly* (1848) 175 ER 342, 342–3; *R v Taylor* (Unreported, Old Bailey Proceedings, November 1882).

[26] *R v Townley* (1863) 176 ER 384.

[27] [1946] AC 588, 598 ('*Holmes*').

[28] *Maddy* (1671) 86 ER 108.

[29] [1946] AC 588, 598. See also Thomas Crofts and Arlie Loughnan, 'Provocation: The Good, the Bad and the Ugly' (2013) 37 *Criminal Law Journal* 23.

[30] *Parker* (1963) 111 CLR 610, 628.

[31] This discussion has also taken place in the United Kingdom. For United Kingdom reforms and debates see Jeremy Horder, *Homicide and the Politics of Law Reform* (Oxford University Press, 2012); see especially 211–22.

legislative reform.[32] The proposed Model Criminal Code, developed by a federal law reform body, proposed abolition of the provocation defence in 1998.[33] Since then, most Australian jurisdictions have reviewed and reformed their provocation laws.[34] Tasmania led the way, abolishing the defence of provocation in 2003.[35] Subsequently a report of the Victorian Law Reform Commission found that the provocation defence, despite the fact that it had been incrementally changed over time in an attempt to ensure that it applied fairly, had continued to reinforce gender inequality.[36] In 2005 Victoria introduced a package of reforms to the *Crimes Act 1958* (Vic) that included the abolition of provocation.[37] In Western Australia, following recommendations of the Law Reform Commission of Western Australia,[38] the defence was abolished in 2008.[39]

However, the defence of provocation and its abolition is a double-edged sword for women. While men have often successfully argued they were provoked to kill by their partner's alleged infidelity, or their partner leaving or threatening to leave the relationship, provocation has also been claimed by women who have killed in the context of a long history of abuse and where self-defence is unsuccessful.[40] With this in mind, other jurisdictions have sought to narrow the reach of the defence, rather than abolish it.[41] More recently, Queensland undertook a review of provocation and defences to homicide[42] and in 2011, changes were introduced in that state. According to the amended Queensland provision, provocation is no longer a partial defence to murder where the provocation is based on anything done by the deceased that indicated a decision to leave, change or end the relationship.[43] There are currently plans to reform, rather than abolish, the law of provocation in South Australia and New South Wales.[44] Whether they achieve their aim of increasing men's culpability for killing wives and women partners remains to be seen.[45]

[32] For some comment on this history see Morgan, above n 21; Howe, above n 13, 40, 44.

[33] Model Criminal Code Officers Committee, 'Discussion paper Model Criminal Code: Chapter five: Fatal Offences Against the Person' (Discussion Paper, MCCOC, June 1998).

[34] For a recent overview see: Crofts and Loughnan, above n 29.

[35] *Criminal Code Amendment (Abolition of Defence of Provocation) Act 2003* (Tas).

[36] Victorian Law Reform Commission, above n 24, xxviii.

[37] Other reforms included the inclusion of a definition of self-defence in legislation, reforms to evidence and a new and controversial offence of defensive homicide. See *R v Middendorp* [2010] VSC 202, included in this collection.

[38] Law Reform Commission of Western Australia, *Review of the Law of Homicide, Final Report*, Project No 97 (2007) 172.

[39] At the same time a defence of excessive self-defence was reintroduced which, if successful reduces murder to manslaughter: *Criminal Code 1913* (WA) s 248(3).

[40] Victorian Law Reform Commission, above n 24, 29.

[41] In relation to English reform see: *Coroners and Justice Act 2009* (UK) ss 54–56.

[42] Queensland Law Reform Commission, *A Review of the Excuse of Accident and the Defence of Provocation*, Report No 64 (2008); Geraldine MacKenzie and Eric Colvin, 'Victims who Kill their Abusers: A Discussion Paper on Defences' (Discussion Paper, Bond University, 14 April 2009). These changes included the introduction of a new partial battered person's defence (*Criminal Code* (Qld) s 304B); see Heather Douglas, 'A Consideration of the Merits of Specialised Homicide Offences and Defences for Battered Women' (2012) 45(3) *Australian and New Zealand Journal of Criminology* 367.

[43] See *Criminal Code* (Qld) s 304, although if 'exceptional circumstances' exist, a provocation claim may succeed – perhaps even where the discovery of adultery is the main provocation. Exceptional circumstances are not defined.

[44] In 2013 the Greens Party introduced a Bill to the South Australian Parliament to exclude homosexual advances as a trigger for the provocation defence: *Criminal Law Consolidation (Provocation) Amendment Bill 2013* (SA). For New South Wales see Select Committee on the Partial Defence of Provocation, Parliament of New South Wales, *The Partial Defence of Provocation* (2013).

[45] Carol Smart, *Feminism and the Power of Law* (Routledge, 1989); Reg Graycar and Jenny Morgan, 'Law Reform: What's in it for Women?' (2005) 23 *Windsor Yearbook of Access to Justice* 393, 401.

[HIGH COURT OF AUSTRALIA.]

PARKER . . . . APPLICANT ;

AND

THE QUEEN . . . . .RESPONDENT.

H. C. OF A. 19621963.

PARKER v. THE QUEEN.

Howe J.

HOWE J. I concur in the opinions of Taylor, Owen and Menzies JJ. that the trial judge did not err in holding that there was no evidence of provocation fit to be left to the jury.

This case highlights a disturbing trend in the application of the law of provocation, particularly in cases concerning husbands killing their wives, in the wake of changes to the common law made by the *Homicide Act*, 1957 (5 & 6 Eliz. 2 c.11) and s 23 of the *Crimes Act*, 1900 (NSW). As Dixon C.J. says, the present case is "a curious one", a curiosity he appears to find in the failure of the accused's defence to argue for an acquittal. In my opinion, its curiosity lies elsewhere, namely in the unprecedented concessions made by the Solicitor General to the applicant. In his address to this court, the Solicitor General pointed out the present case differs "markedly" from the foundational provocation by infidelity case of *R. v. Maddy* (1). Indeed it is, as he said, an "entirely different case". Yet he then proceeded to make major concessions to the applicant, going so far as to agree that the issue of provocation should have been left to the jury. Acceptance of this proposition would appear to represent a significant departure from earlier authorities. Courts, in my opinion, have begun to lose their way in their findings of what should count as sufficient provocation to warrant reducing murder to manslaughter. What always needs to be recalled is Coleridge J.'s observation in *R. v. Kirkham* that although the law "condescends to human frailty" it "will not indulge human ferocity" as it considers "man to be a rational being, and requires that he should exercise a reasonable control over his passions" (2). In my opinion that hallowed concession to "human frailty" has been taken too far and the law of provocation has become unduly expansive, perhaps especially in what were once seen as provocation by adultery cases but which are more properly seen as homicides prompted by wives wanting to leave their marriages. Moreover, in these cases it is always wives who are killed, and who are put at risk by an unduly expansive application of the law of provocation.

In the earliest case of provocation by adultery, *Maddy*, decided in 1671, the court held that killing a man found in the very act of committing adultery with one's wife was "but manslaughter" and directed the executioner to burn Manning gently in the hand, for there "could not be greater provocation than this" (3). This case was approved in *R. v. Mawgridge* which set down four rules, "supported by authority and general consent" regarding "what are always allowed to be suffi-

(1) (1671) 1 Vent. 158 (*Maddy*).
(2) (1837) 173 E.R. 422, at pp. 423-425.
(3) (1671) 1 Vent. 158.
(4) (1706) Kel. 119, at p. 135 (*Mawgridge*).

cient provocations" (4). The fourth rule was this:

> "... when a man is taken in adultery with another man's wife, if the husband shall stab the adulterer, or knock out his brains, this is bare manslaughter: for jealousy is the rage of a man, and adultery is the highest invasion of property" (5).

Property his wife may have been in the eighteenth century, but in an oft-overlooked footnote the court stated that at law a man is not justified in killing a man he "taketh in adultery with his wife" for this "savours more of sudden revenge, than of self-preservation" (6). While the court also noted that this law "hath been executed with great benignity" (7), it is noteworthy that a doubt was registered about the possibility of vengeful motives in such cases right from the start. This doubt can be traced through the nineteenth century cases, by which time the target of such homicidal rages had shifted imperceptibly from interlopers to wives suspected of adultery. Without registering the significance of this shift, English courts continued to confirm the notion that the killing of an adulterer by a husband was the very lowest degree of manslaughter. Mere suspicion was not enough; "strong misgivings" as to a wife's fidelity without proof to warrant "the inference that he was justified in any such feeling" would not do – in *Pearson's Case*, Parke B. said a man had to have "ocular inspection of the act, and only then" (8).

By the mid-nineteenth century it was said that:

> "... to take away the life of a woman, even your own wife because you suspect that she has been engaged in some illicit intrigue, would be murder; however strongly you may suspect it, it would most unquestionably be murder" (9).

This was stated in *R. v. Matthias Kelly* "without the least shadow of doubt. We must not shut our eyes to the truth" – conceiving "a jealousy of the woman" would not reduce the crime to manslaughter (10). As for the man who cut his fiancée's throat when she broke off their engagement, viewing her as if she were an adulterous wife and claiming he had as "perfect a right to deal with her life as he had with any other property", the court saw this as a simple case of insanity (11). The judge told the jury, if his "real motive" was jealousy or a desire for revenge that would be murder. After all, these were "the very passions which the law required men to control". He added: "what would be the consequences to society if men were to say to every woman who treated them in that way that she should die, and carried out such view by cutting her throat?" The defendant's claim that he could exercise "the same power over a wife as he could lawfully exercise over a "chattel" was "the conclusion of a man who had arrived at results different from those generally arrived at and contrary to the laws of God and man" (12). By the late nineteenth century, wife killers were convicted of murder if all that they had to rely on was an "innocent suspicion" – "perfectly sane men

(5) (1706) Kel. 119, at p. 137.
(6) (1706) Kel. 119, at p. 137.
(7) (1706) Kel. 119, at p. 137.
(8) (1835) 2 Lewin 216.
(9) *R v. Kelly* (1848) 175 E.R. 342, at p. 814.
(10) (1848) 175 E.R. 342, at pp. 342, 343.
(11) *R. v. Townley* (1863) 176 E.R. 384.
(12) (1863) 176 E.R. 384 at p. 386.

H. C. OF A. 19621963.

PARKER v. THE QUEEN.

Howe J.

often have a suspicion of their wives having committed adultery" – killing such a wife was very common form of innocent suspicion". But a suspicion was no warrant for murder – and this is the telling point – especially when men admitted that they killed their wives because they had threatened to leave them (13).

Then followed a spate of well-known provocation cases where appeal courts were invited to follow *R. v. Rothwell* (14), an 1871 wife-killing case, one of many departure cases to come – she left because of his violence, he killed her for leaving him. Blackburn J. told the jury that "there may be such heat of blood and provocation as to reduce the crime to manslaughter" but where there are "no blows", there must be "a provocation equal to blows; it must be at least as great as blows":

> "For instance, a man who discovers his wife in adultery and thereupon kills the adulterer, is only guilty of manslaughter. As a general rule, no provocation of words will reduce the crime of murder to that of manslaughter, but under special circumstances there may be such a provocation of words as will have that effect; for instance, if a husband suddenly hearing from his wife that she has committed adultery were thereupon to kill his wife, it might be manslaughter" (15).

It can be seen that finding a wife in adultery remained the paradigmatic and much cited exemplar of sufficient provocation, notwithstanding the fact that it was extremely rare for defendants to claim that they had discovered their wives *in flagrante delicto*. Perhaps it was this very rarity that opened the door for a wife's alleged confession of adultery to count as sufficiently grave provocation to reduce murder to manslaughter. Early twentieth century courts were, however, reluctant to extend the doctrine, refusing to extend it to cover cases of murdered fiancées and unmarried partners. As the court said in *R. v. Palmer* (16), it was "well established by law" that a husband killing a wife found in adultery was guilty of manslaughter, not murder and that had been extended in *Rothwell* to a wife's sudden confession of adultery, a sudden confession being "treated as equivalent to a discovery of the act itself". But while it was a grave offence against the husband for the wife to commit adultery, there was no such offence when the woman was his fiancée or was co-habiting with him (17). Moreover – and this is the critical point as far as the present case is concerned – as the Lord Chief Justice said in *R. v. Ellor*, "no authority can be cited to support" the proposition that if a wife told her husband that she was going to commit adultery a manslaughter conviction was possible (18). That was "not the law of England" – a wife's statement that she was "going to live with another man, or that she was about to commit adultery" would not amount to provocation so as to reduce the crime of killing from murder to manslaughter. Indeed, the authorities supported the "contrary view" (19).

By the mid-twentieth century, it was settled that a man "may conjure up a

(13) *R. v. Taylor*, November 1882, unreported, Old Bailey Proceedings.
(14) (1871) 12 Cox C.C. 145.
(15) (1871) 12 Cox C.C. at p. 147.
(16) [1913] 2 K.B. 29.
(17) [1913] 2 K.B. 29 at p.31 and *R. v. Greening* (1914) 9 Cr. App. R. 105.
(18) (1921) 15 Cr. App. R. 41 at p. 43 citing *Palmer*, *Greening* and *R. v. Birchill* (1914) 9 Cr. App. R. 91.
(19) (1921) 15 Cr. App. R. at p. 44.
(20) *R. v. Gauthier* (1944) 29 Cr. App. R. 113 at p. 118.

motive or reasons sufficient for himself to cause him to kill, but it does not follow that that provides evidence of provocation" (20). Furthermore, "the mode of resentment must bear some relation to the alleged provocation" (21). Thus for example, a Bren gun "which fires bullets in quick succession is one thing, but a woman showing preference for a particular lover is another" (22). In other words, as far as legally sufficient provocation was concerned, finding a wife in adultery was one thing, but finding she wished to leave him for another man was quite another.

The reluctance of the early authorities to permit any extension of *Maddy* (23) or to indulge wife-murderers reached its apogee in *R. v. Holmes'* (24) high point of judicial resistance to expanding provocation in such cases beyond ocular proof of adultery. The court led by Viscount Simon was unanimous: a confession of adultery "without more" was not sufficient provocation to reduce murder to manslaughter. While this court in the present case has paid close attention to Viscount Simon's dicta about "actual intention to kill", his judgment warrants close examination for other reasons, not the least its recognition of the need to balance respect for human frailty with a consideration of the sanctity of human life. Viscount Simon provided cogent policy and legal reasons for the court's unanimous decision to reject the appeal of a man who, on the facts, claimed his wife had committed adultery so that he could continue his adulterous relationship unimpeded by his marriage. The Crown argued that it would be most "unfortunate" if returned soldiers were to believe that on a wife's confession of adultery "there is something like a licence to kill". Viscount Simon found this argument persuasive. After all, no "special quality" attached to confessions of adultery. Words, "whether an insult or an admission of adultery, never constituted provocation" (25). The defence countered with the prediction that in the future "there will certainly be ordinary reasonable men in this country who will hear confessions of adultery from their wives and some of them will be so deprived of their self-control that they will kill them". If the Crown's argument was accepted, these men would be "bound to be convicted of murder" (26). But Viscount Simon was unmoved, reminding the court of the importance of the objective standard: "confession of adultery, grievous as it is, cannot in itself justify the view that a reasonable man (or woman) would be so provoked as to do what this man did". The "actual finding" of a spouse in the act of adultery had always been treated as a "very special exception" to the general rule about sufficient provocation because, as Blackstone put it, "there could not be a greater provocation" (27). For Viscount Simon, it had been "rightly laid down that the exception cannot be extended" and it was not enough to simply repeat Parke B.'s assertion in *Pearson's Case* that ocular observation was essential. He went further, claiming – a claim sure to be cited in future commentaries on the law of provocation: "Even if Iago's insinuations against Desdemona had been true, Othello's crime was murder and nothing else" (28).

(21) (1944) 29 Cr. App. R. 113 at p. 119.
(22) (1944) 29 Cr. App. R. 113 at p. 119.
(23) (1671) 1 Vent. 158.
(24) [1946] A.C. 588 at p. 598.
(25) [1946] A.C. 588 at p. 593-4.
(26) [1946] A.C. 588 at p. 596.
(27) *Commentaries on the Laws of England* (Book IV) at p. 190.
(28) *R. v. Holmes* [1946] A.C. 588 at p. 598.

H. C. OF A. 19621963.

PARKER *v.* THE QUEEN.

Howe J.

With respect to the critical policy issues raised by provocation by infidelity defences, Viscount Simon said:

> "The rule, whatever it is, must apply to either spouse alike, for we have left behind us the age when the wife's subjection to her husband was regarded by the law as the basis of the marital relation . . . when the remedies of the Divorce Court did not exist. Parliament has now conferred on the aggrieved wife the same right to divorce her husband for unfaithfulness alone as he hold against her, and neither, on hearing an admission of adultery from the other, can kill the other and then claim provocation" (29).

Finally, in Viscount Simon's view, and I concur, the application of common law principles in such matters "must to some extent be controlled by the evolution of society" and "as society advances, it ought to call for a higher measure of self-control in all cases" (30).

Of course, the common law has now been modified by s 3 of the *Homicide Act*, 1957 which leaves it to juries to determine whether a "reasonable man" would do as the defendant did in a murder case and to take into account "everything done and said":

> "Where on a charge of murder there is evidence on which the jury can find that the person charged was provoked (whether by things done or by things said or by both together) to lose his self-control, the question whether the provocation was enough to make a reasonable man do as he did shall be left to be determined by the jury; and in determining that question the jury shall take into account everything both done and said according to the effect which, in their opinion, it would have on a reasonable man."

In New South Wales the common law has also been modified by statute, sub-s (1) of s 23 of the *Crimes Act* enlarging provocation to "grossly insulting language" and "gestures". Taylor and Owen J.J. in their reasons for judgment discuss the meaning of sub-s (2)(a), but I wish to draw attention to sub-s (2)(b), namely, that legally sufficient provocation has to be "reasonably calculated to deprive an ordinary person of the power of self-control, and did in fact deprive the accused of such power". This is consistent with the common law and a long line of authorities commencing with Coleridge J.'s observation in *Kirkham* that while the law "condescends to human frailty" it nevertheless considers "man to be a rational being, and requires that he should exercise a reasonable control over his passions" (31).

The reasonable man or objective standard appears to have been first articulated by Keating J. in 1869 when he directed the jury in *R. v. Welsh* that in order to reduce the crime to manslaughter, there should have been serious provocation, "something which might naturally cause an ordinary and reasonably minded man to lose his self-control and commit such an act" (32). The test laid down in *R. v. Lesbini*, namely "the effect of the provocation on a reasonable man" (33) was approved by Viscount Simon in *R. v. Mancini*:

(29) [1946] A.C. 588 at p. 598.
(30) [1946] A.C. 588 at p. 598.
(31) (1837) 173 ER 422 at pp. 423–5.
(32) 11 Cox CC 336 at p. 339.
(33) [1914] 3 KB 1116.

> "The test to be applied is that of the effect of the provocation on a reasonable man . . . so that an unusually excitable or pugnacious individual is not entitled to rely on provocation which would not have led an ordinary person to act as he did" (34).

Here we see a significant bolstering of the notion of an external standard of self-control as an important safeguard against partial exoneration of the short-tempered and the over-sensitive. It is a standard to be met by all individuals, men and women alike, of ordinary self-control. The provocation had to be grave. Subsequently, in *R. v. Duffy* the Court of Appeal approved as "impeccable" a summing up by Devlin J., as he then was, which described legal provocation as some act or series of acts done by the deceased to the accused "which would cause in any reasonable person, and actually caused in the accused, a sudden and temporary loss of self-control" (35). And more recently, Lord Devlin stated in *R. v. Lee Chun-Chuen* that the rule that the act provoked must bear some reasonable relationship to the provocative act is now authoritatively recognised as part of the common law (36). Furthermore, the retaliation had to be proportionate to the provocation. The defence could not require the issue to be left to the jury "unless there has been produced a *credible narrative*" of legal provocation (37).

Yet while the authorities are clear that provocation in law means something more than a provocative incident, that the acts alleged would have caused a reasonable person to lose self-control, credible provocation narratives are rare in wife-killing cases. There the ordinary person test for loss of self-control has a tendency to be overcome by sympathy for the "human frailty" of a man distraught that his wife no longer cares for him. Finding a wife *in flagrante delicto* was a special case, even establishing its own "rule" of what was always regarded as sufficient provocation according to the early authorities. But if Viscount Simon is correct that the application of common law principles in provocation cases must to some extent be "controlled by the evolution of society" and that this entails a higher standard of self-control, we need to guard against provocation following a path that permits it to be discovered in scenarios not imagined or intended by the foundational cases.

In my opinion, the facts relied on in the present case are precisely the kind that successive emphases on the objective or reasonable person standard have been designed to exclude as evidence of provocation fit to be left to a jury. I cannot see how, on the evidence, the applicant had been provoked in a legally relevant sense. That was not the burden of the evidence he gave in any of his contradictory accounts of his conduct on the fatal day. He clearly intended to kill Kelly albeit in a blind rage. Even in his dissenting opinion Dixon C.J. admits that it "might be too hard to credit" the absence of intention given that the prisoner thrust his knife into Kelly's throat. Indeed, there was a great deal of evidence that was damaging to the applicant. His own evidence was contradictory. In his early statements he made admissions that he followed his wife who had left with Kelly with the intention of killing him and the evidence shows that he told several

(34) [1942] AC 1 at 9.
(35) [1949] 1 All ER 932.
(36) [1963] AC 220.
(37) [1963] AC at pp. 231, 232 (emphasis added).

H. C. OF A. 19621963.

PARKER v. THE QUEEN.

Howe J.

witnesses that he meant to kill him. These statements and his subsequent actions in taking weapons in his car and driving his car into his wife and Kelly so as to cause serious injuries and a near double fatality have all the hallmarks of pre-meditated murder. Yet at trial, he changed his testimony, stating that he followed them with the sole intent of getting his wife back. It is difficult to find a credible narrative of provocation as the law requires in these conflicting and self-serving accounts.

I therefore concur with the majority judgments that on neither account should a provocation defence succeed. It strains belief that his frenzied attack on Kelly could be regarded as the product of a continuing emotion of the kind that could ground a successful provocation defence. Upset with himself as he said he was for injuring his wife, he turned on Kelly, transferring the blame to him and killing him in a frenzied attack. Furthermore, far from finding his wife *in flagrante delicto* with Kelly, there was no intimation that adultery had occurred. Rather, the applicant's wife had decided – not without regret and expressed concern for the applicant's feelings – that she wished to end their marriage.

The judge was therefore correct to withdraw the issue of provocation from the jury. No jury acting reasonably could have been satisfied that the deceased's alleged provocative conduct was sufficient to deprive any reasonable or ordinary person of the power of self-control. Indeed, far from displaying the self-control expected of the reasonable man living in the twentieth century, the applicant appears to be a mirror image of that unusually excitable or pugnacious individual whom the authorities have been at pains to prevent from relying on provocation to reduce his murderous act to manslaughter.

Finally, the public policy underlying adoption of the reasonable person test in the common law doctrine of provocation seems clear: it was to reduce the incidence of fatal violence by preventing defendants relying on their own exceptional pugnacity or excitability as an excuse for loss of self-control as the applicant has sought to do in the present case. Allowing them to do so would open the floodgates to provocation pleas in entirely unmeritorious provocation by "adultery" cases. Henceforth, if we are to accept the applicant's and indeed the Solicitor General's submissions, a wife's departure from an unhappy marriage that is aggravated by taunts delivered by her paramour or, presumably, by the woman herself, will be capable of founding a successful provocation plea. These submissions reveal how far we have come since *Mawgridge*, that foundational case requiring ocular proof of a wife's adultery for legally adequate provocation. Whether that is to be regarded as a welcome development, one bearing the hallmarks of a progressive society, is for future courts to decide. It is surely not one of which Viscount Simon would have approved when he delivered his landmark judgment in *Holmes*. Recall the view he expressed there that "as society advances, it ought to call for a higher measure of self-control in all cases". In my opinion, it ought to do so especially in wife-killing cases where the potential to raise successful provocation by "infidelity" defences on the slenderest of evidentiary bases is enormous. When provocation succeeds on slender or spurious evidence justice miscarries. With respect to the facts of the present case, it is essential that if confessed or projected adultery is not to become a licence to kill, courts adhere to a strict objective standard of self-control that recognises *inter alia* the legal right of a woman to leave an unsatisfactory relationship. Women have the same right as men to leave a marital or de facto relationship without fear of serious or fatal violence.

Accordingly, I consider the application for special leave to appeal should be refused.

15

A Well-founded Fear? Giving Context to Self-defence in *Taikato v R*

JULIE STUBBS

Introduction

When Jo-Anne Taikato lost her appeal against a conviction for possessing a spray can of formaldehyde that she carried in her handbag for the purpose of self-defence,[1] there was a strong public reaction. Two days later, on 8 April 1994, the *Sydney Morning Herald* editorial decried the decision as absurd and as evidence of 'the law's inability to come to terms with real differences between men and women'.[2] The editorial noted that the failure of the court to come up with a 'practical, commonsense decision' had increased pressure 'for yet more legislation'.[3]

Criminal justice reforms in New South Wales (NSW) are commonly shaped by law and order politics, and the resultant legislative amendment was no exception. The NSW Opposition Leader, Mr Bob Carr, took up the matter after the government had initially expressed concern that to authorise the possession of irritant sprays might be dangerous for women, since 'hoodlums and louts' could use the sprays against them.[4] Mr Carr proposed 'a special law to allow women to carry police-approved sprays'.[5] By 21 April 1994 the government had changed its position, and amending legislation had been introduced into the NSW Parliament, albeit in different terms than had been proposed by the Opposition.[6] The NSW Attorney General, the Hon John Hannaford, noted the government's concern 'for women and others whose vulnerability to physical attack places them at a disadvantage', and stated that the Bill 'provides greater guidance and flexibility to the court when determining whether a person has a legitimate self-defence need which justifies the carrying of a dangerous article'.[7] The amending legislation was introduced while the matter was on appeal to the High Court of Australia (HCA). The HCA upheld the conviction and dismissed the appeal.[8]

1 *R v Taikato* (Unreported, Court of Criminal Appeal, NSW, Meagher JA, Abadee and Ireland JJ, 6 April 1994).

2 Editorial, 'Needless Legal Absurdity', *Sydney Morning Herald* (Sydney) 8 April 1994, 12.

3 Ibid.

4 Elizabeth Jurman, 'Govt Divided Over Legal Sprays', *Sydney Morning Herald* (Sydney) 8 April 1994, 3. See also Paola Totaro, 'Govt Backflips on Self-Defence', *Sydney Morning Herald* (Sydney) 22 April 1994, 3.

5 Editorial, above n 2.

6 The Crimes Legislation (Dangerous Articles) Amendment Bill 1994 (NSW) inserted new s 545E(3) and (4), which set out the factors to be considered to determine whether, on reasonable grounds, self-defence was available in the circumstances.

7 New South Wales, *Second Reading Speech, Crimes Legislation (Dangerous Articles) Amendment Bill*, Legislative Council, 21 April 1994, 1586 (John Hannaford, Attorney General).

8 *Taikato v R* (1996) 186 CLR 454 ('*Taikato*').

Media commentary on the HCA decision linked the outcome to broader concerns about women's access to self-defence. The decision was reported as a 'setback for women's self-defence',[9] and reference was made to crime statistics on homicides and sexual assaults experienced by women,[10] albeit without indicating that such offences against women are mostly committed by people known to the victims.[11]

Throughout the 1990s as Ms Taikato's case moved through the legal process, there was a good deal of feminist advocacy and scholarship concerning self-defence. However, this focused mostly on self-defence for women who resorted to homicide in response to domestic violence by a partner or ex-partner.[12] Scholars and advocates had welcomed the 1987 HCA decision in *Zecevic v Director of Public Prosecutions (Vic)*,[13] which they saw as having the potential to enhance women's access to self-defence because it had reformulated self-defence to focus on whether the defensive action was necessary in the circumstances. Subsequent to that decision, concepts such as imminence and proportionality, which had been obstacles to women's self-defence claims, no longer had the status of legal rules, but were among the factors to be considered.[14] However, imminence proved to be of considerable importance to how Ms Taikato's case was decided.

There was, and is, a dearth of legal scholarship, feminist or otherwise, on self-defence against non-lethal violence in other contexts or on self-defence as a defence to a charge of possessing a weapon.[15]

The question of whether women should be legally entitled to carry sprays intended for self-defence has gained renewed attention recently, at least as measured by a flurry of material on social media, much of it reacting to the rape and murder of Jill Meagher in 2012.[16] She was attacked by a stranger on a Melbourne street as she walked the short distance from a bar to her home. Some commentators speculated whether she might have survived the attack if she had been armed with such a spray. The public response to Jill Meagher's brutal killing also included a peaceful march of thousands of women and men insisting on their right to use public streets in safety.

On the face of it, *Taikato* seems to demand a different result, one that acknowledges the reality of women's lives and their fears by legitimating Ms Taikato's choice to carry an irritant spray for the purpose of self-defence. For many women and girls, taking precautions against possible threats is routine; they are expected to be prudent, and may be judged

[9] Bernard Lane, 'Setback for Women's Self-Defence', *The Australian* (Sydney) 17 October 1996, 3.

[10] Graham McBean, 'Right to Self-Defence Again in Dispute', *The Canberra Times* (Canberra) 10 December 1996.

[11] Australian Bureau of Statistics (ABS), 'Personal Safety, Australia, 2005 (Reissue)' (Catalogue No 4906.0, 21 August 2006) 9–11.

[12] Examples include: Wendy Bacon and Robyn Lansdowne, 'Women who Kill Husbands: The Battered Woman on Trial' in Carol O'Donnell and Jan Craney (eds), *Family Violence in Australia* (Longman Cheshire, 1992); Julia Tolmie, 'Provocation or Self-Defence for Battered Women who Kill' in Stanley Yeo (ed), *Partial Excuses to Murder* (Federation Press, 1991); Stella Tarrant, 'Provocation and Self Defence: A Feminist Perspective' (1990) 15 *Legal Service Bulletin* 147; Elizabeth Sheehy, Julie Stubbs and Julia Tolmie, 'Defending Battered Women on Trial: The Battered Women Syndrome and its Limitations' (1992) 16 *Criminal Law Journal* 369.

[13] (1987) 162 CLR 645 (*Zecevic*).

[14] Australian Law Reform Commission and New South Wales Law Reform Commission, *Family Violence – A National Legal Response*, Report No 114 (2010) 622–5.

[15] But see David Lanham, 'Offensive Weapons and Self-Defence' [2005] *Criminal Law Review* 85.

[16] *Bayley v Director of Public Prosecutions (Vic)* [2013] VSCA 295 (21 October 2013).

harshly for failing to secure their own safety.[17] Women are more likely than men to curtail their activities due to fears about safety.[18]

However, the case also raises competing issues of feminist concern. These include, inter alia, the need to promote safety without exacerbating fear of crime, situating women as inevitably vulnerable, reinforcing undue concern about 'stranger danger' or holding women responsible for their personal safety. Women too have an interest in removing weapons from public places. Crime prevention approaches and media accounts that hold women responsible for securing their own safety have attracted justified criticism on similar grounds, such as giving undue emphasis to 'stranger danger' when, for most women whose safety is threatened, the risk lies with intimate partners; providing confusing messages that may exacerbate women's fear of crime; and for failing to acknowledge that advice commonly places responsibility on women for avoiding men's violence.[19]

The authorisation of 'defensive sprays' may create a false sense of security, as sprays may be of limited protection, and may be used against a woman who is overpowered by an attacker. Such sprays are also commercial products, and websites that promote their purchase and use often do so by giving [over-]emphasis to women's risk of victimisation and playing on the fear of crime.

The *Taikato* Case

The NSW Court of Criminal Appeal (CCA)[20] considered three stated questions concerning possession of an irritant spray, and whether the facts of the case were capable of establishing a defence under s 545E(2) *Crimes Act 1900* (NSW) (the Act), which at the time provided two exceptions: possession for a lawful purpose or with a reasonable excuse. The defendant carries the evidential burden of proof. Thus, the case involved self-defence, which was then a common law defence, and two statutory defences.

The CCA judges found the argument that self-defence constituted a lawful purpose attractive, but that on the facts it was not available, due to the absence of a reasonable apprehension of imminent attack. In reasons for the decision, Meagher JA said that the Court reached their decision 'reluctantly' because it seemed 'an absurd result',[21] but felt bound to follow the English Court of Appeal decision in *Attorney-General's Reference (No 2 of 1983)*[22] which interpreted a similar statute, and had been followed by Australian courts. Commentary suggests that the CCA was wrong in law and that it was unnecessary to follow the English case.[23] The CCA also found on the facts that the appellant did not have a reasonable excuse.

The matter was appealed to the HCA, which also found against the appellant.

[17] Elizabeth Stanko, 'When Precaution Is Normal: A Feminist Critique of Crime Prevention' in Loraine Gelsthorpe and Allison Morris (eds), *Feminist Perspectives in Criminology* (Open University Press, 1990).

[18] ABS, above n 11, 22.

[19] Elizabeth Stanko, 'Warnings to Women: Police Advice and Women's Safety in Britain' (1996) 2(1) *Violence Against Women* 5.

[20] Pursuant to the *Criminal Appeal Act 1912* (NSW) s 5B.

[21] *R v Taikato* (Unreported, Court of Criminal Appeal, NSW, Meagher JA, Abadee and Ireland JJ, 6 April 1994).

[22] [1984] 1 QB 456 ('*Attorney-General's Reference*').

[23] George Zdenkowski, 'Spraycan Case: High Court May Take A Different View', *Sydney Morning Herald* (Sydney), 5 May 1994, 18. Kirby J was to make a similar finding in dissent: *Taikato* [1996] 186 CLR 454. See also Lanham, above n 15.

There was surprisingly little focus on the elements of self-defence in oral argument before the HCA, but there was an extended discussion of what women carry in their handbags. Hairspray was considered likely to be carried for a lawful purpose, while oven cleaner was not, unless it had been purchased recently and it was in a shopping bag.[24]

As noted above, the CCA gave undue emphasis to the issue of imminence.[25] In oral argument, Kirby J repeatedly pressed counsel for the respondent, Mr Howie QC, to explain the basis on which he presented imminence as a requirement. Counsel replied, 'where there is no actual anticipated violence at the time of the possession or no imminent threat or no perceived imminent threat, it is not lawful. That is the element that is missing. That is the element that must be there to make self-defence lawful',[26] but did not cite any authority for this position.

The HCA sought to limit the scope of any defences so as not to defeat the purpose of the provision. All judges agreed that within s 545E(2) of the Act, a lawful purpose must be one that was 'positively authorised'. However, the judges differed on whether self-defence constituted a lawful purpose. The majority found that attempting to mould self-defence into a lawful purpose was 'fraught with practical and legal difficulties'. They held that possession of an irritant spray for self-defence is not a lawful purpose, since whether a response constitutes self-defence can only be determined 'after the circumstances of the attack and the defendant's response are evaluated'.[27]

The majority considered the meaning of lawful purpose and reasonable excuse and whether each statutory defence extended to the circumstances of self-defence. On one view this was unnecessary, since self-defence 'does not need statutory formulae like reasonable excuse or lawful purpose to bring it into operation'[28] and it would have been preferable to hold the common law defence applicable independently of the statutory provisions.

The paucity of legal analysis of possession for self-defence has been noted above.[29] In *Taikato* much of the analysis imported understandings of self-defence from homicide cases to the consideration of the facts. The absence of any reference to *Zecevic*[30] seems surprising, and is not explained. While *Zecevic* involved homicide, the requirements for self-defence set out in that decision have general application.[31]

In the consideration of self-defence in the feminist judgment, a great deal turns on the interpretation given to the facts. The facts are clearly set out by Crofts and Alexander JJ, and are not in dispute. The majority dismissed the attack on Ms Taikato two years previously as of little relevance to her possession of the spray at the time and place of the arrest. However, as noted below, Crofts and Alexander JJ took a different approach.

On the question of 'reasonable excuse', the majority noted that 'when the legislature enacts defences such as 'reasonable excuse' they effectively give, and intend to give, to the courts the power to determine the content of such defences'.[32] Thus, courts 'have to make what are effectively political judgments by looking for material differences justifying the

[24] *Taikato v R* [1996] HCATrans 201 (24 April 1996).
[25] *R v Taikato* (Unreported, Court of Criminal Appeal, NSW, Meagher JA, Abadee and Ireland JJ, 6 April 1994).
[26] *Taikato v R* [1996] HCATrans 201 (24 April 1996).
[27] *Taikato* (1996) 186 CLR 454, 463–4 (Brennan CJ, Toohey, McHugh and Gummow JJ; Dawson J concurring).
[28] Lanham, above n 15, 95.
[29] But see subsequent analysis by Lanham: ibid 85.
[30] (1987) 162 CLR 645, 661.
[31] Ibid.
[32] *Taikato* (1996) 186 CLR 454, 465–6 (Brennan CJ, Toohey McHugh and Gummow JJ).

distributive operation of the criminal law'.[33] This might have afforded the Court the opportunity to consider issues such as women's fear of crime in public places and the precautions that might be reasonable to take, but they did not do so. Nor were these issues raised in oral argument.

The majority held that it was 'impossible to say that "self-defence" could never be a "reasonable excuse"' under s 545E(2) of the Act, but that it must be based on more than 'mere belief'; a minimum requirement would be 'a well-founded fear of attack in the public place in question' or else 'the purpose of the provision would be too easily defeated'. They held that on the facts, and having regard to the recent amendments of the Act, the appellant had no reasonable grounds for believing that she was in danger of attack at that time.[34]

Other Jurisdictions

Western Australia (WA) has adopted a different approach to the possession of an irritant spray for self-defence. *Taikato* was considered by the WA Supreme Court in *Hall v Collins*,[35] which is distinguishable on the law and the facts. The *Weapons Act 1999* (WA) excludes self-defence as a reasonable excuse for the possession of controlled weapons, except where prescribed by regulation; regulation 7 provides in respect of capsicum spray that self-defence is not excluded if it is carried or possessed 'for the purpose of being used in lawful defence in circumstances that the person has reasonable grounds to apprehend may arise'.[36] The regulation makes no reference to imminence and the circumstances are not limited to the time of possession but are those that 'may arise in future'. Wheeler J found that 'carry[ing it] at all times and in all circumstances' was unlikely to satisfy reasonable excuse although 'where a person envisages on reasonable grounds that circumstances requiring the use of the spray for self-defence may arise from time to time . . . possession on an ongoing basis must be envisaged'.[37]

In *Hall v Collins*,[38] the appellant was the manager of a budget motel who had suffered head injuries following a previous assault at the motel. He kept pepper spray in his office in case of a disturbance, and used it on a person involved in a violent struggle with a guest. He was charged with possession, although not assault or unlawful use of the spray. The conviction was quashed and a verdict of acquittal substituted.

The Feminist Judgment

Crofts and Alexander JJ concur that within the meaning of s 545E(2) of the Act, lawful purpose is a purpose positively authorised by law and they endorse the reasoning of the other judges on this point.

33 Ibid.
34 Ibid.
35 [2003] WASCA 74 [17].
36 *Weapons Act 1999* (WA) s 7(3)–(4); *Weapons Regulations 1999* (WA) reg 7.
37 *Hall v Collins* [2003] WASCA 74 [17].
38 [2003] WASCA 74.

The feminist judges adopt a different approach to the majority by giving separate consideration to whether self-defence may be a lawful purpose and whether self-defence applies in the given circumstances. On the first issue, they follow the reasoning in *R v Fegan*[39] as applied in *Attorney-General's Reference*[40] by the English Court of Appeal, which held that the possession of a weapon for the purpose of protection may amount to a lawful object (or purpose). On the second issue they note that while the court in *Attorney-General's Reference*[41] held that self-defence could not be a lawful object without a reasonable apprehension of an imminent attack, imminence is not a legal requirement of self-defence in Australia. Following the decision in *Zecevic*,[42] imminence is one of several factors relevant in considering whether the accused held a genuine belief on reasonable grounds that it was necessary to do what she did in self-defence.

It is in applying the doctrine of self-defence to the facts that the feminist reasoning of the judges becomes most evident. They also apply the amendments introduced in s 545E(3) and (4) of the Act differently. Those sections provide that a person is not guilty of possession for the purpose of self-defence if the possession is reasonable having regard to all of the circumstances, including (a) the immediacy of the perceived threat to the person charged, (b) the circumstances, such as the time and location, in which the thing was possessed, (c) the type of thing possessed, and (d) the age, characteristics and experiences of the person charged.

The majority endorsed the findings of Rummery DCJ that there was nothing to suggest that Ms Taikato was 'likely to be attacked' and no basis for 'a well-founded fear of attack *while walking in the street where she was found in possession of the canister*' *during the middle of the day* (emphasis added).[43] Crofts and Alexander JJ give greater weight to the appellant's characteristics and experiences and they do not limit their consideration to 'the time and location, in which the thing was possessed'.[44] Having regard to all of the circumstances, they arrive at a different view of the facts.

The feminist judges find it unsurprising that, having been attacked in her home where she is most entitled to feel safe, Ms Taikato 'no longer felt safe at all' including outside her home, and that it was open to a jury to find that she reasonably believed that she faced a threat. In examining whether her response was necessary, they take account of the feared future threat, and not just the circumstances that existed at the time of the possession. They note that in the two years that she had possessed the spray she had not used it and find that this is consistent with her intention to only use the spray in an emergency, and they find that unlike other weapons, because an irritant spray is unlikely to cause lasting injury, it is likely to be a proportionate response to a threat.

The feminist judges apply a similar approach in their consideration of whether Ms Taikato may have had a reasonable excuse. They find that as a woman she is a member of a vulnerable social group, but also that since she has experienced a previous threat of violence in her home, it is reasonable to take precautions against a future attack.

Finally, the feminist judges share the concern raised by the majority of the need to limit the application of the defences so as not to defeat the purpose of the provision, nor to leave open a defence to gangs or to people who might use weapons likely to cause injury. However,

[39] [1972] NI 80.
[40] [1984] 1 QB 456.
[41] Ibid.
[42] (1987) 162 CLR 645.
[43] *Taikato* (1996) 186 CLR 454, 466 (Brennan CJ, Toohey McHugh and Gummow JJ).
[44] Ibid 467 (Dawson J).

they point out that the requirements of self-defence already limit the application of the defence in such circumstances except where there was overwhelming evidence to the contrary.

Conclusion

In *Taikato*, the HCA majority did not repeat the error of the CCA in foregrounding imminence as a necessary pre-condition for the defences, but properly took other factors into account. On one view the amending legislation introduced in 1994 in response to public outcry over Ms Taikato's conviction was largely symbolic, in that it did not change the legal position, but simply gave statutory effect to the factors that were already considerations in such a matter. However, in reaching their finding that there was a minimum requirement of 'a well-founded fear of attack in the public place in question'[45] they focused narrowly on the immediate circumstances of Ms Taikato's possession of the spray and in doing so determined that the attack on her two years previously in a different place did not provide the basis for a well-founded fear of attack.

By contrast, the feminist judges take a fuller view of all of the circumstances, which opens up the possibility that Ms Taikato's fear of attack was not limited to a specific time or place, but arose from more a generalised feeling of insecurity, reinforced by her prior experience of threat.

The outcome in *Taikato* illustrates the challenges that feminist advocates have had in reshaping the manner in which self-defence is applied to better reflect the realities in women's lives. Feminist scholars and advocates in battered women's homicide cases have long argued that a fair application of self-defence requires that the context for her action is fully understood and credited. In *Taikato*, that required recognition that for many women, 'precaution is normal'.

[45] Ibid 466 (Brennan CJ, Toohey McHugh and Gummow JJ).

TAIKATO .... APPELLANT;

AND

THE QUEEN .... RESPONDENT.

ON APPEAL FROM THE SUPREME COURT OF NEW SOUTH WALES

CROFTS AND ALEXANDER JJ. One night, Jo-Anne Taikato and her husband returned home to find an intruder in the process of breaking into their house. On being disturbed in his purpose, the intruder attempted to strike Ms Taikato. Although no harm came to her on this occasion, Ms Taikato was sufficiently disturbed by the incident to seek to take precautions against a future attack. On making inquiries, she was sold a "self-defence" spray in a hotel. She carried this for two years, happily without needing it, until she was stopped and searched in Railway Street, Liverpool, New South Wales, at 12:15pm on 26 March 1992. Upon the spray being discovered in her handbag she was arrested and charged with an offence under s 545e(1) of the *Crimes Act* 1900 (NSW) (the Act). As it transpired, Ms Taikato was a victim of mistaken identity, having been apprehended in the course of a police operation with which she was entirely unconnected.

Section 545e of the Crimes Act 1900 (NSW), at the date in question, provided that:

> "(1) A person who, in a public place, possesses:
> (a) anything. . . capable of discharging by any means:
> (i) any irritant matter in liquid, powder, gas, or chemical form or any dense smoke; or
> (ii) any substance capable of causing bodily harm; or
> (b) a fuse capable of use with an explosive or a detonator; or
> (c) a detonator,
>
> is liable, on conviction before a Magistrate, to imprisonment for 2 years, or a fine of 50 penalty units, or both.
>
> (2) A person is not guilty of an offence under this section for possessing anything referred to in subsection (1) if the person satisfies the court that he or she had a reasonable excuse for possessing it or possessed it for a lawful purpose."

The canister in question was subjected to analysis which determined that it would, when discharged, emit a clear liquid with a pungent odour. The liquid was found to be formaldehyde, which the analyst's report stated is "known to be an irritant substance." In the Local Court, Ms Taikato gave evidence that she had never used the spray, so did not know if it was effective. She repeated in evidence what she had told the police, namely that she had bought it some years before and that her intention was to use it if she were attacked. She explained, "If you spray it in someone's face it's going to give you a few minutes to be able to get away." None of this evidence was contested. The magistrate convicted her under s 545e(1) of the Act and fined her $400.

Ms Taikato appealed to the District Court, where Rummery DCJ upheld the conviction but stated a case for the Court of Criminal Appeal. He asked the

Court of Criminal Appeal to answer the following questions of law:

> "1. Am I correct in concluding that the facts which I have accepted as proved provide no evidence capable of establishing a defence for the appellant under the proper construction of s 545e(2) of the *Crimes Act*?
> 2. Does s 545e(2) of the *Crimes Act*, 1900 render possession in a public place of a thing capable of discharging an irritant liquid illegal where the purpose for which it is possessed was not unlawful prior to the enactment of the section?
> 3. Does s 545e(2) of the *Crimes Act*, 1900 render possession in a public place of a thing capable of discharging an irritant liquid illegal where the purpose for which it is possessed is not proscribed or regulated under any other law or statute?"

The Court of Criminal Appeal answered yes to each question, and upheld the conviction. Its reasons were given by Meagher JA. He held that there was no justification for upholding the defence on grounds of reasonable excuse, as there was no evidence Ms Taikato had any rational fear of another attack. He was more attracted to the second argument, based on lawful purpose, but in the end found himself constrained by the decision of the UK Court of Appeal in *Attorney-General's Reference (No 2 of 1983)* (1). In that case, where the relevant phrase was "lawful object", the Court of Appeal found that it would be necessary for there to be a reasonable expectation of an imminent attack. As there was no evidence Ms Taikato had any reasonable fear of imminent attack, she could not avail herself of the "lawful purpose" defence. We are unable to agree with the findings and reasoning of the Court of Criminal Appeal.

"Lawful purpose"

The phrase "lawful purpose" is ambiguous. It may mean something positively authorised by the law, or something done without breaking the law. We prefer the former construction, for the same reasons given by Brennan CJ, Toohey, McHugh, Gummow, Kirby and Dawson JJ, whose judgments we have had the benefit of reading in draft. However, we do not accept that self-defence cannot amount to such a lawful purpose. Self-defence is a long-standing defence in the criminal law and must therefore be viewed as an action positively authorised by law. We further disagree with the proposition that self-defence cannot amount to a "lawful purpose" within the meaning of s 545e(2) because whether or not it will apply cannot be determined until after the fact of a particular attack or threatened attack. It is clear from the United Kingdom cases of *Attorney-General's Reference* (2) and *R v Fegan* (3), which we discuss in more detail below, that self-defence may amount to a lawful object. For the purposes of the interpretation of s 545e, we do not consider that there is any relevant difference between the terms "lawful purpose" and "lawful object". Assessing whether self defence was in fact a "lawful purpose" in this case will involve a consideration of the rules of self-defence. That is, if the threat did come about and the accused responded as she had prepared, whether she would be able to argue self-defence successfully.

The real question to be determined, therefore, is whether self-defence applies in this situation and this, in turn, necessitates an examination of the scope of

(1) [1984] 1 QB 456 (*Attorney-General's Reference*).
(2) Ibid.
(3) [1972] NI 80 (*Fegan*).

H C OF A
1996

TAIKATO
v
THE
Queen

Crofts J,
Alexander J

self-defence and its relationship with s 545e. As we have just noted, the question has been considered several times in the United Kingdom, in *Attorney-General's Reference* (4) and *Fegan* (5). In *Fegan*, the defendant was a Roman Catholic man married to a Protestant. He had been subjected to threats and beatings. After moving to another area to no avail, the accused had bought a revolver and ammunition to protect himself and his family. He was charged with possession of the revolver. On appeal, the Court of Appeal asserted a distinction between possession and purpose (6):

> "Possession of a firearm for the purpose of protecting the possessor or his wife or family from acts of violence, *may* be possession for a lawful object. But the lawfulness of such a purpose cannot be founded on a mere fancy, or on some aggressive motive. The threatened danger must be reasonably and genuinely anticipated, must appear reasonably imminent, and must be of a nature which could not reasonably be met by more pacific means. A lawful object in this particular field therefore falls within a strictly limited category and cannot be such as to justify going beyond what the law may allow in meeting the situation of danger which the possessor of the firearm reasonably and genuinely apprehends."

It was therefore open to the jury to conclude ". . . that the appellant genuinely and reasonably feared for the life and safety of himself or his family and held the pistol for use if necessary as a protection against this danger" (7).

Fegan was applied in *Attorney-General's Reference* (8). This case arose when the respondent, a man of good character, armed himself with petrol bombs in order to protect himself and his property following two nights of rioting and after his shop had already been looted once. In *Attorney-General's Reference*, Lord Lane CJ and McCowan and Leggatt JJ considered that the defence of lawful object was open to the respondent "if he can satisfy the jury on balance of probabilities that his object was to protect himself or his family or his property against imminent apprehended attack and to do so by means which he believed were no more than reasonably necessary to meet the force used by the attackers" (9). The English Court of Appeal in *Fegan* and in *Attorney-General's Reference* therefore accepted that self-defence may amount to a lawful object (or purpose) in relation to an offence of possession. Attention then focuses on the parameters of that defence.

In the court below, and in the judgment of Brennan CJ, Toohey, McHugh and Gummow JJ as well as Kirby J (concurring in part), the focus is on the criterion of imminence as holding the key to the application of the defence of lawful purpose. This approach relies on the UK cases just discussed. In consequence, they find self-defence cannot be a lawful purpose, or a reasonable excuse, in the present case because that requirement is not satisfied. We disagree and suggest a preferable approach would focus attention on the parameters of the defence of

(4) [1984] 1 QB 456.
(5) [1972] NI 80.
(6) Ibid 194.
(7) Ibid.
(8) [1984] 1 QB 456.
(9) Ibid 471.

self-defence as outlined by this Court in *Zecevic v Director of Public Prosecutions* (10):

> "The question . . . is whether an accused believed on reasonable grounds that it was necessary in self-defence to do what he did. If he had that belief, and there were reasonable grounds for it, or if the jury is left in reasonable doubt about the matter, then he is entitled to acquittal."

In our view, unlike the defences of necessity and duress, imminence is not a legal requirement of the defence of self-defence in Australia. Rather, imminence is a factor relevant to the subjective and objective questions of whether or not the accused believed on reasonable grounds that what she did was necessary in the circumstances. It is relevant because it is often assumed that, if there is no imminent threat, then the legal system is capable of offering protection and this may in turn give rise to an inference that the attack was not motivated by the need to defend oneself but by malice or some other motive. However, imminence is merely one factor of several that may be relevant to an assessment of whether self-defence applies; it is not the only or the chief matter that can be considered.

We consider that, in a case such as this, the imminence requirement should play a much reduced role in the assessment of self-defence for several reasons. The law is not only concerned with whether there was a threat but with what the accused believed. If a person honestly and reasonably believed that X held a loaded pistol against her back, which in all probability would be used if she disobeyed X, then the law would evaluate the person's response in light of this belief. In this case, much has been made of the fact that Ms Taikato was found with the spray in her handbag in the middle of the day in a street in Sydney. The implication is that there are no grounds, reasonable or otherwise, to be in fear of threats in the middle of the day in Sydney. What could be safer? However, for Ms Taikato, even her home, surely a sanctuary for most, has proven to be a place of danger. Her assumption of unsafety is informed by prior experience. If she no longer feels safe in her home, it is unsurprising that she has identified an ongoing threat when she is outside of her home. Her reaction to this perceived threat is both plausible and reasonable. She has not willy-nilly engaged in vigilante justice against ephemeral threats. Rather, she has purchased a purely defensive spray that causes no permanent injury. In *Fegan* the English Court of Appeal asserted that a threatened danger must be "reasonably and genuinely anticipated" (11). It is possible, taking into account Ms Taikato's history, that a jury could find that she honestly and reasonably anticipated a threat, due to the attempted assault in her own home which meant that she no longer felt safe at all.

This leads to the second related argument, about whether or not her fear of a hypothetical threat can be taken into account for the question of lawful purpose. That is, was the accused's response *necessary*? This is a question not only of imminence but of the proportionality and reasonableness of the accused's response. Thus in *Fegan* the English Court of Appeal considered whether a

(10) (1987) 162 CLR 645, 661.
(11) [1972] NI 80, 194.

H C OF A
1996

TAIKATO
V
THE
Queen

Crofts J,
Alexander J

threat "could not reasonably be met by more pacific means" (12). Determining the lawfulness of Ms Taikato's act of keeping the canister of formaldehyde, entails examining the details of when and how Ms Taikato would have defended herself if a hypothetical attack had taken place, and whether this would have satisfied the requirements of self-defence. Ms Taikato was consistent in her claims to the police and the court that she would not have used the spray unless and until she was subject to an imminent threat. Her plan was not that she would use it at any time, but only if she felt genuinely threatened. Given the absence of her use of the spray in the prior two years, her intentions with regard to the spray were clearly that it would only be used in case of emergency. Her use of the spray in these circumstances would be consistent with the requirements of the defence of self-defence.

Moreover, this application of the doctrine of self-defence has the advantage of moving beyond the question of imminence to examining the type of weapon carried by Ms Taikato and her intentions with regard to its use. A central element of a lawful excuse of self-defence is that an accused's reaction to a (perceived) threat is proportionate. This requires assessing the potential harmfulness of different types of weapons. In most situations, spraying an attacker with formaldehyde would be a proportionate reaction to a threat of violence and would thus be consistent with a claim of self-defence. The spray causes discomfort in the eyes for a few minutes and would not cause any lasting injury. The aim of the spray was to assist Ms Taikato to run away. The focus on proportionality addresses concerns that permitting Ms Taikato to carry a formaldehyde spray would open the floodgates to permitting criminals, hoodlums or members of street gangs to carry prohibited weapons such as knives or guns in public places because they had well-founded fears of attacks from other criminals, hoodlums or street gangs. Use of a knife, gun or petrol bomb is far more likely to amount to an excessive and therefore unnecessary response. The United Kingdom cases mentioned above both involved weapons that could only be described as offensive, and the application of which might very well involve lethal force.

This approach would not only be consistent with existing legal doctrine but it would also be consistent with the amendments made to s 545e. Whilst these reforms were introduced after Ms Taikato's trial at first instance, the amendments indicate how the Legislature has intended that the question of lawful purpose should be interpreted. This reforming legislation requires the court to look at the facts of an assertion of self-defence beyond the question of imminence. The legislation refers to the time and location of the event, and the age and experience of the accused. This would require the Court to take into account Ms Taikato's age, her gender, her feeling of unsafety as a consequence of the attack in her home. On this assessment her feeling of unsafety would be both reasonable and credible. In particular, we would return to the very important distinction of a spray that has no potential whatsoever to inflict any lasting injury (unless perhaps an accused hit a victim over the head with it, in which case even a hairbrush could become such a weapon). Other weapons such as guns and knives cause far more serious injury and are extremely unlikely to be proportionate

(12) Ibid.

responses to the majority of threats. We consider that where a weapon is of a potentially lethal nature, such as the weapons involved in *Fegan* and *Attorney-General's Reference*, it is perfectly proper for imminence to play a greater role in the assessment of self-defence. However, where, as here, the weapon is of a defensive nature, the imminence factor is dealt with by Ms Taikato's uncontested evidence that she would only use the weapon if a threat were imminent. The Court of Criminal Appeal erred in dismissing the availability of the defence of self-defence solely on the basis that an attack was not imminent.

"Reasonable excuse"

Notwithstanding the view we have taken of "lawful purpose", we add our view of the second potential defence, namely that Ms Taikato had a reasonable excuse for possessing the weapon. The phrase "reasonable excuse" was clearly intended by the legislature to cover a wider range of situations than the more limited expression "lawful purpose". The words themselves direct us to this conclusion. "Reasonable" is a word which requires the court to make a value judgement in relation to conduct. In doing so, it will be guided by certain considerations to which we will return. By contrast with the phrase "lawful purpose", which implies conduct that is legal and justified, we are now concerned with a defence which excuses what would otherwise be criminal conduct and is sometimes described as a "concession to human frailty" (13).

In considering what would amount to a reasonable excuse, the courts must consider any facts relevant to that assessment. These might include the nature of the perceived threat, whether the threat was genuinely perceived by the defendant to be imminent, the nature of the item possessed, the circumstances of its possession, as well as the characteristics of the defendant, including her age and gender. Imminence is one factor that may be relevant to a finding of reasonable excuse, but it is not the determinative factor. These factors reflect the amendments that have since been made to s 545e, but these amendments simply reflect the pre-existing state of the common law. Again, imminence of harm is one factor that may be relevant to assessing the reasonableness of the excuse, but it is merely one part of the factual matrix which forms the evidence upon which the assessment is to be based.

In considering the reasonableness of the excuse in question, it must therefore be of paramount importance that Ms Taikato was not just a member of a social group particularly vulnerable to violence (other such groups including the elderly, children, ethnic minorities and homosexuals) but that she had personally experienced a threat of violence in her own home. A natural consequence of such an attack is to feel insecure in public and private spaces. A reasonable response to such insecurity is to seek to take precautions against a future attack. The precaution Ms Taikato took was to purchase an item that would allow her the opportunity to retreat from such an attack. She did not arm herself with a potentially lethal weapon (as was the case in many of the cases referred to in the context of imminence) but chose a weapon the effect of which was unlikely to be dispro-

(13) See Lord Hailsham in *R v Howe* [1987] 1 All ER 771, 779–80.

H C OF A 1996

TAIKATO v THE Queen

Crofts J, Alexander J

portionate to any physical attack visited upon her or threatened to be visited.

Furthermore, it can hardly count against her that she possessed the spray in a crowded street in broad daylight. If one is to carry an item to be used in the event of an attack, it must be carried at all times so that it is available and to hand when it is needed. If one goes out in the morning knowing one might return home in the dark, one will need to have taken the item in the morning and to have possessed it at all points up until one is in the potentially dangerous situation of being a female, alone, at night. The reality for many women, and members of other vulnerable groups, is that they simply do not venture out at night or alone. Either personal experience or awareness of the experiences of others has taught them that this would be to expose themselves to potential danger and that the police would be unlikely to have the opportunity to intervene before injury occurs.

It is therefore apparent that when considering whether a defendant might have a reasonable excuse for possessing an irritant substance, the question will be whether the evidence supports the finding that the possession of such an item would be objectively reasonable to a person in the position of the defendant, taking into account their experiences and genuinely held beliefs. If so, she will have a defence under s 545e(2) of the *Crimes Act*.

We have considered the point that a central aim of the legislation is to remove weapons from the street. The concern is that recognising a defence like this could then be extended to a youth who was a member of a gang that regularly carried knives and regularly engaged in acts of violence. Such a person might well have a well-founded fear of attack in a public place. Another concern is that our approach might be the thin end of the wedge and lead to the tolerance or even permission of armed vigilantes to roam the streets. An increase in the number of weapons on the streets would likely make vulnerable groups less safe rather than more so. However, we consider that neither defence would be available in these situations. If the weapon in question were a knife, gun or other kind of detonating device, it would seem that its possession would in almost every situation be disproportionate and excessive, because it would be a disproportionate reaction to most types of threats and assaults. This would create a more difficult situation for a court asked to decide whether the defence were open to such an accused. Fortunately, we are not called upon to decide such a case at present.

The appeal should be allowed. Question 1 referred by Rummery DCJ to the Court of Criminal Appeal should be answered in the negative. Questions 2 and 3 should be answered yes, except where there is a defence of lawful purpose or reasonable excuse.

16

Admitting Legal Wrongs: *PGA v R*

NGAIRE NAFFINE

Legal Background

In 1976, South Australia was the first jurisdiction in the common law world to make rape in marriage a crime, though it confined the new offence to aggravated rape. Before then, the received legal view, derived from extra-judicial writing of Sir Matthew Hale,[1] written some time before his death in 1676 but not published until 1736,[2] was that the husband was immune from prosecution for the rape of his wife because she was legally presumed to consent to sex by act of marriage. The durability of the immunity is perhaps its most striking feature. It was an entrenched part of the criminal law well into the twentieth century. Even the partial criminalisation of wife rape was controversial in the 1970s. A view expressed, without flinching, by some of the most influential legal authorities, was that such an offence would unfairly arm the 'vindictive' wife.[3]

In the 1980s, the various Australian state jurisdictions successively legislated to make wife rape a crime. Then in 1991 the High Court in *R v L* had an opportunity to consider the common law on the marital immunity and declared (by way of dicta) that by 1991, and possibly before that, the husband had lost this protection.[4] In 1992, South Australia, which was now lagging behind the other Australian states, fully criminalised wife rape.

The Facts

In 2009, criminal proceedings were commenced against PGA (Mr P) for the rape of his wife in 1963, when the two were cohabiting. This was not the first time that Mr P had come to the notice of the authorities. There is evidence that 'on numerous occasions during the 1960s' Mrs P contacted the police, complaining of violence, but that they declined to act, regarding it as a private matter.[5]

[1] Chief Justice of the Court of King's Bench, 1671–76.

[2] *The History of the Pleas of the Crown* (1736) vol 1, ch 58, 629.

[3] This was the view of Australia's leading criminal law scholar Colin Howard (*Australian Criminal Law* (Law Book Co, 1965) – the book went through several editions) and it was repeated in the report of the 'Mitchell Committee', of which he was a member: Criminal Law and Penal Methods Reform Committee of South Australia, Parliament of South Australia, *Special Report: Rape and Other Sexual Offences* (1976).

[4] (1991) 174 CLR 379.

[5] Wendy Larcombe and Mary Heath, 'Case Note: Developing the Common Law and Rewriting the History of Rape in Marriage in Australia: *PGA v The Queen*' (2012) 34 *Sydney Law Review* 599, 602.

Some 40 years later, the alleged rapes again came to public attention when the former Mrs P gave evidence before the Mullighan Inquiry into the sexual abuse of children in state care.[6] Action against Mr P proceeded at a measured pace. In August 2006, the former Mrs P gave a statement to the police. In June 2007 Mr P was interviewed, and in September the Port Adelaide Prosecution Service sought the opinion of the office of the Director of Public Prosecutions (DPP) as to whether a rape prosecution of Mr P could proceed; in May 2008 there was an affirmative reply. In 2009, in the South Australian District Court, Mr P was charged, inter alia, with two counts of rape.

There was further delay when (in July 2010) counsel for Mr P sought a permanent stay of proceedings, maintaining that the common law in 1963 did not recognise the crime of wife rape. In response, the DPP sought a temporary stay so that the Court of Criminal Appeal could answer the question: 'Was the offence of rape by one lawful spouse of another . . . an offence known to the law of South Australia as at 1963?' Doyle CJ, who gave the judgment for the majority, declared that it was: that 'even in 1963, a respectable challenge to Mr Matthew Hale's opinion could have been mounted'.[7] The matter went on appeal to the High Court. Again the question was, in effect, whether the crime of rape in marriage was part of the Australian common law in 1963.[8]

PGA in the High Court: The View of the Majority

In May 2012, a majority of the High Court, in a joint judgment,[9] went further still. It determined that the husband's immunity from prosecution for the rape of his wife had ceased to be part of the common law, at least by the time of the enactment of s 48 of the *Criminal Law Consolidation Act* (SA) in 1935,[10] if it ever had been part of Australian common law. Thus the Court remained vague about just when wife rape became an Australian crime, suggesting that possibly it had always been one.

Judgments are steered by the arguments of the parties. The High Court came to its view of the law after a direct affront to the integrity of Australian law, occasioned by Mr Bennett, counsel for Mr P. Our law, he said, had immunised husbands from prosecution for the rape of their wives and consigned the wives of Australia to a pre-Enlightenment condition. In the 1960s, he contended, 'Australia was a very unenlightened and socially backward country'.[11] Solicitous of its forbears (Gummow J suggested that Sir Garfield Barwick's ghost was 'probably stirring' at such a slight),[12] the Court rejected the imputations of Mr Bennett, and

[6] EP Mullighan QC, Presented to South Australian Parliament, *Children in State Care: Commission of Inquiry – Allegations of Sexual Abuse and Death from Criminal Conduct*, 31 March 2008. See discussion in ibid.

[7] *R v P, GA* (2010) 109 SASR 1 [66]. For a critical analysis of this case, see Kellie Toole, 'Case and Comment: Marital Rape in South Australia: *R v P, GA*' (2011) 35 *Criminal Law Journal* 237.

[8] Or as the majority specifically framed the issue: 'whether . . . as a matter of the common law, upon their marriage in 1962 [Mr P's] wife had given her consent to sexual intercourse and therefore could not retract [it]': *PGA v R* (2012) 245 CLR 355 [3] ('*PGA*').

[9] The plurality comprised French CJ and Gummow, Hayne, Crennan and Kiefel JJ.

[10] This was the section which stated, in simple terms, that rape was an offence, leaving it to the common law to spell out its elements.

[11] *PGA v R* [2011] HCA Trans 267 (27 September 2011) (DMJ Bennett QC).

[12] Ibid.

declared wife rape to be a crime known to Australian law for much, if not all, of the twentieth century. And in so doing, it avoided a major concession of moral error.

This was an astonishing determination. It entailed the removal of a well-accepted central, though perhaps negative, feature of one of the two most serious crimes possible, as criminal lawyers themselves calibrate criminal offences. Though the husband's immunity represented a fundamental departure from criminal legal principle, violating the basic right to bodily integrity, it was sustained up to 1976 in South Australia, and up to the 1980s in the rest of the country, in Canada and Scotland, and up to 1991 in England and Wales. It was rock-solid – a basic feature of the criminal legal landscape, so familiar that it was rarely mentioned, yet utterly assumed. Then in 2012, with a minimum of fuss, the High Court simply swept it away.

The reasoning and justification were economical. The majority was receptive to the Crown argument that South Australia was a progressive jurisdiction in a progressive country which would not have tolerated the immunity. By 1930, women in Australia had capacity to act in commercial and professional life, to vote, own property and sue and be sued in their own right.[13] The Court tells a brief and partial tale of the steady modernisation of the legal lives of Australian women, via specific statutory reforms, such that the immunity came to make little sense. Australia had escaped its Imperial past: 'local statute law had removed any basis for continued acceptance of Hale's proposition as part of the English common law received in the Australian colonies.'[14]

Thus there was preservation of the morality and principle of the past and loyalty displayed to past Australian law-makers. And this was achieved with minimal agonising and soul-searching: almost in a perfunctory manner – only 10 pages to change centuries of thought. And hence there was no deep wrong to women recognised, analysed or condemned. There was no critical reflection on past law and practice. There was no 'Nuremberg moment' when a court looks back at a form of behaviour once regarded as lawful and acceptable by a state, and now seen as inhumane, and so condemns it outright. If anything, there was more concern about the legal wrong which might be committed if there were open retrospectivity. Moral outrage at the treatment of women is missing because the mistreatment is denied.

The Dissenting Judges

Heydon and Bell JJ, who gave separate dissenting judgments, tell a less heroic tale of Australian law and its treatment of married women. And yet neither expresses strong disquiet at their misogynist past, though both recognise it, but not as a deep failure of principle – rather as different mores for different times. Indeed, they too are more concerned to defend the great jurists of the past and to insure against the more abhorrent departure from principle which is retrospectivity.

To Bell J, for example, 'It cannot be sensibly suggested that the appellant would have been prosecuted for those offences, had the allegations come to the attention of the authorities in 1963.'[15] She affirms that the immunity was a part of the received common law of Australia.

[13] *PGA* (2012) 245 CLR 355 [63].
[14] Ibid [64].
[15] Ibid [164].

She insists that Hale, who is the provenance of the rule, was a great common lawyer. To Bell J it is not critical that the immunity was defective in principle to modern sensibilities, only that it was law. 'A number of common law rules of liability for criminal offences' she reminds us, 'have their origins in discredited ideas.'[16]

Bell J reflects on the attitudes of 'another age', when a Law Lord could counsel a husband to employ 'some gentle violence' on a sexually recalcitrant wife and so avoid the breakdown of a marriage.[17] She accepts that these were indeed the legal attitudes of Australia in the 1920s. Moreover, distinguished Australian criminal textbook writers of the 1950s and 1960s continued to assert the need for the marital immunity. To Colin Howard: '[A] husband should not walk in the shadow of the law of rape in trying to regulate his sexual relationships with his wife.'[18]

Bell J admits that '[t]he common law was demeaning to women in its provision of the immunity. [But] [i]t is no answer to that recognition to permit the conviction of the appellant for an act for which he was not liable to criminal punishment at the date of its commission.'[19] It would be 'abhorrent to impose criminal liability' retrospectively. There is no shame or disgust at the legal treatment of married women. Though she acknowledges the recent commitment of distinguished legal scholars to the immunity, in her account, this neither weakens the scholar, nor taints the legal tradition.

The Feminist Judgment

Mary Heath and Wendy Larcombe also offer a dissenting judgment: they determine that the rape of a wife by a husband was *not* a crime known to law in 1963, and so Mr P could not be prosecuted for the rape of his wife. But from the outset, they distinguish their position by acknowledging the deep wrong to women and offering an unqualified apology. This is a powerful cathartic moment in their judgment. It is perhaps as unexpected as it is timely.

As a court-ordered remedy in civil actions, the apology has been described as 'uncommon' and 'unorthodox'.[20] The executive apology is rarer still, and can be more a symbolic than legal cure for past injustices, as one government formally acknowledges the wrongs of another.[21] The apology of Larcombe and Heath is a novel and welcome judicial response to the common law wrongs done to married women, one which avoids a rewriting of the past and the erasure of gross injustice.

Our feminist judges arrive at their determination after a close analysis of the available case law. They concede that explicit judicial recognition of the immunity is hard to find, but that the immunity could be inferred from a variety of charging and prosecution practices: husbands were charged as accessories but not as principals; wives who left their husbands, supported by a court order, were taken to have revoked consent; and husbands were

[16] Ibid [214].

[17] Ibid [226]. This is the case of *G v G* [1924] AC 349.

[18] From Howard, above n 3, quoted in *PGA*, ibid [238] (Bell J).

[19] *PGA*, ibid [247]

[20] Robyn Carroll, 'Apologies as a Legal Remedy' (2013) 35 *Sydney Law Review* 317.

[21] On the legal significance of the executive apology of former Prime Minister Rudd to the Aboriginal people of Australia, see Alex Reilly, 'Sovereign Apologies' in Julie Evans et al (eds), *Sovereignty: Frontiers of Possibility* (University of Hawaii Press, 2013).

sometimes charged with false imprisonment and indecent assault of a wife, but not with her rape. These cases show an erosion of the immunity, but not its demise by 1963.

They concur with Heydon J, also in dissent, that a catalyst for reform of the law was second wave feminism of the 1970s and its demand for the equal treatment of women. And it was not until 1976 that South Australia partially removed the immunity. This reform, they say, makes little sense if the immunity had already ceased to be law. The partial decriminalisation necessarily assumed the existence of the immunity.

To Larcombe and Heath, judges are bound to state the legal truth, even if it is harsh. To deny the immunity is to deny the wrongs done to married women. This they will not do.

Postscript

In September 2012 Mr P died and so the matter will never come to trial and we will never know, as a matter of law, whether Mrs P was raped.

PGA.. APPELLANT;

AND

THE QUEEN.................................... RESPONDENT.

[2012] HCA 21

ON APPEAL FROM THE SUPREME COURT OF SOUTH AUSTRALIA

H.C. OF A. 2011–2012

ADELAIDE *Sept* 27 2011

Canberra *May* 30 2012

Larcombe and Heath JJ

249 Larcombe and Heath JJ. The question now before this Court is whether the rape of a woman by her husband was a crime known to the common law of Australia in 1963. In particular, we are asked to determine whether the common law in 1963 provided a husband with immunity from criminal liability for the rape of his wife during the term of their marriage and in the absence of a court order revoking the wife's consent to marital sexual intercourse. It is noteworthy that this question has not been authoritatively answered prior to this case.

Overview

250 The "marital immunity" advanced by the appellant is traced back to a statement of Sir Matthew Hale published in 1736:

> "The husband cannot be guilty of a rape committed by himself upon his lawful wife, for by their mutual matrimonial consent and contract the wife hath given up herself in this kind unto her husband, which she cannot retract" (527).

251 The immunity was assumed to be a common law rule into the 1970s, when it became one focus of feminist pressure for rape law reform. South Australia began the process of abolishing the immunity in 1976 when it passed legislation making rape in marriage a criminal offence in "aggravating circumstances" (528). In the 1980s, other jurisdictions progressively removed distinctions between married and unmarried women in relation to rape (529). South Australia abolished the immunity entirely in 1992 (530). Since then, no Australian jurisdiction has distinguished between rape inside and outside marriage.

(527) Hale, *The History of the Pleas of the Crown* (1736), vol 1, Ch 58, p 629.

(528) *Criminal Law Consolidation Act Amendment Act 1976* (SA).

(529) *Crimes (Amendment) Ordinance (No 5) 1985* (ACT) s 92R; *Crimes (Sexual Assault) Amendment Act 1981* (NSW) s 61A(4); *Criminal Code Act 1983* (NT) s 192(1); *Criminal Code, Evidence Act and Other Acts Amendment Act 1989* (Qld); *Criminal Code Amendment (Sexual Offences) Act 1987* (Tas) s 185(1); *Crimes (Amendment) Act 1985* (Vic) s 62(2); *Acts Amendment (Sexual Assaults) Act 1985* (WA) s 325.

(530) The *Criminal Law Consolidation (Rape) Amendment Act* 1992 (SA) removed s 73(5).

252 The current appeal presents this Court with its first opportunity to determine as a matter of law whether marital rape was recognised as a crime by the common law of Australia in 1963 – prior to the reforms of the 1970s and 1980s.

253 For the reasons that follow, we find that the marital immunity formed part of the common law of Australia until its abolition by statute. It follows that a husband could not be convicted for the rape of his wife in South Australia in 1963.

254 In making this finding, it is important to acknowledge that the incremental processes by which the common law develops proved inadequate to protect the rights of married women. The common law was constrained by official attitudes and policing and prosecutorial practices which did not recognise domestic violence and marital rape as forms of abuse demanding legal recourse. Where judicial opinion on the subject was expressed prior to statutory reform, it acted as a further brake on prosecutions. As a result, for generations, criminal courts failed to offer women redress for rape within marriage. As judges of the final court of appeal in Australia, we extend our sincere apologies to women injured as a result of the common law rule that afforded husbands immunity for marital rape.

Background and issues to be considered

255 The question before us has arisen as a result of rape charges laid against the appellant, PGA, in 2009. The appellant's former wife, GP, alleges that in 1963, immediately before and shortly after the birth of their first child, PGA had sexual intercourse with her using force and against her will. GP and PGA were then cohabiting and no orders were in force affecting the marriage. PGA was charged with rape under s 48 of the *Criminal Law Consolidation Act 1935* (SA). In 1963, the elements of this offence were established by the common law.

256 In 2010, PGA sought a permanent stay of prosecution in the District Court, relevantly contending that rape within marriage was not a crime known to the common law in 1963 (531). On application from the Director of Public Prosecutions, Herriman J sought determination by the Supreme Court of the following question:

> "Was the offence of rape by one lawful spouse of another, in the circumstances as outlined above [where the parties were cohabiting and no legal orders related to the marriage were in force], an offence known to the law of South Australia as at 1963?" (532)

257 A majority of the Supreme Court answered in the affirmative. That decision is now under appeal before this Court.

(531) Transcript of Proceedings, *R v PGA* (unreported, District Court of South Australia, 1418/2009, Herriman J, 5 July 2010) at 38.

(532) *R v P, GA* (2010) 109 SASR 1 at 4 [6] per Doyle CJ; at 20 [95] per Gray J.

258 In our opinion, three issues are determinative of this appeal. First, it must be determined whether Hale's proposition formed part of the common law of Australia. Second, if the immunity was at one time part of the common law, we must determine whether, as the respondent argues, it had ceased to be so by early in the 20th century. Third, if the immunity endured, we must consider whether stating the common law now so as to abolish the immunity would be contrary to principle and policy.

259 First, however, we consider the preliminary matter of this Court's dicta concerning the marital immunity in *R v L*.

R v L

260 This court considered the marital rape immunity in obiter in the 1991 case of *R v L*, stating: "it is appropriate for this Court to reject the existence of such a rule as now part of the common law of Australia" (533).

261 In considering the case now before us, a majority of the South Australian Supreme Court determined that they were bound, following the decision in *Farah Constructions Pty Ltd v Say-Dee Pty Ltd* (534), to apply the dicta from *R v L*. As a consequence, they reasoned that it was not open to them to find that a marital immunity existed in 1963.

262 The dicta in *R v L* were in accordance with then-recent decisions in England and Scotland (535) and emerging criticism of the immunity in Australian courts (536). However, by 1991 the marital immunity had been modified by legislation in all Australian jurisdictions so that the Court's comments could have no prospective effect (537). Moreover, the historical status of the immunity was deliberately left open in *R v L* (538). For these reasons, the dicta in *R v L* cannot be regarded as stating a rule of the common law.

263 The historical status of the marital immunity requires fresh consideration by this Court.

The status of Hale's proposition as a rule of the Australian common law

264 The appellant argues that Hale's proposition provides authority for a husband having immunity from criminal liability for raping his wife. South Australia counters that Hale's extra-judicial statement does not constitute legal authority, and that it is otherwise unsupported.

265 Sir Matthew Hale's eminence as a jurist cannot be doubted. Heydon J and Bell J have outlined the evidence from case law, legislation, commentaries and parliamentary sources demonstrating

(533) (1991) 174 CLR 379 at 389.
(534) (2007) 230 CLR 89.
(535) *S v HM Advocate* 1989 SLT 469; *R v R* [1992] 1 AC 599.
(536) See *R v C* [1981] 3 A Crim R 146.
(537) See fn 469 above.
(538) (1991) 174 CLR 379 at 390, 405.

acceptance that Hale stated a rule of the common law. Whether Hale had stated the law correctly or not, the immunity became widely regarded as "well-settled and ancient law" (539). In this context, it is unsurprising that there are no reported prosecutions for marital rape in England between Hale's time and 1949.

266 However, textbooks, legislative and popular assumptions, and a lack of prosecutions cannot authoritatively state the common law. Prosecutorial practices, in particular, may merely speak to low reporting rates and low prospects of conviction for marital rape, given historic social attitudes to "domestic violence". Nor can Hale's extra-judicial statements, taken in isolation, establish the immunity as a common law rule. This is so notwithstanding the likelihood that Hale stated the common law of his time.

267 As French CJ, Gummow, Hayne, Crennan and Kiefel JJ observe, "common law" relevantly refers to a body of law created and developed by courts (540). Evidence for the immunity forming part of the common law thus needs to be found in its application and development in case law. The paucity of prosecutions means that the immunity is commonly considered only in obiter dicta. In the absence of an authoritative statement of a common law rule, all dicta must be given due attention.

268 Hale's proposition was first discussed in 1888 in *R v Clarence* (541). In obiter, a majority expressed support for the existence of a marital immunity for rape, while a number of judges argued that a wife could lawfully refuse consent to marital intercourse to protect her health. This line of reasoning was not taken up in subsequent cases.

269 Judicial acknowledgment of the marital exemption is then found in three subsequent series of cases. The first series, commencing in 1949 with *R v Clarke* (542), established "exceptions" to the immunity. These cases identified circumstances in which marital consent could be revoked by court orders, allowing rape convictions although the parties remained technically married (543). Second, cases prosecuting husbands for indecent assault and false imprisonment of their wives, but not for rape, suggest that courts would not entertain marital rape prosecutions (544). Finally, cases

(539) *R v Kowalski* (1987) 86 Cr App R 339 at 341.
(540) See above at [267] onward.
(541) (1888) 22 QBD 23.
(542) [1949] 2 All ER 448.
(543) *R v Clarke* [1949] 2 All ER 448; *R v O'Brien* [1974] 3 All ER 663; *R v Steele* (1976) 65 Cr App R 22; *R v Roberts* [1986] Crim LR 188; *R v McMinn* [1982] VR 53.
(544) See above at [107] per Heydon J; *R v Jackson* [1891] 1 QB 671; *R v Miller* [1954] 2 All ER 529; *R v Kowalski* (1987) 86 Cr App R 339.
(545) *Director of Public Prosecutions v Morgan* [1975] 2 All ER 347; *R v Cogan* [1976] QB 217.
(546) Hale stated that a husband who was present and intended to prostitute his wife to a rape by another man should be found equally guilty. Hale, *The History of the Pleas of the Crown* (1736) vol 1, Ch 58, p 628.

involving prosecutions where a husband was charged as an accessory to the rape of his wife by another man (545) appear to proceed on the basis that husbands enjoyed immunity for rape within marriage (546).

270 Each of these lines of cases indicates that Hale's proposition stated a common law rule, even when the inappropriateness and offensiveness of that rule is condemned. We reiterate that acceptance of the immunity in each case is necessarily obiter. Only one case directly applied the immunity prior to 1991: *R v Miller* (547). Heydon J considers that *Miller* remained good law in England until *R v R* and would have been binding had the current case been prosecuted in 1963. However, *Miller* was decided by a single judge and it stands out among the English cases that generated a widening list of exceptions as one of only two decisions finding in favour of the accused (548).

271 Rather than make a finding on the basis of *Miller*, we concur with Bell J's observation that a rule of law need not be applied as a matter of ratio (549). The acceptance and development of a principle across a number of cases can attest to the existence of a common law rule. The "exceptions" cases represent stages in the development of the common law in relation to the immunity, rather than indications of its non-existence or demise.

272 We cannot accept the proposition advanced by South Australia that the immunity never formed part of Australian common law although it has been authoritatively found to have formed part of the English common law. The marital immunity was overruled in England in 1992 (550) and abolished in Scotland in 1989 (551). These decisions recognised the existence of the immunity as a settled rule of law.

273 Although aspects of English matrimonial and ecclesiastical law were not received into Australian law on colonisation, Australia received the criminal common law of rape. We therefore find that, historically, the marital immunity formed part of the common law of Australia.

Did the immunity cease to exist early in the 20th century?

274 The respondent argues that even if the immunity once formed part of the common law, the foundation for the rule and hence the rule itself should be regarded as having "crumbled to dust" by the early to mid twentieth century. In support of their proposition, they observe that in Hale's formulation, the immunity was justified on the basis of a presumption that wives gave irrevocable consent to

(547) [1954] 2 All ER 529 ('*Miller*').
(548) *R v J* [1991] 1 All ER 759 also applied and upheld the immunity.
(549) See above at [222].
(550) *R v R* [1992] 1 AC 599.
(551) *S v HM Advocate* 1989 SLT 469.

sexual intercourse by their husbands. It is then argued that the presumption of marital consent is inconsistent with Australian statutory reforms extending property and franchise rights to married women and amending the "double standard" relating to adultery as a ground for dissolution of marriage.

275 As noted by Brennan J in *R v L*, it is likely that Hale's justification of the immunity misrepresented English ecclesiastical and matrimonial law, which is more accurately understood as never having "embraced the notion of a general consent to sexual intercourse given once and for all on marriage" (552). However, we do not accept the proposition that the immunity ceased to form part of the common law merely because the justification of implied marital consent was either erroneous or rendered fictional by statutory reforms to marriage and women's legal status early in the 20th century.

276 First, it is established principle that changes in social circumstances or erosion of the reasons for the formulation of a legal rule will generally not justify disregarding the rule (553). A common law rule of criminal liability remains in force unless and until it is modified or overruled by judicial authority or expressly abolished by statute.

277 As outlined above, the "exceptions" cases from 1949 onward consistently accepted the immunity as a settled rule even as they restricted its application. Moreover, only one of the "exceptions" cases was decided prior to 1963 (554). It was 1981 before judges in *R v McMinn* commented on the inappropriateness of the immunity – after the statutory reform process had begun (555). It was not until the late 1980s and early 1990s that appellate judges suggested that the immunity should no longer be maintained as a rule of law. Before that time, their remarks reflect a clear acceptance that the immunity formed part of the common law, albeit a distasteful part.

278 Second, in arguing that the presumption of wives' consent had become insupportable, the respondent's treatment of statute law is partial. Inconsistent statutory provisions – affecting divorce, married women's property and the suffrage – are nominated as undermining the presumption of marital consent. However, statutory provisions that are consistent with maintenance of the marital immunity well into the 20th century are overlooked. One example identified by Bell J is the inclusion of the immunity as part of the Tasmanian *Criminal Code* in 1924 which, she observes, was not seen at the time as contrary to advances in married women's rights (556).

279 Third, we concur with Bell J's observation that for much of the

(552) [1991] 174 CLR 379 at 396.
(553) *R v Trigwell* (1979) 142 CLR 617.
(554) *R v Clarke* [1949] 2 All ER 448.
(555) [1982] VR 53 at 59.
(556) *R v McMinn* [1982] VR 53 at 59.
(557) Estrich, *Real Rape* (1987), p 75; Scutt, *Even in the Best of Homes* (1983), p 142.

20th century the immunity may have operated independently of the fiction of wives' consent. For example, the immunity may have been justified as reflecting the principle that the law should refrain from intruding on the privacy of marital relations (557). This is an important consideration, given that this case arises in the South Australian context where the 1976 reforms abolished the presumption of marital consent while preserving a limited form of the marital immunity (558).

280 It follows that even if Hale's presumption of wives' consent to marital intercourse was incorrect or became insupportable early in the 20th century, in our opinion there is strong evidence that the immunity itself persisted as a rule of the common law into the second half of the 20th century.

Should the common law now be stated in terms that abolish the marital immunity?

281 We have determined that the marital immunity once formed part of the common law of Australia and further, that erosion of the fiction of wives' irrevocable consent to marital intercourse did not render the immunity invalid as a common law rule. It remains to be determined whether the common law ought now to be stated in terms that abolish the immunity. In our view, such a course of action would be contrary to legal principle, policy and the historical record. Most importantly, we find that justice for married women is better served by recognising the history of the marital immunity than by erasing it.

282 *Retrospective criminalisation*: The appellant has argued that particular considerations attach to declaring or "clarifying" the criminal common law as any such clarification will operate with retrospective effect. Retrospective criminalisation of conduct is contrary to fundamental rule of law principles. As a consequence, as Heydon J observes, the courts have a very limited role to play in modern times in "creating" offences or extending criminal liability: this is the role of Parliament (559). However, the courts are the guardians of the common law, and it is the task of an ultimate court of appeal to develop the common law so as to ensure that it recognises and protects the liberty and equality of all citizens.

283 In that context, we note that *R v R* and *S v HM Advocate* (560) stated the common law for England and Scotland respectively in terms that abolished the marital immunity with retrospective effect.

(558) In other jurisdictions, abolition of the presumption of marital consent was considered sufficient to abolish the immunity.

(559) We concur with Heydon and Bell JJ that it is improbable that the appellant would have been convicted for marital rape in 1963. Moreover, between 1966 and 2003 prosecution of PGA for the alleged rape offences was statute barred: see above at [12].

(560) *R v R* [1992] 1 AC 599; *S v HM Advocate* 1989 SLT 469.

The courts in both cases were bound by the principles regarding retrospective criminalisation that this Court must now consider. Moreover, they were governed by the European Convention on Human Rights.

284 In *CR v UK* (561), the European Court of Human Rights considered appeals arguing that the House of Lords' decision to abolish the marital immunity breached prohibitions on retrospective criminalisation. After considering the English cases beginning in 1949 that created exceptions to the immunity, the Court stated:

> "There was an evident evolution . . . towards treating such conduct generally as within the scope of the offence of rape. This evolution had reached a stage where judicial recognition of the absence of the immunity had become a reasonably foreseeable development of the common law" (562).

In Australia, we find that there was no such "evident evolution". The process of law reform in South Australia clearly indicates that the common law was not understood as evolving in this manner by 1976. Further, the English and Scottish decisions had *prospective* as well as retrospective effect. Any restatement of the common law immunity by this Court would only have retrospective effect.

285 *The importance of statutory reform:* The intervention of the legislatures to abolish the marital immunity in Australia is another important consideration in now restating the common law. It is desirable not to state the common law in terms that create inconsistency with statutory frameworks. The decision of the majority has the curious effect of rendering the reforms of 1976–1985, intended to limit or abolish the marital exemption, redundant (Victoria and New South Wales) or restrictive (South Australia). Moreover, the codes which included the immunity in order to ensure consistency with the common law as understood when they were created (or amended, in the case of Tasmania) would now, according to the majority, be understood to have maintained an immunity for decades after it ceased to form part of the common law.

286 These inconsistencies flow, in part, from stating the law in terms which differ profoundly from legal and extra-legal sources prior to and after the passage of the 1976 reforms. The decisions in *R v R* and *S v HM Advocate* (563) created no such anomalies in their respective jurisdictions. These anomalies might be overlooked were we not of the opinion that it is inconsistent with all historical evidence to find that the husband's marital immunity for rape "fell away" in the first half of the 20th century.

287 *The historical record*: We have outlined the evidence that the immunity was maintained and affirmed in legislative amendments

(561) [1995] ECHR 51.
(562) [1995] ECHR 51 at [41].
(563) *R v R* [1992] 1 AC 599; *S v HM Advocate* 1989 SLT 469.

prior to 1985 and that Australian judicial opinion did not explicitly turn against the immunity until *R v L* in 1991.

288 Concurring with Heydon J, we find that rejection of the immunity was the result of social and legal developments in the 1970s (564), in conjunction with the sustained feminist activism of this period (565). The marital immunity was only one element of the law of rape that was reformed from 1976 onward. Requirements for corroboration and practices of cross-examination targeting the complainant's sexual history were also reformed. Definitions of rape were extended to recognise penetrative acts beyond penile-vaginal intercourse, and to stipulate circumstances in which sexual consent could not be free and voluntary.

289 The principle of equality before the law underpinned these reforms. Modern rape law acknowledges that sexual penetration without affirmative consent violates an individual's sexual autonomy whether the perpetrator is husband, acquaintance, family member or stranger; whether the victim is female, male, transgender or intersex.

290 Demands for equal treatment on the basis of sex and marital status under the law of rape paralleled demands for equal treatment in other areas of law and life during the 1970s and 1980s. The development of anti-discrimination legislation – in particular the *Sex Discrimination Act 1984* (Cth), which sought to eliminate discrimination on the basis of sex or marital status – is further evidence of the significant changes in legal principles and social values that were occurring during this period.

291 In our opinion, these legal changes, reflecting significant changes in social norms governing gender and sexuality, finally made the marital immunity insupportable as a matter of legal principle. The immunity differentiated arbitrarily between married and unmarried rapists and between married and unmarried complainants. Statutorily removing this immunity thus removed an archaic form of discrimination based on marital status.

292 *Is it better to rewrite or recognise the history of the common law?:* In our opinion any finding in 2012 that marital rape was a crime known to the common law in 1963 would rewrite the legal and social history of the 20th century. While to do so would "remove a blot on the history of the common law" (566), it is our view that that history requires acknowledgment, not revision. The injustices wrought by the immunity, which had undoubted and profound effects on the lives of countless married women, are part of the

(564) See above at [121].

(565) See Scutt, *Even in the Best of Homes* (1983); Sallmann and Chappell, "Rape Law Reform in South Australia", *Adelaide Law Review Research Paper*, vol 3 (1982) 37; Russell, *Rape in Marriage* (1982).

(566) *R v P, GA* (2010) 109 SASR 1 at 17 [85].

history of the common law. The common law's copybook should not be cleaned by erasing the role the law has played in condoning the sexual violence that many married women experienced during the life of the husband's legal immunity for rape.

293 Something of the humiliation and harm that the immunity caused was properly committed to the public record during debate over the South Australian reforms of 1976 (567). For example, the Hon Member for Sturt, NK Foster, after recounting the story of a woman known to his family who was assaulted and raped by her husband more than four years after separating from him, continued:

> "[He] cannot be charged by the police even upon complaint. No lawyer . . . or . . . prosecuting police officer, would be willing to stand up . . . and say, if a woman had laid a complaint that she had been raped by her husband or subjected to serious bestialities, that the police would prosecute" (568).

294 It is important to acknowledge the law's historic failure to recognise married women's dignity and rights. There is ample evidence that, prior to the statutory abolition of the immunity, married women and their husbands ordered their affairs based on a belief that the immunity formed part of the common law.

295 A finding now that the immunity lapsed in the early to mid 20th century would not only be contrary to the legal and social evidence; it would make it appear that the law offered justice to women subjected to spousal rape over a 50 year period in which policing, prosecution and judicial practices offered neither protection nor succour (569). That harm cannot be adequately redressed by this court belatedly enabling the criminal prosecution of a small number of the marital rapes committed during this period.

296 *When did the immunity cease to form part of the common law of Australia?*: It is appropriate for this Court now to state the common law in terms that reject the immunity, as it did in *R v L*. However, we must go further than the dicta in *R v L* and identify as a matter of law when the immunity ceased to form part of the common law. For the reasons above, we hold that the marital immunity remained a rule of the common law of Australia, qualified by expanding exceptions, until its abrogation by statutory reform.

(567) South Australia, *Parliamentary Debates*, Legislative Council, 11 November 1976, 2093 (FT Blevins); South Australia, *Parliamentary Debates*, Legislative Council, 11 November 1976, 2097 (Anne Levy).

(568) South Australia, *Parliamentary Debates*, Legislative Council, 11 November 1976, 2139 (NK Foster).

(569) Allen, *Sex and Secrets* (1990), p 131; Scutt, *Even in the Best of Homes* (1983), p 157.

(570) *R v C* [2004] EWCA Crim 292 at [15] per Judge LJ.

A comment on limitations affecting development of the common law of rape

297 Common law principles cannot be decisively clarified in the absence of judicial decisions, which in turn rely on prosecutions, convictions and appeals raising contentious points (570). In the case of marital rape, the absence of prosecutions has long precluded the expression or development of a clear statement of binding principle. Absent an authoritative statement of the rule, the law as practised effectively authorised the sexual violation of married women until late in the 20th century (571).

298 As an institution responsible for the development of the common law in Australia, this Court acknowledges that reliance on the development of the common law to provide protection for married women raped by their husbands proved misplaced. In particular, since prospects of conviction are lower for rape than for all other comparable offences (572), the process of common law development through appeals against conviction militates against judicial development of the common law of rape.

299 The common law method works fairly and effectively in many areas of life where disputes that enable development of the law regularly come before the courts and are appealed to the highest level. In the case of marital rape, however, it has been exposed as derelict. The few judges who had opportunities in the second half of the 20th century to comment on the antiquated nature of the immunity affirmed it more often than they denounced it, thereby discouraging prosecutions. In this context, victims of marital rape have necessarily relied on legislatures to secure recognition of basic rights.

300 It would be a cruel irony for this Court to rewrite the history of the common law so as to make it appear in 2012 that married women had the protection of the common law throughout the 20th century when this was manifestly not the case. Acknowledging that history, and women's experiences, must serve as a form of justice in this instance: the common law rule affording husbands immunity for rape persisted until it was abolished by statute.

Orders

301 The appeal should be allowed. The decision of the South Australian Supreme Court should be set aside. In lieu thereof, the question of law should be answered in the negative: *the offence of rape by one lawful spouse of another, where the parties were cohabiting and no legal orders related to the marriage were in force, was not an offence known to the law of South Australia as at 1963*.

(571) Feerick and Easteal, "Sexual Assault by Male Partners: Is the License Still Valid?", *Flinders Journal of Law Reform*, vol 8 (2005) 185.

(572) Gelb, *Recidivism of Sex Offenders Research Paper* (2007) 4.

Evidence

17

Commentary on *RPS v R*

KATHERINE BIBER

The Facts and Evidence in *RPS*

RPS was charged with two counts of carnal knowledge and six counts of sexual intercourse with his daughter, ISW, when she was between the ages of 4 and 14. Her sworn evidence was the primary evidence. There were no eyewitnesses, there was no circumstantial evidence and no expert evidence. RPS gave no evidence in his defence. Other evidence came from ISW's mother and grandmother of their conversations with RPS after the daughter first complained to her mother. In those conversations RPS made admissions, as well as a partial denial. When the women had confronted him with ISW's allegations, RPS is alleged to have responded, 'I never had intercourse with her but everything else she said is true'. At trial there was argument about what, exactly, those conversations meant. What, exactly, had he admitted? This was left as a question for the jury. The trial judge directed the jury about the accused's election not to give evidence and how – in the absence of his explanation, contradiction or denial – they might weigh the strength of the prosecution evidence. The jury found him guilty of four counts of sexual intercourse.[1]

The Appeal to the High Court

The trial judge's directions substantially followed the earlier High Court ruling in *Weissensteiner v R*.[2] Following *Weissensteiner*, a trial judge was permitted to direct the jury that there were some circumstances in which an accused might be expected to speak and, if they did not, an adverse inference could be drawn from their silence. However, in 1995 the *Uniform Evidence Acts* were enacted in New South Wales and at the federal level,[3] and s 20(2) of the Act appeared to be inconsistent with *Weissensteiner*. *RPS* was the High Court's first opportunity to consider whether *Weissensteiner*-style directions were still permissible and, if not, what a trial judge might be permitted to say when directing the jury about the silence of the accused. *RPS* now applies in all jurisdictions belonging to the *Uniform Evidence Act* regime.[4]

[1] *RPS v R* (2000) 199 CLR 620 ('*RPS*').
[2] (1993) 178 CLR 217 ('*Weissensteiner*').
[3] *Evidence Act 1995* (NSW) and *Evidence Act 1995* (Cth) (the Act).
[4] These are the Commonwealth, New South Wales, Victoria, the Australian Capital Territory, and the Northern Territory.

RPS introduced a significant restraint upon the trial judge. In rejecting *Weissensteiner*, the Court stated that it is 'seldom, if ever' reasonable to expect an accused person to give evidence.[5] *RPS* says that judicial directions to the jury must protect the accused's right to silence, their presumption of innocence, and must convey that the entire burden of proof rests upon the prosecution. Further, *RPS* says that judicial directions to the jury must make it clear that no adverse inferences can be drawn from the accused's silence.[6]

The majority (Gaudron ACJ, Gummow, Kirby and Hayne JJ) acknowledged 'the difficult task trial judges have in giving juries proper instructions',[7] but they ruled that the trial judge's directions contravened s 20(2) of the Act. They noted that the directions given at RPS's trial contravened the right to silence, but they said that this term (right to silence) obscures the particular principle being applied; that is, restraint upon judicial comment.[8] They interpreted the legislative provision widely: the judicial comment cannot invite *any* adverse inference.[9]

McHugh J agreed, in a separate judgment, that the judicial directions contravened the legislation. He said that the directions 'left to the jury a train of reasoning which implicitly suggested . . . that the accused was guilty of the offences concerned'.[10]

Criticisms of *RPS*

RPS, as I have written elsewhere, represents an attempt by the High Court to gag the trial judge.[11] Further, this gag is most commonly demanded and applied in cases arising from child sexual assault allegations. Notoriously difficult to prosecute, and typically emerging from contexts of secrecy, vulnerability and familial conflict, child sexual assault cases might logically be amenable to *Weissensteiner* directions. They are cases where the accused is the only person in a position to contradict or deny the complainant's allegation, having 'special knowledge' of the offence above all others,[12] and where the accused's failure to explain might reasonably strengthen the prosecution's case.[13] Despite the unique prosecutorial difficulties posed by cases such as these, the High Court has developed many evidentiary principles of

[5] *RPS* (2000) 199 CLR 620 [27] (Gaudron ACJ, Gummow, Kirby and Hayne JJ).

[6] The following year in *Azzopardi v R* (2001) 205 CLR 50, the Court ruled that the circumstances in which *Weissensteiner* might continue to apply would be 'rare and exceptional': [68] (Gaudron, Gummow, Kirby and Hayne JJ). A year later, in *Dyers v R* (2002) 210 CLR 285, the High Court agreed unanimously that an accused person need not give or call any evidence in their defence, and that judicial directions to the jury need to prevent them from drawing any adverse inference from a defendant's failure to do so: [9]–[12], [19] (Gaudron and Hayne JJ); [26]–[27] (McHugh J); [53] (Kirby J); [119] (Callinan J).

[7] *RPS* (2000) 199 CLR 620 [41].

[8] Ibid [22].

[9] Ibid [19]–[20].

[10] Ibid [49]. Significantly, and consistent with his distinctive jurisprudence of silence, including his dissenting judgment in *Weissensteiner*, McHugh J seemed to suggest that there is a difference between the jury's reasoning process ('I see nothing intrinsically wrong with such a reasoning process') ([59]) and a judicial direction about following that reasoning process ([59]–[60]). That is, so long as the jury is correctly directed, they can then go ahead and reason that the silence carries some probative weight when deciding facts that have not been explained or contradicted by the accused.

[11] Katherine Biber, 'On Not Speaking: The Right to Silence, the Gagged Trial Judge and the Spectre of Child Sexual Abuse' (2005) 30 *Alternative Law Journal* 19.

[12] *Weissensteiner* (1993) 178 CLR 217 [17] (Gaudron and McHugh JJ).

[13] Ibid [11]–[14] (Gaudron and McHugh JJ).

general application, arising from the very specific context of child sexual assault allegations.[14] Restricting judicial comments about the silence of the accused represents just one of these principles.

RPS is part of an emerging 'jurisprudence of silence' that appears to mis-recognise the nature, context and meaning of silence. In Australian case law, the 'right to silence' is most commonly litigated in disputes about the words spoken (or mis-spoken) by the trial judge to the jury; these words are supposed to say that silence means nothing. A critical response to this jurisprudence argues that silence frequently means something, that silence demands interpretation, and that context is crucial to grasping – and then relying upon – the meaning of silence. I have written:

> [I]n criminal enterprises and in criminal procedure, speech and silence exist on a spectrum, and in shifting contexts. There are times where silence is impossible, and times where it is irresistible. The law is rarely sensitive to the contexts in which silence falls and those in which silence is broken.[15]

Criticism of such a restrictive jurisprudence of silence need not come from feminist perspectives.[16] However, our contemporary jurisprudence of silence demands that silence be smothered with words:

> Silence, wherever it occurs in law's jurisdiction, must be explained and explained and explained. In this babble of explanation law misbelieves that it protects silence; further, it often misattributes the term 'silence' to certain kinds of noise. Law's commentary forecloses the possibility that silence might be deliberately ambiguous, that it might invite speculation, or that inferences demand to be drawn from it.[17]

The Feminist Judgment

The application, clarification and potential expansion of *Weissensteiner* directions to the circumstances of RPS's trial is central to the feminist judgment. The feminist judgment sees *RPS* as an opportunity to draw upon United Kingdom legislation, which had been in place since 1994. That legislation allows adverse inferences to be drawn from the failure of the accused to give evidence, as explained in the feminist judgment. Further, the feminist judgment reminds the accused that, whilst silence need not be a risk, nevertheless it has consequences. And crucially, it remembers that whilst silence may be the 'right' of the accused, being silenced is typically the experience of victims and complainants.

Whereas *Weissensteiner* ruled that, in some circumstances, it would be adverse for the accused not to explain, contradict or deny facts peculiarly within 'the accused's knowledge',

[14] For examples, see Biber, above n 11, 22–23, many of which have been consolidated by further superior court rulings also arising from child sexual assault allegations.

[15] Katherine Biber, 'How Silent is the Right to Silence?' (2012) 18 *Cultural Studies Review* 148, 149.

[16] Dyson Heydon, long before his elevation to the High Court bench, wrote that drawing inferences from silence was a matter of 'logic and common sense': JD Heydon, 'Silence as Evidence' (1974–75) 1 *Monash University Law Review* 53, 53. Legal scholar and barrister, Andrew Palmer, wrote that there is 'a robust Benthamite common sense' that underlies the reasoning in *Weissensteiner*: 'Silence in Court: The Evidential Significance of an Accused Person's Failure to Testify' (1995) 18 *University of New South Wales Law Journal* 130, 137. *Weissensteiner* has itself been subjected to criticism: 'dangerous precedent', relying upon 'fine distinctions', 'elegant sophistry', and 'gibberish': all cited in David Hamer, 'The Privilege of Silence and the Persistent Risk of Self-incrimination: Part II' (2004) 28 *Criminal Law Journal* 200, 211.

[17] Biber, above n 15, 163–4.

the feminist judgment regards 'the accused's knowledge' as a needlessly narrow focus for the jury. Instead, the feminist judgment differs from *Weissensteiner* by looking to *all* the circumstances of the particular case, and considers whether – given all of those circumstances – an explanation or contradiction would be called for. Further, it is not only the accused's 'knowledge' that ought to be evaluated by the jury, but all of the particularities of the accused. Given RPS's partial admission, the question *What does he know?* is too narrow an inquiry. In fact, the jury was also investigating the questions: *What did he say? What did he admit?* And ultimately *What did he do?* In the absence of his explanation, the answers to these questions *can* be gleaned from the prosecution's case: the evidence of ISW, her mother and her grandmother. It is not that he does not have a right to silence; he does, and he cannot be compelled to testify. But his exercise of the right may yield an adverse outcome for him. The feminist judgment recognises that this is a practical, logical and appropriate outcome in these circumstances.

Significantly, the feminist judgment also encourages the jury to consider the particularities of the accuser and of the crime, in deciding whether or not to draw an adverse inference from the accused's failure to give evidence.

The feminist judgment redefines the fair trial, so that 'fairness' is done to all of those in the courtroom, and not only the defendant. It demands that the courts also take account of the interests of the state, victims, witnesses, and society. The feminist judgment opens up the possibility that there may be a feminist perspective to the debate about whether the right to silence unnecessarily privileges the accused.

The feminist judgment provides a 'model' jury direction which refers to the jury as 'you'. This returns a level of respect and humanity to the trial, and recognises that there is an important dialogue between the trial judge and jurors. There is also a significant omission in the feminist model direction; the direction does *not* require the trial judge to say words to the effect of 'you must dismiss all feelings of emotion or sympathy and prejudice you may feel towards the accused, the complainant and the crime'.

The feminist judgment recognises the importance of context. Context is crucial to understanding what might have happened, what might have been said, what was meant, and what ought to be done about it. Gagging the trial judge prevents the jury from appreciating, and drawing upon, the context in which a crime has occurred. Deciding cases in a factual vacuum, outside of their context, prevents meaningful interpretation of the evidence. The feminist judgment reminds us that context precedes the possibility of justice.

RPS. . . . . Appellant;

AND

THE QUEEN. . . . . Respondent.

[2000] HCA 3

ON APPEAL FROM THE SUPREME COURT OF NEW SOUTH WALES

HC of A 1999–2000

March 4; Sept 8 1999

Feb 3 2000

O'SULLIVAN J

116 O'Sullivan J. This appeal involves an important aspect of criminal law trials – the right of an accused to remain silent. It is also to decide whether the landmark case of *Weissensteiner v The Queen* (90) (*Weissensteiner*) decided by this court in 1993 is still good law.

117 There has been much debate since the decision in *Weissensteiner* about what it said, and whether it went too far, or not far enough, in modifying the common law right to silence at trial.

118 It is therefore incumbent on this court to clarify the current law on the right to silence at trial.

Facts of the case

119 The appellant (Mr S) was charged, in the District Court of New South Wales, with two counts of carnal knowledge of his daughter (ISW) and six counts of sexual intercourse with her. The offences were alleged to have occurred between 6 February 1983 when ISW was four years old, and 31 July 1993, by which time she was 14 years old. He pleaded not guilty.

120 The trial judge directed the jury to acquit Mr S of one of the charges of sexual intercourse; the jury returned verdicts of guilty to four of the remaining five counts of sexual intercourse and verdicts of not guilty to the other count of sexual intercourse and the counts of carnal knowledge.

121 The prosecution case against Mr S depended largely on ISW's evidence. She described various acts of sexual misconduct by him. She swore that, on a number of occasions, he had penile intercourse with her and, on other occasions, had digitally penetrated her. No other eyewitness was called; no circumstantial evidence was given, and expert evidence was not adduced.

122 However, ISW's mother and paternal grandmother gave evidence of their conversations with Mr S. ISW told her mother that her father had, "been fingering me and . . . made me have intercourse with him." ISW's mother swore that in subsequent conversations Mr S said to her: "I never had intercourse with her but everything else she said is true." She asked Mr S, "How long has it been going on?" and he replied, "Since she was about ten." ISW's paternal grandmother gave evidence that she asked him: "Are you saying that you've never touched her with your hands or fondled her or put your penis inside her?" and he replied "That's right."

(90) (1993) 178 CLR 217.

123 Mr S appealed against his convictions to the Court of Criminal of New South Wales, but that appeal was dismissed (91). By special leave, he now appeals to this Court.

The main issue in the appeal

124 The main issue in this appeal is what the trial judge said to the jury about the silence of Mr S at his trial.

The election by Mr S not to give evidence

125 Mr S elected not to give evidence at his trial. In his charge to the jury, the trial judge began by telling the jury that an accused person may, but is not obliged to, give evidence and that the prosecution bears the onus of proof. He said that the jury "must not conclude that [the appellant] has elected not to give evidence because he is guilty of the offences charged against him." He observed that there are many reasons why an accused person may not want to give evidence and told the jury that they "must not speculate as to why [the appellant] has not given evidence." No complaint is made (or could be made) about these parts of the trial judge's charge.

126 This appeal centres upon what the judge then said to the jury:

> (1) "In the present case, however, the Crown asks you when judging the value of, the weight of, the evidence which has been put forward by the Crown as establishing its case against the accused, to take into account the accused's election not to deny or to contradict the matters about which he could have given direct evidence from his own personal knowledge. That is indeed a circumstance which you are entitled to consider in this case. That is, the fact that the accused has elected not to contradict the evidence given by [the complainant's mother] as to his alleged admission – if you construe it as such – and he has been content to rely upon that very brief statement in answer to the detailed allegations made by the complainant."
>
> (2) "You may think that it is only common sense that in a situation where a Crown witness and the accused are directly involved in a particular incident so that they are the two persons best able to give evidence of what happened in that incident, and where the evidence of the Crown witnesses is left undenied or uncontradicted by the accused any doubts which may otherwise have been cast upon the evidence of the Crown witnesses may be more readily discounted and the evidence of the Crown witnesses may more readily be accepted as the truth. That is the approach which the Crown asks you to adopt in this case, in particular with regard to the statement made by him to [the complainant's mother], according to her evidence, in which he denied sexual intercourse but said that everything else that [the complainant] had said was true."
>
> (3) "The accused, however, has met the complainant's allegations. He has not traversed the detail of them, but in his statement which he gave to the police (but not here by evidence) he has denied committing any of these offences. Clearly, it is upon that earlier denial that he now relies. If you are satisfied that the accused could have given evidence from his own knowledge of the events about which [the complainant's mother and the complainant] have given evidence for the

(91) *R v RPS* (unreported; Court of Criminal Appeal (NSW); 13 August 1997).

Crown, if you are satisfied that it is reasonable, in the circumstances, to expect some denial or contradiction to be forthcoming from the accused if such a denial or contradiction is available, then you are entitled to conclude, you do not have to, but you are entitled to conclude, from the accused's election not to deny or contradict that evidence that his evidence would not have assisted him in this trial."

(4) "You may use the election of the accused not to put forward any such denial or contradiction as a circumstance which leads you more readily to accept the evidence given by the witnesses for the Crown the accused was in a position to contradict of his own knowledge."

(5) "Of course, there were a number of witnesses for the Crown and parts of the evidence which he was not in a position to contradict, things that did not take place in his presence or in which he was not engaged. But he certainly was in a position, you might think, to contradict what it was that [the complainant] said happened between him and her and also what it is [the complainant's mother] said had been said on that occasion in August of 1993 in the telephone conversation."

(6) "You cannot however use that election by the accused not to put forward any denial or contradiction in order to fill in any gaps which you think may otherwise be in the evidence upon which the Crown relies. Its relevance relates only to the value or the weight which you can give to the evidence which the Crown witnesses have given. In other words, you may feel more confident in relying upon evidence which is uncontradicted than evidence which is. I do remind you that the accused has made in that statement to the police, (although not in evidence here in Court – he did not give evidence here in Court I should say) which amounts to a general denial of all offences."

(7) "The absence of any evidence from the accused as to the circumstances and details of the incidents also means that there is no evidence to support the particular version which was put to the Crown witnesses in cross-examination by counsel for the accused. All that has been said by the accused is a flat general denial. That version, insofar as it was suggested to [the complainant] that these things had not been done or to [the complainant's mother] that what she said was said had not been said, was denied by each of them when the question was put and the accused has led no evidence to establish that it happened, that his version was correct."

127 The following should be noted about the trial judge's directions:

a) The trial judge told the jury that Mr S's election not to contradict the evidence given by ISW's mother of what was said to be a partial admission could be taken into account by them in judging the value or weight of the prosecution's evidence.

b) He told the jury that in the absence of denial or contradiction of the evidence given of the partial admission they could "more readily" discount any doubts about that evidence and "more readily" accept the evidence.

c) He told the jury that if it was reasonable in the circumstances to expect some denial or contradiction of the prosecution evidence, they were entitled to conclude that Mr S's evidence would not have assisted him in his trial and that the absence of denial or contradiction was a circumstance which could lead them more readily to accept the evidence given by the witnesses for the prosecution.

d) He told the jury that the election of Mr S not to give evidence could not fill any gaps in the prosecution case but could enable them to feel more confident in relying on the evidence tendered by the prosecution.

e) He told the jury that the absence of evidence from Mr S meant that the version of events put in cross-examination of the witnesses for the prosecution was not supported by evidence.

Weissensteiner v The Queen

128 The trial judge's direction in this case was substantially in accordance with *Weissensteiner* which was decided by this Court seven years ago.

129 *Weissensteiner* changed the existing common law right to silence which stated (in summary) that silence proves nothing one way or the other but it does not rebut, contradict or explain the case put forward by the Crown, and the jury is entitled to consider that the silence of the accused permits a more ready acceptance of the Crown case.

130 It changed the law, and it is for this court to decide whether it was an opportunity to be grasped or a mistake to be remedied.

131 In the Supreme Court of Queensland, the trial judge in *Weissensteiner* had given the following directions to the jury:

> "The accused bears no onus. He does not have to prove anything. For that reason he was under no obligation to give evidence. You cannot infer guilt simply from his failure to do so. The consequence of that failure is this: you have no evidence from the accused to add to, or explain, or to vary, or contradict the evidence put before you by the prosecution. Moreover, this is a case in which the truth is not easily, you might think, ascertainable by the prosecution. It asks you to infer guilt from a whole collection of circumstances. It asks you to draw inferences from such facts as it is able to prove. Such an inference may be more safely drawn from the proven facts when an accused person elects not to give evidence of relevant facts which it can easily be perceived must be within his knowledge" (92).

132 It is unfortunate that this Court's decision in *Weissensteiner* was written in three separate judgments and they are not easily reconcilable. It is therefore necessary to deal with each of them.

133 In their joint judgment, Mason CJ, Deane and Dawson JJ said:

> "Not every case calls for explanation or contradiction in the form of evidence from the accused. There may be no facts peculiarly within the accused's knowledge. Even if there are facts peculiarly within the accused's knowledge the deficiencies in the prosecution case may be sufficient to account for the accused remaining silent and relying upon the burden of proof cast upon the prosecution. Much depends upon the circumstances of the particular case and a jury should not be invited to take into account the failure of the accused to give evidence unless that failure is clearly capable of assisting them in the evaluation of the evidence before them" (93).

134 I see no justification for limiting the jury's focus to "facts peculiarly within the accused's knowledge." For reasons which I will develop later in this judgment, this focus is too narrow because it refers only to the accused

(92) Transcript of Proceedings, *R v Weissensteiner* (unreported, Supreme Court of Queensland, Moynihan J, 25 September 1991), 610–11.
(93) (1993) 178 CLR 217, 228.

and only to his knowledge. I consider it should go further, to include all the circumstances of the particular case.

135 Mason CJ, Deane and Dawson JJ pointed out that to adopt the principle that the failure to give evidence bearing upon the probative value of the evidence may be taken into account is not to deny the accused his right to silence: they said "it is merely to recognize that the jury cannot, and cannot be required to, shut their eyes to the consequences of exercising the right" (94).

136 This statement is similar to one expressed by Pincus JA in the Court of Appeal hearing of this case: "It is one thing to say that there is a right of silence and another to say that its exercise shall never be permitted to disadvantage those who exercise it" (95).

137 I respectfully adopt each of these statements.

138 In their joint judgment, Brennan and Toohey JJ took a different approach. They agreed with the trial judge's directions and said:

> "The facts from which an inference of guilt may be drawn are correctly identified [in the charge to the jury] as facts which the prosecution is able to prove. The use to which the appellant's failure to give evidence may be put is correctly restricted to the strengthening of an inference of guilt from the facts proved. And the jury is told not to use the appellant's failure to give evidence unless relevant facts 'can be easily perceived to be in his knowledge'. This additional requirement, which follows a decision of the Court of Criminal Appeal of Queensland in *Reg v Whinfield* [Unreported, Queensland Court of Criminal Appeal, 16 September 1986 at 25] ensures that the drawing of an inference of guilt will not be assisted by an accused's failure to give evidence unless it is reasonable to expect some denial, explanation or answer by the accused to the prima facie case made against him" (96).

139 I see no justification for the limitation on the jury to look only at evidence of facts "easily perceived to be within his knowledge", for the same reason I have discussed above when discussing the phrase "facts peculiarly within the accused's knowledge" in the joint judgment of Mason CJ, Deane and Dawson JJ.

140 Rather, I consider that the jury may take into account any evidence they consider relevant, including the matters which may be the subject of comment from the trial judge. The focus is on all the particularities of the accused, not just his knowledge, and should be widened to also include the particularities of the accuser, and of the crime.

141 In their joint judgment, Gaudron and McHugh JJ took another approach. They said:

> "Directions should be given in terms of the unexplained facts, rather than in terms of the failure to give evidence or to meet the prosecution case generally. Directions shall be precisely framed in terms of the particular facts which call for explanation" (97).

(94) (1993) 178 CLR 219 at 229.
(95) Transcript of Proceedings, *R v Weissensteiner* (unreported, Court of Appeal of Queensland, Pincus JA, 22 June 1992), at 12.
(96) (1993) 178 CLR 219 at [9].
(97) (1993) 178 CLR 219 at [21].

142 The focus of their approach was on the trial judge identifying the unexplained facts calling for explanation. I disagree with this approach, and consider that it is not for the trial judge to identify the unexplained facts because that is for the jury. The trial judge should tell the jury that they may take all evidence into account, and the trial judge should outline the relevant evidence, but it is for the jury to decide what weight should be given to particular parts of the evidence in reaching its decision whether it is reasonable to expect the accused to have given evidence.

Comments and conclusion on Weissensteiner

143 I substantially agree with the trial judge's directions in *Weissensteiner*, but I believe it requires one important change. This change is that the jury may consider more than just "relevant facts which it can easily be perceived must be within his knowledge" or "facts peculiarly within his knowledge." This focus on the accused's knowledge in *Weissensteiner* is unjustifiably narrow. The jury should cast its net more broadly. The jury should be directed that they may take into account any evidence they consider relevant to the question whether it is reasonable to expect an accused to have given evidence. The trial judge should assist the jury in this task by commenting on what evidence may be relevant to this decision, without in any way binding or limiting the jury. The trial judge should stress that it is for the jury to decide whether it is reasonable to expect an accused to have given evidence at his trial.

144 I consider that the judgments in *Weissensteiner* do not give sufficient recognition to the importance of context, and the impossibility of making a decision about silence in isolation from the trial itself, which involved the particular accused [Mr S] the particular accuser [ISW] and the particular crimes alleged against Mr S.

145 The decision whether it is reasonable to expect Mr S to have given evidence at his trial cannot be made by jurors in a "factual vacuum" (98).

146 The jurors cannot ignore the people before the court, and should not be required to do so. The people before the court include Mr S, ISW, and witnesses other than ISW. At the special leave hearing, Defence Counsel said: "It is often difficult to extricate oneself from the human aspects of it [the trial] and confine oneself to the legal aspect" (99). It is of course true that jurors should be instructed not to be biased or prejudiced towards the accused or the accuser or about the nature of the crimes alleged, and to reach their decision on the evidence alone. However, the distinction raised by Defence Counsel is artificial, and disrespectful to the people before the court.

(98) Katherine Biber, "On Not Speaking: The right to silence, the gagged trial judge and the spectre of child sexual abuse", *Alternative Law Journal*, vol 30 (2005) 23.

(99) Transcript of Proceedings, *RPS v R* (High Court of Australia, Ducker J, 8 September 1999) at 39–40.

Law reform proposals for changing the right to silence at trial

147 The decision in *Weissensteiner* led to considerable debate in the courts, the legal profession, and academia. This is understandable, in view of the changes it made to the common law right to silence.

148 It must be remembered, however that proposals for reform of the right to silence at trial have been put forward, even before *Weissensteiner*, and I propose to offer brief comment on each of these.

Legislation in the United Kingdom in 1994

149 Section 35 of the Criminal Justice and Public Order Act 1994 (UK) states:

> "(1) At the trial of any person who has attained the age of fourteen years for an offence, subsections (2) and (3) below apply unless –
> . . . (b) It appears to the court that the physical or mental condition of the accused makes it undesirable for him to give evidence.
> (2) Where this subsection applies, the court shall, at the conclusion of the evidence for the prosecution, satisfy itself in the case of proceedings on indictment, in the presence of the jury) that the accused is aware that the stage has been reached at which evidence can be given for the defence and he can, if he wishes, give evidence and that, if he chooses not to give evidence, . . . it will be permissible for the . . . jury to draw such inferences as appear proper from his failure to give evidence.
> (3) Where this subsection applies, the . . . jury, in determining whether the accused is guilty of the offence charged, may draw such inferences as appear proper from the failure of the accused to give evidence.
> (4) This section does not render the accused compellable to give evidence on his own behalf, and he shall accordingly not be guilty of contempt of court by reason of a failure to do so".

150 Section 38(3) of the same Act states:

> "An accused cannot be convicted of an offence solely on an inference drawn from the failure or refusal to give evidence."

151 This legislation was discussed in a United Kingdom Judicial Studies Board Specimen Direction (100). It includes a direction from the trial judge that the jury may draw a conclusion that the accused has not given evidence because he has no answer to the prosecution's case, or none that would bear examination. They may do so only if they think it is a fair and proper conclusion, and they are satisfied that the prosecution's case is so strong that it clearly calls for an answer by the accused and that the only sensible explanation for his silence is that he has no answer, or none that would bear examination.

152 The United Kingdom law requires the court to make a preliminary finding, and if the finding is that the legislation applies, then the jury is asked to answer a number of nominated questions, as set out in the Specimen Direction quoted above.

(100) United Kingdom Judicial Studies Board Specimen Direction, No 39.

153 I do not agree with the need for the court to make a preliminary finding based on the accused's "physical or mental condition." The jury should be asked to address the question: is it reasonable to expect the accused to have given evidence in the trial before the court? There is no necessity for a preliminary finding by the trial judge.

154 I further consider that to look only at the "physical or mental condition" of the accused is unnecessarily restrictive, and a wider scope of inquiry is warranted. The jury should also have regard to other matters, as outlined below, such as the relationship between the accused and the accuser, the particularities of the accuser, and the nature of the crime.

Western Australian Law Reform Commission

155 Last year the Western Australian Law Reform Commission recommended that:

> "The law on the right to silence at trial should be amended to permit the jury to have regard to a defendant's silence as one of the circumstances or part of the evidence but not, in and of itself, permitting an inference of guilt, so long as the jury is first directed as to the defendant's right to be silent" (101).

156 I have considered this recommendation, and recognise its merit, but I believe that it is desirable to add the pre-requisite that the jury must first be satisfied that it is reasonable to expect the accused to have given evidence, taking into account the particularities of the accused, the accuser and the crime.

Approach suggested by Davies JA

157 Davies JA has suggested reform in a series of articles in the *Australian Law Journal* earlier this year (102). His legislative proposal would allow the jury to draw inferences from the silence of the accused, taking into account certain prescribed matters which may be summarised as: the strength of the prosecution case, whether the facts which call for denial, explanation or answer are within the personal knowledge of the accused, whether those facts are capable of innocent explanation, and any explanation given by the accused.

158 I broadly agree with this proposal, but consider that the goals it seeks to achieve are equally satisfied with the judicial directions which I consider the trial judge ought to have given in this case. Further, the suggested jury directions are less complex, and more likely to be understood by jurors.

159 The jury directions outlined below have a further advantage over the proposal made by Davies JA, namely, they can be adopted by judicial officers immediately, without the necessity for legislation, although legislation may be enacted at a later stage, to provide clarity and reinforcement.

(101) Law Reform Commission of Western Australia, *Review of the Criminal and Civil Justice System in Western Australia Final Report*, Project 92 (1999).

(102) Geoffrey Davies, 'The Prohibition Against Adverse Inferences from Silence: A Rule Without Reason?', *Australian Law Journal*, vol 74 (2000), 26, 99.

Section 20 Evidence Act 1995 (NSW)

160 After the High Court decision in *Weissensteiner*, new provisions were introduced into the Evidence Act 1995 (Cth) and the Evidence Act 1995 (NSW):

> "The judge or any party (other than the prosecutor) may comment on a failure of the defendant to give evidence. However, unless the comment is made by another defendant in the proceeding, the comment must not suggest that the defendant failed to give evidence because the defendant was, or believed that he or she was, guilty of the offence concerned" (103).

161 The Court of Appeal of New South Wales found that the trial judge's directions in the case now before us breached s 20 by his use of the words quoted in paragraph 12(c) above; I agree that there was a breach.

162 The jury directions outlined below, make s 20 redundant.

Fundamental features of criminal trials

163 In view of the uncertainty which has arisen from *Weissensteiner*, it is necessary to state the law which governs the question: in an accusatorial process, in which the prosecution bears the onus of proving the guilt of the accused beyond reasonable doubt, what significance can be attached to the fact that the accused does not give evidence?

> a) In a criminal trial, the accused may not be compelled to give evidence, and the jury must not infer guilt from silence alone.
>
> b) If an accused elects not to give evidence, the jurors may in the circumstances outlined in this judgment, take that into account in reaching their verdict.
>
> c) It is always for the prosecution to prove its case, and to do so beyond reasonable doubt, and the silence of the accused does not shift that onus.
>
> d) The prosecutor "has the responsibility of ensuring that the Crown case is presented with fairness to the accused" (104). This duty means that in many cases the prosecutor would be expected to call a witness who may assist in the defence case. This is part of the duty of the Crown to prove guilt beyond reasonable doubt.
>
> e) It cannot be emphasised enough that in our criminal justice system the accused enjoys the presumption of innocence, and that the onus of proof always remains with the Crown.

Trial judges' directions concerning the silence of the accused

164 The appropriate directions which ought to have been given by the judge concerning Mr S's silence at his trial would have begun with the direction that it was for the jurors (and the jurors alone) to decide whether it was reasonable to expect Mr S to have given evidence.

165 The evidence the jury was entitled to take into account might (but did not have to) include the following:

> The nature of the offences charged;
>
> The fact that they usually occur in secret and therefore with no witnesses;

(103) Evidence Act 1995 (Cth) s 20; Evidence Act 1995 (NSW) s 20.

The ages of Mr S and ISW at the time of the alleged assaults, and at the time of trial;
The relationship between Mr S and ISW at the time, including how frequently they saw each other;
The relationship between Mr S and his former wife, ISW's mother;
The difficulty for ISW in giving evidence of serious sexual assault in these circumstances: they occurred over some years; the assaults were by a member of her family; ISW's possible embarrassment at speaking about such intimate matters; the involvement of ISW's mother and ISW's paternal grandmother; ISW's reaction to her father's conduct at the time; ISW's embarrassment at private matters being aired in public and in a courtroom;
The denial of guilt by Mr S to his mother;
The partial admission – if the jury saw it as such – made by Mr S to ISW's mother;
The words and conduct of Mr S when confronted by his mother and ISW's mother;
What Mr S said in his police interview and whether it was in sufficient detail to make it unnecessary for him to offer any further explanation at trial;
The fact that Mr S's statement to the police was unsworn and not subjected to cross-examination.

166 The jurors might have taken any or all of these pieces of evidence into account, and given them whatever weight they thought appropriate. They might also have taken into account any other evidence they considered relevant to this question.

167 The trial judge ought to have directed the jury about the question for them to address:

> "It is for you to decide whether the evidence I have outlined, together with other parts of the evidence you consider relevant to this question, make it reasonable to expect Mr S to have given evidence at his trial."

168 The trial judge ought then to have directed the jury on what followed from that decision, as follows:

> "If you decide that it is reasonable to expect Mr S to have given evidence, then the fact that he has elected not to do so may mean that you can accept more readily the evidence led by the Crown. It does not of itself mean that he is guilty as charged: you should look at the totality of the evidence and decide whether you are satisfied beyond reasonable doubt that the Crown has proved its case;
>
> If, on the other hand, you decide that it is not reasonable to expect Mr S to have given evidence, then his silence must not be taken into account by you in reaching your verdicts. Your focus should be on the evidence which has been led in the trial, and whether you are satisfied beyond reasonable doubt that the Crown has proved its case."

169 Trial judges should conclude their directions to the jury by stating these important principles which apply in all criminal trials: first, you must consider each charge separately, and reach a conclusion in respect of each count on the indictment; secondly, if you are satisfied on the whole of the

(104) *Richardson v R* (1974) 131 CLR 116 at 119 per Barwick CJ, McTiernan and Mason JJ. See also *R v Apostilides* (1984) 154 CLR 563.

evidence that the Crown has discharged its onus of proving the guilt of the accused beyond reasonable doubt, then you must return a verdict of guilty. If you are not satisfied, then you must return a verdict of not guilty.

Decision

170 The trial judge directed the jury in accordance with *Weissensteiner*, but in doing so breached s 20 of the Evidence Act 1995. A new trial should be ordered to ensure that the jury is appropriately directed, in the manner outlined in this judgment, on the use it may make of the silence of the accused.

Order

171 The appeal should be allowed. The convictions should be quashed, and a new trial ordered on counts 4, 6, 7 and 8 on the indictment.

18

Locating Consent in Similar Fact Cases: *Phillips v R*

MEHERA SAN ROQUE*

Introduction: Coincidence and Credibility

Daniel Phillips was convicted of three counts of rape, two counts of unlawful carnal knowledge, and one count of assault with intent to commit rape. The jury had heard evidence from six complainants, ranging in age from 14 to 18, about assaults that had occurred in 2000–03.[1] He appealed, unsuccessfully, to the Queensland Court of Appeal, but in 2005 the High Court allowed the appeal and quashed the convictions, ordering separate retrials on all counts that had resulted in guilty verdicts.[2]

Phillips' appeal focused on the trial judge's decision to allow all of the charges to be heard together in one trial.[3] This decision depended on the trial judge accepting that in assessing the evidence in relation to each complainant, the jury could take into account, in some permissible way, the evidence from the other five. Allowing the joint trial thus ran up against the common law's stated exclusionary disposition towards evidence that discloses prior, or additional, criminal conduct of the defendant not directly linked to the events giving rise to the specific charge at hand. But courts have developed a number of exceptions moderating this protective posture; in limited cases, this will include allowing fact-finders to rely directly on 'similar fact' evidence. Admitting evidence under this rubric engages two, interrelated, forms of reasoning, both considered dangerous to the conduct of a fair trial.[4] The first, 'propensity' reasoning, allows the fact-finder to take into account that an accused has an established tendency, or propensity, to act or think in a particular way; a propensity that can be mapped so closely onto the events in issue at trial, that it is acceptable to rely on that propensity to find guilt. The second, 'coincidence' reasoning, sees the repetition of events linked in some way to the accused to be so unexpected, so unlikely, that coincidence can be ruled out as a plausible explanation.[5] Coincidence reasoning is most obviously engaged in

* With thanks to Anne Cossins.

[1] *R v PS* [2004] QCA 347 (24 September 2004) [2]. At the time of the 2003 assault Phillips was 18.

[2] *Phillips v R* (2006) 225 CLR 303 ('*Phillips*'). See David Hamer, 'Similar Fact Reasoning in *Phillips*: Artificial, Disjointed and Pernicious' (2007) 30 *University of New South Wales Law Review* 609, 610.

[3] See *Criminal Code 1899* (Qld) s 567 and related provisions. See Anne Cossins, 'Similar Facts and Consent in Sexual Assault Cases: Filling the Gap Left by the High Court in *Phillips*' (2011) 37 *Monash University Law Review* 47.

[4] See, eg, HL Ho, *A Philosophy of Evidence Law: Justice in the Search for Truth* (Oxford University Press, 2008) 300.

[5] Under the Uniform Evidence Law (UEL) the common law's approach to similar fact' evidence is separated into two notionally distinct exclusionary rules. See eg, ss 97 and 98 of the *Evidence Act 1995* (NSW).

a trial involving multiple complainants and charges if those witnesses independently report a (striking) pattern of behaviour, such that it is objectively improbable that they could all, independently, fabricate such details spontaneously.

At Phillips' trial, the jury was directed that it could not use the evidence from the multiple complainants as proof that Phillips had an *established* tendency or propensity to sexually assault young women.[6] Rather, it could be taken into account in assessing the credibility of the six complainants; in particular in assessing how (un)likely it was that all six would have, independently, lied about consent. On appeal, Phillips argued that the evidence did not meet the necessary stringent admissibility threshold for similar fact evidence, such that that the court could be satisfied that the probative value of the evidence was compelling enough to overcome the inevitable risk of (unfair) prejudice that would accompany its admission.[7]

The High Court's Decision

In their judgment the High Court changed the determinative issue, but their application of the conventional test to the facts is nonetheless revealing. For the High Court, the evidence did not reveal the necessary 'striking' or distinctive pattern to justify admission; the circumstances were not exceptional enough to warrant the joint trial. For a feminist reader, the judges' characterisation of the series of assaults, involving as they did, a pattern of escalating violence and intimidation, as 'entirely unremarkable' is startling.[8] Cossins J, in her feminist judgment, says that this reasoning points to a troubling emotional hardening; it suggests also a type of heuristic bias that sees one's own atypical perception or experience of the world, in this case one brought on by repeated exposure to criminal cases involving sexual violence, as the norm.[9] But their characterisation of the events as ordinary is more than a misplaced assessment of typicality, or a failure to empathise and to consider the effects of these experiences on the girls involved, though the erasure or downplaying of the girls' experience is a notable feature of their account.[10] Their ready conversion of the girls' cumulative accounts of escalating violence into a narrative of fumbling romance and frustrated masculine desire is also a failure at a more fundamental level. In the High Court's account, the accused's attempt to engineer consensual intercourse proceeds, unsurprisingly, naturally, to a reckless attempt to engage in sexual intercourse heedless of consent, or of the possibility of interruption. For the High Court it appears that this is what normal, uncontained, impulsive teenage male sexuality looks like.[11] Framed in this way, the evidence of the multiple complainants can never rise above the ordinary.

That the Court takes this approach in this type of sexual assault trial, (re)inscribing as it

[6] The propensity is established by the verdict. See *R v PS* [2004] QCA 347 (24 September 2004) [67], [69], and the feminist judgment [23].

[7] See *Pfennig v R* (1995) 182 CLR 461 and the corresponding, though not equivalent test under s101 of the UEL (see above n 5).

[8] *Phillips* (2006) 225 CLR 303 [56].

[9] See Jeremy Gans, 'Similar Facts after *Phillips*' (2006) 30 *Criminal Law Journal* 224.

[10] See, eg, '[s]omething happened to MM which caused her to run from the isolated house . . . in darkness at 4am. Whatever happened was something she must have found very *unpleasant*': *Phillips* (2006) 225 CLR 303 [72] (emphasis added).

[11] See eg, Kirsty Duncanson, 'Truth in Sentencing: The Narration of Judgment in *R v Webster*', this volume.

goes the common law's traditional wariness towards (young) women who allege rape, is, perhaps, predictable.[12] But in *Phillips* the High Court goes further; they not only interpret the evidence of the multiple complainants to be 'unremarkable', they hold that the evidence can have nothing to say on the question of consent *at all*.[13] In making this unanticipated move, the High Court emphasises that similar fact cases have been conventionally understood as telling us something about the accused and (his) propensities. At best, and tellingly, for the High Court:

> [e]vidence by other complainants that they had not consented [to the sexual conduct with or by the accused] had no more probative value than evidence by them that they had not consented to the performance of sexual acts on them by persons other than the appellant. Like the evidence of the other complainants in this case, evidence of that kind may demonstrate some 'propensity' in particular complainants, but it demonstrates nothing about the appellant.[14]

Converging on this interior perspective – that the evidence speaks only to the girls' state of mind, but tells us nothing about Phillips – exemplifies the High Court's narrow approach to the case, as they extract the moment of consent from its all-important context. And in a moment of surprising self-restraint, they hold that, in the absence of precedent, they are unable to say that the evidence is capable of having a rational effect on the assessment of whether one or more of the girls gave their consent to the acts 'allegedly performed on them by the appellant.'[15]

The Feminist Judgment

In confronting this central question of relevance, the feminist judgment returns to the conduct of the appellant, but in a reconfiguration of its own, also changes the question. The feminist judgment points out that to confine the evidence as being (only) relevant to the question of the probability of whether so many girls would lie, is also to miss the point about the relevance of the evidence to consent. In contrast to the trial court, the Queensland Court of Appeal and the High Court, Cossins J reinstates the full story, holding that the evidence can be used to establish a pattern not of rape, but of 'sexual aggression, force and/or violence', and it is this pattern that can be used, logically, to infer that there was an objective improbability that each of the complainants would consent in such circumstances of violence. It is, perhaps, a decision slightly ahead of its time in allowing evidence of a system or pattern of conduct of this kind to be used in this way.[16] It could be argued that this reasoning is vulnerable to slippages of its own – that it does not entirely escape the

[12] See, eg, the commentary and feminist judgment for *R v A (No 2)* in Rosemary Hunter, Clare McGlynn and Erica Rackley (eds), *Feminist Judgments: From Theory to Practice* (Hart Publishing, 2010); Wendy Larcombe, *Compelling Engagements: Feminism, Rape Law and Romance Fiction* (Federation Press, 2005).

[13] *Phillips* (2006) 225 CLR 303 [56]. Ie, they hold the evidence to be irrelevant. See also *Smith v R* (2001) 206 CLR 650.

[14] *Phillips* (2006) 225 CLR 303 [49].

[15] *Phillips*, ibid.

[16] It is an approach that crystallises in later decisions, such as *R v PWD* [2010] NSWCCA 209 (17 September 2010). See discussion of the competing trends in Annie Cossins, 'The Behaviour of Serial Child Sex Offenders: Implications for the Prosecution of Child Sex Offences in Joint Trials' (2011) 35 *Melbourne University Law Review* 821. See also discussion in Hamer, above n 2, 634–7

impermissible circularity of reasoning, by which the unproved allegations are open to being interpreted as establishing, ahead of the verdict, the propensity that is in issue.[17] In this respect and more broadly, the possibility of *unfair* prejudice remains.[18] And there are risks for the fair trial of defendants in other contexts if such a reconfiguration sits alongside a general reluctance to exclude evidence of low or uncertain probative value.[19]

But these reservations aside, as Christine Boyle points out, '[t]he law of evidence is a rich source of assumptions about human behaviour crystallised into doctrine',[20] and as feminists have argued in relation to this and other areas of evidence law, such assumptions are often wrong.[21] In her judgment, Cossins brings this point to the fore, arguing that the doctrines concerning the admissibility of 'tendency' or 'coincidence' evidence, in cases such as *Phillips*, need to align far more closely with what we know about the nature of sexual assault, and critically, the behaviour of (repeat) sexual offenders.[22] In this respect Cossins' feminist judgment offers the law of evidence some challenging new resources to draw on as alternatives to its own, often un-interrogated assumptions. So in her dissenting judgment, Cossins J points out that precedent does not compel the rejection of evidence of 'ordinary' violence or 'ordinary' sex; that 'striking similarities' can, and should, take into account similarities in context and condition, not merely in the itemised sexual acts themselves. But, more fundamentally, Cossins' feminist judgment takes on, squarely, the assumptions that have concealed themselves within the majority's conception of rational decision-making and relevance. She engages with the difficult implications of framing relevance as inherently subjective; rejecting the attractive but misleading dichotomy of the 'fact positivist', who sees on the one side of the line rational configurations of logical inferences and on the other messy, policy-driven reconfigurations.[23] Cossins' feminist judge knows that relevance is always about managing (competing) values, inferences and policy considerations, and that the common sense so often relied on as providing the grounding for rational inferences is partial, inflected, and very often *un*common.

[17] See the discussion in Annie Cossins, 'The Legacy of the *Makin* Case 120 Years On: Legal Fictions, Circular Reasoning and Some Solutions' (2013) 35 *Sydney Law Review* 731.

[18] See, eg, the discussion in Gans, above n 9, 235.

[19] See, eg, *R v Folbigg* [2005] NSWCCA 23 (17 February 2005). The flawed prosecution of Folbigg is analysed in detail in Emma Cunliffe, *Murder, Medicine and Motherhood* (Hart Publishing, 2011).

[20] Christine Boyle, 'A Principled Approach to Relevance: The Cheshire Cat in Canada' in Paul Roberts and Mike Redmayne (eds) *Innovations in Evidence and Proof* (Hart Publishing, 2007) 112.

[21] See, eg, Kathy Mack and Sharyn Roach Anleu, 'Resolution without Trial, Evidence Law and the Construction of the Sexual Assault Victim' in Mary Childs and Louise Ellison (eds), *Feminist Perspectives on Evidence* (Cavendish Publishing, 2000); Cunliffe, above n 19.

[22] See, eg, Cossins, above n 16, and Hamer, above n 2, 638.

[23] See, eg, Donald Nicolson, 'Gender, Epistemology and Ethics: Feminist Perspective on Evidence Theory' in Childs and Ellison (eds), above n 21. See also Boyle, above n 20.

PHILLIPS . . . . APPELLANT;

AND

THE QUEEN . . . . RESPONDENT.

[2006] HCA 4

ON APPEAL FROM THE SUPREME COURT OF QUEENSLAND

HC of A 2005–2006

Nov 11; Dec 9 2005

March 1 2006

Cossins J

89 COSSINS J: This case comes before the High Court as a test case for an old principle that the prior criminal conduct of an accused (known as propensity or similar fact evidence) should only be admitted in extraordinary circumstances (71), that is, if there are striking similarities between the similar fact evidence and the events leading to the charges against the accused (72). What is "extraordinary" involves an entirely subjective assessment of what is "out of the ordinary". According to my brother judges, whose draft judgment I have had the opportunity of reading, the alleged sexual assault of six girls, aged 14-18 years by the same offender, is entirely unremarkable. One wonders whether we as judges have become so inured to sexual assault that we have lost the ability to appreciate the terrors experienced by women when, faced with threats and violence, they are forced to undergo the ultimate humiliation.

90 Rape is a very serious offence and should never be trivialised. It is indeed, as Kirby J noted in the course of oral argument, a "sorry commentary on our society if there is no distinctiveness or uniqueness in a young man in his own town with [six] complainants engaging in . . . allegedly non-consensual sex" (73). However, distinctiveness is in the eye of the beholder. Before considering these issues further, it is convenient to list the grounds of appeal and the events that led to the appellant being charged with eight counts, including rape and assault with intent to rape.

The grounds of appeal

The appellant argued that the trial judge made an error of law under s 567 of the Queensland *Criminal Code* in ordering that the eight counts be tried in a joint trial instead of six separate trials. Charges may be joined in Queensland where they "are founded on the same facts, or are, or form part of, a series of offences of the same or similar character". The appellant argued the charges did not satisfy these criteria. Even if s 567 is satisfied, a trial judge must consider whether or not "the accused person may be

(71) *Director of Public Prosecutions v Boardman* [1975] AC 421 at 444 per Lord Wilberforce (*Boardman*).

(72) See, for example, *Harris v Director of Public Prosecutions* [1952] AC 694; *Boardman* [1975] AC 421; *DPP v P* [1991] 2 AC 447; *R v Roy* [1992] Crim LR 185; *R v Scarrott* [1991] 2 All ER 796; *R v Wilmot* (1988) 89 Cr App R 341; *Pfennig v The Queen* (1995) 182 CLR 461 (*Pfennig*).

(73) *Phillips v The Queen* [2005] HCATrans 919 at 37 per Kirby J (*Phillips*).

prejudiced or embarrassed in the person's defence by reason of" being charged with more than one offence in the same indictment (s 597A *Criminal Code*). Possible prejudice arises when a jury learns that Phillips has been charged with sex offences against six complainants and concludes that one allegation of rape might be false but six girls alleging rape could not happen unless Phillips was guilty.

92 When considering prejudice or embarrassment to the accused the trial judge cannot consider whether the similar fact evidence was the result of collusion or suggestion (s 597A(1AA)). With no evidence of collusion between the six complainants, the appellant argued that their evidence was not cross-admissible according to the common law rules of evidence governing similar fact/propensity evidence. Argument by counsel largely focused on the probative value versus the prejudicial effect of the evidence. While this is the final consideration for admissibility it is not the first. In fact, at trial and on appeal it was assumed that each complainant's evidence was relevant. Only later did the appellant agree with my brother judges that there was no fact in issue to which the combined evidence of the complainants was relevant.

93 The key issue is the relevance of all of the appellant's alleged sexual misconduct in terms of its cross-admissibility in a joint trial of sex offences involving six complainants. Was the evidence of complainant 1 relevant to the counts involving complainants 2 to 6? Was the evidence of complainant 2 relevant to the counts involving complainants 1, 3, 4, 5 and 6, and so on? Only if relevant, would the next tests of admissibility be applied – the striking similarities and the *Pfennig* (74) tests – before the trial judge could decide whether or not the eight counts should be tried together. The striking similarities test is merely another test of relevance although it imposes a higher threshold to determine the degree of probative value of the evidence which must then outweigh its prejudicial effect. The trial judge must ask, is there "a rational view of the evidence that is inconsistent with the guilt of the accused" (75)? If so, the evidence will be inadmissible.

94 While this is also a test case for that most subjective of tests – relevance, which has no objective, mathematical or scientific criteria by which to measure it – this says little about the psychological and social harm the Court is compelled to consider in relation to Phillips' sexual misconduct. Indeed, to limit the scope of the case by treating the relevance and striking similarities tests as if they were objective tests, somehow scientifically determined, would be an injustice to the complainants in this case.

95 It would also fail to acknowledge those who have campaigned against the sexual exploitation of women and girls. Over the centuries, many have named the unnameable at great personal cost (76). Following in their

(74) (1995) 182 CLR 461.

(75) *Pfennig* (1995) 182 CLR 461 at 482-483 per Mason CJ, Deane and Dawson JJ. This test was first enunciated in *Sutton v The Queen* (1984) 152 CLR 528 at 564 per Dawson J (*Sutton*) and adopted by a majority in *Hoch v The Queen* (1988) 165 CLR 292 at 296 per Mason CJ, Wilson and Gaudron JJ.

(76) See Fawcett and Turner, *Josephine Butler* (2002).

footsteps, it is important to name one of the social evils of our time – the sexual assault of vulnerable, teenage girls.

96 Australian Bureau of Statistics data tell us that girls aged 10–14 and 15–19 years are the age and sex groups most vulnerable to sexual assault (77). Yet court statistics show that sexual assault is more prone to attrition than other serious offences (78) which is partly due to the insufficiency of evidence to prove an offence that occurs in private. These facts raise two questions – is the administration of justice best served by admitting all relevant evidence about a defendant's sexual misconduct? Or as Gleeson CJ noted during submissions, is this evidence *so* relevant it is akin to dynamite such that multiple counts should always be tried separately (79)?

97 Separate trials confer a significant advantage on the accused since each jury remains ignorant of the other allegations while he is able to conduct his trial as if there is no corroborating evidence from other victims. Does the degree of injustice to an accused in a joint trial outweigh the degree of injustice to the victims and the community from having separate trials? Either way, judges must weigh up incommensurables and make decisions that will cause some prejudice or distress to either the accused or the victims.

98 The tension in this case arises from competing public policy issues: the fair trial principle which protects defendants from prejudice, the vulnerability of teenage girls to sexual assault and the incidence of serial sex offending (80). The rights of an accused under the fair trial principle are not absolute and must be balanced against "the interests of the Crown acting on behalf of the community" (81), including the interests of complainants and the public in bringing offenders to justice.

99 Is the test of relevance capable of dealing with these competing public interests? It seems to be a huge task for what is inherently a subjective test.

The problem with facts

100 The subjectivity of the relevance test is exemplified by the way the facts in this case have been interpreted and relevance applied by the majority as if the facts were immutable. The majority have given their interpretation of the facts. I will give mine by recognising that each complainant revealed a pattern of aggression by Phillips when he engaged in sexual relations with them.

101 BS, aged 16, had been invited to Phillips' home for a party. Only he and two other males were present. Phillips "forced her mouth over his penis", "tried to pull her pants down", lay on top of her with his hand over her

(77) Australian Bureau of Statistics, *Recorded Crime – Victims Australia*, 2002 at 12.

(78) NSW Criminal Justice and Sexual Offences Taskforce, Attorney-General's Department of NSW, *Responding to Sexual Assault: The Way Forward*, 2005.

(79) *Phillips* [2005] HCATrans 919 at 12.

(80) Hanson and Morton-Bourgon, "The Characteristics of Persistent Sexual Offenders", *Journal of Consulting and Clinical Psychology*, vol 73 (2005) 1154.

(81) *Dietrich v The Queen* (1992) 177 CLR 292 at 335 per Deane J (*Dietrich*), quoting *Barton v The Queen* (1980) 147 CLR 75 at 101 per Gibbs ACJ and Mason J; see also *R v TA* (2003) 57 NSWLR 444 at [8] per Spigelman CJ.

mouth and penetrated her while she yelled "loudly for him to stop". Phillips was charged with one count of rape and one count of aggravated indecent assault (counts 1 and 2). He admitted to consensual oral and vaginal sexual intercourse.

102 TK, aged 16, was an ex-girlfriend of Phillips. During her birthday party, Phillips carried her to, and threw her onto, a bed, forcibly removed her clothing then held her down as he penetrated her although she cried and told him to stop. Charged with one count of rape (count 3), Phillips denied that sexual intercourse took place.

103 ML, aged 15, was lured away from her sister's party by Phillips to sober up. When he began to kiss and touch her, she protested then passed out. She woke with Phillips having sexual intercourse with her. She shouted at him to stop and was left with grazes, bruises and cuts on her back from the force of the assault. Charged with one count of rape (count 4), Phillips admitted consensual sexual intercourse.

104 SW, aged 14, had consensually engaged in sexual relations with Phillips at a party although when he forced her head down and "made her put her mouth over his penis" she became scared. Phillips then penetrated her although she cried and told him to stop. Charged with one count of rape (count 5), he admitted consensual sexual intercourse.

105 MM, aged 15, was lured away from her boyfriend, who was causing her trouble, with the offer of a lift from Phillips who drove to an empty house on his parents' property. Threatened with a baseball bat and ordered to undress by Phillips, MM performed oral sex after which Phillips pushed her onto a bed and had sexual intercourse with her on two separate occasions despite her protests. Charged with two counts of rape (counts 6 and 7), he denied the sexual intercourse took place.

106 JD, aged 18, met Phillips when he was on bail in relation to the above charges. He invited her to his mother's house for a party although no-one else was there. He touched her without consent, offered her money to take off her shirt then threatened her with a thick chain. When she attempted to leave, he grabbed her and carried her to a garden shed where he tried to push her through the window. JD was saved from further assaults when his mother heard her screams. Charged with one count of assault with intent to rape (count 8), Phillips denied the allegations.

107 Each girl was part of Phillips' circle of acquaintances, was of a similar age and had consumed alcohol or cannabis. As soon as each one resisted either attempts at kissing or touching (BS, ML, MM, TK and JD) or further consensual activity (SW), Phillips' behaviour became threatening and violent.

The facts in issue

108 Before deciding whether each complainant's evidence is relevant to the counts involving each *other* complainant, the facts in issue for each count must be identified, a complicated process because Phillips admitted some and denied other sexual conduct. Because Phillips admitted the sexual conduct the subject of counts 1, 2, 4 and 5, the fact in issue was whether BS, ML and SW consented to sex. SW and ML were below the age of consent

which meant that the defence of mistaken belief as to consent was open to Phillips. This was another fact in issue for counts 4 and 5.

109 Since Phillips denied the sexual acts alleged by TK and MM (counts 3, 6 and 7) as well as the assault on JD (count 8), the prosecution had to prove these acts occurred. Only if the jury was satisfied these acts were proved beyond reasonable doubt would consent become a fact in issue in relation to counts 3, 6, and 7.

110 Because of the common features between each complainant's account, the prosecution argued that the combined evidence demonstrated the objective improbability of six teenage girls independently making a false complaint against the same person. The trial judge informed the jury they were only permitted to use the combined evidence to assess the likelihood of all six complainants telling a similar lie in relation to consent:

> "one girl might deliberately make up a lie that the accused dealt with her sexually without consent; . . . but the chances . . . that all six have made up such a lie . . . becomes remote in the extreme in the absence of any real risk of concoction".

111 The jury were warned not to use the combined evidence on the issue of honest mistake (counts 4 and 5) or the actus reus for counts 3, 6 and 7. Whether the jury was able to make those fine distinctions about the use of the evidence – not as propensity evidence, but to prove the improbability of lies theory – is doubtful. There was a risk the jury would infer that, because of the improbability that six girls would make similar complaints, Phillips had a propensity to commit sex offences. The propensity of Phillips to commit sex offences was not only irrelevant, it was also an impermissible consideration since whether or not Phillips had committed certain acts, or certain acts without consent, were facts up for proof (82). This was the conceptual difficulty in the trial. No argument could be made that the evidence of the six complainants showed that Phillips had a propensity to rape. The circularity of such reasoning was described in *Sutton:*

> "one cannot prove a fact by a chain of reasoning which assumes the truth of the fact. . . . When the Crown seeks to tender similar fact evidence as the foundation for inferring a fact to be proved . . ., it is erroneous to assume the truth of the fact to be proved in determining the cogency of the evidence" (83).

112 Since Phillips admitted sexual intercourse with BS, the fact up for proof in relation to counts 1 and 2 was lack of consent. It could not be argued that Phillips' sexual behaviour with BS illustrated a propensity to rape since, until the jury found him guilty, Phillips was not a rapist. Similarly, because the actus reus for count 3 was a fact up for proof, the evidence of TK could not be used to prove the actus reus for counts 6, 7 and 8. Only a prior conviction for rape or the evidence of a rape victim of Phillips' who was not a complainant in the trial would constitute propensity evidence.

(82) *Sutton* (1984) 152 CLR 528; *Thompson v The Queen* (1989) 169 CLR 1.
(83) *Sutton* (1984) 152 CLR 528 at 552 per Brennan J.

113 Because there was confusion about the facts in issue in relation to each count, my brother judges ask, what is the relevance of each complainant's evidence to the facts in issue associated with each other complainant?

114 Each complainant's evidence had to be assessed in terms of its relevance with respect to each count involving the *other* complainants. The relevance of such evidence is uncontroversial where it is similar in type to the misconduct the subject of the charges, particularly where it consists of a conviction or eyewitness evidence. Its *admissibility*, however, is another question altogether and turns on the *degree* of similarities between the misconduct and the charges in question (a more demanding relevance test), and the probative value of that misconduct versus its prejudicial effect (the *Pfennig* test).

The relevance of the combined evidence

115 The relevance of the combined evidence of six complainants is based, not on propensity reasoning, nor on the prosecution's improbability of lies theory. That theory is only applicable where the sexual conduct (but not consent) is a fact in issue, such as in a child sexual assault case. In cases where lack of consent is the fact in issue, there is now a barrier to the prosecution of alleged serial offenders. This is because my brother judges consider that the combined evidence in this case was irrelevant to any of the three facts in issue listed above because it did not prove any disposition on the part of Phillips, merely the mental state of each complainant. But we must be alive to the reality and vulnerability of girls aged 14–19 years to predatory sexual offending. Lack of consent as an issue should not automatically become a barrier to joint trials and a presumption in favour of separate trials.

116 Contrary to the majority's reasoning, each complainant's evidence shows the improbability of consent being given by each *other* complainant in a particular context. Each complainant revealed a pattern of sexual aggression, force and/or violence on the part of Phillips. Since consent can only be assessed in the circumstances in which sexual behaviour occurs, logic tells us that each complainant's evidence is relevant to a fact (a pattern of behaviour) which, in turn, is relevant to each of the three facts in issue.

117 While not binding, various cases support this reasoning, although the majority feel constrained by the Crown's failure to cite relevant authority to support the admissibility of the combined evidence. I note, however, that the appellant did cite the leading Canadian case on the issue, *R v Handy* (84).

118 In *Wilmot* (85) is so well-known that it would be remiss of this Court to fail to consider the reasoning of the English Court of Appeal which also dealt with the admissibility of the evidence of six complainants. Each woman alleged she was subjected to rape, physical injury and theft of her belongings. Wilmot admitted to consensual sex with each complainant. Glidewell LJ described the similarities in the complainants' evidence as a distinctive pattern which gave the evidence its relevance:

(84) [2002] 2 SCR 908 (*Handy*).
(85) (1989) 89 Cr App R 341 (*Wilmot*).

> "In each case, the defendant . . . picked up a girl [off the street]; he took her to a quiet place . . . one of two places . . . In every case, save one, the girl was a prostitute. So far . . . there is nothing very out of the ordinary . . . But the other features . . . are less usual. They are the use of violence before . . . [sex with] whatever weapon he had to inflict the violence . . . and theft of the girl's belongings. That pattern is consistent . . . [and] is sufficiently unusual and . . . strikingly similar for . . . the evidence of one incident [to be] properly admissible in order to prove the offence in another incident . . . It is the pattern of behaviour . . . which is all important [and its admission] was necessary in the interests of justice" (86).

119 Glidewell LJ did not characterise the combined evidence as proof only of the complainants' mental states. Instead, the pattern of violence and theft was sufficiently similar to be cross-admissible as corroborative evidence – each complainant's account of violence and theft corroborated the evidence of violence and theft of each *other* complainant which was a fact relevant to the fact in issue, lack of consent.

120 In identifying the commonalities between *Wilmot* and this case, we must recognise that similarities are a matter of interpretation and can be expressed at different levels of generality. *Wilmot* and this case concern the same legal issue – the cross-admissibility of several complainants' evidence to prove lack of consent by reference to the similarities in the defendant's behaviour before sex. This evidence shows, not that each defendant had a propensity to rape, but that the allegations occurred in a particular context of violence, aggression or force from which it can be inferred that the complainants did not consent.

121 In a case involving two prostitutes, the Victorian Court of Appeal in *R v Rajakaruna* (87) also held that the evidence of complainant 1 could be used to support the evidence of complainant 2 on the grounds that "the similarity of the *circumstances* of the offending as described by both rape complainants was such as to provide powerful probative force, over and above any prejudicial effect".

122 It is obvious that where a complainant alleges rape while the defendant contends that the sexual intercourse was consensual, other accounts of women being forced to have sex with the accused are relevant, not to show their state of mind or whether they consented, but to show the circumstances in which forcible sex was allegedly committed by the same person since consent is entirely contextual. Without eyewitnesses, consent can only be assessed by reference to the complainant's and the accused's behaviours leading up to and during the sexual incident. My brother judges appear to think that consent is about the complainant's conduct, not the defendant's. But a woman's consent or lack thereof is influenced by what the defendant does. In a word-against-word case, corroborative evidence of the complainant's account will be crucial.

123 The most detailed explanation of why the evidence from two or more complainants is relevant to consent is found in the Canadian case, *Handy*

(86) (1989) 89 Cr App R 341 at 348.
(87) (2004) 8 VR 340 at 365 per Eames JA, Smith AJA agreeing.
(88) [2002] 2 SCR 908.

(88). The accused was charged with sexual assault causing actual bodily harm after the complainant said she had consented to vaginal intercourse but not hurtful or anal sex. Evidence from the accused's former wife that he had a propensity to inflict painful and anal sex, and would not take no for an answer, was admitted at trial. Whether or not the ex-wife's evidence was admissible as similar fact evidence depended on the purpose for which the evidence was adduced.

124 The Supreme Court of Canada held that her evidence was relevant to whether the accused had ignored the complainant's refusal to have anal sex. The Court's reasoning was similar to that used in *Wilmot* since the ex-wife's evidence corroborated the complainant's account, thus increasing the probability that she did not consent in comparable circumstances. The ex-wife's evidence was not relevant to show the accused's propensity but was relevant to a fact (the circumstances in which the alleged rape occurred) which was relevant to the fact in issue (lack of consent).

125 It is obvious, as the Supreme Court of Canada observed, that "sexual activity may not show much diversity or distinctiveness" (89) such that searching for a signature or hallmark sexual behaviour is unrealistic. My brother judges consider that Phillips' sexual behaviour was entirely unremarkable. Is this Court prepared to say to complainants that allegations will only be dealt with in a joint trial where there is something peculiar about the defendant's sexual behaviour? The Canadian Supreme Court recognised the unreality of this approach. Similarities must be drawn from the circumstances of the offending behaviour rather than being confined to the sexual acts themselves. When the Court did so in *Handy*, it rejected the ex-wife's evidence as similar fact evidence because the sexual behaviour described by the ex-wife "occurred in the context of a long-term dysfunctional marriage whereas the charged act relate[d] to a one-night stand" (90). The Court, however, listed a number of "connecting factors" to determine whether or not the probative value of the ex-wife's evidence outweighed its prejudicial effect. While I do not agree with the weight given to each factor in *Handy*, the list of connecting factors is compelling and I adopt them to illustrate the similarities in the evidence of the six complainants in this case:

(i) the proximity in time of the similar events. Phillips' behaviour in isolating each complainant before sex and the use of force or aggression gains cogency because of its repetition over two and a half years and its most recent manifestation (assault with intent to rape) even after he was charged with seven other offences.

(ii) the extent to which other acts are similar in detail to the charged conduct, bearing in mind that "[s]exual activity may not show much diversity or distinctiveness" (91). While different complainants alleged oral or vaginal sex, each said it was accompanied by force, violence and/or threats of violence which also accompanied the assault with intent to rape. In such circumstances voluntary consent cannot be given.

(89) [2002] 2 SCR 908 at [127] per Binnie J (delivering judgment for the Court).
(90) [2002] 2 SCR 908 at [129].
(91) [2002] 2 SCR 908 at [127].

(iii) the number of occurrences of the similar acts, since a pattern of conduct gains its probative strength from repetition. Phillips' alleged behaviour amounted to seven counts of sexual assault and one of assault with intent to rape over two and a half years.
(iv) the circumstances surrounding or relating to the similar acts. Each complainant was within Phillips' circle of acquaintances and all sexual acts and the assault occurred at a party, or an invented party to which Phillips had invited the complainant.
(v) any distinctive features unifying the incidents. The sexual behaviour itself was not distinctive but was associated with distinctive and unusual behaviour in the form of force, violence or threats of violence.

126 These similarities are sufficient to give the six complainants' evidence the required degree of connection to be admissible as relevant similar fact evidence. It is necessary to focus on similarities in the circumstances, rather than just the sexual conduct itself, because this reflects the reality of sex offender behaviour and the reactions of different victims. Although it is likely that judges are influenced by the more graphic cases of sexual assault that come before us, we should not lose sight of the everyday reality of sexual assault in our community. Judges are not qualified to decide that sex offending is notable for its strikingly similar behaviour given the range of sexual behaviour (92) which varies from the ordinary to the bizarre. Searching for similarities in sexual conduct is entirely subjective, cannot be empirically justified and is likely to lead to injustice.

127 Returning to the issue of relevance, does evidence that Phillips was the subject of four other allegations of sexual assault involving aggression, force and/or violence over two and a half years rationally affect the assessment of the probability that BS's complaint (the first complaint) occurred in circumstances of aggression and force? Arguably, it does since relevance is a low threshold test (93). This fact is relevant to the probability of the existence of lack of consent by BS.

128 Furthermore, the evidence illustrates Phillips' pattern of behaviour which is inconsistent with consent having been given by BS, ML and SW because it shows the objective improbability that three girls would describe sexual behaviour involving aggression and force and yet have given their consent. Their evidence is also relevant to whether the sexual acts alleged by TK, MM and JD occurred. The pattern of aggression and force described by BS (forced undressing and forced oral sex) makes it more likely that the sexual aggression described by TK (forced undressing, thrown and held down on a bed), by MM (oral sex and intercourse while threatened with a baseball bat) and JD (assaults accompanied by threats with a thick chain) also occurred.

(92) Smallbone and Wortley, "Criminal Diversity and Paraphilic Interests among Adult Males Convicted of Sexual Offenses against Children", *International Journal of Offender Therapy and Comparative Criminology*, vol 48 (2003) 175.
(93) *Papakosmas v The Queen* (1999) 196 CLR 297.

The striking similarities test

129 As a tighter control for admissibility than relevance, the striking similarities test has been adopted in countless, subsequent cases in both Australia and the UK (94). My brother judges not only conclude that the evidence of each complainant was not cross-admissible due to lack of relevance but also that there were insufficient similarities to produce a strong degree of probative force. But why was it entirely unremarkable for a teenager to use force, violence and/or threats to obtain sex?

130 Previously, this court has held that, in determining the probative strength of similar fact evidence, it is not necessary to find *striking* similarities or an underlying unity (95). Where identity is not a fact in issue, the necessity for striking similarities is even less compelling, as discussed by Lord Mckay in *DPP v P* (96). The striking similarities test was later abolished under the *Criminal Justice Act 2003* in England and Wales. The test is most appropriate in circumstances where it is necessary to identify a stranger such that judges can be sure they are admitting evidence that shows the defendant is the perpetrator and not someone else.

131 The inappropriateness of the striking similarities test is obvious in this case. Phillips appears to have been an opportunist, targeting girls in social settings that were similar but necessarily different depending on what was required to ensure each girl was alone. Rather than discarding the facts as not fitting the test, we should discard a test that has very limited utility in sexual assault cases where identity is not in issue, and which is not supported by empirical evidence. While there is a need to counterbalance the admission of prejudicial evidence, this can be done by careful judicial instructions. Experience shows that juries, properly instructed, have the capacity to deliver different verdicts in relation to different counts as they did in this case.

132 The majority of sexual assaults in Australia are committed by relatives, friends or acquaintances, not strangers where identity may be in issue (97) and there may be a particular modus operandi. Indeed, if striking similarities are required in non-identity cases, only unusual or weird sexual behaviour would pass the test, leaving complainants who are the victim of "everyday" sexual aggression in a disadvantageous position in terms of offenders being brought to justice.

133 Following *Handy*, at the very least there must be a "specific connection" between the similar fact evidence and the events the subject of the charge. The search for similarities is not a scientific exercise but an inquiry that is undertaken through the lenses of judicial experience – higher or lower degrees of similarity will be found depending on what a particular judge knows about sex offending. My brother judges find no specific connection

(94) See fn 72 above.

(95) *Pfennig* (1995) 182 CLR 461 at 484, per Mason CJ, Deane and Dawson JJ; *BRS v The Queen* (1997) 191 CLR 275 at 300 per Gaudron J.

(96) [1991] 2 AC 447 at 462.

(97) Australian Bureau of Statistics, *Sexual Assault in Australia: A Statistical Overview*, 2004.

between the evidence of the six complainants because they are searching for unusual similarities. But they must know from their own experience that sexual activity is not always striking or unusual. Rather than Phillips' behaviour being entirely unremarkable, his behaviour showed all the hallmarks of an opportunistic, serial sex offender such that the six complainants' evidence was admissible on the grounds of sufficiency of connection.

134 The sufficient connection between each complainant's account means their combined evidence had a high degree of probative value, sufficient to outweigh its prejudicial effect according to the *Pfennig* test. There was no rational view of the evidence consistent with Phillips' innocence. Although the *Pfennig* test is not without its difficulties, no argument was made on appeal about whether the test should be overruled or qualified. I agree with the majority that the test does not require the trial judge to assess the evidence using the beyond reasonable doubt standard since it is a test of admissibility not a determination of guilt or innocence.

135 For the reasons stated above, I would dismiss the appeal.

Sentencing

19

Truth in Sentencing: The Narration of Judgment in *R v Webster*

KIRSTY DUNCANSON

Introduction

The judgment rewritten in this chapter is the sentencing of Matthew Webster, who pleaded guilty to the murder of Leigh Leigh. It was delivered by Wood J on 24 October 1990 in the Supreme Court of NSW, Newcastle.[1] Although the judgment did not set precedent, the case holds a place of special, uncomfortable significance in the Australian imagination. Leigh was a 14-year-old girl, brutally raped and murdered during a beachside birthday party. Throughout the party, Leigh was subject to degrading and humiliating treatment by groups of teenaged boys. This appeared to be a response to her complaint of an instance of unwanted sexual penetration. Later, Leigh was raped again, and killed. Her body was found on the beach the following morning. Some concert to the boys' acts is perceptible in a statement made by Webster at the party: 'Hey dude, we are going to get Leigh pissed and all go through her.' Webster's words convey an intent to render Leigh vulnerable and repeatedly rape her. The visciousness of the sexual violence and the collective quality of the boys' acts make the offences against Leigh particularly horrific.

The case attracted a lot of media attention at the time, and since then two plays and a feature film based on the events were produced with reasonable commercial success.[2] Leigh's rape and murder remains strong in the public memory. While feminists have read the events as evidence of a national cultural problem of performative Australian masculinity involving aggressive misogyny,[3] the dominant narratives used to represent the assaults, rapes and murder of Leigh in the public domain have focused on concerns about parental responsibility. Implicit within these narratives is also a pattern of victim blaming. Wood J's judgment is an epitome of such narrations, drawing a causal link between the lack of parental supervision at the party and the underage drinking, drug use and sexual promiscuity he casts as severely impairing the boys' judgements, and thereby leading to their lethal violence. Situating the blame with the parents diminishes the boys' accountability and disregards

[1] *R v Webster* (Unreported, Supreme Court of New South Wales, Wood J, 24 October 1990) ('*Webster*').

[2] Nick Enright, *A Property of the Clan* (Currency Press, 1994); Nick Enright, *Blackrock* (Currency Press, 1996) (first produced by Sydney Theatre Company at Wharf I on 30 August 1995); *Blackrock* (Directed by Steven Vidler, Australian Film Finance Corporation and Palm Beach Pictures, 1997).

[3] Kerry Carrington, *Who Killed Leigh Leigh? A Story of Shame and Mateship in an Australian Town* (Random House, 1998); Jonathan Morrow and Mehera San Roque, 'In Her Death She Remains as the Limit of the System: Notes Towards an Ethical Writing of Collective Sexual Violence' (1996) 18 *Sydney Law Review* 474, 474–502; Felicity Holland and Jane O'Sullivan, '"Lethal Larrikins": Cinematic Subversions of Mythical Masculinities in *Blackrock* and *The Boys*' (1999) 13 *Antipodes* 79–84.

their shared gender beliefs that rendered their acts somehow possible. In the same move, the broader culture tolerating, or even fostering, such attitudes is overlooked. The boys' agency is further reduced by being relocated to Leigh, so that she appears to have caused the violence against herself. In the revised judgment, the authors have rewritten the narratives in order to correct the dilution of the boys' culpability by explicitly identifying the responsibility borne by the defendant in *R v Webster*,[4] Matthew Webster, for the violence he perpetrated against Leigh Leigh.

Legal Truths

The function of a sentencing judgment is the construction of narratives justifying the punishment being handed down. Those narratives become the legal truth of the events in question. Alternative versions are disqualified or silenced. In *Webster*, the narratives presented within the courtroom were already restricted due to Webster's guilty plea, the strong correlation of the prosecution brief with Webster's confession, and the absence of any victim impact statements.

By pleading guilty, Webster circumvented an adversarial trial. Instead, a largely unchallenged account was presented within a sentencing hearing. While the version of events provided in the hearing *does* identify Webster as Leigh's killer, it is an abridged account, and is missing crucial content. The most conspicuous absence is the charge of sexual assault. In Webster's police statement he confessed to digitally penetrating Leigh against her will. He was charged with this offence; however the charge was subsequently dropped. Thus, although his penetrative act was mentioned within the judgment as part of the murder narrative, it did not constitute a separate offence within the legal truth of the sentence.

In addition to the absent charge, evidence potentially contradicting Webster's confession was not presented at the hearing. A four-page post-mortem report was replaced by a one-page interim report.[5] Missing from the interim report was evidence suggesting that Leigh was strangled with the opposite hand to the one Webster claimed to have used in his confession;[6] that Leigh was struck three times from multiple angles, and possibly with different implements, rather than a blow from a thrown rock, as Webster described;[7] and that Leigh acquired injuries to her genitals 'consistent with non-consensual sexual intercourse of an extremely violent nature.'[8] This version of the post-mortem depicts a much more aggressive sexual assault than the unwanted penetration to which Webster confessed. At the same time, the additional material implies that another person was involved in Leigh's murder. The suggestion of a second assailant was also discernible in witness statements observing that Webster was not alone when he followed Leigh onto the beach where he raped and murdered her. These sections of the statements were not included in the prosecution brief submitted to the court.[9]

[4] *Webster* (Unreported, Supreme Court of New South Wales, Wood J, 24 October 1990).
[5] Ibid. Carrington notes that this is not an unusual practice in murder hearings: Carrington, above n 3.
[6] Carrington, ibid 79.
[7] Ibid 79.
[8] Quoting Dr Armstrong's interpretation of the final report, ibid 80.
[9] Ibid. For further discussion of the disparity of evidence, see Kerry Carrington and Andrew Johnson, 'Representations of Crime, Guilt and Sexuality in the Leigh Leigh Rape' (1994) 3 *Australian Feminist Law Journal*

One crucial perspective is always missing within a murder hearing, because the victim is deceased. However, the associated trauma experienced by a victim's relatives potentially reinserts the victim's subjective presence by enabling empathy with that victim. For this reason, a family's victim impact statements are considered to bring 'an otherwise silenced narrative voice' to the legal assessment of an offence.[10] The legislation allowing consideration of a grieving relative's statement was not introduced in NSW until 1996. Thus, no victim impact statements were available for Webster's sentencing. The significance of this particular absence for the capacity to construct a different legal truth about what happened to Leigh is demonstrated in the decision of the victim compensation appeal case, which granted an unprecedented award to Leigh's relatives for *their* suffering.[11] To justify the amount awarded, the civil judgment determined the level of distress endured by Leigh's mother and sister by establishing, applying a balance of probabilities standard of proof, its own narrative of the violence perpetrated against Leigh. This involved assessing evidence from the night Leigh was killed, including evidence not submitted to the sentencing hearing. The resultant decision provides a radically different legal truth from the one asserted by Wood J. The first substantive dissimilarity is a confirmation that Leigh had not consented to the first instance of sexual penetration. Secondly, the decision emphasises the sexual nature of the violence perpetrated against Leigh, and explicitly describes the murder as a continuation of that violence. It also documents the severity of the final sexual assault, and ultimately identifies several young men as responsible for offences against Leigh across the evening of the party.[12] These components of the civil law narrative starkly contrast with the pattern of minimisation discernible in Wood J's judgment, and suggest that consideration of the victim-perspective impels an engagement with alternative versions of what took place.

The structure of the sentencing hearing meant that no counter-narratives were offered to challenge Webster's description of his actions, or to cast a significantly different light on the unfolding of violence against Leigh. Consequently, neither the extent of Leigh's suffering, nor Webster's possible further responsibility for it, could be considered by Wood J – or by the feminist judgment writers.

Facts and Memories

The police investigation into Leigh's rape and murder concluded with the charging of three boys: one with common assault for kicking, spitting and throwing beer bottles at Leigh during the party; the second with carnal knowledge (engaging in sexual intercourse with a person under the age of consent) for the first instance of sexual penetration; and the third,

3, 25–6; Kerry Carrington, 'No Justice for Leigh Leigh: Judicial, Executive and Police Sexism Intersect' (1995) 4 *Australian Feminist Law Journal* 135.

[10] Susan Bandes, 'Empathy, Narrative and Victim Impact Statements' (1996) 63 *University of Chicago Law Review* 361, 362. Note that Bandes is actually highly critical of victim impact statements, particularly in the context of murder hearings. By referencing Bandes, I seek to implicitly endorse her critique, while acknowledging the impact that the consideration of the suffering of Leigh's family had on the civil judgment.

[11] *Jessie Leigh and Robyn Leigh v Victims' Compensation Fund Corporation* (Unreported, District Court of New South Wales, Moore J, 31 May 1995).

[12] Carrington, above n 3, 115–17.

Matthew Webster, with sexual assault and murder. All three pleaded guilty, although as noted earlier, the sexual assault charge against Webster was dropped. Respectively, the boys received: a six-month custodial sentence; community service; and 14 years' imprisonment. Webster sought leave to appeal the severity of his sentence, but although leave was granted, the appeal was dismissed on the day of hearing.

In the end, no one was held legally culpable for non-consensual sexual violence perpetrated against Leigh. Although this has meant that the criminal legal narrative of the events fails to recognise the gravity of the sexual violence against her, it has not erased the spectre of this violence from the public's memory.

Fourteen years after Wood J's sentence was delivered, a newspaper article published on the day of Webster's release described the case as lingering uncomfortably in the public imagination.[13] A teenager's blog attests to the longevity of its legacy, writing in 2012 that although Leigh died before the blogger was born, 'you'd better believe that the story . . . still reverberates up and down this [NSW] coast.'[14] Leigh's treatment during the party has been kept vivid in the national memory not only through the news media, but also by the stage and screen productions, *A Property of the Clan* (1994), *Blackrock* (the play) (1996), and *Blackrock* (the film) (1997).[15] These texts are now part of Australian high school curricula.[16]

Analysing the range of popular, academic and institutional discourses recounting the events of Leigh's murder, Morrow and San Roque found that despite the diversity of formats, a narrow set of narratives have dominated, while alternatives have been eclipsed.[17] The prevailing narratives have demonstrated a tendency for victim blaming, and focusing on parental supervision, while feminist concerns about a 'cultural tolerance for sexual violence' have been largely ignored.[18]

The Original Judgment

The original sentencing in *Webster* repeats the same pattern of representation, focusing on parental responsibility, diminishing the boys' culpability, whilst dismissing suggestions of a broader cultural problem, and blaming Leigh for the violence against herself. Wood J's judgment follows a conventional sentencing template that first narrates his interpretation of the events before considering aggravating and mitigating factors affecting Webster's liability and rationalising the chosen level of punishment. Wood J then reads a moral lesson within the case from which the community might learn, and closes with a commendation of the police investigation.

Wood J explicitly rejects the idea of greater community liability for the violence against Leigh. To do this he quotes at length the expert evidence of psychologist Dr Strum that explained Webster's violence as deriving from a 'tribe'-like rejection of Leigh shared amongst

[13] John Elder, 'A Death in the Sand: Pain that Lives On', *The Age* (Melbourne) 13 June 2004.

[14] 'A Property of the Clan' on Blog by Chally, *Zero at the Bone* (4 January 2012) <http://zeroatthebone.wordpress.com/2012/01/04/a-property-of-the-clan/>.

[15] Enright, *A Property of the Clan*, above n 2; Enright, *Blackrock*, above n 2; Vidler, *Blackrock*, above n 2.

[16] For an example of the way in which these texts are taught in Australian schools see <http://www.curriculum-support.education.nsw.gov.au/secondary/english/assets/pdf/clan.pdf>.

[17] Morrow and San Roque, above n 3.

[18] Carrington and Johnson, above n 9, 25–6.

the boys at the party. In this quote, Webster is described as perceiving Leigh to be a 'property of the clan.' Such a description has the potential to either exculpate the criminal actor or broaden responsibility for the violence across the community – even the nation. Strum uses his identification of a 'clan mentality' to mitigate Webster's personal responsibility. The playwright Enright uses Strum's 'property of the clan' as the title of his first script representing the murder of Leigh in order to emphasise a cultural misogyny as enabling violence against women and absolving male perpetrators of such violence.[19] Enright's interpretation of Strum's words suggests that as a female, Leigh was objectified by the boys, and thereby considered available to them for sex, whether she was interested or not. Her resistance, in this context, can be seen as an unbearable challenge to their belief system that required containment or punishment.

The authors of the revised judgment reject Strum's evidence, insisting that culpability rests with the perpetrator, and responsibility for his actions is not diminished by the existence of any 'clan' culture.

In his narrative of the facts, Wood J cites the actions Webster confessed to performing which ended with him killing Leigh. Wood J also names various acts conducted by other boys at the party, assaulting and humiliating Leigh. However, his particular exercise of grammar functions to lessen all the boys' culpability while attributing liability to Leigh. For example, what Leigh expressed as a boy having 'fucked' her, Wood J describes as sexual intercourse 'taking place with a fifteen year old male person.' Leigh's words resound with the syntactic power of masculinist violence MacKinnon identified when writing 'man fucks woman; subject verb object.'[20] The 15-year-old male person is clearly the agent and the active subject in Leigh's account, performing the action against Leigh, who is simultaneously objectified as a female body. Leigh's portrayal of the sex act reflects the very objectifying operation feminists have detected at the heart of sexual violence and its tolerating cultures. At the same time, it situates responsibility for the sexual act with the boy. Conversely, Wood J's sentence removes agency altogether, so that the male person becomes the grammatical target of the intercourse-action (verb) and thus appears not to have had any control over what happened.

While agency is detached from the boy, it is re-attached to Leigh by the active voice of Wood J's surrounding sentences, which include a misquotation of Leigh's complaint about being 'fucked'. Wood J recounts that Leigh 'went to the sand' where the intercourse took place, and later that 'she spoke of having had sex.' These sentences situate Leigh as an active agent within the scene of carnal knowledge. When woven together with the passively expressed description of the actual intercourse, Leigh is endowed with responsibility for the sex.

Wood J's description of the group assault and humiliation of Leigh at the clubhouse similarly attributes a strange degree of power to Leigh. He narrates: '[Leigh] was also kicked and a bottle thrown at her.' His use of the passive voice disengages the agents from the acts while denoting Leigh as the grammatical subject (which grants some agency to her), even though she is also the target. Additionally, Wood J's surrounding sentences once again cast Leigh in the active role as he recounts: 'she tried to stagger away. She went inside ... She then left the clubhouse ...' Leigh becomes more directly implicated in causing the boys' violence when Wood J explains that Leigh's distress at being fucked '*led* to her being subject to verbal

[19] Ibid. See also Holland and O'Sullivan, above n 3.
[20] Catharine MacKinnon, *Towards a Feminist Theory of the State* (Harvard University Press, 1989) 124.

abuse' (emphasis added). Wood J's organisation of language grammatically exculpated the boys and incriminated Leigh.

This subtle or inadvertent exoneration of the boys involved in the violence against Leigh is confirmed when Wood J rationalises the brevity of the sentence he hands down by evaluating Webster's disposition. The offence of murder, according to Wood J, 'would seem to be out of character.' Rather, Webster is rendered mild-mannered in Wood J's estimation: 'gentle, shy and polite . . . somewhat lacking in self confidence.' For the authors of the revised judgment, this portrayal of Webster sits in contradiction to evidence that Webster suggested that he and his friends 'get Leigh pissed and all go through her', and to his violent assault and murder of her. However, for Wood J, Webster's 'impulsive ferocity' is explained 'to a considerable degree, by the effects on him of alcohol and cannabis.' Once more, Webster's culpability is diminished, and responsibility for Leigh's rape and murder is located elsewhere.

Under-aged drinking, drug use and sexual promiscuity become factors mitigating responsibility for the violence against Leigh. According to Wood J's judgment, these factors situate responsibility with parents. This conclusion is reinforced when Wood J advises parents to organise their teenagers' parties, and ensure that any party attended by their children is appropriately supervised. Parents' responsibility also requires that they counsel their children about 'the dangers of alcohol and drugs and . . . intimate relationships.' Had such parenting been exercised, according to Wood J, the 'tragic killing of Leigh Leigh was . . . totally preventable.' Presented as the moral of his judgment, parental accountability is foregrounded as the main causal factor contributing to the rape and murder of Leigh. Wood J's judgment effectively perpetuates the cultural tolerance of sexed violence, by diminishing and redistributing accountability for it away from the boys who actually committed the acts.

The Feminist Judgment

The authors of the revised judgment have corrected Wood J's moderation of liability for the assaults, rapes and murders of Leigh by resituating it plainly with the perpetrators. They have concentrated their revisions on restructuring the narratives describing the events of the night Leigh was killed. In doing this, the authors have retained the consideration of 'truth in sentencing' that Wood J used in his deliberation over the length of Webster's prison term. While the phrase provides me with a playful way to emphasise the theoretical focus of my commentary and the revised judgment, it also names a policy of sentencing reform instituted by the NSW government in 1989. *Webster* was the first case to apply the reformed legislation. It is thus important that the revised sentence is read within the context of the change. However, the revised consideration of 'truth in sentencing' also represents the particular feminist purpose of the revising authors, and a key assumption underpinning it.

'Truth in sentencing' involved an amendment to the *Crimes Act 1900* (NSW) with the addition of s 19A. The new section rendered 'true' the sentence of 'penal servitude for life' by removing prisoners' access to reductions in the length of their incarceration on the basis of good behaviour. At the time of the reforms, the Australian Institute of Criminology had found that the average duration of a life sentence in Australia was 13 years, significantly shorter than the term of a natural life.[21] The NSW government transformed the life sentence from a symbolic but indeterminate (and potentially 'lenient') sentence to a controversially harsh punishment. By removing the incentive for good behaviour in the form of possible early release, the new 'truth' of the life sentence impeded one of the key purposes of sentencing, by preventing 'any prospect of rehabilitation.'[22] However, the new s 19A(3) protected s 442 of the *Crimes Act 1900* (NSW), which allowed the application of lesser sentences to murder convictions. In fact, no lower limit was set by the new legislation, and no guidance was provided to judges for determining appropriate sentences for individual cases.[23]

The conditions created by the reforms necessitated careful reflection on the objectives of punishment in *Webster* because while the maximum sentence for murder was made inflexible, no principles were yet available for balancing the recently reset 'just punishment' with degrees of culpability. In this context, the revising authors have followed Wood J in prioritising rehabilitation as the paramount consideration. In doing so, they have maintained the 14-year sentence. Under the ominous spectre of a 'true' life sentence, the authors' emphasis on rehabilitation demonstrates that the motivation of their revisions is not retributive but reformative. By recognising the prospect of rehabilitation for Webster, the authors simultaneously implicitly reveal a belief in the possibility of a broader cultural change that would remove the conditions making sexed violence excusable and thereby doable.

The feminist judgment writers have offered the possibility of cultural rehabilitation in their revision of *Webster*. They have done this by identifying, challenging and rewriting the narratives of judgment present in the original sentence that exculpate the perpetrators of sexed violence and blame female victims for the violence they suffer. In the feminist revision of *Webster*, the authors exercise this reform at the greater level of narrative construction, but also down to the very detail of linguistic expression. Such attentive modification reforms legal judgment at the very foundations of what Smart called law's phallocentrism.[24]

[21] Ian Potas, *Life Imprisonment in Australia*, Trends and Issues in Criminal Justice (Australian Institute of Criminology, 1989) 19.

[22] George Zdenkowski, quoted in John Anderson, '"Indefinite, Inhumane, Inequitable" – the Principle of Equal Application of the Law and the Natural Life Sentence for Murder: A Reform Agenda' (2006) 29 *University of New South Wales Law Journal* 139, 141.

[23] Ibid.

[24] Carol Smart, *Feminism and the Power of Law* (Routledge, 1989).

THE SUPREME COURT
OF NEW SOUTH WALES
CRIMINAL DIVISION

TOWNSLEY-VAN RIJSWIJK J

NEWCASTLE: Wednesday 24 October 1990

70012/90 - REGINA V MATTHEW GRANT WEBSTER

SENTENCE

HER HONOUR: Matthew Grant Webster, you have pleaded guilty to the murder of Leigh Leigh (hereinafter Leigh) at North Stockton beach on 3 November 1989. At the time of the murder you were eighteen years old and Leigh was fourteen years old.

You murdered Leigh at a sixteenth birthday party organised by Jason Robertson at a local surf club. Leigh was an invited guest at the party, and was driven to the party by her mother, along with her friend Theresa, who was also fourteen years old. They arrived between 7 o'clock and 7.30 in the evening. Leigh's step-father arranged to pick the girls up at about 11 o'clock, but when he arrived, she could not be found. Leigh's body was found by searchers the next morning.

There were approximately 100 persons who attended the party at various stages during the night, all teenagers. There were no parents present to supervise the event. However, you and another adult, Guy Wilson, attended the party and acted as bouncers, collected money for the provision of food, and checked guests in. This meant that you and Wilson undertook the responsibility of supervising a large group of teenagers.

It is clear that you and Wilson did not take your responsibility seriously: Wilson was involved in fights with young boys at the party; you both took cannabis and consumed large quantities of alcohol; and you both procured cannabis and alcohol for the underage guests. These failures are only the very least of your culpable behaviours on that night, but they are important in setting the context for what followed, and the ways in which you took advantage of Leigh's young age and vulnerability. During the evening, Wilson assaulted Leigh and abused her, and has been sentenced for this assault. You assaulted Leigh, sexually assaulted Leigh, and then killed Leigh. I will now focus on each of these events in some detail.

Shortly after Leigh and Theresa arrived, a youth, at their request, went off and purchased bourbon and port for them. Leigh was an inexperienced drinker. She became affected by alcohol early in the night and continued to drink. Leigh was a virgin, and I mention this because, as will become apparent, she was naïve about sexual matters, and this is relevant to subsequent events. The combination of this inexperience and intoxication meant that Leigh became vulnerable. This vulnerability was firstly taken advantage of by a fifteen year-old youth, who took Leigh to the sand-dunes. Leigh returned from the sand-dunes crying and upset, telling her friends that she had been "fucked", which indicates that she did not consent to the sexual intercourse. As she was under sixteen, her consent was legally irrelevant; the young man was subsequently charged for this sexual assault, and sentenced to community service.

Leigh was obviously distressed after this event. On returning to the clubhouse, she said to people that she had had sex and was "bleeding and pregnant". Leigh was described as being very drunk, crying and depressed. It is fair to infer that Leigh was shocked by the unwanted sexual intercourse, and by the hostile social environment in which she now found herself. She was told to go away by a number of people, and to stop crying, but she stayed, protesting what had happened. Some people, a minority, tried to comfort Leigh and calm her down. Leigh, obviously ill from the effect of alcohol, lay down on the ground.

At this point Leigh was vulnerable, upset, intoxicated, and had just experienced unwanted sexual intercourse. It would be expected that at this point she would be protected, as one of the youngest people at the party that night. But this did not happen; instead, she was taunted, abused, humiliated and assaulted by a number of the people present, including by you and Wilson. In your statement to police, you described Leigh as a "pest", with the inference that this justified your cruel and criminal behaviours toward her. Instead of helping Leigh, as, along with Wilson, you were the two people who had assumed responsibility for the party, it was at this point that you decided to take advantage of her. You and another person called her a "slut" and poured beer on her. You and another person also spat on her, humiliating her further. Wilson then assaulted Leigh, kicking her with some severity. She tried to get away, and a beer bottle was thrown at her. She then returned to the clubhouse and you and another person spat on her again, and poured beer on her.

At this point, Leigh left the clubhouse and sat on a grassed area a short distance away, in an obvious state of physical and emotional distress. It is reasonable to infer that she felt helpless and in a state of deep despair at her humiliating treatment. She would have also been in a lot of physical pain.

You then approached Leigh and walked her to a depression in the sand dunes, about 100 metres from the clubhouse. In your police interview you said that Leigh "carried on with her normal shit and I tried to get onto her". In other words, Leigh was crying, upset and in physical pain, and you decided to take the opportunity that her vulnerability offered to take advantage of her sexually. You forcibly removed her clothes, pulled your shorts down and put your finger in her vagina. Leigh started punching and pushing you away, saying "Don't". You told police that you then lost your temper and grabbed her by the throat. Medical evidence has established that you choked her to the point of rendering her unconscious. You then walked about five feet away, picked up a large rock, walked back to where Leigh was lying, and threw the rock at her head. You struck her twice on the left side of her head with that rock. Leigh sustained massive injuries from your strikes, the blows causing the left side of her head and face to cave in. She died instantly. There were also bruises in the area of her ribs and lower abdomen. When Leigh's body was found she was naked except for socks and shoes; her underwear and shorts were around her right ankle, and the position of her body was sprawled across the ground. She was found on the beach where you had left her.

You ran from the scene to a boat ramp where you washed your hands in a cleaning sink. You then ran or walked through a number of back streets towards your home. On the way you met up with several other people who had attended the party and told them that you had left the party earlier and had been drinking at a local pub. This was an obvious attempt to provide an alibi for your movements.

You were interviewed by police on 5 November 1989 and again on 15 November 1989. On the second occasion you admitted to having lied about your alibi and said that you had done so to "big note" yourself to your friends. During these interviews you sought to shift the blame from yourself by referring to rumours that you had heard about certain other persons who may have been responsible for Leigh's murder.

You were again interviewed on 16 February this year when, after initial denials, you admitted to being responsible for Leigh's death. When asked by the police why you beat Leigh's head with a rock, you replied, "I didn't want to get into trouble can you believe that. I thought she would squeal on me for trying to rape her." In other words, you killed a defenceless fourteen year-old girl for the purpose of concealing a serious sexual assault that you had committed against her. On the following day, after being charged, and after receiving advice from a solicitor, you became co-operative and assisted police with the investigation.

I now turn to the objective gravity of the crime. As I said previously, as a supervisor of teenagers, you did not act responsibly. But in the context of the crime for which you have pleaded guilty, this pales into insignificance. I raise it, though, since the position you assumed is relevant to the premeditation of your behaviour.

In relation to your culpability, you did not supply Leigh with alcohol, but you did take advantage of her intoxication and helplessness. There is evidence that you planned to do so. This is evidenced in a statement you made to a person who arrived at the party shortly before 9 o'clock, to whom you said, "Hey dude, we are going to get Leigh pissed and all go through her." The inference from this statement is that yourself and others intended to make Leigh vulnerable for your own sexual gratification.

It was submitted that your objective criminality was reduced because you lacked premeditation, and because your inhibitions were reduced by the effects of alcohol and cannabis. Whilst I accept you had not decided to kill Leigh earlier in the night and therefore the murder lacked premeditation, there were other premeditated factors leading up to Leigh's death that are relevant, as they contributed to your demeanour, attitude and actions. You told police that you had been annoyed at Leigh during the night – calling her a "pest" for crying in the clubhouse – and that you had abused her both verbally and physically. You took advantage of her at her most vulnerable moments, and, when your sexual advances were rejected, you became extremely angry, strangling her until she was unconscious and then hitting her violently in the head with a rock, twice.

I do not accept that your inhibitions were so reduced by alcohol and cannabis as to explain your behaviour, because this implies that your actions were impulsive, ephemeral and unthinking. Considering the facts, I do not find that you were suddenly overcome by the effects of alcohol and cannabis, but rather that your consumption of alcohol and cannabis enhanced your already aggressive and predatory behaviour toward Leigh. Despite the evidence suggesting that you had consumed a large quantity of beer and cannabis, it is evident that you did have some presence of mind because shortly after killing Leigh, you washed yourself and attempted to set up alibi evidence. It is also obvious from your admission and your actions that you were not so affected by alcohol to lack either an intent to kill or intent to inflict grievous bodily harm, or to lack capacity to cover up your crimes. Additionally, evidence of intoxication comes primarily from you. You admitted to "big noting" yourself to your friends, and to lying to police to protect yourself. This diminishes your credibility regarding your evidence, including the evidence concerning the extent of your intoxication.

I have been asked to consider the evidence of two psychiatrists, Dr Strum, and Dr Barclay, and a psychologist, Mr Taylor, who gave their opinions regarding the significance of intoxication to your crimes, as well as their opinion regarding the role of your personality in the crime, and the significance of other factors. In light of what I have said above, I give little weight to the evidence of Dr Strum and Dr Barclay that the ingestion of alcohol and cannabis "severely impaired" your judgment. I place more weight on the evidence of Mr Taylor that there was some impairment, albeit, in my opinion, minimal.

A further factor, suggested by Dr Strum, in assessing the objective gravity of the crime is the consideration of "clan" mentality and its role in determining your actions. The suggestion seems to imply that the culture of masculinity in this "clan" contributed to, if not endorsed, your violent, appalling and degrading treatment of Leigh, and so diminishes your responsibility. I will not reproduce the opinion of Dr Strum in full here. It is sufficient to say that his argument is not only deeply flawed and unconvincing, even fanciful, it is also unfair to the victim. Indeed, it borders on justifying your behaviour by representing Leigh as the problem. Dr Strum's description of gender violence as a "clan" culture appears to exculpate you and the other participants in this culture of any responsibility for your actions (which would include the collective violence – abuse, physical violence and humiliation – that occurred at the clubhouse earlier in the night) – as though the mentality or culture were outside your control, and the control of others involved that night. This cannot be accepted. Each person that night, including and especially you, was responsible for the actions carried out, and for the production of the culture of gender violence that was operating. I reject the suggestion of Dr Strum that the existence of a clan mentality diminishes the objective gravity of your crime as incorrect and offensive to notions of personal responsibility and moral standards, and as insulting to Leigh. Dr Strum's opinion assumes that a domain of "culture" exists outside the control and agency of individuals and groups. This is not the case. There were people – a minority – who assisted Leigh on that night. There was also a group of males who abused and assaulted Leigh; and you were involved in this collective violence. And then it was you who secluded Leigh and committed a number of violent assaults upon her, and then ended by violently killing her. The criminal responsibility for this murder is a consequence of your attitudes and actions, and yours alone.

I now turn to your subjective circumstances. You are now almost nineteen years old. You left school at sixteen with a school certificate, and then entered a pre-apprenticeship in motor mechanics, but failed to get a job. You have not been in regular employment but have worked on an irregular basis as a fisherman with your father. You have no prior criminal record and you come from a stable and supportive family. It has, however, been established that you abused alcohol and cannabis from an early age.

Although there was substantial evidence given by your friends and family, who have known you for a long time, that you have a reputation of being a gentle, shy and polite young man who can lack self-confidence,

I do not find this evidence convincing. I prefer the evidence of Mr Taylor, who contradicts the character references tendered. Mr Taylor concluded that you have "an unstable personality with some paranoid and obsessional characteristics." I do not find the behaviours and attitudes you showed towards Leigh from early in the evening to be the behaviour and actions of a gentle, shy and polite young man. Early in the evening, and this is evidenced in a statement you made to a person who arrived at the party shortly before 9 o'clock, you said, "Hey dude, we are going to get Leigh pissed and all go through her." You then systematically took advantage of Leigh, humiliating her, isolating her, assaulting her and finally, killing her.

I now turn to considering the penalty to be imposed upon you. In doing so, I have considered the young age of the victim, the interests of the community in protection and deterrence, and the paramount consideration of the rehabilitation of young offenders such as yourself in sentencing. I have also considered the pain caused to Leigh's mother, sister and step-father, as well as her friends and the community of Stockton, through her death. The subjective circumstances suggest that there are prospects for rehabilitation, which will be assisted by your abstinence from alcohol and drugs while incarcerated. Even though your conviction for murder was inevitable, you pleaded guilty to the charge of murder – in doing so, you have saved the community time and expense, but more importantly, you have saved the family of Leigh and the young witnesses who would otherwise be called, from the further distress that would have resulted from going to trial. It is because of this that I accept and accord weight to your remorse and the shame you say you feel for your conduct. You are a first time offender, otherwise of good character. Additionally I account for the impact that imprisonment is likely to have on a person of your age. It is true that you did not supply alcohol to Leigh but, as I have carefully outlined above, you did contribute to Leigh's vulnerable state through actions of verbal and physical violence directed at her, and then you deliberately took advantage of this vulnerability and committed a number of extremely violent acts. Ultimately, you committed a callous, brutal and cowardly murder on a defenceless fourteen year-old girl.

There is also a need for this sentence to demonstrate principles of general deterrence. It is important that the community be alerted that the disregard for Leigh shown on that night is not acceptable and that these actions will be taken seriously by the law. The culture of humiliation and sexual violence apparent on that night is ultimately the responsibility of you and others present. This is, and will continue to be, the legal position.

Because of the date of the committal, section 19A of the Crimes Act applies to the present case. That section imposes a maximum penalty of penal servitude for life for the crime of murder. Under the new legislation a life sentence means the term of the natural life of the prisoner. However, there is a proviso in section 19A permitting the operation of section 442. Previously under section 19 of the Crimes Act the proviso operated where the person's culpability for the crime was significantly diminished by mitigating circumstances. This is no longer required, however because I find the sentencing patterns concerning the proviso under section 19 instructive, I have decided that in considering the mitigating factors and your prospects for rehabilitation, it is appropriate to give you a determinate sentence under section 442 of the Crimes Act. However I do not consider it appropriate to have regard to patterns existing for release on licence of persons previously sentenced to life imprisonment. The licensing scheme is inconsistent with the Sentencing Act which makes it clear that an object of the Act is to provide that prisoners, who have served their minimum terms of imprisonment, may be considered for release on parole for the residue of their sentences. Accordingly, the policy of truth in sentencing requires that prisoners serve a minimum fixed term with the certainty that once they have served that term they may be eligible for parole.

As I have said, I find the sentencing patterns concerning the proviso under the old section 19 leading to the application of section 442 instructive. This is subject to the caution given by the Court of Criminal Appeal on 16 February 1990 in Regina v Maclay as to the way past sentencing patterns should be regarded. I have also determined that because of your age the paramount consideration is your rehabilitation and that this is in the interest of the community. The objective gravity of the crime the need for punishment and the protection of the community are also factors. Accordingly I find that the specified norm in section

5(2) of the Sentencing Act does not apply and that this case falls within the special category considered in Regina v Moffit, Court of Criminal Appeal, 21 June 1990, permitting an adjustment downwards of the minimum term and the extension of the additional term so as to secure your appropriate supervision on parole after you serve the minimum term.

Taking those matters into account, I sentence you, Matthew Grant Webster, to a minimum term of penal servitude of fourteen years to date from 16 February 1990, being the date when you were first taken into custody and to expire on 15 February 2004. I impose an additional term of six years to date from 16 February 2004 during which you will be eligible for release on parole. The earliest date on which you will be eligible for release on parole will be 16 February 2004.

oOo

20

Commentary on *R v Middendorp* (Defensive Homicide)

JANEMAREE MAHER

Introduction

In Western jurisdictions, the partial defence of provocation has provoked legal and social controversies. Criminologists, legal and feminist scholars contend that the intersection of the legal conditions for the defence and socially gendered roles systematically disadvantages battered women while privileging men who argue a 'loss of control' in intimate partner homicides.[1] As Howe notes, the '[d]evastating feminist critiques of the age-old concession to "passion" in the form of homicidal fury unleashed on women by furious men are now legion.'[2] Nonetheless, the mobilisation of gendered assumptions in intimate partner homicides continues to be a critical area of gendered injustice. There have been many law reform campaigns[3] seeking meaningful change in judgments and case outcomes in Australia and internationally. *R v Middendorp*[4] is a 2010 case resulting from one law reform effort in Victoria, which introduced a new category of homicide with the explicit goal of better responding to lethal violence in the context of family violence. The *Middendorp* case exposes the ongoing difficulties of achieving gendered justice through law reform.

Background to the *Middendorp* Case

The background to the *Middendorp* case demonstrates the difficulties historically encountered by criminal justice systems when attempting to achieve equitable protections for women and men in relation to intimate partner violence. In 2004, this issue was graphically revealed in the provocation defence in *R v Ramage*.[5]

[1] Kate Fitz-Gibbon and Sharon Pickering, 'Homicide Law Reform in Victoria, Australia: From Provocation to Defensive Homicide and Beyond' (2012) 52 *The British Journal of Criminology* 159; Danielle Tyson, *Sex, Culpability and the Defence of Provocation* (Routledge, 2013) especially ch 2; Victorian Department of Justice (DOJ), 'Defensive Homicide: Proposals for Legislative Reform' (Consultation Paper, Victorian DOJ, 2013).

[2] Adrian Howe, 'Provocation in Crisis: Law's Passion at the Crossroads? New Directions for Feminist Strategies' (2004) 21 *Australian Feminist Law Journal* 53, 59.

[3] See, eg, Law Reform Commission of Western Australia, *Review of the Law of Homicide*, Final Report, Project 97 (2007); Queensland Law Reform Commission, *A Review of the Excuse of Accident and the Defence of Provocation*, Report No 64 (2008); Victorian Law Reform Commission (VLRC), *Defences to Homicide*, Final Report (2004).

[4] [2010] VSC 202 (19 May 2010) ('*Middendorp*').

[5] [2004] VSC 508 (9 December 2004) ('*Ramage*').

James Ramage was convicted after a trial of manslaughter by reason of provocation. The jury found Ramage was provoked to kill his ex-wife following an argument about his role as a husband and her alleged expression of disgust about their sexual life. At the time of the killing, Julie and James Ramage had been separated for almost two months. On 28 October 2004, Julie Ramage met with James in their previously shared home. According to Ramage, their discussion focused initially on home renovations, which he claimed she devalued. He then claimed that he asked about reconciliation, to which he alleges Julie Ramage responded: 'I'm over you, I should have left you 10 years ago.' In his police interview he claimed that she asserted that the idea of sex with him disgusted her. He said he 'lost control' and was provoked to kill her. Julie Ramage sustained more than 17 injuries that proved fatal. She was buried by her husband in nearby bushland before he returned to the city, sought legal advice and turned himself into police. The *Ramage* case has the most troubling elements of the defence of provocation: the killing occurred post-separation, a key period of danger for women,[6] and James Ramage's account of the victim's allegedly provocative conduct was the only one available at trial. He was convicted of manslaughter on the basis of provocation and sentenced to 11 years' maximum imprisonment, with an eight-year non-parole period.

Legal and Social Context for Defensive Homicide

The jury's decision to convict James Ramage of manslaughter, not murder, provoked sustained social and scholarly critique.[7] The role of provocation in highlighting the actions of Julie rather than James Ramage, showed the inherent injustices of the provocation defence. The gender biases in this case became a key driver for law reform in Victoria, as well as other Australian jurisdictions.[8]

Within Victoria, the *Ramage* case followed the Victorian Law Reform Commission's *Defences to Homicide* Final Report and its recommendation that the partial defence of provocation should be abolished.[9] While the *Ramage* case did not influence the VLRC's recommendations, it is cited as underpinning the Victorian government's willingness to abolish the partial defence, transferring any consideration of provocation to sentencing.[10]

Another key aspect of the 2005 reforms was the introduction of a new offence: defensive homicide. Under s 9AD of the *Crimes (Homicide) Act 2005* (Vic), defensive homicide operates when a person kills another person believing that their act was necessary to defend themselves, or another, without reasonable grounds for that belief. This new offence aimed to address intimate partner homicides, particularly victims of family violence who did not kill in the circumstances of immediate and direct threat that support self-defence. The

[6] Jenny Morgan, 'Provocation Law and Facts: Dead Women Tell No Tales, Tales Are Told About Them' (1997) 21 *Melbourne University Law Review* 237.

[7] See Karen Kissane, 'Honour Killing in the Suburbs', *The Age* (Melbourne) 6 November 2004, 4–5; Graeme Coss, 'Editorial: Provocation's Victorian Nadir: The Obscenity of *Ramage*' (2005) 29 *Criminal Law Journal* 133; JaneMaree Maher et al, 'Honouring White Masculinity: Culture, Terror, Provocation and the Law' (2005) 23 *Australian Feminist Law Journal* 147.

[8] Queensland Law Reform Commission, *A Review of the Defence of Provocation*, Working Paper No 63 (2008) 157; Select Committee on the Partial Defence of Provocation, *The Partial Defence of Provocation*, Final Report (2013) 25.

[9] VLRC, above n 3, xlv.

[10] Fitz-Gibbon and Pickering, above n 1; Select Committee on the Partial Defence of Provocation, above n 9, 25.

VLRC Report acknowledged normative gender roles offered much greater protection to men who killed their female partners in a jealous rage, than to women facing family violence who finally killed their male partners for self-preservation.[11] The Victorian Department of Justice *Review of Defensive Homicide* described the intent of the offence:

> 5. The *Crimes (Homicide) Act 2005* introduced defensive homicide to specifically recognise when a person kills in 'excessive self-defence'. That is, a person might believe it is necessary to kill to protect themself or another but not have reasonable grounds for that belief. The VLRC considered this to be particularly important where there is strong evidence of family violence and the choices realistically available to those who kill in response to family violence are not well understood.
> 6. In this way, the VLRC indicated that excessive self-defence provided an important 'safety-net' for those who kill in response to family violence, for example, where the jury does not consider the response to the threat of harm to be reasonable.[12]

In recommending the creation of the defensive homicide offence, the Victorian government emphasised the need to understand the history of relationship abuse in the relationship prior to the event, and how gender shapes forms of family violence. The VLRC stressed the importance of 'social context evidence' about gendered violence and urged community education about the impacts of family violence, particularly on women.[13] 'Social context evidence' is wider than the type of evidence conventionally accepted in intimate partner homicide cases, and includes targeted attention to the gendered impacts of intimate partner violence. The *Crimes (Homicide) Act 2005* included the insertion of s 9AH into the *Crimes Act 1958* (Vic), extending the definition of family violence to physical, sexual, and psychological abuse (including intimidation, harassment, damage to property, or threats).[14]

In addition, the VLRC recommended ongoing monitoring of judgments to ensure that the objectives of the 2005 law reforms were being achieved.[15] The sentencing decision in *Middendorp* represents an important opportunity for review of the effectiveness of the 2005 reforms.

How the *Middendorp* Case Unfolded

The Victorian DOJ *Review of Defensive Homicide Discussion Paper* found the new offence was primarily used in cases where young men were both protagonist and victim.[16] This pattern evidenced the reinstatement of traditional provocation arguments, where men killed in a sudden rage. This contradicted the original intentions of the legislative reform, to create a safety net for defendants who killed in response to prolonged family violence. In two cases, this offence was applied to lethal violence committed by a man against his intimate partner, including *Middendorp*.

11 VLRC, above n 3, 27.
12 Victorian DOJ, *Review of the Offence of Defensive Homicide*, Discussion Paper (2010) 77.
13 VLRC, above n 3, ii, xxxiv–xxxvi, 188.
14 *Crimes Act 1958* (Vic) s 9AH(4).
15 VLRC, above n 3, xlvii.
16 Victorian DOJ, above n 12, 33–4.

The *Middendorp* case created controversy.[17] The jury's decision to convict of defensive homicide, rather than murder, suggested this homicide was excessive self-defence in the context of partner violence. This decision requires that the defendant, Luke Middendorp, genuinely believed, even if unreasonably, that he was fatally threatened by his former partner Jade Bowndes. A number of reported factors suggested the social context evidence designed to illuminate the nature and dynamics of family violence instead was used to indicate the violence between the parties was 'mutual'. Male violence was legitimated as in the discredited partial defence of provocation. The patterns of family violence are more directly addressed in the feminist judgment, including the defendant's history of intimate violence, a standing Family Violence Order, differences in strength and size, and the defendant's actions after stabbing Jade Bowndes in the back.

The Feminist Judgment

The VLRC *Defences to Homicide* Final Report identified sentencing as crucial for change in the cases of intimate partner homicide following the abolition of the provocation defence.[18] The Executive Summary states:

> [As] current sentencing practices for murder might translate into longer sentences for 'sympathetic' cases of provocation . . . this Report recommends that judges consider the full range of sentencing options for murder where it is appropriate to do so. The Report also calls for greater guidance . . . on how issues such as a history of abuse should be taken into account at sentencing.[19]

It is vital that the gendered problems of provocation do not accompany its transfer to sentencing.

> If the underlying purposes of the proponents of abolition are to be achieved, it is imperative that the problems and flaws of the pre-existing law not be transferred from the substantive criminal law into the law of sentencing . . . Many of the old assumptions will need to be discarded and a new normative framework must be developed.[20]

In this feminist judgment, the authors have chosen to rewrite the sentencing decision in *Middendorp*. This intervention applies social context evidence to reveal the history of abuse in the relationship. The sentence given, 17 years, exceeds previous sentences for this offence, but reflects a more feminist gendered analysis. In the original sentencing judgment, family violence is equally attributed to both parties, supporting Middendorp's access to the lesser charge and sentence. Narratives of a troubled young woman are used to diminish (his) culpability. Here, such mitigations are not accepted, as they reinscribe those flawed older assumptions. This re-imagining of the sentencing judgment with attention to the 'full range of sentencing options' better expresses the aims of the 2005 Victorian law reform process to achieve gendered justice in intimate partners homicide.

[17] Kate Fitz-Gibbon, 'The Victorian Operation of Defensive Homicide: Examining the Delegitimisation of Victims in the Criminal Justice System' (2013) 21 *Griffith Law Review* 556; Danielle Tyson, 'Victoria's New Homicide Laws: Provocative Reforms or More Stories of Women "Asking For It"?' (2011) 23 *Current Issues in Criminal Justice* 203.

[18] VLRC, above n 3, 269–90.

[19] Ibid xxii.

[20] Arie Freiberg and Felicity Stewart, 'Provocation in Sentencing: A Culpability-Based Framework' (2008) 19 *Current Issues in Criminal Justice* 283, 284.

IN THE SUPREME COURT OF VICTORIA
AT Melbourne
CRIMINAL DIVISION

Not Restricted

No. 1487 of 2009

THE QUEEN

v

LUKE JOHN MIDDENDORP

JUDGE:	JUSTICIA J
WHERE HELD:	Melbourne
DATE OF HEARING:	13 May 2010
DATE OF SENTENCE:	19 May 2010
CASE MAY BE CITED AS:	R v Middendorp
MEDIUM NEUTRAL CITATION:	[2010] VSC 202

CRIMINAL LAW – sentence – defensive homicide – killing by stabbing female partner – history of violence - accused in breach of terms of intervention order and conditions of bail – sentence of 12 years imprisonment with 8 years non-parole period.

APPEARANCES:	Counsel	Solicitors
For the Crown	Mr P.N. Rose, SC	Office of Public Prosecutions
For the Accused	Mr T. Walsh	Melinda Walker, Criminal Lawyer

HER HONOUR:

1 Luke Middendorp, you have been found guilty of the offence of defensive homicide. In March 2010, you were charged with the murder of your former partner, Jade Bowndes, at your home at Brunswick on 1 September 2008. She died in the street of stab wounds received at your hands.

2 You were responsible for the death of Jade Bowndes and this fact was not disputed at trial. The trial was contested on the basis that you claimed to have acted in self-defence. By returning a verdict of guilty to the charge of defensive homicide the jury rejected your claim of self-defence. This means the jury were not satisfied that when you killed Jade Bowndes you had a reasonable belief that you were acting in self-defence. However, the verdict indicates that the jury accepted your evidence that Jade Bowndes confronted you with a knife and that you genuinely believed you were at risk of death or really serious injury from a woman who was much slighter than you. I am bound to sentence you in line with this jury verdict.

3 In arriving at a sentence, I have examined the background and context of your relationship to fully explain the circumstances of this killing, a case of domestic homicide. In order to arrive at a just sentence, I have also considered any mitigating and aggravating factors raised relevant to the sentencing guidelines.

Background and context of the relationship

4 The circumstances relating to the killing of Jade Bowndes are taken from the evidence presented at trial and therefore rely heavily upon your version of events. Recent law reforms have sought to enhance the courts' understanding of domestic homicide particularly in the context of separation. Myths and false accounts of women's responsibility for male violence are commonly held within the community. Male violence, particularly fatal violence amongst intimate partners, is often misunderstood and because the victim is dead, she has no opportunity to tell her own story. The facts given in your evidence at trial were almost entirely uncorroborated by any other witnesses. Neighbours witnessed only the final moments of your attack on Jade Bowndes. You were heard by neighbours to say: "You had it coming. You got what you deserved, you filthy slut". You did not call an ambulance for her and she died in the street.

5 You and Jade Bowndes had been involved in a defacto relationship since late 2007. In December of that year you both moved to a house at 18 Rosser Street, Brunswick, where she was later killed.

6 Evidence given in the trial by you and several witnesses referred to a number of incidents involving violence in your relationship that occurred in the period leading up to the fatal incident. I do not intend to mention all the incidents that occurred during this time but it is necessary to mention some of them.

7 There was evidence given by neighbours of your threats and assaults. Ms D'Adam reported your statement some three weeks before Jade Bowndes' death that you would slit Jade's throat. In addition, Jade Bowndes' mother, Shey Beck, said that her daughter complained to her of you hitting, slapping, and punching her.

8 Evidence given at trial relevant to your relationship with Jade Bowndes referred to five 'earlier incidents' involving violence, which was determined to be tendency evidence. That evidence was relied upon by the prosecution to assert that you are a man with a tendency towards violence and might stab a woman regardless of the level of threat presented.

9 Nine months before Jade Bowndes was killed, there was an incident on 19 December 2007 where your neck was slashed. Police officers who attended the scene took a statement from Jade Bowndes which suggested the incident arose in your home together at Coburg in the context of a dispute about her sitting on the couch. The statement reports:

> He jumped on her knees. She hit him on the head with her mobile. He came back with a razor and sliced her on the neck. She called her girlfriend. He thought she was calling the police. He said, 'it doesn't matter if they come because I'm going to slit me throat anyway.' He goes into the bathroom and comes back bleeding heavily from the neck and the police are called. The police attend, take them to hospital, he is taken to the operating theatre while she lays on one of the hospital beds. She was described as being aggressive, affected by drugs and alcohol requiring two orderlies or security guards to restrain her.

10 On 10 March 2008, you hit Jade Bowndes on the arm with a frying pan. She told police who attended the scene that the incident arose out of an argument about or which included threats to kill her dog. The verbal argument got out of hand and you had hit her with a frying pan off the stove causing a red mark on her arm. She said you got the idea she was going to call the police. You pushed or threw Jade Bowndes to the ground, held her by the throat and said, 'You will die before I go to gaol'.

11 The third incident is the 'medical centre in Footscray' incident on 14 March 2008. Jade Bowndes spoke with a police officer on the phone while at the Footscray Medical Centre and said that her boyfriend had come home drunk and wanted sex. She said he had also tried to strangle her, and hit her with a vacuum cleaner pole. Despite the phone call she did not want the police to take any action. The fourth incident is 'Mrs Beck's visit' where Jade's mother, Shey Beck, visited her at home. During the visit they had a mother-daughter chat and Jade said that while she was asleep, you woke her up, you were on top of her and strangling her. Shey Beck also said that Jade had told her that you had threatened to kill her; however there was no formal police report made of this incident.

12 The final incident of the 'steel toe-capped boots' occurred on 31 July 2008. On this evening, there had been a complaint that required police attendance. The police officer found the door locked and there was some difficulty gaining entry. One of the officers then went through the front window. On this occasion, Jade Bowndes was uncooperative about letting the police officers in and said she would set the dogs on them. Consequently, the police used capsicum spray on one of the dogs and once they got past the door, Jade Bowndes then ran past them into the street with blood in her hair, upset and dishevelled. She told them that you, her boyfriend, had hit her with a boot three or four times. She was taken to hospital. You were in the house at the time and the police officer said you were just sitting on the bed, handcuffed. The police officer also said that you had no blood on you at this point but there was blood on the mattress and pillowcase. Dr Grayson, the doctor at the Royal Melbourne hospital who treated her and took a history, gave evidence that Jade Bowndes told him that her boyfriend had molested both her and her young child and that he had become more aggressive so she broke up with him. Then in the evening she was sleeping when he broke into their house and assaulted her. He kicked her with steel toe-capped boots, punched her, broke a bottle over her head, tried to poke her eyes out, threw her around the room and over a coffee table and then assaulted their dogs. Following the attack, Jade lost consciousness, had a throbbing headache, vomited twice and complained of both neck and back pain. When you gave evidence during the trial you denied this. You said that Jade Bowndes had come home after being away for some time, and she complained of having been assaulted by a man or some men who were at the railway station and who wanted money. You asserted that she said she needed money to give them and that she called the police. Your reaction was that you were not going to give them any money and that if they wanted to come round and collect it they would have to settle with you first. This was your version of the 'steel toe-capped boots' incident.

13 Your counsel submitted that episodes of violence and arguments in the relationship between you and Jade Bowndes were 'mutual'. Different versions of this evidence were given in the trial but there are a number of substantive facts that are not in dispute. There was a huge disparity in size and weight between you and Jade Bowndes. On 20 December 2007 there was an intervention order made against you restraining you from assaulting, harassing, threatening or intimidating Jade Bowndes. This order was made in relation to an incident when you and Jade Bowndes were living together at the house in Coburg. That Family Violence Order was still in force at the time you killed Jade Bowndes. There was also another order in force relating to an incident for which you were arrested and charged with the offence of recklessly causing serious injury which an informant, who was a Victoria police officer named Coley, said you committed on 30 July 2008. This charge related to the incident referred to earlier as the 'steel toe-capped boots' incident. You were granted bail on

conditions, which included that you were prohibited from going to the house at Rosser Street where you had been living on your own. At the time you killed Jade Bowndes, you were awaiting trial in the County Court for this offence but it has since been entered as a nolle prosequi. You actions did, however, put you in breach of these bail conditions at the time you killed Jade Bowndes.

14 Family Violence Orders are the means by which the courts, and society more broadly, attempt to deter violent men. Although the orders are equally available to men and women, such orders are most commonly granted to women in Australia experiencing violence at the hands of their male partners. The pattern of such orders challenges extant myths and misconceptions about the nature and dynamics of domestic violence which suggest that both men and women are 'equally violent' or 'as bad as each other'. In this case, as is typical in the vast majority of similar cases, intimate partner violence is committed by men against women and is characterised by a persistent pattern of controlling behaviours. Jade Bowndes had left the relationship prior to your fatal attack. Separation has been identified as one of the most dangerous times for women attempting to leave a violent partner. We must be cognisant of how the experience of violence and control might motivate women to initiate separation, return to a violent relationship or resort to the use of a weapon to defend themselves from further violence.

1 September 2008

15 On the night of 1 September 2008 when you killed Jade Bowndes, you said that she arrived at Rosser Street in the late afternoon with a male companion, Mr Artiz Perez. Shey Beck gave evidence that Jade was attending the house with the goal of feeding her dog. As she did not have a key to the house, she climbed through a window, fed the dog and then left the house. You were not at home during this visit.

16 You said that later in the evening, Jade Bowndes returned to the house at Rosser Street, again accompanied by Mr Artiz Perez. On your evidence you said that you told her this was your house, not hers, and that you told her to 'get her mate and get the fuck out'. You also said that Mr Perez had a knife in his hand. You too had a knife with you and you challenged Mr Perez and then told him to 'get the fuck out of my house' and chased him away. A neighbour who gave evidence in the trial recalls that before Jade Bowndes entered the house, he overheard you threaten to stab her. Despite this, she entered the house and was there when you returned from your pursuit of Mr Perez. The extent to which Mr Perez was present during the subsequent verbal argument and physical assault was contested at trial and it is not necessary for me to decide on this in setting out the facts of this offence.

17 We only have your account about what happened immediately prior to you stabbing Jade Bowndes. Based on the verdict, the jury accepted your

evidence that Jade Bowndes came at you with a raised knife in her right hand and that you formed the unreasonable belief that you were at risk of death or really serious injury and that it was necessary to defend yourself. According to your evidence, you, too, had a knife in your right hand and, in the ensuing struggle you stabbed her over the shoulder in the back four times. You said in evidence that she appeared to be unaffected at first by the stabbing though you were, nonetheless, able to wrest the knife from her grasp before she collapsed. Having collapsed, she was then able to leave the house and to stagger onto the footpath and down the street before she fell and died from the wounds that you inflicted on her.

18 Your claim that you formed the view that it was necessary to defend yourself against the risk of death or really serious injury after Jade Bowndes came at you with a raised knife in her right hand cannot be tested. You were alone with her when you committed the fatal attack, a circumstance typical of domestic homicides. Whilst I am bound to sentence in line with the jury's verdict, I note that the overriding rationale for the introduction of the offence of defensive homicide was to specifically recognise when a person kills in 'excessive self-defence' and in response to prolonged family violence. This offence recognises a person might believe it is necessary to kill to protect themselves or another although they may not have reasonable grounds for that belief. In circumstances of family violence, the actions, beliefs and choices realistically linked to self-defence are not well understood, especially in regard to those who kill in response to family violence. In the offence of defensive homicide, the jury need only be satisfied that the belief in necessity is subjectively held. It is, therefore, a relatively easy claim to make.

19 Your actions against Jade Bowndes would have put you in breach of a Family Violence Order and conditions of bail. You are a man of over six feet tall and weigh about 90 kilograms. Jade Bowndes was much smaller in stature and weighed about 50 kilograms. There was evidence adduced at the trial that the deceased had apparently told her mother, Shey Beck, about the fear she lived with in relation to your violence and threats. The witness recalled that '[i]n February 2008 the Deceased told her that she was afraid that the Accused would kill her. In July the Deceased told her that the Accused said he would kill her if she tried to leave him'.

20 Importantly, following your use of lethal violence you recovered quickly enough from the initial threat posed by Jade Bowndes to follow her outside the house and utter the chilling words overheard by neighbours as she lay dying on the footpath outside: 'you got what you deserved, you filthy slut'. This was a callous remark. It displays no remorse for your fatal violence, pointing instead to your contempt for the deceased.

The offender's background

21 You were born on 23 November 1983 and raised in Frankston, the younger of two children. Your parents separated when you were very young, leaving your mother to bring up your elder sister and yourself. According to the psychological assessment report of Peter Stanislawski, you exhibited insecurity at an early age with a fear of abandonment by your mother.

22 By the age of 12 years you were mixing with older boys at your school, smoking cannabis, using alcohol, inhaling petrol vapours and experimenting with LSD. At this time too you were diagnosed with and treated for attention deficit hyperactivity disorder. In 1977 you left school at age 14, having failed Year 8. You were subsequently unable to hold down a job and commenced using heroin. Your life has been marred by periods of drug dependency and petty crime. In 2002 you commenced a course of methadone treatment. By 2004 you were serving sentences for theft and burglary in youth training centres and by the end of that year you were serving short terms of imprisonment. This pattern continued in 2005 and 2006. In May 2008 you were sentenced to an aggregate term of six months suspended for 12 months for a series of similar charges as well as charges relating to the possession of drugs. Your criminal history discloses conduct of the kind that has brought you before this court, in particular the 'steel toe-capped boots' incident for which you were awaiting trial in the County Court. At the time of the offence you were twenty-four years old and unemployed.

23 Whilst your counsel described your conduct in killing Jade Bowndes as a 'tragedy' which has affected a lot of lives, Mr Stanislawski said that you had not demonstrated a great deal of insight into your behaviour. Your callous remarks as Jade Bowndes lay dying in the street do not indicate remorse or tragedy. They appear rather as gloating over the infliction of fatal injuries on Jade Bowndes, who was only exercising her right to leave a violent relationship when you killed her.

Victim impact statements

24 I have taken into account the victim impact statements that have been tendered by the Crown, in particular, the statement of Jade Bowndes' mother, Shey Beck. Shey Beck described the loss of her daughter as 'the most difficult and painful thing that myself and my family have ever had to find the strength to endure'. Describing 'the needless loss' of her daughter as devastating, she said Jade was 'an amazing, beautiful, loving and gentle young woman [who] is now and forever more just ashes that lie in the cold, dark ground'. Her statement highlighted the all too common experience of the family members of homicide victims after a trial where it is perceived that the life of their lost loved one has been undervalued. Shey Beck said that while her daughter would be remembered by the court as 'just another young woman caught up in an undesirable

domestic situation that led to her death, case file number whatever . . . to me and her family . . . she was a bright light, a warmth, a happy charismatic, extremely lovable, funny and deeply caring human being'.

25 Mr Artiz Perez also tendered a victim impact statement. He described the ongoing effects of your false account to police implicating him in the death of Jade Bowndes. He described his guilt over what he perceives to be the inadequacy of his evidence leading to your conviction for defensive homicide rather than the more serious offence of murder. The statement by Mr Perez, along with the deceased's mother's statement, provides insight into the wide-ranging impact of your lethal actions on 1 September 2008.

26 During the trial, your counsel submitted that it is not in his nature to 'speak ill of the dead, but at times it is our duty to do this. This is one of those times.' Your counsel sought to suggest the pre-existing history of violence between you and Jade Bowndes in some way explained your lethal actions. Provocation has been abolished as a partial defence to murder in Victoria. One of the key reasons for its abolition was that the community perceived that victims were being put on trial and blamed for the violence perpetrated upon them. Jade Bowndes was only 22 years old when you killed her. She had her entire adult life ahead of her. I unequivocally reject any suggestion that because she was, at the time of her death, homeless or misusing drugs that she in some way contributed to her own demise.

27 There is no doubt that all of the people who have submitted a victim impact statement are bereft. You have taken from them someone they loved, someone they cared about deeply and that will never change. Jade Bowndes will not return to their lives. Your actions have ensured that.

28 Equally, it must be understood by all of those involved in this matter that the sentence that is going to be imposed on you, Luke Middendorp, for the offence of defensive homicide is not an indication of the worth of their loved one. That is not how the system of justice works. I am obliged as a matter of law to take into account various matters which I will mention and deal with shortly and determine the appropriate punishment for the offence of which the jury found you guilty. The worth of Jade Bowndes is captured in the statements by those who loved her and is not capable of being reflected by a sentence of imprisonment on the man who took her life. I will take into account the victim impact statements as one of the matters to be considered in determining the appropriate sentence.

Aggravating and mitigating factors

29 Whilst I must take into account all factors including your age, I also have to balance that with other relevant factors such as just and appropriate punishment, denunciation and any aggravating features of this crime.

Your lack of remorse, prior criminal history and that your actions would have put you in breach of bail are of course aggravating factors.

30 That you had previously harmed Jade Bowndes and assaulted her in a significant manner and had a standing intervention order against you, of which your actions put you in breach at the time you killed this young woman, is also an aggravating factor. You should have been alert and aware of your responsibility to ensure that you did not place yourself in a state or situation where you may have caused her harm, such as using violence to resolve domestic conflict. It is unfortunate that the intervention order imposed on you was not taken seriously. Multiple measures have been put in place by parliament and the courts in an attempt to deter persons from seeking to resolve domestic conflicts by means of violence. Actions that put you in breach of the intervention order must be met with a strong message to members of the community that such breaches are viewed gravely by the courts and will be met with serious sanction.

31 Your counsel relies strongly upon your age and lack of premeditation as matters that may mitigate the crime. That is, that you did not have an intention to kill Jade Bowndes before she came into the house at Rosser Street on 1 September 2008. The jury has accepted that you killed Jade Bowndes because of a perceived threat by her. But very shortly after she allegedly approached you with a knife raised in her right hand, it appears that you did form an intention to kill based on your asserted fear. In particular, your conduct, including the words directed at Jade Bowndes as she lay dying, speak to your lack of remorse for causing her death. Whilst it may be possible that you have since developed some regret for your actions, I am unable to conclude that this should be considered as a mitigating factor in this case.

Sentencing principles

32 Sentencing in Victoria is a balance between mitigating and aggravating factors and I must also take into account the relevant sentencing principles referred to in s 5(2) of the *Sentencing Act*. This requires the court to consider five purposes for which sentences may be imposed; these are:

a) to punish the offender to an extent and in a manner which is just in all of the circumstances;

b) to deter the offender or other persons from committing offences of the same or a similar character;

c) to establish conditions within which it is considered by the Court that the rehabilitation of the offender may be facilitated;

d) to manifest the denunciation by the Court of the type of conduct in which the offender is engaged; and

e) to protect the community from the offender.

33 Your future prospects for rehabilitation appear limited given the opportunities already afforded to you by the criminal justice system on several previous occasions. You find yourself here because of your perpetration of one of the most serious of crimes. In 2006 you were involved in the Link Out program conducted by Brosnan Youth Services. Whilst Mr King's report cited your positive involvement in this program as evidence of good rehabilitative prospects, this occurred prior to your killing of Jade Bowndes. Any prospects are thus overshadowed by your lethal actions, which also would have put you in breach of bail conditions and in breach of the Family Violence Order.

34 In Australia domestic homicides represent a risk to women in intimate relationships, particularly to women who exercise their rights by choosing to leave an intimate relationship. Jade Bowndes was one such woman. The sentence imposed upon you for taking her life must reflect the community's condemnation of domestic homicide committed within the context of separation. Such violence represents the ultimate betrayal of trust and in this case, the ultimate exploitation of strength over a significantly smaller and weaker woman. For this reason the need for general deterrence and denunciation is reflected in the sentence imposed.

Sentence length

35 I am required to sentence a man who violently killed a woman with whom he had been in an intimate relationship in which there was an extensive documented history of domestic violence.

36 Defensive homicide is a relatively new offence, and to date sentences imposed have been significantly below the maximum penalty set by Parliament, which is 20 years imprisonment. Despite your counsel's assertion that your actions fall within the upper end of a mid-range offence, I see your use of lethal violence as a very serious example of defensive homicide and for this reason the sentence imposed must reflect the gravity of the offence committed.

37 Luke Middendorp, for the offence involving the death of Jade Bowndes, you are convicted of defensive homicide. I have taken all of the matters to which I have referred into account, including that this was a case in which there was systematic domestic violence over a long period of time. It is important to set a sentence reflective of the level of harm caused and the gravity of your offending. For this reason your term should approach the maximum penalty set by Parliament. I sentence you to a term of 17 years imprisonment. I direct that you are to serve a minimum of 14 years and six months before becoming eligible for parole.

21

Intersectionality and Indigenous Sentencing Courts: *R v Morgan*

HEATHER DOUGLAS

Introduction

In 2009, an Indigenous man named Steelie Morgan was sentenced in the Koori Court Division of the Victorian County Court for crimes of violence against his ex-girlfriend. He later appealed the sentence to the Victorian Court of Appeal, where his sentence was reduced. The feminist judgment provides a dissenting judgment in the Court of Appeal. Before considering the feminist judgment and Morgan's appearances before the County Court and the Court of Appeal, this commentary reflects on the role and development of Indigenous sentencing jurisprudence and Indigenous sentencing courts in Australia.

Sentencing Principles and Indigenous People

Judicial officers who sentence criminal offenders, whether in mainstream courts or in Indigenous sentencing courts, are constrained by legislation and jurisprudence developed by the courts. However, throughout Australia, in considering the appropriate penalty, judges have a wide discretion to consider any factors relevant to the offence and the offender.[1]

In 1982, the High Court in *Neal v R* considered the sentencing principles in relation to Indigenous people.[2] Neal was charged with assault and ordered to serve a period of imprisonment. Ultimately Neal appealed to the High Court, where Justice Brennan held that:

> [T]he same sentencing principles are to be applied ... in every case, irrespective of the identity of a particular offender or his membership of an ethnic or other group. But in imposing sentences courts are bound to take into account ... all material facts including those facts which exist only by reason of the offender's membership of an ethnic or other group.[3]

Many cases followed *Neal*, finding that, while Indigenous people are not an homogenous group, and the individual offender's characteristics must be considered in each case, Indigenous disadvantage and those facts which exist as a result of being Indigenous are

[1] Richard Edney and Mirko Bagaric, *Australian Sentencing: Principles and Practice* (Cambridge University Press, 2007) 16.

[2] (1982) 149 CLR 305 ('*Neal*').

[3] Ibid 307.

material facts that may operate as mitigating factors.[4] One of the key anxieties for policy-makers and courts in sentencing Indigenous people is their overrepresentation in custody in Australia. The rate of imprisonment of Indigenous adults is 13 times higher than for non-Indigenous people.[5] In 1992 Wood J identified the need to consider penalties that supported rehabilitation and proposed that courts need to consider 'more subtle remedies' than imprisonment.[6] Subsequently the importance of rehabilitation as a mitigating factor in sentencing Indigenous people has been restated in many cases.[7]

However the legal system's focus on the rehabilitation of Indigenous men has often contributed, directly and indirectly, to the silencing, trivialising and marginalising of Indigenous women's claims for justice.[8] This silencing extends to Indigenous women's under-reporting of violent crime for fear of reprisals and lack of appropriate response, the under-policing of violence in Indigenous communities and the lack of legal representation provided to women.[9] It also extends to sentencing processes when they focus on the concerns of Indigenous male offenders and fail to hear, or take account of, Indigenous women victims' views and experiences.[10]

Some time ago feminist scholars introduced the idea of intersectionality as a method for interrogating the institutional reproduction of inequality at a range of sites.[11] For example Crenshaw argues that 'feminist and anti-racist discourses failed to consider intersectional identities such as women of colour' and that this approach resulted in their marginalisation by both feminist and anti-racist discourses.[12] More specifically, her analysis is applicable to legal processes that have considered race without considering gender, or gender without considering race. A failure to take account of the multiple grounds of identity leads to the entrenchment of inequality.[13] Such inequality is illustrated by the fact that Indigenous women and children experience disproportionately high rates of violence.[14]

How then can legal processes ensure that in sentencing Indigenous male perpetrators for offences of violence against women, the rehabilitation of perpetrators is supported while at the same time the serious harms experienced by Aboriginal women are heard and recognised? Using an intersectional framework may help to improve criminal justice responses;[15]

[4] Thalia Anthony *Sentencing Indigenous Offenders* (Indigenous Justice Clearinghouse, 2010) 2–3. See also *Bugmy v R* [2013] HCA 37 (2 October 2013) [44].

[5] Anthony, ibid.

[6] *R v Fernando* (1992) 76 A Crim R 58, 62, 63; Anthony, ibid 3.

[7] Anthony, ibid.

[8] Kyllie Cripps, Megan Davis and Caroline Taylor, '*The Queen v BP, DK, MY, PA, Koowarta, Wikmunea, Woola, 2007*' (2008) 7(9) *Indigenous Law Bulletin* 14, 18; see also Kimberle Crenshaw, 'Mapping the Margins: Intersectionality, Identity Politics, and Violence Against Women of Color' (1991) 43 *Stanford Law Review* 1241, 1242–3.

[9] Boni Robertson, Department of Aboriginal and Torres Strait Islander Policy and Development, *Aboriginal and Torres Strait Islander Women's Taskforce on Violence Report* (2000) 13, 98, 186, 189.

[10] Heather Douglas and Mark Finnane, *Indigenous Crime and Settler Law: White Sovereignty After Empire* (Palgrave, 2012) 197–204.

[11] Emily Grabham, with Didi Herman, Davina Cooper and Jane Krishnadas, 'Introduction' in Emily Grabham et al (eds), *Intersectionality and Beyond: Law, Power and the Politics of Location* (Routledge, 2009) 1.

[12] Crenshaw, above n 8, 1242–3.

[13] See Aileen Moreton-Robertson, 'Masking Gender and Exalting Race: Indigenous Women and Commonwealth Employment Practices' (1992) 15 *Australian Feminist Studies* 5, 5.

[14] Kyllie Cripps and Megan Davis, 'Communities Working to Reduce Family Violence' (Brief No 12, Indigenous Justice Clearinghouse, June 2012).

[15] Kathleen Daly, 'Seeking Justice in the 21st Century: Towards an Intersectional Politics of Justice' in Holly Ventura Miller (ed), *Restorative Justice: from Theory to Practice – Sociology of Crime Law and Deviance* (Emerald Group Publishing, 2008) 24.

as Marchetti notes, in a sentencing context 'it is important [for judges] to listen to the voices of Aboriginal and Torres Strait Islander people, particularly the women, when they discuss what types of responses are most appropriate for addressing crimes of domestic and family violence.'[16] Indigenous sentencing courts may provide a model which supports such an intersectional approach.

Indigenous Sentencing Courts

The first Indigenous sentencing court was introduced in Port Adelaide, in South Australia in 1999.[17] Since then they have been developed in all Australian jurisdictions with the exception of Tasmania. These courts aspire to 'increase trust between Indigenous people and white justice and to strengthen Indigenous communities';[18] however other explanations for their emergence have also been identified. Between 1987 and 1990, a Royal Commission investigated the deaths of 99 Aboriginal people who had died in custody from 1980 to 1989. The Royal Commission found that 'facts associated in every case with their Aboriginality played a significant and, in most cases, dominant role in their being in custody and dying in custody.'[19] The Royal Commission's findings provided some of the impetus for the development of a range of alternative criminal justice responses, including the development of Indigenous sentencing courts.[20] These courts aim to help reduce recidivism and the over-representation of Indigenous people in custody.[21] However difficulties have been identified with assessing the effectiveness of Indigenous sentencing courts in terms of reducing recidivism and imprisonment. Justice Wayne Martin of the Supreme Court of Western Australia has commented:

> If we involve the Aboriginal people in the sentencing process, the sentencing process becomes a much more collegiate, constructive, cooperative, positive and collaborative process than merely the imposition of punishment . . . The trouble is that these courts are measured in terms of their impact on recidivism rates, which is a very short-term, blinkered and narrow way of assessing their efficacy.[22]

[16] Elena Marchetti, 'How the Mainstream Criminal Court System is Still Getting it Wrong' (2011) 7(26) *Indigenous Law Bulletin* 27, 30.

[17] Elena Marchetti and Kathleen Daly, 'Indigenous Sentencing Courts: Towards a Theoretical and Jurisprudential Model' (2007) 29 *Sydney Law Review* 415, 416.

[18] Kathleen Daly and Gitana Proietti-Scifoni, '"The Elders Know . . . The White Man Don't Know": Offenders' Views of the Nowra Circle Court' (2011) 7(24) *Indigenous Law Bulletin* 17.

[19] Elliott Johnston, Commonwealth, Royal Commission into Aboriginal Deaths in Custody, *National Report, Overview and Recommendations* (1991) 1.

[20] Kate Auty and Daniel Briggs, 'Koori Court: Magistrates Court (Koori Court) Act 2002)' (2004) 8 *Law Text Culture* 7, 10.

[21] Nigel Stobbs and Geraldine Mackenzie, 'Evaluating the Performance of Indigenous Sentencing Courts' (2009) 13(2) *Australian Indigenous Law Review* 90; Auty and Briggs, ibid 19. Some have considered them to be a form of therapeutic justice and have described them as problem-solving courts: Arie Freiberg, 'Non-Adversarial Approaches to Criminal Justice' (2007) 16 *Journal of Judicial Administration* 196; Bridget McAsey, 'A Critical Evaluation of the Koori Court Division of the Victorian Magistrates' Court' (2005) 10 *Deakin Law Review* 654, 660.

[22] Standing Committee on Aboriginal and Torres Strait Islander Affairs, Parliament of Western Australia, Perth, 30 March 2010 [174] (Justice Wayne Martin, Supreme Court of Western Australia); see also Daly and Proietti-Scifoni, above n 18.

Indigenous sentencing courts vary between jurisdictions and courts; however they share some common features.[23] Generally the offender must be Indigenous, he or she must have entered a guilty plea and agreed to have the matter heard in an Indigenous sentencing court. Indigenous Elders or Indigenous community representatives generally sit with the judicial officer in, primarily, an advisory role. While the magistrate or judge ultimately has control over sentencing and must apply state and federal criminal law and procedure in doing so, the process facilitates Elders discussing the offender's situation with the offender in a culturally appropriate manner and facilitates the incorporation of Indigenous knowledge into the sentencing process.[24] Victims are also encouraged to speak of their experience. By virtue of the inclusion of Elders and the voices of victims and offenders, Indigenous sentencing courts can thus provide the possibility of an 'intersectional race and gender approach'.[25]

Most Indigenous sentencing courts operate in the magistrates' court jurisdiction,[26] but since 2008, an Indigenous sentencing court has operated in the Victorian County Court.[27] This is where Morgan's original sentencing hearing took place. The County Court is the major trial court in Victoria; it has a wider jurisdiction than the magistrates' courts and can hear serious charges which are often associated with domestic and family violence.[28] Similar to other Indigenous sentencing courts, the primary objective of the County Koori Court is to ensure 'greater participation of the Aboriginal community in the sentencing process of the County Court'.[29]

The Case of Steelie Morgan

Steelie Morgan pleaded guilty to several criminal offences that involved serious violence.[30] He appeared for sentencing before the County Koori Court with Lawson J presiding. In sentencing Morgan, Lawson J was able to consider the usual sentencing factors, but she also heard the views of Elders and was able to consider them. As well as considering rehabilitative factors the judge observed that the violence had occurred over a period of months and she also considered the difference in age and size between Morgan and the victim, emphasising the victim's particular vulnerability.[31] While she recognised Morgan's efforts towards rehabilitation and the way in which he had engaged with the Indigenous Elders as part of the County Koori Court process[32] she also observed that engaging with the Indigenous

[23] Marchetti and Daly, above n 17, 421.

[24] Daly, above n 15, 11. Sometimes elders are remunerated: see Roseanne Nettleton, 'Remuneration and Other Conditions for Indigenous Elders in Indigenous Courts' (2010) 20 *Journal of Judicial Administration* 60.

[25] Marchetti, above n 16, 29.

[26] Elena Marchetti, 'Australian Indigenous Sentencing Courts: Restoring Culture in the Sentencing Court Process' in Jane Bolitho, Jasmine Bruce and Gail Mason (eds) *Restorative Justice Adults and Emerging Practice* (Federation Press, 2012) 100, 102.

[27] *County Court Act 1958* (Vic) ss 4, 4a, 4b. See also Zoe Dawkins et al, County Court of Victoria and Victorian Department of Justice, *County Koori Court: Final Evaluation Report* (2011).

[28] See *County Court Act 1958* (Vic) s 36A. See also *Sentencing Act 1991* (Vic) ss 113A–113B.

[29] Explanatory Memorandum, County Court Amendment (Koori Court) Bill 2008 (Vic) 1.

[30] *R v Morgan* [2009] VCC 2013 (3 July 2009).

[31] Ibid [21].

[32] Ibid [42].

sentencing court process was not a matter that could be used in mitigation.[33] Ultimately she imposed a total sentence of three years and six months' imprisonment, with a minimum non-parole period of 18 months.[34]

Morgan appealed against the sentence on the basis that it was manifestly excessive and that the judge had erred in her assessment of the significance of his participation in the County Koori Court process. Unusually the Crown conceded both points and brought the matter on quickly so that Morgan could be resentenced.[35] The Court of Appeal (Maxwell P and Buchanan JA) accepted the Crown's concessions and found that Morgan's 'active participation in the process was a factor that mitigated punishment'.[36] In contrast to the Indigenous sentencing court, the Court of Appeal had not had the opportunity to hear from the Elders directly. The Court of Appeal accepted that 'rehabilitation must be treated as paramount in these circumstances' and reduced the sentence.[37]

There was substantial media interest in the outcome of the appeal.[38] It was suggested that the Court of Appeal had effectively set a precedent that a defendant's engagement with an Indigenous sentencing court was necessarily a mitigating factor.[39] This critique was misplaced, as the Court of Appeal held that engagement in the Indigenous sentencing court process was not inevitably a mitigating factor, although it found it was in Morgan's particular case. It was also suggested that the Court of Appeal's approach to sentencing sent a message that family violence is not taken seriously.[40] One article[41] inferred that it was the Indigenous sentencing court that downplayed the seriousness of Morgan's violence when, actually, the County Koori Court, after considering the harm to the victim, the offender's rehabilitative efforts and Elders' views, had sentenced him to serve a significant period of actual imprisonment.[42]

The Feminist Judgment

The feminist judgment is written as that of a third judge on the Court of Appeal (appeals from the County Court are normally heard by two judges of the Court of Appeal). The feminist judgment, like the original sentencing judgment, emphasises the victim's voice and experience and the Elders' views as key considerations in sentencing. It takes into account the defendant's efforts towards rehabilitation, however it finds that the mere act of participating in a sentencing conversation should not generally affect the sentencing outcome. The feminist judgment reemphasises the intersectional methodology underlying Indigenous

[33] Ibid.
[34] Ibid [56].
[35] *R v Morgan* (2010) 24 VR 230 [7]; there was a third ground of appeal that was not pressed.
[36] Ibid [33], [37].
[37] Ibid [42].
[38] See for example Richard Guilliatt, 'In Black and White' *The Australian* (online), 22 October 2010 <http://www.theaustralian.com.au/news/features/justice-in-black-and-white/story-e6frg8h6-1225942356421>; Norrie Ross, 'Koori Reprieve for Teen's "Shamed" Attacker', *Herald Sun* (online), 22 February 2010 <http://www.news.com.au/national-news/koori-reprieve-for-teens-shamed-attacker/story-e6frfkvr-1225833209499>.
[39] Guilliatt, ibid.
[40] Ibid.
[41] Ibid.
[42] Marchetti, above n 16, 28.

sentencing courts. It stresses that the aim of Indigenous sentencing courts is to make the justice process more culturally appropriate so that Indigenous people's participation in the sentencing process is improved, and so that the process is more meaningful not only for the offender, but for the victim and for the Indigenous community more widely.

R v MORGAN

Court of Appeal

Marsley JA

28 January, 19 February 2010
[2010] VSCA 15

43 Marsley JA. The facts from which this appeal against sentence arises are unfortunately all too common in Indigenous communities, and indeed in non-Indigenous Australian society as well. They involve violence against partners. The facts are outlined below. What makes this case particularly unsettling is the young ages of the people involved, which, although not necessarily uncommon for partner violence offences heard in Indigenous sentencing courts across the country, is indicative of a trend amongst teenagers and young adults to resolve disputes using violence. This trend is even more troubling when it involves situations of partner violence.

44 The original sentencing decision was made in the Koori Court Division of the County Court (the Koori Court) on 3 July 2009. Steelie Morgan pleaded guilty to eight counts of causing injury intentionally, two counts of common assault, one count of threat to kill and one count of false imprisonment. Maxwell P and Buchanan JA in their joint judgment outline the sentences imposed for each charge by the sentencing judge. The sentences imposed resulted in a total effective sentence of three years and six months. A minimum non-parole period of 18 months was imposed. Her Honour stated that had it not been for the guilty plea, she would have imposed a sentence of four years and six months with a non-parole period of two years and nine months. The appellant had already served 57 days in detention prior to his sentencing hearing.

45 This appeal involves three grounds; two are being pressed and are therefore relevant for our consideration. The first ground of appeal is that the original sentence was manifestly excessive; and the second is that the appellant's participation in the Koori Court process should have been taken into account as a mitigating factor in sentencing. Interestingly, the Crown has made concessions in relation to these two grounds of appeal, but as the High Court made clear in *GAS v The Queen*, which involved an appeal from the Supreme Court of Victoria, 'it is for the sentencing judge, alone, to decide the sentence to be imposed'.[1] This is despite any understanding or agreement that has been reached by the Crown and the defence in relation to what submissions will be made regarding the sentence to be imposed. None of that binds the judge tasked with the decision of sentencing. As the High Court observed:[2]

---

[1] (2004) 217 CLR 198 at 211.
[2] At 211.

> In deciding the sentence, the judge must apply to the facts as found the relevant law and sentencing principles. It is for the judge, assisted by the submissions of counsel, to decide and apply the law. There may be an understanding between counsel as to the submissions of law that they will make, but that does not bind the judge in any sense. The judge's responsibility to find and apply the law is not circumscribed by the conduct of counsel.

46 Similarly, while in this case the Crown has chosen to make concessions, this Court is not bound by the Crown's concessions, but must determine the appeal based on an application of the relevant law.

The Facts

47 Although Maxwell P and Buchanan JA in their joint judgment list the facts to which this appeal against sentence relates, it is necessary for me to make reference to some of those facts in order to highlight aspects that typify acts of violence perpetrated by males against their female partners. All too often, such acts occur in private and have therefore historically been viewed as less significant in the eyes of the law. Of course, we now know that the victims of such violence often endure long and torturous treatment at the hands of someone they had chosen to love and trust. Many victims are also unable to seek help, because of fear and powerlessness.

48 The charges in this appeal related to incidents of violence against Steelie Morgan's partner at the time, who was identified as 'X' by the sentencing judge. I will identify the victim in the same way because I trust that Her Honour would have used 'X' after having consulted with the Koori Court Elders, probably as a way to protect her identity in such a close-knit community, as Indigenous communities often are.

49 As with many victims of domestic violence, X did not appear at the sentencing hearing, nor did she provide a victim impact statement, but she did provide statements to the police about how the appellant's actions had affected her. The actions of the appellant occurred between 31 December 2007 and 16 March 2008, not an overly long period of time, but a time during which X was subjected to a number of fearsome and violent attacks by the appellant. X was only 15 years of age when she met the appellant, and the appellant was aged 24, both being quite young considering the seriousness of the trauma and actions experienced and inflicted. Disturbingly, the assaults commenced within the first week of X having met the appellant. The assaults perpetrated against X were born out of jealousy and control, typical of violence inflicted by males against their partners. The injuries were caused by both the appellant's own hands and by using other instruments commonly found around the home, such as tools, cooking pots, knives, forks and garden hoses. On top of the physical abuse, the appellant terrorised X by threatening to kill her, controlling her actions and movements, imprisoning her in her own home, and refusing to let her speak freely with her family. In describing the impact of this abuse on X, the sentencing judge referred to the following distressing statement made by X to the police:[3]

---

[3] *R v Morgan* (unreported, County Court, 3 July 2009) at [20].

> I was scum on the street. I felt dead inside. I felt so low, I thought about walking in front of a car. I never felt this low. I was so scared for my life and my family so I was spinning out thinking that this was how it was going to be. This is how my life turned out.

50 X was therefore paralysed, not only by her fear for her own safety, but also by her fear for the safety of her family. According to the facts outlined by the sentencing judge, X had made attempts to leave the relationship but the abuse that followed at the hands of the appellant had both physically and psychologically stopped her from leaving. It was only when the police arrived at the place at which X and the appellant were at the time living, that X was able to seek their assistance to leave. Had it not been for her parents reporting her missing to the police, X may have suffered many more months or years of abuse.

51 These facts led to 12 charges to which the appellant pleaded guilty. They were quite serious charges, which fell within the jurisdiction of the County Court. The sentence hearing was ultimately transferred to the Koori Court Division of the County Court, where Elders from the appellant's community participated in the process. It is from this culturally appropriate process that this appeal arises.

52 It is convenient to deal first with the second ground of appeal, that is, whether or not participation in a Koori Court process should be treated as a mitigating factor in sentencing, since it involves a question of law that goes to the heart of a Koori Court process. The outcome of this ground of appeal impacts on the determination of the first ground of appeal, namely whether or not the original sentence was manifestly excessive.

Mitigating effect of participation in Koori Court process

53 As noted already, the sentencing in this case took place in the Koori Court Division of the County Court. This involved the appellant participating in a sentencing conversation with community Elders and the sentencing judge. The ground of appeal raised by the appellant is that Her Honour erred in holding that participation in the sentencing conversation was not a matter that could be used in mitigation of sentence. She said:

> You consented to participate in the sentencing conversation and that is not an easy process for any offender. It is a very challenging process. The fact that you did so is not a matter that can be used in mitigation of sentence but your participation is by consent and the mere fact of participation does give some real insight into your present circumstances and also does underscore the genuineness of your expressed desire to change.[4]

54 Her Honour's statement reflected a view that relevant factors which are brought to the sentencing court's attention as a result of an offender's participation in a sentencing conversation with community Elders and other court participants may affect the sentencing outcome but participation in and of itself is not a mitigating factor.

---

[4] At [42].

55 I have had the advantage of reading the reasons of Maxwell P and Buchanan JA in draft. They accept that Her Honour erred, and that the appellant's participation in the process was indeed a factor that mitigated punishment. They do so on the basis that sentencing conversations are designed to further the reformation of Indigenous offenders, and that participation in this process should therefore mitigate punishment. Respectfully, I disagree on this ground of appeal, for reasons I will now explain.

56 In my view, the mere act of participating in a sentencing conversation should be distinguished from relevant facts and considerations that emerge through the conversation which can be taken into account in considering sentencing. I can find no authority for the principle that participating in a conversation, even if it is an 'active' participation in the sense that the offender embraced the spirit of the process, should affect the sentence outcome. It is the information garnered during the sentencing conversation and the effect such a process has on the offender's behaviour that should be taken into account as either an aggravating or mitigating factor.

57 Section 4G of the County Court Act 1958 sets out the sentencing procedure for Koori Court matters, and the statements and other information the court may accept. However, there is no provision in this Act as to the effect this procedure should have on sentencing outcomes.

58 Section 5 of the Sentencing Act 1991 sets out sentencing guidelines, including the purposes of sentencing. Under s 5(2) courts are required to have regard to, inter alia –

> (daa) the impact of the offence on any victim of the offence; and
> (da) the personal circumstances of any victim of the offence; and
> . . .
> (g) the presence of any aggravating or mitigating factor concerning the offender or of any other relevant circumstances.

59 Nowhere in either the County Court Act 1958 or the Sentencing Act 1991 is there any guidance as to the impact the sentencing conversation may have on sentencing outcomes. Given this lack of clarity in the legislation, it is appropriate to seek guidance from extraneous materials. In particular, it is helpful to understand what role Parliament intended for the Koori Court sentencing conversations, and in particular what emphasis it placed on offenders' participation and reformation. Such an understanding can guide this Court's interpretation of whether participation in a sentencing conversation should be taken into account in mitigation of sentence.

60 The Explanatory Memorandum to the County Court Amendment (Koori Court) Bill 2008 sets out the objective for establishing the Koori Court as:

> ensuring greater participation of the Aboriginal community in the sentencing process of the County Court through the role to be played in that process by the Aboriginal elder or respected person and others.[5]

61 In his second reading speech on the Bill, Attorney General Hulls expanded on this:

[5] Explanatory Memorandum, County Court Amendment (Koori Court) Bill 2008 (Vic), cl 1.

> Establishing a Koori Court division in the County Court acknowledges the importance of incorporating indigenous communities' cultural beliefs and practices in our justice system. It is intended that this will produce fair and equitable treatment for indigenous people and address the underlying cause of criminal activity. These aims are best achieved through a partnership between the indigenous community and government which fosters trust, understanding and a commitment through the direct involvement and participation of the indigenous community in the development of justice solutions. . . .
>
> In essence, this model allows for the sentencing process to be more culturally. accessible, grounded in indigenous communities' efforts to promote rehabilitation and promote sanctions which are comprehensible to the indigenous community. . . .
>
> The model is designed to break down the disengagement that many indigenous people have experienced with the criminal justice system. . . .
>
> It is clear from the experience of the Koori Magistrates Court that one of the keys to its success is the participation of the Aboriginal elder or respected person who symbolises that the offence is not condoned by either the indigenous or the non-indigenous community and that any sentence imposed is only carried out after information is provided to the magistrate by the Aboriginal elder or respected person.
>
> In this way, the sentencing process as well as the sentence itself is community owned so that when a crime is committed against the wider community it is also seen as being against indigenous community standards.[6]

62 Hence, while the Attorney General spoke of the Koori Court acting to improve participation of the Indigenous community in the justice system, breaking down disengagement and promoting both rehabilitation and comprehensible sanctions, he made no reference to any intention that participation should mitigate sentencing outcomes for individuals; indeed, his emphasis was on involving and empowering communities. All other speakers on the Bill supported these concerns, and spoke of increasing community ownership of the administration of law, and promoting community awareness of appropriate standards of behaviour.[7]

63 Together these comments indicate that Parliament's intention in establishing the Koori Court Division of the County Court was to encourage greater participation by Indigenous people in the criminal sentencing process, by making that process more culturally appropriate and directly involving Indigenous communities and standards in sentencing decisions. There is also a clear acknowledgement of the importance of sanctions that meet community expectations.

64 Nowhere in the Explanatory Memorandum to the Bill, the parliamentary debates, or indeed the Act itself is there expressed any intention that participation in the Koori Court process should of itself be a factor to be taken into account to mitigate the sentences of individual offenders. And while there are references to the rehabilitation of Indigenous offenders being an important outcome of the Court, there are as many if not more references to its role in incorporating into the legal system Indigenous community

---

[6] Victoria, *Parliamentary Debates*, Legislative Assembly, 31 July 2008, 2884–5.

[7] At 3088–3106.

standards and perspectives. Indeed, the whole process of the sentencing conversation with the presence of community Elders can be seen as designed to achieve this objective.

65 If, on appeal, this Court determines that the offender's participation in the Koori Court process should serve as a mitigating factor, and thereby changes the spirit within which the original sentence was determined, it could in fact be argued that this Court would be undermining the incorporation of Indigenous views, and undermining attempts made to create a process that is more culturally appropriate and inclusive. Such action should occur only in exceptional circumstances where there is clear evidence of an error of law on the part of the sentencing judge. Hence in my view, the role of the Koori Court is multi-dimensional, with the promotion of Koori community standards and values being at least as important as the rehabilitation of individual offenders. The problem, as with all sentencing decisions, is how these goals are to be balanced in individual cases.

66 I turn now to the cases and the extent to which they assist in understanding this issue. *R v Engert*[8] has been referred to as authority for the proposition that sentence determinations involve deciding the influence that various factors will have on discretion in particular circumstances. While it is hard to disagree with this view, it does not touch on the issue at hand – namely, to what extent is participation in a sentencing conversation able to be regarded as a mitigating factor? Similarly, *Rogers and Murray v The Queen*[9] states that social, economic and other disadvantages associated with Aboriginality may be relevant mitigating factors. This also is not in doubt, and in my view, has to a large extent been addressed by the offender's participation in the Koori Court process. This Court also, however, needs to determine how such mitigating factors should be weighed against aggravating factors such as the extent of harm caused and the need to uphold community standards.

67 *Neal v The Queen*[10] recognises the duty of the sentencing court to take into account facts which exist only because of a person's membership of a particular racial or ethnic group, which is a point made in the judgment of Brennan J.[11] Equally relevant however is the judgment of Murphy J, who observed: 'in sentencing the court should consider the offence, the character and record of the defendant and all mitigating and aggravating circumstances'.[12] While it is possible to identify mitigating circumstances, namely the remorse and potential rehabilitation of the appellant, equally important are the aggravating circumstances, namely the cruel and degrading treatment Morgan inflicted on the victim. Following *R v Engert*, both of these important factors need to be weighed in this sentencing determination, and that is precisely what the sentencing judge did in her determination.

---

[8] (1995) 84 A Crim R 67.
[9] (1989) 44 A Crim R 301.
[10] (1982) 149 CLR 305.
[11] At 326.
[12] At 319.

68 Having found that the mere act of participation in a sentencing conversation is not of itself a mitigating factor (even if it is an 'active' type of participation, which in a Koori Court process it normally will be since it is difficult to participate in a sentencing conversation without actively engaging in it), the question I must consider next is whether the conversation revealed other relevant factors sufficient to justify a review of the sentencing decision. In particular, what weight should be given to the victim's suffering in this case, and to the need to denounce widespread domestic violence perpetrated against Indigenous women and children, and how should that be balanced against recognising the rehabilitative efforts made by the appellant as a result of having participated in the Koori Court process?

69 Reference has been made to the reports of the Australian Law Reform Commission and the Law Reform Commission of Western Australia on Aboriginal Customary Laws.[13] These reports acknowledge the importance of 'shaming' as a traditional punishment, and infer that participation in Koori Court facilitates such shaming. There are also many reports that reveal the extent of harm inflicted on Indigenous women and children through domestic violence, and the desire of their communities to have this harm addressed, and condemned, by the Australian legal system. Indeed the Law Reform Commission of Western Australia makes specific reference in its report to the fact that '[i]t has been well documented that Aboriginal women and children are victims of violence and sexual abuse at a much higher rate than non-Aboriginal women and children' and cites a number of statistics and reports in support of this claim.[14]

70 Indigenous women, in particular are often disadvantaged as victims of family and domestic violence because of their distrust of police as an agency that might come to their assistance if they find themselves subjected to such violence. Police have historically assisted in the removal of Aboriginal children, intimidated and mistreated Indigenous people in the carrying out of their duties, and have mistreated perpetrators of domestic violence while they were detained in custody, all matters that the Law Reform Commission of Western Australia identified as having led to the under-reporting of family and domestic violence by Indigenous victims.[15]

71 Additionally, Indigenous victims of family and domestic violence often face cultural barriers that may prevent them from reporting or informing authorities about such violence or abuse. They may not be comfortable with discussing the matter with a male authority figure or their traditional laws may prevent them from doing so. Stories have emerged of situations where victims faced retaliation from family members or the perpetrator if they sought help.[16] These are all factors that make life as an Indigenous

[13] Australian Law Reform Commission, *The Recognition of Aboriginal Customary Laws*, Report No 31 (1986); Law Reform Commission of Western Australia (LRC(WA)), *Aboriginal Customary Laws*, Project 94 (2006).
[14] LRC(WA) at 19.
[15] At 284–285.
[16] At 287–288.

victim of family and domestic violence more complex than that of a non-Indigenous victim.

72 In many ways then, Indigenous women who have domestic violence inflicted upon them are doubly victimised – as female victims of male violence, and as Indigenous people suffering the long-term consequences of dispossession and disadvantage. In addressing one form of disadvantage it is important not to overlook the other. For this reason, it is important to ensure that criminal justice processes are not only more culturally appropriate for Indigenous offenders of family and domestic violence (and of course, of any other type of offence) but also more mindful and reflective of the experiences of a victim of such violence.

73 For many Indigenous communities, the denunciation of violence against women and children is an important consideration. An important rationale for Koori Courts, as I have already mentioned, is to enable Koori community standards to be reflected in criminal court processes. To a certain extent this occurred in the sentencing conversation – the sentencing judge notes that both of the Elders who participated emphasised the importance of the appellant understanding the effects of his behaviour on the victim.[17] They also emphasised the importance of establishing acceptable standards of behaviour by men towards women.[18] By extension, it is important for Australian courts to endorse this message, and not to appear to accept a different standard for Indigenous males simply by virtue of their race and culture. While the historical disadvantage of Indigenous males needs to be addressed, this should not come at the expense of appropriate punishment for the suffering inflicted on their female victims. The sentencing judge noted this when she said: 'It is important for courts to condemn all abusive relationships and domestic violence on behalf of the community'.[19]

74 It could be argued that the appellant voluntarily participated in what might be considered a traditional form of punishment as part of his involvement in the sentencing conversation; that of apologising to the Elders and as a consequence, being subjected to a form of 'shaming' during the hearing. Assuming this is correct, the Law Reform Commission of Western Australia made it clear in its report that:

> traditional Aboriginal law may not have developed adequate responses to family violence and sexual abuse because this type of behaviour did not occur or did not occur to the same extent in traditional Aboriginal societies as it does now.[20]

75 For this reason the Commission recognised the need for strengthening 'both Aboriginal customary law and mainstream responses to family violence', arguing 'Aboriginal people should be encouraged to develop cultural or customary law responses to family violence and sexual abuse'

[17] *R v Morgan* (unreported, County Court, 3 July 2009) at [45].
[18] At [46].
[19] At [51].
[20] LRC(WA) at 22.

while at the same time ensuring 'Aboriginal victims of family violence and sexual abuse . . . have full access to mainstream criminal justice responses'.[21] This further supports the view that participation in the Koori Court process, as a hybrid customary-mainstream sentencing court process, should not be a factor of its own accord to mitigate sentences, particularly those involving family or domestic violence or sexual abuse against women and children. Instead, the Koori Court process is the vehicle through which offenders are given the opportunity to access relevant support and rehabilitation programs. Each individual offender then decides whether or not to embrace these opportunities and make a better life for him or her self. In the case of the appellant, the Koori Court and ensuing sentencing conversation opened up a world where he was able to engage with his community and re-connect with his Indigenous family, get to know and respect his Elders, and address the difficulties which had been plaguing him for much of his young adult life. The appellant courageously jumped into this world feet-first and according to many who gave references in support of the appellant, in a manner which is to be commended. As a result, the appellant has expressed shame and remorse for his actions and has taken responsibility for the pain and suffering caused to X. The fact that the Koori Court's rehabilitative function seems to have worked so well for the appellant, when in the past other opportunities presented through various court orders have failed, speaks volumes about the efficacy of the process. However, this positive outcome does not detract from the need for sentencing decisions to also address victim harm and the fact that the appellant has previously been convicted of offences involving violence. It also does not detract from Parliament's clear intention that the Koori Court should provide a vehicle for Indigenous community views, standards and values to be acknowledged in the legal system, which they were in this case through the sentencing conversation. To overturn the original decision in the absence of clear error would undermine this parliamentary intention, and devalue the role of the Koori Court.

76 The appellant has done well and the sentencing judge acknowledged this and took this fact into account when sentencing. As I outline in more detail below, she did not make an error of law when she balanced the appellant's prospects of rehabilitation as a result of having voluntarily participated in a sentencing conversation irrespective of the sentencing outcome with other matters, particularly deterrence.

Manifestly excessive

77 According to s 5 of the Sentencing Act 1991, when sentencing an offender a court needs to balance the following competing purposes: (1) to punish the offender; (2) to send a message of deterrence to the offender and other people in the community; (3) to facilitate rehabilitation; (4) to send a message of condemnation in relation to the type of offence that has been committed; and (5) to protect the community. Additionally, a court must

[21] At 22 (emphasis added).

take into account the factors listed in s 5(2) of the Sentencing Act 1991, which include matters such as the nature and gravity of the offence; the impact of the offence on the victim and the personal circumstances of the victim; the injury, loss or damage resulting from the commission of the offence; whether the offender pleaded guilty to the offence and, if so, at what stage of the proceedings was the plea tendered; and the offender's previous character.

78 The task of sentencing is often an arduous one particularly when confronted with a set of facts such as those currently before this court, where competing factors are difficult to reconcile. Sitting on the side of a harsher penalty are factors such as the appellant's prior convictions for violence, possibly stemming from the appellant's history of drug and alcohol abuse which he did not take steps to address despite being offered opportunities to do so through previous court orders; the seriousness and gravity of the offences; the psychological harm and physical injury suffered by X; and the fact that the appellant, although quite young, was still substantially older than X. On the other hand, the appellant pleaded guilty at the committal hearing; showed remorse for his actions; has had a difficult family life and upbringing; has suffered substance abuse problems; has accepted responsibility for his actions; and has actively and enthusiastically participated in rehabilitation programs whilst he has been on bail for the current offences, all of which weigh on the side of a lighter penalty.

79 The sentencing judge took all of these factors into account and in my view, balanced the need to punish and deter the offender with the need to appropriately facilitate his rehabilitation. As well as deterring this specific offender from repeating this behaviour, when one considers the importance of combating family and domestic violence, particularly in Indigenous communities, it is necessary to also ensure that penalties properly reflect a denunciation of such behaviour. This denunciation sends a strong message to the Indigenous community and the community generally that domestic violence will not be tolerated in any Australian community. The changes that have occurred in the appellant's life as a result of embracing opportunities for rehabilitation offered as a result of having participated in the Koori Court process are, of course, to be applauded and have quite clearly been taken into account by the sentencing judge as outlined in her Reasons for Sentence.[22] The opportunities for rehabilitation resulted from the appellant having participated in a sentencing conversation during the course of the Koori Court process and his prospects for rehabilitation are therefore closely linked to that process. The manner in which I have accounted for the appellant's prospects of rehabilitation in coming to a decision regarding this appeal, has already been outlined above in my reasons for deciding that the appellant's participation in the Koori Court should not be treated as a mitigating factor.

80 Therefore, after taking into account what I consider to be the relevant factors for making a determination in relation to the ground of manifestly

---

[22] *R v Morgan* (unreported, County Court, 3 July 2009) at [31]–[49].

excessive, I take a different view from that of the majority, in finding that the sentencing judge had properly weighed the various competing purposes of sentencing.

81 I would therefore dismiss the appeal.

Part IV

Interpreting Equality

Family Law

22

Commentary on *U v U*

RACHAEL FIELD

Introduction

The case of *U v U*,[1] decided by the High Court of Australia in 2002, is the leading Australian case concerning international relocation in family law. It involved a mother who, on the breakdown of her marriage in Australia, sought to permanently relocate to her home in India with her daughter. The father, born in India but an Australian citizen, opposed the application and it was refused. The mother appealed to the Full Court of the Family Court, arguing that the court had not correctly weighed up the two proposals put to the court by the parties, and had erred in placing too great a focus on the issue of the father's contact with the child. The Full Court dismissed the appeal. The mother appealed further to the High Court of Australia and again her appeal was dismissed by a majority of 5:2 with Gaudron and Kirby JJ dissenting. The Court held that the Family Court had not erred in weighing up the parties' proposals and reaching a decision in accordance with the best interests of the child. Consequently, the mother and child were forced to reside in the Sydney-Wollongong area, away from the mother's support networks and employment opportunities which were in India. The mother could only return to India if she left the child behind.

Relocation cases in Australia have been acknowledged as 'increasingly controversial',[2] and 'are widely accepted as personally and legally very difficult'.[3] As a subset of post-separation parenting matters dealt with under the provisions of Part VII of the *Family Law Act 1975* (Cth) (the Act), they 'evoke strong emotional responses'.[4] Relocation cases involve a dispute between parents in which one 'parent's wish to move impacts on (existing) parenting regimes',[5] or will 'make it more difficult for a child to spend time with a parent'.[6] Whilst 'relocation cases come before the court with regularity' the Act itself does not have any specific provisions dealing with relocation, and the term 'relocation' is not defined

[1] (2002) 211 CLR 238.

[2] Juliet Behrens, Bruce Smyth and Rae Kaspiew, 'Australian Family Law Court Decisions on Relocation: Dynamics in Parents' Relationships Across Time' (2009) 23 *Australian Journal of Family Law* 222, 223.

[3] Briony Horsfall and Rae Kaspiew, 'Relocation in Separated and Non-Separated Families: Equivocal Evidence from the Social Science Literature' (2010) 24 *Australian Journal of Family Law* 1, 2. See also Patrick Parkinson, 'Freedom of Movement in an Era of Shared Parenting: The Differences in Judicial Approaches to Relocation' (2008) 36 *Federal Law Review* 145, 145.

[4] Janet Richards, 'Children's Rights v Parents' Rights: A Proposed Solution to the Custodial Relocation Conundrum' (1999) 29 *New Mexico Law Review* 245, 245.

[5] Lisa Young, '*U v U*: Reflections on the High Court and Family Law' (2003) 28 *Alternative Law Journal* 78, 78.

[6] Horsfall and Kaspiew, above n 3, 40.

in the Act.[7] This was the case at the time *U v U* was heard in 2002 and remains the case in 2014.

There is now a growing body of Australian[8] and international[9] scholarship on the issue of relocation in family law. *U v U* itself has been the subject of considerable academic analysis and critique.[10] Behrens suggests relocation cases 'provide a focus for political debate about the position of men and women under contemporary Australian family law' because they 'nearly always involve fathers trying to stop mothers from relocating.'[11] *U v U*, an example of a father successfully preventing a mother from relocating, is an apt case for inclusion in the Feminist Judgments Project.

A Feminist Analysis of Relocation Cases Through the Lens of *U v U*

Parkinson claims that 'at the heart of the problem of relocation is the tension between the children's right to maintain a relationship with both parents, and the freedom of movement of the children's primary carer.'[12] This articulation, consistent with the decision in *U v U*, casts the primary care-giver, usually the mother, as someone concerned predominantly with her own personal position and interests, with the father as the party concerned for the best interests of the child.

The Gendered Nature of Relocation Cases

Relocation cases are gendered cases. A recent Australian Institute of Family Studies (AIFS) empirical study of relocation disputes found that 88 per cent of parties applying for orders to relocate were women. It also found that, of the matters studied, relocation occurred in 57 per cent of cases, with 43 per cent of the judgments rejecting the proposed relocation. Eighty per cent of the relationships in the study sample were high-conflict, or involved allegations of abuse or violence. Most of the children in the study sample were in the primary care of their mothers.[13]

[7] Family Law Council, Commonwealth of Australia, *Relocation Report* (2006) 2.

[8] See, eg, literature cited in Behrens, Smyth and Kaspiew, above n 2; Patrick Parkinson, Judy Cashmore and Judi Single, 'The Need for Reality Testing in Relocation Cases' (2010) 44 *Family Law Quarterly* 1; Patrick Parkinson, 'The Realities of Relocation: Messages from Judicial Decisions' (2008) 22 *Australian Journal of Family Law* 35; Joanne Roebuck, '*U v U*: A Chauvinistic Approach to Relocation?' (2003) 17 *Australian Journal of Family Law* 208; Patricia Easteal, Juliet Behrens and Lisa Young, 'Relocation Decisions in Canberra and Perth: A Blurry Snapshot' (2000) 14 *Australian Journal of Family Law* 234; Lisa Young, '*B v B Family Law Reform Act 1995*: Relocating the Rhetoric of Rights' (1997) 21 *Melbourne University Law Review* 722.

[9] See, eg, R George, *Relocation Disputes: Law and Practice in England and New Zealand* (Hart Publishing, 2014); K Waldron, 'A Review of Social Science Research on Post-Divorce Relocation' (2005) 19 *Journal of the American Academy of Matrimonial Lawyers* 337; T Glennon, 'Divided Parents, Shared Children: Conflicting Approaches to Relocation Disputes in the USA' (2008) 4 *Utrecht Law Review* 55.

[10] See, eg, Juliet Behrens, '*U v U*: The High Court on Relocation' (2003) 27 *Melbourne University Law Review* 574; Young, above n 5, 78.

[11] Behrens, ibid.

[12] Parkinson, above n 8, 146.

[13] Rae Kaspiew, Juliet Behrens and Bruce Smyth, 'Relocation Disputes In Separated Families Prior to the 2006 Reforms: An Empirical Study' (2011) 86 *Family Matters* 72, 73–4.

The gendered nature of relocation matters was acknowledged in *B and B: Family Law Reform Act 1995*, where it was recognised that it is only ever the primary care-giver who is stopped from moving post-separation.[14] The parent who does not live with the child is never restricted if they decide they want to relocate. As mothers are most commonly the primary carers of their children, and as the vast majority of applications for relocation orders are made by women, 'the disparate effect this has on women is self-evident'.[15]

The justification for this disparate effect is the statutory principle of 'the best interests of the child'.[16] Preventing a mother from relocating with her child generally ensures that the child remains in close proximity to the father to enable contact. Contact between the father and the child is therefore elevated over the needs or interests of the mother as primary carer; the child's best interests are seen as better served by the child's contact with the father than by supporting the psychological well-being and life opportunities of the mother. Further, in matters where family violence is an issue, denial of an application to relocate elevates father–child contact over the safety of the mother and child.

The Best Interests of the Child in Relocation Matters

In *A v A: Relocation Approach*,[17] the Full Court of the Family Court established guidelines as to how trial judges should weigh up which of the parents' proposals would best serve the best interests of the child. In *U v U*, the mother's proposal to relocate back to India was based on the absence of networks of family and friends in Australia, and also the absence of employment opportunities. She was unhappy, lonely, isolated, had few friends, and was dependent on social security.[18] Requiring her to stay in Australia on the terms suggested in the father's proposal meant that she was forced to make sacrifices not asked of the father. Restricting her relocation compounded her social and economic disadvantage.[19]

It could rightly be argued that imposing such a restriction on a mother's movements is a breach of her human rights.[20] However, human rights, or individual rights, arguments do not support a workable feminist approach to relocation under current Australian law. This is because an argument for relocation based on the individual rights of the mother will inevitably be trumped by a father's argument that ongoing contact with him serves the best interests of the child.

Rather, one feasible feminist approach to relocation decision-making would be based on the interconnectedness of the best interests of the child and the primary carer.[21] Restricting the movement of mothers as primary caregivers will inevitably impact negatively on their children.[22] Kirby J, for example, acknowledged in *AMS v AIF* that preventing relocation may impact on the happiness of the residence parent, and this in turn can impact on the child.[23]

[14] (1997) FLC ¶92-755 [10.64].

[15] Young, above n 5, 81.

[16] At the time of *U v U* this principle was enunciated in s 68F of the Act. It can now be found in s 60CC.

[17] (2002) 26 FamLR 510.

[18] *U v U* (2002) 211 CLR 238 [58]–[65]. See also Behrens, above n 10, 576.

[19] Behrens et al, above n 2, 223.

[20] Family Law Council, above n 7, 24.

[21] See Martha A Fineman, *The Illusion of Equality, The Rhetoric and Reality of Divorce Reform* (University of Chicago Press, 1991); Carol Smart and Selma Sevenhuijsen (eds), *Child Custody and the Politics of Gender* (Routledge, 1989).

[22] Behrens et al, above n 2.

[23] (1999) 199 CLR 160 [145].

Easteal et al refer to *Taylor v Barker*[24] in which 'the mother's happiness and contentment was a determinative factor, based on the Family Report';[25] and in *P and P*, Brown FM stated that the mother's 'level of frustration and unhappiness may have implications for her future psychological health and her capacity to parent to the full extent of her potential.'[26]

Allowing a mother who is a primary carer to relocate to support her needs and interests is therefore not only consistent with her human rights, but is also in the best interests of the child.[27] This is not to ignore the need to weigh other relevant factors in the 'best interests' balance, including the importance of the child's contact with their father. However, it is possible to maintain father–child contact without adversely impacting the mother and child's interests (for example, by requiring the father to move also).

Jonathan Crowe's feminist judgment recognises the interconnectedness of the mother and child's interests as considered above. Crowe also raises a further point about the best interests of the child standard. He considers competing interpretations of the notion that the child's best interests are paramount, and prefers the 'weak' view of paramountcy, which is to say that the court can consider other interests alongside the child's best interests, and the latter will not always be trumps. He rejects the 'strong' view of paramountcy because, in the relocation context, it has a systematically adverse impact on women – a consideration which he has argued elsewhere is a legitimate form of judicial reasoning.[28]

Conclusion

The rewritten judgment proposes a new question for the court in relocation cases: 'Will the child's best interests be affected by relocation to such an extent as to justify limiting the residential parent's freedom of movement?' In finding in favour of the mother's application to relocate, the judgment does not devalue the role of the father in the child's life.[29] Rather, the judgment acts on the reality that in this case, serving the primary carer's interests also served the best interests of the child, while at the same time emphasising the need to consider the primary carer's interests in their own right.

[24] (2007) 37 Fam LR 461 [128].

[25] Easteal et al, above n 8, 20.

[26] Ibid 19, referring to *P and P* [2006] FMCAfam 518 [22].

[27] Adiva Sifris et al, *Submission to the Family Law Council Regarding the Inquiry into Relocation of Children in Family Law* (Castan Centre for Human Rights Law, 2006) 12.

[28] Jonathan Crowe, The Role of Contextual Meaning in Judicial Interpretation' (2013) 41 *Federal Law Review* 417.

[29] Behrens et al, above n 2, 6.

U. . . . . APPELLANT;
APPLICANT,

AND

U. . . . . RESPONDENT;
RESPONDENT,

[2002] HCA 36

ON APPEAL FROM THE FAMILY COURT OF AUSTRALIA

HC OF A 2002

April 11; *Sep* 5 2002

Crowe J

178 CROWE J. This case concerns a young girl, Neha (101). The parties are her parents. Ms Udyavar was born in Mumbai. She trained as a shipbroker in Mumbai and London and has worked in the shipping industry in both locations. Mr Udyavar was also born in Mumbai. He came to Australia as a young man and trained as an accountant. The parties married in Mumbai in August 1989, then took up residence in Sydney. Neha was born in Australia in March 1994. Ms Udyavar acted as her primary caregiver and Mr Udyavar continued with his paid employment.

179 The marriage broke down in July 1995. Ms Udyavar left the couple's home and took her daughter to Mumbai, where her parents live. She left a note for Mr Udyavar, who followed them to Mumbai that August. The Family Court at Bandra, Mumbai, made a consent order that Neha continue to reside with her mother. Mr Udyavar went back to Australia, but he returned to Mumbai on five occasions between August 1995 and January 1998 to visit Neha. Ms Udyavar decided to attempt reconciliation. She returned to Australia with Neha in January 1998. The reconciliation failed and she decided to return to Mumbai. However, Mr Udyavar had commenced proceedings to prevent Neha from leaving Australia, without notice to her mother, and Neha's name had been placed on a watch list. Ms Udyavar was therefore prevented from returning with Neha to resume her life in Mumbai. She instead moved with Neha to Wollongong, where they reside today.

180 The matter was heard by O'Ryan J in the Family Court of Australia. His Honour made a parenting order in favour of Ms Udyavar, but the order requires her to reside in the Sydney-Wollongong area. She cannot return with Neha to Mumbai. Ms Udyavar appealed this outcome unsuccessfully to the Full Court of the Family Court. She now appeals to this Court. The appeal should be allowed. The primary judge failed to properly identify the parties' preferred orders and misapplied the legal principles for deciding between them.

(101) Pseudonyms are employed throughout this judgment to protect the child's anonymity. Names are used in preference to initials to avoid dehumanising the child and the parties.

The impact of the orders

181 It is important in a case like this to be clear headed about the impact of the orders. Parenting orders have life changing consequences not only for the children who are the subject of the orders, but also for their parents and other affected parties. The evidence accepted at first instance indicates that Ms Udyavar's life in Australia is an isolated one with limited social and professional opportunities. She "is unhappy in Australia and misses her family and friends in India". The primary judge noted that Ms Udyavar has no "family in Australia and apart from three or four friends she [has no] other support". She has, by contrast, "a wide and established circle of friends, family members, extended family and past business contacts in Mumbai".

182 Ms Udyavar, as noted above, has trained as a shipbroker and worked internationally in the shipping industry. She has not been able to find employment in that field in Australia, but has rather been limited to casual clerical and data entry work. She has, by contrast, been offered employment in Mumbai, although she indicated in evidence that she proposed instead to undertake legal studies with a view to starting her own business. Further study would be a real option for her in Mumbai, despite being Neha's primary carer, because she could rely on the support of her family. She would be able to live with her mother in Mumbai, which would further assist her to establish financial independence post-separation. She faces serious barriers to establishing similar independence in Australia.

183 I have dwelt on Ms Udyavar's situation, because the disparity between the opportunities available to her in Sydney-Wollongong compared to those on offer in Mumbai is quite striking. The effect of the orders at first instance on Mr Udyavar has not been as profound. He has lived in Australia since his teenage years, as has his immediate family. He has continued to work as an accountant. He travelled to Mumbai on five occasions between 1995 and 1998 to have contact with Neha, but since the orders at first instance he has not had to do so.

184 A counsellor's report obtained under s 65F of the *Family Law Act* 1975 (Cth) (*FLA*) indicated that Neha is attached to both her parents. The counsellor stated that "[i]deally, [Neha's] best interests would be served by her having frequent and liberal contact with both parents". However, he also noted that Neha's welfare would inevitably be affected by her mother's isolation and lack of opportunities in Australia. The counsellor observed that:

> "Should Ms [Udyavar] be ordered to remain in Australia with [Neha] to facilitate contact between [Neha] and her father, it is unclear how Ms [Udyavar's] distress might manifest itself, and what the implications of this might be for [Neha]. It does appear, however, that the degree of distress might be quite debilitating, as evidenced by her current preoccupation with returning to India."

185 The counsellor further noted that if Ms Udyavar were to return to India without her daughter, Neha "would suffer considerable anxiety and distress", while if Ms Udyavar and Neha both moved to India this would

significantly affect Neha's relationship with her father. The situation, then, was "not one where any clear recommendation is possible." This conclusion illustrates the difficulty and, in some cases, artificiality of seeking to decide parenting matters solely by reference to the best interests of the child, which may be unclear. It is therefore appropriate to turn to the legal framework for approaching such matters.

The legal framework

186 Section 65E of the *FLA* states that "in deciding whether to make a particular parenting order in relation to a child, a court must regard the best interests of the child as the paramount consideration." This standard is sometimes called the *paramountcy principle*. The discretion enlivened by the term "best interests of the child" is limited to some extent by s 68F, which sets out a range of matters the court must consider in determining what is in a child's best interests. However, that provision creates its own range of discretions, requiring the judge to determine both how the factors relate to the case at hand and what weight should be given to each. Section 68F(2)(l) additionally gives the court a general discretion to consider "any other fact or circumstance that the court thinks is relevant".

187 What does s 65E mean when it says the best interests of the child are "paramount"? The term admits of more than one interpretation. A useful framework for categorising different possible approaches to the paramountcy principle is provided by the distinction, recently suggested in an extra-judicial article by Richard Chisholm (102), between *strong* and *weak* interpretations. What Chisholm calls the "strong view" of the principle calls for the court to "identify what orders will be most likely to promote the child's best interests" and then "make those orders" (103). In other words, the strong view assumes that the best interests of the child is the *only* factor that may be considered in making a determination.

188 The "weak view", by contrast, "does *not* necessarily require the court to make whatever order it thinks best for the child, regardless of other things" (104). According to this approach, the "best interests of the child" may sometimes give way to other factors. These might include the interests of the parents or children from other relationships. Both views are consistent with the plain meaning of s 65E. The term "paramount" is defined by the *Macquarie Dictionary* as "above others in rank or authority; superior in power or jurisdiction . . . chief in importance; supreme; pre-eminent". The term might therefore mean that the child's best interests always trump other factors, but it might equally mean that the child's best interests are the *most important* or *primary* consideration, although they may be overridden.

(102) Chisholm, "'The Paramount Consideration': Children's Interests in Family Law", *Australian Journal of Family Law*, vol 16 (2002) 87.

(103) Chisholm, "'The Paramount Consideration': Children's Interests in Family Law", *Australian Journal of Family Law*, vol 16 (2002) 89.

(104) Chisholm, "'The Paramount Consideration': Children's Interests in Family Law", *Australian Journal of Family Law*, vol 16 (2002) 89 (emphasis in original).

189 Chisholm argues that Australian decisions since the late 1980s tend towards a strong interpretation (105). This seems correct, but there are tensions in the case law. The Full Court of the Family Court's decision in *B and B; Family Law Reform Act* 1995 (106) clearly favours the strong view. The Court describes the best interests of the child as the "paramount or pre-eminent consideration" (107); it is the "final determinant" of the orders (108). Later in the judgment, the Court affirms that while "a general right of freedom of movement is a right recognised by Australian law", nonetheless "in proceedings under Pt VII [of the *FLA*] it is a right that cannot prevail over what is considered to be in the best interests of the children in a particular case" (109).

190 This Court had occasion to consider its approach to the paramountcy principle in *AMS v AIF* (110). That case, like *B and B* and the present case, required the Court to decide whether to permit the residential parent to relocate with her child. Kirby J's leading judgment in *AMS* summarises the existing legal principles governing relocation cases (111). A number of these principles are relevant in determining the strength to be attributed to the paramountcy principle. At first glance, however, the principles do not all point in the same direction.

191 Kirby J observed that while the best interests of the child is the paramount consideration in parenting matters, it is not "the 'sole' or 'only' consideration" (112). His Honour went on to say that "a statutory instruction to treat the . . . best interests of the child as the paramount consideration does not oblige a court . . . to ignore the legitimate interests and desires of the parents" (113). Nonetheless, if there is a conflict between the interests of the child and those of the parents, "priority must be accorded to the child's welfare and rights" (114). This last direction seems an endorsement of the strong view, an impression bolstered by the later statement that "the touchstone for the ultimate decision must remain the . . . best interests of the child and not, as such, the wishes and interests of the parents" (115).

192 The Court's decision in *AMS* was subsequently followed by the Full Court of the Family Court in *A v A; Relocation Approach* (116), which took the opportunity to set out general guidelines for dealing with issues of parental relocation. The judgment of the Full Court (comprising Nicholson CJ, Ellis and Coleman JJ) began by noting that "the welfare or best interests of the child as the case may be under the relevant legislation, remains the

(105) Chisholm, "'The Paramount Consideration': Children's Interests in Family Law", *Australian Journal of Family Law*, vol 16 (2002) 87, 89.
(106) (1997) 21 Fam LR 676 (*B and B*).
(107) (1997) 21 Fam LR 676 at [9.32].
(108) (1997) 21 Fam LR 676 at [9.51]. See also [9.58].
(109) (1997) 21 Fam LR 676 at [10.43].
(110) (1999) 199 CLR 160 (*AMS*).
(111) (1999) 199 CLR 160 at [141]–[151].
(112) (1999) 199 CLR 160 at [143]. A similar comment is made by Gaudron J at [95].
(113) (1999) 199 CLR 160 at [144].
(114) (1999) 199 CLR 160 at [144].
(115) (1999) 199 CLR 160 at [145].
(116) (2000) 26 Fam LR 381.

paramount consideration but it is not the sole consideration" (117). Later, however, it is stated that "the ultimate issue is the best interests of the children and to the extent that the freedom of a parent to move impinges upon those interests then it must give way" (118).

193 The interplay between the best interests of the child and parental freedom of movement is complicated by the later statement that "in determining a parenting case that involves a proposal to relocate the residence of a child, the process of evaluating the proposals must have regard to . . . the importance of a party's right to freedom of movement" (119). This direction was somewhat undercut by the subsequent discussion, which made it clear that the parent's freedom of movement will never be permitted to prevail over the best interests of the child. The precise sense in which this is to be treated as a factor of "importance" is therefore rather unclear.

194 The cases cited above reveal a tension in the legal principles relevant to relocation matters. In what sense are the best interests of the child not the sole consideration in parenting matters, if they must nonetheless always prevail over all other interests? One answer might be that the interests of parents and other parties may be taken into account *as long as* they point to the same conclusion as the best interests of the child. However, this interpretation renders the "paramount but not sole" formulation empty of meaning, since the child's best interests is elevated to a position where no other factor can compete with it.

195 This tension can be partially resolved by emphasising the inherent overlap between the interests of the child and those of the residential parent. Section 68F of the *FLA* lists the matters that the court must consider in determining the child's best interests. The matters listed in that section include "the nature of the relationship of the child with each of the child's parents", "the likely effect of any changes in the child's circumstances" and "the capacity of each parent . . . to provide for the needs of the child, including emotional and intellectual needs". The effect of any proposed orders on the emotional well-being of the parents, particularly the residential parent, is therefore a relevant matter for the court to consider.

196 The best interests of the child, considered in light of the factors identified in s 68F of the *FLA*, will often favour allowing the residential parent to relocate if she or he wishes to do so, particularly where this will significantly improve the parent's employment prospects, access to support networks and financial independence. Nonetheless, the question still arises as to whether the residential parent's autonomy is a factor that can potentially be considered in its own right, apart from its impact on the child's best interests.

197 There is a clear gendered dimension to this issue (120). The strong view of the paramountcy principle, according to which the best interests of the

(117) (2000) 26 Fam LR 381 at [64].
(118) (2000) 26 Fam LR 381 at [93].
(119) (2000) 26 Fam LR 381 at [96].
(120) This point was noted by Kirby J in *AMS* (1999) 199 CLR 160 at [140] and is reiterated in his reasons in the present case at [141]–[143], [145]–[146].

child trumps all other factors, is ostensibly gender neutral. However, considered against a social backdrop where the bulk of domestic labour, including child rearing, continues to be borne by women, its practical implications are far from evenly distributed. It is no coincidence that in each of the relocation cases discussed above the residential parent was the mother. The point is illustrated further by a recent study of relocation cases in the Canberra and Perth regions during 1997 and 1998 (121). That study recorded thirty-eight cases where a parent was seeking to move residence with the children; in thirty-six of the cases, the parent seeking to move was female.

198 The implications of this disparity are worth spelling out. Residential parents seeking to change living arrangements may be compelled to seek approval from the courts; contact parents planning to relocate are rarely required to do so. The residential parent is usually the mother (122). This empirical factor, when combined with the strong view of the paramountcy principle examined above, means that mothers in such cases are regularly submitted to a legal process that subordinates their interests to those of their children; the father, by contrast, does not generally have to justify his choices in this way. The strong view is therefore socially regressive. Its practical consequence, if not its intent, is that women are obliged to compromise their interests in favour of their children in a way that men generally are not.

199 The weak view of the paramountcy principle, then, offers a preferable route to reconciling the tensions in the previous case law. The key characteristic of the weak approach is that it allows the courts to consider the interests of other parties alongside those of the child. This does not mean the court must exhaustively consider all the possible interests affected by a parenting order, but where the case affects a parent's basic right to choose her or his place of residence, this should be taken into consideration. The question in relocation matters then becomes: "Will the child's best interests be affected by relocation to such an extent as to justify limiting the residential parent's freedom of movement?"

Identifying the proposals

200 There are many possible orders in any parenting matter. However, the courts do not actively consider all of them. The framework is set by the orders proposed by the parties. It therefore becomes important how these proposals are identified. A further question is whether the courts are limited to the orders proposed by the parties. If they are not, it becomes important how they decide what other proposals to consider. This should be done transparently and in a way that affords procedural and substantive fairness to both parties.

201 I turn first to the orders proposed by the parties. Ms Udyavar sought orders that Neha reside with her in India on a permanent basis. Mr Udyavar

(121) Easteal, Behrens and Young, "Relocation Decisions in Canberra and Perth: A Blurry Snapshot", *Australian Journal of Family Law*, vol 14 (2000) 234.

(122) Figures cited in *AMS* indicate that "the mother is reportedly the residence parent in approximately 84 per cent of cases": (1999) 199 CLR 160 at [140], per Kirby J.

was then to have unlimited contact with Neha in India at the mother's residence, as well as contact with Neha for two months each year in Australia, with the costs of travel shared between the parents. The proposal anticipated that Mr Udyavar would continue to live in Australia. Mr Udyavar, by contrast, sought orders that Neha reside with him in the Sydney-Wollongong area, except for specified periods on weekends, school holidays and other special occasions, when she should reside with her mother. The proposal anticipated that Ms Udyavar would continue to live in the Sydney-Wollongong area. Mr Udyavar also sought secondary orders in the event a residence order was made in favour of Ms Udyavar. These orders required Ms Udyavar to continue to reside in Sydney-Wollongong and provided for Neha to spend time with her father for substantially the same periods detailed above.

202 The orders sought by the parties were therefore mutually incompatible in fundamental respects. Ms Udyavar anticipated that she would live in Mumbai and Mr Udyavar would live in Australia. The orders sought by Mr Udyavar anticipated that both he and Ms Udyavar would continue to reside in the Sydney-Wollongong area. The parties were each asked at trial about their attitudes to the proposals put forward by the other parent. However, this questioning took significantly different forms in each case. Ms Udyavar was cross-examined as follows:

> "Is it the case, ma'am, that you have deliberately avoided dealing with the possibility that you won't be able to go [to India]? — No sir, I haven't. But I would like to think that we will be able to go.
>
> Let's deal with what I asked you before. Have you thought [about] the possibility that you won't be able to move to India? — I haven't given it much thought yet, sir.
>
> Don't you think you should? — I think I would like to give it much more weight as the case proceeds and as the judgment – I get the judgment, sir.
>
> What, when you're finished in the witness box you will give it some thought, is that right? — No, no, I wouldn't – not that.
>
> I will ask you [to] think about it now. Assume that his Honour says you can go to India any time you like but you can't take your daughter. Assume that's the situation. What could you do then to make life as good as it can be for your daughter here in Australia? — I have to think about it, sir.
>
> You don't have the capacity if you sit in the witness box to think about that, is that what you're saying to his Honour? — I'm sure I have the capacity.
>
> Or is it that you won't do it, you won't think about it? — I will think about it but –
>
> I'm asking you to think about it. What can you do – what could you do to make life for your daughter as good as possible here in Australia? — I would be doing the things that I'm doing now, sir, but it would be –
>
> Don't say you would continue to ensure she has a good and full activity session at school and out of school? — That's right, but I would rather that she be brought up in a more loving atmosphere in Bombay.

> . . .
>
> Ma'am, in the event of you not being permitted to take the child to Mumbai with you, is it your intention to remain living in the Wollongong area? — Yes."

203 Mr Udyavar, by contrast, was cross-examined in the following terms:

> "Did you read in your wife's affidavit of a regime of contact which she proposes if [N] goes to live in Bombay? — I did.
>
> She proposes that on a number of times during the year for holidays [N] would come to Australia with your wife? — Yes.
>
> For several weeks, and at other times you could have access to [N] in India? — Yes.
>
> Would you be prepared to travel to India for that purpose? — Well, in the event that she did go to live in India I would have to.
>
> Well you would want to, wouldn't you? — To keep up my continuing association with her, yes.
>
> Yes, and you would anticipate, wouldn't you, that your wife would keep sending you the things I asked you about earlier from [N], cards and presents and the like? — I would hope so, yes.
>
> To keep you up to date as to what she is doing and what is going on in her life? — Correct."

204 Both parties, then, expressed a willingness to change their lives to maintain contact with their daughter in the event that orders were made against them. The respective lines of questioning reflected the orders sought by the other party. Ms Udyavar was asked about the possibility of being forced to live in Australia, because that was what Mr Udyavar had asked the court to do. Mr Udyavar, on the other hand, was not asked about whether he would consider locating permanently to Mumbai. This was not something that had been canvassed in the proposed orders. He might have been asked anyway, but the question was never directly posed.

205 The Family Court is obliged to give due consideration to the proposals put forward by the parties. However, the Court is not limited to those proposals. This is implied by the duty to consider the factors listed in s 68F of the *FLA* and, in particular, the open ended discretion conferred by s 68F(2)(l). Other possible orders not proposed by the parties may emerge in the course of proceedings and the Court is not obliged to turn a blind eye to them. On the other hand, the Court need not and, indeed, cannot consider every possible proposal (123). The reality is therefore that the attention of the Court will be focused on different possibilities in an organic fashion, as they arise through argument and evidence. The primary judge must be willing to scrutinise this process with an eye to procedural and substantive fairness. It cannot simply be assumed that proposals will emerge in a neutral and equitable way.

(123) (1999) 199 CLR 160 at [284], per Callinan J.

206 The primary judge in the present case, however, did not merely turn a blind eye to the way that the competing proposals emerged. He considered that the answers given by Ms Udyavar under cross-examination amounted to an "alternative proposal" that she and Neha continue to reside in Sydney-Wollongong (124). This interpretation cannot be supported. The proposal that Neha continue to reside with her mother in Australia was originally raised by the alternative orders sought by Mr Udyavar. Both parties were questioned about how they would react if the other's proposals prevailed. However, the judge did not regard Mr Udyavar's comment that he would be willing to travel to India to visit Neha as an alternative proposal by him.

207 It is hard to escape the conclusion that the primary judge was unwittingly influenced by his implicit conception of the gender roles of Neha's parents. It seems to have been assumed that Ms Udyavar would be willing to compromise her well-being in order to maintain close contact with Neha in a way that Mr Udyavar would not. Ms Udyavar was therefore interpreted as making a voluntary proposal that she would remain in Australia with Neha, whereas similar comments by Mr Udyavar about the prospect of visiting Neha in India were viewed as less significant. The fact that the mother's comments were viewed as suggesting a compromise, while the father's remarks were seen as a mere concession, may itself reflect gendered stereotypes about the willingness of women and men to compromise in response to domestic and other forms of conflict.

208 Furthermore, it is at least possible that the primary judge's decision to transform the secondary orders sought by Mr Udyavar into an "alternative proposal" of Ms Udyavar was the product of a deliberate litigation strategy. Thorpe LJ commented in *Payne v Payne* on a common tactic in relocation cases (125):

> "In very many cases the mother's application to relocate provokes a cross-application by the father for a variation of the residence order in his favour. Such cross-applications may be largely tactical to enable the strategist to cross-examine along the lines of: what will you do if your application is refused? If the mother responds by saying that she will remain with the child then the cross-examiner feels that he has demonstrated that the impact of refusal upon the mother would not be that significant. If on the other hand she says that she herself will go nevertheless then the cross-examiner feels he has demonstrated that the mother is shallow or uncaring or self-centred."

209 The cross-examination of Ms Udyavar in the present case bears striking similarities to this description. It is notable that Ms Udyavar was never directly asked what she would do if a residence order was made in favour of Mr Udyavar. Rather, the questioning focused on how she would respond if she were prevented from relocating to India. This might have raised a question in the mind of the primary judge as to whether the application for a residence order in Mr Udyavar's favour was merely a tactical manoeuvre

(124) Decision of the primary judge at [152].
(125) *Payne v Payne* [2001] Fam 473 at 488–9.

to secure Mr Udyavar's preferred option of forcing Ms Udyavar to remain in Australia to serve as the primary carer for their child.

210 It is easy to see why Mr Udyavar would prefer that option, as it would secure him easy access to Neha without having to abruptly assume the responsibilities of the residential parent. However, parenthood is not a slave contract (126). The law should not force a woman to remain in Australia against her wishes purely so that she can bring up her child in a convenient location for its father. The primary judge would have done better to focus squarely on the contrasting orders sought by the parties: namely, Ms Udyavar's proposal to relocate with Neha to India and Mr Udyavar's proposal that a residence order be made in his favour or, alternatively, that Ms Udyavar be compelled to remain in Sydney-Wollongong.

211 These competing proposals should have been examined using the test articulated above: "Will the child's best interests be affected by relocation to such an extent as to justify limiting the residential parent's freedom of movement?" This question would have focused attention on the details of Ms Udyavar's proposal. A negative answer would suggest acceptance of Ms Udyavar's proposed orders, perhaps with some modifications, while a positive answer would shift focus to the issue of who should act as the residential parent if Neha was to remain in Australia. However, the primary judge side-stepped the central question in the case by wrongly identifying an "alternative proposal" by Ms Udyavar to remain in Sydney-Wollongong. Ms Udyavar's true preference to relocate to Mumbai was effectively disregarded in favour of the convenient fiction that she was willing to fundamentally compromise her interests to facilitate Mr Udyavar's contact with Neha.

212 The primary judge compounded his error by criticising Ms Udyavar for giving "very little thought" to arrangements for residing with Neha in Australia (127). This standard, if applied equally to the parties, would have required Mr Udyavar to have given detailed attention to how he would maintain contact with Neha in the event that she moved to Mumbai. However, the answers given by Mr Udyavar in cross-examination do not reveal any greater level of detail than was disclosed by Ms Udyavar in her responses. The primary judge therefore failed to properly identify the proposals of the parties and evaluate them in a fair and balanced fashion. This error went uncorrected on appeal to the Full Court.

Conclusion and orders

213 The appeal should be allowed. The order of the Full Court of the Family Court dismissing the mother's appeal should be set aside, as should the parenting orders made by O'Ryan J at first instance. The matter should be remitted to a single judge of the Family Court for reconsideration.

(126) Compare Pateman, *The Sexual Contract* (1988), ch 5.
(127) Decision of the primary judge at [176].

23

Goode and Goode: The Practice of Feminist Judgment in Family Law

ANN GENOVESE

Introduction

Goode and Goode[1] is an exemplar of the everyday experience of family law. The case concerned contact arrangements for the parties' two sons after separation. Before Collier J, at an interim hearing, the father sought orders that the boys spend equal time with both parents. The mother argued that the children should remain living with her, although they should continue to spend time with their father, as agreed. The mother also described to the Court instances of family violence. Collier J made orders in favour of the mother. That decision was the subject of the father's appeal to the Full Court of the Family Court of Australia. The Full Court's judgment was significant because of the timing. It was the first appeal to be heard after the passing of the *Family Law Amendment (Shared Parental Responsibility) Act 2006* (Cth). This was a legislative reform that added to the paramountcy principle in the *Family Law Act 1975* (Cth) (the Act) – that the Court should make orders in the best interests of children – a rebuttable presumption that those best interests included the child's parents having equal shared parental responsibility.[2] The amendments further provided that where the presumption of equal shared parental responsibility applied, the Court must consider whether it was in the best interests of the child to spend equal, or substantial and significant, time with each parent.[3] In *Goode*, the Court gave these two provisions central importance, with the result that shared parenting time took precedence over the children's existing routine at an interim stage. This altered previous jurisprudence that it was usually in the best interests of children to maintain certainty in their living and contact arrangements, until final hearing at least. Although this is not to be overstated, preservation of the status quo involved children remaining with their primary care givers, usually their mothers, and having contact with their fathers to the extent appropriate.[4]

[1] (2006) FLC ¶93–286 ('*Goode*').
[2] *Family Law Act 1975* (Cth) s 61DA.
[3] Ibid s 65DAA.
[4] *Cowling v Cowling* (1998) 143 FLC ¶92–801.

The 2006 Amendments to the *Family Law Act*

The 2006 amendments followed a period of heated debate in Australia concerning the role of the Act and the Family Court in governing the lives of men, women and children after separation. Although the primary *legal* objective of the Act remains the best interests of children, the *political* objectives of some members of the community have been oriented instead toward prioritising the interest of parents. Specifically, since the 1990s, a politically active fathers' rights lobby had been vocal in claiming that the Family Court discriminated against men. This was based on a perception that the essence of the concept of the status quo was to privilege mothers, rather than to maintain stability for children. It was also influenced by a hostile critique of feminist research which had highlighted the effects of family violence on women and children, and the need for the Court to consider those effects when making contact orders.

These fathers' rights lobbyists were extremely effective in generating a heightened gendered political context for the operation of family law.[5] They were also effective in eliciting a response from the state in those gendered terms; so much so that during this period there were two significant parliamentary inquiries that occasioned important changes to the Act.[6] Among other things, the fathers' rights lobbyists argued that the Act ought to include a specific direction that children should spend equal time with both their parents after separation.[7] In 2003, a reference was made to a House of Representatives Standing Committee to consider that question.[8] The Committee's final recommendations, in the *Every Picture Tells a Story* report, acknowledged that there is no 'one size fits all' solution to the individual experiences of families post-separation.[9] However, in 2006, the Howard Government amended the Act to include the rebuttable presumption of equal shared parental responsibility.[10] It could be rebutted if a Court considered that such an order would not be in a child's best interests, and it did not apply where there were reasonable grounds to believe there had been child abuse and/or family violence or, in interim proceedings, where the Court considered it would not be appropriate in the circumstances to apply the presumption. If an order for equal shared parental responsibility was made, the Court was now required to consider making orders for the child to spend equal or 'substantial and significant' time with each parent.

[5] Ann Genovese, 'Family Histories: John Hirst v Feminism in the Family Court of Australia' (2006) 21(50) *Australian Feminist Studies* 173; Miranda Kaye and Julia Tolmie, 'Discoursing Dads: The Rhetorical Devices of Fathers' Rights Groups' (1998) 22 *Melbourne University Law Review* 162; Miranda Kaye and Julia Tolmie, 'Fathers' Rights Groups in Australia and Their Engagement with Issues in Family Law' (1998) 12 *Australian Journal of Family Law* 19.

[6] Genovese, ibid. For a full discussion, see Helen Rhoades, Reg Graycar and Margaret Harrison, *The Family Law Reform Act 1995: The First Three Years* (University of Sydney and Family Court of Australia, 2000); Reg Graycar, 'Family Law Reform in Australia, or Frozen Chooks Revisited Again?' (2012) 13 *Theoretical Inquiries in Law* 241; Helen Rhoades, 'The Dangers of Shared Care Legislation: Why Australia Needs (Yet More) Family Law Reform' (2008) 37 *Federal Law Review* 279.

[7] Graycar, ibid, 253.

[8] Ibid 250–1.

[9] House of Representatives Standing Committee on Family and Community Affairs, Parliament of Australia, *Every Picture Tells A Story: Report on the Inquiry into Child Custody Arrangements in the Event of Family Separation*, 29 December 2003, [2.4], [2.39].

[10] *Family Law Act 1975* (Cth) s 61DA.

The Decision in *Goode and Goode*

Goode was the first opportunity to examine the connection between equal shared parental responsibility and equal time. When interpreting legislation, courts are guided by common law and statutory principles of interpretation. The central principle is to give legal effect to parliamentary intent, and this is done by reading the new provision in the context of the Act as a whole.[11] Courts may also have recourse to extrinsic materials – documents outside the text of the statute itself – to assist them.[12] These materials include government reports, explanatory memoranda, or reading speeches that accompany legislative change. It can also include academic research.[13] In *Goode* preference was given to scholarship that was critical of feminist research on shared parenting and domestic violence. The work of Patrick Parkinson offers an example.[14] In 2006, before *Goode* was decided, Parkinson outlined in the *Australian Journal of Family Law* his opinion of how the Court should interpret the new legislation.[15] Although conceding that no two families' experience of separation could be the same, Parkinson advocated that the Court needed to be 'directed' by parliament's intent in enacting the reforms. And that intent was to change the emphasis in the Act, so that the objective of ensuring children have a 'meaningful involvement' with both parents was robustly adhered to by the Court.[16] Parkinson argued this would provide certainty to family law and that judges had a duty to implement the legislative mandate.[17] This argument is in fact how the Court interpreted the reforms. The Court neither read the sections on shared parental responsibility and equal time as contingent; nor emphasised the importance of judicial discretion and individualised consideration of the best interests of children (interpretations that were equally open in the context of the legislative schema as a whole). They also did not consider the full gamut of research that offered different insights into the reforms.

The ongoing significance of the judgment is that instead of clarifying the ways in which the law might operate to promote the best interests of children, and their parents, it has drawn the knots of legal interpretation more tightly around individual facts. *Goode* is now precedent in all family litigation, and casts a shadow over all private dispute resolution processes concerning children. The lived reality of the law for individuals – and the recommendation in the 2003 report that every picture might tell its own story – is obfuscated as a

[11] *Project Blue Sky Inc v Australian Broadcasting Authority* (1998) 194 CLR 335; *Acts Interpretation Act 1901* (Cth) s 15AA.

[12] *Acts Interpretation Act 1901* (Cth) s 15AB.

[13] This has been a contested question. See Zoe Rathus, 'A Call for Clarity in the Use of Social Science Research in Family Law Decision-Making' (2012) 26 *Australian Journal of Family Law* 81; Graham Mullane, 'Evidence of Social Science Research: Law, Practice and Options in the Family Court of Australia' (1998) 72 *Australian Law Journal* 434.

[14] See, eg, the veiled exchange on gender politics and family law research agendas after the publication of research on the impact of the 1995 reforms: Helen Rhoades, Reg Graycar and Margaret Harrison, 'Family Law Update: The First Three Years of the Family Law Reform Act' (2001) 58 *Family Matters* 80–3; Patrick Parkinson, 'Letters' (2001) 59 *Family Matters* 78; Lawrie Maloney, 'Researching the Family Law Reform Act: A Case of Selective Attention?' (2001) 59 *Family Matters* 64–8; Helen Rhoades, Reg Graycar and Margaret Harrison, 'The Authors Respond' (2001) 59 *Family Matters* 69–75.

[15] Patrick Parkinson, 'Decision-Making About the Best Interests of the Child: The Impact of the Two Tiers' (2006) 20 *Australian Journal of Family Law* 180, 191–2.

[16] *Family Law Act 1975* (Cth) s 60B(1)(a).

[17] Parkinson, above n 15, 191.

result. In the *Goode* case itself, when the case was remitted for re-hearing, Altobelli FM (as he then was) made orders for the children to spend 'substantial and significant time' with each parent, although his Honour found, 'the evidence overwhelmingly demonstrates that the parents lack the capacity to implement an equal time order, lack the capacity to communicate, and . . . it is generally not in the best interests of the children for there to be equal time'.[18]

The Feminist Judgment

In their feminist judgment, Rathus and Alexander give an indication of how the amendments might have been interpreted differently.[19] They hold to the practices of statutory interpretation more closely than the Full Court (in part by paying closer attention to the actual wording of the statute and the Explanatory Memoranda). They also pay attention to the particularities of the individual case, by reintroducing facts – the story – stripped from the appellate decision. They use these facts to shape the exercise of their discretion in deciding the best interests of the children. Importantly, they refer to well-recognised research to inform the interpretation of when, and in what limited circumstances, 'equal time' could ever equate to the best interests of the child. The return to personal narratives of family life reminds us that the desire to 'guide' courts to provide 'consistent' solutions in accordance with legislative principles should not detract from the need to determine the particular matter – and lived experience of law – that is before the court. This judgment speaks of two loving parents. It uses pseudonyms rather than the more usual initials, to give identity to their children. It includes a table to explain clearly how the children's daily lives would be disrupted if the father's proposal were to be ordered. These are rare techniques in family law judgments. It also reminds us that there are procedures by which family violence allegations can be brought to the Court's attention as a relevant consideration, and queries why that did not occur in this case.[20]

In conclusion, it is important to note how this is a feminist judgment. The enactment of the *Family Law Act* in 1975 was contemporaneous with the assertion by feminists of the need to rethink law in a way that responded to the social experience of women. By taking law's doctrines and techniques seriously, feminist jurists have shown many times that to change law – to reform its practice or alter its perceptions – does not necessarily involve a polemical position that would force feminists to sit outside the door of the court. Instead, the task has been to master law, to understand its rehearsed movements and its rules of interpretation, as well as to monitor its lived effects. It is only through that form of engagement with how law is practised that alternative versions of seeing how law might be lived, how it might be experienced, become possible. Rathus and Alexander, by making that gesture in their judgment, reconnect the mode of judging in family law back to the social, and the political. In doing so, they offer a tacit reminder that connecting those realms back to law has been, and remains, an important feminist project.

[18] *Goode & Goode* [2010] FMCAfam 14 [103].

[19] Zoe Rathus and Renata Alexander wish to acknowledge the comments of Jacqueline Campbell, partner at Forte Lawyers, Melbourne.

[20] The Full Court in *Goode* did not discuss the failure to file the new Form 4, which was intended to alert the Court to allegations of family violence and trigger procedural responses. It has been suggested that these provisions were not well employed by lawyers after the commencement of the amendments and it is arguable that judicial discussion of their advantages in this first appeal may have unseated that malaise.

[¶93–286] GOODE & GOODE
(2006) FLC ¶93-286

Alexander and Rathus JJ

INTRODUCTION

119. The case before this Court is one of two loving parents who cannot agree on the parenting arrangements to put in place since their separation. This is an appeal by the father against an interim decision made by Collier J on 10 August 2006. The father sought orders which enabled the parties' two sons, Tandeep and Jai to spend equal time with each parent. The respondent mother sought orders that the father spend time with the children each alternate weekend and half the school holidays and, in respect of Tandeep only, for two additional days during the week.

120. The *Family Law Amendment (Shared Parental Responsibility) Act 2006* ("the amending Act") came into effect on 1 July 2006 so that was the law that governed his Honour's decision. This court is therefore required to interpret the amendments and determine how they apply to the facts of this case – to the extent that they could be established at an interim hearing.

BACKGROUND FACTS

121. The father was born in Kenya and is now 39 years old and the mother was born in Uganda and is now 37. They met in the United Kingdom and married there in 1996. In 1997 they migrated to Australia with the father's parents. Tandeep was born in November 1997. He is now nine years old. Jai was born in April 2004. He is 2½. After a brief separation in 1999 the parties separated in late May 2006 when the father left the former matrimonial home and moved to his parents' home.

122. Although there is some dispute as to detail, it seems clear from the evidence that during the marriage the mother was the primary carer of the children. She took maternity leave, worked part-time and generally arranged her life around the care of the children. She continues to work part-time. That said, because the father works in his parents' business, he has had flexibility. The children spent some afternoons with him and his parents and the father was actively engaged with Tandeep's various activities. His parents also cared for both children at times.

123. Tandeep is at primary school. He attends scouts on Monday evenings, has piano lessons on Tuesdays, special tutoring on Wednesday nights and swimming on Thursdays. He plays cricket on Saturdays in summer and soccer in winter and sometimes has other scouts-related activities on the weekend. He clearly has a rich and full life. It is also no doubt demanding for a young boy. Jai attends day care on Mondays, Thursdays and Fridays when the mother is at work as a part-time accounts assistant. He has swimming lessons on Tuesdays and music classes on Wednesdays.

124. The father's evidence was that since separation the mother determined contact. He says he was given no contact for the first two weeks and that since then he has had two weekends per month, Monday and Tuesday afternoons with Tandeep and half of the July school holidays. Since June he has paid child support. The father's application seeks equal time – with a five day / two day alternating roster.

Week No	Monday		Tuesday		Wednesday		Thursday		Fri	Saturday		Sun
1	F	T scouts	F	T piano J swim	M	T tutoring J music	M	T swim	F	F	T cricket / soccer	F
2	F	T scouts	F	T piano J swim	M	T tutoring J music	M	T swim	M	M	T cricket / soccer	M

125. Given the newness of the amendments, their connection to specific time outcomes, and the young age of Jai, it is useful to provide a diagram to represent the father's proposal. It assists in envisaging how these quite complex arrangements would play out in the busy lives of the children.

126. The mother's case is that since separation the father's contact has been by agreement and she is seeking that the current arrangement continue – every second weekend, two extra evenings each week (Monday and Tuesday) for Tandeep, and half the school holidays.

127. The mother claims that the father has perpetrated family violence against her. She deposes to physical abuse by the father during the first few months of marriage; details being pushed onto the floor during her pregnancy in 1997 and describes other violent incidents between 1997 and 1999. She claims there was a more serious incident in January 2006 when the father physically abused her and threw her around the bedroom resulting in her being unable to attend work the following day.

ANSWERS TO QUESTIONS POSED BY THE FATHER

128. The father's amended notice of appeal contains six grounds, but his counsel also identified nine discrete questions that fell to be answered in a consideration of the amending Act and the grounds of appeal. The respondent mother's counsel replied in kind. We have only dealt with those questions which are relevant to our findings in this case.

129. We have taken the view that it is permissible for us to turn to a range of extrinsic material. *B and B: Family Law Reform Act 1995*[1] was heard in early 1997, just over six months after the *Family Law Reform Act 1995* (Cth) had commenced operation. The Full Court relied on s 15AB *Acts Interpretation Act 1901* (Cth) to make reference to a number of inquiries, reports and explanatory memoranda in examining the context of the amendments and interpreting the new provisions.

Question 2: Does the presumption that equal shared parental responsibility is in the best interests of the child carry with it any presumption about time?

130. The presumption is set out in s 61DA:

> **Presumption of equal shared parental responsibility when making parenting orders**
>
> (1) When making a parenting order in relation to a child, the court must apply a presumption that it is in the best interests of the child for the child's parents to have equal shared parental responsibility for the child.
>
> Note: The presumption provided for in this subsection is a presumption that relates solely to the allocation of parental responsibility for a child as defined in section 61B. It does not provide for a presumption about the amount of time the child spends with each of the parents (this issue is dealt with in section 65DAA).
>
> (2) The presumption does not apply if there are reasonable grounds to believe that a parent of the child (or a person who

lives with a parent of the child) has engaged in:

(a) abuse of the child or another child who, at the time, was a member of the parent's family (or that other person's family); or

(b) family violence.

(3) When the court is making an interim order, the presumption applies unless the court considers that it would not be appropriate in the circumstances for the presumption to be applied when making that order.

(4) The presumption may be rebutted by evidence that satisfies the court that it would not be in the best interests of the child for the child's parents to have equal shared parental responsibility for the child.

131. The amending Act was the product of a lengthy and extensive consultation process commencing with an Inquiry on "child custody" which was referred to the House of Representatives Standing Committee on Family and Community Affairs in June 2003. One of the terms of reference of the Inquiry was:

> "... given that the best interests of children is the paramount consideration ... should there be a presumption that children will spend equal time with each parent and, if so, in what circumstances could such a presumption be rebutted?"

132. In its Report *Every Picture Tells a Story* tabled in December 2003, this bi-partisan Committee rejected any presumption of equal time and concluded:[2]

> "In the end how much time a child should spend with each parent after separation should be a decision made either by parents or by others on their behalf, in the best interests of the child concerned."

133. The Explanatory Memorandum to the amending Act circulated in the House of Representatives in 2004–2005 confirms[3] that the "presumption of equal shared parental responsibility is not a presumption of 50:50 joint custody". The words used in s 61DA(1) as set out in full above are unambiguous. Therefore the answer to this question is that there is no presumption about time.

Question 3: Can one make an order for equal shared parental responsibility or equal time, other than by application of the presumption?

134. We will deal with the issues of equal shared parental responsibility and equal time separately.

Equal Shared Parental Responsibility

135. Recommendation 1 in *Every Picture Tells a Story* was that a presumption of equal shared parental responsibility be "the first tier in post separation decision-making" but recommendation 2 was for a "clear presumption against shared parental responsibility" where there was "entrenched conflict, family violence, substance abuse or established child abuse, including sexual abuse".

136. Although no presumption *against* shared parental responsibility was enacted, the legislature has drafted the amending Act in a way that anticipates some circumstances in which equal shared parental responsibility should not be ordered. Those circumstances are when the presumption has not been applied or been rebutted.

137. So our answer to this part of the question is that when the presumption has been rebutted or not applied then an order for equal shared parental responsibility cannot be made because the legislative pathway to making such an order has not been triggered.

Equal Time

138. We think the position is somewhat different and more complex when it comes to orders for equal or substantial and significant time. For the purpose of this discussion we set out the critical sub-section of

s 65DAA, the provision which deals with making orders for equal or substantial and significant time:

> **Court to consider child spending equal time or substantial and significant time with each parent in certain circumstances**
>
> Equal time
>
> (1) If a parenting order provides (or is to provide) that a child's parents are to have equal shared parental responsibility for the child, the court must:
>
> (a) consider whether the child spending equal time with each of the parents would be in the best interests of the child; and
>
> (b) consider whether the child spending equal time with each of the parents is reasonably practicable; and
>
> (c) if it is, consider making an order to provide (or including a provision in the order) for the child to spend equal time with each of the parents.
>
> Note 1: The effect of section 60CA is that in deciding whether to go on to make a parenting order for the child to spend equal time with each of the parents, the court will regard the best interests of the child as the paramount consideration.
>
> Note 2: See subsection (5) for the factors the court takes into account in determining what is reasonably practicable.

139. If the court does not make an order for equal time then s 65DAA(2) sets out a similar process to follow to determine whether an order for substantial and significant time should be made. A statutory set of criteria for determining reasonable practicability is contained in s 65DAA(5) which we discuss later.

140. In their Reasons for Judgment, which we have had the advantage of reading in draft, the majority consider that the amendments evince a legislative intent in favour of substantial involvement of both parents in their children's lives after separation, in respect of both parental responsibility and time, except where it is contrary to the children's best interests.

141. Although this may be so, the legislature has provided clear limits to this intent by providing exceptions to making an order for equal shared parental responsibility in sections 61DA(2), (3) and (4). There is also a strong link between the presumption (s 61DA) and the time provisions (s 65DAA). Both s 65DAA(1) and s 65DAA(2) commence with the phrase:

> "***If*** a parenting order provides (or is to provide) that a child's parents are to have equal shared parental responsibility . . .".

142. One view of what this means is that ***if and only if*** an order for equal shared parental responsibility has been made can a court consider equal or substantial and significant time orders. However, another view is that parenting orders are ultimately discretionary[4] and, as there are no provisions which explicitly prohibit the making of equal or substantial and significant time orders in specific circumstances, such orders can always be made if they are in the best interests of the child.

143. We note that the latter approach creates a rather incongruous outcome. In cases where the presumption has been applied and an order for equal shared parental responsibility has been made, equal or substantial and significant time orders can only be made *after* the court has considered the reasonable practicability factors set out in s 65DAA(5). These cases will tend to involve families with some history of co-operation and ability to communicate.

144. However, in cases where there is evidence of family violence or abuse or other circumstances which have caused the presumption to be rebutted or not applied and no order for equal shared parental responsibility is made, s 65DAA does not apply and therefore there is no requirement for the court to consider reasonable

practicability factors before making an equal time or substantial and significant time order.

145. We cannot comment on whether the legislature intended this bifurcation or not. We are merely applying rules of statutory interpretation. We prefer the following approach:

a) Where a court makes an order for equal shared parental responsibility then it must consider making orders for equal or substantial and significant time – but must only make these orders if the court is satisfied that this is in the best interests of the children and reasonably practicable (sub-ss 65DAA(1)(b) and (c) and sub-ss 65DAA(2)(c) and (d)).

b) Where a court does not make an order for equal shared parental responsibility, then it is not obliged to consider equal or substantial and significant time orders but it is not prohibited from doing so.

146. In light of the legislative structure, a court should no doubt exercise caution if considering making equal or substantial and significant time orders when it has not applied or has rebutted the presumption. Again the legislative pathway has not been triggered in this situation but the court is not prohibited from exercising discretion to make such orders, depending on the facts and the overarching paramount consideration of "best interests".

Question 5: What does "consider" mean?

147. This question arises in the context of s 65DAA when the Court is required to consider making orders for equal or substantial and significant time.

148. We agree with the majority that administrative law cases provide little assistance in interpreting the *Family Law Act*, so we have turned to a dictionary definition to ascertain the ordinary meaning of the word. *The Australian Oxford Dictionary*[5] defines "consider" as: "contemplate mentally, especially in order to reach a conclusion; give attention to"; "examine the merits of (a course of action . . .)" and "take into account; show regard for".

149. We are unable to agree with the majority's view that the combination of sub-ss 65DAA(1)(a), (b) and (c) suggests a need to consider making orders for equal or substantial and significant time *positively*. The requirement for the court to "consider" making equal time or substantial and significant time orders under ss 65DAA (1) or (2) in no way suggests any particular outcome. The court is to do exactly what the words say and examine the merits of those options (as indicated by the dictionary definition) by applying the paramount consideration of the best interests of the child which is specifically reiterated in this section and the Notes. *If* such orders are in the child's best interests, then the court must give attention to the additional criteria regarding reasonable practicability set out in s 65DAA(5) before making any specific time order.

Question 6: To what extent does *Cowling* continue to apply [in interim parenting proceedings]?

150. Before answering this question we set out relevant provisions of the applicable new law. One of the most significant amendments to Part VII is that when determining what is in a child's best interests, the Court must consider matters in two tiers: two primary considerations and then 13 additional considerations. The primary considerations are set out in s 60CC(2) and are aligned with the objects in s 60B. These must be given careful attention. The primary considerations are:

(a) the benefit to the child of having a meaningful relationship with both of the child's parents; and

(b) the need to protect the child from physical or psychological harm from

> being subjected to, or exposed to, abuse, neglect or family violence.

151. The additional considerations are contained in s 60CC(3) and include:

> (d) the likely effect of any changes in the child's circumstances, including the likely effect on the child of any separation from:
>
> (i) either of his or her parents; or
>
> (ii) any other child or other person . . .

This is often referred to as the consideration about "status quo".

152. The question to be answered raises an interesting point about the possible tension between the first primary consideration (sub-s 60CC(2)(a)) and the existing case law regarding "status quo" at interim hearings. Does the amending Act have an impact on the determination of interim applications? Does the case law beginning with *Cilento and Cilento*[6] through to the most recent Full Court decision of *Cowling and Cowling*[7] still apply? It is always important to remember that at interim hearings, evidence cannot be tested; allegations and counter-allegations cannot be tried and witnesses are not examined and cross-examined.

153. In *Cowling* the Full Court developed six principles for application in interim hearings. These will be discussed in more detail when we examine the father's grounds of appeal but, in summary, they provide that where a child is living in a well-settled environment at the time of an interim hearing and there are no welfare concerns, the best interests of that child will normally be met by ensuring stability in the child's life and preserving those arrangements. These are well established principles in the jurisprudence of family law and there is nothing in the amending Act which suggests they are to be discarded.

154. In their Reasons the majority takes the view that many elements of the Act as amended militate against the continued application of the principles in *Cowling,* particularly regarding the importance to the child of a stable environment.[8] For example, while the ultimate goal of the legislation is to provide for an outcome in the best interests of the child, if the presumption in s 61DA applies, then the Court is obliged by s 65DAA to consider equal or substantial and significant time outcomes. In the majority's view, the presumption "trumps" the *Cowling* principles at interim hearings.

155. Again we must respectfully disagree. Although "status quo" is now an "additional" consideration in the second tier of considerations, sub-s 60CC(3)(d) is an exact repetition of the former sub-s 68F(2)(c) factor, suggesting that the impact of change of "status quo" remains *one* relevant consideration in an expanded list. Nothing in the new provisions dictates that maintaining the status quo is a priority and we are not saying that the benefits of maintaining the status quo are absolute. Clearly there are cases where maintaining the status quo is not in a child's best interests.

156. We are fortified in our view by the fact that the legislature saw fit to include two separate provisions in the amending Act which deal with interim hearings and the application of the presumption. First of all, s 61DA(3) provides an exception to the operation of the presumption at interim hearings. This will be discussed in more detail later.

157. Secondly, s 61DB provides that:

> "If there is an interim parenting order in relation to a child, the court must, in making a final parenting order in relation to the child, disregard the allocation of parental responsibility made in the interim order."

158. Here the legislature appears to have accepted that orders made at an interim

stage may not be relevant to orders to be made after a final hearing when all of the evidence is put and tested before the Court – an acknowledgment that preserving the status quo at an interim hearing should in no way be considered determinative of the final outcome.

159. The principles from *Cowling* were never legislatively entrenched but the judgment has not been challenged. It reflected what was known from the social sciences about children and parental separation at the time. Although the legislation has now changed, and there is a clear legislative intent to encourage children to have meaningful relationships with both parents after separation, subject to being protected from harm (sub-ss 60CC(2)(a) and (b)), nothing has changed about children and the likely unsettling effects of frequent alterations to their living arrangements whilst disputes between their parents await final judicial determination.

160. Therefore our answer to this question is that, at interim hearings, the principles in *Cowling* regarding status quo are still applicable and, of course, remain subject to the paramountcy of the best interests of the child under s 60CA.

Question 7: In what circumstances will s 61DA(3) of the Act be properly invoked?

161. In our view s 61DA(3) is properly invoked when the state of evidence at an interim hearing does not enable the judge to make important findings of fact. This will often be the case. Here the trial judge could not make a finding as to whether the allegations of family violence were true and therefore could not rely on s 61DA(2) to rebut the presumption as to equal shared parental responsibility as was argued by counsel for the mother.

162. Instead his Honour relied on s 61DA(3) and held that an interim order applying the presumption as to equal shared parental responsibility was not appropriate in the circumstances. We do not believe the trial judge erred in this respect. It was a matter for his Honour's discretion.

GROUNDS OF APPEAL

163. We now turn to the father's amended grounds of appeal.

1). That his Honour erred in finding that section 65DAA did not apply in the circumstances of the case, including where the mother had herself sought that both parties have "joint long term" parental responsibility.

164. As discussed above, in the proceedings at first instance, the trial judge determined not to apply the presumption of equal shared parental responsibility based on s 61DA(3). Although both parties had applied for "joint" parental responsibility in their initiating material (the applications having been filed under the old law), Collier J did not address those aspects of the applications, and simply made orders regarding the practical parenting arrangements. Given that decision, s 65DAA was not triggered.

165. If the father's argument is that an order for equal shared parental responsibility should have been made and therefore s 65DAA would have been triggered, no automatic outcome can be assumed. Given the early interlocutory stage and factual vacuum of this case when it came before Collier J, it would have been almost impossible for his Honour to apply the presumption in s 61DA and then follow the pathway through s 65DAA and the two tiers in s 60CC.

2). That his Honour erred in failing to apply *Cowling* appropriately.

166. We have considered this ground and now apply the two most relevant principles from *Cowling* to the facts as known and find that no appealable error occurred.

167. The first is that, given the mode by

which interlocutory proceedings are conducted, the child's interests will normally best be met by ensuring stability in their life pending a full hearing of all relevant issues. Although there was only a short period from separation to the first hearing there was a caregiving routine in place for the two children.

168. In our view, the trial judge made an interim order promoting stability and predictability for the two children based on the material available. It was in accord with existing arrangements, avoided the need for the father's parents to care for the children when the mother was unavailable and limited the frequency of changeovers.

169. The second principle is that the Court is entitled to place such weight upon the importance of retaining the child's current living arrangements as it sees fit in all the circumstances. As noted above, the new sub-s 60CC(3)(d) retains "status quo" as one of the additional considerations. In our view, maintaining the current parenting arrangement pending a final hearing does not offend against the primary consideration in sub-s 60CC(2)(a). Even if we accept the father's affidavit material that this arrangement was in place through the unilateral actions of the mother, the arrangement does not prevent nor inhibit the continuation of the benefit of the meaningful relationship which the children already have with their father.

170. Given the fact that the children were in a reasonably well-settled environment at the time of the interim hearing and there were no welfare concerns raised concerning those arrangements, we do not consider it necessary to canvass the other principles of *Cowling*.

3). That his Honour erred in failing to apply Part VII of the Act as it now exists.

171. It is correct to say that in the *ex tempore* judgment delivered by Collier J on the day of the hearing, no attention was paid to a range of significant aspects of Part VII. In particular there was no discussion of the new two-tiered best interests considerations contained in ss 60CC(2) and (3). We nevertheless consider that the order that Collier J made satisfied those considerations and therefore his Honour's failure to articulate the detail of the provisions does not amount to appealable error.

172. The new primary considerations introduce the notion of the benefit of a child having a "meaningful relationship" with both parents. Here the challenging tension of the aims of contemporary family law are juxtaposed – the ideal for children to have on-going meaningful relationships with both of their parents post-separation whenever possible and the need to protect children from a range of harms which may occur if they spend time with an abusive and / or violent parent. In the case before us, on the limited evidence available at the interim hearing, it would seem that the children would benefit from a meaningful relationship with both parents, although the allegations of family violence sound a warning note. In our view, Collier J's interim orders struck an appropriate balance.

173. However, perhaps the implicit assertion in this ground of appeal is that the amending Act somehow creates or encourages a link between meaningful relationships and equal or near equal time orders. We think this overstates the new law. Section 61DA(5) sets out criteria for determining whether equal or substantial and significant time would be reasonably practicable. This demonstrates that the legislature recognised that shared care only works for some families. The criteria are:

a) how far apart the parents live from each other; and

b) the parents' current and future capacity to implement an arrangement for the child spending equal time, or substantial and significant time, with each of the parents; and

c) the parents' current and future capacity to communicate with each other and resolve difficulties that might arise in implementing an arrangement of that kind; and

d) the impact that an arrangement of that kind would have on the child; and

e) such other matters as the court considers relevant.

174. It is clear from case law that court-imposed shared care orders (ie equal or near equal time) are uncommon because of widely held notions that children benefit from the stability of one home and general routine. In addition, there may be practical difficulties and different parenting styles as well as a range of contra-indicators discussed below. Cases prior to the 1995 amendments set the tone,[9] and judicial reluctance to impose shared care continued after those amendments.[10] Where it is appropriate and workable, those parents are likely to agree and co-operate, not resort to litigation. Imposing co-operation by court order may do more harm than good.[11]

175. Due to the interim nature of these proceedings to date, no family report was prepared and therefore the court had no assistance from any expert or other social science evidence in relation to this family. Although published social science research cannot be drawn upon to make any findings in this case, we take some comfort that our cautious view about shared care is well supported by literature from the United Kingdom, the United States and to a lesser extent Australia since the 1990s.[12] This makes it clear that shared care is not in the best interests of many children, including those from families with high conflict, allegations of family violence and / or child abuse, poor communication, lack of mutual trust and respect and differing parenting styles. We are also mindful of research that frequent changing of overnight arrangements and multiple caregivers can be contrary to the best interests of or even detrimental to young children especially under three years of age.[13]

176. Referring back to the diagram set out earlier, the father is proposing shared care with multiple transitions, where one of the children is under three years. There have been allegations of family violence; there is a lack of mutual trust and co-operation and parental conflict is on-going as reflected in the different accounts of the post-separation arrangements to date. At the interim stage, the trial judge was not in a position to determine whether or not the parents had the "current and future capacity to communicate with each other and resolve difficulties that might arise in implementing" a shared care arrangement in accordance with sub-s 65DAA(5)(c). Perhaps one fact that was clear was that the father did not have the "current capacity" to implement shared time (sub-s 65DAA(5)(b)) without enlisting considerable assistance from his parents to provide child care at a range of times – particularly for Jai.

177. Therefore it is our view that even if the trial judge had applied the presumption under s 61DA and made an order for equal shared parental responsibility, and then applied the considerations in ss 60CC(2) and (3) and the criteria in s 65DAA(5), it is doubtful that an order for equal or even substantial and significant time could have been the result at that stage. No appealable error is demonstrated on this ground.

FAMILY VIOLENCE

178. The only other matter on which we need to comment regards family violence. Numerous sections in the Act now make reference to family violence and are

relevant to decision-making both in terms of procedure and the nature of orders to be made. Critical sections for this case include s 4(1) (definition), sub-s 60B(1)(b) (objects and principles), sub-s 60CC(2)(b) (the primary consideration dealing with protection from harm), sub-ss 60CC(3)(j) and (k) (additional considerations) and s 60K which requires the Court to take prompt action where there are allegations of family violence and obliges the Court to make appropriate procedural orders.

179. In respect of s 60K the Explanatory Memorandum states[14] that:

> "This is an important provision as where issues of violence and abuse are raised there is a process in place to ensure that there will be adequate information provided to the court so that it can make appropriate orders and so that necessary steps can be taken to ensure appropriate protections are in place."

180. We do not know why the mother did not file a Notice of Child Abuse or Family Violence (Form 4) under the *Family Law Rules 2004* which would have triggered the operation of s 60K. However, the failure to file a Form 4 does not mean that the Court can ignore the question of family violence.

181. It is unfortunate that Collier J did not refer to s 60K and consider adjourning the proceedings so that a Form 4 could be filed. That may have even averted this appeal. However, although this section was not directly referred to by his Honour, this further supports our view that his Honour's interim decision maintaining the status quo rather than increasing the father's time was the most appropriate decision on the available evidence.

CONCLUSION

182. For all of the above reasons, we would dismiss the father's appeal.

Footnotes:

1. [1997] FamCA 33.
2. at para. 2.44
3. at para. 120.
4. *CDJ v VAJ* (1998) CLR 172.
5. 2nd ed, Oxford University Press (2004).
6. (1980) FLC ¶90–847.
7. (1998) FLC ¶92–801 ("*Cowling*").
8. (1998) FLC ¶92–801 at 85,006.
9. *H and H-K* (1990) FLC ¶92-128; *In the Marriage of Padgen* (1991) FLC ¶92-231; *Forck and Thomas* (1993) FLC ¶92-372; *H and H* (1995) FLC ¶92–599.
10. *T and N* [2001] FMCAfam 222; *H and H* (2003) FLC ¶93–168; *M and G* [2003] FamCA 796; *M and M* [2005] FamCA 207.
11. See P Stahl, *Co-operative Parenting or Parallel Parenting*, Impact Publishers (2000).
12. For example, E Hetherington and M Stanley-Hagan, *The Adjustment of Children with Divorced Parents: A Risk and Resiliency Perspective* (1999) 40 Journal of Child Psychology and Psychiatry 129; J Kelly, *Children's Adjustment in Conflicted Marriage and Divorce: A Decade Review of Research* (2000) 39 Journal of Child and Adolescent Psychiatry 963; B Neale, J Flowerdew and C Smart, *Drifting Towards Shared Residence* (2003) 33 Family Law 904; J McIntosh, *Enduring Conflict in Parental Separation: Pathways of Impact on Child Development* (2003) 9 Journal of Family Studies 63.
13. J Solomon and C George, *The Development of Attachment in Separated and Divorced Families: Effects of Overnight Visitation, Parent and Couple Variables* (1999) Attachment and Human Development 1; MK Pruett, R Ebling and G Insabella, *Parenting Plans and Visitation: Critical Aspects of Parenting Plans for Young Children: Interjecting Data into the Debate about Overnights* (2004) Family Court Review 39.
14. at para. 110.

Discrimination Law

24

Commentary on *JM v QFG*

PAULA GERBER

Introduction

The beginning of wisdom is the definition of terms.

Socrates

The Queensland case of *JM v QFG*[1] was all about the definition of terms – 'lawful sexual activity', 'infertility', 'direct discrimination', 'indirect discrimination' and 'reasonableness' – but alas, did not demonstrate the getting of wisdom. Rather, the three privileged male judges of the Court of Appeal engaged in spectacular linguistic gymnastics in order to define these terms in such a way as to defeat the objects and purpose of the *Anti-Discrimination Act 1991* (Qld) ('ADA').

When the Queensland Court of Appeal handed down its decision in *JM v QFG* in August 1998, Queensland was still carrying the legacy of a period of extreme conservatism, under the reign of its longest serving premier, Sir Joh Bjelke-Petersen (1968–87). Indeed, one of the Court of Appeal judges who decided this case had been appointed by Bjelke-Petersen (Thomas JA), as had the lower court judge (Ambrose J), with whom the Court of Appeal agreed. Queensland had a reputation for being a homophobic, redneck state where equal rights and non-discrimination were not priorities. It is against this backdrop that the case of *JM v QFG* should be understood.

JM v QFG was the first Australian case to specifically deal with the question of whether a self-identifying lesbian was entitled to access assisted reproductive technology (ART). JM was raising a child with her same-sex partner. They wanted to expand their family by having another child. In order to achieve this, JM required access to ART (insemination with donor sperm, rather than IVF). The respondents, a doctor and a medical company offering reproductive services, were only willing to provide services to JM if she suffered from the medical condition of infertility, which they defined as 'the inability of a couple to conceive after 12 months of intercourse without contraception'. The Anti-Discrimination Tribunal[2] held that the provision of ART services based on such a definition breached the direct and indirect discrimination provisions of the ADA, in that it excluded JM from accessing the services based on her 'lawful sexual activity', that is, being in an exclusive lesbian relationship.

[1] [2000] 1 Qd R 373.

[2] At the time of *JM v QFG* it was the Anti-Discrimination Tribunal. However, in December 2009, the Anti-Discrimination Tribunal was, along with 22 other tribunals, amalgamated to form the Queensland Civil and Administrative Tribunal.

It is not surprising that the feminist judgment written by Anita Stuhmcke comes to a contrary conclusion than that reached by the Court of Appeal. It is also not surprising that subsequent jurisprudence, legislation and societal attitudes reflect the approach adopted in the feminist judgment, namely that lesbians and single women are entitled to access ART services to the same extent as infertile heterosexual women.

The Supreme Court Decision in *QFG v JM*

The matter initially went on appeal from the Anti-Discrimination Tribunal to the Supreme Court. Ambrose J allowed the appeal, finding that JM had not been discriminated against, either directly or indirectly.[3] His Honour held that the Anti-Discrimination Tribunal erred in finding the appellants had engaged in discriminatory conduct simply because they provided their 'expert medical treatment only to those women who had attempted unsuccessfully to become pregnant in the *normal* way' [emphasis added]. His Honour made frequent reference to 'normal heterosexual intercourse'. The addition of the adjective 'normal' does nothing other than to suggest that His Honour considered heterosexual conduct to be normal and homosexual sexual conduct to be abnormal. His lack of understanding of sexual orientation is clearly on display in the following comment:

> There is no evidence whatever to suggest that the respondent was physically or psychologically incapable of engaging in heterosexual intercourse. The evidence indicates that because of her lesbian sexual orientation she had chosen an exclusive sexual activity which excluded the possibility of achieving pregnancy in the normal way.

Ambrose J ultimately disagreed with every aspect of the decision of the Anti-Discrimination Tribunal, in that he found there had been no indirect discrimination, no direct discrimination and that the Tribunal had failed properly to consider whether the doctor's refusal to treat JM was reasonable.

The Court of Appeal Decision in *JM v QFG*

JM appealed this decision to the Court of Appeal, where she was met with very similar attitudes to those displayed by Ambrose J. The Court of Appeal judges drew conclusions that are inconsistent with a feminist approach to the facts of the case. Like Ambrose J, the three male judges appear to have a limited knowledge or understanding of lesbianism, which led them to draw some questionable conclusions (even taking into account that the decision was made over 15 years ago). Some examples of their very naïve, masculinist, heteronormative approach are exhibited in the following extracts from the Court of Appeal judgments:

> The true basis of the doctor's refusal to provide services to the patient was not because of her lesbian activity but because of her heterosexual inactivity.[4]

[3] *QFG v JM* [1997] QSC 206 (24 October 1997).
[4] [2000] 1 Qd R 373, 396 (Thomas JA).

> [T]here was no policy of excluding from services women who engaged in lesbian activity. It was the absence of heterosexual activity which mattered.[5]

> [C]ommon sense suggests that many lesbians are also prepared to engage in heterosexual activity.[6]

> I do not think that this, or any other court, can reach the conclusion, as if it were a notorious fact, that a person who engages in lesbian sexual activity is generally exclusively lesbian.[7]

These opinions were not based on any research findings, and the subtext appears to be that 'infertility was JM's choice – that she could, if she wished, have sex with a male and become pregnant'.[8] The Court of Appeal unanimously endorsed an exclusively medical definition of infertility, with no recognition of the fact that lesbians and single women need sperm in order to conceive, to which they may not have ready access. It is worth noting, that unlike other Australian states, Queensland did not have any legislative prohibition on single women accessing ART services. However, there was a tacit agreement between medical practitioners and the Queensland Health Department that infertility services would only be provided to married women. The Court of Appeal's decision upheld this practice.

Ultimately, the Court of Appeal was satisfied that the refusal to treat JM was not directly discriminatory, because it was based on the doctor's opinion that the appellant had failed to satisfy the definition of infertility, rather than because of the attribute of 'lawful sexual activity'[9] (being lesbian activity). The Court held that the word 'activity' did not include inactivity, and since the doctor's refusal to provide fertility treatment was based on JM's inactivity – in not engaging in heterosexual intercourse – it could not amount to discrimination. The Court also agreed with Ambrose J that the Tribunal had not properly considered whether the refusal of treatment was 'not reasonable', and remitted the question to the Tribunal for reconsideration.

A final point worth noting about the Court of Appeal judgments, is that the all-male bench seemed to have more respect and esteem for the male doctor, than for the women involved in the case – the female appellant and the female President of the Anti-Discrimination Tribunal, the Honourable Justice Roslyn G Atkinson. There is a long-standing protocol among appellate judges not to identify or personally criticise the decision-maker whose judgment is being appealed. Thus, courts of appeal generally refer to the maker of the decision under appeal as the 'lower court' or 'tribunal'. This practice was evident in the Court of Appeal's judgment in *JM v QFG*, when they referred to Ambrose J's decision, which was under appeal, as simply that of 'a judge of the Court'. However, that same practice was not followed when referring to the original decision of the Anti-Discrimination Tribunal. Rather than simply referring to the decision-maker as 'the Tribunal', the Court of Appeal judges constantly identified the decision-maker as 'The President', and singled her out for sharp criticism. One of the more glaring illustrations of the lack of respect shown to Justice Atkinson was the assertion by Thomas JA that the President engaged in 'leading and argumentative cross-examination' of the doctor. Similarly, Davies JA stated that the President's decision was 'neither logically nor legally correct'. One

[5] Ibid 373 (Pincus JA).
[6] Ibid 396 (Thomas JA).
[7] Ibid 385 (Davies JA).
[8] Anita Stuhmcke, 'Limiting Access to Assisted Reproduction: *JM v QFG & GK*' (2002) 16 *Australian Journal of Family Law* 245, 252.
[9] *Anti-Discrimination Act 1991* (Qld) s 7(1)(l).

can speculate whether the same degree of disrespect would have been shown to a male President of the Tribunal.

Subsequent Developments

The Court of Appeal judgments in *JM v QFG* have not withstood the test of time. Within a few years of the decision, courts and legislatures in other jurisdictions were considering whether access to ART should be limited to married or partnered heterosexual women, and reaching the conclusion that such a restriction amounted to unjustified discrimination.

The landmark judgment in this area is undoubtedly the Federal Court decision in *McBain v Victoria.*[10] Unlike the respondents in *JM v QFG*, Dr McBain wanted to provide ART services to a single woman but was not able to do so because of a legislative prohibition on the provision of such services to single women. Section 8 of the *Infertility Treatment Act 1995* (Vic) imposed a requirement that a woman must be married or living with a male de facto partner in order to be eligible for ART. It was argued that such a provision was inconsistent with s 22 of the *Sex Discrimination Act 1984* (Cth) (prohibition on discrimination based on marital status), and therefore inoperative by reason of s 109 of the *Constitution* of the Commonwealth of Australia. The State of Victoria declined to defend the Victorian legislation, but the Australian Catholic Bishops Conference and the Australian Episcopal Conference of the Catholic Church were given leave to intervene to make submissions in favour of upholding the Victorian legislation. Sundberg J found that the Victorian prohibition on providing ART to women who were not married or living in a heterosexual de facto relationship was inconsistent with the *Sex Discrimination Act 1984* (Cth) and therefore ineffective to the extent of the inconsistency.[11] The Catholic Church's application for leave to appeal to the High Court was rejected.

There was significant public outcry in response to this judgment, including from the then Prime Minister John Howard, who threatened to amend the *Sex Discrimination Act 1984* (Cth) to overcome the decision.[12] However, such amending legislation was never passed.[13] Rather, Victoria and other jurisdictions set about amending their legislation regulating ART to remove discrimination against single women and lesbians. Thus, the position across Australia now is that lesbians can access ART either because it is expressly mandated in legislation, or because there is no explicit legislative prohibition.[14] However, ART remains beyond the reach of many because of the high costs associated with treatment. Whilst

[10] [2000] FCA 1009 (28 July 2000).

[11] A similar decision had been reached a few years earlier by the Full Court of the Supreme Court of South Australia in *Pearce v South Australian Health Commission* (1996) 66 SASR 486 regarding a similar restriction in the *Reproductive Technology Act 1988* (SA).

[12] See, eg, Australian Broadcasting Corporation, 'PM Moves to Close IVF Access for Single and Lesbian Women', *7:30 Report*, 1 August 2000 (Kerry O'Brien).

[13] Kristen Walker, 'Should There Be Limits On Who May Access Reproductive Services?' (2002) 6 *Flinders Journal of Law Reform* 67.

[14] Note that the National Health and Medical Research Council's *Ethical Guidelines on the Use of Assisted Reproductive Technology in Clinical Practice and Research* (2007) do not address eligibility. These Guidelines refer to those seeking access to ART as 'participants', which obviously applies equally to lesbians, single women and married women.

Medicare covers part of the cost, it has been estimated that out-of-pocket expenses are likely to be in the range of $2000 per cycle.[15]

Although JM was denied the opportunity to have a child with the help of ART, she can take some small comfort from the fact that some 15 years later, law and society have evolved to such an extent, that not only can lesbians access ART in every State and Territory across Australia, but their same-sex partner will be recognised as a parent of any child born following ART, and can be named as a parent on the child's birth certificate.[16]

Feminist Judgment

The writing of the feminist judgment in *JM v QFG* was not Stuhmcke's first encounter with this case. In 2002, she was one of the few academics to provide a scholarly analysis of the decision.[17] In her previous writing about this case, Stuhmcke focused on the Court of Appeal's failure to recognise infertility as a social construct or to consider in any way the best interests of children. She noted that the Court of Appeal judgments appear to encourage lesbians and single women wanting to have a child to have a one-night stand in order to get pregnant, with little thought as to the welfare of any child conceived in such a manner. For example, would such a child be able to identify their 'father' and access information about his medical background?[18]

In her feminist judgment, Stuhmcke takes as a starting point the purpose of the legislation. In stark contrast to the approach of the Court of Appeal judges, she begins by considering the objects of the ADA. She lays a solid foundation for this approach, citing High Court authorities such as *Waters v Public Transport Corporation*[19] and *IW v City of Perth*[20] which held that with anti-discrimination legislation, courts have a 'special responsibility to take account of and give effect to the statutory purpose' and should employ a 'generous construction'.

Stuhmcke notes that the long title of the ADA is 'An Act to promote *equality of opportunity* for everyone by protecting them from unfair discrimination in certain areas of activity and from sexual harassment and certain associated objectionable conduct' (emphasis added). By relying on the objects and purpose of the Act, Stuhmcke is able to approach the case from a human rights perspective and to apply the legislation in a way consistent with the stated intention of Parliament. As a result, her judgment is fundamentally different from

[15] See Julia Medew, 'Women Put Off IVF After Costs Rise' *Sydney Morning Herald* (online) 26 October 2011 <http://www.smh.com.au/national/health/women-put-off-ivf-after-costs-rise-20111025-1mi5i.html>.

[16] See, eg, *Family Law Act 1975* (Cth) (s 60H: child born via ART is conclusively presumed to be the child of woman who gives birth and her de facto partner, defined to include same-sex couples – s 4AA(5)(a)); *Status of Children Act 1978* (Qld) (ss 19C(3), 19D(3), 19(E): the de facto female partner of a woman undergoing ART is presumed to be a parent of the child; this presumption is irrebuttable – s 19F); *Artificial Conception Act 1985* (WA) (s 6A: same-sex de facto partner of woman who undergoes ART is conclusively presumed to be the parent of the child); *Status of Children Act 1974* (Vic) (s 13: the female partner of a woman undergoing ART is presumed to be a parent of the child; this presumption is irrebuttable) and *Births, Deaths and Marriages Registration Act 1996* (Vic) (s 17A(2): if the Register only names the mother of the child, the mother and her partner may apply to amend the Register to name the partner as a parent of the child).

[17] Stuhmcke, above n 8, 252.

[18] Ibid.

[19] (1991) 173 CLR 349, 359, 394.

[20] (1997) 191 CLR 1, 22, 27.

those of the majority, and she alone considers JM's right to dignity and equality before the law.

Another point of departure of Stuhmcke's judgment from the majority is her recognition that the heterosexual nuclear family is only one form of family structure and that 'lesbians and gay men are having children outside of the context of heterosexual relationships and sexual reproduction'. This acknowledgement assists her to approach the facts of the case with more sensitivity and less disdain than the other judges.

Overall, Stuhmcke's feminist judgment concludes that the respondents' refusal to provide ART to JM contravened the provisions of the ADA. Her findings uphold JM's right to dignity and equality; concepts entirely absent from the judgments of both the Supreme Court and the Court of Appeal, but which are now well entrenched in the ART practices of all Australian States and Territories.

JM v. QFG

[1998] QCA 228

[App. 10523/1997]

Court of Appeal (Davies J.A., Pincus, J.A., Thomas J.A., Stuhmcke J.A.)

19 May; 18 August 1998

STUHMCKE J.A.:

The appeal to this Court

At issue in this appeal is the meaning of certain sections of the *Anti-Discrimination Act* 1991 ("the Act") as that legislation applies to the provision of medical treatment for infertility. Because of the sexuality of the individual seeking fertility treatment, the case has given rise to a contest between an approach to the provision of medical treatment which is focused upon the treatment of sexually active heterosexuals, and one which would make medical services for assisted fertility treatment available to lesbian couples. For the reasons which follow, the application of the Act means that the latter approach is correct.

I have had the advantage of reading in draft the judgments of Davies, Pincus and Thomas JJ.A., with whom I disagree. A comprehensive overview of the relevant facts and circumstances of the case, including disputed facts, are set out in the reasons of Davies J.A. An understanding of the medical context of the parties' interaction, and the procedural path of this case, is necessary to gain an appreciation of the competing arguments.

Background

This case concerns the seemingly straightforward situation of the appellant before this Court, a 24 year old woman, JM, wanting a child, a mainstream desire actively sought by many and one often characterised as 'normal' and 'natural'. Being in a lesbian relationship, JM desired to use assisted reproduction services to achieve pregnancy. JM was refused access to assisted reproductive services offered by the second respondent, Dr GK, a practising obstetrician and gynaecologist and a member of the group of medical practitioners in QFG. Dr GK gave JM a consent form to be completed before undergoing treatment. The consent form required signatures from the "wife" and the "husband". JM was unable to comply with that requirement and return the form signed by her "husband" as her partner was female and not her husband.

Due to her inability to complete the form, assisted reproductive services were refused by the second respondent. JM made a complaint to the Queensland Anti-Discrimination Commission, and subsequently brought a successful action in the Queensland Anti-Discrimination Tribunal ("the Tribunal"). The Tribunal found in favour of the appellant on the basis of direct and indirect discrimination in the provision of services based on the attribute of "lawful sexual activity" (prohibited under ss. 7(1)(*l*), 10, 11 and 46 of the Act), holding:

> "The discrimination against JM is both direct and indirect. It is direct in that Dr GK has refused JM service because of her lawful sexual activity of being engaged in an exclusive lesbian relationship. It is indirect discrimination under s. 11 of the Act because of the imposition of the term that she would not receive treatment unless she returned the form stating the name of her male partner and signed by her 'husband'."

The Tribunal ordered payment of costs by the respondents and a compensation payment to JM of $7,500, an amount far from punitive. This payment was to compensate JM as "she felt humiliation due to being treated less than equal to heterosexual/married women in regard to her right to choose parenthood". The relatively small amount also took into account the lack of malice of Dr GK and was made in order for JM "to have a continuing therapeutic relationship with Dr GK or the other doctors in QFG".

The first and second respondent refused to accept that decision and appealed to the Queensland Supreme Court. There, a single judge of the Court overturned the Tribunal's finding on direct discrimination, finding that the appellant was refused treatment due to her "heterosexual inactivity", "and had therefore not been discriminated against on the basis of being in an 'exclusive and stable lesbian relationship'". The original finding of indirect discrimination was remitted to the Tribunal for further consideration with respect to the reasonableness of the requirement that JM return the form signed by her "husband".

The appeal before this Court is against the decision of the Supreme Court setting aside the findings of the Tribunal. For the reasons that follow I would allow the appeal and reinstate the decision and orders of the Tribunal.

The issues

Three issues are before this Court:

(i) whether the Tribunal made an error of law in determining that the second respondent directly discriminated against JM under the Act by refusing to provide her with artificial insemination services;

(ii) whether the Tribunal made an error of law in determining that the second respondent indirectly discriminated against the appellant under the Act;

(iii) whether the Tribunal made an error of law in determining that the second respondent is the agent of the first respondent, resulting in a finding of vicarious liability on the part of the first respondent.

Statutory interpretation of anti-discrimination legislation

As the Act does not include a definition of "lawful sexual activity", nor of "attribute", the preferred meaning must, with regard to s. 14A(1) of the *Acts Interpretation Act* 1954 (Qld), be one which best achieves the purpose of the Act. Section 14A(1) of the *Acts Interpretation Act* provides that "In the interpretation of a provision of an Act, the interpretation that will best achieve the purpose of the Act is to be preferred to any other interpretation." The term "purpose" is defined to include "policy objective" in s. 36 of the *Acts Interpretation Act*.

Turning to the purpose of the Act, it is then important to observe that the Act states that it was enacted in recognition of "the need to protect and preserve the principles of dignity and equality for everyone". As per the long title, this is an ". . . Act to promote equality of opportunity for everyone by protecting them from unfair discrimination in certain areas of activity . . .". The Act provides that this purpose is to be achieved by prohibiting discrimination that is on specified grounds, of specified types, and in specified areas of activity, unless a specified exemption applies. This includes discrimination based on the "attribute" of "lawful sexual activity" under s. 7.

In *Waters v Public Transport Corporation* (1991) 173 C.L.R. 349 the High Court considered the *Equal Opportunity Act* 1984 (Vic), a piece of remedial legislation with similar aims to the Act. In that case, Dawson and Toohey JJ. stated that a "generous construction" (394) must be given to the legislation. As Mason C.J. and Gaudron J. similarly observed:

> "... the principle that requires that the particular provisions of the Act must be read in the light of the statutory objects is of particular significance in the case of legislation which protects or enforces human rights. In construing such legislation the courts have a special responsibility to take account of and give effect to the statutory purpose" (at 359).

The High Court in *IW v City of Perth* (1997) 191 C.L.R. 1 recently confirmed this approach with respect to the Western Australian *Equal Opportunity Act* 1984 (WA). Dawson and Gaudron JJ. stated that "In construing legislation designed to protect basic human rights and dignity, the courts 'have a special responsibility to take account of and give effect to [its] purpose'" (at 22). In that case, albeit in a dissenting judgment, Kirby J. agreed with Dawson and Gaudron JJ. when he observed:

> "The purpose of anti-discrimination legislation, such as the Act, is to ensure that, within the areas prescribed by Parliament, equals are treated equally and human rights are not violated by reference to inappropriate or irrelevant distinctions. Especially where important human rights are concerned, protective and remedial legislation should not be construed narrowly lest courts become the undoers and destroyers of the benefits and remedies provided by such legislation. Courts will not unduly stretch the language of such legislation. But they will be very slow to find that the effect of something which is discriminatory falls outside the ambit of the legislation, given its purpose. This is especially so where a complainant, who can establish unequal treatment, falls within the category of persons for whom anti-discrimination legislation has apparently been enacted. It is legitimate in giving effect to such legislation, to keep in mind its broad purposes and, to the full extent that the text permits, to ensure that the Act achieves its objectives and is not held to have misfired. To the extent that, in legislation such as the Act, courts adopt narrow or pernickety approaches, they will force parliaments into expressing their purposes in language of even more detail and complexity. This will increase the burden and costs of litigation. It will obscure the broad objectives of such statutes and frustrate their achievement" (at 58).

I emphasise here the warning of Kirby J. against applying meanings to words which are overly literal and technical. This warning is particularly apposite in light of the exuberant use of dictionary definitions in this case. Indeed, as shown in the Court below and in the Tribunal, the application of different versions of dictionaries to interpret the words that comprise "lawful sexual activity" has done little more than result in starkly divergent outcomes for the appellant. While dictionaries perform a necessary role in statutory interpretation, in this case their use illustrates the dangers of straying into what Kirby J. correctly characterised as "narrow or pernickety approaches". In my view, selective use of particular versions of dictionaries to find definitions which will fit preferred interpretations of legislation is contrary to what the High Court means by a liberal interpretation such as that preferred in *IW v City of Perth* (1997) 191 C.L.R. 1. For example, the use of the Macquarie Dictionary in the Tribunal resulted in the finding of direct discrimination while the use of the Shorter Oxford English Dictionary in the Supreme Court resulted in a finding of no direct discrimination. The consequence has been to propel this case through the appeal process. Finding conflicting dictionary definitions of words such as "sex", "sexual", "hetero", "homo", "homosexual", "lesbianism" etc. does little to advance the correct interpretation of the Act.

Waters v Public Transport Corporation (1991) 173 C.L.R. 349 and *IW v City of Perth* (1997) 191 C.L.R. 1 direct this Court to approach the construction of the Act with particular attention to its purpose. In so doing, I heed Kirby J.'s warning in *IW v City of Perth* (1997) 191 C.L.R. 1 of the well-worn "difficulty of obtaining the successful application of anti-discrimination legislation to simple facts" (at 52).

The attribute of "lawful sexual activity"

It was accepted by the Tribunal that an exclusive lesbian relationship is included within the attribute of "lawful sexual activity" as set out in s. 7(1)(*l*) of the Act. In my opinion the finding of the Tribunal was correct in law.

As noted above, "lawful sexual activity" is not defined in the Act. In light of this the ordinary meaning of the term must be used. This is clearly the intent of the legislature given that those attributes listed in s. 7 of the Act which mention activity – "political belief or activity", and "trade union activity" – are not defined, suggesting that they are activities within their ordinary meanings. As the ordinary meaning of "lawful sexual activity" will capture all forms of lawful sexual activity, it follows that the purpose of the Act is to include lesbian sexual activity, a lawful sexual activity in Queensland.

Direct discrimination "on the basis of an attribute"

Much has been made of the question whether JM was refused fertility treatment on the basis of her attribute of lawful sexual activity, i.e. of being in an exclusive lesbian relationship. The majority of this Court and the court below hold that the refusal of the second respondent to provide medical services to JM was not because of her lesbian activity but rather because of her heterosexual inactivity. As such it is found that there was no direct discrimination under the Act. The court below held that the appellant was refused services not "because of her lesbian activity but because of her heterosexual inactivity" and it "was her heterosexual inactivity which put her outside the guidelines which the second appellant had adopted for the provision of his specialist medical services". Aided by a list of readings set out in full in Appendix A to His Honour's judgment, including material such as "Passions of the Cut Sleeve: The Male Homosexual Tradition in China" and "Immodest Acts: The Life of a Lesbian Nun in Renaissance Italy", the judge likened the appellant's inability to comply with the second respondent's definition of infertility to that of a virgin, stating that "it would be ridiculous to describe a woman as 'infertile' merely because she was a virgin".

It is wrong, however, to characterise this case as turning on an absence of heterosexual activity. The outcome of such an approach is that if JM can physically comply with the requirement to be heterosexually active she has not been unlawfully discriminated against. This is clearly not the intention of the legislature in the Act. It is unconscionable to prohibit someone from accessing a service because they do not perform an activity by reason of an attribute and then to tell them that it is a simple case that if they perform the activity despite their attribute they will be allowed to access that service. If we follow the reasoning to its logical conclusion, an individual who is refused employment because they will not join a trade union or a person who is refused government benefits because they fail to profess a political belief or activity under s. 7 of the Act will not be unlawfully discriminated against as it is that person's choice to either refrain from or to engage in the relevant activity. To adopt such an approach would fatally frustrate the purposes of the Act.

Moreover, to construe this as a case concerning "heterosexual inactivity" not only reinforces lesbian invisibility but positively denies the legitimacy of lesbian sexual activity. Such exclusion in this instance fails to protect lesbians from discrimination with respect to reproductive services and forces lesbians who wish to have children to either engage in heterosexual intercourse against their will or to use medically unsafe semen through home insemination. In this case the appellant gave evidence before the Tribunal that her wish to access clinical donor insemination services was based upon her not wanting to "pursue alternative means of conception which would pose unacceptable risks to her mental and physical health." Such risks may include: difficulty in conceiving; difficulty in finding a known donor; preference for an anonymous donor because of concern about potential conflict with a known donor over contact or parental responsibility in later years; access to safer sperm; and different legal consequences of using anonymous versus known donor insemination. The approach of the court below and of the majority of this Court to the interpretation of ss. 7 and 10 of the Act not only fails to protect from unlawful discrimination, it positively reinforces discriminatory behaviours through supporting the dominant conditions of society – a result which is wholly contrary to the remedial purpose of the legislation.

Application of the High Court decisions in *Waters v Public Transport Corporation* (1991) 173 C.L.R. 349 and *IW v City of Perth* (1997) 191 C.L.R. 1 requires this Court to have regard to the purpose of parliament in passing the Act which is, as stated in the preamble to the Act, to "promote equality of opportunity for everyone". In his Second Reading Speech on the *Anti-Discrimination Bill*, before the Queensland Legislative Assembly, the Attorney-General, the Honourable DM Wells, stated:

> "For too long, Queensland has been in the Dark Ages with respect to human rights. This Bill not only brings Queensland up to the present but also goes further than any of the other States in that it implements the spirit of the International Covenant on Civil and Political Rights beyond what even the Commonwealth has done." (Hansard, 26 November 1991, 3193)

In addition, the preamble to the Act states that the Queensland Parliament, in passing this legislation, supports the Commonwealth ratification of the International Covenant on Civil and Political Rights (ICCPR). A recent decision by the United Nations Human Rights Committee on 4 April 1994 (*CCPR/C/50/D/488/1992*) determined that Articles 17 and 26 of the ICCPR extend to protect homosexuality. If, therefore, it appears that a person, because of their attribute of "lawful sexual activity", is unable to live with the same dignity as other people, or to enjoy the public benefits of that society to the same extent as others, there is a prima facie nullification or impairment of human rights and fundamental freedoms, which it is the purpose of the Act to address.

"Less favourable treatment"

Section 10(1) of the Act states that direct discrimination on the basis of an attribute will occur if a person treats or proposes to treat a person with an attribute less favourably than another person without the attribute in circumstances which are the same or not materially different. The Tribunal held that JM was clearly treated less favourably because she possessed the attribute of "lawful sexual activity" which was to engage in sexual activity exclusively with her partner who happened to be a woman. It was on this basis that she was refused medical treatment. I agree with the finding of the Tribunal that this refusal constituted direct discrimination under s. 10 of the Act. In refusing to treat the appellant, the second respondent clearly stated that he would treat other women engaged in lawful sexual activity, as long as it was the type of lawful sexual activity that he prescribed – that is, heterosexual activity for a 12 month period. In refusing to treat JM, Dr GK treated her, under s. 10, less favourably than he would another person without the attribute, in circumstances that are the same or not materially different.

In summary, the Tribunal did not err in finding that the second respondent directly discriminated against the appellant.

Indirect discrimination

The meaning of indirect discrimination is set out in s. 11(1) as occurring when:

> ". . . a person imposes, or proposes to impose, a term –
> (a) with which a person with an attribute does not or is not able to comply; and
> (b) with which a higher proportion of people without the attribute comply or are able to comply; and
> (c) that is not reasonable."

Section 11(2) states that

> "Whether a term is reasonable depends on all the relevant circumstances of the case, including, for example –
> (a) the consequences of failure to comply with the term; and
> (b) the cost of alternative terms; and
> (c) the financial circumstances of the person who imposes, or proposes to impose, the term."

Under s. 11(1)(a) the appellant was unable to comply with the term imposed by the clinic and the doctor (the requirement to return the form signed by her "husband") due to her lesbianism. Under s. 11(1)(b), a higher proportion of people who are not lesbians are able to comply with that term. The issue before this Court is whether the Tribunal erred in failing to take into account all relevant circumstances in determining that the term was not reasonable under s. 11(1)(c) and (2).

The key relevant circumstances going to the question of reasonableness in this case were the reasons for the adoption of the term by the respondents. The first reason for the adoption of the term was the respondents' adherence to a medical definition of infertility, wherein a woman is deemed infertile only if she has had sexual intercourse with a man over a period of 12 months without using contraceptive devices and has failed to conceive a child.

As the Tribunal correctly identified, however, there are alternative, more inclusive definitions of infertility. The Tribunal observed that the World Health

Organisation describes infertility as "the incapacity of a man, woman or couple to participate in reproduction, i.e. the production of a live child", noting that in this definition "there is no reference to the gender of the couple or the reason for the incapacity to participate in reproduction". It was noted by the Tribunal that this more expansive definition of infertility is incorporated into draft Australian Health Ethics Committee guidelines which would cover the appellant and her partner to allow them to access fertility treatment.

The second reason for the adoption of the term was the respondents' adherence to requests from the Queensland Department of Health that they should follow the guidelines for treatment set out in the Demack Report, which recommended restricting artificial insemination services to married couples and those in stable de facto (heterosexual) relationships. The Tribunal, however, also considered this rationale, noting that the Department's position had no legal status, and that while there was no legislation governing or limiting the provision of assisted insemination services in Queensland, the respondents were bound by the terms of the Act. Further, the Tribunal noted that no conditions concerning the definition of infertility attached or related to the first respondent's private hospital license.

It is clear, then, that the Tribunal did take all the relevant circumstances into account, and did not err in finding that the term was not reasonable.

In my opinion, in the absence of legislation regulating access to fertility services, the imposition of sexual preference as a basis for controlling access to such services is, as described by Mason C.J. and Gaudron J. in *Waters v Public Transport Corporation* (1991) 173 C.L.R. 349, an "irrelevant and impermissible condition" (at 363). As observed by the Canadian Law Reform Commission in a paper titled *Medically Assisted Procreation* (Working paper No. 65) 1992:

> "Making access to medically assisted procreation conditional upon the existence of pathological conditions (sterility, physiological and genetic infertility) may seem normal, since the technologies were developed to circumvent these problems. However we cannot ignore the fact that establishing such a condition with respect to artificial insemination would deny access to single people and to homosexual people . . . For the moment, taking current social conditions into account, the Commission is of the opinion that with regard to artificial insemination, protection for the traditional family should not be incorporated in legislation at the expense of the right to equality."

The medical definition of infertility adopted by the respondents contradicts the purpose of the Act which is to respect and promote the principles of dignity and equality. A woman's choice of sexual partner should not determine when and if she is able to receive the medical treatment she seeks.

The legislature is the appropriate body to determine whether certain classes of individuals should be prevented from accessing fertility treatment, as any such limitation carries potentially serious public health risks. As increasing numbers of lesbians and gay men are having children outside of the context of heterosexual relationships and sexual reproduction, it will, in light of these risks, become increasingly important for parliament to pass clear laws in this area of access to medical services. It may be said that the tides of community opinion are turning in this case, from being largely unsympathetic to increasingly seeing the desire to have a child by any individual as normal and usual.

Vicarious liability

The Tribunal held that the first respondent, QFG, was vicariously liable for the actions of the second respondent, Dr GK. The first respondent contends, however, that the second respondent did not act as its agent and therefore it should not be held liable for his actions in discriminating against the appellant.

Agency may be established by actual, implied or ostensible conduct. Here the agency of Dr GK is established ostensibly. To a lay person, such as JM, the supply of a letterhead bearing the name of the first respondent with a list of clinicians including the name of the second respondent is sufficient (in the absence of any other facts) to establish ostensible agency. It is not necessary for the appellant to establish that she acted in the belief that the second respondent was the agent of the first respondent – indeed, I agree with Davies J.A. that the appellant was entitled not to give any thought to that matter at all. A reasonable person in the appellant's position, presented with a consent form bearing the letterhead of QFG and the name of Dr GK, would objectively believe that QFG had conferred authority on Dr GK to act on its behalf.

Conclusion

In answer to the questions raised in this case I find that the Tribunal did not err in holding: (i) that the respondents directly discriminated against the appellant; (ii) that the respondents indirectly discriminated against the appellant; and (iii) that the first respondent is vicariously liable for the actions of the second respondent.

Orders

1. Allow the appeal against the orders made by Ambrose J.
2. Reinstate the orders made by the Tribunal.
3. Order the respondents to pay costs.

25

Commentary on *McLeod v Power*

KATHARINE GELBER

Anti-vilification Laws in Australia

The complaint in *McLeod v Power*[1] was lodged under federal anti-vilification legislation.[2] Anti-vilification laws also exist in every State[3] and Territory[4] in Australia except the Northern Territory. The common ground on which complaints may be lodged in all relevant jurisdictions is race, with other grounds varying between jurisdictions, but including sexuality/homosexuality, transgender/gender identity, religion, HIV/AIDS status and disability. The State and Territory laws utilise a mixture of criminal and civil laws, with only civil provisions existing federally and in Tasmania, only criminal provisions in Western Australia, and a mix of the two in all other relevant jurisdictions. Criminal laws have rarely been enforced in practice – there have been three successful prosecutions under Western Australia's idiosyncratic criminal laws.[5] In practice, therefore, the emphasis in Australia is on the civil provisions whose location within anti-discrimination law animates civil mechanisms of complaint resolution. Under the federal law, if conciliation by the Australian Human Rights Commission is unsuccessful, the Commission terminates the case and the complainant may take the matter to a federal court for determination, with the court able to order remedies such as an order to desist, a corrective notice, an apology, or payment of compensation.

The Feminist Judgment

McLeod v Power concerns a complaint of racial vilification lodged by a prison officer of Anglo-Celtic descent (Neale McLeod) against an Aboriginal woman (Samantha Power) who, with her children, was denied entry to the prison to visit her partner. The rewritten judgment primarily addresses the issue of whether the use of the word 'white' as an epithet

[1] *McLeod v Power* [2003] FMCA 2 (14 January 2003) ('*McLeod*').

[2] *Racial Discrimination Act 1975* (Cth) ss 18B–18F.

[3] *Anti-Discrimination Act 1977* (NSW) ss 20B–20D, 38R–38T, 49ZS–49ZTA, 49ZXA–49ZXC; *Anti-Discrimination Act 1991* (Qld) ss 124A, 131A; *Racial Vilification Act 1996* (SA); *Civil Liability Act 1936* (SA) s 73; *Anti-Discrimination Act 1998* (Tas) ss 17(1), 19; *Racial and Religious Tolerance Act 2001* (Vic); *Criminal Code* (WA) ss 76–80H.

[4] *Discrimination Act 1991* (ACT) ss 65–67.

[5] Katharine Gelber, 'Hate Speech and the Australian Legal and Political Landscape' in Katharine Gelber and Adrienne Stone (eds), *Hate Speech and Freedom of Speech in Australia* (Federation Press, 2007) 8; Office of the Director of Public Prosecutions (WA), correspondence with the author and Professor Luke McNamara, 11 November 2011; *O'Connell v Western Australia* [2012] WASCA 96 (4 May 2012).

by Ms Power constituted prohibited conduct on the ground of race. The original judgment found that the moniker 'white' did not represent a race. Brown FM recognised the obligation that derived from the International Convention on the Elimination of Racial Discrimination (ICERD) to prevent racial discrimination.[6] He took this to mean the prevention of discrimination against minority groups who are vulnerable to prejudice. Despite the term 'white' denoting a colour, he argued, first, that this term in Australia did not denote a particular 'ethnic, national or racial group', and secondly, that white people are dominant historically and culturally, and therefore 'not in any sense an oppressed group'.[7]

The feminist judgment, written by Jennifer Nielsen,[8] takes issue with the first element of this finding, holding instead that white *can* be used to denote a race within the meaning of the *Racial Discrimination Act 1975* (Cth). It does this by drawing from critical whiteness literature, where race and racism are seen as constructs that profoundly affect both those who are marginalised and those who are privileged by them, even if those affected in either way are not aware of it.[9] The successful construction of the 'Other' is necessarily dependent on the construction of members of the dominant community, who benefit in myriad and often unseen ways from the racial hierarchies in which they are situated.[10] Thus, to suggest that 'white' does not denote a race in a racialised society is to ignore reality.

The feminist judgment agrees with the original judgment, however, in finding that Mr McLeod did not suffer from racial vilification. It draws that conclusion based on an understanding that he was in a position of direct authority over Ms Power, because he could make the decision not to permit her entry to the prison. This aspect of the rewritten judgment is also feminist, to the extent that it openly acknowledges institutionalised and often invisible power inequalities, and incorporates that understanding into an examination of whether the conduct in question could have constituted vilification, that is, speech that enacts harm.

Feminist thought has exposed the operation of unequal power relations in both private and public domains.[11] Understanding the often invisible role that power inequalities play in enabling and perpetuating unequal gender relations has been a core feminist contribution to understanding social relations, and has generated the view that achieving gender equality requires contesting and changing those power relations.[12] The feminist judgment seeks to make visible the power relationships that are germane to considering how race and gender are constructed and operate in Australian society. In acknowledging that Ms Power was responding to the unequal power relationship in which she had been placed, it views her use of epithets and name-calling as an expression of frustration with those inequalities. These inequalities were magnified by her positioning as an Indigenous woman, who faced power differentials generated both by her gender and by her race. She was not simply angry at being denied entry to the prison to see her partner, after travelling on a bus for hours with

[6] *McLeod* [2003] FMCA 2 [54].

[7] Ibid [59].

[8] Jennifer Nielsen would like to acknowledge the constructive feedback on drafts and the support provided by Professor Katharine Gelber and Marcelle Burns from the Queensland University of Technology.

[9] See, eg, Woody Doane, 'Rethinking Whiteness Studies' in Ashley 'Woody' Doane and Eduardo Bonilla-Silva (eds), *White Out: The Continuing Significance of Racism* (Routledge, 2003) 3; Ruth Frankenberg, 'White Women, Race Matters: The Social Construction of Whiteness', in Richard Delgado and Jean Stefanic (eds), *Critical White Studies: Looking Behind the Mirror* (Temple University Press, 1997) 632; Belinda McKay, *Unmasking Whiteness* (Queensland Studies Centre, 1999).

[10] See, eg, Aileen Moreton-Robinson, 'Whiteness, Epistemology and Indigenous Representation' in Aileen Moreton-Robinson (ed), *Whitening Race: Essays in Social and Cultural Criticism* (Aboriginal Studies Press, 2004).

[11] See, eg, Carole Pateman, *The Sexual Contract* (Stanford University Press, 1988).

[12] RW Connell, *Gender and Power* (Allen & Unwin, 1987) 34–5.

four young children to discuss a matter concerning the possible removal of her children (although that would have been understandable); she was also expressing anger at the gender- and race-based power inequalities that were represented by Mr McLeod refusing her entry. She was, arguably, 'entitled to be an agitator'.[13]

Finally, one might argue that there is a risk posed by acknowledging whiteness as a racial construct; namely, that people of Anglo-Celtic descent in Australia would attempt more often to utilise the neutral language of racial discrimination statutes to their own benefit, although their racial group is by and large not the intended beneficiary of such legislation. This risk is mitigated by the operation of anti-vilification laws, which require a reasonable likelihood that the conduct offends, insults, humiliates or intimidates. As the rewritten judgment shows, drawing from legal authority extant at the time the *McLeod* judgment was handed down, such prohibited conduct does not amount to merely offending someone or hurting their feelings, but it is restricted to substantial harm.

Other Racial Vilification Cases

Since *McLeod v Power* there has been a small number of racial vilification cases adjudicated in Australian courts, two of which I will discuss briefly. The first is *Toben v Jones*[14] which concerned a Holocaust denier, Frederick Toben, who hosts a website. A complaint was lodged under federal anti-vilification laws in May 1996 regarding the site's material by Jeremy Jones on behalf of the Executive Council of Australian Jewry and the Australian Jewish community. The complaint was substantiated by the then Human Rights and Equal Opportunity Commission (HREOC) in 2000, and Toben was required to remove the material from his website and desist from further publishing it. Due to a failure to comply, proceedings were commenced in the Federal Court in 2001 to enforce HREOC's determinations. An injunction was granted, against which Toben appealed. Toben lost his appeal. This case became well-known when he then refused to comply with over 20 court orders to remove the prohibited material from his website. Finally, in August 2009 Toben was jailed for three months for contempt of court. This case concerned Holocaust denial, a type of speech that was found to be actionable under racial anti-vilification laws, on the ground that it enacts harm against its targets. This stands in contradistinction to the speech in *McLeod* that was found not to be actionable.

A second important case was that of *Eatock v Bolt* in 2011,[15] a representative complaint made in the Federal Court on behalf of nine named individuals in relation to newspaper articles written by journalist Andrew Bolt, in which it was alleged that 'fair-skinned Aboriginals' were not genuinely Aboriginal, but chose to identify as such in order to access benefits for Aboriginal people. The complaint was upheld, and a corrective notice ordered to be placed with the offending material on the newspaper's website. In judgment, Bromberg J drew from previous authority that the words 'offend, insult, humiliate or intimidate' were intended to cover consequences more serious than 'personal hurt'. They were intended to protect against conduct that has 'profound and serious effects, not to be likened to mere

[13] *Neal v R* (1982) 149 CLR 305, 317 (Murphy J). My thanks to Mary Crock for pointing me to this citation.
[14] (2003) 129 FCR 515.
[15] (2011) 197 FCR 261 ('*Bolt*').

slights'.[16] The importance of this case lies in the decision by Bromberg J that the language of Andrew Bolt – which did not contain overt epithets or crude insults – nevertheless constituted language that constituted vilification.[17] This is in contradistinction to the language used in *McLeod*, which did comprise crude epithets, but was not actionable under racial anti-vilification laws. These two cases together make it clear that the law is not designed simply to address crude epithets and name-calling, but rather the substantive harms occasioned by hate speech.

After the *Bolt* decision was handed down, Bolt's employer, the Herald and Weekly Times, subsequently campaigned against the federal racial vilification legislation.[18] Then leader of the Opposition, Tony Abbott, committed to repeal the federal racial vilification legislation if elected,[19] and after the September 2013 election both the Prime Minister and the Attorney-General, George Brandis, with the support of the new Human Rights Commissioner Tim Wilson, restated this commitment.[20] However, in August 2014, following considerable public opposition to the draft Freedom of Speech (Repeal of S. 18C) Bill 2014, the commitment was withdrawn.[21]

[16] Ibid [268].

[17] Katharine Gelber and Luke McNamara, 'Freedom of Speech and Racial Vilification in Australia: "The Bolt Case" in Public Discourse' (2013) 48 *Australian Journal of Political Science* 470.

[18] David Marr, 'Bolt's "Freedom of Speech" Crusade Won't Right His Wrongs', *Sydney Morning Herald* (Sydney) 20 October 2011; 'Editorial', *The Australian* (Sydney) 29 September 2011, 13; Gary Johns, 'Cultural Identity Open for Discussion', *The Australian* (Sydney) 29 September 2011, 12.

[19] Dennis Shanahan, 'Abbott to Champion Freedom of Speech', *The Australian* (Sydney) 5 September 2013, 1.

[20] Chris Merritt, 'A-G's First Task: Repeal "Bolt Laws" in Name of Free Speech', *The Australian* (Sydney) 8 November 2013, 1; Tim Wilson, 'The Building Blocks for a Free Society', *The Australian* (Sydney) 18 December 2013, 12.

[21] The Canberra Times, 'PM Bows to Public Opinion', *The Canberra Times* (Canberra) 7 August 2014, 1, 4.

[FEDERAL MAGISTRATES COURT OF AUSTRALIA]

McLEOD v POWER
[2003] FMCA 2

Nielsen FM

11 December 2002; 14 January 2003

Introduction

1 On Sunday 8 April 2001 Samantha Power attended Yatala Labour Prison to meet with Adam Wilson, an inmate. She wished to discuss with him a care application concerning their four children, and was upset with him because he had supplied information to the relevant government department. The trip from the family's home involved two buses and took approximately two hours, and she traveled with the four children, all under the age of six.

2 At the prison gatehouse, Ms Power spoke with Kenneth O'Leary, a correctional officer and the visits booking officer that day, responsible for ensuring visitors to the prison provided appropriate identification and for recording the details of each visit. Ms Power had visited the prison on approximately 20 prior occasions and each time had gained entry by using her Medicare and pension cards for identification purposes. However, in her haste to travel that day, she had forgotten these documents; instead, to gain entry for the visit, she presented the only documents she had brought which named her (and Mr Wilson) – the court documents associated with the children's care application. Mr O'Leary, however, refused her entry advising that these documents were inadequate. When Ms Power reacted stridently to Mr O'Leary's refusal, Neale McLeod, the senior correctional officer in charge of the gatehouse that day, intervened and repeated to her that she was refused permission to enter the prison on that occasion.

3 Perhaps unsurprisingly, Ms Power became agitated and angry, and although extremely upset, she left the gatehouse of her own accord. Even though she did not have to be forcibly removed, Mr McLeod and another officer, Mr Farquharson, elected to leave the gatehouse and follow her to ensure that she left correctional services property. She continued to voice her anger as she walked with her children down the concrete walkway and then along the driveway.

4 I have heard evidence from each of the three prison officers and from Ms Power. Mr McLeod's complaint specifically states that Ms Power said to him, "you white piece of shit", "you fucking piece of white shit" and "fuck you whites you're all fucking shit", and that she made these statements during her discussion with Mr O'Leary inside the gatehouse, and again while she was outside leaving the prison premises. In her testimony, Ms Power conceded that she was "cursin' " but disputes that she used the words "white" or "whites" at all. In her affidavit, however, she indicates

she took a prescribed dose of methadone that morning, which made her feel "spaced out" and unable to "think clearly"; in my view this may have affected her recollection of these events. In his testimony, Mr McLeod stated that she used the alleged words only outside of the gatehouse; accordingly, I accept Ms Power's evidence that she did not use these words inside the gatehouse. However, the two other officers corroborated Mr McLeod's testimony that she used these words outside of the gatehouse, and so I accept his evidence on this point and find that the words "white" and "whites" were used by Ms Power during the exchange outside of the gatehouse.

5 Mr McLeod states that he was offended by this incident because, in his view, Ms Power, an Aboriginal woman, used these words to portray him unfairly as a stereotypical white, racist prison officer. As a consequence, and with the backing of a Legal Fund established by the South Australian correctional services officers' professional association, of which he is a member, Mr McLeod brings to this court a complaint that he has been racially vilified by Ms Power contrary to the *Racial Discrimination Act 1975* (Cth) ("the Act").

What is racial vilification?

6 The claim of racial vilification, inserted into the Act by the *Racial Hatred Act 1995* (Cth), is set out in s 18C(1) which provides:

> "It is unlawful for a person to do an act, otherwise than in private, if:
> (a) the act is reasonably likely, in all the circumstances, to offend, insult, humiliate or intimidate another person or a group of people; and
> (b) the act is done because of the race, colour or national or ethnic origin of the other person or of some or all of the people in the group."

7 Section 18D sets out exemptions to protect – in certain contexts – a personal right to freedom of speech; I note that none of these exemptions are claimed or apply to this case.

8 To establish his complaint Mr McLeod must prove on the balance of probabilities that Ms Power's behaviour outside of the gatehouse ("the act"):

(i) occurred because of his race, colour or national or ethnic origin; and
(ii) that it was reasonably likely to offend, insult, humiliate or intimidate a person with his race (etc); and
(iii) it occurred otherwise than in private.

I will consider each of these matters in turn.

Was there a causal connection between the act and the complainant's race, etc?

9 Mr McLeod argues this complaint comes within the scope of the Act because Ms Power used the words "white" and "whites", which demonstrates she abused him "because of" his "race, colour, or national or ethnic origin".

10 The first question is, then, does the term "white" refer to a race, colour, or national or ethnic origin? The Act does not define these terms so their meaning must be derived by reading them in the context of the Act as a

whole and the words that surround them: *Project Blue Sky v ABA* (1998) 194 CLR 355 at 381. Section 15AA of the *Acts Interpretation Act 1901* (Cth) also requires regard to be had to the Act's purpose, while s 15AB permits the enquiry to be informed by extrinsic material, including the Act's Second Reading Speech, Explanatory Memorandum, or an international agreement referred to in the Act, and s 13 enables consideration of certain material that is part of the Act.

11 The Explanatory Memorandum to the *Racial Hatred Bill 1994* (Cth) explains that the word "race" will "include ideas of ethnicity so ensuring that many people of, for example, Jewish origin would be covered" and that while it "connotes the idea of a common descent, it is not necessarily limited to one nationality and would therefore extend also to other groups of people such as Muslims" (p 3). There is no specific comment on the meaning of "colour" or "national origin", but it is noted that the words "race" and "ethnic origin" are "complementary" and "intended to be given a broad meaning" (p 2).

12 Looking then to judicial consideration of these words, Driver FM has described the word "race" as a "broad term" (*Williams v Tandanya Cultural Centre* [2001] FMCA 46 (23 July 2001) at [21] ("Williams"), and beyond that the meaning of "race" has attracted very limited judicial comment. Perhaps this is because, as Lord Simon of Glaisdale observed in *Ealing London Borough Council v Race Relations Board* [1972] AC 342 ("Ealing") at 362, it is an "unprecise" concept and anthropologists might disagree that it is "biologically at all relevant" to human beings. Its ordinary meaning is described by the Macquarie Dictionary (3rd ed, 2001) as including "a group of persons connected by common descent, blood or heredity" and "a group of tribes or peoples forming an ethnic stock".

13 The meaning of "ethnic origin" has attracted more significant judicial consideration. The leading authority is the New Zealand Court of Appeal's decision in *King-Ansell v Police* [1979] 2 NZLR 531 ("*King-Ansell*"), which held that Jews in New Zealand formed a group with common ethnic origins within the meaning of the Race Relations Act 1971 (NZ). Richardson J said, at 542, that:

> "The real test is whether the individuals or the group regard themselves and are regarded by others in the community as having a particular historical identity in terms of their colour or racial, national or ethnic origins. That must be based on a belief shared by members of the group."

He went on, at 543, to say that:

> ". . .a group is identifiable in terms of its ethnic origins if it is a segment of the population distinguished from others by a sufficient combination of shared customs, beliefs, traditions and characteristics derived from a common or presumed common past, even if not drawn from what in biological terms is a common racial stock. It is that combination which gives them an historically determined social identity in their own eyes and in the eyes of those outside the group. They have a distinct social identity based not simply on group cohesion and solidarity but also on their belief as to their historical antecedents."

14 This interpretation was endorsed by the Bill's Explanatory Memorandum, noting it would "provide the broadest basis for protection of peoples such

as Sikhs, Jews and Muslims" (pp 2-3). It was also approved by the House of Lords in *Mandla v Dowell Lee* [1983] 2 AC 548 ("*Mandla*") where, at 562, Lord Fraser of Tullybelton explained that it was characteristic that an ethnic group was "a minority or an oppressed group or a dominant group within a larger community".

15 The meaning of "national origin" was considered in *Ealing*, and found to be distinct from, yet related to, the concept of race (per Lord Cross of Chelsea, at 366). Viscount Dilhorne observed, at 338, that it means "national in the sense of race and not citizenship".

16 The final word, "colour" has not attracted specific judicial consideration. The *Macquarie Dictionary* states that its primary definition is "the evaluation by the visual sense of that quality of light (reflected or transmitted by a substance)", but may also indicate "racial complexion other than white, esp Negro". I return to this point below.

17 It is significant that the terms in s 18C(1)(b) are separated by "or", so that the act complained of must impart the meaning of any of these terms separately or a number of them read together. Indeed, each of these words must be read in the context of the other words that surround them in s 18C and in context of the Act itself, so as to be read to reflect the meaning and purpose of the Act as a whole. Reading these terms together, each imparts some racial connotation by which people are delineated into some form of social grouping or class – whether by choice or otherwise – in accordance with their common biological or social origin, their historical antecedents, their skin colour or common physical or other traits, or through shared customs, beliefs, traditions and characteristics, and whether or not any of these things are real or perceived. Nonetheless, to bring a matter within s 18C, its "racial" tone need not be *all* of these things.

18 So, is "white" any of these things? Some might say that as "white" is not *even* a "colour", it imparts no racial connotation. Yet according to the *Macquarie Dictionary*, the word "white" can refer to race as its meanings include having "light skin; marked by comparatively slight pigmentation of the skin", "denoting or relating to the Caucasian race" and "dominated by or exclusively for only members of the white race". Nonetheless, I accept that "white" people are not a homogeneous group in terms of the test of "ethnic origin" put forward by Richardson J in *King-Ansell*, as they may well have many different languages, religious beliefs, countries of origin and cultural practices.

19 Moreover, skin colour or pigmentation is not determinative of racial origin or how an individual understands their racial identity. Nonetheless, it is often used to refer to racial identity. For instance, "black" is commonly used to refer to Aboriginal and Torres Strait Islander peoples, even though this grouping encompasses diverse peoples who originate from many nations, with distinct languages, cultural practices and territories; as Driver FM noted in *Williams* at [21], even those with "a rudimentary understanding of Aboriginal culture and history" would be aware that "Australian Aborigines are not a single people but a great number of peoples who are collectively referred to as Aborigines".

20 It is no leap to suggest, then, that "white" has the same potential to import "racial" identity into conversation, even though those regarded as – and indeed who may regard themselves as – "white" encompasses a large array of possible ethnic and national origins. To suggest otherwise is to ignore our history. For instance, immigration in this country was governed from the time of federation to the mid-1970s by a policy infamously known as the "White Australia Policy", and in its decision to apply equal award wages to Aboriginal workers in the pastoral industry, the Conciliation and Arbitration Commission distinguished this group of workers from "white workers" and "white labourers" and discussed at length how Aboriginal workers would engage with the "white community" and "white economic society": *The Cattle Industry (Northern Territory) Award 1951* (1966) 113 CAR 651.

21 As this indicates, the inclusion of the word "colour" in the Act reflects the continued social practice of distinguishing different groups by skin colour, described by academic David Hollinsworth as a practice inspired by the now discredited taxonomical system of racial classification that categorised and ordered humankind according to "unique" social and/ or physical distinctions, including skin colour (*Race and Racism in Australia*, 2nd ed, 1998, p 29).

22 And despite their differences in language, religious beliefs, countries of origin and cultural practices, white people are understood as the dominant peoples historically and culturally within Australia (since colonisation). They are not in any sense an oppressed group whose political and civil rights are under threat. But as Lord Fraser of Tullybelton stated in *Mandla*, an ethnic group may comprise a "dominant group" as well as a "minority or an oppressed group" within a larger community. Thus the social understanding of racial identities is not limited to those in the minority, but equally encompasses those who enjoy a privileged position within a larger community (see, for instance, Aileen Moreton-Robinson in *Unmasking Whiteness: Race Relations and Reconciliation*, 1999). Thus, I find that Ms Power's reference to "white" does involve a reference to colour and race within the meaning of those terms in the Act.

23 However, the Act demands more, as it requires proof that an impugned act is done "because of" the complainant's race, that is, proof of a causal connection or nexus between the act about which Mr McLeod complains and Ms Power's reference to his race and colour. Section 18B of the Act provides that where an act is done for two or more reasons and only one of the reasons is the race (etc) of the complainant, even though that reason is not necessarily the dominant or substantial reason for the doing of the act, the act is still taken to have been done because of the person's race (etc). Thus, that Ms Power's purpose was to make known her anger does not preclude her act also being connected to Mr McLeod's race.

24 Mr McLeod complains about Ms Power's use of the word "white" and "whites" in conjunction with the words "fucking", "fuck" and "shit". It is not enough if Ms Power's use of the word "white" or "whites" was merely incidental because to establish the necessary causative connection, Mr

McLeod must establish sufficient connection between Ms Power's act of swearing and race (etc) to show the swearing occurred *because of* his race.

25 In *Creek v Cairns Post Pty Ltd* [2001] FCA 1007 (31 July 2001) ("*Creek*") Kiefel J examined this test at some length (see especially [17]-[27]). Her Honour noted, at [15], that the Explanatory Memorandum to the Act described s 18C as "the proposed prohibition on offensive behaviour based on racial hatred", and, at [8], that Part IIA of the Act (within which s 18C etc are contained) is titled "Prohibition of Offensive Behaviour based on Racial Hatred". However, while Her Honour acknowledged that "hatred of other races is an evil spoken of in the statute", she concluded that the Act's references to "racial hatred" do not create a separate test requiring proof that the behaviour had a basis in actual hatred of race; instead, Her Honour pointed out at [18], s 18C (and s 18B) makes clear that a breach will occur "if the basis for the act was the race, colour, national or ethnic origin of the other person or group". After outlining the main authorities on this question, Her Honour stated the relevant test, at [28], as whether "anything suggests race as a factor in the respondent's decision" to undertake the impugned act.

26 As the facts demonstrate, Ms Power is an Aboriginal woman who was subjected to an unwelcome decision by officers of a state-run correctional facility, which prevented her from seeing Mr Wilson about their children's welfare, a matter that was of significant and urgent concern to her. It seems she regarded this decision as arbitrary and unreasonable in nature. Whether or not that was true, I can understand why she felt aggrieved: she had been admitted to the prison on numerous occasions without incident in the past; I am also told that sometimes visitors are admitted to the prison without providing identification where they are known to the correctional services staff on duty at the relevant time. What is abundantly clear is that the officers' decision made her extremely angry and her response then, was to protest this decision and to do so vociferously. Her swearing voiced that protest.

27 But what do the words "white" and "whites" add to her protest? In essence, they infused into it considerations of race: from her perspective, this event was a product of an imbalance of power that was connected to race – not just her own race, but also his. It is my view that she referred to Mr McLeod as "white" to bring attention to what she perceived as a racialised hierarchy with which she found herself in conflict.

28 Thus, I find that Ms Power's use of the words "white" and "whites" did impart a reference to race and that this reference was directed at and was because of Mr McLeod's race. However, this of itself does not prove that Mr McLeod was subject to racial vilification, as the question then is whether this act was reasonably likely to offend, insult, humiliate or intimidate.

Was the act reasonably likely to offend, insult, humiliate or intimidate?

29 Mr McLeod testified that he was offended by the incident, although he did not have any time off work as a result; nor did he seek counselling or any psychological treatment. However, more than a year after the event, his

lawyers arranged a medico-legal examination by Dr Christopher Griffin, a psychiatrist, who gave evidence at the hearing. Dr Griffin diagnosed Mr McLeod as suffering from an "adjustment disorder unspecified (that is, with angry mood)", which included symptoms that "predominantly involve a sense of outrage and indignation". However, the authorities are clear that Mr McLeod's subjective perception cannot itself satisfy the test in s 18C.

30 In his Second Reading Speech for the Bill, then Attorney-General Lavarch said:

> "The Racial Hatred Bill is about the protection of groups and individuals from threats of violence and the incitement of racial hatred, which inevitably leads to violence. . .The bill is intended to close a gap in the legal protection available to the victims of extreme racist behaviour. No Australian should live in fear because of his or her race, colour or national or ethnic origin."

He also said that the Bill requires "an objective test" to determine whether an act is likely to offend etc, so that "community standards of behaviour rather than the subjective views of the complainant are taken into account": *Hansard* (15 November 1994) at 3336 and 3341.

31 The accepted statement of this test was given by Drummond J in *Hagan v Trustees of the Toowoomba Sports Ground Trust* [2000] FCA 1615 (10 November 2000) ("*Hagan*") at [15], as being an objective test to determine "whether the act complained of has the necessary offensive, insulting, humiliating or intimidatory quality". This must be considered from the view of the "reasonable victim" (*Corunna v West Australian Newspapers Ltd* (2001) EOC ¶93-146 ("*Corunna*")); that is, a person possessing the racial, ethnic or other relevant attributes of the complainant in the matter but not particularly susceptible to being roused or incited. This avoids the real risk that the standards of a different person or group to that of the victim of the impugned act are adopted without any sensitivity to cultural differences between groups in the community.

32 Thus, the test to be applied to Ms Power's words is whether a "reasonable white prison guard" would be "likely to be offended, insulted, humiliated or intimidated". I note from the outset my view that there is simply no evidence to suggest Mr McLeod – who was in a superior position of authority and under no real or perceived threat – was likely to have been intimidated.

33 As to the rest of the possible effects, looking to the words used, the words "fucking", "fuck" and "shit" might be unpleasant but are not necessarily so, in that they are used frequently with a range of meanings in daily life, and would be common lingo in any correctional facility. Given the frequency of their use in this setting, I do not accept that a reasonable white correctional services officer would be offended, insulted or humiliated by the use of these words alone. Therefore, the question is whether the character of this exchange is transformed to any significant degree by the addition of the words "white" or "whites".

34 It is important to note that it is not the purpose of this law to prevent all types of offence or quell every expression of anger or discontent. Instead,

the Explanatory Memorandum states that the Bill was intended to "strengthen and support" the "social cohesion demonstrated by the Australian community at large" and was "based on the principle that no Australian need live in fear because of their race, colour or national or ethnic origin" (p 1).

35 It is also relevant to consider Australia's obligations pursuant to the *International Convention on the Elimination of Racial Discrimination* ("ICERD"), the Convention given effect by the enactment of the Act. Part IIA of the Act (and thus s 18C) relates specifically to Article 4 which calls on state parties to the Convention to:

> ". . .condemn all propaganda and all organizations which are based on ideas or theories of superiority of one race or groups of persons of one colour or ethnic origin, or which attempt to justify or promote racial hatred or discrimination in any form, and. . .to eradicate all incitement to, or acts of, such discrimination".

Clearly the Article does not articulate the purpose of the Act but is instructive in delineating the mischief that Part IIA was designed to address. What Article 4 suggests is that one of the characteristics of racial hatred and discrimination is a belief in or theory of the superiority of one race or group of persons of one colour or ethnic group over another.

36 As explained, the Act does not require proof of racial hatred but it does require proof that, objectively viewed, the act "has the necessary offensive, insulting, humiliating or intimidatory quality": per Drummond J in *Hagan*. Kiefel J explained this further in *Creek* at [16], stating that to "'*offend, insult, humiliate or intimidate*' are profound and serious effects, not to be likened to mere slights". Endorsing Kiefel J's statement in *Jones v Toben* [2002] FCA 1150 (17 September 2002) at [92], Branson J explained that her Honour was referring to the:

> ". . .legislative intent to render unlawful only acts which fall squarely within the terms of the section and not to reach to '*mere slights*' in the sense of acts which, for example, are reasonably likely to cause technical, but not real, offence or insult".

In *Jones v Scully* [2002] FCA 1080 (2 September 2002) at [102], Hely J also noted that the Attorney-General's Second Reading Speech stated "that the HREOC was familiar with the scope of such language and has applied it in a way that deals with serious incidents only: *Hansard* (15 November 1994) p 3341". As stated by Commissioner Wilson in *Bryant v Queensland Newspapers Pty Ltd* (unreported, Human Rights and Equal Opportunity Commission, Wilson P, 15 May 1997) the assessment of whether a particular action is reasonably likely to offend is a "question of fact in every case, depending on the context in which the allegedly offensive word or words" are used (cited in *Corunna*, at 75,466).

37 Looking at the context in this case, and the effect of Ms Power's use of the words "fucking" etc in connection with the words "white" and "whites", I have already explained that "white" refers to racial identity, and specifically to the group of peoples who form the dominant group in Australia. Ms Power called attention to Mr McLeod's membership of this group, not to express an attitude of racial superiority but, as I have indicated above, to express her frustration with what she saw as the imbalance of racial power

in the situation. In effect, Ms Power invoked the terms "white" and "whites" to express her frustration that this decision was made against her by the white prison officers because she was an Aboriginal woman. Put another way, she was pointing out her view that Mr McLeod had subjected her to an act of racial discrimination.

38 In fact, Mr McLeod's evidence suggests he formed the same view in that he expressed indignation at Ms Power's suggestion that he had been racist and not performed his duties fairly. While I accept his feelings on this were genuine, I do not accept that the effect of Ms Power's statement meets the requirements of the legislation. Considered in the context of the incident as a whole, and in light of the Act's purpose, it is my view that the likely effect of Ms Power's statement upon the reasonable white prison guard does not have the "necessary offensive, insulting, humiliating or intimidatory quality" referred to by Drummond J in *Hagan* and nor does it meet Kiefel J's test in *Creek* of being likely to have a "profound and serious" effect.

39 From his evidence, I understand that one source of Mr McLeod's indignation is his view that if he were to refer to Ms Power as "black" in an abusive tone, he would be brought to account by correctional services authorities. I agree that he would face action in those circumstances, but I do not agree that the events can be considered as equivalents. The *National Inquiry into Racist Violence* (HREOC, 1992) – one of the reports that inspired the introduction of the *Racial Hatred Act 1995* – found that Aboriginal and Torres Strait Islander peoples "are faced with racism in almost every aspect of their daily lives" and that violence against them is "endemic" (p 1). The experience of an act of race discrimination or vilification by an individual Aboriginal person cannot be understood in isolation from the pervasiveness of racism in their daily life, and so its impact is likely to be profound and serious. Conversely, we white Australians do not face the daily prospect of being discriminated against or subject to violence because of our race, colour or national or ethnic origin.

40 I have no doubt that Mr McLeod and his colleagues must regularly enforce unpopular decisions and in doing so attract the ire of prisoners as well as affected members of the public. However, those who exercise authority might well expect to encounter resistance and critique, and more particularly, in such an emotionally complex environment as a prison, might expect such resistance and critique to take robust forms. Even though it is not an act of racial vilification, I accept that Mr McLeod found the experience unpleasant. In that regard, it is significant that Mr McLeod and his fellow officers have other avenues to pursue their concerns, and have already made a complaint to prison authorities that resulted in Ms Power being banned from visiting the facility at Yatala for 3 months.

Was the act done 'otherwise than in private'?

41 For completeness, I note that it is clear that Ms Power's words occurred "otherwise than in private". The area outside the gatehouse where the words were said is a public place as defined by s 18C(2) and (3). Though Ms Power may well have intended her words to be private, she was

speaking loudly enough for the officer to hear her, and her words were capable of being heard by someone else. In my view, then, the quality of this act is that it is one that occurred "otherwise than in private" (see *Korczac v Commonwealth of Australia (Department of Defence)* (2000) EOC 93-056).

Conclusions

42 Accordingly, for the reasons outlined I find that the act complained of does not contravene the Act so that Mr McLeod's complaint must fail.

43 As this was in effect a "test case" brought by the Legal Fund, it is appropriate to state my view that, even if successful, this case would not have been an appropriate one for a grant of relief under s 46PO(4) of the *Human Rights and Equal Opportunity Act 1986* (Cth), which makes it discretionary to grant relief for proscribed acts of discrimination and vilification. As explained above, the Act was enacted to give effect to Australia's obligations under the ICERD, including those obligations related to eradicating acts "based on ideas or theories of superiority of one race or group" over another. The Act is not intended to shut down a conversation simply because it refers to race, but instead is clearly directed to protecting those within Australian society who are affected by harassment and fear as a result of their race, colour or national or ethnic origin.

44 I will take submissions on the issue of costs.

26

The Indirection of Sex Discrimination: *State of New South Wales v Amery*

MARGARET THORNTON

Introduction

A separation between public and private life is a central tenet of liberal legalism which has been accepted in the case of anti-discrimination legislation no less than in other instances of state regulation. This is despite the fact that inequities in the private sphere have long been recognised by feminist scholars as the primary cause of discrimination against women in public life, albeit not by judges, as is apparent from *New South Wales v Amery*.[1]

Although the last remnants of coverture, whereby a woman's persona merged with that of her husband on marriage, were removed over a century ago, the seeds of invidiousness associated with the deference of women to their male partners linger on in the contemporary social script. The question of where to live, for example, is likely to be influenced by *his* career, not hers. Women are also expected to assume the major responsibility for housework and caring for children, as well as for sick and elderly relatives.

The private location of these social practices has placed them largely beyond the limits of the law, although indirect discrimination on the ground of sex has corroded, if not eviscerated altogether, the private sphere immunity. A complaint of discrimination, however, has to arise in an area of public or quasi-public life, such as employment, and the complainant needs to establish the existence of an unbroken causal thread linking the respondent employer and the alleged discriminatory harm. Systemic discrimination buried deep within the social psyche does not suffice, as 'society' is not a suable entity; the harm must be sheeted home to an identifiable wrongdoer. Even then, it may be averred that a woman's decision to change from full-time to part-time or casual work, for example, is a matter of individual 'choice' not connected with the employer's work practices.

Given the contradictions besetting the conjunction of women, work and family in the discourse of gender equality, it is perhaps unsurprising that 'work/life balance' has become '*the* topic of the 21st century for families, employers and government',[2] a manifestation of which is thrown into high relief by *Amery*.

[1] (2006) 226 ALR 196 ('*Amery*').

[2] Sarah Squire and Jo Tilley, *It's About Time: Women, Men, Work and Family* (Human Rights and Equal Opportunity Commission, 2007) xi.

The Facts

This case involved a group of 13 female casual high school teachers in New South Wales who alleged that they had been subjected to sex discrimination because they were paid less than permanent staff, despite performing essentially the same work. All complainants were located at the top of the casual scale and were subject to a 20 per cent differential in pay compared with those at the top of the permanent scale. There were five steps in the casual scale and 13 in the permanent scale, with the top of the casual scale equating with Level 8 of the permanent scale.

The nub of the sex discrimination complaint was that access to the higher rate of pay required the women to satisfy the permanency requirement, which involved accepting a post anywhere in the State. As intimated, relocation because of family commitments is more difficult for women than for men because of the well-entrenched norm that women give priority to the needs of their families over their own careers. This norm induced the women to opt for casual positions close to their homes rather than relocate. The statistics adduced by the complainants graphically bear out the intransigence of the gendered norms. Although 70 per cent of all teachers in the New South Wales Teaching Service were women, only 59 per cent were permanent employees, compared with 79 per cent of men. Of the casual staff, approximately 83 per cent were female.

However, disproportionality alone does not establish discrimination. The social rationale for women's lower representation among the ranks of permanent teachers also needs to be established. It is this issue that goes to the heart of substantive equality. As feminists have long recognised, cognisance must be taken of the history of exclusion, past injustices and skewed social norms; formal equality (same treatment or equality before the law), which conveniently sloughs off the historical and contextual factors, is inadequate.[3]

The Litigation

The complaint was lodged under the *Anti-Discrimination Act 1977* (NSW) ('ADA (NSW)') in 1995 but was not decided by the High Court until 11 years later. In accordance with the typical model of anti-discrimination legislation in Australia, there was an initial attempt to effect a settlement through conciliation, but this proved unsuccessful. There were then four hearings within the relevant hierarchy of tribunals and courts, which alternated between findings in favour of the complainants and the respondent.

The primary hearing was before the NSW Administrative Decisions Tribunal (ADT), which found in favour of the complainants and awarded them damages of $250,000.[4] In the second instance, this decision was overturned by the ADT Appeals Panel in favour of the respondent.[5] Thirdly, the NSW Court of Appeal reinstated the decision of the ADT in favour

[3] Margaret Thornton, *The Liberal Promise: Anti-Discrimination Legislation in Australia* (Oxford University Press, 1990).

[4] *Amery v New South Wales* (2001) EOC ¶93-130.

[5] *New South Wales v Amery* (2003) 129 IR 300.

of the complainants in a 2:1 decision.[6] Finally, the High Court in *Amery* upheld the respondent's appeal in a 6:1 decision.

Underscoring the adjudicative volatility are the leeways of choice open to judges in their interpretative role.[7] Normally, they would have an array of binding precedents and persuasive decisions from which to choose. However, when the legal issues are novel, judges invariably fall back on their own normative universe to create meaning.[8] The element of judicial subjectivity determines whether they will look to the past in order to uphold the status quo, or look to the future to create a more imaginative and beneficent interpretation of the legislation. This dichotomy is sharply depicted in the *Amery* judgments.

The Jurisprudence

In common with most Australian anti-discrimination legislation, the ADA (NSW) distinguishes between direct and indirect discrimination. Direct discrimination sets out to deal with the simplest manifestation of discrimination, such as treating another person differently by virtue of (inter alia) sex when in the same or similar circumstances. Indirect discrimination attempts to go further by considering a practice that appears neutral on its face but disproportionately impacts on a group by virtue of sex. While well intentioned, the inclusion of indirect discrimination in anti-discrimination legislation resulted in a complex test that has become more convoluted with the aid of powerful and well-resourced respondents, such as State governments, as was the case in *Amery*. In addition, the neoliberal turn, which was very much in evidence during the period of the Howard Coalition Government (1996–2007), was reflected in conservative judicial appointments, the revival of employer prerogative in labour relations[9] and a preference for a strict equal treatment approach in discrimination jurisprudence.[10] *Amery* stands in stark contrast to the landmark indirect sex discrimination decision of *Australian Iron & Steel Pty Ltd v Banovic* in 1989,[11] a decision of the Mason Court (1987–95) when social liberalism was in the ascendancy and there was a greater willingness to endow remedial legislation with a beneficent interpretation.

The four-part test for indirect discrimination under the ADA (NSW) involves addressing: (i) the relevant requirement or condition; (ii) its disproportionate effect on the ground of sex; (iii) the reasonableness of the requirement or condition; and (iv) the ability of the complainants to comply with the requirement or condition. The probative burden on complainants is onerous under the ADA (NSW), as they have to prove that the requirement or condition is not reasonable. This contrasts with other Australian legislation where the burden rests with the respondent to prove the reasonableness of the requirement or condition.

Despite the complex constellation of issues that emerged in the case, the condition of permanency was accepted by the ADT and both appellate bodies as the relevant requirement or condition with which the complainants had to comply, but this was overruled by the High

[6] *Amery v Director-General, Department of Education and Training (NSW)* [2004] NSWCA 404 (15 November 2004).

[7] Julius Stone, *Precedent and Law: Dynamics of Common Law Growth* (Butterworths, 1985) 4, 109 *et passim*.

[8] Robert Cover, 'Nomos and Narrative' (1983) 97 *Harvard Law Review* 4.

[9] As reflected in the body of legislation known as 'WorkChoices' incorporated in the *Workplace Relations Act 1996* (Cth) and *Workplace Relations Regulations 2006* (Cth).

[10] Margaret Thornton, 'Sex Discrimination, Courts and Corporate Power' (2008) 36 *Federal Law Review* 31.

[11] (1989) 168 CLR 165. Cf *Waters v Public Transport Corporation* (1991) 173 CLR 349.

Court. The majority (Gummow, Hayne and Crennan JJ (Callinan J agreeing)) held that the terms or conditions of employment offered by the employer referred to the 'actual employment' in which the complainants were engaged,[12] that is, their employment as casual teachers, not their employment as teachers more generally. The bifurcation between casual and permanent employees meant that the terms and conditions of employment could apply to only one category of employee at a time, not both. The majority regarded the conflation of the casual and permanent categories as an error of law bordering on the incongruous.[13]

The narrow construction of the requirement or condition meant that the High Court had no need to progress to the second issue of reasonableness, which is frequently the sticking point in indirect discrimination litigation. It was discussed only by Gleeson CJ (Callinan and Heydon JJ agreeing), who was of the view that it had not been established by the complainants that it was unreasonable to pay casual and permanent staff at different rates.[14] The technocratic approach adopted by the majority, which treated the casual and permanent classifications as discrete, accords with the formal equality model. It meant that the overarching legislative aim of effecting equality between men and women in public life was accorded short shrift.

The majority judgment stands in sharp contrast with that of Kirby J, the sole dissenting judge. He lambasted the majority judges for their 'narrow and antagonistic' stance in light of the beneficial and purposive approach mandated by the legislation. He was even more censorious of the majority's deference to the historic and gendered categorisations, which he asserted had the effect of defining the discrimination complaint 'out of existence'.[15]

Amery was greeted with dismay by feminists, who felt that the High Court had frustrated the potential for claims of indirect discrimination in the same way that it had dealt a major blow to direct discrimination in *Purvis v New South Wales (Department of Education and Training)*[16] shortly before.[17] It was apparent that indirect discrimination could not be relied upon to address entrenched gender inequities in the workplace associated with pay, casualisation and family responsibilities.[18] The neoliberal turn with its favouring of employer prerogative, has resulted in technocratic judgments that pose a daunting challenge for heroic complainants in the future.

The Feminist Judgment

Beth Gaze carefully considers the arguments of the State of NSW relating to the characterisation of the requirement or condition, particularly the contention that there were two

[12] *Amery* (2006) 226 ALR 196, 213–14.

[13] Ibid 214.

[14] Ibid 203.

[15] Ibid 230.

[16] (2003) 217 CLR 92.

[17] K Lee Adams, 'Defining Away Discrimination' (2006) 19 *Australian Journal of Labour Law* 263, 278; Belinda Smith, 'Rethinking the *Sex Discrimination Act*: Does Canada's Experience Suggest We Should Give Our Judges a Greater Role' in Margaret Thornton (ed), *Sex Discrimination in Uncertain Times* (ANU EPress, 2010) 254.

[18] Beth Gaze, 'The *Sex Discrimination Act* at 25: Reflections on the Past, Present and Future' in Thornton (ed), ibid 120; Belinda Smith, 'What Kind of Equality Can We Expect from the Fair Work Act?' (2011) 35 *Melbourne University Law Review* 545; Fiona MacDonald and Sara Charlesworth, 'Equal Pay under the *Fair Work Act 2009* (Cth): Mainstreamed or Marginalised?' (2013) 36 *University of New South Wales Law Journal* 563, 568.

different jobs – casual teacher on the one hand, and permanent teacher on the other. She argues that to support the State's view would privilege form over substance. Furthermore, she suggests that the interpretation of the requirement or condition in the ADA (NSW) to refer to 'a particular kind of employee', viz, permanent *or* casual, would involve reading words into the Act. She rejects the technocratic interpretation of the majority judges of the High Court in favour of the liberal construction of the Court of Appeal.

Hence, unlike the majority judges of the High Court, Beth Gaze was compelled to consider the second prong of the indirect discrimination test – that of the reasonableness of the requirement or condition. She accords short shrift to the State's decidedly specious arguments, which included the contention that casual employment was a matter of individual 'choice' and that acceding to the women's claims would create an industrial problem by disturbing the settled expectations of (male) teachers. She therefore concluded that the imposition of the requirement or condition was not reasonable, and found for the complainants.

In common with the dissenting judgment of Kirby J, Beth Gaze evinces a willingness to move beyond the narrow interpretation of the ADA (NSW) adopted by the majority judges to pay attention to the context in accordance with the intention of the legislature. However, whereas Kirby J was primarily concerned with the deleterious impact of *Amery* on anti-discrimination legislation generally, Gaze's judgment is sensitively attuned to the ongoing workplace disadvantages experienced by women, particularly those with family responsibilities. Both judgments highlight Julius Stone's thesis that the leeways of choice are always open to judges; there is never just one right answer.

Postscript

One positive outcome to emerge from *Amery* is that supply casuals (temporary teachers) under the NSW Teaching Award are now paid at the same rate as permanent staff, and it is only relief casuals who are paid according to the casual award.[19] It is notable that this change was effected in January 2001 prior to the initial hearing before the ADT, but it was too late to alter the course of the litigation.

[19] Industrial Relations Commission of New South Wales, *Crown Employees (Teachers in Schools and Related Employees) Salaries and Conditions Award*, IRC 1027 (7 December 2012) ss 22–3.

THE STATE OF NEW SOUTH WALES............ APPELLANT;
DEFENDANT,

AND

AMERY AND OTHERS........................ RESPONDENTS.
PLAINTIFFS,

[2006] HCA 14

ON APPEAL FROM THE SUPREME COURT OF NEW SOUTH WALES

HC of A 2005-6

Nov 15,16 2005

April 13 2006

Gaze J

211 GAZE J. This appeal is brought by the State of New South Wales (the State) against a decision of the New South Wales (NSW) Court of Appeal in favour of thirteen women who claimed that the NSW Department of School Education (the Department) had indirectly discriminated against them on the basis of sex. All the women held appointments as permanent teachers in the Department earlier in their careers but resigned their positions, most (but not all) for reasons of family responsibilities, when they had children. All sought to rejoin the Department as teachers, but because of their family commitments to children and partners they had limitations on the areas in which they could work. Because they could not move as the Department directed, they were offered only casual teacher positions.

212 The salary scale for casual teachers was substantially lower than that for permanent teachers. Its maximum rate was the equivalent of level 8 of the 13-point permanent teachers' salary scale. Maximum pay for a permanent teacher was $50,000 at 1 January 1999 while for a casual teacher it was $40,576, a difference of almost 20 per cent. A senior casual teacher could be paid 20 per cent less than a permanent teacher with the same experience and responsibilities working in the next classroom.

213 The Department employed casual teachers in two categories: "relief casuals" were short term casual staff employed on a daily or hourly basis to cover absences by other teachers due to illness or other commitments, and "supply casuals" were casual staff employed on a long term basis (for at least eight weeks) to cover longer absences such as maternity leave or long service leave, or even sometimes as part of the regular staffing complement of a school. The women respondents were all supply casuals, who generally took the same responsibilities in a school as the permanent teachers they were replacing.

214 The situation facing the women in this case is not unusual for women who want to retain and pursue their careers while also taking primary responsibility for care of children. Social convention, and women's generally lower pay mean that women's jobs are often regarded as secondary to their husband's job, and that once children arrive, it is the mother who is likely to work part time or take some years out of the workforce to accommodate child care responsibilities, while the man takes over as main breadwinner and his career advances. As his employment is given priority, the

family is more likely to move to accommodate his employment than hers. A man whose wife is not working, working part time or has returned after a career break has mobility that a woman with a working husband does not (174), giving him an advantage where an employer requires mobility.

215 Women combining employment with care responsibilities seek work compatible with their care obligations. Although the teaching workforce is predominantly female, the Department's employment practices make no allowance for teachers during, or seeking to return after, taking responsibility for family care. Experienced teachers who seek to return and whose partner is not able to move are offered employment only as casual teachers, which is both insecure and lower paid. The Department benefits through access to a pool of cheaper but experienced employees who have few other options. These structural constraints on teachers who are mothers reinforce their workforce marginalisation.

The appeal

216 The appeal to this Court is an appeal in the strict sense, so to succeed the appellant must establish that the Court of Appeal made an error of law. This is not a merits review that would enable the court to substitute its own view without identifying an error made by the Court of Appeal. The legislative context of indirect sex discrimination is defined in s 24 of the *Anti-Discrimination Act 1977* (NSW) (the ADA) as follows:

> "(1) A person (the perpetrator) discriminates against another person (the aggrieved person) on the ground of sex if, on the ground of the aggrieved person's sex or the sex of a relative or associate of the aggrieved person, the perpetrator:
>
> . . .
>
> (b) requires the aggrieved person to comply with a requirement or condition with which a substantially higher proportion of persons of the opposite sex . . . comply or are able to comply, being a requirement which is not reasonable having regard to the circumstances of the case and with which the aggrieved person does not or is not able to comply."

All four elements mentioned in s 24(1)(b) must be established by the plaintiff to make out a case of indirect discrimination.

217 By s 5, the ADA binds the Crown. Section 25 specifies the areas of activity in which discrimination is unlawful:

> . . .
>
> "(2) It is unlawful for an employer to discriminate against an employee on the ground of sex:
>
> (a) in the terms or conditions of employment which the employer affords the employee."

218 When the ADA was adopted in 1977, s 54(1)(e) expressly excluded from its scope:

> "anything done by a person if it was necessary for the person to do it in order to comply with a requirement of . . . an order or award of a court or tribunal having power to fix minimum wages and other terms and conditions of employment."

(174) Joan Williams, *Unbending Gender* (Oxford University Press, 2000); Sandra Berns, *Women Going Backwards* (Ashgate, 2002); Barbara Pocock, *The Work-Life Collision* (Federation Press, 2003).

In August 1995 this provision was amended to expressly remove the exclusion of such orders or awards. As a result, a claim such as this became possible, and this claim was lodged in November 1995. The claim was upheld by the NSW Administrative Decisions Tribunal (the ADT) (175), overturned on appeal by the ADT Appeal Panel (the Appeal Panel) (176), and restored by the NSW Court of Appeal by a 2-1 majority (177). The only disagreements to this point have been on whether the onus of proof of "not reasonable" has been correctly applied.

Background: employment practices and salary scales

219 The *Teaching Services Act 1980* (NSW) (the TSA) authorises the Department to employ teachers in two categories: permanent teachers, known as "officers" and casual teachers, who are paid by the hour. The different salary scales for permanent and casual teachers are set by the teachers' award (178). The pay differential can be traced to a 1983 Industrial Commission decision (179) that treated all non-permanent staff the same, despite recognising that the value of long term "supply" casual teachers' work was closer to that of permanent teachers, since they took on after hours commitments corresponding with their longer term appointments, such as camps, parent teacher interviews and curriculum development (180).

220 The value of the work of long term casuals was the subject of evidence in the ADT, which found that it was equivalent to that of a permanent teacher (181).

221 The disproportionate impact on female teachers was addressed by evidence from the Department about staffing numbers for the period relevant to this case:

Classification	**Male**	**Female**	**Total**
Permanent	18,125	32,692	50,817
Casual	4,828	23,182	28,010
Total	22,953	55,874	78,827

Although 70 per cent of teachers were women, only 59 per cent of women teachers held a permanent position, compared with 79 per cent of men,

(175) *Amery v New South Wales* (2001) EOC ¶93–130. In *Amery v New South Wales (No 2)* [2001] NSWADT 187 (13 November 2001), the complainants' application for costs was denied, with the opinion of the judicial member on a question of law prevailing over the two dissenting non-judicial members.

(176) *New South Wales v Amery* (2003) 129 IR 300.

(177) *Amery v State of New South Wales* (2004) EOC ¶93–352 per Beazley JA and Cripps AJA, Hodgson JA dissenting.

(178) *Crown Employees (Teachers and Related Employees) Salaries and Conditions Award* made under the *Industrial Relations Act 1996* (NSW) from August 1996. Before then pay scales were in the Teachers and Related Employees Enterprise Agreement made under the *Industrial Relations Act 1991* (NSW).

(179) [1983] AR 672.

(180) *Amery v New South Wales* (2001) EOC ¶93-130, 75,283 at [32]–[33].

(181) (2001) EOC ¶93–130, 75,287 at [35].

leaving 41 per cent of women but only 21 per cent of men employed as casuals. Of casual teachers, 83 per cent were female and only 17 per cent male. Men held more permanent positions because they could more readily agree to move than women. Women were much more likely than men to be casuals and limited to the lower pay scale. There is a clear and substantial disproportion in the type of position held and hence pay rates according to the sex of the teacher.

The State's arguments

222 The State put two main arguments to this court. First, it argued there was no requirement or condition, because two different job categories were involved rather than one job with a requirement or condition attached to access the higher pay scale. Secondly it argued that if there was a requirement or condition, it was reasonable in all the circumstances. The State argued that the Court of Appeal had erred in law in finding that there was a requirement or condition, and that it was not reasonable.

The requirement or condition

223 Identifying the "requirement or condition" claimed to be discriminatory is central to an indirect discrimination case, as it determines the formulation of the other elements that must be proved by the complainant, such as ability to comply, disproportionate impact, and assessment of whether or not the requirement or condition is reasonable. In the ADT and the Appeal Panel the requirement or condition was loosely referred to as a requirement to have permanent status to access the higher pay scales. The Court of Appeal noted that the requirement to hold a permanent position to access the higher pay scale was not imposed by any law but resulted from the Department's practice of not making over award payments (182). This practice primarily affected supply casual teachers whose work was of the same value as permanent teachers.

224 Neither the TSA nor the teachers' award requires the Department to follow a policy or practice of not making over-award payments. Neither the TSA nor the award determined the requirement or condition involved, which was the Department's decision not to make over-award payments to provide equal pay for equal work.

225 In this court the appellant argued that there was no requirement or condition, even if it was formulated as a practice of not making over award payments to supply casuals. It said there are simply two different jobs, permanent teacher and casual teacher, not a single job of teacher to which people are appointed as permanent or casual staff. Since the difference between the jobs is part of their nature, it could not be separately identified as a requirement or condition.

226 The Department supported this argument by pointing to several provisions in the TSA that treat "officers" (permanent teachers) and casual teachers differently. As noted above, "officers" can be directed to work in

(182) (2004) EOC ¶93-352 at [11]–[12].

a particular location and be dismissed if they refuse; there is power to ensure the salary of an officer matches the duties performed: s 73(1); an officer who becomes ill can be retired or transferred: s 76; officers have an entitlement to leave: s 79; and may not engage in certain commercial activities without consent: s 89. Only officers can seek promotion to leadership positions in schools. In reality, however, these differences have little practical effect. Casual teachers are only offered specific work for a limited time and accrue no leave, so there is no practical need for the powers like those in the ADA.

227 To accept the State's argument that there are simply two different jobs would privilege form over substance. The focus of indirect discrimination law is on the effects of practices, not their form. The fact that supply casual teachers actually carry out the work of permanent teachers for more than eight weeks at a time and in some cases longer, strongly suggests that the jobs are regarded in practice as the same.

228 In further support of its argument, the state contended that the reference in ADA s 25(2)(a) to prohibiting discrimination in the "terms and conditions of employment" must refer to employment *as a particular kind of employee*, which had to be either permanent or casual, and therefore under the ADA there are two different kinds of employment rather than a requirement or condition. This argument rests on reading words into the ADA that are not present, requiring a "particular kind of employment", and interpreting that employment in a very narrow, formalistic way. If accepted, it would preclude any inquiry into whether the Department's practice regarding casual teacher pay is "not reasonable".

229 The ADA's prohibitions on employment discrimination are not formulated in terms of specific jobs. Instead, the formulation of "employment" used throughout s 25 is quite general and refers to the general nature of the relationship between the parties. The reference to "terms and conditions" suggests that varying terms and conditions of work such as full or part time, casual or permanent, categories were intended to be covered. Nothing in the ADA indicates that only a specific and narrowly defined job category was intended, which would protect differential treatment of employees engaged in the same work from challenge. To the contrary, the 1995 amendment of s 54 that opened industrial awards to challenge for discrimination suggests that Parliament's intention was to expose all aspects of employment relationships to scrutiny under the ADA, to better serve the ADA's aim of preventing and remedying discrimination.

230 The authorities indicate that it is not appropriate to take a narrow approach to identifying the requirement or condition, and a broad interpretation should be given. In *Australian Iron and Steel v Banovic* (183), this court approved the comments of Browne-Wilkinson J in *Clarke v Eley (IMI) Kynoch Ltd* (184) on the correct approach to interpreting the words "requirement or condition". Dawson J said of the NSW ADA that (185):

(183) (1989) 168 CLR 165.
(184) (1983) ICR 165.
(185) *Banovic* (1989) 168 CLR 165 at 185.

"[Section 24(1)(b)], which defines indirect discrimination, has a much wider application [than the provision which defines direct discrimination] and covers discrimination which is revealed by the different impact upon the sexes of a requirement or condition. The starting point with [s 24(1)(b)] must be the identification of the requirement or condition. Upon principle and having regard to the objects of the Act, it is clear that the words 'requirement or condition' should be construed broadly so as to cover any form of qualification or prerequisite demanded by an employer of his employees: *Clarke v. Eley (IMI) Kynoch Ltd.* (1983) ICR 165, at pp 170–171. Nevertheless, it is necessary in each particular instance to formulate the actual requirement or condition with some precision".

231 McHugh J also approved the comments of Browne-Wilkinson J, noting that in *Clarke*, an employer retrenching part time workers first in a redundancy situation was held to be applying a requirement or condition (186):

"[in *Clarke* the] Employment Appeal Tribunal rejected the submission that 'requirement' meant something which calls for or demands something of the person to whom it is applied and that 'condition', while including a qualification for holding a position, did not include a qualification for immunity from a disadvantage. Browne-Wilkinson J., giving the judgment of the Tribunal, said (187):

'In our view it is not right to give these words a narrow construction. The purpose of the legislature in introducing the concept of indirect discrimination into the Act of 1975 and the *Race Relations Act 1976* was to seek to eliminate those practices which had a disproportionate impact on women or ethnic minorities and were not justifiable for other reasons. The concept was derived from that developed in the law of the United States which held to be unlawful practices which had a disproportionate impact on black workers as opposed to white workers: see *Griggs v. Duke Power Co.* [1971] USSC 46; (1971) 401 US 424. If the elimination of such practices is the policy lying behind the Act, although such policy cannot be used to give the words any wider meaning than they naturally bear it is in our view a powerful argument against giving the words a narrower meaning thereby excluding cases which fall within the mischief which the Act was meant to deal with.'"

232 In *Home Office v Holmes* (188), a challenge was brought to a requirement to work full time, and in defence it was argued that the nature of the work was full time, not part time work, so there was no requirement or condition. The defence argued that the employment should be characterised as incorporating the requirement, so that it was simply the nature of the employment rather than a separate requirement, and the indirect discrimination claim must fail. The United Kingdom Employment Tribunal rejected this approach, holding that full and part time work were not different work; the legislative words were

"plain clear words of wide import fully capable of including any obligation of service whether for full time or for part time, and we see no basis for giving them a restrictive interpretation in the light of the policy underlying the Act" (189).

233 The style of argument put unsuccessfully by the defence in *Holmes* was also rejected by this court in *Waters v Public Transport Corporation* (190),

(186) *Clarke* (1983) ICR 165 at 196.
(187) (1983) ICR 165 at 171.
(188) (1994) ICR 678.
(189) (1994) ICR 678 at 682-3.
(190) (1992) 173 CLR 349.

a challenge to the removal of conductors from the Melbourne tram system. The plaintiffs claimed that the service in question was a public tram service on which a requirement for commuters to use it without the assistance of conductors was being imposed, which would have a disproportionate effect on people with a disability. The Corporation's argument that the service provided was simply a tram service without conductors, and no requirement or condition was involved, was rejected by the majority of the High Court (5-2). Dawson and Toohey JJ cited with approval Dawson J's comment in *Banovic* and continued (191):

> "It is true that for something to be a requirement or condition in relation to a matter it must be separate from that matter. However, whether such a requirement or condition is in fact separate from the matter to which it relates will clearly depend upon how the matter is described and how the requirement or condition is characterized. Given that the legislation should receive a generous construction, we do not think that the respondent can evade the implications of s. 17(5) by defining the service which it provides so as to incorporate as part of that service what would otherwise be a requirement or condition of the provision of that service".

234 McHugh J reiterated that "the phrase 'requirement or condition' [should] be given a broad interpretation to enable the objectives of the Act to be fulfilled" (192) and continued (193):

> "In the context of providing goods or services, a person should be regarded as imposing a requirement or condition when that person intimates, expressly or inferentially, that some stipulation or set of circumstances must be obeyed or endured if those goods or services are to be acquired, used or enjoyed".

235 In both *Banovic* and *Waters* this Court has held that a broad approach should be taken to interpreting "requirement or condition" in accordance with the objectives of the legislation. In *Waters* where it was argued that the alleged requirement or condition was part of the nature of the service or employment, this Court specifically warned against determining the service so as to exclude cases that fall within the mischief the Act is intended to deal with. By analogy, the same should apply to identifying the employment concerned, as *Holmes* illustrates.

236 The State has not convincingly argued that these precedents are not applicable or are no longer authoritative. Its argument would undermine the purpose of the ADA and the concept of indirect discrimination, and would prevent consideration of the very issues that Parliament has specified as relevant to assessing whether indirect discrimination has occurred. This Court should follow the approach adopted in *Banovic* and *Waters*. No error has been shown in the Court of Appeal's decision identifying the requirement or condition.

Was the requirement or condition "not reasonable"?

237 Two other elements of the indirect discrimination claim are clearly established. The disproportionate impact of the requirement is clear from

(191) (1992) 173 CLR 349 at 394.
(192) (1992) 173 CLR 349 at 406.
(193) (1992) 173 CLR 349 at 407.

the Department's data. The inability of the complainants to comply with either the requirement to be available for relocation in order to qualify for permanent status, or to be paid over-award by the Department, is not contested.

238 The State argued that the requirement or condition had not been shown to be "not reasonable", pointing to a range of factors that were said to make it reasonable. The assessment of reasonableness is a question of fact, although determining what factors are relevant to assessing it is a question of law: *Waters* (194). The Court of Appeal's decision cannot be set aside merely because of disagreement with its assessment and weighting of the factors considered. It can be overturned only if legal error can be shown.

239 The State made a number of arguments in support of its claim that the requirement or condition had not been shown to be not reasonable. To show error of law by the Court of Appeal, the State would have to establish that the factors were relevant and were not considered by the ADT in making its assessment. The Court of Appeal did not undertake its own assessment of reasonableness. Instead, in setting aside the Appeal Panel's determination that the ADT erred in law, and rejecting all other arguments, it restored the ADT's decision. First, the State said, it was the respondents' own choice to limit the area in which they could work and hence they limited their own ability to access the higher pay scale. Further, a finding of indirect discrimination would be unreasonable because it would disturb existing industrial relativities in pay, and finally, it would benefit only the plaintiffs in this action, not all other women or employees who were supply casuals.

240 *Choice:* It was argued that it was the respondents' own choice to restrict their geographical availability that was the reason for their casual status and lower pay. However, as Beazley JA held, the subjective preferences of the respondents were not a relevant factor in assessing reasonableness (195). The issue is the reasonableness of the requirement or condition that the Department not make over-award payments to supply casuals. The choices made by individuals to impose limitations on their job applications that prevent them from obtaining a permanent position are not relevant to this requirement or condition, as they do not influence it in any way. No error of law has been shown.

241 In practice the respondents had little choice. If they wanted to return to professional work using their qualifications and experience, and could not undertake to move their family as the Department required, their only option was to accept casual work. The essence of the disadvantage of indirect discrimination in this situation is that the employer's practices constrained long term casual teachers to "choices" that disproportionately disadvantaged them on the basis of sex. Such a "choice" is not a defence to a discrimination claim.

(194) (1992) 173 CLR 349 at 378 per Brennan J; at 396 per Dawson and Toohey JJ. The Victorian Supreme Court had held that excluding the financial situation of the Public Transport Corporation from assessment of reasonableness amounted to error of law: *Public Transport Corporation v Waters* [1992] 1 VR 151.

(195) [2004] NSWCA 404 at [81]–[86].

242 *Industrial relativities*: The State argued that relativities in the industrial relations system would be disturbed if it made over award payments to the respondents. However, this argument could apply to all indirect discrimination cases that affected payment practices, as any remedy would disturb existing pay practices and therefore relativities. This argument would negate the 1995 amendments to the ADA by which Parliament indicated that a discriminatory industrial instrument was no longer to be an automatic defence to a discrimination claim. It cannot be accepted.

243 The State further argued that it would not be reasonable to pay every potentially affected teacher on the permanent salary scale because it would be too costly. It was recognised in *Waters* that the cost to the employer of compliance is a relevant factor, and in *Waters* it was decisive (196). But the context is different when considering pay inequity than the reduction or variation of government services for budgetary reasons. While both can seriously affect individuals in protected groups, the ongoing personal injustice of pay inequity makes it more difficult to regard it as reasonable.

244 The 1995 amendment of the ADA that brought industrial awards and agreements within the scope of the ADA's prohibitions on discrimination was a major change. It shows a clear legislative policy to remove discrimination in or arising from awards or agreements. This change exposed to scrutiny longstanding and widespread practices that had developed in an environment protected from challenge for discrimination.

245 Of its nature, indirect discrimination poses a challenge to existing ways of doing things and is likely to disrupt some settled practices (197). As a result, decisions on indirect discrimination claims can be controversial and unfamiliar. With the large scale movement of women into the workforce since the 1960s, employment practices designed for the paradigm "unencumbered" worker (198) who can readily move at his employer's direction can operate unfairly to them. Indirect discrimination law provides a means for this to be addressed.

246 The lower pay rate for casual teachers originated in 1983 when awards were protected from challenge for discrimination, but the State seeks to continue this approach despite its discriminatory effect. To allow this would fail to give due weight to the injustice experienced by the respondents, and to Parliament's 1995 decision not to continue to protect industrial practices from challenge for discrimination.

247 Lower pay for work of equal value is a serious, substantial, and ongoing injustice. Lower pay for a work category dominated by women where the work is of the same value is both intrinsically unjust, and also contributes to the reinforcing cycle of women's disadvantage at work. In particular it positions mothers as a cheaper, reserve labour force.

248 The challenge facing the Department in resolving any industrial relations issues that might be caused by remedying this injustice is a factor that deserves consideration. But if it were to outweigh the injustice identified

(196) (1992) 173 CLR 349.
(197) Hunter, *Indirect Discrimination in the Workplace* (Federation Press, 1992).
(198) Williams, above n 1.

here, gendered pay inequity could never be resolved through a discrimination claim. This cannot have been the intention of Parliament in adopting the 1995 amendment.

Remedy would benefit only these claimants: The 13 women who brought this claim should not be denied a remedy for proven discrimination against them because others in a similar position may also have experienced discrimination. Speculation about possible consequences of this decision cannot be a reason to refuse a remedy where a breach of the law has been established.

249 The test of reasonableness provides a mechanism for moderating the impact of indirect discrimination law and allowing change to occur while ensuring that other interests are also considered, but not for halting it altogether. It should not be a means for condoning a serious and ongoing discriminatory injustice. Courts must be careful, in weighing up the circumstances, not to devalue the disadvantage suffered by the complainants in the existing system merely because it is familiar and longstanding. The State has not succeeded in showing that any error was made by the ADT in its assessment that the requirement was not reasonable, or by the Court of Appeal in upholding that decision.

250 I would reject the appeal and uphold the decision of the Court of Appeal.

Treaty Law

27

Commentary on *In the Matter of Djappari (Re Tuckiar)*

THALIA ANTHONY

Background

The judgment of *Tuckiar v R*[1] has acquired a reputation as a moment when the High Court provided justice for Indigenous defendants and the accused more generally. The case is celebrated by evidence and criminal lawyers as vindicating the right to a fair trial because it upheld principles of judicial impartiality and independence (including from prejudicial publicity), the presumption of innocence, the right to silence and a lawyer's duty to his/her client and the court.[2] The High Court overturned the Indigenous defendant's conviction for murder on a number of grounds, including that the Northern Territory Supreme Court trial judge, Wells J, exhibited bias against the defendant in his remarks inter alia about the need to retain the memory of the deceased white police officer through finding the defendant guilty.

The *Tuckiar* trial took place during the high-water mark of protectionism, when social Darwinist ideas about the inferior status of Indigenous people prevailed.[3] Aboriginal Protection Acts governed Aboriginal lives across Australia – placing control in the hands of Aboriginal protectors, including control over Aboriginal work, residence, money, marriage and legal matters.[4] These discriminatory Acts excluded Aboriginal people from Australian society. The judge in the case, Wells J, was a proponent of Aboriginal protectionism and their exclusion from cities and towns, and viewed the prison system as an inadequate punishment for Aboriginal offenders.[5] He feared that prisons would bring Aboriginal people within white domains. Rather, he promoted corporal punishment (a sentencing option that was unavailable by the time of Wells J's term) and capital punishment for Aboriginal offenders.[6] He routinely ordered the death penalty for Aboriginal offenders who committed

[1] (1934) 52 CLR 335 ('*Tuckiar*').

[2] Robert Hayes and Michael Eburn, *Criminal Law and Procedure in New South Wales* (Lexis Nexis, 3rd ed, 2009) 39.

[3] For the context and critiques of this case, see Ted Egan, *Justice All Their Own: The Caledon Bay and Woodah Island Killings 1932–1933* (Melbourne University Press, 1996); Peter Read, 'Murder, Revenge and Reconciliation on the North Eastern Frontier' (2007) 4 *History Australia* 09.1.

[4] See, eg, *Aboriginal Protection Act 1869* (Vic); *Aborigines Protection Act 1886* (WA); *Aboriginal Protection Act and Restriction of the Sale of Opium Act 1897* (Qld); *Aborigines Protection Act 1909* (NSW); *Aborigines Act 1911* (SA); *Aboriginals Ordinance 1911* (Cth); *Aboriginals Ordinance 1918* (Cth).

[5] Heather Douglas, *Aboriginal Australians and the Criminal Law: History, Policy, Culture* (VDM Verlag, 2009) 153.

[6] Ibid.

serious crimes, notwithstanding that it was not a mandatory penalty for homicide.[7] Wells J was vocal in his opposition to 'do-gooders' who sought to recognise Indigenous cultural issues in the criminal justice system, as well as the 'sloppy sentimentality' of those who believed that Aboriginal people should be able to administer their own punishment without interference from the courts.[8] His perception of the backwardness of Aboriginal people meant that Wells J believed that they required harsh physical punishment to teach them a lesson.[9]

The 1930s – the period of Tuckiar's trial – is also considered a time when concern was mounting over the 'annihilation of full-blooded Aborigines' and there was international pressure for Australian governments to revise the Aboriginal Acts in order to 'embrace Black Australians with varying degrees of Aboriginal blood'.[10] At the same time, there was a substantial 'increase of mixed-blooded Aborigines' in the Northern Territory, approximately 60 times the growth rate of the 'white population', leading to the conclusion that 'miscegenation between blacks and whites was widespread, the typical sexual union being between European men and Aboriginal women', with men seldom accepting and recognising their offspring.[11]

Historians describe the courtroom dramas at Tuckiar's trial and appeal as involving the church, the state, the judiciary, various pressure groups and foreign governments.[12] In response to pressure exerted by the British Dominions office, Prime Minister Lyons sought to ascertain from groups critical of the trial, such as the Association for the Protection of Native Races, led by Professor Elkin, the truth of the allegations against Tuckiar.[13] At the time, the Australian government was particularly sensitive to international opinion regarding its treatment of 'native peoples'.[14] Missionaries, on the other hand, were in favour of apprehending Tuckiar, presumably to counter widespread evidence that white men were entering into sexual relations with Aboriginal women.[15] Surrounding Tuckiar's trial, the media 'demand[ed] vengeance'.[16] The media omitted reference to what historian Peter Read describes as McColl's attempted rape, namely, that the deceased police officer, McColl, had taken 'Tuckiar's women' with the intention of committing sexual assault, which was consistent with McColl's previous encounters with Aboriginal women.[17]

The Trial

The trial involved Tuckiar, a Yolŋgu man, who allegedly killed Constable Albert McColl, a white policeman, on Woodah Island, Gulf of Carpentaria in 1933. Tuckiar was described by

[7] Dean Mildren, *Big Boss Fella – All Same Judge: A History of the Supreme Court of the Northern Territory* (Federation Press, 2011) 24.

[8] Read, above n 3, 09.5.

[9] Wells J regarded the death penalty as condign punishment for Aboriginal people guilty of homicide: Mildren, above n 7, 111.

[10] Adam Shoemaker, *Black Words White Page: Aboriginal Literature 1929–1988* (ANU e-press, 2004) 20.

[11] Ibid.

[12] CD Rowley, *The Destruction of Aboriginal Society* (Penguin, 1978) 290–7.

[13] Richard Broome, *Aboriginal Australians: Black Response to White Dominance, 1788–1980* (Allen and Unwin, 1982) 165.

[14] Ibid.

[15] Rowley, above n 12, 290–7.

[16] Read, above n 3, 09.2, 09.5.

[17] Ibid.

the High Court as 'a completely uncivilised aboriginal native',[18] which echoed the view of Wells J. The only evidence against him at trial were confessions that he allegedly made to two other Aboriginal people who could not speak English. One confession was to Parriner, another Yolŋgu man, that Tuckiar had hidden in the bushes and signalled to one of 'his women' [wives] (who had been taken away by McColl along with two of his other women/wives) to move away from the constable so he could spear him. The other confession was to an Aboriginal boy named Harry in which Tuckiar claimed he had seen McColl having sex with one of his wives and consequently McColl fired at him four times and Tuckiar retaliated by spearing McColl. Forcibly taking Aboriginal women and having sexual relations outside of customary marriage are both serious breaches of Yolŋgu law.

Tuckiar did not speak English and did not submit any evidence at trial. His legal representative was appointed by the Protector of Aborigines. The lawyer told Wells J that he had not obtained instructions from Tuckiar about what Parriner had to say. The judge adjourned the trial so the lawyer could speak with Tuckiar, and the lawyer could then speak privately with the judge in the presence of the Protector of Aborigines. Subsequently no evidence was called on Tuckiar's behalf. Trial judge Wells, nonetheless, commented that he believed Parriner's evidence over Harry's, stating that he believed Harry's statement to be 'so utterly ridiculous to be an obvious fabrication'.[19] By contrast, the Crown's story 'sounds highly probable, and fits in with all the known facts', according to Wells J.[20]

The jury asked the trial judge how to form a position if they are not satisfied that there is enough evidence for the Crown to prove guilt beyond reasonable doubt. In directing the jury on how to treat this issue, including due to Tuckiar exercising his choice not to give evidence in court, Wells J said that the jurors should not be swayed if they thought the Crown had not done its duty, and to make whatever inference they choose from Tuckiar's silence. Rather than informing the jury that the correct position would be to acquit the defendant, he stated that a 'verdict of "not guilty"' may 'mean a grave miscarriage of justice' because it 'would be a serious slander on [the police officer]'.[21] In other words, an acquittal would harm the reputation of the officer because it would imply that he had engaged in 'sexual relations with the lubra'.[22] In seeking to maintain the virtue of the white police officer, Wells J pointed to McColl's good moral character.[23]

In relation to the inference to be made from Tuckiar's silence, Wells J commented that the jury could draw any inference: 'For some reason Tuckiar has not gone into the box and told you which [story] is true, and that is a fact which you are entitled to take into consideration. You can draw from it any inference you like'.[24] Tuckiar was convicted. After the verdict, Tuckiar's counsel informed the Northern Territory Supreme Court that Tuckiar had told him that Parriner's account was true.[25] Wells J sentenced Tuckiar to death. In doing so, the judge refused to take account of the defendant's background and customs, despite recent legislation specifically allowing him to do so.[26] This refusal to account for mitigating circumstances led to a large public meeting in Sydney in 1934 and the involvement of the

[18] *Tuckiar* (1934) 52 CLR 335, 339.
[19] Cited in ibid 351.
[20] Quoted in ibid 343.
[21] Quoted in ibid 342.
[22] Cited in ibid 341.
[23] Quoted in ibid 341.
[24] Quoted in ibid 343.
[25] Quoted in ibid 354.
[26] *Criminal Procedure Ordinance 1933* (NT) s 6; *Crimes Ordinance 1934* (NT) s 6A.

Prime Minister and the Australian High Commissioner in London.[27] Public pressure would influence the decision to appeal the case to the High Court.[28]

High Court's Reasoning

Tuckiar appealed to the High Court on the grounds that Wells J had misdirected the jury. The five judges unanimously upheld the appeal and quashed the conviction. They found that Wells J acted in a way prejudicial to the defendant.[29] He defied the presumption of innocence that was embedded in Northern Territory statutes.[30] The Court did not order a new trial due to the widespread prejudicial publicity surrounding the statement made by Tuckiar's counsel that imputed his guilt.[31] In these circumstances, the Court considered that it would be 'impossible' to afford Tuckiar a fair trial.[32] Burgess describes *Tuckiar* as a 'landmark decision in Australian criminal law as it represented the first instance of a defendant's conviction being quashed, and a verdict of acquittal being entered, on account of the potential prejudicial effect of pre-trial publicity'.[33]

In relation to the right to silence, the majority, Duffy CJ and Dixon, Evatt and McTiernan JJ, held in a joint judgment that Wells J's observations in relation to Tuckiar's failure to give evidence 'amounted to a clear misdirection and one which in the circumstances was calculated gravely to prejudice the prisoner'.[34] The judgment held that the defendant was not obliged to give evidence in his own defence.[35] Further, Wells J should have disallowed the admission of evidence of McColl's 'good character and moral tendencies' on the basis that it was irrelevant: 'the purpose of the trial was not to vindicate the deceased constable but to inquire into the guilt of the living Aboriginal'.[36]

The majority joint judgment was critical of Tuckiar's counsel's conduct, especially in relation to disclosing confidential communication with his client, and failing to pursue the possibility of an acquittal or a verdict of the lesser charge of manslaughter.[37] The High Court regarded the lawyer's disclosure of Tuckiar's confession as a 'grave breach of confidence'.[38] In relation to pursuing the lesser charges, the majority stated that the lawyer's duty is 'both to his client and to the Court', which includes pressing rational considerations as the evidence provides in favour of acquittal or a verdict of manslaughter.[39] The majority held that a lawyer has a duty to act honestly and fairly in the client's best interests and to present the

[27] AP Elkin, 'Aboriginal Policy 1930–1950: Some Personal Associations' (1957) 1 *Quadrant* 29–30, cited in Rowley, above n 12, 295.

[28] Australian Law Reform Commission, *The Recognition of Aboriginal Customary Laws*, Final Report No 31 (1986).

[29] *Tuckiar* (1934) 52 CLR 335, 344.

[30] Ibid.

[31] On the issue of prejudicial publicity, see Craig Burgess, 'Prejudicial Publicity: When Will it *Ever* Result in a Permanent Stay of Proceedings?' (2009) 28 *University of Tasmania Law Review* 63.

[32] *Tuckiar* (1934) 52 CLR 335, 337, 347, 355.

[33] Burgess, above n 31, 65–6.

[34] *Tuckiar* (1935) 52 CLR 335, 344.

[35] Ibid.

[36] Ibid 344–5.

[37] Ibid 346.

[38] Ibid 354.

[39] Ibid 346.

evidence fairly, and the lawyer's opinion about the matter or what he may have uncovered as the 'truth' is irrelevant.[40]

Transforming *Tuckiar* Through a Feminist-Oriented Indigenous Judgment

Ultimately, the High Court's majority judgment employs a traditional doctrinal or legalist approach, focusing on the trial judge's decision and whether the statutory and common law principles were correctly understood and applied. It does not consider the relevance of Tuckiar's background or culture in interpreting the situation he was facing. The minority judgment, delivered by Starke J, does this to a greater extent by applying a 'realist' and 'purposive' approach. He attempts to consider the personal perspective and environment that came to bear on the interpretation of the law. He also highlights different facts, placing greater emphasis on the circumstances facing Tuckiar and his community at the time of McColl's death. Starke J notes the 'wild, excited and frightened' nature of the Aboriginal people, given the increased police presence and police apprehensions, and how the Aboriginal people may have perceived the police as attacking them and their women.[41] Starke J underscores the dangers of relying too heavily on the witnesses' statements, especially given that neither understood English, as over-riding proof that Tuckiar had confessed to murdering Constable McColl. However, even this broader reading is circumscribed by the limited capacity of the courts to account for Indigenous perspectives.

Nicole Watson's feminist-oriented Indigenous judgment attempts to bridge the gap between the white legalist approach in *Tuckiar* and Indigenous laws. It envisions a future society where a Treaty Act governs relations between Indigenous and non-Indigenous Australians and an Indigenous court has jurisdiction over Indigenous matters. The approach of the Indigenous court draws on the lived experiences of Indigenous peoples and is not constrained by evidence or legal doctrine. The court has been tasked not with deciding the culpability of Tuckiar, but rather with piecing together the historical story of Tuckiar's widow, Djaparri. It rectifies the invisibility of Djaparri's experience in the *Tuckiar* proceedings – an invisibility that has been attributed to Indigenous women's experiences generally in the criminal justice system.

Watson's feminist judgment shifts the legal approach, including by its reliance on more diverse sources and means of analysis, and through its critical use of language and Indigenous terms. It positions Djaparri as a sovereign of Yolŋgu law, rather than a mere victim. It details her experiences of colonisation and the white police and legal system with brutalising effect on an empowered Yolŋgu society. The feminist judgment condemns the Australian legal system for its disregard of the alleged sexual assault of Djaparri and its derogatory characterisations of her sexuality. It conveys the damage that the criminalisation of Indigenous men has on Indigenous women. Watson's judgment does not provide justice through a finding in law, but through findings of historical fact and the rewriting of the historical record.

[40] Ibid 346.
[41] Ibid 349.

IN THE MATTER OF DJAPARRI (RE TUCKIAR) [2035] FNCA 1

FOLEY CJ and WATSON J

11 December 2034; 14 January 2035

FOLEY CJ

1 This is an application brought by the Aboriginal Women's Rights Foundation pursuant to s 25 of the *Treaty Between the Republic of Australia and the Confederation of Aboriginal and Torres Strait Islander Nations Act 2028* (*Treaty Act*). Section 25 requires the Court to critique decisions that have had significant impacts on the ability of Aboriginal and Torres Strait Islander people to exercise their right to legal equality. The purpose of s 25 was elucidated by Mansell J in *Re Anderson*:

> "The Court's function under s 25 is but one dimension of the decolonisation process that began with the enactment of the Treaty Act. Section 25 requires the Court to re-examine the histories of those Aboriginal and Torres Strait Islander people whose names appear in our law reports. By going beyond the relevant facts considered by the original decision-maker, and casting a light on the lived experience of Aboriginal and Torres Strait Islander people, this Court writes back to a legal system that was once the bulwark of colonisation."[1]

2 In fulfilling this role the Court is constrained by neither the rules of evidence, nor established doctrine. The Court's deliberations will have no legal impact upon the actual parties, some of whom may be deceased. The absence of tangible outcomes notwithstanding, the Court's role under s 25 has proven to be a meaningful contribution to the national healing process that began with the enactment of the *Treaty Act*. It has created a medium for the inclusion of Aboriginal and Torres Strait Islander narratives in the common law. This process of "outsider storytelling" has long been recognised to be empowering for groups who have, historically, suffered oppression.[2] Storytelling is also the most "primordial meeting ground"[3] that we human beings possess, and therefore, the Court's function under s 25 can promote greater understanding between all citizens of the Republic.

3 This application requests the Court to consider the decision of *Tuckiar v The King* (1934) 52 CLR 335 (*Tuckiar*). It is unusual in that the Court has not been asked to unearth the prisoner's story, but rather the story of his widow, Djaparri Bulinjun Wirrpanda (Djaparri).

The facts before the High Court

4 The prisoner was charged with the murder of Constable Albert Stewart McColl, at Woodah Island off the coast of Arnhem Land, on 1 August 1933. He was convicted before

[1] *Re Anderson* [2030] FNCA 1 (1 February 2030), [25].
[2] Richard Delgado, "Storytelling for Oppositionists and Others: A Plea for Narrative" (1988–1989) 87 *Michigan Law Review* 2411.
[3] Ibid 2438.

the Supreme Court of the Northern Territory and sentenced to death. The High Court granted the prisoner leave to appeal against his conviction and sentence.

5 Chief Justice Gavan Duffy and his brother judges described "Tuckiar" as a "completely uncivilised aboriginal native".[4] In reality, however, this Yolŋgu man was properly called Dhäkiyarr.[5] Out of respect for him and his family, this Court will refer to the prisoner by his real name. Little else appears to have been known about Dhäkiyarr, other than that he neither understood nor spoke English.

6 Immediately prior to his death, McColl had been a member of a police party that travelled to Woodah Island for the purpose of investigating the deaths of five Japanese fishermen. Soon after its arrival the party stumbled upon a group of Aboriginal women, who were described in the judgments as "lubras"; a term that is now regarded as derogatory.

7 The women were handcuffed and taken back to the party's camp. The police were subsequently notified of some "natives" nearby. The party splintered, with some members leaving the camp to intercept the new arrivals. However, McColl and two trackers remained with the women. By the time the other members of the party returned to the camp, McColl and the women had disappeared. McColl's body was found the following morning, approximately 400 metres away from the camp. He had died as a result of a spear wound to the chest.

8 Dhäkiyarr was later induced to sail to Darwin where he was charged with the murder of McColl. The Crown's evidence consisted of confessions allegedly made by Dhäkiyarr while on his voyage, to two Aboriginal men; Parriner and Harry. As was the practice in 1930s Australia, those Aboriginal men were referred to as "boys" in the judgments of both the majority and Starke J.

9 According to Parriner's evidence, Dhäkiyarr told him that he had seen the police party take a group of Aboriginal women to their camp, some of whom were his kin, including Djaparri. He hid in the jungle nearby and waited. Eventually, one of the policemen and a "lubra" walked away from the camp. While they were separated from the others, Dhäkiyarr threw his spear at the officer, causing the fatal wound. Although she was not named in the judgment, Djaparri was the woman who was with McColl at the time of his death. Harry's evidence differed somewhat from Parriner's. Crucially, Harry alleged that Dhäkiyarr told him that he had seen McColl having sexual relations with Djaparri.

10 Dhäkiyarr's disadvantage stemming from being unable to understand the proceedings, which were conducted in English, was compounded by the trial judge and his own counsel, WJP Fitzgerald. The desire of both to protect McColl's reputation from what they considered to be a grave slur resulted in a number of irregularities, which ultimately caused the trial to miscarry. Those anomalies included the wrongful admission of evidence of McColl's good character. The trial judge also made a number of directions that were calculated to prejudice Dhäkiyarr, including a direction to the jury that it was open to them to draw "any inference you like"[6] from his failure to give evidence. Perhaps unsurprisingly, in light of the conduct of the trial, Dhäkiyarr was found guilty. Fitzgerald then disclosed, in

[4] *Tuckiar* (1934) 52 CLR 335, 339 (Gavan Duffy CJ, Dixon, Evatt, McTiernan JJ).
[5] Richard Trudgen, *Why Warriors Lie Down and Die* (Aboriginal Resource and Development Services Inc, 2000) 37.
[6] *Tuckiar* (1934) 52 CLR 335, 343.

open court, privileged communications between Dhäkiyarr and himself, to the effect that the confession made to Parriner had been truthful.

11 The High Court quashed the conviction and directed that a verdict of acquittal be entered. Freedom for Dhäkiyarr, however, was short-lived, as he disappeared soon after he was freed from Fanny Bay Gaol on 9 November 1934, the day after the High Court handed down its decision. Over the years there has been much speculation that Dhäkiyarr was murdered by police, who disposed of his body in Darwin Harbour.[7] That mystery, however, has never been solved.

The Court's approach to s 25 *Treaty Act*

12 This Court defers to the view of esteemed literary critic and public intellectual Edward Said that "reading and writing texts are never neutral activities".[8] In interpreting colonial texts, Said urged for a "contrapuntal" analysis; that is, an analysis that identified the shadow of empire in English novels, while simultaneously considering the repressed histories of the colonised:

> "In practical terms, 'contrapuntal reading' as I have called it means reading a text with an understanding of what is involved when an author shows, for instance, that a colonial sugar plantation is seen as important to the process of maintaining a particular style of life in England. Moreover, like all literary texts, these are not bounded by their formal historic beginnings and endings. References to Australia in *David Copperfield* or India in *Jane Eyre* are made because they *can* be, because British power (and not just the novelist's fancy) made passing references to these massive appropriations possible; but the further lessons are no less true: that these colonies were subsequently liberated from direct and indirect rule . . . The point is that contrapuntal reading must take account of both processes, that of imperialism and that of resistance to it, which can be done by extending our reading of the texts to include what was once forcibly excluded . . ."[9]

13 Contrapuntal analysis is a useful tool for creating a medium for Indigenous voices to be heard, while also interrogating the histories and assumptions that provide the backdrop of court decisions. The end result presents the whole picture of an episode in the trajectory of Australian law, told through Indigenous and non-Indigenous voices.

14 In exercising its function under s 25, this Court applies a contrapuntal analysis. That is, the Court reaches beyond the legal text and tries to cast light on the lived experiences of the Indigenous parties. The Court considers the forces that made oppressive laws possible, the likely impacts upon the individuals concerned, and the legacies that remain in the shadows of Australian law.

A contrapuntal analysis of *Tuckiar v The King*

The pervasiveness and normalisation of racial oppression in Northern Australia

15 Racism was firmly embedded in the early criminal laws of the Northern Territory, and the cultures of the institutions that would have such profound impacts upon the lives of Dhäkiyarr and Djaparri. White male privilege and a widely held belief in Aboriginal inferiority provided the ideological foundations for the colonisation of what is now known as the Northern Territory. Nineteenth century police officers on the frontier were largely concerned

[7] Ted Egan, *Justice All Their Own: The Caledon Bay and Woodah Island Killings 1932-1933* (Melbourne University Press, 1996) 192.

[8] Edward Said, *Culture and Imperialism* (Chatto & Windus, 1993) 385.

[9] Ibid 78–79.

with protecting settlers whose mining and pastoral activities resulted in the dispossession of traditional owners. Such protection included punitive expeditions. A few years before the fateful events on Woodah Island, a police patrol was responsible for the killing of at least 31 Aboriginal people in Central Australia, in what is now known as the Coniston Massacre.

16 Those who were spared retributive justice were subject to inhumane and degrading treatment, such as being forced to wear neck chains. Gray suggests that not only Aboriginal prisoners but also Aboriginal witnesses were escorted in neck chains as a matter of practice.[10] Punishments imposed on Aboriginal prisoners who managed to survive for long enough to be sentenced included whipping, flogging and death by hanging. Of the latter, Aboriginal prisoners were regularly executed at the scene of the crime, in order to provide an example to their countrymen. Gray has referred to the execution of one man, Moolooloorun. The 50 Aboriginal people who witnessed his death were instructed not to grieve and were then provided with tobacco, blankets and food.[11]

17 The brutal and retributive justice regularly meted out to Aboriginal people reflected the view that they were a threat in need of control, and as such, unworthy of the law's protection. This view was so pervasive that the right to trial by jury was abolished in the Northern Territory in 1921, partly in response to the unwillingness of juries to convict Europeans charged with committing offences against Aboriginal people.[12] Members of the judiciary, however, were not unaffected by the society to which they belonged. Judge Thomas Alexander Wells, who presided over Dhäkiyarr's trial, believed that Aboriginal prisoners should be flogged rather than incarcerated. In sentencing "Packsaddle", an Aboriginal man convicted of indecent assault, Wells J said:

> "This boy should be given a good flogging. Then he should be sent back to Bathurst Island and made to stay there. Unfortunately, the existing law compels me to send him to gaol. It is going to do him more harm than good. Imprisonment is no punishment to the natives, and it will not deter them from repeating the offence. They get a good bed, meals and tobacco there, and when released boast of it to their friends. Corporal punishment is the only form of punishment they understand."[13]

18 Beliefs in Aboriginal inferiority and an attendant need for punitive measures were not confined to the criminal justice system, but appear to have permeated everyday life in the Northern Territory. At the time of the events in question, the *Aboriginals Ordinance 1918* (Cth) (the Ordinance) comprehensively deprived Aboriginal people of personal autonomy. In Darwin, where Dhäkiyarr's trial was heard, Aboriginal people were subject to a curfew, compulsory medical examinations, and issued with identification tags that they were compelled to wear around their necks.[14]

19 In an affidavit filed in the High Court in support of Dhäkiyarr's appeal, his counsel, Fitzgerald, attested to "substantially true characteristics of the average Aboriginal".[15] These

[10] Stephen Gray, "Law in a Lawless Town: The Development of the Criminal Justice System in the Northern Territory from 1869 to 1911" (2006) 17 *Journal of Northern Territory History* 1, 3.
[11] Ibid 7.
[12] Dean Mildren, "The Role of the Legal Profession and the Courts in the Evolution of Democracy and Aboriginal Self-Determination in the Northern Territory in the Twentieth Century" (1996) 7 *Journal of Northern Territory History* 47, 50.
[13] Originally published by the *Northern Standard*, quoted by Dean Mildren, "The Administration of Justice in the Northern Territory During the War Years" (1994) 5 *Journal of Northern Territory History* 21, 23.
[14] Fiona Paisley, "Race Hysteria, Darwin 1938" (2001) 16(34) *Australian Feminist Studies* 43, 44.
[15] Egan, above n 7, 158.

included suppositions such as "[t]he Aboriginal is first and foremost a liar to the white man", and "[t]he Aboriginal has the mind of a child."[16] As Fitzgerald claimed to be "sincerely interested"[17] in Aboriginal people, one can only imagine the beliefs of those whose leanings towards Dhäkiyarr and his fellow Yolŋgu were less than sincere.

20 Characterisations of Aboriginal people as childlike and deceptive were essential to dispossession and colonisation. Likewise, they facilitated the micro-management of Aboriginal lives through protectionist legislation, such as the Ordinance. By the time that the police party arrived on Woodah Island, such beliefs had imbued the criminal justice system for decades, so that those who would go on to play pivotal roles in the ensuing saga were inured to racism.

Finding the voice of Djaparri Bulinjun Wirrpanda

21 Although much could be said about the injustice suffered by Dhäkiyarr, this application is concerned with Djaparri. Far from being a seemingly powerless "lubra", Djaparri was a sovereign Yolŋgu woman. According to Yolŋgu history, the world was created when the Great Creator Spirit sent women to make the physical features of the land and the Yolŋgu people. Those deities also gave the people a comprehensive code of existence, called Maḏayin.[18] It is inferred that Djaparri's early life was governed by this system.

22 It can also be inferred that at the time of the events in question, Djaparri's life had been affected by decades of warfare between the Yolŋgu and Balanda. For centuries the Yolŋgu had enjoyed cordial relations with visiting Macassans. However, their mostly positive experiences of outsiders changed dramatically with the arrival of pastoral lessees in the latter part of the nineteenth century. Yolŋgu history is replete with stories of poisonings and massacres during this time.[19]

23 A later threat to the Yolŋgu came in the form of boats, manned by Asian crews, in search of trepang. Like the Balanda before them, these crews were notorious for their ill treatment of Yolŋgu women. At first, the men tried to protect the women from abuse, but as times grew more desperate, Yolŋgu women became active participants in skirmishes that left fishermen dead and their boats destroyed.[20]

24 We know from the author Ted Egan that Djaparri lived on her country at GarnGarn until her death in 1986.[21] However, little else is known, at least on the public record, about Djaparri. Crucially, we do not know what she thought of her treatment at the hands of the police in August 1933.

25 Together with three other Aboriginal women, Djaparri was handcuffed and taken to the police camp for questioning. The length of time of the women's detention remains unsettled. According to a missionary who spoke to Dhäkiyarr in March 1934, the women were held for two days.[22] When Egan interviewed Djaparri forty years later, she told him that she was detained for, "[o]ne day. That afternoon the policeman was killed."[23]

[16] Ibid.
[17] Ibid 157.
[18] Trudgen, above n 5, 13.
[19] Ibid 12-38.
[20] Ibid 28.
[21] Egan, above n 7, 212.
[22] Ibid, 67
[23] Ibid 204.

26 In common with the other women who were held, Djaparri was denied the respect of a name in both the proceedings in Darwin and the subsequent appeal to the High Court. But at least one member of the High Court recognised that their detention was without legal basis. Starke J wrote:

> "It was, no doubt, necessary for the police to capture and handcuff the lubras if they were to achieve the object of their expedition, but the rules of English law cannot be cited in support of their action."[24]

27 The detention of an individual for mere questioning is not only unlawful;[25] it can also give rise to liability for false imprisonment. That it was apparently acceptable for police officers to hold innocent women unlawfully, for up to two days, is a powerful demonstration of the racism that imbued Australia's legal system in the 1930s. Djaparri and her kin may have been subjects of the Crown, but their denial of the protection of the rule of law aroused no real controversy.

28 In the Acknowledgements of his book, *Justice All Their Own*, Egan ponders why "the many other people who have written around these events did not see that she [Djaparri] was the most important person of all".[26] I wholeheartedly concur. With the exception of Dhäkiyarr, Djaparri was possibly the only person who witnessed the killing of McColl. Fortunately, historians have been able to retrieve some of the pieces of the story that never made it into the judgments of the High Court.

29 The death of Constable McColl was the last of eight killings in Arnhem Land, from 1932 to 1933. What became known in the press as a "Black War" began with the deaths of five Japanese fisherman in Caledon Bay on 17 September 1932.[27] Months later, two itinerant men from Sydney were killed at nearby Woodah Island. Those tragedies provide the background to Constable McColl's death.

30 In September 1932, the man who would persuade Dhäkiyarr to sail to Darwin, Fred Gray, was collecting the highly lucrative trepang, in Caledon Bay, north of Woodah Island. On 4 September two luggers manned by an Aboriginal and Japanese crew sailed into Caledon Bay. While Gray enjoyed friendly relations with the Yolŋgu, there had been earlier tensions between the crew and the traditional owners, and some of the Yolŋgu complained to Gray that the Japanese had fired guns at them.[28] On 17 September Gray was confronted by the aftermath of a clash between the two groups, which left five of the fishermen dead.

31 The motive behind the killings has been subject to debate. Most commentators believe that they were motivated by the deceased's alleged sexual abuse of Yolŋgu women.[29] Egan has also interviewed a son of one of those involved in the skirmish, who said that the victims had humiliated a senior Yolŋgu man, who tried to counsel them against breaching strict rules governing interactions between men and women.[30]

[24] *Tuckiar v R* (1934) 52 CLR 335, 352.
[25] *Ex parte Evers; Re Leary* (1945) 62 WN (NSW) 146.
[26] Egan, above n 7, xx.
[27] Mickey Dewar, "Death in the Gulf of Carpentaria: A Look at the Motives Behind the Caledon Bay and Woodah Island Killings: Eight Men Killed by Aborigines in 1932/1933" (1993) 4 *Journal of Northern Territory History* 1.
[28] Ibid 2.
[29] Ibid 5.
[30] Egan, above n 7, 15.

32 In December, two itinerant Europeans, Frank Traynor and William Fagan travelled through the area on their way to Thursday Island. After urging them to abandon their journey, Gray warned them against interfering with the Yolŋgu, to which one allegedly responded: "One white man is worth sixty natives."[31] Traynor and Fagan's journey, however, ended at Woodah Island.

33 Traynor and Fagan took Djaparri and other Aboriginal women to their boat where the women were sexually assaulted. While the women were still on the boat a group of Yolŋgu men, which included Dhäkiyarr, conducted a surprise attack. Traynor and Fagan fell overboard during the melee and perished. When Egan interviewed Djaparri several years later, she confirmed that Traynor and Fagan had been killed because "they took Aboriginal ladies".[32] When the police party left Darwin months later, in order to investigate the earlier killings, they were unaware of the deaths of Traynor and Fagan. Arguably however, those events explain the anxiety felt by the Yolŋgu when the police party arrived and detained their kin.

34 Before she died, Djaparri told Egan that the "policeman [McColl] who was handcuffed to us did not do anything to the Yolŋgu ladies."[33] Of the moments before McColl was killed, she said that the "handcuff was open then. Only chain (holds her wrist). Like puppy dog. We were sitting quietly. Only one white man. I got a signal from my husband . . . He talked to me on his fingers. He said 'I will kill him'."[34]

35 Dewar has cast doubt on the reliability of Egan's interview with Djaparri:

> "Ted Egan interviewed Tuckiar's wife, Japarri, just before her death and questioned her about whether sexual intercourse had taken place. Japarri apparently stated clearly that it had not (Egan 1989). But whether a male questioner would receive an accurate answer to such an intimate question after Japarri had been living for some forty years at the Methodist Mission at Yirrkala seems doubtful. McColl's behaviour in separating himself and another woman from the rest of the party is difficult to explain as it was surely both dangerous and failing in the duty with which he was charged, that is, the guarding of all the women."[35]

36 The account told by Djaparri to Egan also conflicts with notes taken by a missionary, Dyer, who spoke with Dhäkiyarr through an interpreter, during his journey to Darwin:

> "One policeman is left in the camp with Takera's young lubra, he has three wives he said. Takera comes to look at the camp but cannot see anyone. He looks further and sees this policeman away from the camp in the scrub she is calling out for help. He finds them in the act of intercourse with his wife. We charge how important it is that he tells us truly through Harry, he said it is true, he saw it with his eye, pointing to it. He hid behind a tree watching. As he did up his clothes he Takera showed himself to take her away. The policeman fires three shots at him & when he stops to attend to his gun, he throws the spear that kills him . . . the spear hit him in the chest . . . he pulled out the spear & went a little way and fell down (Dyer nd c1934, CRS A1 36/4022)."[36]

[31] Dewar, above n 27 8.
[32] Egan, above n 7, 203.
[33] Ibid 204.
[34] Ibid.
[35] Mickey Dewar, *The Black War in Arnhem Land: Missionaries and the Yolŋgu 1908-1940* (Australian National University, North Australia Research Unit, 1992) 57.
[36] Quoted by Dewar, ibid 54.

37 The precise chain of events on that day in August 1933 will presumably remain unknown, because those involved have since perished. However, it is incontrovertible to say that the Yolŋgu people in this story suffered terribly at the hands of outsiders. It is a certainty that the Yolŋgu women, including Djaparri, had been sexually assaulted by Balanda who were travelling through the area.

38 Dewar describes a "double standard" in relation to inter-racial sexual relations, at the time of Dhäkiyarr's trial. Sex between Europeans and Aboriginals was proscribed by the Ordinance. Furthermore, there was a stigma attached to European men who openly consorted with Aboriginal women. In reality however, it was the "usual practice" for European men on the frontier to do so privately.[37] So when the allegation that sexual intercourse had taken place between Djaparri and McColl received its first public airing, Darwin's European population rallied to the cause of protecting McColl's reputation.

39 Journalists who attended the coronial inquiry into McColl's death made a pact that Harry's allegation of "misconduct with a lubra" would be omitted from news reports.[38] According to one journalist, the coroner, the prosecutor and even Fitzgerald, were parties to this agreement.[39] Soon after Dhäkiyarr had been committed for trial, Darwin's establishment turned out in large numbers, for McColl's funeral. Egan estimates that "more than 90 per cent" of the mourners had not known McColl, including Wells J who featured prominently at the graveside.[40]

40 The trial itself miscarried due to irregularities, referred to above, which were grounded in an attempt to protect McColl's reputation. Other than Dhäkiyarr, the person who bore the brunt of this collective endeavour was Harry. Perhaps, the only frank reporting of Harry's evidence came from the Communist Party newspaper, the *Darwin Proletarian*, which claimed that "the Judge did everything to intimidate this witness".[41]

41 In his summing up to the jury, Wells J was vociferous in his attempt to discredit Harry's evidence:

> "It may be that he [Harry] has put it up himself or somebody may have suggested it to him. I put it to you that this story is a concoction. Give it very careful consideration. If you agree with my view, I ask you to say so. I see the real improbability of it. It is so improbable as to be incredible. The story is so ridiculous that you should not have the slightest difficulty in coming to the conclusion that it is a fabrication from start to finish. One story is highly probable, the other utterly ridiculous and a fabrication."[42]

42 Lost in the struggle to preserve McColl's reputation was not only Dhäkiyarr's right to a fair trial, but also Djaparri's humanity. The possibility that Djaparri had been the victim of sexual assault appeared to be of no concern to anyone. Furthermore, she should have been kept informed of her husband's welfare while he was in custody, but that too appears to have been overlooked. It is likely that no one even bothered to inform her when Dhäkiyarr had been sentenced to death.

[37] Dewar, above n 27, 5.
[38] Egan, above n 7, 145.
[39] Ibid 145–146.
[40] Ibid 81.
[41] Ibid 147.
[42] Ibid 142.

43 Rather than being remembered as the victim of abuse, Djaparri has often been painted as a calculating jezebel who lured an innocent police officer to his death. This theory was taken further by McColl's colleague on the expedition, Constable Victor Charles Hall. In his novel based on the actual events, *Dreamtime Justice*,[43] Hall made the extraordinary claim that Djaparri not only spoke English, but also tricked McColl into following her into the jungle.[44] Given that the police have long been suspected to have killed Dhäkiyarr, it seems unlikely that any genuine attempt was made by the authorities to solve the mystery of his disappearance. Such apathy was perhaps the final insult dealt by the criminal justice system to Djaparri.

Contemporary legacies

44 The final element in this Court's analysis is a consideration of the contemporary legacies of Djaparri's story. In many ways, Djaparri's experiences of the law fell within the "binary of invisibility and control".[45] That is, her right to be protected from sexual assault became invisible. At the same time, the colonial state exercised extraordinary control over Djaparri, as evidenced by her unlawful detention.

45 Like Djaparri, Aboriginal women over the supervening decades continued to grapple with invisibility, while at the same time, being subject to excessive control by the state. In the early 1990s, researchers such as Bolger powerfully elucidated the invisibility of female victims of Aboriginal family violence.[46] At the dawn of the twenty-first century Aboriginal women continued to suffer terrifying levels of violence.[47] That many Aboriginal women did not report such violence to police, and still refrain from doing so, can be explained in part by the state's historical use of police as conduits of racially discriminatory laws and policies. Under-reporting of violence has also been attributed to systemic racism.[48]

46 Throughout the twentieth century, Aboriginal women were invisible not only as victims of family violence, but also as offenders. Although the now historic Royal Commission into Aboriginal Deaths in Custody investigated the deaths of eleven Indigenous women, it declined to make any specific recommendations concerning women.[49] It was not until a decade after the Commission handed down its National Report, that attention was given to the needs of Indigenous women in the criminal justice system.[50]

47 More recently, the binary was manifest in a body of measures under the rubric of the Northern Territory Intervention, also known as the Northern Territory Emergency

[43] Victor Charles Hall, *Dreamtime Justice* (Angus and Robertson, 1962).
[44] Ibid 92.
[45] Nicole Watson, "The Northern Territory Emergency Response: Has it Really Improved the Lives of Aboriginal Women and Children?" (2011) 35 *Australian Feminist Law Journal* 147.
[46] Audrey Bolger, *Aboriginal Women and Violence*, Report for the Criminology Research Council and the Northern Territory Commissioner of Police (1991); Boni Robertson, Queensland Government, *The Aboriginal and Torres Strait Islander Women's Taskforce on Violence Report* (1999).
[47] Dorinda Cox, Mandy Young and Alison Bairnsfather-Scott, "No Justice Without Healing: Australian Aboriginal People and Family Violence" (2009) 30 *Australian Feminist Law Journal* 151, 152.
[48] Chris Cunneen, *Conflict, Politics and Crime: Aboriginal Communities and the Police* (Allen & Unwin, 2001) 176.
[49] Greg Gardiner and Tina-Maree Takagaki, "Indigenous Women and the Police in Victoria: Patterns of Offending and Victimisation in the 1990s" (2002) 13(3) *Current Issues in Criminal Justice* 301.
[50] Rowena Lawrie, "Speak Out Speak Strong: Rising Imprisonment Rates of Indigenous Women" (2003) 5(24) *Indigenous Law Bulletin* 5; Elena Marchetti, "Indigenous Women and the RCIADIC – Part 1" (2007) 7(1) *Indigenous Law Bulletin* 6; Elena Marchetti, "Indigenous Women and the RCIADIC – Part 2" (2008) 7(2) *Indigenous Law Bulletin* 6.

Response. Although the Commonwealth Parliament introduced such measures for the ostensible purpose of protecting Aboriginal women and children,[51] some diminished Aboriginal women's rights, such as the freedom of movement.[52]

48 Although it is the contention of this Court that the binary of invisibility and control continues to be manifest in the application of the law to Indigenous women to this day, it is also the profound belief of this Court that the binary is capable of being severed from the law. But this crucial goal can only be achieved when the stories of Aboriginal and Torres Strait Islander women are heard. Through exercising its role under s 25 *Treaty Act*, this Court wades through historical records in an attempt to listen to the ghosts of women such as Djaparri.

49 This Court has inferred that Djaparri was a victim of assault. Instead of receiving the protection of the rule of law, however, Djaparri was unlawfully detained at the hands of police officers. At her husband's trial and subsequent appeal, Djaparri was not even afforded a name, but referred to as a "lubra". In a final insult, Djaparri was never told what became of her husband after his release from gaol, although it has long been suspected that police officers were responsible for his death. This Court has attempted to rectify some of the harm that was inflicted on Djaparri's humanity. We have recognised her sovereignty as a Yolŋgu woman. We have also cast a light on the pervasive roles of race and patriarchy in the evolution of Australian law. By doing so, we hope to play but a small part in rebuilding the legal system from its colonial origins to one that affords genuine equality to all citizens of the Republic.

WATSON J

50 I agree with the judgment of Foley CJ.

[51] Commonwealth, *Parliamentary Debates*, House of Representatives, 7 August 2007, 6 (Mal Brough, Minister for Families, Community Services and Indigenous Affairs and Minister Assisting the Prime Minister for Indigenous Affairs).
[52] Watson, above n 45.

INDEX

Lightning Source UK Ltd.
Milton Keynes UK
UKHW030604230120
357471UK00004B/52

9 781849 465212